D1006120

SISTER NOVELISTS

BY THE SAME AUTHOR

The Daily Jane Austen: A Year of Quotes

The Making of Jane Austen

Women Writers and Old Age in Great Britain, 1750–1850

British Women Writers and the Writing of History, 1670–1820

SISTER NOVELISTS

THE TRAILBLAZING PORTER SISTERS, WHO PAVED THE WAY FOR AUSTEN AND THE BRONTËS

DEVONEY LOOSER

BLOOMSBURY PUBLISHING
NEW YORK • LONDON • OXFORD • NEW DELHI • SYDNEY

BLOOMSBURY PUBLISHING
Bloomsbury Publishing Inc.
1385 Broadway, New York, NY 10018, USA

BLOOMSBURY, BLOOMSBURY PUBLISHING, and the Diana logo are trademarks of Bloomsbury Publishing Plc

First published in the United States 2022

LIBRARY OF CONGRESS CATALOGING-IN-PUBLICATION DATA IS AVAILABLE

ISBN: HB: 978-1-63557-529-3; EBOOK: 978-1-63557-530-9

2 4 6 8 10 9 7 5 3 1

Typeset by Westchester Publishing Services
Printed and bound in the U.S.A.

To the librarians, archivists, and collectors who preserve materials that make the stories possible

CONTENTS

PROLOGUE

Two Sisters of Blazing Genius

I was sitting in the reading room at the Huntington Library in San Marino, California, during the summer of 2004. Any scholar fortunate enough to have worked at its pristine desks knows it's a beautifully silent place, save for the low-grade clacking of fingers on keyboards and the occasional clearing of a throat. In front of me there was a folder—number 839 out of 2,662—from the Jane Porter Papers. It contained a long letter written in a sharp, half-curvy hand, dated July 15, 1820. It began, "Dearest Jane!" and was signed, "your Maria."

As I read, I found myself needing to stifle laughter. The letter's pages were filled with delightfully snarky gossip. One sister was writing to another about how she'd "escaped alive" from a boring, gluttonous dinner party hosted by neighbors. So much food was served that, as Maria put it, "I was literally crammed with as many different things as there were animals in the ark." Maria decided to approach the meal like a soldier heading into battle, circumventing the meat in favor of a sophisticated attack on fine fruit.

The other guests were described with unsparing mockery. One man, she joked, must have fallen "desperately in love with me, as he sat gazing either with horror or admiration at me all the time he was playing whist." Another man, choosing conversation over card games, "went off like an alarum at particular words." The scene was ridiculous. Maria confessed, "I longed for Miss Austin's now buried pen (alas that it is!) to have immortalized the whole company."[1]

What struck me as I read Maria's words was that this letter could go head-to-head with any of the 160 or thereabouts that survive from Jane Austen. The sarcasm was dripping, the comic timing was impeccable, and the implicit social criticism was pointed. With a light touch, Maria deftly eviscerated the meal, the silly human-alarm man, and the inscrutably staring boor. No doubt he was gawking at her because she was "an authoress," as celebrated women writers were called. At the time, Maria Porter was far more famous than Miss Austen, who'd died just three years before and wasn't yet a household name.

I was savoring every detail in Maria's letter when I was jolted back to the present. The walkie-talkie sitting on the desk in front of me buzzed. For a split second, I couldn't remember what year it was. Okay, I couldn't remember what *century* it was. This kind of cognitive lapse may be hard to imagine for some, but for those of us who spend countless hours in libraries reading unpublished letters by long-dead people, our work is a time-traveling excavation of lost stories. It sometimes proves difficult to dig yourself out.

The walkie-talkie's buzzing required my attention. It was a signal from my husband, asking me to meet him outside the library because our infant son was crying from hunger. The buzz was noisy proof that I lived in the twenty-first century, that it was time to nurse our baby, and that the labor of a man was making possible my archival work on the history of nineteenth-century women. I could imagine what some of the writers I study might have had to say about my priorities and this unusual role reversal.

To women writers then, including the sisters whose vast correspondence I was reading, how wondrously jumbled, and impossible to pull off, would my identities as scholar, professor, writer, wife, and mother likely have seemed. The risks that Jane and Maria Porter took to publish—obstacles faced, criticisms endured—had absolutely paved the way for me and other scholars to recover their life stories. Reading their correspondence sometimes felt like voyeurism. It also felt like repaying a debt.

I began to mention these brilliant literary sisters to anyone who'd listen. Few had heard of them. It sounds clichéd, but I felt called to scour the Porter family's thousands of letters gathering proverbial dust on shelves. I got grants to travel to dozens of libraries. When I began to read from the sisters' remarkable output of twenty-six books, I was upset to learn how they'd lost the credit they'd been given, and deserved, for creating the historical novel as we know it. Jane

Porter's books had sold not just thousands, or hundreds of thousands, but more than a million nineteenth-century copies in the United States alone![2] Why had we lost sight of her?

In the months after that walkie-talkie moment in 2004, I got pregnant again, and our second child was born. We've now raised our two Gen Z sons almost to adulthood. But rarely has a day gone by during those chaotic years of childrearing when I haven't thought about the Porter sisters. It felt so unfair that the sisters never had the benefit of a full biography, while hundreds of books on Austen and the Brontës—many with little new information to recommend them—churn from presses. I decided to do something about it.

A biography of the Porter sisters could be written as a surface-level tale, recording an impressive litany of their once-heralded literary achievements. The sisters published innovative novels that many nineteenth-century readers worshipped, although skeptics criticized these books as outlandish and improbable tales. But the fact is that the Porter sisters' lives, beneath the surface, were often outlandish and improbable. Their real-life adventures read like funhouse-mirror versions of Austen's famous characters and plots.

For the Porter sisters, there were few conventional happily-ever-afters. As they supported their widowed mother and three chronically disappointing brothers, the sisters fell hard for impossibly handsome and deeply flawed men. Nearly every major decision Jane and Maria made in the hope it would bring them requited love, or domestic comfort, did exactly the opposite. During the writing of this book, I had moments when I wished I could shake these brilliant sisters by the shoulders and ask, "What are you doing?"

But as I grasped the complex contours of their overtly polite but covertly audacious lives, I saw the Porter sisters as learned women whose judgment understandably ricocheted between wise and naïve. I made the decision to center the sisters' own voices in this first telling of their stories, both to honor their significant achievements and to showcase their personal strengths and faults. This centering also reflects the imaginative-meets-real world the sisters had built around themselves and inhabited together since childhood—a world that propelled them to create great historical fiction. The Misses Porter were single women without fortunes whose dreams and schemes helped and hampered them by turns. They made their way together in settings where they were never meant to compete, much less to triumph.

In the following pages, I've used the sisters' private correspondence and other sources to piece together the true stories of their daily dramas as they unfolded. Jane and Maria often exchanged letters with long sections of reported dialogue, as if their lives were the stuff of plays or novels. They were so closely connected that they wrote each other long letters even when they were separated for a day or two or even if that separation was by just a few miles (as was often the case), as one sister accepted an invitation to stay overnight with nearby and more well-off friends, while the other stayed home in cramped circumstances with their widowed mother.

From the conversations recorded in these manuscripts, I've reconstructed their stories of experiencing authorship and fame, as well as hidden and forbidden love. But what I hope this biography shows is that it was the sisters' unshakeable love for each other that proved their most significant, enduring relationship. It provided their alternative happy ending, as each one encouraged the other to keep writing, book after stunning book.

Jane and Maria deserve to be put prominently back into our literary histories for their central roles in creating historical fiction. But they may be even more important to posterity for their exceptionally moving unpublished letters, which reveal not only their skills as writers but also the overwhelming challenges that nineteenth-century women writers of genius faced, in public and private. Jane Austen's life remains a myth-laden mystery because most of her correspondence was apparently destroyed by her family in the years after her death in 1817. But the Porter sisters lovingly preserved their letters. In them, these long-forgotten sister novelists not only immortalized each other. They also immortalized the whole company they kept, in the dazzling, perilous era during which they shined so brightly.

MISS JANE PORTER and Miss Anna Maria Porter were the most famous sister novelists before the Brontës. People went to great lengths to see these female curiosities, who were hailed as literary wonders in Regency London. The sisters were known to be beauties; they'd sat as models for famous painters. They traveled in the same circles as celebrity actors, poets, activists, publishers, and politicians. They hobnobbed with nobles and royalty. A marquess, it was said, once paid to get a glimpse of them.

But not everyone approved. At the beginning of their careers, anonymous reviewers repeatedly told the ambitious sisters they should give up on novel-writing—and on having ambitions. Yet most readers ended up in awe of their literary powers. Their dozens of romantic, uplifting novels of love and war were seen as so true to life that it seemed impossible the sisters hadn't been on battlefields themselves.

The Misses Porter gained global renown, with Jane the more famous and Maria (as she was called) the more prolific sister. Jane's bestselling historical novel *The Scottish Chiefs* (1810) was said to be Queen Victoria's favorite book.[3] Across the Atlantic, it was President Andrew Jackson's favorite.[4] Novelist William Thackeray, author of *Vanity Fair*, remembered *The Scottish Chiefs* as the first novel he'd read as a boy. He'd so cherished it that he couldn't "read to the end . . . of that dear delightful book for crying," because finishing it would have been "as sad as going back to school."[5] Jane's earlier novel of war-torn Poland, *Thaddeus of Warsaw* (1803), was also a literary phenomenon. Emily Dickinson's well-worn copies of Jane's two bestselling novels have dozens of folded-over page corners, showing intense engagement with the books.[6] Fans told Jane they stayed up all night reading *Thaddeus of Warsaw*, losing themselves in its pages. Her signature books about history's underdog war heroes in nations fighting off tyrants were considered politically dangerous enough to be banned by Napoleon.[7]

Until the end of her life, Jane's novels were widely read, rarely out of print, and translated into many languages. After she died, her works lived on, although they were shortened, and then relegated to children's literature. *The Scottish Chiefs* was abridged with illustrations by N. C. Wyeth in the 1920s. In the 1950s, it was featured as a Classics Illustrated comic book. Later still, Jane's novel served as the probable, though uncredited, source text for Mel Gibson's Academy Award–winning film *Braveheart* (1995). But by then, the name Jane Porter was best known as Tarzan's wife, and the original Jane Porter's less celebrated sister, Anna Maria Porter, was no more than a footnote.

None of this was predictable, neither the rapid rise to fame nor the gradual forgetting. The Porter girls came up in the world from what the late eighteenth-century elite would have called "nothing." Such girls, born portionless, had few prospects. Then the sisters became fatherless. Without male relatives to depend on, downwardly mobile single girls might hope to become seamstresses or, with some education, governesses. If attractive and good with numbers, they might marry tradesmen. The world might have expected the Porter sisters to become wives to struggling medical men like their late father.

But the Porters, who loved reading books, broke the mold. From a very early age, the sisters began to amuse each other with the products of their pens. They wrote long, loving letters, full of silly jokes and make-believe intrigue. They chose outlandish pseudonyms and scrawled playful postscripts to each other at the end of dutiful letters to their uneducated, widowed mother. In her early teens, Maria teased Jane about her melodramatic prose and bad handwriting, declaring that her sister's topsy-turvy commas looked drunk.[8]

Soon the sisters were exchanging letters in rhyming verse. In one poem-letter, Maria closed with, "I'll sheath my pen, then stir my fire / and sign myself your fond Maria-r."[9] It's how we know she pronounced her name with a low back vowel, to sound like Mariah. Maria grasped early on that the life of the mind and pen could serve as a pleasure-filled battle of rapier wit, even for struggling girls confined to the domestic routines of stoking household fires. For Maria and Jane, their pens were their swords. The Porter family's shabby series of rented hearths and homes were places that lit up their imaginations. When Mrs. Porter, their plainspoken mother, declared their London lodgings looked like a dog hole, Jane disagreed. She said it was the manner of a place that determined its elegance, not its size.[10] The sisters imagined greater things, then almost wrote them into being.

Jane and Maria, armed with no more than a few years of charity school education, had little help in learning how to write. They became each other's first audience. Together they built word-worlds, took oaths of sincerity, and expressed mutual admiration.[11] One of the sisters' favorite words was "blazing." In their letters, passions blazed.[12] Gossip blazed. Beaux blazed. Each sister told the other that her fiction blazed with genius.[13]

They decided, against all prevailing advice, to seek print. In 1790, Jane, at age fourteen, wrote a poem about a young female author who stayed up late, writing by candlelight. The author dreamily records her visions of mythical gods, muses, and cupids. She writes about Venus's eyes shooting forth a fatal blaze that inspires creativity in the girl-author. But in the middle of this reverie of night-writing, the poem's speaker is interrupted by a knock on her door. Her male friend has come to report disappointing news. His efforts to sell her writings have been in vain. The booksellers have risen up against the girl's attempt to publish. Nevertheless, she's undeterred.

"One cries I'm fool or rather mad," she complains of the booksellers. "Others my works are cursed bad. / I start and vow it can't be true, / And then sit down to write to you."[14]

That trusted "you" for Jane—the one who kept her writing, despite the criticisms of the male-dominated publishing world—was Maria. The young sisters soon turned from writing childish letters and light verse to serious poems, short stories, essays, histories, novels, pamphlets, and plays. They wrote of the horrors of war, the beauties of the natural world, moral philosophy, classical history, friendship, and families. They befriended young editors of newspapers and magazines. The once-skeptical book publishers were eventually won over.

Jane and Maria grew up similarly as authors but became distinctly different women in looks and personality. Maria—the more impulsive, younger sister—was a social being, lively and loquacious. Those who knew her best worried that she fell in love too readily, not only with attractive men but also with children, dogs, cats, birds, and breezes. She was thought pretty, with a round, girlish, pleasing face, azure eyes, and blonde hair, producing bright, sunshiny good looks.[15] She could draw people in with her gentle, joyful enthusiasm.[16]

Jane was called the more beautiful sister—tall, with long, auburn hair and striking features. She projected a graceful, calm placidity.[17] Later in life, she could command rooms upon entering them, with her conspicuous good looks and quiet authority. It took her some years to leverage that power, due to an early, awkward shyness that masked her great inner strength. From a young age, Jane was a sought-after adviser. Her own mother relied entirely on her eldest daughter's sound judgment.

Jane's and Maria's opposite personalities could have inspired Jane Austen's sister-heroines, Elinor and Marianne Dashwood, of *Sense and Sensibility* (1811), although there's no proof of connection. In situations where Maria rushed in, Jane carefully considered. From their youth, the Porter sisters were likened to two contrasting poems by venerated seventeenth-century author John Milton. His "Il Penseroso" describes the serious man in deep thought—learned, melancholy, and pensive—while "L'Allegro" investigates the happy man of mirth and play. Jane's nickname was "Il Penseroso," and Maria's was "L'Allegro."[18]

It was understandable that the sisters would find nicknames in the male-authored literary canon. Both revered history's great men. In their books, they advocated for what then seemed a pressing need in Britain—inspiring rudderless young men of talent to become upstanding sons, brothers, husbands, and military heroes who might lead nations and slay villains, particularly during the Napoleonic Wars. Yet, as much as they revered heroes, the sisters recognized how cruelly limited their own options were in not having been born male.

"But my love, had you been born a Man with your head & heart what an ornament to society you would have been," Maria wrote to her sister. "I love you more than ever, Jane!"[19]

The sisters worshipped history's great women, too—although there would have seemed fewer of them. They also sought out living examples of female greatness. In their teens, they formed friendships with famous and infamous learned women. By their late twenties, the sisters were known as female geniuses themselves. Jane's and Maria's brilliant literary careers helped transform the "authoress" into a more respectable, formidable type. The obstacles they faced in doing so were unintentionally captured in a single sentence from a male literary acquaintance. He wrote, "I liked these two sisters exceedingly, although they were authoresses."[20]

Female authorship in the early nineteenth century was fraught. Educated women weren't supposed to do anything for pay because it was said to tarnish femininity and jeopardize fragile middle-class standing. Elites couldn't decide whether a scribbling woman was a wonder or a monster. Once such a woman published under her own name, the die was cast. Although fame had been something the Porter sisters prized in their youth, especially Jane, it came at a price.[21] "I seriously and sincerely declare that nothing but necessity ought to have made me an authoress," Maria confessed after publishing her sixth book. "I see that I was never meant for one."[22] She often felt she wasn't cut out for public life.

The necessity that compelled her to authorship was financial. The Porter family's three chronically debt-saddled brothers offered little help to their widowed mother and unmarried sisters—a dereliction of traditional masculine duty. The conventional way for the Porter sisters to secure their future—and the future comfort of their "dearer than self" mother—would have been to marry well. But neither sister took a mercenary approach to love. They refused the prevailing idea that securing a well-off husband was a necessary business transaction. At the same time, they boldly negotiated the sale of their own writings.

There's no question that the perfect heroes Jane and Maria dreamed up in the pages of their books had an impact on the men they imagined marrying. The sisters' ideals for male intelligence, charisma, and virtue were high, but the men they fell for proved very wide of the mark. And both sisters fell hard—often for colorful, charismatic men who were living double lives—in an era when a polite woman wasn't supposed to discover her own feelings for a man until he'd revealed his own first. Another problem was that most educated men of the time had their own visions of a perfect wife, and she bore little resemblance to a clever, talented literary woman. It was thought unseemly to sully a polite reputation by immodestly publishing works.

For the Porter sisters, it was a catch-22: While single, they needed to write to support themselves. They maximized profits by publishing under their own names. But pursuing literary careers made it less likely they'd find the heroic husbands they desired. Extraordinary men were sometimes fascinated by strong intellectual women with public reputations, but such men were encouraged to marry subservient, delicate, and unworldly helpmates.[23] Ideally, these self-effacing innocents were also rich.

These limiting beliefs carried over into the literary world. Female authors relied on fathers or brothers to sell their writing to publishers, most of whom were male, because it was polite and expected. Jane's early poem describing her male friend's unsuccessful attempts to sell her writing acknowledges that custom. But without the benefit of effective help from a father, brother, or male friend, Jane unconventionally stepped into the role of literary agent. She got the best deals she could for herself and Maria. The sisters took care of their own business, although, as Jane put it, "Men of Business are not always at the command of our sex."[24]

The sisters used both stereotypically masculine and feminine traits in their negotiations. They felt they had to. "Booksellers, are like Lovers," Jane once wrote to Maria. "We must be coy-ish, if we would keep advantage."[25] Maria, too, understood the publishing game. "At present, money is our aim, and everything that is fair and honest must be attempted to obtain it," she told Jane.[26]

With this philosophy, and pressing economic need, Maria published book after book, to collect the sums each title brought. Jane faithfully recopied and lightly edited Maria's rapidly crafted works and painstakingly composed her own. The sisters worked so hard, with their different habits of composition, that they often wrote themselves sick. Despite difficult circumstances, their talents found expression. Their achievements were immense.

Jane and Maria's groundbreaking fiction was historically researched, morally uplifting, and brilliantly inventive. Their signature sensitive male protagonists cried at home and battled abroad. They married resilient, chaste women, after having fought off desirous femmes fatales. The stories involved deception, cross-dressing, madness, imprisonment, and murder. These novels were meant to entertain but also to lead readers into the further study of history. Most of all, their books were meant to inspire admirable behavior and good character.

The Porters' fiction was exceptionally important in its time. Their stories are sprawling, and their characters well drawn, the result of minute social observation and extensive historical research. Yet the descriptions and coincidences might sometimes strike today's readers as laying it on a bit thick. The good characters are unbelievably good. The moral lessons are pat. That was the expectation then for higher sorts of literature, especially from polite female pens. The sisters dutifully followed those conventions.

But the place where Jane and Maria weren't afraid to step off the beaten path, to show life as it was, was in their private letters. Because their emotionally raw and confessional correspondence wasn't designed for other readers' eyes, the sisters often went to great lengths to conceal its contents. They used initials and mythological names to hide the identities of suitors, rivals, and enemies. That way, if a letter were intercepted before delivery, or its pages seen by a curious brother, their communications might be concealed. The sisters sometimes used banal phrases as secret codes. They plotted the use of invisible ink. They trusted, encouraged, and advised each other, in affairs of authorship, as well as the heart.

"With sisters, who are together all day, and generally all night—they cannot look nor move without observation," Jane once described her relationship with Maria. "Hardly a thought can pass in their minds, but must be seen to each other."[27]

Jane called herself "the Echo" of Maria's "feelings and sentiments."[28] Maria boasted that no one who ever met "my Jane" lost sight of her again willingly.[29] When one sister made a new friend, the other longed to be introduced. "Is there any person, dear to my Mother and sister," Maria wrote, "that can fail of becoming so to me?"[30]

Their letters proved a training ground, not only for lifelong, sisterly love but also for practicing the craft of novel-writing. Jane and Maria recorded scenes they witnessed, and entire conversations they overheard, to capture the adventures of their daily lives. Their letters became a storehouse from which to craft fiction. When Maria wrote to Jane from Brighton about the way moonlight shined on the ocean, Jane encouraged her to save the passage, to insert in some future book. "All such contemplations are as useful to us, as they are delightful," Jane wrote, "for they form the veins of gold from which we work our future fabricks in 'fairy land.'"[31]

The sisters wrote often, too, to friends and family. Jane shared with Maria her secrets of success as a correspondent. When she wrote to people, Jane said, it was generally just as she talked to them—more in their strain than in her own.[32] Jane tried on voices and identities to please listeners and recipients.

One famous and wealthy friend, Thomas Hammersley, who served as banker to the Prince of Wales, told Jane people would want to save the letters of "such a mind like yours." He predicted, "Every paper which comes from you will be worth preserving." He wanted her to think of posterity and collectors as she composed them. "May I take the liberty of making a remark which will be to the advantage of your other correspondents as well as myself," Hammersley wrote, "to leave a margin in the folding part of the paper where I have marked. Your letters may then be pinned or stitched together without any of the writing being obscured."[33]

Of that suggestion, Jane wrote to her sister, "I could not but smile at his hint . . . I, who would wish to have them all burnt as soon as the receiver has read them!"[34]

It's fortunate they weren't destroyed. Two distinguished literary men once declared that Jane's private letters would put her on a par with eighteenth-century literary greats like Jonathan Swift and Lady Mary Wortley Montagu. These male friends believed Miss Jane Porter would someday be ranked among the illustrious females of her country, if her letters were collected and published.[35] So far, very few have been.

Jane was amused that her correspondence was so prized, but she came to acknowledge its value. She once wrote to Maria about their letters, "We ought to collect these histories of our own times."[36] By the end of their lives, the sisters had exchanged thousands of pages of observations and reports about their acquaintances and friends, including the era's most famous novelists, poets, artists, actors, and military men, as well as several royals and many others of rank and title. Jane and her admirers fanned the flames of her celebrity into the Victorian era. At her death, she was called "one of the most distinguished novelists which England has produced, [deserving] the lasting respect and gratitude of her country."[37]

The pathbreaking experiences of the Porter sisters made possible the careers of Austen, the Brontës, and George Eliot, until each of these followers outpaced the sisters in fame and reputation. Memory of their literary achievements in historical fiction, which gradually faded, deserves to be reignited. Yet posterity may decide that their greatest masterpiece is a vast, uplifting, and heartrending correspondence, filled with stories of literary intrigue, financial disasters, and secret suitors. The Porter sisters describe it all in throbbing detail, giving it to us straight—what it was like to try to live and love as brilliant, accomplished, and cash-strapped women writers, in the whirl of the late eighteenth and early nineteenth centuries in Britain. The lives of these remarkable sisters may sometimes read like a novel, but it's a true, blazing history.

CHAPTER 1

Five Fatherless Porter Children (1779–90)

To be the daughters of a penniless widow is a romantic but not a propitious way to come into the world.

Jane and Anna Maria Porter were two of the five surviving children born in the 1770s to Mr. William Porter and Mrs. Jane Blenkinsop Porter. Before she became Mrs. Porter, Jane was known as Jenny Blenkinsop, the lively youngest daughter who helped her father run his Durham inn, the Star and Rummer. Peter Blenkinsop's inn was a popular stop on the Great North Road, a stagecoach route connecting London and Edinburgh. The Star and Rummer was just a stone's throw from the city's majestic cathedral and served as a hub of town activity. Jenny worked there alongside her loyal older sister, Ann, known as Nanny. Their mother had died when Jenny was in her early teens, leaving Nanny to help manage the inn with her father and raise her younger sister.[1]

The Blenkinsop daughters had no education to speak of. As innkeepers' daughters, they belonged to a class of females regularly made the butt of jokes—caricatured either as sexually loose strumpets or as innocent, easy marks for unscrupulous men. But Jenny and Nanny avoided these stereotypical fates and instead proved to be like their father: clever and musical. Peter Blenkinsop made money on the side as a concert promoter. He also sang at the cathedral, with his rare talent of being able to hoot through his nose like a penny trumpet.[2] He must have encouraged his daughters' creativity, since "Love Is a Joke, a Song, by Miss Blenkinsop" was either Nanny's or Jenny's original work.[3] Love became quite serious, however, when Jenny Blenkinsop met the Irish army surgeon who'd become her fiancé.

William Porter was almost thirty and Jenny nearly twenty when they fell in love. He served with the Inniskilling Dragoons, the famed cavalry regiment. As a younger brother of a minor landowning family in Guystown, County Donegal, William didn't have the money to marry his Durham sweetheart right away. To make matters worse, his work as a military surgeon required extensive, unpredictable travel to care for sick and injured soldiers wherever they were convalescing. Surgeons were seen as the crude butchers of the medical profession, and military injuries could be especially gruesome. Treating them was considered perfectly honorable but not genteel.

William and Jenny's engagement lasted almost five years. During that long period, he was often far away, fulfilling his duties, and attempting to please his commanding officers, Lieutenant-Colonel Lord Robert Ker and Coronet William Ogilvie, the eighth Lord Banff. These two men were significant enough to the Porters that the couple eventually named sons after them, in a bid to gain future favor. Such patronage was needed, because advantages were unlikely to come from their own families.

The couple found a way to afford to tie the knot. William and Jenny married on July 17, 1770, at Durham's St. Mary-le-Bow, the little church next to the grand cathedral across from her father's inn. A Newcastle newspaper announced the wedding of "Mr. William Portair, surgeon to the Inniskilling Dragoons, to Miss Jenny Blenkinsop, of Durham, an amiable young Lady, with a handsome fortune."[4] The amiable part must have been true. The handsome fortune part fell between an outright lie and wishful thinking.

The newlyweds built a more-than-common marriage. William wrote tender, loving letters to his wife while he was away. Whenever they could manage it, she joined him on his military postings in rented lodgings, but it wasn't always convenient or practical to have Jenny with him. So the couple—and child after child—often lived apart.

Six children came from William and Jenny's marriage. A year after they married, the Porters had and lost an infant son named William. Their next five children—John Blenkinsop, William Ogilvie, Jane, Robert Ker, and Anna Maria—were born in quick succession over six years.[5] The eldest surviving three of them—John, William, and Jane—would have remembered Grandfather's Star and Rummer as one of their first homes. Jane and Robert were probably born there, in the same room.[6]

When William Porter was away, Mrs. Porter and the children stayed at her father's inn, with Nanny and Grandpapa Blenkinsop. William was proud to pay his father-in-law a fair price for his growing family's room and board. "You need not be ashamed to look anyone in the Face," William wrote to Jenny, "as you pay your way like a Gentlewoman, & so you are, as the mother of my Children, & by the good Behaviour of yourself."[7]

William hated these separations. Fond letters described his deep longing to be home. He called Jenny "the best of Wives and Mothers" and vowed to be the best guardian and husband. He told her he was moping and stupid, day and night, so anxious and miserable was he without her. At least he knew his father-in-law was taking tender care of the Porter grandchildren.[8]

Peter Blenkinsop oversaw his older grandsons' educations and hired their tutors. He referred to the little Porters by loving nicknames. John was called Jacky, and William was Billy. Little Jane he called Jenny—a next-generation Jenny to him. Robert Ker was always Bobby. But a loving grandfather was no substitute for a distant parent traversing the country on horseback with his regiment. Eldest son John once asked Grandpapa Blenkinsop to pass on a message to his absent father.

"Pray tell Pappa when he has done with his Poney to remember poor Jack," the little boy said.[9]

But William Porter, who had vowed to travel to the farthest part of the world to get his wife and children bread, accepted a promising invitation to go abroad.[10] Lord Robert Ker asked William to accompany him to the Continent as his private physician. William hoped to be generously repaid for his trouble, then sell his military commission, leave the regiment, and set up his own medical practice.

Much was hoped for, but little was gained. After some months in Europe, Lord Ker returned healthy to England, but he made no grand gesture to compensate William. To make matters worse, Jenny was pregnant again and Grandpapa Blenkinsop had taken ill with jaundice and dropsy. All the old man wanted, he told his son-in-law, was to have his family live together in peace.[11]

He didn't get his wish. On December 4, 1778—the day after his little granddaughter Jane turned three—Peter Blenkinsop died at age seventy-five. He was buried in Durham's St. Oswald's churchyard, near his late wife. He left no fortune. His remaining business debts were thirty pounds and his unpaid medical bills ten more.[12] That was as much as a middle-class person might expect to make in a year.[13]

As one life ended in the struggling family, another began. Anna Maria Porter was born two weeks after her grandfather's death, on December 17, 1778.[14] By late December, William and Jenny Porter were in Salisbury, where Maria (as she'd always be called) was quietly and privately baptized on Christmas Day.[15] Older sister Jane, age three, later claimed to remember being in Salisbury, with her father, mother, and new baby sister.[16]

When the family returned to Durham, in the first months of 1779, Mrs. Porter noticed that something seemed wrong with her husband. First she observed his memory loss. They had access to the best medical advice and would have sought it. But then things took a worse turn. Mrs. Porter's beloved husband seemed to have descended into madness. He began to lose every other rational faculty, including, finally, the ability to speak.[17] By April 1779, it was clear he couldn't return to work, so they sold his military commission.[18] For a time, the Porters had this small sum to live on.

By autumn, the situation had become very grave. On September 7, 1779, baby Maria was taken to St. Mary-le-Bow, to be baptized a second time. The very next day, her father, William Porter, passed away. He left behind a widow, three sons, two daughters, and less than forty pounds.[19]

Mrs. Porter, having lost her father and her husband in less than a year, was desperate enough to look for supernatural solace. She sought out a fortune-teller, who wrote out a prophecy divining her future on a small piece of paper. It predicted the widow's happy longevity, although in far from perfect English: "Madam, Your nativity shews as followeth your Life will be of no short Duration."[20]

The seer foresaw the widow's good fortune, too. There would be "unexpected advantages," which "fortune . . . shall throw in your way," between 1779 and 1780. The fortune-teller said the widow's luck would turn, thanks to her open, free, and lofty temper and aspiring disposition. Her good character would always bring her honor and merit. But for Mrs. Porter, the most uplifting part of the prophecy must have been the predictions about her five fatherless children. "Your children," the fortune-teller proclaimed, "will live to honour and abe you honourable indeed."

"Abe" or "abee" was a Scottish word that meant "to let be." The five children would leave their widowed mother honorable, indeed. Mrs. Porter preserved the fortune-teller's prophecy as a relic of that devastating year. She kept it across decades and distant moves, even apparently when the paper became tattered, with its folds well worn. She talked with her children about these predictions. As they grew up, the fortune-teller's words became a running joke, as well as a serious expectation. Their bright future was fated.[21]

In late 1779, good fortune would have seemed highly unlikely. As a distant family member later put it in a letter to Mrs. Porter, "You were left with a small Family, without Friends, without Money, and I may safely say without the smallest ray of Hope to Support them with the Common Necessarys of Life."[22] Mrs. Porter wrote to the War Office to request a military widow's pension, in recognition of her late husband's twenty-three years of service to the army.[23] The clerk who responded was encouraging, but when the pension was granted, its ten pounds a year weren't enough to support a middle-class household of one, much less six.

Relatives didn't come to her aid. William Porter's large Irish family did little. One week before William died, Mrs. Porter wrote to a brother-in-law in Strabane, asking if there was any history of lunacy in the family. She must have asked him for money, too. His refusal to help her and his little nephews and nieces was, at least, full of apology. He had his own large family to support. And no, he reassured her, there was no history of madness among the Porters. It was true that, when a child, William had gotten a violent cut on his head. But nothing else could explain his condition. It was uncharacteristic. It was unfortunate! He wished her well. He was terribly sorry.[24]

Some of Mrs. Porter's begging letters received better replies. Her two oldest sons were accepted as scholarship students to the prestigious Durham School, just as some of their Blenkinsop uncles had been years before. Eldest son John enrolled in 1780. Second son William joined him by 1782.[25] These scholarships not only covered the cost of tuition but also provided stipends to pay room and board.

That left Mrs. Porter needing to support herself and the three youngest children. She made the bold decision to leave her hometown behind. Two months after her husband's death, she moved them across the border to set up a boardinghouse in Edinburgh, where her late husband had trained and had medical contacts. As a landlady, she could use the knowledge she'd gained working at her father's inn.

Moving would have been complicated. The hundred-mile stagecoach journey took some fourteen hours, with stops to switch tired horses for rested ones. It was an expensive trip. Mrs. Porter may have paid for her and the children to be among the six passengers inside the coach. To save money, however, they may have taken half-price seats on the roof or in the box. It's hard to imagine even an experienced traveler like Mrs. Porter protecting an infant and small children on the roof of a stagecoach.

This mode of transportation offered few comforts. On cold days, tightly packed travelers put straw around their feet to keep warm.[26] Some passengers found the ride so jostling they felt almost seasick.[27] The Porters were traveling as autumn turned to winter. The roads were becoming less passable, the days shorter, and the drivers perhaps too daring. Yet the widow and her three youngest children set off. When they arrived in Edinburgh, Mrs. Porter would have had a great deal to do to establish a boardinghouse with furniture, linens, and dishes, which she'd have had to purchase with credit or receive as gifts, unless the house in question were already appointed with such things. Once she'd assembled a household, she advertised in the newspaper, on November 10, 1779:

> MRS. PORTER, from England, Widow of Mr. William Porter, late surgeon to the Inniskilling regiment of Dragoons, begs leave to acquaint her friends and the public, That she has entered upon a convenient House in *Buccleugh-street*, an airy and pleasant situation, in which she means to accommodate Students of Physic, and other Gentlemen, with LODGING and BOARDING, on reasonable terms. She hopes for the patronage of those who have already honoured her with their friendship; and will make it her study to merit the countenance and recommendation of them and the public in general.[28]

Work as a landlady was no easy road to prosperity. The elite looked askance at single women running boardinghouses, with strange men coming in and out of their homes. Yet a landlady who was known to be widowed, taking in male medical students, in her time of grief and need, might appear maternal and almost gentlewomanlike.

The transition didn't go smoothly. Within a month, Mrs. Porter left Buccleugh Street. She ran a second advertisement, telling the public she'd moved to a convenient house in the "Surgeon's Area in the High School Yards," in another airy and pleasant situation.[29] The "airy" part mattered. Those who could afford it lived in places with good air, as bad air brought disease. Close conditions created opportunities for contagion. Deaths of infants and children were rampant.

One doctor estimated half of Edinburgh's children died before their second birthdays.[30] Jane and Robert had made it through infancy, but little Maria had a delicate constitution. Mrs. Porter later ascribed it to her baby's being nursed on widow's tears. Yet Maria grew gradually stronger.[31] The Porter children were inoculated against smallpox, a benefit of having had a medical father.[32] That the siblings survived their childhoods stemmed in part from Mrs. Porter's maintaining her late husband's medical connections.

Mrs. Porter's second Edinburgh boardinghouse was better located. Surgeon Square was home to the Royal College of Surgeons and Surgeons' Hall. It was next to the Royal Infirmary, a teaching hospital, and near the High School Yards. The Edinburgh Medical School, considered the best in the English-speaking world, enrolled several hundred students. Many came from great distances, and they needed someplace to live.

Mrs. Porter set up for business on the south side of Surgeon Square, in the western half of a long house. She created a shrine to her late husband, placing his regimental sword over their fireplace, along with a sketch of the Battle of Minden, in which he'd served, when British forces gained victory over the French in the Seven Years' War.[33] Their new neighbors included members of the Kerr family of Chatto—relatives of Lord Ker, whom William had nursed back to health in France. The strong possibility is that the Ker/Kerr/Carr family (all three spellings were used) helped Mrs. Porter get her start in Edinburgh.

A landlady's work had a reputation for being "a slavish business and very unprofitable," as one nineteenth-century gentleman put it.[34] Proprietors went into debt, hours were round the clock, and profit margins were slim. Once she could afford it, Mrs. Porter would have hired someone to help care for her children so she could focus on running the house.

For young Jane, Robert, and Maria, growing up in a boardinghouse must have been lively and interesting. A description of a woman-run Edinburgh boardinghouse for medical students from this era offers a window onto the Porter children's daily world. The boardinghouse was described as a commodious home on a square—much like Mrs. Porter's—with a furnished, shared parlor. A forest of empty bottles gave evidence of past revelries. Meals included courses of haggis, barley-broth soup, cheese, radishes, "*a parton tae*" (the claw of a crab), and dessert. After dinners, the proprietor joined her boarders for a "nice pickle *whusky toddy*."[35] "So merrily did they live," said the visitor about the students, "that my only wonder was how they found time to study."[36]

The Porter children would have watched their busy mother serving young men, who spoke in a rarified language of scientific terms. They likely spoke many other languages, too. Edinburgh, as a world medical center, had students coming from all parts of the globe and a racially diverse population.[37] In these cosmopolitan surroundings, the three youngest Porter children were becoming attached to Scotland. Little Maria's first words were said to have been spoken in its dialect.[38] Later, she'd write poetry in dialect, too.[39] But Jane, who was almost four when they arrived, looked around her for reminders of Durham.

One day, Jane saw a thin, elderly man in the square wearing a light-colored coat with a plaid—the traditional body-covering tartan of Scotland. She innocently told him how much he looked like her late Grandpapa Blenkinsop. She took his small, blue hand into her own and insisted he come home with her. There Jane guilelessly introduced the stranger to her mother, as looking so like her grandfather.

What Mrs. Porter must have thought! The old man wasn't in his right mind. But perhaps remembering her late husband's mental disability, she invited him to sit down. He told them long stories about himself and his life's painful adventures. Afterward, he made an exit. Some days later, the Porters learned he was tragically run over by a wagon in the streets. He was taken to the infirmary, gravely injured.

There it was discovered, to the surprise of the medical staff, that he had been born female. He told his caregivers he was Jenny Cameron, the famous cross-dressing warrior-heroine of the 1745 Jacobite rebellion, who had, in fact, died more than fifteen years earlier. This injured man soon died in the hospital.[40] His painful story stuck with Jane. It fired her imagination from girlhood, along with the story of Cameron herself. Jane's later fiction featured many cross-dressing figures in wartime.

The imaginative Porter children craved knowledge, but Mrs. Porter wouldn't have had the time or ability to teach them. Uneducated herself, she wanted more for them. The problem was cost. Schooling was a privilege afforded primarily to boys from families of means. The elder Porter boys had won scholarships, but precious few girls of any class were given the opportunity to study. Mrs. Porter could no longer afford a private tutor for youngest son Robert, like the one John had in Durham in better economic times. However, an opportunity arose. A charity school was willing to take not just the Porter boy but also the two girls. The Niddry Street School, known as the City's Charity School, was highly experimental.[41] Its young head teacher, George Fulton, was innovative and systematic. His classroom brought out remarkable things in Jane, Robert, and Maria.

The school was located deep in a gorge, near a fish market in one of the most densely populated and oldest sections of the city. The children's walk to their new school would have involved going down a set of the city's famous stairs to a neighborhood called the Cowgate. It was known for its narrow, torturous, sunless alleys, and was sometimes described as a slum, although this doesn't capture its vitality.[42] It was dark and crowded—known as picturesque but squalid—and teeming with life.[43]

The place would have seemed something out of a gothic fairy tale to the three curious Porter children. Streets in the Cowgate had once been traversed by royalty, including King James VI. Its houses were featured in shocking legends, like the "Banishment of Lady Grange," a tale about a wife who is violently removed from a mansion by her powerful husband and forced into seven years' imprisonment on a remote island.[44] The Porter children would have grown up hearing such stories. Maria began translating them into her own original storytelling with encouragement from her new teacher.

Education was young Mr. Fulton's second profession. He'd started out as a printer's apprentice and risen in the ranks to serve as a journeyman printer. He drew on his knowledge from the publishing world in the classroom. His students used the print shop's moveable letters, mounted on pieces of wood, to memorize the alphabet. The students organized their letters in the kind of type cases used by compositors in printing houses. After learning each letter separately, they'd organize them into words and, from there, into sentences. As a method, it proved remarkably successful. Fulton's scholars were said to have gained a surprising proficiency, not only in spelling but also in pronouncing and reading English.[45]

Jane, Robert, and Maria met Fulton very early in his career, when he was an untested pedagogical innovator. He made an enormous impact on them. Fulton went on to become one of the most notable and prosperous teachers in the city, eventually educating Edinburgh's elite. He taught elocution to boys who grew up to be famed orators. He published textbooks that trained other teachers. He compiled a dictionary used in schools across Britain. Yet he well remembered the three studious, creative Porter children, who were among his very first pupils. "Jane," he recollected decades later, "might be represented (in her slender form and dignified mien,) reciting some beautiful ode; Master Robert stealing an opportunity of sketching a horse or dog, with a lead pencil, on a blank leaf of his book; and the little lovely Maria receiving a kiss of approbation from her delighted Preceptor."[46]

But Maria wasn't just the adorable, affectionate youngest child and teacher's pet. Under Fulton, with whom she started studying by age four, her literary and intellectual powers grew to be formidable. She proved a prodigy. At age five, it was said she could recite Shakespeare with precision and emphasis. She had a firm voice unmatched by her classmates. At a public examination of Fulton's students by Edinburgh's high authorities, Maria was put above a sixteen-year-old girl and named Head of the Class.[47]

Jane and Maria would have soaked up knowledge from Fulton, from their mother's medical student boarders, and from Edinburgh's historic streets, but they also had an openness to learning from those without the benefit of an education. In Scotland, as Jane later put it, it wasn't just "pastors and masters" who educated the people. She found "a spirit of wholesome knowledge in the country, pervading all ranks, which passes from one to the other like the atmosphere they breathe."[48]

Jane learned Scottish legends from the maids in the nursery and the servingmen in the kitchen. Their folk songs put baby Maria to sleep. Working-class caregivers' bedtime stories kept the Porter children up far too late and left them dreaming afterward of long-ago heroes and tall tales. The Porter family wove tall tales about itself, too. Later in life, the family would claim Robert had received his first lessons in history painting from the real-life Jacobite heroine Flora MacDonald. According to Porter family lore, they visited her, and she regaled them with an account of her glorious adventures. She'd helped Bonnie Prince Charlie (grandson of the deposed King James II) escape from the decisive Battle of Culloden in 1746. It was said young Robert became distracted during MacDonald's storytelling as his attention was drawn away by a work of art on the wall.

He couldn't take his eyes off the painting. MacDonald noticed his curiosity, stopped her narration, and asked him what he was looking at. She put Robert up on a chair to get a close-up view. She told him it was the Battle of Preston and gave him a little lecture about the earlier Jacobite rising of 1715.[49] Robert was said to have discovered there his first desire to become a history painter. Whether this encounter happened in the way the Porters later claimed or not, this much is true: they were acquainted with the MacDonald family, and Robert eventually studied and excelled in history painting.

Other brushes with greatness in Edinburgh were recorded in the Porters' accounts. Jane, Robert, and Maria said the future-famous poet and novelist Walter Scott had been their playmate. Years later, Jane would say she remembered his face from childhood.[50] Later still, Jane would write a letter to Sir Walter, calling herself and Maria his "old Scottish acquaintances of the High School-yards."[51] She didn't say friends, and Scott didn't leave any record of his early connection to the Porters.[52]

It's clearly the case that the Scotts and Porters shared a social circle in the 1780s, although the children's upbringings were completely different. Walter Scott, four years older than Jane, was a student at the tony Royal High School of Edinburgh in the High School Yards, just next door to Mrs. Porter's boardinghouse. He crossed to and from his comfortable home to his elite school, translating Horace and Virgil into English and sitting among the best minds and future leaders of Britain. The Porters' experiences were hardscrabble by comparison.

After five years, Mrs. Porter called it quits in Edinburgh. She and the youngest children moved back to her hometown of Durham, around 1785. Perhaps the boardinghouse for medical students hadn't proved profitable. More likely, it was a move made for Robert's sake, in the hope that he, like his older brothers, would win a scholarship to Durham School.

Durham had its advantages. Mrs. Porter once again had the help of trusted women. She reconnected with an old friend, Mrs. Brocket, who'd helped look after the Porter children as infants. For a short time, all five siblings would have been reunited, with William, age eleven, and John, nearly thirteen. It might have been a happy time, if their mother hadn't been destitute.

Mrs. Porter described her poverty when she approached Lord Crewe's charity. In pleading for assistance, Mrs. Porter wrote of having been "left for these six years past, to struggle with the world, & its inconveniencys, upon the poor pittance of Ten Pound a year from Government, which (tho a blessing) scarce able to afford me the means of supporting myself & children."[53] She tried to be resourceful, but her efforts gained her nothing. As she confessed, "Was I to tell all my distress to the world part of it might pity me, but few assist me." The charity sent Mrs. Porter two pounds and two shillings in October 1785.[54] That amount wasn't nearly enough to set up a new household or to launch her oldest boys into careers. They needed "situations," as they were called. Apprenticeships of some kind were necessary for aspiring middling-class boys, and these situations were rarely free.

She found a way to get her son William apprenticed to Dr. James McDonnell in Ireland. The plan was that William would follow in his father's footsteps to a medical career. Dr. McDonnell, a recent Edinburgh medical school graduate, was a talented physician who later became known as the Father of Belfast Medicine. He was probably a friend from Mrs. Porter's landlady days. In securing this apprenticeship, she successfully put young William on a path to self-sufficiency. He'd train to become an apothecary, dispensing medicine.[55]

Son John must not have inherited the talent or temperament for medicine. Mrs. Porter tried to get him into her late husband's dragoon regiment as a soldier, but her request was denied twice.[56] She wrote again to Lord Crewe's

Charity, in November 1786. She asked for money to send John to Antigua, the West Indian colony. She told the trustees the boy had the promise there, through a family friend, of a six-year position as a mercantile apprentice.[57]

This faraway situation was probably a favor from the Kerr family. The Kerrs, as Mrs. Porter would have known, profited from business interests built on the forced labor of enslaved people. John would have been hired to do work alongside, and in support of, that family's brutal exploitation of people. Lord Crewe's Charity awarded ten pounds and ten shillings to send John off to build a career in colonial trade.[58]

The situation put John on a ship, exposed to disease and a new climate, and far beyond his mother's care and influence. Mrs. Porter must have sought it out of desperation. It didn't match her politics, either. She and her late father had openly avowed radical causes. They'd supported the rights of men and the abolition of slavery as devoted followers of radical writer and politician John Wilkes. Wilkites advocated for people's liberty, freedom of expression, and full enfranchisement—for men.

Before she became Mrs. Porter, Miss Jane Blenkinsop paid a visit to the famous John Wilkes at his home in London. She later sent him a fan letter, which still survives among Wilkes' papers. She included a parcel of comforts for him, with some of her needlework, as well as words of strong support for Wilkes. He was by then in the King's Bench Prison on a charge of seditious libel. "Never a day pass's but your health is Drank by," Miss Jane Blenkinsop wrote to Wilkes, "by a set of Gents who meets at my Father's house for that purpose."[59]

Fifteen years later—as a widow and struggling mother of five in 1786—Mrs. Porter sent off her eldest son to a life that undermined her early progressive politics. With her two elder sons gone, she set up again as a landlady on Dun Cow Lane near Durham Cathedral and Durham Castle, the formidable Norman structures built on the orders of William the Conqueror in 1072, atop the high banks of the River Wear. Jane, Robert, and Maria played on its banks and in the Cathedral's cloisters.

Nestled nearby, too, was a fine library, which held the large book collection of a forward-thinking seventeenth-century bibliophile, John Cosin, Bishop of Durham. Bishop Cosin's Library was designed for clergy and scholars, not children—and certainly not for daughters of widows who kept boarding-houses. In this era, only the wealthy owned books outright, which made access to a private library an enormous privilege. Mrs. Porter had somehow used her influence to wrangle access for her precocious children to roam freely among the library's five thousand volumes, nearly whenever they pleased.[60] Jane, age ten, and Maria, age seven, would have been able to dash from their lodgings to the library in minutes. The sisters read books from "sunrise to sunset, in total abstraction from everything else."[61] Jane described it as their knowledge-seeking season.

The girls would have appeared as tiny figures in the library's enormous main room, with its high ceilings, striking windows, and ten-foot bookshelves. Atop the shelves were portraits of Aristotle, Plato, famous historians of Rome, saints, and philosophers.[62] There were full-length portraits of King Charles I and Bishop Cosin himself, the son of a tradesman who read avidly, despite having only one good eye.[63] All were men.

Over the door of the library was a Latin inscription: *Non minima pars eruditionis est bonos nosse libros*. Jane and Maria, without any classical training, would have had to be told what it said. It translates as "Not the least part of erudition is to know good books." The sisters read eyewitness histories that transported them to an idealized medieval past. Robert, when with his sisters, made drawings from prints he found in old books while the girls sat on the floor next to him, reading greedily.[64]

The Porter sisters each discovered a favorite author. Maria's was Shakespeare, whose plays she revered and regularly read aloud to family and friends. She studied his portrait for clues to the man himself. Then she and Jane would look for resemblances to Shakespeare's face among their male friends.[65] Comparing anything favorably to Shakespeare was Maria's highest praise. She may have read Shakespeare from Bishop Cosin's first folio.

Jane declared she felt as intimately acquainted with the heroes of Greece and Rome as she did with her nearest neighbors in Durham.[66] But what she cried over were the works of the sixteenth-century courtier, warrior, poet, and romance writer Sir Philip Sidney, who became her lifelong favorite and almost a living person to her. He wrote a famous cycle of love sonnets, *Astrophel and Stella*, and published a sprawling prose romance, *Arcadia*. He is known for *The Defence of Poesy*, his argument for literature's value as a moral teaching tool. Sidney claimed that literature—"poesy"—was superior to history and philosophy for moral education. Jane took that to heart. She saw Sidney as the perfect

Renaissance man, whose life and writings were virtuous and exemplary. She wanted to marry a man like him, but she also wanted to be him. Jane once joked that she was so inclined to moralizing that there must have been a mistake made at her birth. Surely, she said, she was intended for a parson.[67]

"I never thought of becoming a writer at all," Jane claimed about these years in Bishop Cosin's Library. "To learn, was my sole ambition."[68] This wasn't quite true: Jane, who rose as early as four in the morning to begin reading a book, also began writing poems, stories, and letters.[69] The sisters' earliest compositions were painstakingly copied over in their mother's handwriting, with names, titles, and dates. Jane later called hers "My Rhyming Follies." Her early sonnets are often melancholy, describing youthful days passed in adversity and "grief's black cave."[70] Maria's work was more cheerful. One of her first literary efforts, at age seven, was a poem of several stanzas in honor of her mother's birthday.[71] It became a family tradition for Maria to write a poem to her beloved parent each January eighteenth.

Getting away to read and finding time to write wasn't a given, because plucky Mrs. Porter was of unsteady health. In September 1786, she struggled with an undiagnosed condition that produced periodical excruciating pains in her stomach. She wrote to Edinburgh's famed Dr. William Cullen, who admitted he couldn't be sure what was causing her symptoms, although the word "periodical" may imply they were menstrual concerns. Her Durham doctor had prescribed the highly addictive opium-and-alcohol painkiller, laudanum, but Dr. Cullen thought Mrs. Porter might try acid drops, designed to make patients break out in a profuse sweat.[72] Neither treatment would have allowed for a solid day's work.

During Mrs. Porter's illnesses, her children's labor would have been relied upon. Maria knew at a young age how to prepare an adult's tea or dinner, and air the sheets and put them on a bed.[73] In a boardinghouse, there was always more work to do. Mrs. Porter's Durham boarders may have been visitors to the city or perhaps boys attending school with Robert. Robert, like John and William, was named a King's Scholar at Durham School after attesting, as required, that his family wasn't wealthy. These scholarships came with a coveted annual stipend for living expenses.[74] Between Robert's stipend, Mrs. Porter's army widow's pension, and the boarders, the family must have just made ends meet.

Jane and Maria, who would have regularly walked by Robert's school, could only look on with envy. It was difficult for intellectually ambitious girls to be taken seriously. But among Mrs. Porter's boarders, Jane found an older man eager to teach her. Percival Stockdale, a clergyman and a minor literary celebrity, stayed with the Porters on Dun Cow Lane when church business brought him to Durham.[75] In his fifties—almost forty years older than Jane—he was a married man, although separated and estranged from his wife, with whom he had no children. He befriended Mrs. Porter and her clever offspring.

It would have impressed the Porters that Stockdale personally knew great men of letters of the previous generation. He befriended not only the legendary Samuel Johnson—responsible for the famous milestone English Dictionary—but also the actor and theater manager David Garrick and the playwright and poet Oliver Goldsmith. During his stays in Durham, many years later, Stockdale became especially taken with young Jane. He offered advice about what she should read. She consulted with him about a planned course of study. The two exchanged letters regularly. He had a reputation for being difficult and frequently criticized the teen girl's writing style, but Jane thanked him for it.

As Jane and Maria came of age, the sisters' personalities began to diverge more strongly. Practical Jane would tie up the family's loose ends, make things work, and set things right. She learned about philosophies of education and teaching and created a book of favorite extracts from Plato and Aristotle.[76] She kept careful records of what she read. Maria, sprightly and spontaneous, loved reading aloud, especially to local little ones, delighting them with fairy tales, like "Little Red Riding Hood."[77] She doesn't seem to have kept records of her reading or to have approached her learning with the discipline of her sister, but she was a quick study, eager to share knowledge and to entertain.

Although it was brother Robert who was seen as the family's genius, its future hope, and a protector in training, all three Porter children attracted notice for their talents. One Durham neighbor, young Anne Robinson (later Mrs. Henderson), spent countless hours with the Porters as their mothers sat doing needlework while the children played on the floor before them. As an adult, Mrs. Henderson shared her myth-laden memories of the talented Porters. She remembered Robert drawing a grand battle scene on tissue paper, in order to display it in the front window of their lodgings to passers-by. Next to him on the floor, Jane, Maria, and young Anne Robinson were often wordlessly active. Maria's voice would break the silence. She'd pull a manuscript out of her pocket with one of her original compositions and hold the room in thrall as she recited it.[78]

Among the stories Maria may have been working on at this time was "Sir Alfred; Or, The Baleful Tower," a surreal story about a knight, a virtuous heroine, a sylph goddess, a bewitching woman, and a hermit. The story ends in a happy marriage between hero and heroine, after the death of an avaricious father. Maria was also writing a surprisingly worldly story, "The Noble Courtezan," featuring a married, half-dressed femme fatale, who tries to seduce a young, virtuous orphan-hero. The hero rebuffs the passionate, beautiful woman, even after she reveals her breasts and propositions him. A mysterious cross-dressed page, who warns the hero about her, ends up being a chaste heroine who loves him. The two marry in the end.

Jane, Robert, Mrs. Porter, and the Robinsons became Maria's trusted audience for reciting her stories. One day, after Maria read aloud, everyone praised her achievement. Then, according to Mrs. Henderson, Jane rose as if she were a tragic actress on the stage. She told Maria, "You have written well." Then Jane paused for some moments before declaring, with authority, "When I write, I shall write history." It was said she swept out of the room with the air of a duchess.[79] Mrs. Henderson's story suggests the Porter children were remarkably self-possessed and unafraid to perform.

After Robert graduated from the Durham School, Mrs. Porter moved her family yet again. At first, they traveled to Coleraine, perhaps trying to gain favor with Porter family relatives there, and no doubt to check on William and his Belfast physician-mentor. Mrs. Porter made connections that eventually allowed her to place William in a new situation with one of his Porter uncles, a wealthy medical man in Jamaica. Eldest son John remained in Antigua with the Kerr family. The vicious environment of wealth and slavery in the colonial West Indies would shape each boy's character and life course—for the worse.

Securing this situation for William must have seemed a small success, but the move to Ireland proved a disaster, filled with what Mrs. Porter called "misery and tears."[80] Early in 1790, she packed up the children and moved to London, where she schemed with them about how make their creative talents pay. Robert drew, painted, and promoted his artwork, trying to win over powerful patrons. Jane and Maria readied fiction and poems to submit to publishers and editors.

"I am very busy writing the story's," Jane reported to her mother, "Maria says they will do very well."[81]

CHAPTER 2

London's Covent Garden and Maria's Teenage Tales (1790–96)

The goal in moving to London in the summer of 1790 was for Robert to be accepted into the renowned school at the Royal Academy of Art. The odds of a boy of Robert's age and background gaining admission were long, but Mrs. Porter placed a bet on her talented son. If he found success, it would secure the family's future. Jane and Maria were proving strikingly beautiful girls, but they had no fortunes. Robert's advancement might forward his sisters' marriage prospects.

When the Porters first came to London, Jane was fourteen, Robert was thirteen, and Maria was eleven, yet Robert could have been mistaken for a younger boy. His artistic talents were considered astonishing even for thirteen, but it must have seemed helpful for him to pass for younger, to appear more of a prodigy. A year or two shaved off Robert's age—and then Maria's, too, since the two weren't twins—were little white lies the family began to tell.

In relocating to London, Mrs. Porter left behind every solid support system, although friends and family may have provided contacts to smooth her way. Percival Stockdale, Mrs. Porter's former boarder and Jane's literary mentor, occasionally visited London to negotiate with publishers and printers. He called on the Porters whenever he was in town. The fact that he didn't stay under their roof suggests Mrs. Porter didn't try to set up again as a landlady. Needlework, and her small army widow's pension, served as her means of support.

As Mrs. Porter tried to make ends meet, she contemplated dressmaking schemes. She explored ways to sell ready-made gowns at home or abroad.[1] Rightly anxious, and occasionally desperate, she couldn't shield her children from these financial worries. Around this time, Maria wrote a story, "The Children of Fauconbridge," about two brothers and a sister of a widowed mother, all of them starving. The girl tries to make a living by taking in mending. She's denied further work when her employers wrongly suspect she's a thief. To feed her sick mother, the girl turns to begging on the streets. Her brothers worry that their beautiful sister will end up prostituting herself. It must have cut close to the bone for a girl of twelve or so to be writing about these subjects. The story shows an intimate knowledge of poverty and pain.

Mrs. Porter, in her struggle to provide for her family, had written a letter to a faraway nephew in Jamaica in July 1790. She must have begged for money, because he wrote back to tell her he had none.[2] He was a mere clerk, although he did eventually send twelve pounds, a sum he'd scrimped and saved. In a later letter, he also delivered unwelcome news that her son William was in debt to local shopkeepers. He tried to offer his aunt words of consolation.[3] Nature had been kind and blessed her with extraordinary children, with talents to compensate for their lack of fortune, he wrote.

The family's first years in London brough frequent setbacks and moves from one modest apartment to the next. Mrs. Porter eventually landed in rented lodgings at 38 Bedford Street in Covent Garden, a vibrant center for London's art, theater, and culture. Acrobats, actors, and entertainers mingled in the streets, alongside sellers of fruits, vegetables, and flowers. It was home to celebrated coffeehouses and taverns. Covent Garden was also notorious for drunken revelry, property crimes, and sex workers. To many mothers, it wouldn't have seemed an ideal place to raise poor, vulnerable teenagers, especially daughters.

It was, however, nearby to the Royal Academy Schools. Robert entered the grueling, high-stakes process that offered admission to just twenty students a year, on average.[4] He passed each successive test. He was formally admitted as a pupil on February 18, 1791. The schools provided its boys and young men—many in their late teens and twenties and a few in their thirties—with free studio space, a community of up-and-coming artists. and a widely publicized opportunity to exhibit their best work. The art students had to provide their own materials but were allowed up to six years of training, tuition free. If they exhibited work that won a prize, then they were granted a studentship for life. Jane and Maria once again would have looked on as Robert gained educational opportunities denied to girls.

The times were tumultuous. People in France were shifting the course of history, having stormed the Bastille prison in Paris in July 1789, and initiating a revolution against the corrupt monarchy, church, and state. Revolutionaries put forward a new vision for the future, with their *Declaration of the Rights of Man and of the Citizen*. The British watched events in France with rapt attention and, for some, with great hope. The Porter family, with their history of supporting radical politics, considered themselves friendly to the French Jacobin philosophies advocating for a more inclusive, equitable society. To Jane's view, the vocal opponents of these ideas, called "anti-Jacobins," were practicing a kind of bigotry.[5]

Artists in London also tended to be sympathetic to the revolutionaries in France. Benjamin West—regarded as the founder of English historical painting—was an open supporter of political rebels, although King George III was his patron.[6] For a time, West's revolutionary sympathies were tolerated by the government, and he'd soon become the second president of the Royal Academy. West took a special, almost parental interest in young Robert Ker Porter.[7] It was said West appreciated the vigor and spirit of the boy's artwork.[8] Vigor and spirit weren't only artistic labels then but political ones, too.

Robert's rise as an artist proved remarkable. He'd gone from a dreamy, doodling Edinburgh charity schoolboy to a wunderkind at the toniest art school in the country in less than a decade. He was a diligent student. At the Academy schools, Robert often signed in first in the attendance book and helped in the classroom. He was said to be a very intelligent-looking and gentlemanly lad, whose childlike appearance, compared to the rest of his older classmates, attracted notice.[9] He was treated by the other artists with a familial tenderness.

The Porter sisters benefited from the social and intellectual world opening up to their talented brother. Robert, known at the school as the darling of his mother, was eager to introduce his new acquaintances to his family.[10] Fellow student Martin Archer Shee (another future Royal Academy president) was asked several times by young Porter to take tea at his nearby home. At first, Shee hesitated, worried it was a boy's unwelcome imposition on an unsuspecting parent.

But one night, after class, Shee agreed to go home with Robert. He found Mrs. Porter to be a widow of amiable manners. The greater surprise was the boy's two stunning sisters, in the first bloom of youth. When Shee walked into the Porters' small and humble sitting room, he found Jane seated in deep and earnest study of a favorite author. He was thunderstruck.

"Never," he would say, in years afterward, "did I see any living face, the outline and expression of which bore so strong a resemblance to the Venus de Medici."[11]

Other artists who met the Porter sisters were similarly moved. Soon Jane and Maria were sitting as models not only for their brother but also for many Royal Academy artists. Their new friend, the melancholic Thomas Kearsley, painted a portrait of Jane, which was said to capture her rapt soul through her expressive eyes.[12] Maria's and Jane's likenesses appeared uncredited in works by famous painters—Maria as Hebe, the Greek goddess of youth, and Jane as the biblical Jephthah's virginal daughter.[13] New artist friends, taken, at first, by the Misses Porters' beauty, were impressed by their minds and characters. The sisters were clever, confident, lively, and eager to share their opinions—innocent but not naïve.

At the Royal Academy, Robert quickly proved his talents. By 1792, at age fifteen, he'd won his first silver medal, judged just behind fellow student J. M. W. Turner's work in its quality. Jane saw her fair-haired brother bend his head to receive the medal around his neck from the hands of Benjamin West.[14] Robert later called it a time when the "*Light* and *Chaos* of the fine arts" were first breaking on him. He lamented that the chaos often governed his actions.[15]

The Porter household had its chaotic elements, too. There seem to have been few rules, which meant there was little for the teens to rebel against. But when Percival Stockdale visited the Porters' lodgings, he was horrified to see the girls surrounded by young coxcombs, who fluttered around them. He was insulted Jane would choose the company of these insincere, insensitive boys over his own. Of course, Stockdale must have been jealous. Their fluttering made it impossible for him—an old married man—to capture young Jane's full attention, as he felt was his due.[16]

In general, Jane, Robert, and Maria were respectful toward their elders, especially their selfless, permissive, plainspoken mother. They dearly loved and wanted to please her. Maria signed one letter to Mrs. Porter, "Your Affectionate and Dutiful Child, A. M. Porter," preferring androgynous initials. Perhaps she was copying Robert, who'd taken, for a time, to signing the attendance book at the Royal Academy Schools as "R. K. Porter, Esq.," pretending to a landownership status he didn't have.[17] All three teens sought respectable ways to add to the family's desperately small income.

Robert drew and painted while his sisters made up playful, powerful female identities and experimented with writing under invented names. As Jane Austen's narrator once put it in *Northanger Abbey* (1818), "What young lady of common gentility will reach the age of sixteen without altering her name as far as she can?" In August 1793, Jane, seventeen, wrote to Maria, fourteen, as if she were living in a Gothic novel, describing cloisters, turrets, and meadows. She called Maria "Lady Grease." "My dear Grease!" she addressed her, "I make bold to tell your Ladyship that the elements are up in arm's against me, the Wind's are whistling behind the Arras, and the rain beating against my casements, the murky clouds gather o'er the Welkin, and yet, I write to thee."[18]

Maria wrote back using the name "Idalia," and dubbed Jane "Arethusa." Idalia and Arethusa were carefully crafted alter egos that matched their personality traits. Idalia was the rule-breaking, drama-attracting heroine of an old racy romance, *Idalia; or The Unfortunate Mistress*, published by the bestselling fiction writer Eliza Haywood in 1723. Beautiful teenage Idalia inspired fatal duels, cross-dressed, and accidentally caused a woman to fall in love with her. She experienced catastrophes from shipwrecks to stabbings.

Jane's taken name emphasized her as Idalia's opposite. Arethusa was the chaste, lovely wood nymph from Greek mythology who tragically caught the eye of a river god while bathing. She escaped from the god with the help of a goddess but was transformed into a spring. Arethusa was depicted on coins as a stately looking beauty, with wild, curly locks, just like Jane's hair. (Maria would later publish a story, "Tour of the Lakes," featuring a heroine named Arethusa.) "Dear Arethusa," Maria wrote to Jane in 1793, "Idalia desires her love to you, and begs you will write to her, a very, very long Epistle. She commands it: and as she is your Queen obey."[19]

Maria easily moved from her mock-royal voice to that of a taunting sister. She poked fun at Jane's letter-writing, acknowledging her occasional well-written lines but skewering her sister's bad handwriting. It was all in good fun. "I never was less in Humour for writing lord bless me!" Maria-as-Idalia proclaimed, despite recording page after page of high-flown rhetoric that shared gossip of the whereabouts of their boy-admirers.

That summer of 1793, as the sisters exchanged teasing letters under fanciful pseudonyms, a momentous step was taken by the family to try to make money from Maria's fiction. Five of Maria's short stories about family strife, thwarted romance, and happy reunion were collected. Among them was that heart-rending tale of youthful poverty, "The Children of Fauconbridge," as well as a fanciful, supernatural story, "The Cottage of Glen: A Wizard Tale."

Maria's stories feature innocent but surprisingly sexually knowing heroines. Some characters' names are drawn from Shakespeare—Ophelia, Olivia, Henry, Edward. Other names were inspired by romance, including Olerelgin, Kilwarlock, and Milderine. Outlandish as they were, the stories were rooted in the places of her youth. Experiences of Scottish poverty feature in a story about a tartan-hooded widow on a pension who catches fish and geese for food while her only daughter fashions sandals out of rabbit skins. The book's dedication lists Maria's address as Bedford Street, Covent Garden, which is fitting, because London's sights and sounds clearly inform the stories, too.

Someone decided it was wise for Maria to publicly avow her authorship. Perhaps Mrs. Porter agreed with the late Samuel Johnson's quip: "No man but a blockhead ever wrote except for money." Maria, though so young, understood why she was selling her stories. "From the first time I published, money was my object," she later privately confessed, "support for myself and for others dearer to me than self."[20]

The title of her first book was *Artless Tales. By Anna Maria Porter. Ornamented with a frontispiece, designed by her Brother, R. K. Porter.* It signaled the debut collaboration of gifted siblings. The word "artless" was no doubt carefully chosen. It was meant to communicate the innocence of the stories and the author. Yet advertising Maria's real name involved risks. Half of the fiction writers publishing books then signed their names and half didn't. Using a real name was an irrevocable choice. By age fourteen, Maria was indelibly in the public eye as an author, or rather, as an authoress, as she styled herself.

The Porters sold Maria's book "by subscription," an early form of crowdfunding that raised money to bring out an as-yet-unpublished book. The author, who assumed all financial risk, might reap the full reward, depending on copies presold. The Porters would pay a printer to produce the volume. Any money collected above costs would be theirs. For the method to pay off, the Porters became salespeople, asking supporters to pay up front for an eventual copy of the future work. These buyers, referred to as subscribers, expected public recognition for their investment, with their names printed in the book's subscription list.

The cost to publish a typical edition of five hundred copies for one slim volume might be fifty pounds. Ten more pounds might have been needed to have Robert's frontispiece design engraved, unless a friend did the work for free. Sixty pounds was an enormous sum, but if the Porters got enough subscribers, they could collect even more in advance. Opportunities for further profit were possible after publication through sales in shops. The Porters partnered with three booksellers in London, Northampton, and Durham.

The family's efforts were successful, attracting an impressive 466 subscribers, some of whom bought as many as a dozen copies. If *Artless Tales* sold for three shillings, the likely price subscribers were asked to pay, then the book was profitable. Assuming the Porters and their agents collected diligently and struck a good bargain for printing costs, they may have cleared thirty-five pounds—enough to live on for several months.

The subscription list is a telling document that helps trace the family's circles of support. Robert's artist friends and mentors subscribed in droves. Benjamin West subscribed, as did Martin Archer Shee. In Jamaica, Maria's brother William may have collected names and funds from two dozen subscribers, including the lieutenant governor and the multigenerational Betts family, a widow and daughter. Through these wealthy white colonial subscribers, Maria's book took some portion of its profits, secondhand, from the labor of enslaved people. At the same time, Maria's book was patronized by some of the country's most important antislavery activists, including Granville Sharp and his daughters.[21] By the age of fifteen, Maria's own attitudes toward the institution of slavery may have been continuing to take shape. Her earliest stories describe inequities of gender and class but not yet of race.

Maria's dedication to *Artless Tales* signaled that she understood the humility and modesty expected of a young female author. It was common for a woman writer to claim she didn't want to publish her book or that someone talked her into it, which allowed the author to deflect charges of ambition. It was also common to apologize for a book's quality, lowering reader expectations and forestalling criticism, conventions Maria closely followed for the rest of her career. Maria also apologized for her youth and inexperience. She humbly asks readers to point out errors, so that she might correct them in future works, if any should appear.[22] She says her stories were written at age thirteen and dates her preface December 16, 1792—one day before she turned fourteen. But by the time *Artless Tales* was finally published in autumn 1793, Maria was nearly fifteen. This subtle subtraction of two years from her age, whether her own idea or her mother's, cleared the way for her to pass herself off as younger than she was for the rest of her life.

Maria's book was, by many measures, a remarkable success. Had *Artless Tales* succeeded only with its subscribers, it would still have been something, but the notice it got in the main review periodicals of the day was a coup for a first-time author. The Whig-leaning *Monthly Review*'s brief notice calls the stories deficient but extraordinary "effusions of childhood." It invites Miss Porter "sedulously to exert those talents of which she has given these early proofs."[23] This was strong encouragement in the pages of one of the top review periodicals in the country.

The notice in the Tory-leaning *Critical Review*, by contrast, was cutting. The anonymous reviewer took issue with the book's title, which he suggests is nonsensical. Tales require art, and art implies labor, so there can be no such thing as an artless tale, he says. The reviewer pauses to acknowledge that his reflections may be thought severe, but he feels he must be severe, not only for this one author's sake, but also for all those of her deluded type—the young writer "misled by an early genius, and the praises of partial friends." Miss Anna Maria Porter, and others like her, make the dangerous mistake of plucking "the blossoms for a gaudy nosegay, which, by being left upon the tree, might have matured into wholesome and well-tasted fruit."[24]

The sexualized Garden of Eden overtones are positively sickening. Maria's mistake, in this thinly veiled rhetoric, was not retaining her literary innocence. As an avowed author, she'd now been ruined, with her unripened fruits of the mind plucked too soon. The reviewer slyly suggests she's prostituted herself, like the sex workers of her Covent Garden neighborhood. Young female authors, to this reviewer, can't become mature, wholesome women, or, it would seem, respectable wives.

The first of the five Porter children to marry was William, in his twentieth year, to Miss Lydia Helen Betts.[25] Mrs. Porter would have learned of it by letter, months after it happened in October 1794, in Spanish Town, Jamaica. At the time, the groom was a sailor on the frigate HMS *Success*, under the command of a brutal and sadistic captain who flogged half of his eighty-five-member crew that year, killing two of them.[26] Because William understandably didn't stay long in this post, it turned out to be a less than ideal moment to marry, from a career standpoint.

William's new wife was a stranger to his immediate family, although the marriage had been approved by its nominal patriarch, eldest brother John, still in Antigua. Robert feared William had chosen his bride too hastily. Jane and Maria would have known their new "sister" (as a sister-in-law was then called) by name, thanks to her widowed mother and older sister having been among *Artless Tales*'s subscribers in Jamaica. Lydia Betts was a younger daughter of a minor landowning military man who'd been dead for fifteen years. He'd come from an extended family of British enslavers in Jamaica. Mrs. Lydia Porter (as she was now called) wasn't rich, but she brought some ill-begotten small fortune to the marriage.[27] The Betts family must not have insisted on a financially advantageous marriage, because William brought no assets at all.

William, after having separated somehow from the disastrous HMS *Success*, traveled with Lydia to Rochester, England, on a newlywed trip, early in 1795. Rochester was probably chosen for the nuptial visit because a prosperous cousin on their mother's side, William Blythman Blenkinsop, had settled there with his wife. After leaving Durham, this cousin had risen in the world as a tradesman, military man, and liberal friend of reform.[28] Blenkinsop was kind to his Porter relatives. There must have been a hope he'd do something generous for William and Lydia, who didn't have sufficient funds to live on or raise a middle-class family.

William was contemplating looking for a post in the East Indies or Africa.[29] Once he passed his naval surgeon's examinations, as he'd do in the spring of 1795, he'd seek a situation on a ship.[30] Where this would have left Lydia was a question mark, but there were greater obstacles. William lacked the resources to take up such a situation, even if it were offered. He'd have needed not only the Royal Navy's appointment or commission but also an initial outlay of cash to purchase the needed instruments and medicines. William required patronage.

Among the London branch of the Porter family, money was, as ever, painfully short, so it was decided that Maria, age sixteen, should be the family's sole emissary to greet the newlyweds. She would travel alone for thirty miles by stagecoach to Rochester. Once Maria arrived in Rochester, she'd stay with her mother's friend, who ran a boardinghouse and school. That was a welcome novelty. It would be the very first time Maria slept in a bed by herself.[31] There in Rochester, in April 1795, Maria would reunite with William and welcome his bride.

Maria would have been a useful person to have on hand in Rochester, because she could serve as a female companion to Lydia. The two women could go about town together in ways either one of them alone wasn't supposed to for propriety's sake. But for the Porters the idea that genteel women ought to travel in twos was more polite pretense than actual practice. Maria's unaccompanied travel on the stagecoach became a money-saving habit she and Jane would continue throughout their lives, although they didn't advertise it.

Rochester was a pleasant, navigable town, situated in a valley, known for its healthy air and spring water. Maria had loved spending time there in the past. Walks on the nearby banks of the River Medway were beautiful and suited her bucolic tastes. On previous visits, she had enjoyed the city's concerts, balls, and parties, too. She welcomed leaving behind the smoky bustle of London for the delights of Rochester, Kent. It was a pleasant surprise to discover, too, that she was in great social demand in this smaller city in ways she never had been in the metropolis.

Her good looks attracted attention. Maria often wore her long, fair hair braided back, like a Madonna, and sometimes knotted it up in a Grecian style.[32] She wrote home to Jane and her mother about her social conquests in Rochester and said she was surprised and pleased at the stir she was causing. When Maria went out with her cousin's family to see a concert, she decided to wear her yellow turban, which captured the attention of young men with roving eyes. Mothers with unmarried sons—ladies and soldiers alike—were trying to find out who she was.

Then the introductions began. Her brother William presented her to a fellow sailor he thought Maria might like. The sailor was pleasant enough, but she didn't admire him back. At one ball, she told Jane she was asked to dance by five frightful-looking men and three redcoats, attractive for their uniforms, if nothing else. She rejected them all. To her amazement, her selectivity drew her even more attention. The fashionable set must have marveled at this girl who could afford to turn down so many dance partners and would-be suitors.[33] The flattering attention was becoming unwelcome.

A visit that had started off as a social triumph began to sour further when Maria found herself drawn into William and Lydia's already struggling marriage. One day, William took Maria aside to ask for help. He wanted Maria to instruct Lydia. To *correct* her, he said. William had discovered his wife had little solid knowledge. "Judge my dear Jane both of my surprize, and my distress," Maria wrote home, "when he told me . . . to take Lydia on a long walk, and give her a long lecture, upon her wilful ignorance; to advise her to pay more attention to her mind, and to study."

He thought she made an idiotic appearance in public. William confessed about his wife, "I find it is impossible to raise her from her mental sloth, she can understand nothing, nor will she read anything." He wanted Maria to intervene. He asked his sister to pretend that she'd noticed Lydia's intellectual shortcomings. By no means, William said, should Maria suggest Lydia's flaws were observed by her husband. Maria's pleas for Lydia to improve herself should seem as if they came from her new sister alone. "Represent to her," William told Maria, "the danger she is in of losing my affections forever."

William cried as he asked for this great favor, and Maria was moved. She felt for him and was deeply worried for them both. She decided to try to do what her brother asked and soon found an opportunity to see Lydia alone. Their private interview lasted for an hour and a half, during which Maria delivered William's messages by proxy, as if they were her own.

Lydia listened in stony silence. She responded to Maria only twice. Once she said, "I will." A second time she said, "Yes to be sure." Otherwise, Lydia gave no hints as to her thoughts. When Maria ended this long lecture, she gave her new sister an assignment. From henceforth, Lydia must spend three hours a day in reading books, in order to eventually render her a suitable companion for her educated husband. With a steady diet of reading, Lydia would acquire more fitting things to contribute to conversations, in private and public. What man, Maria said, would want to be married to a woman with but a commonly pretty face to recommend her!

Finally, Lydia responded by blurting out a more substantial remark. She defiantly told Maria, "Reading wouldn't make me talk." Maria was shocked that Lydia was so unmoved. She vowed to change nothing, and felt no shame in herself. If Lydia didn't want to improve her mind, despite these warnings and admonitions, then there wasn't much that could be done. Lydia showed no interest in her husband's happiness. Maria broke the bad news to William in a conversation that must have solidified the emotional bond between brother and sister, despite confirming the rift with his wife.

When Maria wrote home about it to her sister, Jane was appalled. "Poor William," Jane wrote back, "Oh what a dreadful, irksome life lays before him, to be tied to such an ugly, idiotical, unfeeling woman forever." The sisters couldn't imagine why William had done it—why he'd brought this woman into their learned, curious, ambitious, attractive family. Lydia wasn't even that rich, and her mother owned enslaved people. Jane and Maria had pity for the world's Lydias and understood very well how they were born and bred. What Jane and Maria couldn't understand is why anyone with their sister's deficiencies would refuse to improve, given the chance. William had chosen his wife poorly, but Lydia had dug in her heels, refusing to better herself, even if only to please her new husband.

Another predictable outcome was that William, by sending Maria to do his bidding, made it a challenge for his wife to grow closer to his sister. Lydia may have been jealous of Maria's social triumph at Rochester, but after this failed lecture, there was little hope of a friendship between them. Maria reported that William had become very dejected. She rightly predicted about Lydia, "I fear he will soon hate her." Even worse, Maria told Jane, "Everyone here appears to despise her." Maria pulled no punches in summing up the newest member of their family: "It is in vain to dissemble her real character. I am obliged to own she is stupid."[34]

Sending Maria to Rochester to play the role of female companion to Lydia had been a disaster. The Porter sisters would soon come to a righteous cynicism about men's romantic and marital dealings. But Lydia's example proved that women, too, could be culpable for failed marriages. Her case cemented the idea that properly educating girls was necessary to their own happiness, as well as to their potential future husbands and entire families. One positive thing to come out of the trip was that it added to Jane and Maria's growing observations and fund of knowledge to use in their novels.

Maria was working on a new collection of tales that year, which would come to be called *Artless Tales II*. Its lead story was "Elinor, or the Errors of Education." It was set in Kent. There Elinor, a heroine from a once-wealthy family now in reduced circumstances, is described as a young woman born with a lofty soul that would have been capable of noble exertions, if her wrong education had not perverted her. She indulged in foibles that grew into serious errors of judgment. The fictional Elinor felt deep envy. She was thoughtless, credulous, and full of resentment, although affectionate and dutiful to her parents. But that loyalty, too, turned out to be a problem, because her parents were both deeply flawed. Elinor lets her family's ambitions dictate her choices. She marries a nobleman, who "fancied that he loved her with an unalterable ardour," but possessing her as his wife convinces him what he'd felt wasn't a lasting attachment. His love for Elinor dies away by degrees.[35]

Elinor's fictional tale resembles the experiences of William and Lydia in many ways. In the story, however, things lurch toward a happy ending after Elinor's marriage, steering clear of the messiness Maria observed in Rochester. Maria gave her heroine a second chance. Elinor finds her way back from this ill-chosen marriage through a love of books and poetry-writing. Her selfish nobleman husband dies, which leaves her free to wed the untitled man she truly loves—and who loves her in return. Along with "Elinor," Maria included two other short stories that featured strong, complicated, passionate, book-loving heroines. The heroines' original verses (actually Maria's) are woven into the story's pages.

In the fall 1795, *Artless Tales, by Anna Maria Porter, Vol. II*, was printed for the author and published by London's Hookham and Carpenter. It was reprinted in 1796, under a slightly different title, *Artless Tales; or, Romantic Effusions of the Heart*. This time, the book wasn't published by subscription but rather at the author's expense and financial risk. Her family would have paid for the printing but hoped to recoup costs through sales that might come after publication.

Maria's publishers, Hookham and Carpenter, were known for running a circulating library, a popular type of local business that allowed its paying members to rent out books. Maria must have hoped her book would do well in this market. Hookham and Carpenter had a good track record, having published works by the reclusive bestselling Gothic novelist Ann Radcliffe—whom the Porters revered—as well as the society novelist Susannah Gunning, and the teenage poet Elizabeth Benger, with whom the sisters would soon become close friends.[36]

By calling her book *Artless Tales* a second time, Maria was ignoring the *Critical Review*'s complaints about her original title. It was a bold move, defying a powerful reviewer. It was also clever marketing, because her second book could function as a continuation volume. It made her into an author one might follow from book to book. Readers were accustomed to renting and reading volumes of novels in quick succession, so after renting *Artless Tales*, they might take up *Artless Tales Volume II* next to it on the circulating library shelf.

In the preface to the 1795 printing of *Artless Tales Volume II*, Maria claimed her friends talked her into keeping the title. She refers to her previous cruel reviewer, trying to placate him. She writes that, since she's now sixteen and has undertaken three further years of study of the best authors, she hopes her book is improved and stripped of the gaudy tinsel he perceived in the first volume. In the subsequent 1796 edition, she scales back that deference.[37] For all her declared modesty, Maria presents herself as an author who isn't going away.

The attempts to please her first hostile reviewer didn't work. The passionate, sexually knowing stories of *Artless Tales Volume II* proved too much for some prudish critics, including the *Critical Review*. Its reviewer again damned Maria's book in a strongly worded takedown. The reviewer reminded the public of the author's history and remarked that, two years before, he'd hoped that, one day in the future, her genius might, "with assiduous cultivation reward the care bestowed upon it." This is far more generous than what he'd previously said. Yet he declared, in the royal third person, "We are sorry this care has *not* been bestowed." With this second volume, he believed, she'd overstepped in every way. *Artless Tales II*, the reviewer concludes, "disgusts us with the most extravagant language of a passion which at present she ought scarcely to be acquainted with, even by name." This young female author, the reviewer implies, must be disgustingly passionate, too. The reviewer's final advice to Maria is harsh and clear: "We sincerely advise this young lady to lay her pen entirely aside for ten years, and to apply herself to the serious improvement of her mind."

It's a lecture similar to what Maria had once been asked to give to her sister-in-law, Lydia, although the reviewer's desired outcome is different. William wanted Maria to tell Lydia to improve her mind to save her failing marriage. Maria's reviewer wants her to give up authorship in order to become eligible as a conventional, good wife. If Maria reads serious things, the reviewer states, and acquires some useful knowledge, then, at the end of her decade of sequestering, "we hope she will find something better to do than write at all."[38]

Maria, sixteen, and Jane, nineteen, must have read this advice. They ignored it.

CHAPTER 3

Two Girls Masquerading as Society Gentlemen

Jane's and Maria's Early Fictions and the Caulfield Brothers (1794–97)

"I am afraid you are jesting about this Mr. Wade," Robert wrote to Jane. "He is only a child of your own brain, to raise the curiosity of your B[rothe]r Bob."[1]

Whatever Jane had written to Robert in praise of her new friend Wade wasn't a joke. In late 1794, brothers Wade and Henry Caulfield came into the Porter sisters' lives like a revelation. Robert must have been gone from London, painting portraits or small church altar pieces, when the Caulfields entered the scene. Jane and Maria both thought sensitive eldest son Wade the nearest thing to male perfection they'd ever encountered. His witty, lively younger brother, Henry, was also devastatingly attractive.

Wade Caulfield was closer to Jane's age and Henry Caulfield to Maria's. In the earliest days of their friendship with the boys, the Porter sisters would stroll teasingly by the Caulfields' father's house on College Street near Westminster Abbey. The boys would stare out the window at the girls or call out to them on the street. Then they'd meet up in nearby St. James's Park, seemingly by chance. Once, when Wade was passing by on horseback, he bowed to Jane, so she approached him, kissed his hand, and smiled.[2] If Maria ever failed to bow to Wade, he'd fly off in disappointment.[3] Another time, when Jane was mistreated by a brutal fellow in the park—verbally and perhaps physically assaulted—Wade rescued her as if he were her brother.[4]

Just coming into manhood at fifteen and seventeen, Henry and Wade Caulfield were capturing Jane and Maria's hearts, minds, and imaginations. The Porters and the Caulfields not only shared in the first stirrings of romantic desire but also matured together as writers and budding public figures. The Caulfields were at the center of the Porter siblings' group of ambitious, talented teenage artists, poets, writers, editors, and intellectuals. For Jane and Maria, Wade and Henry Caulfield would inspire hero worship and serve as models for fictional heroes for the next decade and beyond.

Wade Francis Caulfield and Henry Edwin Allen Caulfield had been born into an old Anglo-Scots-Irish family of property and status. The surname Caulfield (sometimes spelled Caulfeild) may come from anglicized Gaelic words for "battle" and "chief." Their military father was Wade Toby Caulfield, Esq., of Raheenduff, Ireland, a captain in the Prince of Wales's Dragoon Guards and a great grandson of a viscount. The two families, Porter and Caulfield, shared one connection: Their fathers had served at the Battle of Minden against Prussian forces in 1759, during the Seven Years' War, Mr. Caulfield as a captain and the late Mr. Porter as a surgeon.[5]

Like Jane and Maria, the Caulfield brothers knew what it was to lose a parent at a young age. The boys lost their well-born mother, Janet Ruthven Caulfield, daughter of a Scottish lord, after she'd given birth to more than a dozen children, many of whom died in infancy. After her death, old Mr. Caulfield remarried another woman of property and had more children with her. The two sons of his first marriage somehow lost his paternal affection. Mrs. Porter took in the emotionally neglected Caulfield teens at a time when her own sons were far from home.

Wade had expectations of an independent fortune when he reached twenty-one. At age sixteen, he'd followed his father's footsteps into military life. He became an ensign in the First Regiment of Foot Guards and served under the Duke of York in Holland, early in the French Revolutionary conflict. He advanced to lieutenant.[6] Wade would regale Jane and Maria with colorful stories about his dangerous military service on the Continent. They must have stored up these well-told tales in their memories, for future use in their fiction.[7] Although sensitive Wade may have seemed destined to become a future war hero, he had a wicked sense of humor. He wrote clever poems ridiculing fellow officers. Wade had thick, dark hair and a countenance so fine that Jane thought it could imprint itself on the heart of others.[8]

His younger brother Henry was even more gorgeous, if less heroic. Henry had followed in Wade's footsteps and obtained a commission in the foot guards, but military life never suited him quite so well.[9] He was just as clever yet was livelier, earning a reputation as the gayest of the gay. Henry was also athletic, an accomplished skater whose feats on ice could attract crowds.[10] A surviving portrait reveals a tall man, with brown eyes, an aquiline nose, bright cheeks, and full lips. Wavy brown hair and sideburns frame his angular face. His tight breeches accentuate long, muscular legs, then called "well turned." Henry looks dramatically off into the distance, relaxed and confident. Artists sought him out as a live model.[11] Robert would end up painting portraits of the attractive Caulfields, as well as of his beautiful sisters.[12]

The Caulfield brothers became Jane and Maria's male muses in poetry and prose. Maria wrote "Beauty: Sonnet to H. Caulfield," describing his perfect face and the bloom of his rosy cheek. This unpublished poem records Henry's glowing aspect and his "lip's tint" on which she loved "alone to gaze." It describes how his beauty steals the poet's ardor-filled heart and puts her in raptures. "Unsated still I look," the poem's speaker confesses.[13] This was exceptionally forward, passionate language, beyond anything Maria had included in *Artless Tales*.

The Porters and Caulfields expanded their circle to include other talented literary teens. Poet-editors Richard Davenport and Peter Courtier helped to shape Jane's and Maria's writing. The witty future-famous literary brothers James and Horace Smith served as another set of beloved companions. Jane and Maria developed brief crushes on the Smiths. The sisters made friends among their own sex, too. They began to spend time with Wade and Henry's sisters, Kitty and Jessie. They also formed a female trio with the flirtatious Selina Granville Wheler. This friend group wrote poems to and about each other and helped one another move forward in the literary world. Once they began publishing books, Robert and his artist friends would illustrate their works.

The Porters, Caulfields, and Smiths, along with Wheler, regularly met up for walks in the park and in Westminster Abbey, where they wandered together, admiring its rich history and fine objects. One day, Wade was so affected by viewing a work of art that he burst into tears, then found it impossible to shake his melancholy. Others in the group moved on, but Jane remained behind, choosing instead to comfort Wade for the rest of the day. "So much sensibility in one so young," Jane wrote in her diary, "has impressed me with the strongest interest in the future fate of so fine a heart."[14]

These teens spent countless hours together at the Porters' lodgings. Mrs. Porter's home served as an all-hours salon, with no curfew and rarely any pretense of chaperoning. Sometimes Wade and Henry called twice a day—morning and night, for two to three hours at a time. Jane's diary from August 1796 includes four entries in a row: "Wade and Henry," "Wade and Henry," "Wade and Henry," and "Wade & Henry as usual."[15] Wade's regiment was quartered in greater London. Its officers had time on their hands while they awaited orders as the French Revolution unfolded.

Jane and Maria were doing less than they should have (according to the polite world) to hide their feelings for these young male friends, although they did begin to use code names for them in their private letters, such as "Agamemnon," "Endymion," "Apollo," and "Lindor."[16] Commander Agamemnon was war hero Wade. Endymion—the irresistible, captivating hunter—may have been Henry. Apollo was their nickname for their wise, melancholy artist friend Thomas Kearsley, who'd begun to show a growing preference for Maria. Lindor was probably one of the brilliant, cherubically beautiful Smith brothers.

Handsome men also inspired Jane to write poetry. She composed a "Sonnet to Lindor," praising the lovely boy's starry eyes, Corinth-berry lips, pearly teeth, waving hair, and luring voice.[17] Another of Jane's poems describes Endymion's gaze and friendship. If the sisters shared these poems with others beyond their circle, few would have been the wiser about the real men they described. But even without naming names, the sentiments Jane and Maria expressed in verse were risky. They so plainly revealed an overpowering sexual attraction that young women weren't supposed to feel or admit—and certainly not supposed to advertise.

The sisters' more conventional poems and essays began to come into print in 1794–95, thanks to their friends Courtier and Davenport, who published the group's efforts in their new magazines, the *Monthly Visitor* and the *Pocket Magazine*. Jane's and Maria's verses were published under real names and playful pseudonyms. Maria most often published poetry under her own name, including verses on soldiers going off to war, actresses she'd seen perform on stage, and seasons of the year.[18] Jane's writings are more difficult to trace, because she published under unlikely disguises, like the weighty, masculine pen name "Classicus."

In daily life, the Porters and Caulfields behaved with a freedom usually confined to siblings. When Maria was away in Rochester with William and Lydia, Jane told her sister she'd been tying Wade's cravats. Once Wade stood over Jane's shoulder as she wrote without trying to interrupt her. Later, Maria grew close to Henry, too, who seemed to show as much joy in greeting her as Jane. For a time, Henry tried to teach Maria to reform her sloppy handwriting, so Jane wouldn't any longer have to recopy her sister's love tales for the press.[19] Perhaps Henry held Maria's hand to do it. But these pairings would soon reverse. For the Caulfield brothers and Porter sisters, when it came to romance, opposites attracted: Sensitive Wade became lively Maria's object of affection and dramatic Henry became solid Jane's preferred man.

Problems arose in their little group when Jane discovered a rival for Henry's affections. Selina's attempts to win Henry away from Jane and Maria had begun shortly after they'd all met. The three girls had much in common. Selina's impoverished but genteel upbringing was almost a mirror image to Jane and Maria's—although a motherless version to their fatherless one. But her father, the great nephew of a famous travel writer, would prove unreliable.[20] Selina may not have understood yet that she was an illegitimate child. If it were known she was a so-called natural daughter, polite society would have declared her all but unmarriageable.

Jane apparently didn't know this secret but had learned another: Selina had been trying to ruin Jane's reputation in Henry's eyes with malicious gossip. When his affections toward Selina cooled, she blamed her friend Jane and began to spread lies about her. This must have been the first time Jane experienced defamation and the possible loss of a man's affections. She steadfastly denied doing anything to interfere in Selina and Henry's budding relationship in response. "Heaven is my witness," she wrote to Selina, "in proportion as I saw his preference for you increase . . . I sought to withdraw myself from him." She continued, "If Henry has altered his behaviour, to you—I do assure you, by every thing that is sacred, that I am ignorant of the cause . . . If you had not so often, so very often, written things of my family, things, which your heart must reproach you with being false, how readily should I have caught at every affectionate expression in your letter."[21]

Jane told Selina that it was her practice to love others for their virtues. She wanted to regard Selina as the friend she once was, but trust had been lost. When confronted, Selina was chastened, confessed, and apologized. She pleaded for forgiveness. She begged Jane to treat her as she had before, declared herself wretched, and said she valued Jane's friendship more than life.[22] But just as it had taken time to remove Selina from Jane's heart, so it would take time for Selina to regain it. This experience of female competition with a manipulative, talented woman, fighting over a man's affections, would inform almost every novel Jane later wrote. Echoes of Jane's experience with Selina appear in her deceptive (and often later contrite) femme fatale characters.

After the drama with Jane and Henry, shrewd Selina was unfazed. She inspired strong feelings among others in their group. Richard Davenport published a sonnet "To Serena," a close cognate of Selina, praising the woman as a muse and lamenting his poor powers as a poet in comparison to her perfections.[23] Jane published a story, "Youthful Imprudence," featuring an indiscreet, passionate protagonist named "Serena Granville," further evidence that these fictional Serenas were inspired by Selina.[24] In that story, Jane had named one of Serena's male suitors "Richard Wade," melding Davenport's and Caulfield's names. Jane published this story under the clever, self-aggrandizing, and self-deprecating French pen name "Miss St. Leger," which translated to a "light" or "slight" saint.

The romantic connection that bloomed next in the group was between Maria and Wade. Privately, Jane teased Maria about her growing attachment to the eldest Caulfield brother, suggesting that, because Selina had an extra name—Selina Granville Wheler—perhaps Maria should add one, too. Jane suggested "Anna Maria Wadepha Porter."[25] Selina, although encouraging Davenport, had developed new crushes on Robert Ker Porter and Wade Caulfield. It became very clear that Wade had begun to prefer Maria above all others.

In March 1796, Jane's diary records a day that she, Maria, and Selina took their usual walk in St. James's Park to see and be seen amid its fashionable throngs. There they'd met Wade, who was walking with a male friend. Wade and Maria caught each other's eyes, but this day, she had merely curtseyed and proceeded, without paying him any special attention. Wade stood gazing at her. As he watched her from a little distance, his male friend stepped away to catch up to the three women. Maria loudly told Selina that she had an extreme happiness at the sight of Wade—so loudly that it could be overheard by Wade's friend. This was encouragement enough. Wade's friend flew forward to Maria. He begged her pardon for his intrusion but declared that Wade's situation demanded it. Wade, he said, loved Maria to madness. "Maria burst into tears," Jane wrote, and "Selina stormed."

Wade's friend apologized for upsetting Maria, but still he swore Wade had a passion for her. This drama—a declaration of love by proxy—unfolded on a busy public walkway. It wasn't an offer of marriage. Jane's diary doesn't record further details of the day but concludes with this charged question: "How will this end?"[26] Maria and Wade came to be accepted among the members of the group as specially attached to each other, although not engaged. Maria's lack of fortune, and Wade's lack of financial independence, no doubt played a role. Their half-declared love remained in limbo.

Jane's romantic status with Henry was even more ambiguous. For her own part, she idolized him, took him on as a project, and told him she was certain they'd be friends their whole lives. She cheered him on. "It is impossible that talents like yours were born to waste in oblivion," she once told him. "You might as well suppose that an all-wise Deity would create a Sun, without placing one world near it, to be cherished by its beam." Jane also tried to correct his behavior. She admonished him to spend one or two nights a week at the home of his father, who'd complained about Henry's evenings being given over too often to the Porters. She didn't really want Henry to spend any less time with her. His absence any night would be felt as a privation by her whole family. But Jane began to worry that she might be trying to hold on to Henry too tightly and told him so. She feared she might inspire his contempt by the level of interest she took in him.[27] Henry chose to stay close to Jane but didn't publicly declare his love for her, the way Wade had for Maria.

Love must have been in the air among the teens in 1796–97, because the group experienced several more declarations of it, some by women to men—a thing that wasn't supposed to happen. Henry and Wade's unsteady sister Kitty declared her love for Robert Ker Porter. Things had gone far enough between them that she somehow ended up with Robert's hair in a locket. Robert must have put a stop to her attentions. That was welcome news to Jane and Maria since they didn't approve of her as a match for their darling brother—especially with the disastrous marriage of William and Lydia fresh in their minds. Kitty wasn't as clever as Robert or her Caufield brothers. It was a pity, the sisters thought, that Kitty's head was so weak and her temper so querulous.[28]

Selina—not to be left out after apparently failing to capture the attention of both Caulfields—also set her sights on Robert for a time. Robert had openly admired Selina's letters, which he found sublime and playful. (Then again, Robert's letters to Jane from this time include such lines as "Damn your writing / Mind your shiting," so perhaps his sense of sublimity isn't entirely to be trusted.[29]) Yet Robert seems to have pushed away Selina, too. She would soon declare that her romantic connection with Robert was dissolved forever. Money may have been at the root of it. Selina wrote to Jane with her earnest wish that Robert might marry a woman of title and riches—if that would ensure his happiness.[30]

Instead of defying convention by entering into engagements while lacking the means to marry, the group threw themselves into creating a once-a-week magazine. Starting in 1797, *The Quiz* ran for a respectably successful fifty-one issues, until it folded the following year. It came to be described as an editorial project led by Thomas Frognall Dibdin, but its contents were collaborative. *The Quiz* was written by a collective that called itself "A Society of Gentlemen," echoing satirically the phrase used by the eminent Tory magazine, the *Critical Review*. Jane and Maria, along with Robert and the Caulfields, produced a great deal of the contents of *The Quiz*, under amusing pseudonyms.

Jane wrote under the name Arthur Hildebrand (meaning "battle mark"), who was said to be a sixty-year-old recluse. Maria chose cheekier pseudonyms, like Charles Chickenheart and Philip Harmless. Robert wrote as Reginald Steinkirk—combining words for "beer mug" and "church." He created frontispiece designs for the magazine and further essays under the name Anthony Serious.

The Quiz's fictional society of gentlemen was described in its pages as being made up of five members, including the pseudonyms of Robert, Jane, and Henry Caulfield. They wrote as if they were wizened, learned gentlemen, while poking fun at the stereotype. They claimed to write with quill pens that had been grasped by John Milton as he finished *Paradise Lost* and inkwells once the property of Edward, the fourteenth-century Black Prince. The society of gentlemen described their wigs and three-cornered hats, their stockings worn around their heels, and being known around town as "fine old cocks." Each detail was a comic caricature of the previous generation's privileged men.

Jane's first identifiable contribution to *The Quiz* introduces Arthur Hildebrand as a loving father who went into seclusion after the tragic death of his son in the American Revolution. The son died a hero, but his father regrets, rather than celebrates, his loss. Hildebrand declares that he's lost "my only comfort . . . my only prop, to my country." The tale questions the sacrifices of war. Jane also wrote about a heroine named Aspasia, who openly criticizes the era's young men because they rarely use their reflective powers.[31] Her pieces were the magazine's most narrative, detailed, and morally upright, although Robert and Henry were its most frequent contributors.

Other friends also found their way into the mix of authors in *The Quiz*, including Edward "Ned" Warren, the literary son of a wealthy physician. There were exclamation-mark-filled and long-winded pieces on religion, signed "W. T. C.," the initials of Wade and Henry's father, Wade Toby Caulfield. They may have been the work of the man himself, but they could have been written by Wade or Henry, comically pretending to speak in their father's voice. It was Henry who, in his persona as Isaac Fitzhakary (meaning "son of a light carriage"), was described as the most knowing member of their society of gentlemen. That adjective "knowing" may have meant experienced, rather than wise.

During this experiment in magazine making, Jane was quick to praise her male collaborators, although rarely as willing to concede her own growth as a writer. Through Jane's contributions to *The Quiz*, Maria's to *Artless Tales* and the *Pocket Magazine*, and other periodicals, the teenage Porter sisters were young veterans of the London publishing world. Their developing talents also shine brightly in their letters to each other. They regularly spent time apart and took turns making visits to friends and family in the country. The sister who stayed in the metropolis helped to keep their mother company and sought ways to observe fashionable life. The sisters' letters rarely lose an opportunity to capture social ridiculousness. When Maria was away from home, Jane's descriptive and dialogue-rich letters were so good they could make Maria cry from envy over everything she was missing.

Once, Jane wrote Maria a long description of a vocal and instrumental music concert held at Willis's Rooms. "I'm sure," Jane wrote, "if all concerts are like it, I never wish to see another." She told Maria with high energy about its disastrousness, as well as about her own spectacular performance. Jane had worn her white dress with a green sash, tied on the left side. She'd put on a borrowed locket, its gold chain wrapped twice around her neck, with the loose end hanging down several fashionable inches. Her turban, too, was white, with one green bushy feather and one long white one, gracefully towering over it. It was elegant, simple finery, but Jane was nervous about how her appearance would measure up.

She was escorted by her mother and their friend Mr. Jameson. The point in Willis's Rooms wasn't just to hear music but to see and be seen. The trio arrived fashionably late, to make a grand entrance. They took a spot on the front sofa, with a commanding view. Jane was so anxious about the figure she'd cut upon entering that she told Maria it took five minutes for her to gather the courage to raise her eyes. When she looked up, she took a careful survey. She realized she needn't have worried. Everything and everyone was garishly overdone.

"No female appeared there under less than five colours," she wrote, "Skirts white, trains worked, bodies red, trimmings yellow & all in this stile—feathers of a hundred hues and shapes—and their behavior suiting their habits . . . Judge how unembarrassed, how lofty I felt," Jane told Maria, "when I found that I was the most elegant woman in the room, saving Miss Courtney, and she was not in the least my superior." There were so many risible figures. Jane relished describing to Maria "a lady with a head so loaded with feathers, flowers, ribbons, & c. & c. that I should have expected to have seen her [fall over] had it not been for the size of her bottom."[32]

In this flurry of new daily drama and colorful, humor-filled letters, Maria and Jane each began to write their first full-length novels. Maria worked faster. By autumn 1796, she was transforming their talented circle's knotty emotional experiences into fiction. She did it with Henry Caulfield sometimes standing over her shoulder as she wrote, just as Wade had once stood over Jane's. Maria's first novel was later said to be founded "on some incidents in real life, in which the fair and youthful author was in some measure personally interested."[33] These incidents concerned young men in the Guards—Wade and Henry's regiment.

Maria named her hero Walsh Colville, and she made him a beautiful young man, with blue eyes and silken, thick, light hair, as well as a figure that gives "indescribable attraction to his every movement." The significance of the initials of her protagonist wouldn't have been lost on anyone among the Porters' friends. Walsh Colville, like Wade Caulfield, was a W. C.—the very way their friend signed his letters.[34] Other real-life references made their way into the novel's pages, including the character Bob Ker, a play on her brother's name. A female character was named Jessie St. Leger, echoing the surname from the pseudonym Jane used and the Christian name of a younger Caulfield sister. The events of the novel were said to have fictionalized the life of a young man of Maria's acquaintance. There's little doubt that the broad brushstrokes of what happened to Walsh Colville in the novel were experienced by Wade Caufield in real life.

Maria's Walsh Colville convinces his reluctant father to let him join the fashionable Guards. His father warns him that he'll never pay off any of his son's gaming debts, but the unworldly Walsh falls immediately into a crowd of heedless soldier-gamblers. Walsh, who'd never had a drink in his life, is tricked into drunkenness by villainous men. They set their sights on this sensitive, trusting young man of fortune as easy prey. Walsh is made vulnerable to their machinations after a scene in the park. His female love interest, Lady Frances—Wade's middle name was Francis—refuses to acknowledge his bow to her, and it devastates him. Walsh, upset, gets drunk and loses the enormous sum of three thousand pounds gambling. Although his wealthy father breaks down and pays the young man's debts, he declares it will not be repeated. Alas, soon enough, Walsh is shamefully fleeced out of sixteen thousand pounds more, becoming the victim of his supposed best friend, a secret libertine. The false friend also successfully passes off his own kept mistress as Walsh's. For a time, the virtuous hero is mistakenly thought to be the villain.

Walsh, without the protection of his family and friends, takes ill with shame and attempts to live on nothing. There is, however, a happy ending. The false friend's father pays off Walsh's debts. Walsh's father forgives his contrite son. Lady Frances, the young woman who'd denied Walsh in the park, finds out he never kept a mistress. She learns this thanks to the helpful interference of Jessie St. Leger and Bob Ker. When Walsh turns twenty-one, he and Lady Frances marry. In the end, there are four marriages, with even the novel's flawed young men and women gaining their happily-ever-afters.

This must have been Maria's first transformation of personal experience into a novel. There is every indication, though no solid proof, that the false friends, the gambling debts, the estrangement from the father, as well as the illness—and certainly the drama in the park—came from Wade Caulfield's (and Maria's) life. But the ending Maria gave to her story couldn't yet have come true, because Wade wasn't yet twenty-one, the age at which he'd become financially independent. The possibility of Wade following in the footsteps of the fictional Walsh to marry his beloved woman from the park—Maria—would have been a hoped-for future at the time the novel appeared in print.

At first, the sisters referred to the book as Maria's "novel of The Guards." The day after Maria completed a draft, in February 1796, Jane copied it for the press. In the guise of a scribe, Jane's hand was more readable than her sister's.[35] It was the first of many of Maria's novels that Jane would transcribe and lightly edit for the press. Maria's *Walsh Colville; or A Young Man's First Entrance Into Life* was anonymously published in 1797. Maria found a new publisher—one of the men who'd printed *The Quiz*.

It's likely Maria decided to publish anonymously because of her known connections to these drawn-from-life characters. No doubt after the reviews of *Artless Tales*, she'd also have been skeptical of the ability of a seventeen-year-old girl to win praise for publishing a novel featuring depredation and vice. How shocked her reviewers would have been to learn their worst suspicions were partly true. Maria hadn't just read about men's flirtations, temptations, and near ruinations. She was a close witness to them and sometimes a participant.

Reviewers liked *Walsh Colville*. The *Critical Review*, previously so full of bile for Maria's work, had only positive things to say. It praised *Walsh Colville* for the way in which it "exposes in lively colors the dangerous dissipation, of which the higher ranks of the army have (we fear too justly) been accused."[36] The reviewer in the *Monthly Visitor*, the magazine edited by my friend Peter Courtier, gave *Walsh Colville* much praise. It concludes that "*Walsh Colville* will be admired wheresoever he is known," in a double entendre the Porters' circle must have laughed at.[37]

As the romantic and family entanglements that Maria's novel had begun to narrate from the raw materials of real life continued beyond the book's pages, events lurched sharply away from her fantasized happy ending. Not long after *Walsh Colville* was published, late in 1797, Wade became very ill. He traveled in search of a cure. He seems to have had little money. "I feel that all of his expectations are vanish'd," Maria wrote to Jane, about Wade. "I feel that for his sake and for that of his family we must long, and perhaps ever experience nothing but sorrow."[38]

Wade's symptoms were described as a consumption. His friends believed he'd fully recover.[39] But then he wrote letters that seemed like goodbyes. He thanked Mrs. Porter for taking him in once, when he was shut out, and for feeding him when he was hungry. He spoke of his present difficulties—illness and aloneness, except for the occasional male companion. "My strain is so melancholy," he wrote to Mrs. Porter, that there was "a reluctance in making those unhappy, to whom I should wish to render every joy—every Day informs me, my end is near."[40] His wish to "render every joy" might be read as an unfulfilled hope to marry Maria.

He was right that his end was near. Wade Francis Caulfield died on May 6, 1798, at Hotwells, near Bristol, just before his twenty-second birthday. He was buried at nearby St. Andrew's Church in Clifton. An unsigned magazine obituary remembers Wade as manly and beautiful, with a cultivated and polished mind, and a heart rich with grace and virtue. It alludes to his having endured "family dissensions" and lauds his love of a sister and brother. Wade's loyalty to his siblings after "a parent's unjustifiable resentment" is what the obituary claims hastened his "commendable affliction" and death.[41] A surviving note from Jane suggests she may have been the obituary writer, as it also describes Wade's sickness brought on by the "cruelty of a parent" and his honorable heart.[42]

More of this complicated story is revealed in the will Wade had made the previous January. He divided his estate and personal belongings among his brothers and sisters. But the will declares a problem. Wade bequeathed money he said he was owed—the promised fortune he'd never received, after he'd turned twenty-one. He'd named two friends as his executors and pledged to pay each of them twenty pounds for their trouble to try to extract his family money to give to his siblings after his death.

Absent from these end-of-life documents is Wade Caulfield's father. In Maria's novel, the benevolent father of Walsh Colville forgives his repentant son. In real life, Wade Caulfield died estranged from his only remaining parent, who presumably obstructed his eldest son's receiving his inheritance.[43] Old Mr. Caulfield died two years later, in 1800. His will—which named his son James as the principal heir—complained about the long trial of the conduct of his children.[44] If Maria had hoped *Walsh Colville* might inspire a real-life rapprochement between strict fathers and repentant sons, it hadn't worked out for Wade.

Somehow it fell to devastated Maria to write Wade's epitaph. Not only was Wade's body kept out of the Caulfield family vault in London's tony St. James's Church in Piccadilly, but also his family seems to have left the work of his faraway gravestone to others. Years later, Robert, on a visit to his old friend's grave, copied Maria's memorial verse into his notebook. It read,

> *"O! if Thou e'er hast loved" one friend most dear*
> *And o'er his early grave has pour'd the tear;*
> *If to that friend each tender grace was given,*
> *From those soft eyes, beam'd purity and heaven;*
> *Whose angel smiles still spoke the angels' heart.—*
> *Ah! Do not, do not, from this spot depart—*
> *Now stranger pause and on the cold stone weep.*
> *For here, youth, valour, sense, and sweetness sleep.*
> *A. M. P. W. F. C.*
> *died May 6th 1798 Aged 21.*[45]

Wade's death was an enormous blow. The literary collective of *The Quiz* fell apart, as did the exuberant, romantic sibling pairs that had fired the sisters' early writing lives. Even Jane dreamed that she'd died and joined Wade. She also wrote a poem, "To the Spirit of Dear Wade," in which the female speaker calls him the "gentle Brother of my love." She imagines being touched by his cold hand, which she'd so often pressed and laid upon her heaving breast in life. Jane writes of his brother Henry's tears and imagines all of them meeting again, when they burst from their mortal holds.[46] Jane's poem suggests Henry leaned on the Porters in his grief.

Walsh Colville ends with several marriages among a group of friends, but in real life, only one couple from their little literary circle tied the knot just after coming of age. The first moment Selina was free to do it, without parental permission, at age twenty-one, she married Richard Davenport. It was said she chose him to disoblige her father.[47] The marriage would prove a disaster. But even before Selina married the poet and editor, the Porter sisters had become skeptical of her. Maria called Selina a "very ungrateful creature" and predicted "she will come to no good."[48]

Maria hoped not to follow in Selina's footsteps in another way. "God keep me from a literary husband, at least a professed author," Maria declared to Jane, "for they are of all stupid, formal, affected wretches the most hateful."[49]

CHAPTER 4

In Spite of the Prudish World

The Sister Novelists and the Great Historical Picture (1798–1800)

Maria's intense grief over Wade's death didn't slow down her writing. In 1798, she threw herself into her next book about the adventures of two sisters with opposite personalities. During this period, Jane, too, would complete a novel—her first. She'd decided to write about a lonely heroine, in dark and stormy Gothic circumstances. Robert, meanwhile, was scheming up ways he might join his art to public spectacle. The Porter siblings' frenzied labor as the eighteenth century came to a close would also prove a climax of ambition, fame, and fortune—for a short time.

As Jane, Robert, and Maria moved into young adulthood, things were still proving financially difficult for Mrs. Porter. She continued to rely on her talented children to help cover family expenses. Home life could be unstable. A problem with their landlord left Jane questioning the false friendships her mother experienced during their first years in the metropolis.[1] Some unnamed calamity compelled the Porters to leave their lodgings on Bedford Street, Covent Garden. Mrs. Porter found a new place to rent at 66 St. Martin's Lane.[2]

The new friendships made on that street would prove more lasting and true. Jane and Maria grew close to the neighboring Middletons, a family who ran a lucrative color shop, which sold paints and supplies to artists. Robert and fellow students from the Royal Academy would have bought materials there. Jane and Maria discovered in the wealthy shopkeeper's daughter, Anna Middleton, a trusted confidante.[3] Anna remained a friend even after the Porters found they needed to change lodgings once again.

After St. Martin's Lane, Mrs. Porter rented a shabby place on Great Newport Street in Leicester Square. It proved a vibrant, if sometimes frightening, location. One night, when a mob assembled, presumably in response to British crackdowns on revolutionary activism, the Porters worried that their house might be in danger from rioting. As protection, Maria took Robert's portrait of Polish hero General Tadeusz Kościuszko and arranged it in their window, illuminated by a candle.[4] It was a sign to activists that the inhabitants were friendly to the revolutionary cause.

Robert made use of this new apartment in advancing his career. He'd helped found a watercolor society, in which fellow artists worked on historical landscapes inspired by poetic passages. Its members, calling themselves "The Brothers," met for evening drawing sessions. They gathered for the first time in the Porters' lodgings on Great Newport Street in a room said to have formerly been used by Joshua Reynolds and Samuel Johnson. Jane, who often watched her brother and the young artists at work, was occasionally put in charge of choosing the poetic passage and theme to guide the session.[5] Although Jane's learned reputation was well known among these men, they may not have known that she published her writing anonymously.

After Great Newport Street, the Porters moved to nearby Gerrard Street in Soho.[6] The poet John Dryden had died on Gerrard Street, and the philosopher-statesman Edmund Burke had once lived there, but the lodging wasn't much of an improvement, as far as Mrs. Porter was concerned. Although she described their new home as "a dog-hole," Maria thought it far better than the other dismal places they'd lived.[7] Here the sisters set to work on new novels.

Maria's next book—her fourth—was *Octavia*. Its two orphaned sisters, Octavia and Antonia Rochford, ages sixteen and seventeen, had a spoiled brother, George. Octavia was the more lively, self-educated, and charming sister, and Antonia was the more serious, detached, and beautiful one, although she was a budding coquette. Maria put her fictional sisters among a group of flawed and worthy young people, with names like Miss Ferrars and Captain Mansfield. The two heroines faced everyday problems—some of their own making—until the characters finally sorted themselves out into three happy marriages. Remarkably, Maria seems to have dashed off her three-volume novel in a year.

Perhaps her speed was a result of not having to start from scratch. In *Octavia*, Maria wrote about the flirtations and machinations of a group of clever but error-prone young people. She mined private letters for material. Early in *Octavia*, the sisters attend a concert with their maiden aunt as a chaperone. The scene directly echoes the London concert in Willis's Rooms that Jane had written home about several years before. Maria has her three Rochford women enter the room together, strikingly dressed, with turbans and feathers. The young sisters, despite having small fortunes, captivate men. The Rochford sisters, as the narrator explains, "knew well the difference between finery and elegance; and their dress powerfully displayed it."[8]

For *Octavia*, with its emphasis on virtue over passion, Maria acknowledged her authorship. The book was brought out by Thomas Longman, who ran an established and respected publishing house. Avowing her authorship, however, meant a return to mistreatment from reviewers. The *Monthly Review*, despite praising *Octavia*'s well delineated characters and sprightly dialogue, called its incidents and personages "trite and trifling."[9] The *Analytical Review* had mild praise but took issue with the novel's use of fashionable slang.[10] The most damning assessment came once again from the *Critical Review*. It had been in the business of discouraging Maria's authorship, painfully and publicly, since she was scarcely fifteen, and was still trying to stop her pen at almost twenty. Its reviewer offered the opinion that Maria ought to "relinquish the task of writing novels."[11]

Maria and Jane were gaining firsthand understanding of institutional sexism. In the process of trying to make sense of these responses to their writing and to their own difficult life experiences, the Porter sisters had discovered and devoured the writings of the late Mary Wollstonecraft, author of the feminist treatise *A Vindication of the Rights of Woman* (1792). Wollstonecraft had died in 1797, from complications giving birth to her daughter, who would become Mary Shelley, the author of *Frankenstein*. After her death, Wollstonecraft became a polarizing figure. Jane and Maria still admired her.

The word "feminism" hadn't yet come into the English language, but Wollstonecraft was at the vanguard of eighteenth-century proto-feminist thought, along with another progressive writer who'd soon become the Porters' close friend and mentor, Mary Robinson. Jane and Maria were compelled by their righteous arguments, especially by the claim that women were just as capable of genius as men, that the sex had been wrongly devalued as mentally weaker just because it was supposedly physically weaker, and that females had been denied a proper education.

Maria was so moved by Wollstonecraft's writings that she'd written two poems in her honor, which she seems never to have published.[12] To praise the late Wollstonecraft publicly was too much of a risk, because in his 1798 memoir of his late wife, Wollstonecraft's husband, William Godwin, had revealed she'd had a child out of wedlock and had attempted suicide. He also lauded her gifts in philosophy and literature. The conventional world ignored the praise and damned the woman, her supposed sins, and most of all, the progressive philosophy said to have caused them. Maria was more forgiving. Some years later, she saw Godwin at the theater with his second wife and his children, as well as the late Wollstonecraft's daughter. Maria thought the second wife couldn't compare to Wollstonecraft and felt her heart move while looking at her idol's illegitimate daughter.[13]

Jane didn't approve of the sexual freedom in lives like Wollstonecraft's, but she believed in repentance and forgiveness and admired female genius. When she first read Madame de Staël's *A Treatise on the Influence of the Passions, upon the Happiness of Individuals and Nations*, she went wild for it. "Each line is a gem to me," she wrote to Maria, "while I look after the immortal flight of such minds as hers, and Mary Wollstonecraft, and Madame Roland—I am more convinced that there is a sex in souls."[14]

Jane thought there was a difference in the spirit of man and woman—that men had more pride, and women had more sublimity. Women were the link between men and angels. Her belief provides the framework to understanding her involvement in one of the first pieces of writing to imagine Mary Wollstonecraft as a ghost—as a speaking spirit among the feminist greats of Western history. Jane may not have written it, but she edited the manuscript and kept it among her papers. It was a story set in the heavens, looking down on a London debating society.

Debating societies boomed as paid entertainment in 1790s London. A keepsake in a Porter family scrapbook is an admission ticket to the School of Eloquence, a popular debating society run by their friend Peter Courtier.[15] Money was made by impresarios and speculators who knew how to gather popular debaters and thrill a crowd. Robert, who designed the art on the admission ticket for Courtier, must have paid close attention to this entrepreneurial venture. "Political questions are not debated," the ticket declares to its holder, "And no Visitor is allow'd to speak."

The reality, however, was different from the rules. One ad tells the public that the School of Eloquence will next debate Alexander Pope's assertion that every woman was at heart a rake. The ad predicts, "It is not to be doubted but some Lady will on this occasion interfere, if in behalf of the sex."[16] Jane attended the School of Eloquence many times. Maria writes about having gone to a rival debating society. Women were welcome in the audiences but weren't included as official speakers, being limited to supposedly forbidden—but advertised—female heckling.

These societies advertised their controversial subjects in advance, often choosing gendered topics, such as "In the Marriage State, which constitutes the greater Evil, Love without Money, or Money without Love?" or "Which is the greater crime, to seduce a Married or an Unmarried Woman?"[17] Sometimes the questions tied into current scandals. Maria was sure the debate about seduction was inspired by a local man known to have seduced at least six girls under the age of fourteen and who was said never to have kept them beyond that age.[18] She and Jane would have understood that these debated questions had real consequences. After each side was given its chance to persuade, a winning side was declared.

In March 1798, Jane was involved in the creation of a fictional piece that used the School of Eloquence as its setting, the cumbersomely titled "Ithuriel, the angel of truth, thus restateth an event of the Heavens," a remarkable dialogue of the dead that ends with a rousing hymn to female liberty.[19] It imagines a public debate about women's rights, in which living, mortal men speak but history's immortal women—including Sappho, Boadicea, Lady Jane Grey, and Wollstonecraft—pass judgment. After overhearing the flawed earthly arguments men make about the rights of women at the School of Eloquence, the great women predict the future triumph of women's rights. "Ithuriel" was never published, and it isn't in Jane's handwriting. But her markings, corrections, and suggestions on the manuscript demonstrate her commitment to its ideals, and her keeping a copy of it throughout her life suggests she valued it.[20]

She came to understand men's abuse of power over women through hard experience. Jane's understanding of the daily workings of sexism, and of how power over women's bodies was routinely taken away from them, came from daily life. Her first kiss was a sexual assault. It came from an acquaintance during a military review at Wimbledon—a public government propaganda performance and recruiting tool that featured colorfully dressed marching soldiers.

Jane had recently taken to wearing a thin lace veil in public, which may have simultaneously drawn and averted attention. It allowed her to cultivate a new persona of devout Gothic mystery and extreme modesty. More practically, it prevented others from seeing her facial reactions and from judging her by her looks. She could watch others, too, with greater freedom. What any observer of her could easily perceive, with or without her veil, was that Jane was a tall, stately woman who uttered few words yet wasn't timid. When she spoke, she did so forcefully.

At the Wimbledon military review, Jane joined in a lively conversation with a group of friends about the practice of kissing on the lips. She told her companions she'd never been kissed on the lips by a mere friend, because she made it a habit to turn her cheek if she were approached in that way. Some hours later, a gentleman from the group walked directly up to her.

"Why do you wear this?" he said, taking hold of her veil.

"Because I like it," she replied.

"It is too low. Let me raise it for you," the man said.

Jane wrote out the story of all that happened next, in moving dialogue, to share with Maria.

"I let him lift it up as high as my mouth, when he fairly kissed me," Jane reported. "I was monstrous mad, but every body laughed."[21] To the rest of the group, this seemed a harmless entertainment to pass the time at the military review. To Jane, it held no humor; this day affected her deeply.

She reminded Maria, "You know, from Baby-hood, *we* were taught to believe that *Danger* lurks beneath a *scarlet coat*—We *see It threatening* on the smart cockade, the dazzling epalette, and all the gay etceteras of the Soldier.—But, when we *do not* see It, under the quiet vest of sober-suited Blue, or Brown, or Black—*then*, it may pop out, and chop us up in a moment." Jane was telling her sister that girls and young women must be on their guard against clergymen and schoolmasters, those sober-suited and supposedly respectable men in blue, black, and brown clothing. Jane saw through their respectable positions to the harm they might cause.

Experiences like these led Jane to consider that she might not take a husband. Maybe, Jane said, she wouldn't marry, because she was too much like her warlike, martyred, virginal namesake, Joan of Arc, "fearlessly marching on, to advance my waving colors on the walls."[22] But Jane and Maria, both in their early twenties at the turn of the century, were charged by their brothers with the task of making advantageous marriages. Robert had told Jane, half in jest, that she could have until age thirty to marry.[23] John and William were more straightforward. They wanted Jane to marry soon, no doubt to reduce their financial responsibilities.[24] To her credit, Mrs. Porter doesn't seem to have put pressure on her daughters to marry.

The sisters joked with each other about whether they were on a path to becoming old maids. "Old maid" was not only a term of derision, but also a category of person popularly imagined as risking a damned afterlife. A familiar saying had it that "old maids were destined to lead apes in hell," and the two wondered if they were on a path to "leading apes" since female authorship and advantageous marriages were not seen as compatible.[25]

They were still publishing poems and prose in newspapers and magazines at fast clips. Maria regularly published in half a dozen magazines. In the pages of the *Monthly Visitor*, she was prolific, with as many as forty separate poems published under the names Anna, Anna Maria, Anna Maria Porter, A., and A. M. between 1797 and 1804.[26] Jane took on classical pseudonyms, including Veritas, the Roman goddess of truth. She published as E., N., P., Censoricus, Atticus, K. Clever, and Ronald. Maria, if she wrote under a pseudonym, chose Candidus, Varicipus, M. A. Honestus, C. Common-Sense, Julia, or Cyrus, although she preferred to identify her published poems as her own more often than Jane.[27] "In spite of the prudish world, I shall put my name to my verses," she once declared to her sister. "Do with your essays as you please."[28]

By 1798, Maria had published four books. Jane had yet to publish one, although her first full-length novel was taking shape, having grown out of a story she'd begun two years earlier, with the working title "Mysteries of the Black Forest."[29] Jane imagined herself on a path to becoming a prolific novelist. She even wrote out a list of titles, with the heading, "Imitations, Which I intend to write—of living female authors." It was probably more of an inside joke than a serious plan, but it demonstrates how closely Jane studied the genre.

In imitation of one bestselling Gothic novelist, Jane claimed she'd write a book called *The Father: Some Ghost Story*. In imitation of proto-feminist Mary Robinson, Jane said she'd write a book about an Italian girl with the subtitle *Enthusiastic*. Her comic imitation of the works of upright Hannah More would be called *Hints to Old Ladies*, an amusing turnaround from the moralizing, preachy guides that More published, which often told working-class children how to behave. In a stroke of good humor and gentle ribbing, Jane ended her list of planned imitations with the author Anna Maria Porter. Jane's one-word title in imitation of Maria's books was *Arpasia*, a classical sounding send-up of her sister's *Octavia*.[30]

When it came time to title her own first novel, Jane called it *The Spirit of the Elbe: A Romance*. Although it wasn't an imitative title, it was steeped in the Gothic tradition. The story begins with a dramatic carriage ride. Orphaned heroine Rosamund Petrie travels on a dark and stormy night from the convent in Hungary in which she was raised to the home of her aunt, the Countess Blackenberg, who lives in a imposing castle in Saxony. After being shown by the servants to a room in the castle, and finding no one comes to greet her, she opens a casement window in the room. She discovers just below it a raging river in the rain, and she's soaked from head to toe in brine.[31]

The Gothic tone of dejection, cheerlessness, inhospitality, and bewilderment continues throughout in rich, direct, and anxiety-ridden diction and action. Gothic novels regularly featured evil, titled scoundrels and worthy, put-upon aunts, as well as restricted young heroines in danger. *The Spirit of the Elbe*'s plot serves up villains, a ghost, a dungeon, a trapdoor, a bloody injury, a threat, a poisoning, and an adulterous affair in its two volumes. There were also long-lost children, parents, and sisters, separated and reunited. The story is fast paced and consistently dark. It features an almost dizzying number of characters.

Jane published *The Spirit of the Elbe* anonymously in March 1799, with the same publisher Maria had used for *Octavia*: Thomas Longman, in partnership with Owen Rees. It was the beginning of Jane's and Maria's decades-long relationship with the respected house of Longman and Rees—and its many additional future partners. Jane's novel was advertised alongside works by Jane West, Mary Robinson, and (in translation) Madame de Genlis.[32] This was exceptionally good literary company for a first novel.

Yet Jane's *Spirit of the Elbe* failed to win over the critics. The *British Critic* sarcastically applauded the author's choice of anonymity, writing, "We think it fortunate for the author, that it is presented to the public without his name; and we think he will be wise, not to subject himself to discovery by any future attempt."[33] Jane could now join Maria in having been admonished by a reviewer never to publish again. Other reviews sprinkled in a few compliments. Each morsel of praise was countered by a devastating adjective: wild, extravagant, inflated—even destitute of grace.

Novels of the time regularly faced vitriolic critical response. Reviewers operated under the conventional, privileged cloak of anonymity. Old-fashioned, gatekeeping skeptics dismissed prose fiction as literary trash. They saw poetry, drama, and nonfiction as the higher status genres and fiction as the low. Even knowing this much about how different genres were valued wouldn't have taken the sting away from being publicly advised to stop writing. Coping with the psychological and financial effects of devastating reviews would have been a challenge for any emerging author.

Ebullient Maria seems to have taken it in stride more easily than sober Jane. After what she'd endured earlier, Maria tried to assure her sister that at least her reviewers were phlegmatic and civil. As Maria mock-cheerfully put it, "Well, patience and perseverance; and then we succeed—and then if we do not—why, we drop into our graves, and all our unsuccessful attempts are forgotten by the head and heart that once ached in making them."[34]

Whether it was Jane's aches in completing *The Spirit of the Elbe* or the upsetting reviews, something brought on illness after the book was published. The tendency to work to exhaustion was becoming a dangerous pattern for both sisters, as they took turns pushing their pens to the point of physical breakdown. They'd reach the end of writing a book, get their promised payment, and go into a total collapse of energy and spirits.

There had been, perhaps, no sense of irony, when in August 1799 the Porter family decided to send Jane away from home, alone in a stagecoach, just like her heroine at the opening of *The Spirit of the Elbe*. In search of better health, Jane traveled to the small town of Grantham in Lincolnshire, a 110-mile journey that would have weakened even a strong person. But Jane, at twenty-three, couldn't have been described as strong. She wondered in a letter whether she should just resign herself to being thin and pale.[35]

When trying to regain health, country air was preferred to dirty, smoky London, but Grantham was a welcome destination for another reason. It was home to the Porters' old family friends, the Rawlinsons. When the widowed Mrs. Rawlinson learned from one of her five daughters that dear Miss Porter was in a weakened state, she'd dispatched an invitation, telling Jane to come. The Rawlinsons insisted Jane convalesce there for three months, to properly relax and recover.[36] They'd read books aloud together. When Jane was stronger, they'd roam the fields, on foot or horseback.

"No study—I forbid it," Maria warned Jane. "Remember you have left London not to acquire Learning, but to acquire health."[37]

The long stagecoach journey to Grantham would offer plenty to study. Jane found herself seated near a drunken farmer. All day long, she looked on as the man made what she called "ocular love," as he ogled another female passenger. In such close quarters, everyone in the coach, even if watching with only half an eye, would have seen the farmer's alcohol-fueled lust and the female passenger's obvious pleasure at his attention.

But Jane's half-observation turned to shock when nightfall came. The man and woman used the cover of darkness in the stagecoach to explore each other's bodies, heedless of the presence of their fellow passengers. The ride itself was bumpy, but everyone inside would have been further jostled as the lusty couple tumbled into each other's arms. Jane wrote to Maria, "They began pulling each other about so abominably, that I wished myself any where but where I was."

Jane found the best way to distract herself was by watching the moon out of the coach window. She imagined the moon itself was turning pale, observing such wanton conduct happening below on earth, in its chaste lunar presence. Jane thought her best course of action among this "foul company" was to pretend to be asleep. She tried.

Her busy mind considered her options, weighing them alongside behavior of heroines in novels. Heroines held captive in vehicles were subjected to far worse things, Jane had to admit. She wasn't being abducted or assaulted. She imagined herself instead as an updated version of the heroine in Samuel Richardson's novel *Sir Charles Grandison* (1753).[38] Perhaps, she told Maria, she was a new-style Harriet Byron, half a century later—a different kind of main character, for a new era in history.

In Richardson's sprawling book, the virtuous, worthy Harriet is kidnapped and held against her will in a carriage by a rapacious villain. Her screams prompt another man to rescue her. Like Harriet, heroic Jane in the stagecoach was, in a sense, being held against her will. She was compelled to watch, or at least listen to, passengers making love. Instead of being attacked herself, she was merely being dragged along into the sordid sinning of others. Unlike heroine Harriet, Jane chose not to scream.

The stagecoach arrived safely in Grantham. Jane remained unharmed and untouched, if not exactly untainted. The episode—which Jane wrote about to Maria in full detail—reinforced how closely the polite and the impolite, the innocent and the lewd, could collide in their lives. The two sisters lived on this razor's edge of respectability and besmirched reputation.

Jane's arrival in Grantham, to relative comfort, quiet, and friendship, proved, as everyone had expected, a welcome departure from London life. She found her health strengthened and spirits restored almost immediately.[39] Hospitable and kind Mrs. Rawlinson was the widow of a successful butcher. She remained in fortunate circumstances, thanks to earnings from her investment shares in the nearby turnpike, a growing and popular toll road.[40] Her younger daughter Lucy Rawlinson's maturity impressed Jane. She was no longer the giddy, wild girl they'd last seen but had become reflective, sober, cheerful, and beautiful. Lucy, who treated Jane as if she were another sister, was someone Jane felt resembled Maria, in mind if not body. Reflecting on that gave Jane a chance to tell Maria how much her sister meant to her: "No *compliments* you know between sisters—it is my *pride* that *you* are *mine*."[41]

Jane regaled her hosts with stories. She told the Rawlinsons about her adventures in worldly London. Her anecdotes made her provincial Grantham acquaintances laugh to the point of tears. The group took turns reading aloud to one another. One of the first books they chose was Jane's *The Spirit of the Elbe*. Here, Jane discovered an ideal, enthusiastic, and approving audience for her novel. Its details stuck with them, especially with little Fanny Rawlinson, with whom Jane was sharing a bed. One night, her bedfellow exclaimed, "La, Miss Porter . . . how they cry away in your book!"[42]

Perhaps the family hoped Jane's trip to Grantham would end like it did for her novel's heroine—in marriage. But since Jane or the Rawlinsons had let the fact of her authorship slip, her beaux in Grantham feared her as much as they loved her. They dreaded her caricaturing them with her pen and behaved exceptionally politely around her.

"You did not know your daughter was so terrific a personage, such a medusa," Jane wrote to Mrs. Porter, "*admired* for her *features*, *feared* for her *snakes*."[43]

Maria joked that Jane ought to be on the lookout there for a good husband for her sister, too, describing her fantasy man as decent, reputable, sober, warm, and North talking. She advertised herself as a woman who could cast accounts and keep reckonings as clear as the best "she" that wears a head.[44] During Jane's three-month absence, Maria had reason to wish she were living quietly in Grantham: A ladder fell on her head in the street, injuring her.[45] Their friend Ned Warren accidentally broke Maria's arm from the shoulder to the elbow during some kind of horseplay.[46] And while Maria could still hold a pen, the physical setbacks became financial setbacks, with lost writing time and unexpected doctor's fees.

Money was so short that Mrs. Porter and Maria couldn't easily come up with funds for Jane to travel back to London. Jane looked for a way to return before winter weather made roads less passable, and somehow she found the means. She made plans to leave Grantham late in 1799. One of her last social events was a private ball. Jane had been disappointed by Grantham's young people, finding the women ordinary and without ideas and the water-gruel men clumsy, leafy-legged, and heavy-headed.[47] But at this last ball, Jane noticed quite a few smart beaux.

Jane had recently become intrigued by the young heir of Heath Hall, a former convent where it was said the ghost of a bleeding nun appeared at night. Jane desperately wanted to wander its grounds at midnight.[48] It's hard to say if she was more intrigued with Heath Hall's heir or his family's supposedly haunted home, which reminded her of the setting she'd created for *The Spirit of the Elbe*. The young heir had shown some interest in Jane, and the ball might bring things forward.

At this momentous ball, however, Jane attracted little notice. All attention, she reported, was focused on a "monstrous fat woman, habited in a red and gold brocade, with earrings stolen from the chandelier." She turned out to be a very rich widow who, it was whispered, had started her life as a procuress, helping debauched men find girls to deflower. She'd been elevated to the rank of nurse, taking care of a rich, elderly man, who'd married her and then conveniently died.

Jane relished describing her rival in full color and cruelty, down to her immense, menacing ostrich feather that waved back and forth in the lights as she leered on passing gentlemen. She wasn't just ridiculous looking, Jane discovered. She was flatly ridiculous. At one point, the wealthy woman lost her bracelet. Upon realizing it, she started up and exclaimed, "I've lost my *Brasslet*—my *people* put it on—its very *valuable*—I am so *frighted*, it has thrown me into a nervous fever, altho I only drink Barley-water—but to be sure lately, I have sipped a little raison wine!"

The rich widow refused to dance because she said she had a little gout in her toe. She bragged about where her late husband would and wouldn't allow her to bathe. She praised her groom's driving. Others laughed, but Jane was struck dumb.

"How I longed for you to enjoy the scene," Jane told Maria. "I never was more gratified with an original in my life."

As Jane's time at Grantham came to a close, there was talk of her being escorted back to London by the heir of Health Hall. It would have signaled his desire to become her suitor, leading some there to expect an imminent engagement. But at the last minute, the heir changed his mind about taking the trip with her.[49] Such things weren't surprising to Jane. As she opined, most men of talents liked to discourse with learned women, but few liked to marry them.[50]

Jane would return alone to London on the stagecoach. She asked her family if they might make a fire in her bedroom the night she arrived, as she was sure she'd be chilled to the bone from the winter ride. At other times, they might have done it, but Maria informed Jane there was just one box of coal left in the house and no money to get more.[51] Jane would have to go without.

"We must think of nothing but how to keep money when we have it," Maria told Jane, in autumn 1799.[52]

In middle-class and wealthy families, adult men would have been expected to provide for widowed mothers and unmarried sisters, but the two eldest, absent Porter brothers habitually fell short.[53] William had the best excuse. He and Lydia were living in Scotland, expecting a child, and dangerously in debt as William tried to set up as a medical man.

Eldest brother John, in his twenty-seventh year, sent his mother very welcome but very irregular money.[54] His prospects took an unexpected turn for the worse when his mentor, the wealthy Charles Kerr, died in Antigua of a nervous fever. The obituary called him an "eminent merchant," a euphemistic term pointing to his status as an enslaver.[55] At his death, all of Kerr's wealth went to his wife and daughter. John Porter, although a witness to the rich man's will, was otherwise unremembered in it and eventually ended up in the army.[56]

So it was Robert, then twenty-two, to whom the Porter women looked for financial support. He'd been taking artistic work wherever he could find it, as a book illustrator and as a scene painter at the Lyceum Theatre.[57] He'd also become a volunteer member of the Royal Westminster Militia, supplying drawings for a manual of military instructions.[58] The three Porter brothers served in different branches of the military in wartime.

All Britain was paying close attention to daily reports of deadly battles against France and Napoleon, but the Porters didn't mistake war for mere entertainment. They understood its great costs to families and the nation. Maria wrote poems to fallen soldiers. Jane read accounts of battles with voracious interest and began to consider military themes for her next novel. Yet it was Robert who first realized that visions of war might be transformed into a rousing spectacle for paying audiences.

Late in 1799, Robert made a plan to paint a recent battle on a gigantic scale, to capitalize on the vogue for the art of war. The painting was striking in scope and entrepreneurship. Robert would have had firsthand knowledge from the School of Eloquence about just how much money could be made from paid admissions to advertised events in rented spaces. One venue for staging such a public art spectacle, which Robert knew well, was the Lyceum Theatre in the Strand, near Somerset House and the Royal Academy. Once used for art exhibitions, it had been transformed into a theater that its proprietors let out to enterprising showmen.[59] The space was used for a popular light show, the *Phantasmagoria*, which displayed moving images on an enormous sheet, at a cost at four shillings for a box seat or two shillings to stand in the rowdy pit. Madame Tussaud's waxworks ran for a time at the Lyceum, without financial success at first.

Robert's familiarity with the Lyceum must have helped him recognize its potential. It could be used to display an enormous painting in the round—a panoramic painting of war, to delight, awe, and instruct. Panoramic paintings were already fashionable. The father-son team of Robert and Henry Aston Barker had coined the term "panorama" and created large-scale pictures of city-scapes in the late 1780s. Exhibiting panoramas had proved so lucrative that the Barkers constructed their own building to hold them. Perhaps to differentiate his work from the Barkers, Robert decided to call his three-quarter, circular canvas a great historical picture.

He planned a grand painting to illuminate the glories and horrors of war and took as his subject the exceptionally bloody British victory in the Kingdom of Mysore, in what is now southern India. This battle of colonial subjugation looks different to today's eyes, but in 1800, Britain's 1799 victory over the French-leaning Kingdom of Mysore was seen as a triumph. Privately, Jane and Maria didn't quite think so. Tipu Sultan "died in a manner that ought to bring a blush over European kings," Jane told Maria.[60]

The British—using fifty thousand soldiers drawn from the East India Company, European mercenaries, and "native troops" from Hyderabad—stormed the walls of the fortress at Seringapatam on May 4, 1799. Victory was declared, as the British suffered just one hundred casualties to Mysore's ten thousand, in an attack led by Major General David Baird. The attack may have been personal as well as strategic, because Baird had been held captive by Tipu Sultan two decades earlier. After killing Tipu Sultan, British troops seized the kingdom's treasure and jewels. The total prize money was one hundred thousand pounds—the equivalent of twelve million today.[61] One of the most famous spoils of war was a mechanical tiger, depicted in the act of attacking a British soldier and created for the tiger-loving Tipu. The automaton tiger, which held a pipe organ inside its belly, was taken back to Britain.

Robert must have seen immediately that this story had every element required for a grand history painting—a home-crowd victor, a vanquished enemy, a strategic location, a devastating battle, and a robotic, musical tiger. Robert painted the battle scene, re-creating soldiers crossing bridges, storming a fortress, and leaving behind piles of corpses, on a 120-foot, life-size canvas that wrapped three quarters around the space.

He wrote to potential investors for his "Indian picture." One, the Earl of Warwick, was straightforwardly skeptical, replying, "You mention painting a Picture 106 feet long & 20 feet high—where are you to stand to see the effect of such a Picture." It was bold, but the Earl asked if it was prudent, telling Robert he'd be happy if he *didn't* undertake this great attempt without further consideration.[62]

Robert did it anyway. He had the silent help of another investor and many painters. One was an artist of African descent, a Black man who frequently served as an uncredited and probably exploited partner in Robert's artistic work.[63] Robert also relied on the help of young artist William Mulready, who later claimed that on *Storming of Seringapatam*, he was painting three full-length figures a day.[64] They did their work in secret, with Jane being one of the few granted the privilege of seeing it. Robert always claimed he did it by himself.

It would later also be claimed Robert did it in six weeks—excepting Sundays, as Jane was quick to add. His own account recorded it taking eight weeks and mentions nothing about Sundays. But Robert had started some version of the painting in October 1799, more than six months before it was declared completed.[65]

Once the work was finished, the Porter family enlisted the support of friends to advertise it.[66] When Robert was ready to show the painting, he went right to the top, asking Benjamin West to visit.[67] West promised this pupil he'd known since boyhood he'd come render an opinion. He may have planned to take no more than a passing glance, but once he got there, he lingered. And lingered. It was said he was an hour late to his next appointments at the Royal Academy. Legend has it that Sir Thomas Lawrence asked West what detained him so long.

West replied, "A wonder! A wonder of the world! I never saw anything like it!—a picture of two hundred feet dimensions, painted by that boy Ker Porter, in six weeks! and as admirably done as it could have been by the best historical painter amongst us in as many months!"[68]

With that incredible endorsement, and word of mouth set in motion, the advertisements set out to lure the public, telling them that from nine to dusk each day, they could see this great historical picture, the *Storming of Seringapatam*. The public was assured it was designed from correct information. It promised explanatory descriptions. These statements were, unsurprisingly, marshaled in support of British interests rather than South Asian ones. The charge of admission was one shilling.[69]

Jane was indefatigable in supporting Robert's venture. She was also becoming his editor and ghostwriter. Always a careful student of history, Jane was deeply interested in detail and accuracy, as well as in how to tell a good story. Her research into the East Indies and the battle itself may have helped Robert design the enormous painting. Or her assistance may have come later, once the painting was nearly complete. Jane put into words the images Robert and his hidden team captured with their brushes. A creative partnership between Jane and Robert was forming, although Jane neither got—nor took—any credit either.

When Robert's "Great Historical Picture" opened on April 17, 1800, viewers were astonished. They poured in by the hundreds each day and by the thousands over months. Standing before the painting, they felt they were there on the battlefield. The Porters' old friend Thomas Frognall Dibdin, a collaborator on *The Quiz*, said that people did nothing after seeing it but think of it, talk of it, and dream of it. There were reports of women having to be carried out swooning.[70]

Robert himself became a swoon-worthy figure. He wore his hair loose, in wavy brown curls. He was sure of himself yet interested in others. He could sport a full-lipped pout while cutting a fine figure. He might have been mistaken for a dandy, if his dark eyes weren't so piercingly intense, if he didn't sometimes blush at being praised, and if the world hadn't declared him a genius. Some claimed the artist was then only eighteen or nineteen, although he was almost twenty-three.[71] Overnight, he was a famous wunderkind, declared one of the country's greatest living artists.

One critic speculated Robert might turn out to be the first English Raphael or Michelangelo. The anonymous claim was written by the fascinating poet, novelist, and feminist Mary Robinson, who'd taken an interest in Robert and his sisters.[72] Other connections to fame followed. The Princess of Wales herself began to visit Robert's studio, perhaps testing the waters for a more intimate connection with the artist.

"*The Porter*"—that is, Robert—"is in great request" everywhere, Maria told Jane.[73]

Crowds kept coming to see the painting. In the summer of 1800, a further enticement was advertised—a *Narrative Sketches* pamphlet, collected from what were touted as authentic and original sources about the battle, along with a description of the design and execution of the painting, followed by explanatory notes.[74] Jane's name appeared nowhere on it, but her hand is everywhere in its 134 pages. The pamphlet, which sold for two shillings—twice the price of admission—moved enough copies to go into a second edition.

While Jane was ghostwriting part or all of Robert's pamphlet, another author was rewriting Jane's first novel, *The Spirit of the Elbe*, into a theatrical spectacle. There was no law against adapting someone else's story, however much Jane may have wished she'd thought to do it herself. The grand ballet pantomime, *Blackenburg; or, the Spirit of the Elbe: Founded on a Favourite Romance*, by the prolific composer and dramatist Charles Dibdin, had a respectable run of performances at Sadler's Wells Theatre.[75] Although Jane didn't benefit from it financially, it would have been gratifying to her to see her anonymous novel live on, especially after dismissive reviews.

Robert's painting exhibited in London for thirty-eight weeks, until January 1801. His total expenses were 1,093 pounds, including 200 pounds of rent to the Lyceum Theatre. Total receipts came to a staggering 3,499 pounds, which meant the picture cleared a profit of 2,406 pounds. Half of that was Robert's to keep, with the other half going to his investor. Having earned 1,203 pounds, Robert was rich and famous.[76]

Many pressed him to share the wealth. He loaned his desperate brother William three hundred pounds, to keep him out of debtors' prison. But Mrs. Porter was rightly panicked when Robert began to loan friends large sums, too. One man swindled him out of hundreds of pounds. Robert also spent freely on new investments and ventures. When the Lyceum Theatre's leasehold came up in May 1800, a month after *Storming of Seringapatam*'s runaway success, Robert joined a group of men who signed onto a new long-term lease. It was done to secure himself future use of the premises. He'd already begun to sketch his next great work. But the agreement meant Robert had future financial responsibilities for the Lyceum Theatre, too, in sharing the rent, along with any profits.[77] He became a famous painter, property manager, and theatrical producer. Because the *Seringapatam* was succeeding so wildly, the responsibilities would have seemed perfectly manageable.

Robert's good fortune transformed Jane's sense of their present and future prospects. She began to chide Maria about her anxieties about money. "O silly Maria!" Jane wrote, "Why do you fret about Moma's representation of our finances?—Have you not long ago experienced her timidity in these matters?" Jane continued, "Do you think if our purse was so near worn out, as fundamentally to cause all this clatter, I should be gay—and thinking of literally nothing else, but the nearest way to be happy?"[78]

CHAPTER 5

Cut My Heart

Jane and Maria's Rival Mentors (1798–1801)

At the turn of the century, Jane's and Maria's novel-writing hadn't yet made them famous or made them a fortune, but Robert's efforts as an artist of a great historical picture had done both, with the help of powerful mentors and secret investors. His sisters, too, had cultivated powerful advocates, including notable women writers. It meant Jane and Maria wouldn't need to manage the pressures of female authorship on their own since their mother had no experience of such matters.

For her earliest literary advice, Jane had drawn on the wisdom and guidance of an older man, the irascible poet Percival Stockdale, but both sisters had begun to make important new connections in London. Their precocious talents had caught the attention of female mentors, from whom Jane and Maria took inspiration and gained advice. Unfortunately, two of these mentors were opposites who were entirely at odds with each other—the wealthy, high-society moralist Mary Champion de Crespigny, and the dazzling actor, writer, and former courtesan Mary Darby Robinson.

Because both mentors were exceptionally complicated figures, in personality and reputation, their notice of Jane and Maria would prove a mixed blessing. Yet these female mentors were also life-changing figures. The Porter sisters would end up publicly connected to them in their own books and in the press. Maria dedicated *Octavia* to "Mrs. Crespigny," by permission, in 1798, praising her virtues and talents and declaring respect and love.[1] Mrs. Robinson's name would become connected to Jane's and Maria's through her own published poetry. These relationships with Crespigny and Robinson proved joyful, formative, and painful for the sister novelists.

Mrs. Crespigny, handsome, clever, and rich, had been known to Jane and Maria for several years. She was an only child and an heiress who served as a strict but generous mother figure to the Porter sisters, although closer to them in age, at ten years younger than Mrs. Porter. She was married to a wealthy, well-connected man, Claude Champion de Crespigny. By the time Mrs. Crespigny met Jane and Maria, she'd already raised her only child, to whom she'd addressed her moralizing book, *Letters of Advice from a Mother to Her Son* (1780).

Mrs. Crespigny had recently published an anonymous novel, *The Pavillion* (1796), although she was widely known to be its author. *The Pavillion* was Gothic fiction with good morality, featuring long-sealed letters, an attempted abduction, a burning cottage, a forged will, and a modest heroine who's restored to high birth and large fortune. The story also revealed its author to be a writer with a tin ear for dialogue, which seems only fitting, as Mrs. Crespigny wasn't much of a listener. She was known as an august matron with an imperious temper and an insipid mind.[2] Yet learned Mrs. Crespigny supported many young women writers' books. She was a powerful force any young authoress would rather have in her corner than not.

She had the means and the space to entertain lavishly. Her husband's property, Champion Lodge, sat on a thirty-acre park in Camberwell, Surrey, four miles south of London. It had a famed garden and a grotto, which was dedicated to contemplation, as well as a private theater for staging amateur plays. The Prince of Wales became a frequent guest at her parties, and she set up elaborate gatherings for his amusement.

Jane, Maria, and Robert had become favorite guests of the Crespignys, too. Mrs. Crespigny was a dedicated toxophilite since her girlhood. She found Robert valuable because he, too, was good with a bow and arrow. Jane and

Maria became trusted female companions, and soon the sisters were being invited for overnight stays. Mrs. Crespigny kept a stable of young women at her home, as adoring company. Jane later showed her appreciation of her host by publishing an anonymous, glowing character sketch of her for a magazine. There Jane dubbed Mrs. Crespigny the patroness of talent and the benefactress of those in distress.[3]

Time with Mrs. Crespigny could be very happy. Female companions were given the opportunity to eat, sleep, and stay in comfort on lavish pleasure grounds, among highly interesting people. Maria remembered her days at Champion Lodge as among the most agreeable of her life.[4] There the sisters had much-needed access to the family's private library. But serving as Mrs. Crespigny's female companions also involved tedious labor. Jane and Maria were at the society matron's beck and call, reading aloud to her to entertain her, or following her to wherever her whims took her, almost as a personal assistant. She rarely gave her female companions one moment to themselves.[5]

As a hostess, Mrs. Crespigny did things on a grand scale and needed helpers. She held breakfasts for droves of fashionable Londoners, to which a ticket to attend was a prized thing. She organized archery contests for both sexes on her property. The competition was all in good fun, but guests were forced to take it seriously because she made losers pay a fine to support the local Sunday school. Accounts of these gatherings regularly ended up in the newspapers. In June 1798, a printed report mentioned the handsome country girl who never left Mrs. Crespigny's side and was admired for her rustic dress and animated looks. That unnamed girl was Jane, who'd declined to wear the shepherdess costume Mrs. Crespigny had chosen for her. Jane, having selected her own outfit, received public compliments in return for her defiance.[6]

As important as she was to their being introduced into society, Mrs. Crespigny wasn't the Porter sisters' only source of literary support. Another role model who took an interest in Jane and Maria was Mrs. Crespigny's opposite, in reputation and habits. By the time the Porters met the notorious Mary Robinson, she was living a secluded life, after having been a famed actor and royal mistress. She remained one of the most recognized women of her generation, publishing poems, feminist essays, and novels. Her beauty was captured in portraits by the era's most famous artists. But while officious Mrs. Crespigny sat at the zenith of fashionable female politeness, the iconoclastic Mary Robinson had become a pariah.

Mrs. Robinson, as they called her, was twenty years older than Jane and Maria. She was known to the sisters as a disabled mother living in genteel poverty. They thought she'd been used and discarded by powerful men and had reformed. Jane and Maria believed in redemption and forgiveness. Others scorned Mrs. Robinson as an unredeemable sinner, but Jane and Maria idolized her as a wronged genius.

In the first half of 1799, nearly every private letter Jane and Maria exchanged mentioned Mrs. Robinson in some way. They couldn't stop talking about her. The sisters shared reports on her health, especially when it was fragile, as well as on her lovely daughter, Maria, who was just their age. The Porter sisters began regularly to visit the Robinson women—visits apparently made with Mrs. Porter's knowledge and approval. They would have heard Mrs. Robinson's remarkable story from her own mouth.

Mary Robinson's colorful life is difficult to capture on the page. As a successful young married actress, she had, twenty years before, played Perdita in Shakespeare's *The Winter's Tale* in a royal command performance before the Prince of Wales. He was seventeen, and she was twenty-two or twenty-three. Her husband was a swindler, and she was already the mother of daughter Maria, then age five. The Prince, after watching Mrs. Robinson's performance, sent her a love letter. She responded. They connected. Mrs. Robinson left her debt-ridden husband to become a royal mistress.

The Prince of Wales dubbed her "Perdita," after the Shakespearean role she'd played. It was a nickname taken up by the public, too, signaling something lost or fallen. When the young prince discarded Mrs. Robinson, a year later, it was without having married her, as she'd apparently once hoped. The Prince did, however, settle on her an annuity of five hundred pounds a year, with which she could have raised her daughter in comfort, if it had been enough to clear her already substantial debts.[7]

So Mrs. Robinson took other lovers, whether out of financial urgency, romantic feelings, or an adherence to the new radical philosophy of sexual freedom. She connected herself to a nobleman, then a politician, and then a warmongering, slavery-supporting army colonel. These alliances were well known by the gossiping public. Many years later, when Mrs. Robinson began to face health challenges after what was called a "violent rheumatism," she gave up the stage to seek a literary life.

Financial concerns led to her publishing at a rapid pace. She built a successful career as an author. Writing had long been part of her identity. Like the Porter sisters, Mrs. Robinson had published verses as a teen. She wrote about the injustices of slavery and debtors' prison in *Captivity: A Poem* (1777). She published the feminist treatise *A Letter to the Women of England, on the Injustice of Mental Subordination* (1798). By the time the Porters came into her life, Mrs. Robinson was known as a woman of once-extraordinary—and still extant—beauty and intellect.

Jane and Maria knew who Mrs. Robinson had been in the past, and they didn't approve of her choices, but she was a sympathetic a character to them, particularly when her health took a turn for the worse. Once, when Mrs. Robinson was gravely ill, Jane wrote to Mrs. Robinson's daughter, Maria, to express deep concern, telling her, "those I esteem are always particularly endeared to me, when they are in sickness."[8] Jane wished she could transport herself to their neighborhood to stand as a handmaid to her mentor and friend. She longed, she said, to throw "a few smiles over the languid lips of your estimable mother."

Jane and Maria saw Mrs. Robinson for the best of what she was: a strong, independent woman and a gorgeous literary genius. She grew fond of the Porter sisters, too, despite the skeptical coolness toward female friendship she'd once expressed to Jane. It was understandable. Mrs. Robinson had been held at arm's length, or worse, by most of the intellectual women of her generation. Her illicit love affairs had cut her off from polite society, especially women's society. For a woman to openly visit her, even to secretly visit her, was to court guilt by association.

Jane and Maria were eventually forced to see their own peril in knowing Mrs. Robinson. The upright Mrs. Crespigny pulled Robert aside at Champion Lodge and questioned him closely about his sisters' degree of intimacy with Mrs. Robinson. She told him that not only ladies but also many gentlemen had expressed to her their concern and surprise at Jane and Maria's supposed association with a woman who'd once lived in so disgraceful a manner. Mrs. Robinson, she reminded him, was now shunned by every person of character.

"Good Heavens!" Maria wrote. "How astonished I was, when Bob told me, that no woman visited her . . . that it was a talk among the officers, our being seen in her company."

Robert believed Mrs. Crespigny was a sincere friend of his sisters, who had their best interests at heart. She'd praised Jane's and Maria's fine persons and elegant manners. But these lovely qualities, she believed, made the world *more* observant of their conduct. She begged Robert to urge them to break their connection to Mrs. and Miss Robinson. The Porter sisters could *not* be on visiting terms with those Robinson women, and especially with the mother. Maria, upon hearing this, was shocked into submission. "No urging I am sure will be required with me," she told Jane. "I see the danger we are in."

Maria and Mrs. Porter devised a plan to drop the Robinsons' acquaintance by degrees. Maria also canceled her plans to eat at the soldiers' barracks on Sunday, lest she give them further occasion to gossip about her. Maria railed at herself for her naïveté, at the world for its narrowness—and at Robert, too. "He never used to talk calmly of the injury our characters would sustain," Maria complained to Jane. "It is the only thing I have been angry with him for, but I will say no more."[9]

It shouldn't have been up to Mrs. Crespigny to warn them about the damage to their reputations, Maria thought. Robert should have been the one to point it out. Mrs. Robinson was his friend, too. Two years earlier, he'd presented her with verses and a picture to show his admiration.[10] In return, she'd admired Robert enough to publish that anonymous sketch touting his greatness as an artist.[11]

But no one in the family loved Mrs. Robinson more than Jane, who, in the months following Robert's and Mrs. Crespigny's admonitions, was unable to end the friendship. She continued to write secretly to the Robinsons, under the cover of another friend. She'd hide her risky letters to Mrs. Robinson underneath a second envelope, addressed to someone she could acknowledge writing to, which would be hand delivered by that go-between.[12]

Adding insult to injury, Robert, despite telling Maria and Jane to end all visits with the Robinsons, hadn't done so himself. Once he and a friend went to their cottage but found only Miss Robinson at home. She reported her mother was on an airing in a carriage. When Robert told Maria about this meeting, she felt a pang of regret that she couldn't visit the mother and daughter herself.

Maria summed up her conflicted love in a letter to Jane: "With all her frailties, nay immoralities, Mrs. Robinson is interesting and painfully so, to me."[13]

Late in 1799, the situation with the Porter sisters' female mentors underwent another revolution. Lurid gossip was revealed. Mrs. Robinson was said to have taken a new lover. His identity came as a shock to Jane and Maria. It was Mrs. Crespigny's brother-in-law, Philip Champion de Crespigny, a married lawyer and politician. He and Mary Robinson were said to be living together, although it was supposed to be a profound secret. Her daughter, Maria, in an act of self-protection to save her own reputation, was said to have left her mother's house.

Jane and Maria stayed as far away from the secret scandal as they could, but Robert had the luxury of behaving as he always had. Thanks to the different expectations for male and female behavior, Robert accepted an invitation to join a small supper that included both Mary Robinson and Philip Champion de Crespigny. Robert's reputation wasn't damaged by dining with his famous friend and her new lover, although he surely wouldn't have wanted to advertise it to his upright friend, Mrs. Crespigny.

Robert got away with it, but Jane and Maria found themselves subject to new scrutiny for their friendship with Mrs. Robinson. Their connection to her was revealed, in all places, in the pages of a widely circulating newspaper. In June 1800, Mrs. Robinson had done what she no doubt thought was a favor to the literary sisters. She'd named them in two short poems published under her byline in the *Morning Post*: "To Miss Porter, in the Character of a Nun" and "To Miss Maria Porter, as Roxalana."[14]

The titles of the poems referred to Jane's and Maria's costumes worn at a fashionable masquerade party, called the most select and brilliant of the season.[15] Mrs. Robinson hadn't been invited, but the young Porters had. On June 12, 1800, a newspaper report provided a list the evening's prominent characters and costumes. Guests who came dressed as opposites often traveled together through the party in pairs. Maria and Jane, too, came as opposites of a sort. According to the *Morning Post*, Miss Porter came as a Carmelite nun and Miss A. M. Porter as a Turkish girl. Circulating reports had it that all three Porters—Robert had come as an old squire—were among the most distinguished characters present.

Jane and Maria wore costumes to suit their personalities. Jane's nun's habit was in keeping with her serene piety, as well as her penchant for veils. Maria's costume was not precisely of a Turkish girl but in the character of Roxalana. It was copied from a stage role made famous by several actresses, including one of Maria's then-favorites, Mrs. Dorothy "Dora" Jordan, mistress of the Duke of Clarence, the future King William IV. Roxalana was a turban-wearing, free-speaking Englishwoman, who'd been kept as property by a sultan, in Isaac Bickerstaff's play *The Sultan*. This costume meant Maria would have had opportunities to play the saucy-tongued, flirtatious part with the other guests, perhaps alongside her piously dressed (and well-behaving) sister.

The event must have been a who's who of royal, noble, literary, and theatrical life. The Porter sisters left a record of the night through their own poetry. If Maria's enjoyment came from playing actress for a night, then Jane's pleasure was in her work on her written accessories created for a friend's costume. The Porters' friend, Miss Myers, planned to go dressed as a flower girl, so Jane decided to compose original verses for her friend to carry in her basket. The handwritten poems were tied onto flowers that Miss Myers would hand out to guests. Jane wrote nine poems and Maria wrote one. The sisters paired each short verse with a designated flower, said to be associated with one host, guest, or illustrious personage.

For the host Lady Dashwood's flower-poem, Jane chose to pair her original verse with a columbine, declaring her host the night's "presiding goddess." For Sir John Dashwood, Jane tied her poem to a branch of elm and described him as a sturdy tree, the pillar and crown of his house. Jane's longest poem, a sonnet, was written for the Prince of Wales, Mrs. Robinson's former lover. Jane paired the poem with white and red roses. The poem fulsomely explains that the verses are in honor of the respected historical princes who came before him, including in the War of the Roses, and the country's good fortune in having so good a prince again.[16]

Jane must have taken pride in her flower-girl masquerade poems, because afterward she sent copies of them to her friend Mrs. Robinson, who decided to publish them in the poetry section of the *Morning Post*, which she edited. Jane had declared in her letter to Mrs. Robinson that she didn't want her verses published, but Mrs. Robinson did it anyway. It's possible Jane even half-wished for this result. She was sending her poems to a known editor. Jane wouldn't have anticipated or desired that Mrs. Robinson would mingle the sisters' verses on the page with her own. Two of Mrs. Robinson's signed poems, in praise of Jane as a nun and Maria as Roxalana, followed Jane's and Maria's masquerade poetry.

Mrs. Robinson's verse called Jane "sweet maid! in holy guise" and said she was "more lovely than the sun." She also declared Jane "A mild and beauteous star." Mrs. Robinson wrote that Maria was "So sportive! so lovely! so witty! so chaste!" and declared that she must be able to overcome a tyrant with her beauty.[17] These were flattering tributes—high praise of both beauty and brains—from the pen of a woman said to be one of the most attractive and talented writers of her generation. What a shame, then, that seeing the names "Miss Porter," "Miss Maria Porter," and "Mrs. Robinson" printed together in the newspaper would have been devastatingly unwelcome attention for the sisters.

Mrs. Robinson seemed unaware of or unconcerned about what she'd done to her young protégées. She told Jane afterward, "I sent your charming lines to Stuart," the *Morning Post*'s publisher, "and I am certain that, both he and the public, will rejoice in my having *done* what your graceful diffidence declined doing." Mrs. Robinson, in her next letter to Robert, reports that Jane's and Maria's verses were much admired.[18]

In the months that followed, the Porter sisters tried to distance themselves from their admiring mentor. Only Mrs. Robinson's side of the correspondence with the Porters has survived. What it shows is the older woman's increasing desire, even desperation, to reconnect with the sisters. She had invited a series of friends to stay with her that summer at her well-situated, tasteful, and quiet home at Englefield Cottage. Most were young women writers, including the novelist Eliza Fenwick, a financially struggling and unhappily married friend of the Porters.[19] Mrs. Robinson repeatedly invited Jane and Maria to be her guests, too.

"All my friends," she writes, "excepting your family, and none do I *love better*, have been in turn to see me."

When that approach didn't work, Mrs. Robinson tried another form of encouragement. She wrote out predictions for Jane's future.

"Lovely and highly-gifted as you are," she wrote, "you will rise in the gay mazes of Society, but for a Time; for your Soul is to[o] finely organised, your heart too sensitive, to enjoy for a long period of time the artificial Beings you will meet with.

"Yet," Mrs. Robinson told Jane, "you should not be secluded. You are one of those who are created to embellish, to refine, to charm a vile unfeeling world."[20]

Despite the flattery, Jane didn't come to see her. Of all the interactions with Mrs. Robinson that Robert might have tolerated, his sisters staying overnight at Englefield Cottage was the last he'd approve. She had harbored male lovers under her roof—recently even. Perhaps Robert knew more there than he could say himself: Mrs. Robinson referred to Robert, who didn't come to see her then either, as her truant, saucy Raphael.[21]

Jane and Maria filled their days that year with new writing and bustling social activity. But in December 1800, they were painfully reminded of their neglected friend when they learned Mrs. Robinson had taken seriously ill. Maria was the first to receive news of it. She wasn't sure how to respond, whether directly to Mrs. Robinson, through their secret courier to her, or at all. On Christmas Eve, Maria told Jane, "I have written to poor Miss Robinson offering her every attention in our power. Was it not right?"[22]

The following week, Jane accepted an invitation to stay for an indeterminate number of days at Champion Lodge, as the companion of Mr. and Mrs. Crespigny. Maria stayed behind in London with Mrs. Porter. But no sooner had Jane traveled to them in Surrey than her hosts decided to attend a dinner in town. They brought Jane with them back to London. Just before the meal was served, another guest, a wealthy widow, announced a piece of celebrity gossip. The infamous Mary Robinson had died.

Jane, shocked, tried to conceal how grieved she was. Some in the group must have known a Crespigny brother was rumored to have been Mrs. Robinson's lover. There would have been disparaging remarks made about her as they ate. During this chatter, Jane was able to regain some composure. After dinner, Mrs. Crespigny noticed something was wrong with her young friend. There was a hint of tears.

Mrs. Crespigny asked Jane directly, with a frown, if she were acquainted with Mrs. Robinson. She asked Jane whether it was true that some lines of verse in the newspaper, supposed to have been written by Mrs. Robinson, were about Jane? When Jane said little in reply, Mrs. Crespigny continued her attack. If

Jane had been a friend of the now-dead Mrs. Robinson, then all the world would have to cut her. Indeed, Mrs. Crespigny herself would have to drop Jane. She'd be shunned by all decent people, the powerful society woman proclaimed, threatening to do it then and there, in front of the whole company.

Jane, terrified, chose to betray the memory of her beloved, morally flawed mentor. She blurted out a lie. She told Mrs. Crespigny and the rest of them that she didn't know Mrs. Robinson. The reason tears wouldn't stop pouring down her cheeks, she explained, was because she had a nervous headache. Somehow, Jane carried on through the rest of the evening. At the end of the night, the party returned, as planned, to Champion Lodge. Jane went to bed with an indescribable feeling of sadness. She was ashamed.

"Oh! how did it cut my heart, that I was thus forced to hide a regret which I thought laudable!" she wrote in her diary. "One moment I despised myself, for being ashamed to avow feelings, which I could not condemn; and the next I excused myself, from the conviction that it was only a prudence."[23]

What Jane did next was what she knew best. She tried to write her way out of the shame. She stayed awake and wrote two things, a tribute to Mrs. Robinson and a letter of condolence to her surviving daughter. Then Jane secretly sent them off inside a sealed letter to her sister. Jane wanted Maria to read them, and if she approved, to post them—the letter of condolence to Miss Robinson and the tribute to Mrs. Robinson to a magazine, for anonymous publication.

In the letter of condolence, Jane told Miss Robinson, "My heart deeply participates in the grief which you now suffer; and from an unrestrainable impulse of the heart." Jane's letter, although sermon-like, is filled with praise for Mrs. Robinson, envisioning her as a saint, now in heaven with her sister-angels. Jane asks the grieving daughter if she might call on her. She promises the Porter family's everlasting affection and signs herself "very faithful friend."[24]

The second piece Jane sent to Maria to read was the anonymous tribute. Jane's "Character of the Late Mrs. Robinson, Who is Usually Stiled the British Sappho. Extracted from a letter to a lady" staunchly defended her friend. Her moving memoir was the riposte Jane might have offered had she responded honestly to judgmental Mrs. Crespigny, without fear of social retribution.

Jane's "Character" presents itself as if composed by a lady writing a letter to a female friend, just after learning about Mrs. Robinson's death. The letter doesn't mince words about Mrs. Robinson's former fall from morality. It describes the failings of her youth and her seduction by the Prince of Wales. But the letter writer forgives her these youthful indiscretions because she later redeemed herself. Mrs. Robinson improved her own mind. Her strongest passions in later life were for genius. Jane's "Character" describes how Mrs. Robinson made money by writing and editing and helped authors who came to her, advising them on how to correct the faults in their verse and prose. The tribute claims Mrs. Robinson's "charms and talents attracted the envy and malevolence of most vain women; while they excited the proud boasts of men." Jane condemns those who circulated malicious stories, repaid Mrs. Robinson's friendship with slander, and left her to scrape by. The piece ends with a plea to the arrogant world not to extend its prejudices from the unfortunate parent to the blameless child—her daughter, Miss Robinson.

Maria read Jane's tribute and the letter of condolence and reflected on them. She wrote back informing Jane that she'd decided not to send out either document. She wasn't sure the letter of condolence would be welcomed since a cold, repulsive reply to the Porters' offer of help had arrived from Miss Robinson. So Maria held back Jane's letter to the bereaved daughter.

Maria also held back from sending the tribute because she feared her sister would be suspected as its author. Maria also questioned whether Jane would be able to withstand Mrs. Crespigny's close questioning a second time. Either Jane would confess to lying or would tell another one, and Maria thought her sister was more likely to confess.

Jane saw the wisdom in everything Maria had written. She regretted her lie.

"I would have given worlds to have recalled it," she wrote. "I never again would have raised my head." Her regret brought on a resolution. She vowed to correct her future conduct in moments when her headlong enthusiasm might damage veracity. Whenever she found that her violent candor was hurrying her to calumny, she wrote, she'd remember Mrs. Robinson. She was filled with regret.

"That I admired her talents, that I pityed her sufferings, that I loved her virtues, that I forgot her errors, as I hope Heaven will forget mine; that I visited her, that I wrote to her, that she called me her 'sweet Friend!'" she wrote. "And yet, that I could, when taxed with it deny that we were acquainted! I ought not to have accepted her friendship, when I was ashamed to assert it."[25]

In the weeks that followed, Jane's denial of Mrs. Robinson weighed heavily on her mind. She wrote a poem, "Lines supposed to be written in Old Windsor Church Yard, at the Grave of the Celebrated Mrs. Robinson."[26] It's likely she did what the poem's speaker reports having done—wandering around the gloomy churchyard, praising her dead friend, with a bereaved heart. Eventually, Jane's guilt was too great. She confessed her betrayal of Mrs. Robinson, although not to Mrs. Crespigny. She confessed to a third party, one of Mrs. Crespigny's other female companions, Miss Elizabeth Ogilvy Benger. Jane had known Miss Benger only slightly before, but during the winter of 1801, the two young women were staying at Champion Lodge and expected to share a bed. There Jane made her new acquaintance into a confessor and confidante.

Elizabeth Benger (pronounced "Ben-jay") had published her first book in her teens. She had, like the Porters, come into the literary world from almost nothing. Her friends called her by her surname, and she had a reputation for a melodious voice, charm, and lively conversation.[27] On this night in bed with Jane, however, Benger was called on to be a sympathetic listener. Jane poured out her shame in having lied to Mrs. Crespigny about knowing Mrs. Robinson. Jane and Benger stayed up talking until past one in the morning.

Once she'd listened to the entire story, Benger told Jane she'd acquit her conduct.[28] Jane's response under pressure was understandable. With her new friend's approval, Jane forgave herself for wronging the memory of Mrs. Robinson. After Jane's confession, and Benger's forgiveness, the two women's intimacy was sealed. Benger promised to visit Jane and Maria often when they returned to London and promised, too, to include the sisters in the interesting literary salon she hosted at her modest home. Jane couldn't wait to meet Benger's friends. Many were celebrities, or on the cusp of becoming so, including the poet, critic, and editor Anna Letitia Barbauld; the playwright and novelist Elizabeth Inchbald; and the poet Robert Southey. Jane admired them from their writings, but she'd never met them.

"This is the society that I love," Jane wrote in her diary. "It is amongst such beings, that I feel the dignity of man. For the liberty of listening one day, to the wisdom and wit, of such a circle, I would surrender up, a year's homage, from the silly *Great*, who so arrogantly think and say, that there is no word out of *their* sphere."[29]

Jane vowed to leave behind the "silly great," among whom she would surely have included Mrs. Crespigny, to connect herself to a new set of brilliant authors. She also became increasingly disciplined about her writing. She created an exacting daily schedule for herself. She'd rise at 6. Breakfast at 8. Write from 9 until 2. Dine at 2. Read from 3 until 4. Walk from 4 until 6. Tea at 6. Write letters or read from 7 until 9. Supper at 9. And from 10, to rest. As Jane calculated it out in hours, "Reading, 3. Writing, 5, Rest, 8."[30]

In the early months of 1801, Jane traveled back and forth often from London to Camberwell, to stay with the Crespignys, but she did so with increasing aversion. She found revolting all the tasteless Gothic novels that her host insisted Jane read aloud to her. "Hour after hour spent in wading through pages of sheeted ghosts, and goblins dire," Jane complained, "not one of whose 'names on earth' I now remember."[31] She called it a "torture" that wearied her to death. But when Mrs. Crespigny summoned Jane to read, she obeyed. In her diary, however, she could record her true opinion that the book of choice, Regina Roche's *The Nocturnal Visit*, was execrable. Of reading such garbage aloud, night after night, Jane wrote, "My lungs hold out longer than my patience."[32] But the moment they finished *The Nocturnal Visit*, Mrs. Crespigny had Jane begin reading aloud another just like it.

"I have been so cloyed, or rather *bored*, with such visits lately," Jane confessed in her diary, "that I don't believe I shall be able to look into a novel for a century, when I return home. Indeed, I am so disgusted with the trash which I nightly run through, that in the daytime, I have not patience to add to the heap, by writing one line of my own."[33]

This pledge to swear off writing fiction didn't hold. Reading trash to the judgmental Mrs. Crespigny somehow proved a literary inspiration to Jane. During the first week of February 1801, she finished writing the opening to what would become her next novel, *Thaddeus of Warsaw*.

"It pleases me more than anything I have written," Jane recorded in her diary, with uncharacteristic self-satisfaction, "because it is the most simple. I detest the common fustian air of my stile. How I got it, found it, or come by it, I am yet to learn! I am sure; I never sought it."[34]

Maria, on the other hand, was displeased with her own literary efforts. She was producing books more than twice as fast as Jane and wrote in manic spurts.

She confessed to Jane that she now thought that a learned man's prediction to her, that she'd one day produce something very great, wouldn't come true.

"I am very easy about it," Maria admitted to her sister, because "to be happy, not celebrated, is my aim, whether I become so by making a pudding or making a Book, is all one to me."[35]

CHAPTER 6

Gone Theatrical Mad

Maria's Plays, Jane's New Romance, and the Enchanting Kembles (1801)

In the wake of Robert's newfound fame, the three youngest Porter siblings were happily thrust into the colorful, dramatic, and mercurial London theater world in 1801. Robert had emerged there as a major player—a fellow entertainment impresario, with throngs of people visiting his great historical pictures at the Lyceum Theatre, in which he also had a production stake. He'd become sought-after company and was followed around by attractive actresses as he created his next great work. His sisters, often by his side, had become devoted fans of the theater in their own right. As close observers of its stars, they were budding critics of the stage. They had already proved their worth among thespians by publishing an anonymous pamphlet in defense of the profession of an actor the previous year.

At first, this theatrical immersion was a welcome thing. The Porters went to plays. They befriended famous actors. They made their amateur acting debuts, performing farcical scenes Maria had written. Eventually, the Porters would transform a room in their home into a private theater. But by the end of 1801, Jane, Maria, and Robert were experiencing dramas—verging on melodramas—in their personal lives. Maria, left alone one momentous night with a theater-loving male friend, would find herself questioning where adoration stopped and love began.

Jane, too, would experience a romantic crisis. Her beloved Henry Caulfield, after the death of his disapproving father, had surprised his friends by reinventing himself as an actor. He was also proving a rake, with gossiping reports connecting him to a series of women. As Jane tried to wrest her heart back from roving Henry, she discovered a yearning for another man. The object of her secret affection was a member of the most famous acting family of the day, the powerful Kembles. Jane, newly intimate with this circle of celebrity actors, was slowly pulled into a painful love triangle. It would prove an event-filled year, as confusing and complicated as the plot of any five-act play or five-volume novel.

The turning point that brought on the enormous changes and challenges of the year might be dated back to one night in March 1801. At first, Jane thought she might go to the theater to see a favorite actress, Dora Jordan, starring in *The Country Girl*. The play was merely a tame rewriting of a Restoration romp, but Jane and Maria took every opportunity to see productions at the two great theaters within walking distance—Covent Garden and Drury Lane. The sisters often gained free access to excellent box seats, thanks to a growing circle of actor-friends, including, soon, Mrs. Jordan herself. Robert's success as an artist meant the sisters would sometimes even be able to pay their own way to the theater. Money was flowing more freely than ever before.

But on that March night in question, Jane found herself feeling languid. Instead of going to see *The Country Girl*, she decided to stay home on Gerrard Street for dinner with Maria and Robert. It was a fortunate choice, because the conversation proved transformational. The siblings' probing exchanges about their hopes and dreams were more important to her than watching any play. The Porters were joined that night by their friend Ned Warren—the friend who'd once accidentally broken Maria's arm—who was on intimate terms with all of them. Ned's late father, Dr. Richard Warren—physician to the Prince of Wales and King George III—died a wealthy man. Maria suspected Ned must be the one behind the anonymous, mysterious love notes Jane had recently been receiving, but no one ever stepped forward to claim authorship.[1]

As the four of them shared a meal, Robert described his fantasies for the future. If he ever made a fortune, he wanted to build a structure to hold his enormous paintings. He'd exhibit *Seringapatam* along with the new great historical picture he was working on, *The Siege of Acre*, and any others he might paint. At his death, he mused, he'd bequeath the building and its paintings to the nation. Jane, Maria, and Ned assured him his dreams were within reach. Robert's genius was worthy, they said, of the nation's admiration and posterity's gratitude. After dinner, Ned and Robert went their own way, and Jane and Maria fell into a private conversation.

Having just spent the night listening to Robert's grand plans, the sisters dared to talk about their own. Maria was torn about her path forward. At age twenty-two, she'd published four books, three under her name, but she wanted to try something new and was beginning to write a comic play. Her love of the theater prompted the attempt but so did a hope to make money. A playwright might make much more than a novelist.

Maria would have known that the celebrated writer Elizabeth Inchbald had enjoyed several stage successes and had recently been paid five hundred pounds for her adapted play *The Wise Man of the East*.[2] At its unfortunate debut, Maria had been in the audience. She watched as the actors were nearly booed off the stage.[3] Perhaps its failure inspired her to try her own hand at an adapted play. Maria, a literary prodigy with a knack for capturing dialogue, would have seemed a good bet to become the next Inchbald.

Jane, at age twenty-five, was notably behind Maria in literary output and achievement. She'd published one anonymous novel, only to have her next two works rejected by Longman and Rees. One was the pamphlet defending the profession of an actor, co-written with Maria, which had eventually found another publisher. The other was a fictional work for children, which Jane was in the process of selling elsewhere. Maria had been outraged on her sister's behalf at Longman's rejections, having declared, "One might as well attempt to 'move a dish of skimmed milk with sugar' as teach a *bookseller* to feel genius"—a riff on a Shakespearean line.[4] Maria rightly believed Jane's talent was immense.

But apparently unspoken that night, even between these closest of sisters, were the ways that love, romance, and marriage might go along with their literary work. A young woman's having, much less expressing, romantic feelings for men—especially before being told she was beloved—was vigorously discouraged then. Jane was skeptical of the wisdom of this advice, touted by their moralizing mentor Mrs. Crespigny, who believed no delicate woman should ever love a man until she was sure of the return of his affections. Jane believed differently. "I rather think, with Lord Lyttleton," she wrote, "not loving first, but loving wrong, is blame!"[5] Lyttleton's original quotation used the word "shame," not "blame," but Jane gets the substance right. She found it neither shameful nor blamable to love first. Yet among Jane's papers, too, is another scrap with this quotation: "If a woman wishes to fix the affections of any man, she must carefully conceal from his view the hold that he hath upon her heart."[6] Neither of these would-be pieces of wisdom covered the question of whether a woman should acknowledge *to herself* when she had romantic feelings for a man—or whether she should try to deny or ignore them.

That was the very problem Maria diagnosed in her sister that night. It must have started with Maria's suggesting Jane lacked candor, because of a refusal to admit, even to herself, her hopes and dreams. Maria encouraged Jane to pour out her whole heart into a journal of her life. Jane had started keeping a diary that year, at Mrs. Crespigny's suggestion. Maria thought her sister should register every thought—every feeling—in private writing. That's how this night's conversation survives. Jane recorded as much of it as she could in her new diary, including not only dialogue, like a playwright would, but also the finer points of character and performance. There were musings, too, on the mysteries of her own character—mysteries even to her.

Many women in this era kept diaries, recording a line or two about activities of the day. Jane had previously kept that sort of factual record. Some women writers composed longer narrative accounts of their lives. The late Mary Robinson had left behind her *Memoirs* at her death, to justify her unconventional behavior to the world. Jane's case was different. Maria thought Jane should keep a journal not to be candid with the world but to improve her self-candor—to engage in self-discovery.

"I believe that she is right," Jane reflected later that night, about Maria's admonitions. "But yet my heart is a churl; it will not, even to myself, allow the extent of all it feels. It is continually to my own investigation, expanding and contracting: and when it thus shrinks at the touch of my own finger, how can I expose it naked on paper, before mine eyes!"

Jane thought she might be made up of two reasoning spirits, the scholar and the teacher. Constantly at odds with each other, these warring spirits prevented her from understanding her own heart. At first, she'd resolve to investigate her feelings on the page, like a scholar might do, trying to dig deep. But then she'd suddenly shift to writing about common subjects, like a teacher might do with guileless students. The teacher inside Jane would prevent her pen from going beyond the surface of a subject, saying, "Alas! I dare not! Though no eye should see these sheets but my own, I dare not."[7] This entry reads almost as if it's Jane's soliloquy on a polite woman's life. She mused on her inscrutable, conflicted personality. She considered how best to perform her role in a world of admonitions, as a fear-filled but deep-feeling female. She did it in the medium she loved—the written word.

She admired those who could speak feelings. By 1801, Jane and Maria had come to worship the daring talents of actors, plumbing the depths of the spirit, through lines put into their mouths by talented writers. Maria couldn't get enough of the theater, her favorite subject.[8] Once, in a letter, Maria had begun to make fun of the theatrical obsessives among their acquaintance. Then she stopped herself, to self-deprecatingly declare, "So theatrical-mad a creature as I am, I have no right to laugh at others."[9]

The sisters had their personal favorites among the day's celebrated actors. Maria praised to the skies the wonderful acting of Mrs. Sarah Siddons in *Jane Shore* at the Drury Lane theatre. Mrs. Siddons—born into the famous Kemble acting family and then in her forties—was considered the best actor alive. Both Porter sisters wholeheartedly agreed.[10] Jane and Maria had dedicated their forty-page pamphlet *A Defence of the Profession of an Actor* (1800), to Mrs. Siddons, describing her as a steadfast lady and a star irradiating life on the stage.

Jane knew a great deal about the theater. The pamphlet (which Jane wrote, with Maria's help) begins with a brief history of the stage.[11] Then it argues that the theater, despite its bad reputation, has a positive effect on society's morality. *A Defence* doesn't deny the theater is sometimes the scene of vice, but it claims the problem isn't the corrupting influence of playwrights, theater managers, or actors. Instead, Jane argues, aristocrats are more to blame.[12] Titled men who make actresses into mistresses are the problem, not the actresses. Adding insult to injury, the pamphlet argues, these same guilty elites then turn around and wrongly shun the actors they've corrupted. Jane offers a revolutionary reverse take. Although it goes unmentioned, the actor Mary Robinson's mistreatment by the Prince of Wales may have prompted Jane's anger.

The genre of the defense is one Jane knew well. Her favorite author, Sir Philip Sidney, wrote *The Defence of Poesy* (1595) to argue against the common sixteenth-century belief that imaginative literature contributes to vice. Jane's defense of actors follows in the same vein: It's ridiculous that dramatic texts are admired by privileged readers, while the theater is insulted. Worst of all, she argues, actors who are applauded onstage are then socially shunned off it, by hypocritical, unfair elites.

Reviewers weren't impressed with the pamphlet. Dr. Charles Burney (father of famous novelist Frances Burney), writing anonymously in the *Monthly Review*, called Jane's *Defence* a "*tweedle dum* and *tweedle dee* quarrel" by a "pompous and labouring author." A few actors have always been welcomed into the higher social circles, Burney argues, but actors largely deserve the poor treatment they get. So many, he writes, are "ignorant, vulgar, without knowledge of the world, good morals, good-breeding, wit, or any of the necessary talents for conversation; and would be at best a dead weight on good society, if admitted into what is *truly* called good company."[13] This perfectly summed up the bigoted attitudes toward actors that Jane's pamphlet was fighting against.

At the time of the *Defence* publication, in spring 1800, Robert's fame was accelerating with his first great historical picture. By the following year, his network had grown to include notables in the professional theater, as well as in amateur private theatricals, thanks to society hosts like Mrs. Crespigny and the wealthy eccentric, the Margravine of Anspach. By 1801, the Porter sisters, too, could count actors as close friends.

The husband-and-wife team of Henry and Amelia Johnston were the sisters' current on- and offstage favorites. Jane and Maria were on familiar visiting terms with the Johnstons, affectionately calling them "Harry" and "our sweet Amelia."[14] Mrs. Johnston and the Misses Porter sat together in hours-long visits. Once Mrs. Johnston confessed to Maria that she'd feigned illness so as not to have to play an immodestly revealing breeches part. She dreaded playing one of the cross-dressed roles in which she'd have to wear pants and show the contours of her figure on stage, although she knew her avoidance couldn't last long.[15] Maria felt deeply for her poor friend and the evils of managers who forced such costumes and roles on reluctant female performers.

It wasn't just with actors that the sisters talked incessantly about the theater. Maria had non-thespian friends who shared her theatrical mania, too, especially the artist Thomas Kearsley, one of Robert's Royal Academy classmates. Kearsley—as they called him—had been on visiting terms with the Porters for five years and was thought of as Maria's admirer. He lived as many hours a day as he could in audiences, or backstage, or offstage. He also painted portraits of actors and theater managers.

Kearsley came from a notorious bookselling and publishing family. He was the younger son of a radical bookseller known for having betrayed John Wilkes (the politician and Porter-family favorite) to the government in order to escape charges of having publishing seditious libel. Wilkes was imprisoned. The elder Kearsley had gone bankrupt, escaped to the Continent, and endured a brief imprisonment himself upon his return, ultimately being forgiven by Wilkes.[16] The bookseller rebuilt his business and started a family. When he died in 1790, he left nearly everything to his widow and namesake eldest son to continue the business. To his artistic younger son, Thomas, he left a modest twenty-five-pound annuity, to be paid out yearly until twenty-five, the age he would turn in 1801.

Although Kearsley had few prospects, he'd earned a solid reputation as a good young man, despite his occasionally intense melancholy. The Porter sisters believed Kearsley's personality was more sweetly sad than darkly brooding. He was, to them, in every other respect, the complete specimen of male beauty, grace, proportion, and attitude.[17] Theater roused this otherwise quiet artist to excitement, just as it did Maria.

A little over a year before, in late 1799, Kearsley had invited Maria to come view the two actors' portraits he was working on in his studio. Kearsley's inviting Maria to see his paintings in progress was a sign of respect for her opinion, as well as a gesture of intimacy. The subjects of both portraits were his close friends. One was a professional actor, Charles Kemble. The other was a rising amateur actor, none other than Henry Caulfield, who was then a captain in the military but also proving a phenomenon on the private stage. Unfortunately, Maria hadn't been as impressed with Kearsley's artwork as both of them would have hoped. While she was mildly disappointed in his portrait of Kemble, she wrote to Jane that his portrait of Henry resembled a cur.[18] Her negative judgment may have been meant to lessen the disappointment of what she needed to tell Jane next: Kearsley's portrait of Henry wasn't destined to become a gift to her sister. Maria wrote to Jane, with pointed directness. "Do not flatter yourself about Henry's portrait; if Kearsley gives it to him—it most assuredly will not come to us—we must remember that we are only Henry's friends—and that he has now a dearer connection."[19]

In the years since his brother Wade had died, Henry's behavior had changed. He hadn't wavered in his fondness for the Porter family, but he'd been spending time elsewhere. Jane had been forced to confront Henry's romantic feelings for other women. The sisters had looked on as Henry indulged in infatuations that lasted for one, two, or three months. One of Henry's faults, Jane thought, was inconstancy. Town gossip reported once he'd entertained feelings for a married woman.[20] There was a rumor of an attachment to some girl in Huntingdon. Maria told Jane she couldn't learn the woman's name from Henry or anyone else but that the attachment had swayed Henry very much.[21]

Maria thought Kearsley's portrait of Henry was surely destined to go to this woman with whom he was then in love. "It is but natural—as far as I know the business," Maria wrote to Jane about Henry. "You shall know when you come to town—it is not very pleasant I assure you—but we must now make up our minds to bear evils with calmness; would to God! I could do so, as easily as I say so."[22] Jane and Maria continued to exchange cryptic gossip about Henry's erratic choices. He'd once shocked his family and friends by temporarily abandoning his regiment, potentially forfeiting his honor as a soldier and risking future poverty. He declared he hated the military. He wanted to move beyond amateur theatrical performances to make a living on the professional stage.[23] Jane had her doubts about the wisdom of it. She feared her own family had coddled Henry too much, and Maria agreed. But, still, in the Porter women, Henry found the unconditional love that rarely came from his own family. Although he was persuaded to return to his regiment and patch things up, he began to make serious moves to change careers.

No one questioned Henry's talent for the stage. Although nominally an amateur—he wasn't paid—he was gaining renown. He was working to form a private theatrical society among his fellow officers of the Guards, which would later become known as the Pic Nic Club. It set up temporary theaters in rented spaces and threw parties that attracted royalty, audiences of hundreds, and legitimate reviews.[24] Subscribers would pay to see a full-length play performed by the officers with short, often farcical afterpieces, followed by a supper. Henry was regularly cast as the lead and took on emotionally complex parts, including Othello and Hotspur in *Henry IV, Part I.* He earned good reviews.[25] What had once seemed like a pipe dream—Henry's giving up a military career for the stage—would soon begin to seem within reach. The sisters didn't record where, or with whom, Kearsley's portrait of Henry, in his guise as an actor, had ended up after 1799. Kearsley, as the sisters' ideal specimen of manhood in grace and attitude, seems rarely to have served as the conduit of gossip.

Kearsley had a habit of coming and going from the Porters' inner circle, but on a winter's evening in 1801, something happened that promised to transform the theater-loving friendship between him and Maria into a more significant connection. It was just after Kearsley had been to see a play. In the late-night hours, as lively audiences spilled into London's streets, he decided to walk west to call on the Porters on Gerrard Street.

It was late for a visit, but Kearsley was enough of a fixture at Mrs. Porter's that he'd have known he was unlikely to be turned away. There he'd be able to talk about the play he'd just seen with eager listeners. When he arrived, he found only Maria and Mrs. Porter at home.[26] Jane was at Champion Lodge again, and Robert was temporarily away. Kearsley, invited in, sat talking for some time on "indifferent subjects"—little nothings, small talk. Around eleven, he had delighted Mrs. Porter long enough, though she didn't send the young man home. She simply walked upstairs to bed, leaving the artist alone with her daughter. It wasn't strictly allowable, but a level of trust had been built up, and Mrs. Porter must have been very tired. For a time, Maria and Kearsley sat in the room and just looked at each other in complete silence. He studied her earnestly. Finally, he spoke.

Maria later wrote down their conversation in a letter to Jane as a captured dialogue, with quotations written out just as she remembered them. To break the silence, Kearsley said something blunt and odd: "I think you have mistaken my character."

"I think not," Maria replied. "If studying a man's character for years, *can* bring one acquainted with it—I certainly know *yours*."

"You consider me cold hearted?" he asked.

Maria thought he'd said it with a look that expressed the pain he'd experience if she said it were true.

"I don't," blurted out Maria, in a tumult of delight, wanting to move his sensations.

"Then you think me inconsistent?"

She told him that he confused her, because each time he reappeared, she felt as if they were renewing their acquaintance. They might part from each other in conviviality, but then the next time they'd meet again in coldness.

"Ah!" Kearsley said, "That is my unhappy infirmity."

Maria, feeling the weight of this moment with him, decided to answer him boldly. She said, "Do you at these times really meet us with coldness?"

"Never," he said. "But my sad state makes it suspicious. At such periods, all my feelings are deadened, and I am not alive to any sensation.—I am sure you believe me to be cold hearted."

Maria detected something in his manner that made her eyes swim in tears. "I do not *indeed*," she said. "I have warmly and uniformly asserted to the contrary."

"Then others think me so," he said to her. "Tell me what *am* I considered!"

"Cold hearted," Maria was forced to admit to him.

"Ah! And you think so. I know your sister does not!"

"My sister gives you credit for a stronger use of reason in your attachments than I do," Maria replied. "I have always said you had more impetuous feelings than you would allow."

Kearsley declared it wasn't true. He just wasn't as indiscriminately loving and optimistic as Maria. He couldn't just see *every* fine quality in a person who might possess only two or three of them. Yet, he told her, he never deceived himself in the characters of those he loved. This was even more dangerous conversational ground. It was the kind of ground on which a man might make a declaration of love, which was supposed to be followed by a proposal of marriage.

Maria didn't shut down the conversation. Instead, she asked him, "Then you have an affection for some people?"

"For many," he said. "And I can like, and endure, a great number more."

"Can you *endure us*?" she asked Kearsley, pointedly.

Kearsley looked down for a few moments at this loaded, audacious question. Suddenly, he came forward and snatched Maria's hand.

"Yes," he said, his eyes burning with ardor, "I can *endure you*!"

The pressure on Maria's hand was intense. Then, just as quickly as he'd grabbed her hand, Kearsley let it go. He rose again and wished her good night.

She got up, too, and followed him to the door. But he turned back and began to talk to Maria on some random subject, as if none of this momentous interaction had just happened.

Maria's heart was in a flutter. She wouldn't have been able to tell if Kearsley might suddenly declare or propose and perhaps didn't know herself what she might say in response. She froze in the moment. She couldn't retain in her memory the words he was saying. She admitted to Jane afterward that she saw the extreme friendship of Kearsley's look, his apprehensions, but she remembered so little of what he said next.

She recalled just one line of his. Kearsley admitted that he came to the Porters, after an absence of weeks, with a distanced air, because he feared he might not be remembered by her. Maria's answer was only a significant expression on her face. She felt she had no proper words to use to disagree with him. The only response she could offer would have been far too strong. It would have created a predicament.

Kearsley seemed to be trying to get Maria to share the extent of her own feelings for him, before he'd properly declared his own to her. It was supposed to be up to the man to reveal his romantic attachment first, which put Maria in a bind, but Kearsley would have been in a bind of his own. He must have been pondering whether saying too much might provoke Maria's rejection of him and the end of their precious friendship.

"I must suppose I was wrong," he finally said, in response to her continued silence.

"You ought *never* to have thought it!" she blurted out. "Have not my sister and I shown ourselves *obtrusively* fond of your society?"

"I entertained you, perhaps," he said. "I was strange, and you were amused."

"I wish you could read our hearts! You *have* read them very ill," she said.

Kearsley took Maria's hand again. This time, she returned the pressure he gave. She walked with him into the front passage of their home. She'd always found Kearsley to be such a noble mixture of frankness, reason, feeling, and sadness. But as she watched him prepare to leave this time, she thought him radiant. His countenance looked exactly like a sunny April day, in the middle of the night, she wrote. A smile of delight began to play on Maria's lips, as her eyes overflowed with tears.

"What a strange conversation we have had!" he exclaimed to her, stepping out into the dark street. It was half past twelve. Then he darted away and was gone.

Maria told Jane that she wished to remember this night—the unconnected parts of it that she wrote down for her sister, to try to preserve it—"*for ever.*" Surely, she told Jane, a man never approached so near a god as Kearsley did at that moment. Maria wished Jane had been there. She wanted her sister to observe Kearsley and help interpret everything that had passed in this emotion-laden, almost-romantic exchange, in which too much and not enough had been said.

Maria found herself confused about Kearsley's meaning, even after having written it all down in dialogue for Jane, as best she could. It was almost as if Maria were composing a scene in a play—a moving, intimate, difficult scene. In a play, the scene would have ended with a falling curtain, moving the plot quickly forward. Perhaps Maria didn't know how she wanted this act to end. An inscrutable near-declaration of love had come from an attractive, admirable man, for whom she cared very deeply, with whom she shared interests. Yet she told Jane she couldn't understand why she was so agitated. "Do not mistake me," Maria wrote to Jane, "I am not *in love* with him, tho' I *adore* him I think."

What marked the distance between love and adoration? Maria seemed to be asking Jane, her confidante and first reader. She wanted Jane to explore and discern it with her, from this carefully recorded scene. Maria told Jane she wished such an exalted creature as Kearsley, although he was just a few years older than she was, had been her father, that he would have been sent to her twenty years earlier, when her own father had died, to have guided her through life.[27] But what was the proper distance between a protector, a father, a teacher, an interlocutor, a friend, and a husband?

Maria admitted to Jane that she didn't have the courage to reveal to anyone else the follies and weaknesses of her heart. She valued Kearsley because he was a man who forced her to reflect before she addressed him. He prompted her to criticize her own thoughts, so that she made them worthy of her companion's hearing. She thought he'd done more service to her mind than all the books she'd ever read or any friends with whom she'd conversed.[28]

As Maria poured out her heart on the page to her sister, she insisted on one thing. Jane must not mention Kearsley in her next letter home. Because it was customary for letters to be read aloud to everyone in the family after they were opened, Maria didn't want to risk having to try to hide Jane's words from their mother. The sisters would have to wait to talk about Kearsley in person.

When Jane received Maria's letter at Mrs. Crespigny's and read the description of this conversation, she was stunned. She admitted to herself that Maria's letter amazed and delighted her. This was the right word if, by "delight," Jane meant its definition as a potent mingling of pleasure and pain.

"There is a fervor on his part and an emotion on Maria's, that makes me tremble for the future peace of both," Jane recorded in her private diary. "At present, I am surer of the safety of my sister, than I am of him."

Jane could easily believe melancholy Kearsley was in love with her sister. What she couldn't believe was that Maria might return his feelings. No one questioned Kearsley's worth. Reticent as he could be, everyone sang his praises and believed him to be virtuous. When he did speak, he was impressive and exquisite in describing things and characters.[29] But Jane confessed in her journal that she secretly wanted to prevent the intimacy with Kearsley from growing on her sister's side. "To what may not these sentiments, when nourished by the confidence which this explanation has brought between them; into what may it not betray her heart!" she mused. "I shudder for the event of this . . ."

Weighing her next steps, Jane decided to tread carefully. She didn't want to reveal to Maria her true opinion of this potential match. Jane was fearful of putting Maria too suddenly on her guard. She decided she'd try to separate Maria from Kearsley by degrees. Jane realized how strangely destinies could be marked. She was contemplating whether to shape her sister's destiny, by not encouraging this worthy man's further declarations.[30]

Jane gave herself a night's sleep to consider how best to respond to the dramatic scene written out in Maria's letter. In the morning, she wrote a long letter back that didn't mention Kearsley at all, just as she'd been directed.[31] But she spent the day thinking about the two of them, replaying in her mind, and in her journal, some lines of Shakespeare's Juliet about being a woman whose heart had little joy in the disclosure of this night.

These are the lines Jane was paraphrasing from *Romeo and Juliet*: "I have no joy of this contract tonight. / It is too rash, too unadvised, too sudden; / Too like the lightning, which doth cease to be." It was Jane who played the Juliet in this scenario. Maria's letter had expressed joy. It was Jane receiving it who found it rash. She saw Kearsley and Maria's potential coupling not as the stuff of a comic happily-ever-after, as Maria herself had drafted it, with Kearsley's joyful look, darting off into the street. Jane read it as a tragedy.

The next morning, Maria must have told her mother some part of what had happened with Kearsley, because Mrs. Porter prohibited his visiting their home again until Jane returned to town to serve as a chaperone.[32] There would be no repeated scenes of inappropriate intimacy or half-declaration. But Mrs. Porter and Jane needn't have worried overmuch. Kearsley was no bold Romeo. In the next visit he made to their home, he found other men present, trying to commandeer Maria's attention. He said fewer than twenty words.[33]

Jane and Mrs. Porter seem to have decided that Kearsley was wrong for Maria. His temperament was too melancholic and Maria's too lively for it to have been imagined by her family as a good match. Jane appears to have tried to keep her sister and Kearsley apart, to stop their intimacy from growing, just as she'd strategized in her diary.

Maria, in her contact with Jane, had been asking for guidance. She declared that she thought Kearsley too exalted a creature to be comprehended by anybody but her. She laughed at herself, in admitting this to Jane, joking, "There's humility for you!" But then, taking on a tone of greater seriousness, she admitted that he had become "the glass by which I dress my mind, whose reflection shews me exactly what I am, and unlike any other glass, tells me what I ought to be."[34] Maria was describing her relationship to Kearsley with language that echoed the function of the theater. It was said the theater served as the entertaining mirror that audiences looked on each night to better understand themselves.

But at this moment, it was Jane to whom Maria gave the power of self-reflection. Jane successfully discouraged Maria from greater intimacy with Kearsley. While Maria and Kearsley's close friendship continued for many years after March 1801, it gradually cooled, at least on her side. It appears never again to have progressed to such a climactic scene. Whether she was conscious of it or not, Maria allowed Jane write this drama's last act.

What Maria increasingly immersed herself in that year was playwriting. She was writing shorter works for the amateur stage but also drafting one longer play, adapted from *The Story of Henrietta* (1800), a novella by Charlotte Smith. *The Story of Henrietta* was an improbable Gothic melodrama about the rebel daughter of a West Indian enslaver. Maria retitled her dramatic adaptation *The Runaways*.[35]

In the early months of 1801, Maria worked diligently to improve her craft as a playwright. She tried to keep her own expectations low. She wanted to write a play for the challenge of the thing, and the love of the theater, not just for the hundreds of pounds it might eventually bring her and her family. "I am convinced, I shall make little, at first," she later told Jane, speculating about her possible future as a successful playwright.[36]

During the period of months when Maria was theatrical-mad—and wondering how far she should allow herself to imagine her own reflection through Kearsley—Jane was plunging into her new historical romance, *Thaddeus of Warsaw*, and her diary of attempted self-candor. Remarkably, almost as soon as Jane vowed to be more honest about the state of her heart in her private writing, she fell in love, quite hard.

On March 12, 1801, the day after the Porter siblings' conversations about their ambitions, hopes, and dreams, the actor Charles Kemble made a long visit to Gerrard Street. Robert was a new close friend of the famous Kemble theatrical family, especially Charles. Robert had socialized, too, with Charles's former love interest, the stunning Austrian-born actress Marie-Thérèse De Camp, who went by Therese and performed as Miss De Camp. Because Kearsley was also a good friend of Charles's, the Porter sisters had heard much of the actor and seen him perform. They'd known him personally only a short time. That's what made Charles's visit to Gerrard Street that day so remarkable. With his relationship with Miss De Camp at an end, he was designedly making a visit to Robert's sisters.

Such a visit would have been understood by many as Charles's investigating whether he might court Jane or Maria. Both had become intrigued with this youngest Kemble son. His visit opened up possibilities in Jane's imagination, especially after he sat talking with them for a three and a half hours. At the end of the day, Jane admitted something momentous to herself in her diary. She was beginning, as she put it, to long for Charles's company and to fear its effect on her.

Charles Kemble, the eleventh of twelve children, was the same age as Jane. His family had already risen from strolling players to theatrical royalty by the time he was born in 1775. Charles's oldest siblings, John Philip Kemble and

Sarah Kemble Siddons, were the reigning stars of the Drury Lane theatre during his childhood. His other siblings and their spouses were actors, too. It had been decided, however, that little Charles shouldn't be destined for an actor. The Kembles seem to have concluded early on that he lacked the family talent for the stage.

With his supposed "rustic plainness"—a euphemism that suggests his perceived lack of an actor's charismatic attractiveness—Charles was sent off by his family to be educated at a strict religious boarding school in Flanders.[37] His first job thereafter had been at the post office, where he discovered he wasn't suited to that work. Against his family's wishes, he abandoned it to take the stage in the provinces, where enterprising managers snapped him up, eager to advertise a new player with the Kemble surname. His family eventually relented, and they brought Charles into the fold on the London stage.

By the time the Porters met him, he had been playing supporting roles at Drury Lane theatre for several years, while his siblings successfully starred and his brother managed. No matter how small the part, Charles faced devastatingly poor reviews. One critic described him as "a tall, awkward youth," with "a hatchet face" and a "badly proportioned" figure, "weak in his limbs," whose "acting was even worse than his appearance."[38] Another described his acting as unqualified, cold, languorous, and monotonous.[39] Several years in minor roles had, however, somewhat improved Charles's abilities. He'd had one of his plays produced, which met with tepid critical applause. The Porters would have known him by reputation before they'd known him as a friend.

Jane didn't see him as plain. In an unpublished poem, she writes of his fragrant lip, tender and feeling eyes, and voice that enchains and enchants. The poem talks about how Charles inspires passion in women.[40] The Porter sisters knew of Charles's recent failed courtship with Miss De Camp. She was a year older and very different from him in looks and personality, with an assertive air and the fine, lithe figure sought for breeches roles. Miss De Camp was also known for her excellent singing voice. She'd shared the Drury Lane stage with Charles, he'd fallen in love with her, and they'd become engaged. Yet he'd been forbidden by his family to marry her, supposedly because of her class background, lack of fortune, and profession, and because she was more "worldly" than Charles.

Everyone knew the painful reasons why she was thought worldly. It was the subject of salacious, open gossip. Part of her reputation, and part of the family's objection to her as a wife for Charles, must be laid at the feet of his brother, John Philip Kemble, who'd sexually assaulted Miss De Camp five years earlier, in 1795. She'd forcibly resisted him. There were witnesses. Some said Charles himself pulled his older brother off the actress. Others said it was Miss De Camp's brother who did.[41] The evidence of his crime must have been incontrovertible, because John Philip Kemble took the rare step of issuing a public apology, carried in the newspapers. Sadly, and predictably, the fashionable world found it a matter of comic mirth and moved on to the next scandal.

After the attack, Miss De Camp remained in the acting company, and Charles fell in love. But faced with the family's objections to his marrying her, he couldn't merely defy their wishes. There were promises made and perhaps threats. Anyone could see that if Charles went against his powerful elder siblings it would mean the end of his London theater career and Miss De Camp's, too. The Kembles succeeded in pulling the couple apart. By the time the Porters were keeping company with Charles, there was no longer talk of him marrying Miss De Camp. The two actors still worked together, and although there was continued contact and tension, offstage they'd officially separated.

Miss De Camp's response was to throw herself in the path of other men, including Robert Ker Porter. Maria wrote to Jane, in December 1800, "Bob sups with Miss de Camp on Sunday. I think she sets her cap at him. She wants to give C. K. a celebrated rival."[42] A desire to get closer to the newly famous and dashing Robert may be what led Miss De Camp to seek out Maria's friendship, too. She'd written to Robert, hoping to solicit the honor of his sister's acquaintance. After such a letter, Maria couldn't refuse to meet her without making Miss De Camp her enemy. Yet the Porter family was concerned that this would prove yet another frowned-upon social connection for Maria among their morally upright friends, especially Mrs. Crespigny.

It was decided that Maria would accompany Robert to a party at the De Camp sisters' home on Tottenham Court Road. There Maria found Miss De Camp to be an excellent, attentive host, both fascinating and good-natured. She watched the actress flirt with her brother but was unable to tell whether she was really charmed with him or if she were a practiced coquette offstage, too. What Maria was sure of, she told Jane, was that Miss De Camp's attachment to Charles Kemble was over. Maria was surprised it had ever existed.

She wrote, "I can see no part of her character or manners that can unite with the softness, and dignity of Kembles. She is lively, free, commanding, and self-assured—exactly what she appears on the stage, only losing twenty per cent in the person, as you approach nearer." But Maria admired her bewitching singing and liked her, on the whole—perhaps a little too well, she admitted.

Mrs. Porter's approval was gained for Maria's continuing friendship with the actress. Next, Miss De Camp called on her friends at Gerrard Street for a brief visit. Maria duly returned it the following day. She found her new friend to be animated, ardent, and affectionate, with a powerful intellect, an independent spirit, and an apparently feeling heart.[43] Even so, she couldn't tell exactly what to make of her. Robert seemed quite susceptible to her charms. Miss De Camp wrote him a note after the party, asking, "How are we to come together on Saturday? Do you call upon me, or I upon you?"

Robert let Maria read it, and she declared it a very tender epistle. Its main subject was Miss De Camp's intention to accompany Robert for a special private viewing of his *Seringapatam*. This seemed proof of her romantic interest in him, as well as of his willingness to be made a public talk by squiring her.

"So much for conquests," Maria wrote to Jane.[44]

It was two months afterward that Jane had had that three-hour conversation with Charles Kemble in their home. She hadn't yet met Miss De Camp, having been away so often that winter, reading dreadful Gothic novels aloud to Mrs. Crespigny. How perfect it might have seemed to the Porters, if Robert were to end up with Miss De Camp and Jane with Charles Kemble. It would be just like a comic play, in which mismatched former lovers realize they'd each be made happy with other worthy spouses who happened to be brother and sister.

Charles's visit to Gerrard Street was everything Jane could have hoped. At first, they'd talked about their mutual close friend, Thomas Kearsley. Jane told the actor how grateful her family was that he'd had such a positive effect on Kearsley's mind and mood. It led to their animated conversation on the subject of friendship and the affections. Charles spoke cryptically of the perfidy he'd once endured, which Jane thought gave a peculiar pathos to his words and manner. It also gave her a closer view of the workings of his mind and heart.

By degrees, the sisters drew out of Charles a full account of his early life and education. His tutors, he said, were so fearful of the harmful effect poets might have on their pupils that the room in which poetry books were kept was commonly referred to as "Hell." During his three formative years at this school, he never beheld a woman within the walls of the university. Yet this strange schooling had done him some good, he admitted. He thought it had given a solidity to his soul. This line struck Jane forcibly—the idea of a man with a solid soul, gained through virtuous, sheltered education. She was incredibly moved by his life story.

She wrote in her journal, "Wealth, fashion, personal elegance, learning, accomplishment, without religion and virtue, whether separately or collectively, I feel, (and I trust I feel truly,) would have no effect on my heart: but this man, pious, good, and fascinating! I should be formed of some other principles and feelings, than those of which I am, not to wish, and fear his society."

When he finally left their home that March day, Maria and Jane exchanged a look. They saw it in each other's eyes: hours had flown like moments. Within twenty-four hours, Charles Kemble's long visit to the Porter sisters became a subject of gossip and speculation. Mrs. Porter, out shopping, had run into Ned Warren. He expressed curiosity about Charles's interest in her daughters and told her Charles must be in love with Jane. He reported that Charles had called Jane a "*very pleasing girl*." Ned asked if Jane would marry Charles Kemble. Mrs. Porter told her daughters she'd replied, "No."

After recording this exchange in her journal, Jane wrote what she hadn't dared to say aloud: "Dear mama! thought I, be not so hasty." With her own sense of this man with a solid soul, and his report of finding her *very pleasing*, Jane's heart was now fully engaged. She confessed to herself alone that she'd rather be called "very pleasing" by Charles Kemble than be called the "most charming woman in the world" by any other man.[45]

Three days later, on March 16, 1801, Jane and her family went to Drury Lane to see *Deaf and Dumb*, a historical drama featuring both Charles and Miss De Camp. Miss De Camp was the lead, an orphaned deaf-mute, in a breeches part. Charles played the hero in a romantic subplot. Jane watched the play with special interest. She liked it well enough, particularly because, as she put it, "Charles cannot fail in a part of feeling."

The other actor she watched very carefully that night was Miss De Camp. Jane thought her far too lively for the circumstances of the character. She also watched the two actors perform together. As Jane wrote in her journal, "I wish I knew whether he still loves her. I am much mistaken if she cares so much for the loss of his affections, as for the loss of her adorer." As soon as Jane wrote it down for herself, though, she worried that she was being ungenerous to Miss De Camp. She was tortured by the idea that she might be unfair to any woman genuinely in love, in order to advance her own prospects.

The next day, Jane felt ill. She was physically spent, probably from worry and anxiety, yet had no choice but to rally. There was author business to take care of. Her new publisher, Benjamin Crosby, had decided to make an unannounced house call. He came to ask a favor of his new author. Despite his own illness, he'd come in person, on a matter of great importance. Crosby asked Jane to change her mind and agree to put her name on the title page of her next work. Jane's new book for children was to be called *The Two Princes of Persia: Addressed to Youth*, featuring a series of connected, moral stories for the young. Crosby couldn't be blamed for making the special request. He'd have known Maria published under her own name. There couldn't be any family objection. At first, Jane refused.

"But the man seemed so impressed with the injury I was doing him by withholding it," Jane wrote later in her diary. Crosby told her that she was going to do him monetary harm by publishing anonymously. She was moved enough by this plea that she offered him a compromise. She told him he might put the gender-ambiguous "J. Porter" on the title page—and nothing more. But when the publisher continued to press her for her name on her work—to reveal her sex—she relented further still. "He struggled hard for the *Miss* in the advertisements," she continued. "And as they are only things of the day, to oblige him, who tho' ill, had taken the trouble to walk thus far to ask the favour, I gave him leave." Jane didn't look forward to the judgmental response she anticipated from Mrs. Crespigny, who disapproved of women's publicly avowed authorship.

Jane's one-volume book features chapters on pride, procrastination, and vanity, as well as honor, justice, and ancestry. The two princes of the title, Omra and Behauder, are joined by their old sage and teacher, Sadi. The stories follow the fictional formula of brother-opposites. Omra, the elder—who ascends to the throne—proves humble and gentle. Behauder, the younger, starts out lazy and superficial, but reforms to activity and energy, happy for his brother's rule. The introduction to *Two Princes of Persia* sets out to differentiate Jane's stories from other books like it. She claims to intentionally avoid tripping fairies, witches on broomsticks, turbaned giants, and sheeted ghosts, because they're hallmarks of the past that dangerously repeat false traditions and notions.

The rest of her introduction lays out her theory for educating children, boys and girls together, because "the grand outlines of duty are the same to man and woman." "Were this truth more universally inculcated," Jane writes, "we should see men less weakly prone to vice, and women, more firm in the higher ranks of virtue."[46] She dedicated the work to Percival Stockdale, which was only fitting, as he'd been educating her since her youth.

Later in that momentous month of March 1801, after Jane had published a book with her name on it and was falling in love with Charles Kemble, the sisters had another late-night tête-à-tête. Maria steered the conversation. She wanted to talk to Jane about good character, conduct, and principle. Charles Kemble had once described to Maria the character of the woman he wanted to marry, and Maria thought it sounded like the opposite of Miss De Camp's. She wanted to tell Jane the story. Of his ideal future wife, Kemble had said, "Her beauty should not be of the obtrusive kind; her dress should be quiet; her manners retiring; and her temper the gentlest of the gentle," because a bad temper "was a horror to him."[47]

Every word Maria shared made Jane worry she'd spoken too unreservedly to Charles and hadn't measured up to his moral ideal. She panicked that her own character deviated too far from his wishes in a wife. Unlike the heroine Elizabeth Bennet to Mr. Darcy in Jane Austen's *Pride and Prejudice* (which would be published a dozen years later), Jane could not make fun of Charles's list of desirable qualities in a wife. But she could almost laugh at herself, she wrote, for admitting on the page her hopes of the two of them ending up together. At this point in her diary, long passages begin to be vigorously scratched out, usually after sentences devoted to her feelings for Charles, as she tried to erase what she'd dared to record.

Several days later, Jane's thoughts of Charles Kemble were set aside temporarily for another object of her affection. Henry Caulfield had reemerged, under dramatic circumstances. He and Ned Warren were fighting with each other, and they put Jane in the middle of it. The two men had recently had a falling out and stopped speaking. Now they were sworn enemies, and each wanted to claim Jane for his own side. Each used her as his confidante to try to gain her allegiance.

It was perhaps not coincidental that Henry and Ned wanted to pull Jane closer at the precise moment she was being gossiped about as the romantic interest of Charles Kemble. Henry played the field, but he seems to have thought of Jane as his own. Ned may have been secretly in love with Jane and would probably have thought an actor-husband unworthy of her strong moral fiber. At a delicate moment in her growing closeness to Charles, Jane was pulled away from him to deal with Henry and Ned's squabbling—and likely jealousy.

In her diary Jane tried to re-create the dialogue of this drama as faithfully as she could. She tried to capture these men's voices, their feelings, and her own. To read Jane's rendering of the scene is almost to be a fly on the wall in a London drawing room. It shows how deeply enmeshed she was with Henry, despite her professions of having moved her heart on to Charles Kemble. Her diary entry was also a training ground for capturing on the page the sensitive hero in the new romance she was writing, whether she realized it or not.

Jane heard Ned's side of the story first. It led her to think Henry must be in the wrong. A day later, Henry knocked on the Porters' door and asked for a quarter of an hour with Jane. Henry trembled before her, and burst out, "Jane, I would not lose your esteem. I come, to explain what has passed between Warren and me." By the end of his explanation, Jane was unable to think Henry was at fault. "I made a vow to myself," Jane wrote, "from this day forth, dear Henry! No second person shall make me think you otherwise than true and constant in your friendships!"

Jane told him she'd try to fix the breach between him and Ned. Afterward, they discussed books and reflected together on their favorite authors and ideas.

He stayed and stayed and stayed. When the rest of the family left to see a play, they remained, just the two of them, alone in her home. Even when Jane's friend Mrs. Elizabeth Dillon came to tea, Henry stayed. When Mrs. Dillon left at nine, he was still there. When he finally rose to go, he said, "Good night my loved Jane. I shall leave town tomorrow, but will see you first."

He'd used the phrase "my loved Jane." Jane recorded in her journal, "O Henry, my friend, my brother! Be ever thus, and while breath, and reason, are in my body, I will be as a sister to thee! . . . Who is there, that reading my soul, would say, that the purest and most lively affection in the breast of woman, cannot exist without love?"[48] Even in a diary designed to explore a learned woman's deeply buried feelings, this line stands out for its tortured exploration of what is, and isn't, romantic love.

This overwrought scene laid the groundwork for everything that happened the following night. Mrs. Porter decided to host a dinner of theatrical luminaries. She'd invited to their home the most brilliant actors of the day. Among them were Henry Johnston, Charles Holland, John Emery, and William Thompson. Included, too, were Ned Warren and Henry Caulfield.

But the point of the whole dinner was obviously to host Charles Kemble. Mrs. Porter seated her daughter Jane between Charles and Ned. She'd kept Henry farther away. This dinner was an opportunity. If Jane and Charles needed a way to deepen their connection to each other, this dinner could do it. And if Charles had doubts about Jane's suitability, then seeing her among his theatrical brethren—along with proof the Porters were beloved by many other actors—might convince him of her fit in his world.

From the start of the night, Jane was out of sorts. Although seated right beside Charles, she found she couldn't concentrate on him. All she could think about was the painful falling out between Henry and Ned and the role she ought to take in mending it. Jane could hardly move for trembling or speak for tears. She was sure she seemed strange to Charles. She couldn't eat dinner. During dessert, he tried to talk to her. He was amusing, she thought, and she recovered a little.

But when the ladies withdrew and the gentlemen remained below, as was the custom, rebellious Henry set arrangements askew. Against protocol, he joined the women upstairs in the drawing room. He stayed for two hours. Jane was in a panic. The conflict between Henry and Ned had been kept at a simmer throughout the dinner and after it. Jane didn't want a scene to erupt to ruin the evening. She left the room and met Robert in the passage to try to come up with a plan. He told her Ned knew very well that Henry was upstairs with the women and resented it. In fact, Robert said, Ned had twice burst into tears in front of the rest of the men, worried about losing Jane's esteem, because it seemed she was choosing Henry's side over his. Charles Kemble would have witnessed all this tear-filled man-drama over Jane, playing out in the Porters' home.

Whether that would have raised or lowered Jane in his esteem is anyone's guess. Seeing a woman desired by other men may inspire some suitors to greater efforts to win her. But if Charles's ideal wife was retiring and gentle, then this little conflict would seem proof that Jane could provoke fierce feelings in men. He had experienced far more difficult moments of real-life drama when he was with unpredictable Miss De Camp, not to mention having acted many more such things on the stage. But this little spectacle at the Porters' home was hardly a scene of calm.

When the time came for the men to rejoin the women, Jane did her duties as a host. She'd have been closely watched for her talents at serving, poised at the tea table, pouring coffee for all of them. Instead of watching Jane at work, however, as the rest of the men were no doubt doing—this was, after all, a feminine performance—Ned bolted from the room. Robert immediately followed him. Thirty minutes later, Ned sent for Jane. When she went to him, she found him worse off than she ever could have imagined.

"Ned was in such agonies, convulsed in every limb, drowned in tears and uttering such piercing groans & exclamations, that my very soul was torn," Jane wrote. In vain, Jane tried to tell him how much she respected him. It wasn't until Robert wept, and Jane clasped Ned's hand, washing it with her own bitter tears, declaring that she regarded him as a brother, that Ned was pacified. After drying their eyes for several minutes, the three of them went back upstairs. Jane's eyes were still red. "Kemble," Jane wrote, "was gone."[49]

The dinner at which she'd been seated next to Charles, to test their attachment, had been entirely given over to Henry and Ned's argument and Ned's violent tears. Charles Kemble had been made the regular audience—not the star, or even a supporting player—at Jane's unanticipated, and surely unwelcome, domestic theater.

"These mental blows, don't agree at all with any of us," Jane wrote in her journal, a day after trying to manage these histrionic, possessive men. She recorded that their last guests had left at four A.M.

Jane was merely exhausted at first, but then exhaustion progressed to miserably ill. Mrs. Porter, too, took ill, with what they'd at first feared was a paralytic fit. Jane had given her mother laudanum to help her sleep. None of the principal players seem to have gotten what they'd wanted out of the evening.

The underlying, unspoken reasons for Ned and Henry's fighting with each other might have become clearer to Jane in the weeks that followed. By April 1801, gossip about Henry's latest risky activities filtered back to the Porters. A friend wrote to inform her that Henry was living with a married woman, separated from her husband. This must have been the woman that previous gossip had linked him to. Jane finally learned her name. She was also a Jane: Mrs. Jane Rodney Chambers. Henry stayed under the same roof with Mrs. Chambers, ostensibly as her lodger. They kept separate bedrooms, but their cover story of her as his landlady was little believed. It was a highly unusual household, without her estranged husband around. Jane abhorred the "principles, or whatever it may be, in his character, which induce him to continue this disgraceful connexion."

Nevertheless, Jane decided she'd continue to write letters to Henry. She just wouldn't acknowledge or sanction his choices by writing to him at Mrs. Chambers's address. As she wrote in her journal, "I felt my writing to him there, an outrage to the delicacy of my own mind." Yet she refused to give into the dictates of convention, which said she ought to shun him. Jane vowed that her sisterly feelings would remain for Henry, no matter what. In agreeing to write him, despite this moral lapse, she wanted to convince him of how truly *fraternal* her affection was for him.[50] Given their seven-year history of intimacy, this might seem like protesting too much—or acting a part.

At this moment when Henry was no longer casting his lot with Jane, it seems understandable that Jane would try to take an emotional step forward with Charles Kemble. She revealed her feelings for him to Maria, her "other self." The next time the sisters found themselves alone, before Jane was quite aware what she was saying, she let down her guard. Jane told Maria she thought "from the virtues of Charles Kemble, if I durst, I could prefer him to all men living." This was a feminine euphemism that substituted for a declaration of love: I *could* prefer him to all men living, if he could prefer me first.

She told her sister, with a trembling heart, that she had a deep fear that Maria would think her indelicate. Although Jane had made efforts to stop Maria from indulging in tender feelings for Kearsley, Maria responded in the opposite way when Jane sought her help. She encouraged her sister to express and explore her feelings. She told her she approved of the object of Jane's affections. She even gave Jane advice on how to manage the next steps with Charles to secure his affections. Maria wasn't entirely sanguine about it all. There was the matter of his previous attachment to Miss De Camp. Where Jane's heart was concerned, Maria warned, "Be wary."

When Charles Kemble again visited the Porters' home, he announced he was about to leave for Bath for a week. Jane seized an opportunity to plant an idea in his mind that she'd recently had. She suggested Charles and Robert ought to travel to Germany together that summer, on what was called a Grand Tour. He listened with interest and agreed to ask her brother about it. Jane mentioned it to Robert, too.

The Grand Tour was a rite of passage for British gentlemen to sow their wild oats before becoming engaged and marrying. Jane would have had several hopes for this trip. One would have been that Robert could be pulled away from his idle, archery-obsessed male friends who went from party to party and were "all beastly drinkers."[51] If Charles and Robert were to take a tour together, it might also forward a more selfish design of Jane's. It could advance the intimacy of Robert and Charles and their two families, the Kembles and the Porters. It would ready Charles for his expected next step in adult life—marriage—and might help Jane's chances as a potential wife.

With the idea for that European trip communicated, and Kemble temporarily gone to Bath, Jane had time to refocus on the business of authorship. She went to Crosby's office to receive her payment of fifteen pounds for *The Two Princes of Persia: Addressed to Youth*, then in press. The amount she received was five pounds more than what Crosby would pay two years later to the anonymous author of *Susan: A Novel*, who turned out to be the as-yet-unpublished Jane Austen. For ten pounds, Crosby bought but mysteriously refused to print Austen's novel, which the world eventually came to know as *Northanger Abbey*.

Jane Porter's experience with Crosby went more smoothly. He brought out Jane's *Two Princes of Persia* with good speed. Someone, however, got confused about the byline they'd agreed should be used. Instead of "J. Porter," the title page listed it as the work of "I. Porter." This was probably a printer's error, but it meant Jane's identity was cloaked more than Crosby wanted. The book's advertisements did identify her, as they'd agreed, as "Miss Porter." The reviews were mildly approving, if lukewarm. For a change, critics weren't telling a Porter sister to put down her pen and give up writing. There was little to object to in a moralizing work for children.

During the period when Kemble was absent from town, a group of friends had gone to preview Robert's next great historical painting, *The Siege of Acre*, before its public opening at the Lyceum Theatre. Robert had invited only his family, friends, and some notable guests. Jane's diary shows she had more interest in who was there than in describing the painting. Maria and Kearsley walked through the great room together, which left Jane to her own devices. One of the people she saw there among the invited was the old Corsican war hero General Pasquale Paoli. Jane studied him closely. She was fascinated by seeing a war hero in person. She described him in her diary in minute detail. She'd end up using the material to create a character in *Thaddeus of Warsaw*.

The next day, when Kearsley, Jane, and Maria took tea together, their conversation turned to plans for an upcoming celebration for Robert's work. Mrs. Porter had agreed to allow her three children to host a large dance in their home, to celebrate the opening of *The Siege of Acre*. Jane and Maria went over the guest list with Kearsley. One of the people they mentioned was Miss De Camp. When Kearsley heard her name, he thanked Maria and Jane for giving him notice of her being invited. He told them he wouldn't come. Anywhere Miss De Camp would be, Kearsley said, he tried to avoid.

He told them flatly that he had an antipathy to her. Kearsley thought her fascinating, very fascinating, he said, but "not so much so that any man would run into her tails unless she purposely spread them." He found her dangerous. He believed she adored power. Kearsley had once spent hours in her company, painting her portrait. On the last day she sat for him, he said, she'd offhandedly remarked something to the effect of "Perhaps we shall never meet again!"

"I thought it so excellent an idea," Kearsley told the sisters, "that from that moment, I determined we never should meet again—and we have not."

Kearsley monitored Maria's growing friendship with Miss De Camp with deep concern, not only for Maria but also for Robert. Kearsley listened to Maria describe how she'd gradually changed her own first impression of the charming actress, from seeing her as a coquette to believing her a true-feeling female friend. After listening to this description, Kearsley said he read the situation differently: Miss De Camp wanted something from Maria. She'd found she could win over Maria by exciting her gratitude. So she'd adopted a show of warm kindness. She'd wanted to draw Maria under her influence. Maria had to admit that the tactic, if that's what it was, was indeed working.

Jane, overhearing the two of them, boldly told Kearsley, "She never can [win] me! I think her enchanting, but I think her a mere coquet; and I doubt, of the tenderness of her heart!" As soon as she'd said it, Jane worried Kearsley might think her too severe, but on the contrary, he wanted her to say something more severe still. He wanted her to tell Maria to drop Miss De Camp's acquaintance. Maria made an excuse about why that couldn't be. How ungrateful and cold would it look if she were to withdraw from her now? Kearsley didn't argue further, saying he believed Maria must be right.

Thinking about it afterward, Jane noted, "Not a word of Charles Kemble passed in this conversation," although Charles was one of its subtexts. Kearsley feared either Charles or Robert might be ensnared by Miss De Camp.[52] Jane decided she needed to know more about this woman Charles had once loved and with whom her brother was becoming increasingly romantically entangled. Later that week, Jane went, by invitation, to see "'Kemble's enchantress' in person." Jane watched Miss De Camp with astonishment and admiration. What she discovered, on the surface, was a woman of grace, vivacity, and intelligence.

"But," Jane thought, "it goes no deeper than to dazzle others, without illuminating her own mind & heart. I am amazed that she should have fixed Charles Kemble."[53] Jane didn't think Miss De Camp was good enough for him.

A week later, after Charles's return from Bath, a vague report circulated that Miss De Camp and Charles Kemble had reconciled.[54] The rumor made its way to the Porters. Then further reports seemed to confirm it. Charles and Miss De Camp had made a plan to meet at the Lyceum Theatre, presumably to see Robert's new painting together. What a strange visit to have arranged—a rendezvous with a former love interest to tour the great new artwork of a current one. Things took an even more surprising turn when it was said Charles had been stood up by Miss De Camp. She'd even said, in front of witnesses, that she wouldn't tell Charles *why* she didn't come. The very idea that Charles had waited for her, at the door to see Robert's new picture—Robert, with whom Miss De Camp had so assiduously flirted—must have pained the Porter sisters in many directions.

It certainly worried Maria, who began to suspect that she'd been Miss De Camp's pawn to bring about a reconciliation with Charles, in a manufactured chain of gossip. As Maria recounted to Jane what happened, it seemed to add up. She'd been duped into repeating rumors that Miss De Camp wanted spread, to precisely the parties she'd wanted to hear them. "We shrank at the idea of having really been puppets in her hands," Jane wrote in her journal.

If it were true, then the Porter sisters felt they should have only compassion for Charles's future—and gratitude for their brother's escape—to be united to such a woman. Maria was coming around to the conclusion that Miss De Camp was a selfish creature who loved exerting power over others. She was starting to believe Kearsley had been right. The sisters recognized another likely outcome of all this seeming manipulation. If Miss De Camp and Charles Kemble were reconciled, then not only would Jane be removed from Charles's sights as a romantic prospect. Kearsley, who so hated Miss De Camp, also would lose one of his few friends. The sisters, and Maria especially, feared what this would mean for Kearsley, who'd relied so much on the company of Charles.

Given all that the sisters were recognizing was happening offstage, it shouldn't have been a surprise when Miss De Camp came next, quite directly, for Jane—the woman with whom Charles had been spending so much time and the one Ned Warren was telling people Charles wanted to marry. Jane was Miss De Camp's most visible rival. Over the next week, Miss De Camp spent nearly every day cultivating Jane's friendship. She took both Porter sisters on a walk to her little cottage, invited Jane to dine, and called constantly on the sisters at Gerrard Street. Maria and Jane naïvely wondered where this persevering attention might be leading.

All was revealed when Jane found herself alone one afternoon in Miss De Camp's drawing room. The enchanting actress started a conversation with Jane on the problem of people with cold dispositions. She said the Kemble family was remarkable for its coldness. One member of the family, she said, could be at first all ardor and then all ice. Miss De Camp didn't have to mention Charles's name; Jane knew that she'd been making veiled references to him all along.

Perhaps seeing her opening, Miss De Camp poured out to Jane "the whole history of their mutual situation," describing her long romantic attachment to Charles. It was as if she were acting a scene from Austen's as-yet-unpublished *Sense and Sensibility*, with Miss De Camp playing Lucy Steele to Jane's Elinor Dashwood.

Jane remained strong in the face of this unlooked for and painful confession of how Miss De Camp and Charles's relationship first became romantic and then began to fall apart. During her monologue, the two women were interrupted by the return of other guests. But after dinner, as they prepared to leave for the theater—some to act and others to watch—she surreptitiously passed Jane a letter to read. "There," she said to her. "Read that, and tell me what you think of it." Jane opened the letter. She saw that it began, "My dear Therese." She turned it over to look at the signature. It had none. But Jane immediately knew it was a letter from Charles. By all standards of propriety, Jane should have refused to read it. Yet she couldn't look away. Here was her opportunity to know exactly what Charles thought of her rival for his affections. Later, Jane recorded the contents of the letter, word for word, in her diary.

"My dear Therese!" it said, "What I have long doubted; that your affections to me have never been equal to mine for you; is now confirmed by the eagerness of your demand, that I will release you from your vow of faith to me.—I do release you—but as I have sworn—I will abide by my oath, that unless I possess you, to go single to my grave.—You are free—but I hold myself bound, untill I cease to live."

This would have been a slap in the face. Jane, in love with Charles, read over this very painful letter twice before returning it. It told her everything she needed to know. She wasn't Miss De Camp's rival. Miss De Camp had no rival. Whatever Charles was doing with Jane, it wasn't exploring romantic feelings. His own feelings he had declared set for life.

Jane needed to retain her composure, rousing her best acting skills at that moment, as would be required of any heroine. As the group of them left for the theater, Miss De Camp coolly put her arm through Jane's to walk beside her. Ned Warren hovered near them. He tried to talk to Miss De Camp. As Jane was going over everything that had passed, she began to realize how thoroughly she'd been used, by Miss De Camp certainly, but perhaps also, if she'd allowed herself to admit it, by Charles.

"I felt as if I were entangled," Jane wrote later in her diary. "As if she had caught me.—However, there was but one way for me to act—and though I had declared to Kearsley, that she never should get me under her influence, I found that she had just gained the same end, for she had completely put me under my own."[55]

Jane realized she couldn't be the sort of woman who'd try to get in the way of a man's professed love for another. In life, she cast herself as the modest heroine, not the femme fatale. Miss De Camp had given Jane knowledge that, had she been dishonorable, could have been used to her own advantage. But Jane was honorable. By bringing Jane into her confidence, Miss De Camp was betting, correctly, that her friend would hold the secrets of the letter sacred. By showing Jane the letter from Charles, Miss De Camp had, in one fell swoop, killed off her romantic rival and compelled her to transform into an ally.

From that moment, Jane began to selflessly separate out her own interests and feelings for Charles. She even began to feel sorry for him. Miss De Camp's spirit, she thought, was vain and violent. Jane felt sure the actress could never make Charles happy and felt uneasy about having been pressed into furthering her possession of him. As Jane was mulling all this over during their walk, Miss De Camp leaned in to speak to her. Jane later recorded the conversation. She'd cemented it into her memory, as only a brilliant novelist could, communicating the tone of manipulation and compliance in each recorded line.

Miss De Camp whispered, "What do you think of the letter . . . Is it not cold?"

"No," replied Jane. "It is the letter of a broken heart; he thinks that you are eager to break your bonds with him, else why ask it! . . . He generously gives you up the freedom you ask, while he tells you, that himself is bound till his death."

Jane continued, "What can be more generous, more gratifying, than this? You know his character.—He is not like most young men, of a disposition to be dissipated. He is retired and contemplative.—What seizes on his heart, takes strong possession, and trust me, what he says, he will do—*you* are free, but *he* is yours forever."

Having wrung this declaration of Charles's deep love for her out of Jane, Miss De Camp smiled and looked pleased at her friend's explanation. She said she doubted it. She granted the strength of Jane's argument about Charles's character, but she doubted the rest.

Ned Warren, who must have overheard them both, distanced himself from the two women, as Miss De Camp continued to tell Jane the story of her courtship with Charles. They'd become engaged last August. John Philip Kemble was violently against it. The rest of the Kembles joined in. They threatened Charles with their everlasting displeasure if the marriage took place.

The Kembles finally got Charles to agree to stop visiting at Miss De Camp's house. If he still wanted to marry her when he turned thirty—six years later—then they'd give him their consent. Charles and Miss De Camp had submitted to this plan. They'd vowed to stay together. At first, Charles wrote her two or three letters a day. But lately, he'd been avoiding her at the theater. She wrote to him that perhaps they should give up their engagement. The letter she'd shown Jane was his reply. Miss De Camp asked Jane what she thought now. Jane said, with cutting honesty, she thought Charles's letter to her was much better than Miss De Camp's letter to him merited.

All that happened in the following weeks must have seemed to Jane to be merely going through the motions. Jane, Maria, and Robert were busy preparing for the large dance to celebrate Robert's new great historical picture, on the day after his twenty-fourth birthday, April 27, 1801. When the night arrived, it was magical. Fifty guests packed their Gerrard Street home to the walls. The poetic Smith brothers were there. Mrs. Henry Johnston, dear Amelia, came and, of course, Therese. Robert thought both Mrs. Johnston and Miss De Camp looked like divinities.[56]

Despite the feelings she tried to steel herself with that week against Miss De Camp, Jane found she couldn't resist her. Her attractive sweetness and affectionate manner had caught a fast hold on Jane. She was entirely susceptible to the great actress's acting. At one point, during the dance, she found herself standing next to Miss De Camp, who took up Jane's hand.

She asked Jane, "I would give the world to know whether you love me or not?"

Jane was silent for a moment. She reflected later, about her short silence. She thought to herself that the cruelest thing the human tongue can do is to make others suspect our sincerity. In that second of silence, so many things passed through Jane's mind. Was Miss De Camp's love of power and control imposing on Jane?

"Such a creature should never have me under her influence," Jane wrote in her diary. She doubted Therese loved her. "But should she really feel as she says?—I am almost a devil to doubt it." It was like the work of a novel's narrator, investigating her characters' minds and innermost thoughts.

After that pause, Jane had answered Therese, "I do."

"Upon your honour?" Therese probed further.

Jane hesitated again. She found herself, she thought, called upon to seal the doom of her sincerity. Jane had received Therese's confidence, and told her she loved her, because Jane felt she did, although she acknowledged to herself that she hadn't yet a fixed opinion on Therese's own steadiness.

"Yet I loved her," Jane thought to herself, "and in defiance of the doubts which yet lurked about me—the Judgement of Kearsley, which I ever had respected as without appeal—I felt an irresistible impulse to be her *friend*."

So Jane lifted up her hand and laid it on her own breast. She answered Therese, "On my heart."

It's impossible to know if Therese understood the fine slippage Jane had introduced, between her honor and her heart. If it had been a line spoken in a play by an actor, the sleight of hand in changing words might be delivered almost imperceptibly. In the pages of a diary, or a novel, the distance between these two words is more easily seen.

In the weeks that followed, Therese kept Jane very close and eventually credited her friend with saving her relationship with Charles Kemble. She said it was Jane's interpretation of Charles's letter that convinced her not to break it off with him. Thanks to Jane's advice on how to read the emotions behind the letter, Therese had been unusually kind to Charles. It had brought about a reconciliation. Jane, having sealed her friends' love, tried to put aside her own feelings for Charles. She soon found herself so completely won over by Therese that she forgot her own emotional needs.

"Indeed, Maria, I am devoted" to Therese, Jane wrote later, "She has perfectly blotted me out of my own eyes."[57]

Jane compared her admiration and love for Therese to what she'd once felt in the presence of the late Mary Robinson. She admitted that, of the two women, she preferred Mrs. Robinson but was now determined to help Therese secure Charles's hand in marriage.

That summer, from June to September 1801, Robert and Charles explored the Continent together on their Grand Tour, just as Jane had suggested. The young men were armed with letters of introduction to meet Europe's celebrated intellectuals and high fashionables and to see sights in Denmark, Saxony, Bohemia, Austria, Hungary, and beyond.[58] From time to time, Robert wrote home to London. After visiting Koenigstein Castle on the Elbe River, near Dresden, he informed Jane which details she'd gotten right and wrong in her novel *The Spirit of the Elbe*. His letter was also unsatisfyingly short, for which he apologized.

"Charles is waiting for me to go out with him," Robert told Jane.[59]

Jane, back in London, set aside her diary of self-candor for six months. During this period, Maria and Kearsley continued to run hot and cold with each other. Ned Warren began to fade from the sisters' lives while Henry remained central to it. Jane began to write new fiction. One of her unpublished pieces was a short sequel to *Two Princes of Persia*, featuring two brothers named Robert and William. She gave it the subtitle "Traveling at Home," which suggests some insight into her own life's static circumstances at a time when her brother was off exploring the world.[60] Then she abandoned the project.

Instead, she redoubled her efforts on *Thaddeus of Warsaw*, her novel about a worthy, sensitive, defeated Polish war hero who becomes a destitute refugee and rebuilds his life in England. Her hero often breaks down in tears. In one scene, he attends a play at a London theater and watches Charles Kemble perform. Jane, instead of trying to make Charles Kemble into her husband, gave him up to Therese and made him a minor character in her next book.

Five years later, when Charles Kemble turned thirty, he and Therese De Camp married, as they'd pledged. They became one of the most powerful couples on the London stage. They had several children, who also grew up to become theatrical celebrities. The Porters and the Kembles—although their friendship had its ups and downs—would remain affectionately connected for the rest of their lives.

CHAPTER 7

"The Fire! The Splendour!"

Maria's Opera, Jane's Bestseller, and the War Hero, Sir Sidney Smith (1802–3)

In the first years of the nineteenth century, Robert's career as an artist seemed secure and his fame permanent. Privations and going without would have appeared a thing of the past. Although Britain's war against France remained alarming, the Porter family's better future seemed secure. Jane and Maria were in the most comfortable situations they'd ever experienced domestically, socially, and financially. Both sisters would have felt, too, as if they were completing the most important writing of their lives.

When Jane began writing again in her diary in December 1801, after an unexplained hiatus of six months, it was to record what she called a rare day of the "highest felicity." Her soul was "throbbing with bliss" after meeting the Royal Navy's Sir William Sidney Smith, who went by Sir Sidney Smith. Jane compared his coming to their home to being visited by an angel. "We had heard of Sir Sidney Smith," Jane wrote, "as all the world has heard of him, as the bravest most intrepid of men—we had read of his glorious actions, both by sea and land."

Smith came to Gerrard Street to meet Robert, who had invited the war hero to sit for his portrait in the small studio he kept upstairs. Smith agreed, and the two men arranged a meeting. But when Robert's return to London was unexpectedly delayed, Jane, Maria, and Mrs. Porter realized they'd have to receive Smith themselves. Their plan was to explain that Robert was unable to keep his appointment and to apologize profusely. The sisters were incredibly anxious. They no idea how a war hero might behave when disappointed. Once Smith arrived, was welcomed, and received the news of Robert's absence, Jane realized their worries were needless. Smith's graciousness surprised them. Although a stranger to them, with his appointment in their home canceled, Smith stayed to talk with the Porter women for hours.

Smith was a celebrity of wartime. His name was in every newspaper and on every tongue. In military honor and fame, he was the equal of Admiral Lord Nelson. The two men were Britain's leading living naval heroes, each renowned for victories against Napoleonic France. Smith and Nelson may have been compatriots—two ambitious men heedless of danger—but they weren't friends. Those who preferred Nelson found him to have greater gentility or claimed Smith was too self-regarding. Nelson would achieve the longer-lasting fame, but some at that time might have predicted Smith would be the one to end up most prominently featured in the history books. Napoleon, looking back on his failed rule, was said to have declared of Sir Sidney Smith, "That man made me miss my destiny."[1]

When Jane met Smith in late 1801, he was a single man in his late thirties whose destiny was still in progress. She was a budding novelist, just turned twenty-six, writing her next book, *Thaddeus of Warsaw*, about a fictional war hero on the losing side of a real European conflict. Her historical romance about the second partition of Poland would explore not only how that hero fought, survived, and escaped the Russian enemy, but also how he rebuilt his life, discovered half his family, fell in love, and married in England. It must have seemed almost providential that a real-life war hero like Sir Sidney Smith had been thrown in Jane's way at this moment in her writing process. More than that, Jane was simply in awe of him.

Sir Sidney Smith had, while very young, fought with the British in the American Revolution. He'd served in a foreign war, fighting for Sweden against Russia, earning a knighthood for his efforts. With King George III's permission, he began to use the foreign title, styling himself Sir Sidney Smith. Fellow officers, however, ridiculed him as the "Swedish Knight." The public, by contrast, treated him as a legend in his own time, especially after his capture and imprisonment by the French. He'd spent two years in Paris, held as something between a criminal and a prisoner of war, before he'd dramatically escaped. The story was so much a part of the national consciousness that his adventures were turned into a pantomime play, *The Lucky Escape, or The Return to the Native Country*, performed an astounding eight hundred times.[2]

From there Smith's fame grew. His leadership was decisive in the momentous victory at the Siege of Acre in 1799, a battle that turned the tide on Napoleon's Egyptian campaign. Robert, who'd chosen it as the subject of his second great historical painting, had previously painted Smith in action. A descriptive sketch had been published to accompany *The Siege of Acre* when it opened in April 1801. Jane had once again ghostwritten the pamphlet, while Robert focused on the art. One of Robert's diaries includes fifty-four pages of material about Smith in Jane's most meticulous handwriting. She knew a great deal about the hero before meeting him in the flesh.

Robert's enormous *Siege of Acre* hadn't been nearly as popular an attraction as *Seringapatam*. He'd fixed some trouble with the poor lighting, but it didn't help admissions. Then he put the new painting into a traveling exhibition, hoping to make it profitable on the road. Its showing in Liverpool had been a complete disaster, leaving a three-hundred-pound debt.[3] Robert needed a financial win. He'd begun work on another great historical painting, *The Battle of Alexandria*, which depicted the British victory over the French in Egypt, where valiant Sir Ralph Abercromby had tragically fallen, on March 21, 1801. Smith had fought there, too, and had been sent home a hero to recover from a shot in the arm.

While painting Smith's portrait, Robert would have a chance to gather ideas about recording the Alexandria battle on canvas. For Smith, a new portrait by a celebrity artist was in his own interest. If done right, it would be displayed, engraved, subscribed to, printed, and sold for a profit—for Robert. It would also advertise, cement, and immortalize Smith's military exploits. Although Smith had accomplished much in his thirty-seven years, he wasn't born to wealth and had contracted debts. He would have seen the benefit of taking an interest in his own good publicity.

Jane was surprised that day in their drawing room because she hadn't expected Smith to be so winning a man in looks and personality. As she wrote in her journal, "We were prepared to see a noble creature, tho' with these drawbacks—we had been told, that his person was insignificant, his features sharp, and that much of his bravery, was mere madness." His victories were seen by skeptics as crazy good luck, the result of one man's willingness to take inadvisable military risks with ships, sailors, and troops.

But Smith proved elegant-looking to Jane. A decade seemed to have been removed from his age, as he appeared no older than twenty-five. He stood five foot nine, was finely proportioned, and had a dignity of air, and a noble chest and shoulders. What struck her most was his graceful manner. He set them all at ease about Robert's absence. He visited for two full hours, during which he'd engaged the Porter women in conversation on Egyptian affairs. Jane must have been as conversant on this subject as any nonmilitary expert because of her ghostwriting.

Smith described to them the famous, tragic moment of the Battle of Alexandria when Sir Ralph Abercromby received his fatal wound. He told the women how Abercromby had pulled a sword out of his side and handed it to Smith, who'd then mounted a wounded Abercromby on his horse and rushed him off to be treated. Yet that hadn't been the man's undoing. The blow Abercromby died from was in his upper thigh, Smith explained.

"That," observed Jane to him, "was the wound of which Sir Philip Sidney died."

"Ah!" he replied, "I did not know that circumstance."

This would have pleased Jane, that she could teach Sir Sidney Smith something about war and her favorite sixteenth-century soldier-writer, who shared a part of his name. She would start connecting the living Sir Sidney Smith and the dead Sir Philip Sidney in her mind. Both, to her, were models of male perfection.

Smith told the Porter women that perhaps there was something fortunate in Abercromby's death in battle in old age, because he never had to return to civilian life and outlive the public's memory of his great actions.

"He ought to be remembered for ever!" Jane insisted.

Smith replied, "So he will . . . by all but the thoughtless; and they are the most numerous of mankind."

Jane was entranced. Smith promised to return there the next day to meet Robert. A moment after he left, Charles Kemble arrived. He'd had to listen to the Porter women rave, for a full hour, about the graces of Smith. In her diary, Jane recorded the scene in dialogue, capturing his every word, look, and gesture. It was her second brush with living military greatness, after having observed the Corsican hero General Paoli at the Lyceum Theatre some months before.[4] Jane was taken with patriots who tried to liberate their countries and the people from invaders and corrupt rulers.

The next day, Robert returned home. He waited for Smith to come until two, at which point he gave up and went out. At just that moment, Smith arrived and dismounted from his horse. Again, the Porter women offered a thousand apologies for Robert's absence. Smith drew up his chair and sat down, complaining of cold. They offered him wine and cake. He stayed. The Porter women showed Smith a sword used at the Siege of Acre, given to their brother by a friend. Smith gallantly asked for permission to draw it. Jane was once again in raptures, watching him deftly remove the weapon from its silver sheath. He explained to them how it was used, what it was called. Its name was a "launcher," he said, and narrated more stories of former battles.

The sisters asked if he might tell them about the two years he'd spent as a prisoner of war in Paris. What they most wanted to know, they said, was if it were true he'd escaped with the assistance of a lady. He said it was true. He told them about the failed attempt to dig a mine underneath the ground and up into his cell, followed by a dramatic escape, in which rebel forces dressed up as French guards whisked him out of the prison and out of France. Jane meticulously wrote out Smith's story, to preserve it. She also recorded her own feelings hearing it.

"I felt the lustre of his character in every nerve; and whether my inward feelings gave any illumination to my looks, I cannot tell," Jane wrote.

It certainly must have, because Smith turned to Jane and asked, "Have you ever been told that you are like Mrs. Siddons?"

Jane, confused, admitted that yes, she had been told she had a resemblance to that family, the Kembles.

"You are very like her indeed," Smith returned.[5]

It was a great compliment to Jane's striking looks. Smith, who'd made a point of telling the Porter women how many places he had to go that day, stayed with them again for two hours. When Robert didn't return, Smith arranged to come back again on Monday, after his planned breakfast with Mr. William Wilberforce, the politician and champion of the antislavery movement.

When Smith returned to the Porters' home for the third time, Robert met him at the door. Smith went upstairs to Robert's studio and sat briefly for the artist. Before he left, he told Jane and Maria that Robert's quick sketch was more like himself than any he'd ever seen. After that, Jane couldn't help praising Smith to anyone who'd listen. Of Robert's capturing the man's face, Jane raved, "The fire! The splendour! . . . I never have seen anything like it—he is all soul, within & without, a perfect hero!"

The next day, Smith returned to their home for the fourth time. Jane was vexed he'd arrived with company. It gave her no chance to talk to him. But toward the end of his sitting for Robert, he came down to the women to ask for supplies to write a letter. To close the note, Maria offered him a wax seal. The design on the seal was an antique head of a vestal virgin.

"Ha!" Smith said of it, turning it over in his hands, "this is a fine antique!"

"Yes," said Maria, "it is thought very beautiful."

"It is the very transcript of your sister," Smith said, "a perfect facsimile!"

In her diary, Jane tried to write down every word Smith uttered. She professed she didn't record these things because she wanted to preserve the compliment to her.

"I write them," she declared, "because Sir Sidney said them."

She decided to compose an anonymous sketch of Smith's life for the *Union Magazine*. Maria wrote an animated ode to him. The sisters sought ways to learn about him and talk about him, even in his absence. They had dinner twice with Smith's secretary and heard more stories, including one about Smith's learning on the battlefield that his mother had died, finishing the fight, and then breaking down to cry. Jane would end up using the story in her fiction writing.

Over the next month, as Robert completed Smith's portrait, the hero was frequently in the Porters' home. Sometimes he brought guests. Once, he surprised them by coming with the Duke of Gloucester, nephew of King George III. Smith could have taken his friend directly upstairs to Robert's studio, bypassing the women, but he made a brief stop to introduce him to Jane and Maria. This was a favor indeed. The Duke of Gloucester would later become Jane's great supporter and friend.

Four months after they'd first met him, in March 1802, Smith arrived very late for his appointment with Robert. He galloped up to the door, alighted from his horse, and said he'd rushed directly from the Princess of Wales's home at Blackheath. He'd made the eight-mile trip in a mere forty minutes to give Robert as much notice as possible. He told the Porters that the Princess of Wales herself would soon be arriving at their home.

Her Royal Highness arrived ten minutes later in her phaeton, a light, swift vehicle she rode in about town at top speeds. She wore an immense wig and painted her eyebrows in a way that gave her face a fierce look. She often wore very high-heeled shoes that made her lean forward.[6] Both the Princess and her phaeton would have been unmistakable on Gerrard Street. When she entered their home, she must have gone directly upstairs, without stopping to attend to Mrs. Porter, Jane, or Maria. They wouldn't have expected otherwise. That Her Royal Highness was in their home at all was a great and surprising honor. She stayed with Robert and Smith for a perfunctory fifteen minutes, as a crowd gathered outside next to her fine vehicle. Then the trio left to go to the Lyceum to see Robert's great historical picture in progress.

Of all the things Jane had seen in that short span of minutes—the Princess of Wales in their modest home!—one brief vision was seared in her memory: Smith's departure. She saw him standing by the royal carriage without a hat. His hair was blowing about, and his eyes and forehead were glowing. Jane wondered that the mob in the street could stare at the Princess but look at him with such indifference. How quickly, she thought, their eyes would have turned from the splendor of royalty, if they knew they were looking on the defender of their country's honor. "Every blast of wind that lifted his hair, I felt blow through me," Jane wrote.[7]

After that day, from March to December 1802, Jane saw Sir Sidney only twice more, once at their home and once at the theater. She was disappointed he hadn't called on them more often. She comforted herself by acknowledging that such a being was too resplendent to come very often into her sphere. Jane may not have heard or paid any attention to the idle gossip that Smith was privately spending a lot of time at Blackheath with the Princess of Wales, who was, in turn, making frequent visits to the neighboring home where Smith was staying as a guest. Her Royal Highness was said to have had several male favorites, and it was common knowledge that she and her husband, the future King George IV, weren't on good terms. Jane focused only on the hope for humanity that Smith inspired in her. "The sight of his Excellence," Jane wrote in her diary, "has renewed in my breast all its ancient belief in the grandeur of man—I think on him, and I can neither see nor hear anyone else.[8]

During the years 1801 and 1802, when Jane's hero worship of Smith was at a fever pitch, and as she was capturing her own fictional Polish war hero on the page, Maria continued to work on her adapted play *The Runaways*. It had come together with much difficulty, over the course of two years. She fretted about the work so much, she told Jane, that her mind was exhausted.[9]

Maria had been encouraged to write the play by none other than Mr. Thomas Harris, the powerful manager of the Theatre Royal in Covent Garden, who wanted to stage her play. He was related through marriage to the Longman publishing family and would have known Maria's talents in fiction. It was said Harris made a visit to her home to encourage her—a rare, and almost unheard of, honor.[10] An enthusiastic response from Harris was an incredible prospect for a beginning playwright. Her previous dramatic work was limited to short pieces performed in her home. When he read her draft, "His opinion seemed to be pretty much in its favor," Maria told Jane. The problem was that he believed her play was better suited to opera. Maria didn't mince words with Jane: "I hate the thought of an opera."[11]

Yet an opera was what Covent Garden wanted from her, and a musical project wasn't outside of the scope of Maria's talents. She'd been working with a male friend on a few compositions, back when *The Runaways* was going to be a play with a few songs. She'd written the lyrics, and her friend composed beautiful music. Maria, whose singing was said to be just as skilled as Miss De Camp's, decided to give in to Harris's vision. She transformed *The Runaways* into a comic opera, writing more lyrics and adding grand flourishes to the adapted story.[12]

She completed another draft. But then, despite initial encouragement, Harris kept delaying putting Maria's opera onto Covent Garden's schedule. In the middle of 1802, he raised more objections. He scratched things out that struck him as too political. He didn't think Maria's opera should take a strong abolitionist stance. She struggled with his commands, but she told Jane, "You will perceive on reading my Runaways that I have blotted out, some speeches about the slaves—they were too full of the spirit of wide benevolence for Mr. Harris—the piece itself will insinuate, what might not be so well, to say broad out."[13]

Maria knew her play needed to please the public. She wasn't opposed to satisfying an audience. But she wanted the play to expose the tyrant enslaver as the problem in a corrupt system that hurt all people. This she found difficult to do. She'd been directed to write material she thought of as nonsense.[14] When

Jane read the draft of the opera to offer feedback, she objected to the nonsense. But Maria, sounding quite tired, uncharacteristically overruled her sister's suggestions. "You will be amazed after all I wrote in my last, to see the MS so like what you sent me down," she wrote to Jane. "The fact is, I have thought, and thought, and so I find *I* can not make it better, am resolved it shall take its chance as it now stands."

She admitted, with resignation, "Those scenes which you marked *abominable* I have preserved;—as public taste runs, they are reliefs to the piece, and will I am sure succeed—let them stand, *still*."

The plot and characters of Maria's play followed trends of the London stage. Her play's heroine, Julie, raised in a Portuguese convent, sails across the ocean to the island of her birth, Guadeloupe, in the French West Indies to rejoin her father, an enslaving tyrant. When Julie and her orphan friend Adelaide arrive on the island, they dream of lavish balls and beautiful men. What they discover is a place of nightmarish hardship.

Julie then discovers her father plans to treat her, too, like an object. He has designs to marry her off, by force, to a man of his choice, rather than allowing her to marry her beloved, the absent Theodore, who has secretly followed her to the island. The only protector Julie has against her father is the enslaved man Ornubo, who tells Julie that the man her father has chosen for her husband is a bad white man, one who beats and kills poor Blacks.

Horrified, Julie tells Ornubo she hopes the English will soon take charge, show compassion, and drop the chains of slavery, dissolving his and others' bonds. Julie then becomes "the Runaway" of the title, leaving her father for Ornubo's protection. He doesn't turn out to have her best interests at heart, either. By the end of the play, the military camp has gone up in flames, the rebelling enslaved people voluntarily choose peace and re-enslavement, and the tyrant father is vanquished. Julie marries Theodore, and her friend Adelaide also gets the European man of her choice for a husband.

Little of this sounds like comedy, but as a comic opera, the piece needed to end happily, in marriages and songs. The chorus declares everything ends in a blessed happy night. The total control of allegedly benevolent white male Europeans is reinstated, save for the removal of a few bad actors. The institution of slavery remains intact, although supposedly with less brutality. The white women are put under the control of nicer husbands than the previous generation's male tyrants would have chosen for them. This ending didn't do much to challenge West Indian enslavement of Blacks or compulsory marriages of white European women. Although Maria had tried to draw attention to the unfairness of violent systems, it would be difficult now to label her opera more than tepid abolitionism or proto-feminism. By making the outliers in the system the problem, not the system itself, the opera's message might more widely please—or so Harris seems to have convinced Maria.

She waited for Harris to set a date on which her opera's fate would be decided before an audience. Some plays then never came to the stage at all, even from this advanced point. Others might be performed only once, if opening-night audiences revolted with shouts or boos, until the piece was announced as withdrawn from the stage. A few productions went on to great applause, performed many times. This might result in a playwright's earning hundreds of pounds through an eventually scheduled benefit performance, in which the night's profits were shared. Maria asked Jane to copy out her opera in a neat book. They needed Harris to see the work as finished and ready. But Harris kept postponing and postponing. "If Harris should fly from his promise after all!—but I won't pause on the thought," Maria wrote to Jane. "God bless you, and bless me in my present undertaking—my success is the success of the whole family, and so I repeat again, God bless me."[15]

As Maria tried to get Harris to schedule her opera, Jane set out to complete her historical romance. She did so, at first, without Maria's usual support. Maria wanted to convince Jane to stop writing fiction, because her uncredited efforts with the historical pamphlets accompanying Robert's paintings had proved successful. Jane should pursue real historical writing, Maria thought, not works of mere imagination so little respected by elite readers. It gave Jane pause. This novel would be her last, she thought, although she still felt very interested in its story, or she wouldn't have continued it.[16]

While writing this book, Jane almost didn't recognize herself because she was so insecure about the process. As she grew older, she was no longer the writer who, as Maria used to say, always took things so coolly. Jane found herself instead horridly timorous. She was unable to get out a sentence without literally shuddering. She told Maria she threw down her paper ten times an hour. She drove herself to headaches with anxieties about how ridiculous everything she wrote might appear to readers. Sometimes, she confessed, she considered quitting. "I continually cry to myself,—'I won't write another line.'—Then I take the paper up again, 'Yes I will, for when it is done, if I don't like it, there is nobody will compel me to expose myself.' "

Writing the sections narrating wartime made her feel like a fraud. She'd never witnessed a battle. She worried military men would laugh at her presumption. She declared that, in defiance of all the headaches, she'd go on and print or not print, by Maria's judgment.[17] When Jane shared her work, Maria approved. Jane sent the manuscript to Longman and Rees. They accepted it and put it into production. It would be a four-volume novel—Jane's first of that extended length.

Thaddeus of Warsaw follows the adventures of fictional war hero Thaddeus Sobieski, a Polish nobleman who survives a devastating loss in battle to the invading Russians. Thaddeus immigrates to England, in nameless poverty, to try to put his life back together. Although there was no such person as this Sobieski, Jane did take a real surname from Polish history and transformed famous people into fictional characters. She placed them in actual circumstances of war in the 1790s, narrating the battles in gruesome detail. Then she told dramatic stories of her noble Polish hero as a mistreated, penniless refugee in English society. She wove fictional domestic scenes together with real political events. She presented morally uplifting outcomes.

Jane was doing something new in fiction. Many previously published novels incorporated real people as characters or used real events as the jumping-off point for fictional stories. They'd appeared for at least a century, from Daniel Defoe's *Robinson Crusoe* (1719) to Sophia Lee's *The Recess* (1783–85). What was new about *Thaddeus of Warsaw* was its mingling of climactic historical events with the conventions of biographies, romantic tales, and probable domestic novels. Jane innovated when she "introduced the fundamental form of the historical novel to British readers," and "placed her protagonists in the midst of military upheaval," as a recent critic puts it.[18]

Jane's worship of Sir Sidney Smith also flowed into the novel's pages. What Jane had heard, felt, and experienced with Smith became material for fiction. But more importantly, it became her inspiration and motivation. Although her story was set in the 1790s, *Thaddeus of Warsaw* wasn't directly about the French Revolution or the Napoleonic Wars, yet every page indirectly commented on them. The book illuminated the devastating effects of war and its accompanying poverty on survivors and explored the plight of refugees facing xenophobia, through the eyes of its protagonist hero.

Thaddeus of Warsaw has a plot so intricate that providing a summary is difficult. It would have been an easier story for readers to follow while Russia's brutal aggressions on Polish soil remained fresh memories. The most prominent war hero of the failed bid for Polish independence in the 1790s was General Tadeusz (or Thaddeus) Kościuszko, a man as celebrated as Britain's Sir Sidney Smith. Kościuszko's valiant efforts resulted in battle injuries. When Poland was ultimately partitioned, Kościuszko emerged a hero of the people and an international celebrity.

Admiration for the Polish general was well established in the Porter family. Robert had exchanged letters with him during his visit to England in 1797. In the sisters' papers, there are poems dedicated to Kościuszko and Poland. Jane decided Poland's fight against Russia was the right canvas for her, perhaps with the recognition that any story about a power-hungry nation's bullying would have brought special satisfaction to British readers during the Napoleonic Wars. As the narrator described the hero's thinking early in the novel, "He well knew the difference between a defender of his own country and the invader of another's."[19]

General Kościuszko appears as a character in *Thaddeus of Warsaw*, and may have been an inspiration, but he's not the novel's hero. Jane's protagonist is Count Thaddeus Constantine Sobieski, fictional descendant of the real-life King John Sobieski, who is young, highborn, and impossibly attractive. At the beginning of the book, he loses his family in wartime, after learning his father was an unnamed Englishman who mysteriously deserted his mother, shortly after their secret marriage. The novel's first volume puts Thaddeus into combat on Polish battlefields, in a panorama of horrifying violence. Jane's earlier work researching and writing descriptions and pamphlets to accompany Robert's great historical pictures would have been solid narrative training.

As the story proceeds, Poland's attempts to defend itself against invading Russian forces prove futile, and Thaddeus rushes home just in time to watch his mother die. He cries with her before she breathes her last. He manages to escape as the Russians burn his family's castle to the ground. With no home, no family, and little money, he goes to London to build a new life and to be reunited with a young Englishman whose life he'd spared in battle. Pembroke Somerset was first made a prisoner of war by Thaddeus but then became a friend. In England, the hero attempts to contact Somerset but mistakenly believes his friend spurns him. Next, Thaddeus tries to make his way as a poor immigrant artist in the London neighborhoods the Porters lived in during the 1790s. By the end, he finds his long-lost friend, Somerset, who turns out to be his younger brother. He's reconciled with their father. He's given a fortune and marries his virtuous, independent-thinking cousin, Mary Beaufort, whose surname is French for "beautiful" and "strong."

Thaddeus of Warsaw mixed two popular literary genres, the old-style, fantastical, and highly entertaining romance, with the weighty, fact-based, and (it was hoped) ennobling accounts of great men found in history writing. In Jane's morally uplifting mix, the hero is too perfect and the good characters too good. The story's culminating events are filled with impossible coincidence. All the reunions! Economic problems are brushed away in a stroke. These things require the reader's suspension of disbelief. That suspension is perhaps at no moment more needed than when Thaddeus regains possession, across the English Channel, of his lost horse from Poland.

But the novel is also a tour de force. The dialogue is spirited. The satirical young flirts, desperate femmes fatales, and wise, hard-hearted female mentors in its pages are drawn with vivid discernment and human sympathy, as well as the requisite moral judgment. Jane announces in her preface that her book has "made no ceremony of making Truth the help-mate of Fiction." The events of real history are narrated as compelling stories, as if they were told by a brilliant eyewitness. The novel "introduced the fundamental form of the historical novel to British readers," as one critic puts it, by placing its protagonist in the midst of bloody battle.[20]

The years of training Jane gained in her diary and letters—especially by setting out to capture the overheard dialogue of real people—were also put to impressive literary use. This was precisely the kind of innovative book, combining fact, fiction, and moral lessons, that Jane's immense literary talents and polite character made her seem almost destined to create. Even the domestic scenes are presented as if they are true stories told by an observer. In her preface, she writes, "I have sketched no virtue that I have not seen, nor painted any folly from imagination." She claims her characters are drawn from "living evidence."

The incredible details of her family's and friends' lives made their way into *Thaddeus*'s pages.

Sympathetic Thaddeus cries frequently throughout the novel. He displays as much emotional sensitivity as he does bravery in war. This sort of sentimental hero was prevalent in the day's popular fiction, but Jane also witnessed everyday scenes featuring emotionally overwrought men. She'd comforted sensitive, crying Wade Caulfield for a full day, after he'd broken down looking at a work of art. She'd comforted Ned Warren in sobs, as he fought with Henry Caulfield over Jane's allegiance. She'd heard secondhand about Sir Sidney Smith's stoicism, postponing his emotional response to a battlefield revelation about the death of his mother. Jane used these experiences in her fiction. She knew men like Thaddeus—strong, fighting, sensitive, tearful.

Jane's literary inspirations, too, are marshaled in her book. She refers throughout to her favorite authors, including William Shakespeare, Sir Philip Sidney, and Samuel Richardson. She also mentions recent favorites, like Frances Burney and another dear friend and mentor, Mrs. Susannah Gunning. Jane made some friends into characters, too, having included that scene with Charles Kemble. He takes the stage as a Polish exile, a role he'd played, although anachronistically placed in Jane's story.[21] The actor's magnificent performance moves sensitive Thaddeus profoundly, which makes the women around him go wild, especially the virtuous Mary. The character of Mary is very Jane-like. She's easily emotionally moved but just as easily frozen in place by her strong feelings.

Jane mined details from her mother's years running an Edinburgh boardinghouse, likely serving foreigners, for the novel's landlady Mrs. Robson, who tends to down-and-out Thaddeus. It must have been a Porter family inside joke that Jane gave Mrs. Robson's poor, precocious grandchildren the names William and Nanny. Nanny was a nickname for Anna, as well as the name of one of Jane's aunts. Another character, a "daring girl" with a "satirical spirit," was named Maria.

Jane drew on Mrs. Crespigny for aspects of her novel's powerful society women. Miss De Camp may have inspired the beautiful, drama-seeking coquette, Eugenia Dundas. Thaddeus's wronged mother, Therese Sobieski, has shades of Mary Robinson, although she shares the first name of Miss De Camp. Even Jane's complicated femme fatale seems to have been drawn from a distant acquaintance. Jane created a beautiful, neglected married woman who fruitlessly pines for Thaddeus, Lady Sara Roos. Lady Sara eventually throws herself at the hero in the same way Mrs. Chambers was said to have done to seduce young Henry Caulfield.

But the most significant decision Jane made, as she completed the book, was in its title page and dedication. First, she put her name and gender on display on the title page. The decision to acknowledge it as the work of "Miss Porter" (as the eldest unmarried daughter in a family was called) was financial. Jane believed she and Maria would both "stand a good chance for a better price" in selling their books to Longman and Rees by putting their names on their works.[22] Her dedication, too, took a risk. She'd once planned to dedicate it again to her mentor, Percival Stockdale, but she threw aside that plan to choose instead Sir Sidney Smith.

Jane's motivations for dedicating the book to Smith were complex. In the dedication, she connects fictional Thaddeus, living Smith, and the long-dead soldier-writer, Sir Philip Sidney. Jane lauds Smith as a man of taste, feeling, and candor, of whom the future will speak with honor and the present times boast as their glory. The dedication concludes, "To Sir Sidney Smith I submit this humble Tribute of the highest Respect which can be offered by a Briton, or animate the Heart of his most obedient and obliged Servant The Author."[23] These were audacious words for an unmarried woman, naming an unmarried man as her dedicatee. It was daring to address him in print at all, much less to refer to her animated heart.

When Jane's novel was published in April 1803, it was advertised as *Thaddeus of Warsaw*, in four volumes, by Miss Porter. Publishers Longman and Rees advertised it alongside Jane's *The Spirit of the Elbe* (as yet uncredited), in two volumes, and Anna Maria Porter's *Octavia*, in three volumes.[24] The Porter family could have an advertisement to themselves with their works, although the world wouldn't have grasped that yet. The Porter sisters, young as they were, had published enough to begin to fill a shelf.

Sales for *Thaddeus* were unremarkable at first. Longman and Rees, having printed a standard run of five hundred copies, didn't immediately send the book to reviewers. But word of mouth began to build. The novel seemed poised, in spring 1803, to be at least a moderate success. Jane learned that a general had said, "No one could have described so well the horrors in Poland, who had not been an eye-witness."[25] Many couldn't believe a woman had written it.

It was a pivotal moment in their lives. In May, just a month after *Thaddeus*'s publication in May, Maria's opera was finally scheduled for its Covent Garden debut. The work had undergone a name change from *The Runaways* to its advertised title, *The Fair Fugitives*. Harris had engaged the well-known composer Dr. Thomas Busby to set Maria's songs to music. Leading actors were cast, including the best singer of the day, famed tenor John Braham. But then, at the last minute, Braham withdrew from the role. Harris replaced him with a respectable tenor of far less talent and renown. Maria was devastated. She'd written the lead specifically for Braham. There was nothing to be done. Then yet another actor pulled out, claiming illness, right before the opening.

When *The Fair Fugitives*, a musical piece in three acts, had its opening night on May 16, 1803, it must have been a thrilling milestone for Maria. On the first evening, it was said to have been received with great applause.[26] But this report was in her friend Peter Courtier's magazine, the *Monthly Visitor*, where Maria and Jane were sure to get sympathetic reviews. Other reviewers paint a less rosy picture. The scenery and pleasing music were praised, but there was said to be nothing else new, striking, or interesting in the opera.

"It was upon the whole tolerably well received," reported one newspaper, "and announced for repetition with few dissenting voices."[27]

A less sympathetic critic claimed *The Fair Fugitives* lived to a second night only because the manager John Philip Kemble tried to step in, shorten, and improve it.[28] If so, then Kemble's dramatic triage wasn't enough. *The Fair Fugitives* was withdrawn from the stage on the second night.[29] How the audience condemned Maria's opera isn't recorded, but it's probable that it was booed and that she'd witnessed it.

A gentle account of the condemnation was later published in the *Monthly Visitor*. The reviewer said the ill-success of the piece shouldn't be blamed on the playwright but on the principal actors, who refused to take their given parts.[30] Another reviewer, too, blamed the cast for the opera's failure, saying none of them seemed right for their roles. There was a report that whole sentences were ad-libbed and that one performer was heavily intoxicated.[31]

But not every reviewer was so ready to blame the players. *The Fair Fugitives*, one source reported, lacked coherence and was a silly, feeble piece.[32] Another thought the materials were good but that this first dramatic effort of Miss Anna Maria Porter had the faults of inexperience one might expect from a talented young dramatist.[33] That supportive critic also notes that the piece was rumored not to have been originally conceived as an opera and that its incidents were therefore probably much distorted from the author's first conception. This review, filled with insider knowledge, was a gentle elegy. *The Fair Fugitives*, the work of years, died a quick death. When its songs were later published separately in a pamphlet, Maria's name was left off.[34]

The month of May 1803 was momentous for Jane and Maria for different reasons. For Jane, the first notices of *Thaddeus of Warsaw* appeared. Some reviewers seemed unable to get beyond the book's dedication, remarking on Jane's unusual address to Sir Sidney Smith, occasionally with ridicule.[35] Gossip circulated that Miss Porter must be about to marry Smith, which would have been a simultaneously distressing and thrilling prediction to Jane. The rumors probably helped boost sales. The critical assessments began to shift to absolute raves. Reviewers focused on the novel's innovative form—remarking that it was "a novel founded, in part, on historic facts" and "a very interesting historical novel."[36] "Thaddeus is a work of genius," one reviewer eventually declared.[37]

Historical novels, like novels in general, were greeted with suspicion. Historical fiction was declared problematic by readers and critics, who believed it was dangerous to confound truth and falsity. Yet even the skeptical acknowledged Miss Porter had mixed them in *Thaddeus* in a way that worked. *Thaddeus of Warsaw* would be listed as one of the year's best novels and a national treasure, "entitled to notice, as the original production of our own country."[38] Within six months of its publication, Jane would have known she had a literary phenomenon on her hands. Almost overnight she changed from the least to the most famous Porter sibling. "I know how precious Fame is to *you*," Maria wrote to Jane, "and therefore I prize it for your sake."[39]

As Jane's celebrity grew, so did Robert's private troubles. In the early months of 1803, as Jane was bringing *Thaddeus of Warsaw* to press and success, and Maria was seeing *The Fair Fugitives* to stage and disappointment, Robert was sliding further into debt. He'd burned through most of his large *Seringapatam* earnings. To keep money coming in, he needed to paint constantly. It became clear his next great historical pictures weren't going to succeed as well as the first one had. The mad vogue for his enormous, panorama-style paintings had run its course.

To make matters worse, Robert and the other investors were in arrears on their lease at the Lyceum Theatre, with a five-hundred-pound debt, an amount that only increased with interest. Robert wrote to his brother William, asking if he could immediately repay the three-hundred-pound loan Robert had previously provided. Robert had given his brother money in order to keep William, in Scotland with his wife, Lydia, and infant son, Charles, out of debtors' prison. For more than a year, William said he couldn't repay.[40] William would successfully abscond from his Scottish debts and take his family to Durham. His non-payment left Robert in danger.

Robert needed to find new capital to pay old debts. He took out loans and began writing what were, in effect, postdated checks—bills for amounts to be paid in the future, for which he was given a lesser portion in immediate cash. The sums ballooned to three figures. Then they began to come in at four figures.

"No money," Robert wrote in his diary in 1803. "Infamous times."[41]

Jane, Maria, and Mrs. Porter had thought it would be Robert's genius and connections among the titled and wealthy that would lead them to prosperity, but Jane's was the star on the rise. Her success brought her acclaim, readers, and fans, although not wealthy patrons, investors, or profits. Newfound fame did, however, make Jane resemble a victorious war hero, at least to Maria's mind.

"See what it is to be a Beauty!—and a hit—and the author of Thaddeus of Warsaw!" she wrote to Jane, "Truly you take the field, with such a Battery of destruction before you, that is it no wonder you slay thousands and tens of thousands!"[42]

CHAPTER 8

Hearts and Darts

Maria's Sighing Soldier (1803–4)

In the summer of 1803, Maria accepted an invitation to travel to the Isle of Wight to visit her good friends the Asplands. The trip promised an opportunity to regain health and strength—and her footing as a writer. It had been two months since *The Fair Fugitives* had been performed only twice on the Covent Garden stage. Maria's change of scene ought to have brought an escape from metropolitan bustle and family financial anxieties. The reality would prove less soothing than the fantasy.

It was an eighty-mile journey from London to the Isle of Wight off the southern coast of England. Maria's hosts, the Reverend Robert and Mrs. Sara Aspland, lived in Newport, the capital at the island's center. Maria knew the couple well, having been the witness at their London marriage two years earlier. She traveled from London with Sara Aspland's sister and brother, Anna and Jesse Middleton, their old neighbors from St. Martin's Lane. Jesse was expected to step into the thriving family art supply business. Anna, the dearest Middleton to Maria, reminded her of the late Mary Wollstonecraft.[1]

Their trip took two days by stagecoach and boat, which resulted in Maria's sunburned arrival in Newport.[2] The three travelers would have been warmly welcomed by the Asplands, who'd moved to the island for Robert's position as preacher in a small, lively General Baptist/Unitarian congregation.[3] By all reports, the Asplands were happy. Robert expressed gratitude for his "equal wife," "liberal friends" and "smiling babe!"[4]

Maria's escape from London brought a welcome change of air. The compact Isle of Wight had abundant natural beauty. The Asplands took their guests out in the carriage to see picturesque views. Maria wrote home describing how her eye could catch the bright gleams of the sea in the openings between the island's verdant hills and how green roads skirted around their undulations. She relished sharing these descriptions with Jane. While on the island, Maria wrote a poem addressed to Jane, happily recollecting a time the two of them had taken a quiet trip to the country. As much as Maria loved Anna and the Asplands, she sometimes wished she were traveling with her sister instead.

The island might have seemed a more relaxing place if it hadn't been such an anxious moment for Britain. Every town was filled with soldiers. The Isle of Wight was temporary home to a large barracks as extensive as a small city. Soldiers were at the ready, should Napoleon decide to cross the English Channel and attack. Rumors of a French invasion kept the island on full alert, yet most days were peaceful, and their sightseeing trips undisturbed.

When Maria had time to herself, she worked on a new novel, *The Lake of Killarney*. She was again in a rush to finish, since Robert's and William's debts were overwhelming the family. Despite the promise of quiet time to work on the island, Maria was finding her new novel very painful to unravel.[5] It would be set in Ireland's County Kerry in the 1790s, with scenes of war on French soil in 1794, following the adventures of an admirable young heroine, an adopted foundling who avidly reads and writes poetry.

Like her heroine, Maria often found herself more interested in observing nature and writing poetry than in forwarding her complex novel's plot in prose. One day, Robert Aspland rescued a glowworm from a ledge and gave it to Maria. It prompted her to write a poem, in which the speaker looks tearfully down on the lost worm held in her confining hand, and bids it to find its beloved friends and embrace its freedom. The world's cruelties and injustices, and the unfair confinement of living things, were on Maria's sympathetic mind. Her host Robert Aspland would publish the poem several years later in a magazine he began to edit.[6]

Maria also struggled to focus on *The Lake of Killarney* because she was preoccupied with the people around her. One of her companions especially tried her patience: the absurd, boring, and vexatious Jesse Middleton. He was civil, yes, but then there were his vulgarisms and his officiousness. The biggest problem Maria had with him was that he found eating and drinking unpleasant. He tried to control everyone's appetite and access to food and drink, especially the women.

At breakfast, Jesse would hand Maria bread and butter with the unencouraging remark, "I suppose you don't feel any inclination—this supping out last night must have taken away all your appetite.—*I* can't eat; I wonder who can?" When they stopped at midday to open a bottle and share cake after sightseeing, he would declare, "Of course the ladies can't eat.—one has but just breakfasted." He actively stood in the way of Maria's drinking wine. Maria told Jane that she silently fumed at Jesse's refined temperance. She considered herself a poor, fainting creature who needed refreshment. But Jesse was insistent he knew best what ladies should do.

"But I say Miss Porter," Jesse would tell her, "Wine alone is so strong.—it makes the head ache. You'd better have water in it."

Maria would insist she didn't want her wine diluted. She wasn't ashamed of her healthy, unfeminine appetite for eating and drinking, even alcohol. The others with her were at least on her side and joined her in taking exquisite pleasure in annoying Jesse.[7]

"If he did not provoke me sometimes almost out of myself," Maria admitted, "I could be egregiously entertained."[8]

Maria was further provoked to discover everyone on the island assumed Jesse was destined for her husband. That gossip transported her into a rage of rudeness.[9] But Jesse's sisters were so gloriously kind that Maria tried to remain calm about people's loose talk. Anna and Sara even nursed Maria when she took sick. She was temporarily seized with pains and tremblings, likely menstrual, a problem that was becoming chronic.

When Maria wasn't convalescing or trying to write a novel or railing against Jesse's strictures and the gossip about her marrying him, she discovered a new sight to catch her eye. It happened at her window. She noticed a very handsome soldier, marching by the Asplands' home, with his regiment. What struck Maria wasn't only this soldier's incredibly good looks but the fact that he'd noticed Maria in the window, too, watching him. Feminine politeness would have dictated her looking away, but she didn't. He didn't take his eyes away from her, either. A grand flash of acknowledgment passed between the two of them, Maria thought, before he marched off, into the distance.

It might have ended there, but Maria noticed when her soldier returned. At first, it wasn't clear what his purpose was, but Maria concluded it was no coincidence. He seemed to be marching back and forth near *her* window, looking for her. Then she became sure of it. The soldier stationed himself in front of the Asplands' window, where he'd first seen her, at all times of the day and night, marching some lengths near the house. Maria began to watch for him at certain times, with growing interest and curiosity. Sometimes he saw her noticing him, although she now tried to pretend not to care.

In letters to Jane, Maria began to call him "the military Adonis." Soon, the most interesting sightseeing Maria was doing on the Isle of Wight was out of her hosts' window. She took in the striking view of his carnation complexion and his azure eyes. But Maria not only saw her Adonis. She also began to hear him, too, thanks to his constant sighs.[10] Here was a handsome young soldier, in the bloom of youth, at such a period as *this*—in wartime—marching, gazing, and sighing—and for her, it seemed.

A uniform alone might have made a man handsome. This soldier would have worn a red coat on top of a white waist coast. The jacket would have been short in front with tails hanging down in back, accentuated by a yellow collar and epaulettes with decorative fringe. His pantaloons would have been white and tight-fitting, tucked into black half-boots. It was meant to be an arresting look. The soldier's black sash and his coat's many buttons would have been brilliantly set off by the uniform's reds and yellows.

Maria admitted to Jane that the soldier never failed to excite some pitying emotion in her as she watched him. She imagined him going off to some dangerous battle. But perhaps the pity was for herself, too. The Middletons were planning to return soon to London. Maria's time on the island, and being transfixed by her attentive, sighing soldier, would come to an end. "Call it gratitude, call it vanity, call it what you will," she wrote to Jane, "I must honestly confess, that I cannot leave even my military Adonis, without a feeling of regret."[11] The soldier, of course, had no idea Maria was preparing to leave, and Maria wasn't ready to let him go. In her head, she'd been making up empty, amusing stories about him, when she was in the mood for idle writing. She shared them with Jane.

What she had to acknowledge was that her soldier was also a very clever man. The next day, as he sauntered by her window, in his usual pattern, he found a way, without talking to her, to let her hear his name. Speaking to her directly would have been beyond all decorum. It would have been a sign of disrespect. The two of them hadn't been properly introduced, so it wasn't okay for a strange man to notice a polite woman in public. What the clever sighing soldier did instead was to pretend to talk, very loudly, to a friend of his who was half a mile ahead on the street. In whatever manufactured message he'd mock-shouted, the soldier had said his own name loudly enough for Maria to hear it: "*Lieutenant Frederick Cowell.*"

After that, there was rain. Then more and more rain. Robert Aspland wouldn't let his guests leave the island with such unsafe conditions on the water. Maria's stay was extended several times. When the weather finally cleared, and Jesse declared his plan to return to London before the others, no one suggested he stay. Maria and Anna Middleton decided to remain behind. After Jesse left, Maria quickly regained her appetite for the Isle of Wight. The Asplands' household was a respite. They gave Maria time alone to write, and their conversation gave her such pleasure. She wrote for most of the day, took long walks with Anna, and agreed to return to London whenever her friend decided to go back.

This further delay turned out to be a very good thing for *The Lake of Killarney*. She wrote home to Jane, "I suppose it will give you some pleasure to hear that my novel is finished—so it is—I have laid about me in a most furious manner, with no other weapon than a very blunt pen, and have succeeded in giving life and death, madness and reason, to a whole colony of notable Worthies."[12]

In *Killarney*, Maria worked with dramatic, and sometimes bloody, family conflicts, as well as mistaken identity, cross-dressing, and mysterious parentage in Ireland and France. Maria's orphaned heroine, Rose de Blaquiere, is said to be the niece of her guardians, but the truth, as she knows, is that she was left an infant on their doorstep. As the novel opens, Rose—artless, chaste, well-read—is reunited with a male friend of her youth, Felix Charlemont, the novel's hero and the son of the Earl of Roscommon.

In choosing the two Irish surnames Charlemont and Roscommon, Maria was paying homage to two sets of friends. Charlemont was a maternal surname in the Caulfield family tree. The city of Roscommon was a place connected with another of the sisters' female mentors and close friends, the novelist Mrs. Gunning. Hero Felix Charlemont—impetuous and passionate—had many similarities to the sisters' beloved Henry Caulfield.

In the novel, Rose can't control her feelings for Felix, and she struggles with her emotions for him on their reunion. Maria made her vivacious heroine into an avid and skilled archer. Added drama came in the form of a few light fainting fits, several violent fevers, a man's head injury, a masquerade ball, many tear-filled scenes, and picturesque descriptions of boats on the lake. The novel also has moving and funny dialogue and a cast of characters who represent the best and the worst in the fashionable world. Their voices come alive on the page.

In her novel, Maria was also indirectly commenting on the day's debates about female authorship. Rose is a poet who accidentally drops her papers with handwritten verses outdoors. Felix finds the pages and reads them, prompting him to fall in love with her. Rose's brilliance and sensibility make him cry, although Rose is embarrassed. Later, a well-born but poor literary man teaches Rose "that to be ashamed of showing honestly the limits of any talent she possessed," especially her writing, "was to give way to a species of vanity which sullied character, and made it unjustly withhold its quota of pleasure from mankind." Women of genius must share its fruits.

By putting feminist ideas into the mouth of a male character, Maria may have been attempting to make them more palatable. When the literary man later writes a tragedy for the stage, it allows Rose to step in to rousingly defend his work. This minor plot point also gave Maria a chance to insert her real theatrical friends, including John Philip Kemble, into scenes in *The Lake of Killarney*.

But women's creativity is the book's focus. The literary man gives a rousing speech about the superiority of literary women. His arguments echo those of Mary Wollstonecraft, although she's never named. "If it be an acknowledged truth," the literary man says, "that reflection is the nurse of wisdom, as well as of virtue, then we may safely infer, that women are not merely better, but wiser than we." He argues that women should be able to direct and decide on their own actions, concluding, "Where can love subsist, but in perfect equality of soul?"[13]

That's the sort of relationship the heroine and hero end up in, after requisite hardships. But the novel doesn't end there. Once they marry, they're briefly separated when Rose temporarily goes mad. In writing this last dramatic section of her novel, Maria may have drawn on stories of her late father's mental incapacity, as well as on her love of Shakespeare and *Hamlet*'s Ophelia. The happy ending arrives when Felix discovers Rose and gets her medical help. She's restored to her senses and to motherhood.

When Maria wrote home from the Isle of Wight, she joked to Jane that the hero of *The Lake of Killarney*, Lord Tyrone (the former Felix Charlemont) was now as ready as she could make him to join Jane's hero Count Thaddeus Sobieski of *Thaddeus of Warsaw*, although she acknowledged her hero couldn't possibly join Jane's on any equal footing. Her sister's success with *Thaddeus of Warsaw* was prompting her to reevaluate her future. Jane had achieved the fame she'd long desired at age twenty-seven. Maria, twenty-four, had published far more without gaining nearly as much acclaim, while having endured consistent, bile-filled remarks from reviewers.

After the failure of her opera, she became convinced Jane was the more talented sister and began to ask if she was really cut out for a life of authorship. Maria wrote to Jane that she thought she might renounce future attempts to gather laurels. She confessed that *Thaddeus of Warsaw* made the patterns of men she envisioned in her own creative brain appear as "puny whipsters" by comparison. "I will therefore magnanimously relinquish the Quill and taking up a good darning needle, strive to mend my errors," Maria wrote. "If some honest man will marry me, then will I give up the muses;—but if not, authorship and old maidism shall go together. Happiness or Fame, that is the alternative."

This was playful banter, but it had a serious edge. Maria's doubts that she could outdo Jane's literary achievements encouraged her to look more critically at possible futures. The paths were so starkly different. The world wasn't set up to allow women conventional domestic happiness and unconventional public fame. The sisters knew few women writers who'd succeeded without having been born into money or a title. After finishing *The Lake of Killarney* and watching her military Adonis through the window for weeks, Maria began to lean in a new direction. "I cry, Happiness!" she declared to Jane, "but I'm afraid Fame and crabbed celibacy, are all that will be offer'd me.—every body has their fame, somehow or other; and if mine, don't extend beyond a circle of booksellers clerks and milliners apprentices, still it is Fame."[14]

Jane's next letter to her sister jokingly warns her that being discovered as a writer won't help her case with the attractive soldiers there. "What would the gay officers you speak of think," Jane teased Maria, "if they knew that you were a Poetess, and one that dedicated her muse only to her own sex, and what is worse a sister!—I fear they would cut you for your antiquated notions."[15]

Jane wanted Maria to use these attentive soldiers as inspiration for her next fictional work, which they referred to as "The Green Griffin," already begun. She included a scene in it where two male heroes serenade two lovely women under their window in the moonlight. The heroines, Violante Willoughby and her friend Helen, listen to the heroes in their nightclothes and thrust their heads out the window, before rattling it back down. As Maria wrote in the story, which she titled "The Serenade; or, Green Griffin," "The serenade roused their imaginations, and occupied their thoughts." The two heroines, who'd been raised in seclusion from society, didn't understand the impropriety of encouraging the serenade's repetition. "To talk to the charming serenaders, and to see the charming serenaders, became, shortly, the sole business of their unguarded solitude," she wrote.[16]

Maria's daily life on the Isle of Wight resembled that of her naïve heroine, Violante Willoughby. She watched so obsessively for her charming officer that the Asplands began to catch on. Once, when Maria and Anna were returning home from the post office, three soldiers followed them down the street, and Anna noticed it. At the Asplands' home, Maria's sighing soldier so often passed and repassed under the window, murmuring appreciative things under his voice, that Robert Aspland noticed, too, and asked Maria if she'd brought home soldiers to look at her. With that insinuation, she gave up the pleasure of listening for her soldier's soft sounds. She started up from her seat by the window and vanished from the Adonis's sight.

"There is heroism for you," she joked to Jane, "from a poor girl who is thought little better than a homely wench in the metropolis."[17]

Maria worried that if she met her Adonis on the streets, and if he said something admiring to her in front of her hosts, she'd lose her good reputation. Had the soldier been disrespectful, Maria thought, she'd have had to avoid him ever after.[18] But he hadn't disrespected her. These musings prompted the self-realization that she might have a little of what Methodists then called "carnal mindedness." The inwardly good man wasn't enough to please her. She needed him also to be outwardly rather handsome and perfectly graceful. "Shall I fall under your censure for this confession?" Maria asked her sister. "Seriously, I often censure myself for it, most liberally."[19]

Maria must not have censured herself too severely, because the next step she took was a radical one. She knew her time on the island was ending and heard rumors that regiments were preparing to leave, too. She made use of her knowledge of the sighing soldier's real name. She wrote a letter, using a false name, addressed to Lieutenant Frederick Cowell.

In her letter, Maria would have given the soldier some way to write back to her under that false name. She justified this brazen act of writing to a male stranger by telling herself she was never bold with him *in person*. She'd given him no inappropriate encouragement. In writing to him, she was only doing what she often did—taking up her pen in the service of romance. But this time, the romance was her own, and her forwardness put her polite reputation on the line. Maria was in uncharted emotional and morally dangerous territory.

As she put it later, "I never gave him the slightest idea that he had interested me in the least, and he never had the vanity to suppose it, till he received my first letter."[20] Maria would come to refer to it as "that first *sermon* of a letter."[21]

She may have taken a playfully high-handed tone. Perhaps she dressed him down for pacing and sighing in front of her window or muttering flattering things, in danger of being overheard by others. Whatever it was that Maria wrote, her shame in doing it was mixed with a little bit of pride. She later called this "indiscretion" of hers "so wild a thing."[22]

She eventually learned her soldier had tried to learn her name, too. Once, when they'd been walking a little distance from each other in the street, he'd asked a woman he knew if she was acquainted with the woman he pointed to. Some confusion led him to believe Maria was the sister of the Asplands.[23] He mistakenly thought he was pining for Anna Middleton, sister-in-law of a well-respected young preacher, not Anna Maria Porter, the authoress.

But Maria didn't then have any notion her soldier believed her to be someone else. She didn't sign her letter, and he didn't hint that he thought he already knew *her* real name. Perhaps Maria had her soldier leave a letter at the Newport post office, also under a false name, which she'd have been able to pick up when she fetched letters addressed to her from London. At the post office, one could ask for letters on behalf of another person, even a fictitious person, without raising much suspicion, especially because recipients paid for letters.

Maria somehow learned her soldier was leaving the island, too. Lieutenant Cowell's regiment would remove from one city named Newport to report to duty at another with the same name, four thousand miles away. The regiment made the arduous trip from Newport, Isle of Wight, across the Atlantic Ocean to Newport, Jamaica. Before leaving, the sighing soldier must have given the woman in the window an opening to write to him again.

Maria hardly dared to breathe a word of this reckless romantic adventure in her letters home. But once she and Jane were alone together, she would have revealed all, no doubt with trepidation and excitement. Jane must have approved of her sister's wild actions. Maria wrote her own letters to Lieutenant Cowell—to Frederick—but Jane began to help direct their contents, once again becoming Maria's romantic counselor.[24]

For the correspondence to continue between Maria and Frederick, utmost secrecy was required. An illicit courtship by letter needed to be kept hidden from her mother and brothers, as well as the rest of the world. Robert had disapproved of it when they had openly visited the late Mrs. Robinson, worrying her stained reputation would rub off on his spotless sisters by association. Imagine what such a brother would think of Maria behaving like a forward, loose woman herself, in writing to a man—a stranger—and inviting further exchanges.

Maria and Frederick's relationship by secret correspondence blossomed. From the autumn of 1803 and through 1804, Maria would come to know him from his monthly letters, sent from Jamaica. He told her he was Irish, not a Scottish Highlander, as she'd once fantasized. He'd been in the army since age fifteen and had no great fortune or prospects. He was a younger brother, in a family of many sons, and worse still, his advancement in the army was uncertain.

His posting in the West Indies was thought highly undesirable. He was an officer in the Second West India Regiment, otherwise known as the Black Troops. The Black Troops were an unusual regiment. Its officers were white, but its soldiers were Black. Some of the regiment's first soldiers were formerly enslaved men who'd served on the side of the British during the American Revolution. Then freed Blacks in the West Indies were recruited to grow the West India regiments. Unsurprisingly, few were interested in a British military career, so recruits were sought from West Indian plantation owners. These enslavers rarely wanted to accept the government's offered prices for enslaved men.[25] When these recruiting methods didn't raise enough soldiers, the government turned to slave traders. The eight West India regiments were made up principally of soldiers purchased by the British Army from slavers. The British government may have been the largest individual buyer of enslaved people from 1795 to 1807, paying for more than thirteen thousand enslaved Africans for its West India regiments.[26] Lieutenant Cowell's job would be to arm, train, and lead them.

The regiment's Black soldiers weren't necessarily welcomed by the island's wealthy whites. Locals feared the British Army's organizing formerly enslaved men into a permanent armed corps might send the wrong message to enslaved Blacks being forced to work on the plantations. It was especially controversial that the Black Troops were uniformed in the same way as white troops and served alongside them. There was, too, a great deal of confusion about whether Black soldiers were subject to local laws. The position of the government was that the Black Troops were subject to military regulations, over and above local laws. In Jamaica, armed Black soldiers might be called in to guard white deserters, standing over them with weapons—and the complete support of the British Army. White colonizers feared the optics of this sanctioned use of military force. There were brutal, deadly confrontations.[27]

Even before going to Jamaica, Frederick would have known that being posted to this regiment wasn't an enviable assignment. Many British-born soldiers sent to the West Indies never acclimated. Some died of disease. It was believed that one benefit of the Black Troops was that its soldiers got sick less often, accustomed as they were to exertion in hot climates. Frederick's regiment had been in Jamaica for two years when he was assigned to it, and its numbers were expanding. It would shortly grow from six hundred to one thousand soldiers. The directives sent down from the British Army were that Black soldiers were to be treated just the same as white ones. It wasn't precisely true. Both Black and white soldiers were eligible for retirement pay, but Black soldiers were purchased for life, whereas whites enlisted for a more limited period. Black soldiers were supposed to serve as long as they were uninjured and able bodied.

Frederick would have found himself in the center of many kinds of conflict. He didn't take to the work very well. After a short time, he wrote to Maria about how desperately he wanted to leave Jamaica. He was miserable there, he said, as well as miserable not to be nearer to her. Everything he shared with her pulled at her heart strings. He was mysterious about his past conduct, too, admitting to her that in his teens, he'd done things he regretted. He assured her he'd entirely reformed. His experience in Jamaica was transformative, as was watching her from afar in the Isle of Wight.

Maria's hard-won experiences told her she couldn't judge a man solely by his stated principles and opinions. The same man might talk like a philosopher but act like a fool. She worried Frederick might have habits that would offend her. She shuddered to think she knew nothing of his conduct or manners.[28] "I take them all upon trust," she admitted. "I may hereafter bitterly regret having surrendered myself to my Imagination."[29]

Yet it took just a handful of monthly letters for Maria to begin to fear their breakup and then a few more to imagine matrimony. When a letter from Frederick didn't materialize, Maria was sure he was ending their connection, had gotten sick, or died. Instead, she might discover his previous letter had miscarried. Frederick jumped to conclusions, too. Sometimes each skipped a monthly opportunity to write, out of fear or petulance. They managed to have disagreements, arguments, and disappointments, even in a forbidden relationship consisting of infrequent trans-Atlantic letters.

Maria discovered she was older than he was. She acknowledged there were four years' difference in their ages, but it was at least six and perhaps eight. He may have added as many years to his age as she shaved off. He appears to have been born around 1786, and she was born in December 1778.[30] In the summer of 1803, when they first saw each other, he may have been seventeen or eighteen to her twenty-four. Maria didn't want there to be a thunderstrike when they met again one day and he realized she wasn't so pretty as he imagined.

She also thought it possible Frederick misremembered her. Their relationship began with so little time in each other's presence and no exchanged words. He'd only seen her while animated in a window, or after exercise on a street, not in a hum-drum room. She asked Jane to look for a slight drawing of her done by one of their old painting friends, to send it to Frederick, so he could discover her defects.[31]

Maria worried that every day made her older, sadder, and less agreeable. She felt a woeful change taking place in herself, she confessed to Jane. By contrast, she thought Frederick's eyes and heart must be finding fresh charms in life. A man's morning of existence lasted so much longer than a woman's, she thought. She worried that when they finally met all she'd have left to attract him would be her virtue.[32] Frederick tried to assure her of his preference and her perfections, especially her virtuous character. He admitted he was astonished by her first indiscreet letter, although confident it was uncharacteristic of her. He read and reread her letters and believed her indiscretion was the first and last she'd ever commit.

Maria's anxieties over Frederick were taking a physical toll. During a period in 1804, when Maria was at home and Jane far away, Maria's letters to her sister about Frederick verge on manic. In one, she celebrated that "the very fluctuations of grief and joy which Frederick causes me, seem to unite my soul more intimately with his;—his dangerous profession, his yet more dangerous station in Jamaica, his unsettled fortune, his rash but interesting character all conspire to keep up a sleepless solicitude for him, in my thoughts."[33]

The couple worried, too, about being caught. If he were about to die, he promised, he'd protect her reputation. He kept her letters under his pillow in the barracks, ready to be burned the instant he might breathe his last.[34] And when she wrote to Jane about Frederick, Maria used euphemism and code, in case her letters needed to be read aloud or were intercepted. She was right to be cautious. A month after she'd come back from the Isle of Wight, her older brother John—himself newly returned from the West Indies—had scooped up and read a letter that fell out of her pocket.[35] Fortunately, it wasn't about Frederick. Once Robert had torn open Maria's letter to Jane. But thanks to the sisters' cryptic language, he didn't understand it. All he grasped was Maria's outlandish wit.[36] Another time, he'd come into the room while Maria was reading one of Frederick's secret letters, but she successfully hid it.[37]

Jane and Maria employed clever methods for stealth in their letters. As in the past, they used brackets around any material they were signaling shouldn't be read aloud to their mother. Jane called it writing that was hidden between "hooks and hangers."[38] But communications about Frederick required even greater ingenuity. The sisters plotted the use of invisible ink. Maria told Jane, "You must write your reply to me in milk or lemon, over the ink lines of your letter here—before you send it off, so, that it cannot be seen.—I shall make it visible to myself, by holding it to the Fire.—no one knows that I write to you."[39] Perhaps they never used this method, because Jane replied she was unable to get these ingredients.[40]

Another way the sisters kept their exchanges secret was by receiving letters through a third party. They brought trusted friend Elizabeth Benger, the author Jane met while sharing a bed at Mrs. Crespigny's, into Maria and Frederick's secrets. They used Benger's address as a clandestine way station, especially when the Porter sisters could get a frank, which was a cost-free method of sending a letter through the post office when signed by a member of parliament.[41] Sometimes the sisters couldn't find an MP for a frank. Then Benger agreed to pay to receive the letters and wait for repayment. There are repeated references in the sisters' letters about the need to settle with Benger.[42] They often owed her small sums of money that were nevertheless difficult to scrape together. Ongoing communication with Maria's overseas lover was proving expensive at a time the Porter family couldn't afford it, because every shilling was being counted.

Frederick sometimes conveyed his letters back to England through a particular friend of his uncle who traveled to and from the West Indies. A letter hand-carried back to England had the advantage of being inexpensive. It could either be brought directly to the addressee or dropped in the penny post once the traveler arrived in London. But private hands could be unreliable—and not very private. Letters might be damaged, forgotten, lost, destroyed, or intentionally opened. Once, such a letter took five months to reach Maria. She worried others in a similar strain hadn't yet arrived and wondered if they were being read by curious, impertinent people.

This fear began to affect Maria in other ways, too. Maria told Jane she'd burned "millions" of verses, plays, and stories she'd written at ages eleven, twelve, and thirteen. She'd laughed when she'd reread them but then set fire to them.[43] Her immature productions would no longer be able to be read, sniggered at, or surreptitiously published by future prying eyes.

It seems incredible, but more than a year into their correspondence, Maria still hadn't told Frederick her true, full name. Frederick had no idea his woman in the window, with whom he envisioned a future life, was Miss Anna Maria Porter—well-known poet, fiction writer, and playwright—the sister to Jane Porter the famous novelist, and Robert Ker Porter the famous painter.

Jane urged Maria to disclose her name and identity, to "at once reveal to him who you are, and as much of your feelings as you deem proper. I think you ought to understand each other clearly."[44]

Maria struggled with herself over writing him this letter of revelation. She reread it a thousand times, wavering as to whether it was too warm or too cold. She decided to reveal everything to Frederick—not only her identity as an author and an explicit account of her family and name, but also the true state of her loving heart.[45] She declared her future peace was in his hands. She told him she'd either have happiness with him or complete failure of it from him. She declared there was one heart in Europe that beat only for him. "What would I not give to see absolutely into his heart," Maria wrote to Jane, "or rather, what would I not give to be able to believe that it is possible for me to be loved as much as I can love."[46]

When Frederick wrote back, he sent Maria a lock of his hair. On first seeing it, she was languishing in bed in the morning. She'd been waiting anxiously for his letter in the packet from Benger and for a private moment to read it. When she tore open the letter and saw the hair, the blood froze in her veins. It looked, she thought, absolutely *dark*. She worried for a moment she'd been writing to the wrong soldier. "I tore open the curtains, the light fell upon it, and then I saw the same bright, beautiful-colored hair, I used to admire so in Newport," she wrote.[47]

She thought it was the color the god Apollo's would have been—the same color she'd given her hero in *The Lake of Killarney*. It was similar in color to her own, except his hair had a divine, golden glow, rather than her pale silvery tint. Frederick admitted nothing could appear more ridiculous and incredible than a man being wholly ignorant of the name and connections of a woman in whom he professed to have so strong an interest, yet such, he confessed, was his case. But with that exchange of letters, her confessed identity and feelings, and his gift of hair, Frederick and Maria reached a mutual understanding. They formed a secret engagement to be married.

Maria's betrothal to Frederick should have brought her happiness, despite its being unknown to everyone else in England but Jane. The reason it couldn't make her happy was because the year 1804 was bringing the Porters to the brink of financial collapse. All three brothers were dangerously in debt. Robert called it the Porter family's "season of inconveniences" and blamed William's first large debt to him as the origin of their problems.[48] But Robert had gone just as deeply into debt himself. And John, in trying to help manage traveling exhibitions of Robert's paintings, was now so foolishly enmeshed in his brother's business affairs that he was proving more of a hindrance than a help.

The Porters considered more drastic ways to retrench. They looked for cheaper lodgings outside of London. Jane and Maria tried to find more ways to earn money. Maria was poised to earn thirty guineas for *The Lake of Killarney*, when it was finally published.[49] She hated how it had turned out and professed herself eager to give up on authorship to become Frederick's wife. Maria wrote to Jane, "I abominate my Lake of Killarney, because it is nothing but *Hearts and Darts.—seriously*, I am absolutely sick of it."[50]

Then Jane and Maria found a way to attack both problems at once—to earn money from writing and cheaply receive Frederick's letters. They entered into an agreement to anonymously edit a new magazine. It was work they'd already seen up close as a part of *The Quiz* collective. Many other friends had become editors in the years since. When the sisters pitched a new magazine to a Mr. Dale, he approved it, in partnership with the publisher Thomas Ostell.

The sisters called their magazine *The Sentinel; or British Miscellany and Review*, which was to appear monthly, starting in August 1804.[51] Jane and Maria would produce almost all the contents themselves. For their trouble, they were promised four guineas per month, along with another four guineas and a half per month to Robert to produce its illustrations. Jane calculated it out very carefully, down to the shilling, for six issues. A guinea was a pound and a shilling, and there were twenty shillings to a pound. So they might earn twenty-nine pounds, eighteen shillings, and six pence for six months' work.[52] Every penny mattered.

This new labor of being editors gave Jane and Maria a few unusual freedoms. They arranged to receive *The Sentinel*'s editorial correspondence through their printer. It was widely done in the magazine world—publicly naming a printer's or bookseller's shop as a place where editors would receive letters and submissions. It was Jane who ingeniously suggested their printer should be told to receive all letters for the editors from a friend in the West Indies who'd contribute to the magazine.[53] Frederick would pretend to be one of their authors, the sisters would receive his letters, and then they'd reimburse the postage to publisher and printer, presumably out of their earnings. Maria was supposed to communicate to Frederick the need to sign his future letters as from the author of "The Green Griffin," addressing them as official correspondence to the magazine's editors. These packets would be held for Maria or Jane to pick up in person. No one would have suspected Maria's carrying away illicit love letters, just as no one would have suspected *The Sentinel* was edited by two young women.[54]

Even with this clever arrangement, Maria and Frederick's love letters came dangerously close to discovery. Jane wrote to Maria, "By the way, pray tell Mr. Dale, that the communications of your Jamaica friend, are not to be opened by any hands but yours or mine.—I got a pacquet of letters for the Sentinel yesterday and to my surprize found them all opened—if they should perform this way, upon the Epistles of our *literary Soldier*, what a discovery would take place."[55]

Jane and Maria pretended that the man who wrote from the West Indies was the author of "The Green Griffin," which would actually appear unsigned in parts in the issues of *The Sentinel*. It was an amusing lie, since Frederick had played a part in inspiring the serenading soldier in Maria's novella.[56] As they pretended he was their author, however, the sisters discovered Frederick wasn't literary at all. That, too, began to worry Maria. She became convinced he needed to take more active steps to get ahead in his military career—and find a way to get transferred out of the Black Troops. Maria had doubts about his ability to forward himself.[57] She encouraged him to use every means to advance by patronage. She also wanted him to study. She sent him lists of books to read and, someday, when she could afford it, she hoped to send actual books. One title she wanted to send, *The Military Mentor*, was a self-help manual for young soldiers seeking to further their careers.

Jane did what she could to assuage her sister's fears about Frederick's talents and potential. There was no mental inferiority in Frederick, Jane told her sister. Any lack of learning in him was no obstacle. Jane reminded Maria that they themselves enjoyed early advantages in self-improvement that Frederick didn't. The Porters had had to fake it to make it. Jane admitted "a very *little* reading, with a *great* knowledge of calamity, has made us what we *are*—has set us on the same bench with people whose actual *Book-Learning*, might overwhelm us."[58] Frederick, Jane wrote, was like them, a virtuous autodidact who'd learned calamity's lessons. He just needed to complete that very little reading that he now lacked, under Maria's tutelage. "I often think, how absurd we must both appear, in your eyes," Maria told Jane, about her and Frederick. "Two people that only know one another by sight, that have precipitated themselves into the most serious engagements and professions, merely upon *a liking for one another's looks*."[59]

But in Maria's dreams, it was all happily settled.

She told Jane, "I dreamt last night you were married secretly to Henry—and I, as secretly to somebody else—it was quite ridiculous."[60]

CHAPTER 9

How Wild Is the World

Celebrity Jane's Suitors and a Defense of Crim. Con. (1804)

As Maria looked to Jane for help navigating her secret correspondence with Lieutenant Frederick Cowell across 1804, Jane entered a whirlwind year of her own. She had accepted an invitation to travel to the spa town of Bath that winter and spring, as the female companion to a newlywed novelist friend. It was a trip many would have seen as an active attempt to get her married off.

No sooner had she arrived in Bath, in February 1804, than she wrote home to Maria, "Stop before you read the succeeding and marvel! I certainly must be married before I leave Bath, for I was not here a morning before I opened an offer of marriage!"[1]

Jane cleared up the mystery. When she'd left London by coach the previous day to travel the hundred miles to Bath, it was without realizing she was carrying a letter that included a declaration of love. Their longtime friend Charles Rivers had handed Jane a letter when she left and told her to read it at her leisure. She'd thought nothing of it but finally opened it in Bath. She was vexed to discover it was a very odd declaration of love and an unwanted proposal of marriage. Jane had absolutely no idea that Mr. Rivers thought of her in that way. She'd never entertained the slightest romantic thought of him. The sisters believed this painter of miniatures who'd come into their circle through brother Robert to be an honest man but a bit of a dullard.[2] Once, Jane had asked him, "What news?" and he'd replied, "Really, Miss Porter, I never trouble myself about news."[3] After that, whenever they met, Jane cheekily greeted him by asking, "What news, Mr. Rivers?"[4] He must not have understood he was being teased.

That Mr. Rivers could think Jane would welcome a marriage proposal from him seemed incredible. His lugubrious response to her refusal of the offer of his hand was an embarrassment, full of clichés. His second declaration of love began by quoting a maudlin line from John Gay's poem "A Thought on Eternity": "Ah! What is life with ills encompassed 'round." Rivers followed up with melodramatic statements about his romantic feelings. He told Jane that if she continued to reject him, "Far very far away must I remove from this once happy spot, never to intrude myself again in your presence."[5]

His purported love was far, very far from welcome news to Jane, although she pitied Mr. Rivers a little. She asked Maria to please inform their mother about this turn of events. Meanwhile, Jane would consider how to let the young man down gently. But it would end up taking greater efforts to get Mr. Rivers to understand he'd been rejected. He was convinced Jane must be concealing an attachment to him. He told Maria he'd had conversations with five different Porter acquaintances, all of whom thought that Jane's kind letter of rejection was actually an encouragement. His subsequent letters to her were a mixture of arrogant pretension and roaring misery. Maria begged Jane to communicate even more plainly to Mr. Rivers, rejecting him again with greater force and urgency. They were becoming enraged at the man's stupid obstinacy.[6]

No doubt Mr. Rivers worried that Jane, heading off to Bath, might return an engaged or even married woman. Jane also understood the expectations of going off to Bath. She told Maria teasingly, "I mean to give you and my dear Mother, a short account of the sort of folk I meet here, that you may have timely notice . . . when I am likely to be in danger of falling in love with any of the charming Beaux who are presented to my sight."

It took just two days for Jane to find herself not only fascinated with but also disgusted by what she saw there. Nothing could be more absurd, she wrote, than the marrying mania absorbing every imagination in Bath. Men would look at one woman and then another, without any warmth or emotion, and merely take one for better or worse, because they wanted a pretty, good-natured wife. Jane's position on wife-shopping was unequivocal: "I would just as soon jump into a boiling cauldron, as marry, in one of these Matrimonial-Warehouses."[7]

Her invitation to Bath had come from a close friend, the former Miss Elizabeth Gunning. Jane had dedicated her first anonymous novel, *The Spirit of the Elbe*, to her. Miss Gunning's late mother, the novelist Mrs. Susannah Gunning, had been another important early mentor to the Porter sisters. The Gunnings were notorious public figures, who'd been through an almost incredible scandal that involved alleged forgery and supposed love triangles, in what seemed to some a failed bid to manipulate a nobleman into a marriage. The fallout from that failure pitted Miss Gunning against her military father, General Gunning. He took the nobleman's side. It also pitted husband against wife, with General Gunning and Mrs. Susannah Gunning at odds over their daughter's character. Mrs. Gunning insisted Miss Gunning was innocent.

The fight spilled over into a pamphlet war and from there to newspaper coverage that divided elite households. The women often sided with the mother and daughter. The men sided with General Gunning, who soon disowned his wife and daughter. The abandoned Mrs. Susannah Gunning, capitalizing on her fame, returned to publishing novels to make a living. Her daughter Elizabeth then followed in her mother's footsteps to authorship. The surname "Gunning" drew in curious readers, and the novels sold well enough.

This scandal had occurred years before the Gunnings met the Porter sisters, but it meant Mrs. Gunning was well poised in the late 1790s to help Jane and Maria navigate their early literary careers. When Mrs. Gunning became deathly ill, Jane came to their cottage to nurse the old woman and support her daughter. Jane was at her bedside when Mrs. Gunning took her last breath in August 1800.[8] In the three years following that devastating loss, Miss Gunning had built a new life. She'd completed and published one of her mother's unfinished novels and wrote some of her own. But in November 1803, she'd taken a step in a different direction. She'd become Mrs. Plunkett at age thirty-four.

Her new husband was Major James Plunkett, an Irish Catholic widower ten years her senior. Major Plunkett's first wife had died suddenly of an apoplectic fit.[9] He'd observed the appropriate mourning period of one year and then taken a second wife. "Married," the newspapers announced, "Major Plunkett, to Miss Gunning, Authoress of several interesting productions."[10]

Miss Gunning's past notoriety may not have bothered Major Plunkett—or at least not as much as it might have other men. He'd had his own problems, after being implicated in what the British called the Irish Rebellion of 1798, a failed uprising. Plunkett was charged, arrested, and examined for high treason but escaped a death sentence by slipping off to France. He was eventually cleared and returned quietly to England. Miss Gunning, like her new husband, had Irish family roots. And like his wife, Major Plunkett had faced gossip questioning his character. Some said he'd fabricated his military title. This much Jane was sure of: her friend wasn't in love with the major. She'd married him for money.[11]

The newlywed Plunketts, to celebrate their nuptials and settle into married life, had rented comfortable lodgings in Bath. As was customary then, Mrs. Plunkett invited along Jane as a female companion and, in return, would introduce her friend into fashionable society and serve as her chaperone. Mrs. Plunkett had married at an age considered late, and Jane, at twenty-eight, was nearing the age at which she'd be presumed an old maid.

Jane's invitation to Bath had come at an opportune moment for her family. Brother John had returned to London late in 1803. After fifteen years in Antigua, he'd come back as almost a stranger to his mother and siblings. Robert felt guilt about the financial disasters John discovered there, admitting to his brother, "You should have found a happy and easy home," instead of shared miseries. At least, Robert promised, he'd find among them a sure return of his love and affection.[12] But even if love were in abundance, room in their lodgings was not. Jane's temporary absence meant freeing up household space. She believed she could live very cheaply in Bath as a guest of the Plunketts. While there, she planned to continue her writing. She was under deadline for Robert's pamphlet for his new great historical picture, *The Battle of Alexandria*. His agent had sent Jane to Bath with a packet of paper, specifically for writing it.[13] Jane was waiting, too, for Longman and Rees to call for the second edition of *Thaddeus of Warsaw*. As soon as they gave the word, she'd turn to correcting and revising it.

The Plunketts took lodgings in a convenient and central part of Bath, in Kingston Buildings, just across from the stately Bath Abbey. Each morning, Jane could hear its musical chimes from her bedroom.[14] Kingston Buildings—regular, neat, and magnificent—were a good address, even if not among the most prized.[15] From there, the group could walk to any of Bath's desirable places in a moment. It was Jane's first trip to Bath, and she declared she'd never seen a more charming place, with the beauty of its buildings and its landscape of hills surrounding and intersecting the town.[16]

Any trip to Bath started in the famed Pump Room, so that's where Jane and Mrs. Plunkett began. "Taking the waters" there was widely believed a curative medical treatment. Its mineral water had a unique, acidic, and not entirely pleasant taste. It was also a spot for visitors' arrivals to be recorded, for later newspaper publication. Well-dressed sightseers could promenade around the room in their finery. On the brief walk from Kingston's Buildings to the Pump Room, Jane learned that Mrs. Plunkett had an agenda. She prepared Jane to meet a man likely to be there waiting for her. He was Major Henry Holditch. This major, Mrs. Plunkett told Jane, was the admiration of the ladies and an admirer of them in return. He was resolved not to leave Bath unmarried. Mrs. Plunkett implied that Jane should be the woman to help him fulfill his resolution. As a further sweetener, Mrs. P. (as Jane began to call her) told Jane why Major Holditch would be worth catching. He had two thousand pounds a year—enough to support a wife in style, with houses in town and country, a carriage, a houseful of servants, and parties. Major Holditch was, from a financial standpoint, a desirable husband.

When Jane entered the Pump Room, she noticed the fine rotunda looked a lot like the great room she knew from London's Vauxhall Gardens. She was pleased with the room and thought it poised to be filled with loveliness. But when she looked around, she discovered nothing could have been further from the truth. "Never in my life," Jane wrote, "did I behold such a collection of frights, men and women, all uglier, one than another."[17] The beauty of the room, she thought, set its people off to very bad advantage. Jane and the Plunketts hadn't been in the Pump Room more than a few moments when a smartly dressed, conceited man hopped toward them, with an affected kind of limp. Mrs. P. introduced him to Jane. *This* was Major Holditch. At first, Jane chose to say very little in conversation with him. "You know I never say much for the first quarter of an hour in which I see people for the first time." Jane wrote home. "In a few minutes of listening, I heard enough to assure me of the affectation and folly of the rich Major."

When their party decided to leave the Pump Room to walk in town, it gave Mrs. P. a moment for private exchange with Jane. She whispered that Major Holditch found her *wonderfully* handsome and longed to hear her speak. Jane decided to extend this man's *wonderment*. She answered only yes or no to his barrage of questions as they walked. Mrs. P. next steered all of them to the house of a gentleman who'd promised to show off his pictures. On viewing them, Jane, who knew fine art, saw at a glance these pictures were very bad. Once they'd left the gentleman's home, Major Holditch asked Jane how she liked these pictures. She replied that she thought some of them good. How many, he'd asked her, to which Jane tersely replied, "Two."

"Then how can you make out *some*?" he pompously answered. "*Three* may be *some*, but *two cannot*."

Jane thought he'd looked round with a glance that said, "See how clever I am! How wise she thinks me!" So she replied, coolly, "I would thank you sir to *explain why two* cannot be expressed by the word *some*, as well as *three*? I should think, that as *some* is a word to express the *plural* number, it may as well express *two*, as a *hundred*—If you can *prove* to me otherwise, I shall consider myself obliged."

Poor Major Holditch went silent and took a hasty leave. Later, Mrs. P. told Jane all the fine things he had said about her, but Jane was sure that, after hearing her speaking powers, he'd never recommence his attacks on her.[18] Major Holditch, she later learned, believed every woman he saw wanted to marry him, so she was glad to have drawn daggers at her first interview with him, as she told Maria.[19] In return, her sister teased Jane that she expected too much: "It is a dreadful thing that you should require so many ingredients in the beverage of matrimony."[20] After all, she wrote, other women they knew could contrive to be happy with wealthy fools or handsome rakes. Perhaps Jane should try out this Holditch for a few years as an experiment, Maria joked, so she could decide whether to follow Jane's example into such a marriage.[21]

The men were disappointing, but Jane made one new female friend, a pleasant and genteel Irish relation of Major Plunkett's named Mrs. Carrol.

Mrs. Carrol was in Bath, at first, without her husband, although he planned to join her some weeks later. The two women arranged to go see a play together, while the Plunketts were otherwise engaged. Jane was excited to take her new friend to the theater, because that night, Henry Caulfield would perform.

That spring Henry had taken a place among the actors at a respected provincial theater in Bath. His presence there had surely added to Jane's sense of the likely attractions of the city. Jane thought Henry a marvelous actor. A year before, she and Maria had used their connections to get Henry an audition with Covent Garden's theater manager, Thomas Harris. Henry had proved himself. He'd made his professional stage debut as Hamlet, on February 2, 1803. Jane was there in the audience, and she wrote a long diary entry about the day that would determine the earthly fate of "our dear Henry."

Henry was an iconoclastic actor. He took parts out of their received performance traditions and remade them. His Hamlet was enthusiastically received. Jane had hoped—expected—genius from Henry that night, but this was beyond everything. Jane had seen John Philip Kemble in this role. She'd seen his nephew, Henry Siddons. Henry Caulfield outdid both. "He was the perfect Hamlet," Jane had recorded. "Every feature spoke the contention of his mind, his limbs trembled, his hair seemed to elevate itself, and the colour fled from his face, untill his lips were of a deadly paleness.—Peals after peals of applause succeeded."

Jane felt she was seeing theater history in the making. Henry, she was sure, was the next David Garrick—the most famous and talented actor, manager, and playwright of the eighteenth century. The audience followed Henry's every move and responded with energy. At the end, it gave bravos and huzzahs for ten minutes. After this triumph, Jane and Maria hurried home to Gerrard Street. No sooner had they gotten there than Henry appeared with Robert. He'd come to them directly. Both sisters reached out for him at the same time. "Maria caught him in her arms—I did the same, I clasped him to my breast with a joy that almost suffocated me.—Our happiness could only be seen in our eyes—our tongues had no power to tell it."[22]

Henry held them both. He stayed with the sisters and Robert, talking and laughing, all night. The next day, reports from the theater were everything they should have been. Harris said he'd never witnessed such a debut. Even Henry's enemies had been won over. Henry proposed he next play the hero-rake Ranger in Benjamin Hoadly's *The Suspicious Husband* and then Hotspur in Shakespeare's *Henry IV, Part I*, two parts with the late Garrick's imprint on them.

"Choose what you like," Harris approvingly told Henry, as Jane recorded it.

After several more turns at Hamlet, Henry got his chance as the lead of *The Suspicious Husband*, a play in which Ranger climbs a ladder into a married woman's bedroom. She rejects his wooing to remain faithful to her husband. Expectations for Henry's performance were high, and audiences were pleased. Reviewers, however, proved harder to impress. One made fun of Henry, slyly pointing out that perhaps he was so good in this role because of his real-life experience in seducing married women.[23]

Jane and Maria knew this hearsay had a basis in truth, but they gloried in Henry's theatrical success. Audience enthusiasm propelled his new career. The Duke of York agreed to allow Henry to sell his captain's commission and leave the military. Harris engaged Henry for the season, at eight pounds a week. But over the summer of 1803, the contract wasn't renewed. Rumor had it that John Philip Kemble's jealousy forced Henry out. Henry had to resort to acting in the lesser theaters in the provinces.

So in the spring of 1804, Henry was there in Bath, reprising his London performance of the hero rake Ranger in *The Suspicious Husband*, as well as performing Young Wilding, the man with a talent for embellishment, in Samuel Foote's *The Lyar*.[24] During her stay with the Plunketts, Jane would again have a chance to see Henry perform, alongside her new friend Mrs. Carrol. That night, audience members praised Henry's performance as exceeding even Kemble's, as Jane overheard it, as they called him a "pretty young man." Their next comments pleased her far less. "What a pity it is," she overheard someone say, "that he'd run through such a large fortune!"

This was the sort of loose talk Jane was compelled to listen to. At least Jane had the promise of more of Henry's company. Much to her delight, he called on her at the Plunketts'. The next evening, Jane and Mrs. Carrol went to see him perform again, as Octavian in George Colman's *The Mountaineers*. Henry was wondrous, Jane thought. In one moving scene, Jane bit her lip almost all the way through, to check a scream from bursting from her mouth. The next day, Henry called on Jane again and stayed all morning—and then again the next. His visits to Jane were noticed by the gossips.

Jane came to the conclusion that the nuances of Henry's performance were lost on Bath's audiences, which lacked taste and reveled in rumors. The elite of the town were Henry's advocates. The Duchess of Devonshire was said to go to the theater every chance she got to see him perform.[25] But the second set in Bath—of slightly less importance, wealth, or title—had nothing but malice and envy toward Henry. With the Plunketts, Jane often found herself in the gossip-mongering second set. She couldn't abide the shallowness. Indeed, Bath was proving disappointing to her, despite its natural beauties, reasonable prices, and delicious air.

"Every man," she wrote home, "I think a fright and a dunce; and almost every woman, as empty as can be."[26]

To Jane, Henry would have seemed above them all. He wasn't quite as notable as Jane, the bestselling novelist, but his name had become recognizable, not only as an actor but also as an amateur athlete. For years the London newspapers had been full of his head-turning exhibitions of ice skating on the Serpentine, a lake in Hyde Park. Each winter, crowds of thousands watched Henry skate, forming a large circle around him, twelve people deep. He could skate on one foot without allowing the other to touch the ice, and make the finest half circles.[27]

Fashionable London showed up in droves to see him, with the women in their finery, wearing velvet, silk pelisses, muffs to warm the hands, and fur tippets as scarves. Jane and Maria would have been among them. Jane had set a scene in *Thaddeus of Warsaw* in Hyde Park and made brief reference to its ice skaters. Maria would give her handsome hero an ice-skating scene in *Lake of Killarney*, comparing him to a Grecian statue on the ice.[28]

Henry's many attractions and talents didn't win everyone over. In conversation in Bath, Jane was forced to listen to him being criticized, till she became pale and red by turns, with suppressed indignation. She sometimes took up his cause. At others she sat in resigned contempt.[29] She never breathed a word of this to Henry, whose visits to her were also beginning to cause a stir. "I am lectured an hour every day," Jane wrote home, "for fear I should intend to marry him.—'It would be a shame'—'I certainly could not be such a fool'—'You may do so much better for yourself'—'He is a very nice young man but it would be ridiculous to think of liking him!'"

He was an actor, they said! He'd been born into a good family, yes, but he had no regular fortune. It wasn't just that he was likely broke. He was said to be a debauched rake who had to drag himself hungover to the theater each day. Mrs. P. and the other busybody women around Jane tried to push her toward so-called proper matches, like Major Holditch.

Jane couldn't bear the way Mrs. P. and her friends held up these men—"nothings" to her—and declared *them* and not Henry the sort of husbands a woman should jump at. Jane found herself repeatedly assuring them she wasn't going to marry Henry. She told them he'd never thought of *her* as a wife, nor did she think of him as a husband. They didn't believe her. "I laugh at all this," Jane wrote. As for these other nothing-men, Jane would tell her female friends, "I would not marry one of them, if they were kings of the world." After this declaration, Jane wrote, "I am generally called a thousand fools—and I am well content to wear the title."[30]

Major and Mrs. P. thought Jane more nice—meaning more discriminating—than wise. They were kind to Jane, but her friend wasn't the Miss Gunning she'd once known. Jane thought Mrs. P. almost too happy. She seemed to have no deep thoughts anymore. She'd married without love yet was now declaring she wouldn't exchange her husband for any man in the world. "Her advice to us as young ones, ever runs thus—If a man be rich, no matter what he is—you will be a fool if you do not marry him."

Jane despised this base homage to riches. She found she had a most animated detestation against the whole mercenary plan of prudential matches. She mostly laughed at the women who recommended them. There was only one friend Jane could count on to laugh along with her: Mrs. Carrol. It was with Mrs. Carrol alone that Jane might make fun of Major Holditch behind his back.

Within weeks of meeting each other, Miss Porter and Mrs. Carrol were going not just to the theater but everywhere together.[31] The more they went out together, the more notice they attracted. Then Jane discovered, much to her surprise, that *she* was the attraction—not just as a potential wife in a vast matrimonial warehouse but as a noted authoress in a fashionable place that reveled in popular books and gossip. This celebrity treatment was a novelty she hadn't experienced in London. "I find my Romance is in high vogue in Bath," Jane wrote home to Maria in London. "Two gentlemen told me the other evening at the Ball, that they had separately remained awake in their beds till two in the morning reading it."[32]

This would have been gratifying praise—and unusual flirtation. Young men sought opportunities in Bath to worship the author of *Thaddeus of Warsaw*. Each time Jane and Mrs. Carrol entered the assembly rooms, the men would fly to them. "I suppose there was something very extraordinary playing about our two figures," Jane wrote. "On entering the Ball-room, we were whirled into such a blaze of Beau! There was nothing of fashion or youth, that did not crowd round us—in a moment, the ladies began to make wry faces, and our names flew about the room, like wild-fire."

It seemed as if the gallant youths were ready to seize them, the moment Jane was beyond the eye of her chaperone, Mrs. P. "In all my life, I never listened to so many fine things, never received so much attention," Jane told Maria. "Had all my words been oracles, they could not have been hearkened to with greater veneration.—All this is very ridiculous—What matters it, what will it avail?—The lovely Carrol and her friend, will depart—and in a few days, their very names, perhaps, will be forgotten."[33]

Jane understood the attention as ephemeral and sporting, but she didn't deflect or reject it. Mrs. P. looked on with concern at the behavior of her charge and worried about the notoriety of Miss Porter in the rooms.[34] This dig at notoriety is especially rich, coming from the once-notorious Miss Gunning, but Jane understood some of Mrs. P.'s feelings arose from jealousy.

The Plunketts took Jane to endless balls, although she didn't like them.[35] She drew attention to herself because she wouldn't dance. It was a tactical decision. She dressed carefully in her new silk gown and felt she was admired, but she preferred to walk about and entertain herself by watching other dancers. Rather than being compelled to say yes to dancing with the likes of the detestable Major Holditch—who still wouldn't take a hint that Jane hated him—she didn't dance at all. It was a line in the sand that ought to have allowed her to escape pestering from Bath's pests, but it didn't fully protect her.

One man she needed protection from was Sir Essex Edgeworth, cousin to the famous author Maria Edgeworth. The polite world debated whether he was actually a baronet, but he styled himself "Sir." Edgeworth "took a most ugly fancy to me at first sight," Jane complained to Maria. "When he dined here, he made such consuming love to me, that I was obliged to fly to all ends of the room to escape his impertinence."

At a subsequent ball, he found a moment when her chaperone's back was turned. Jane was alone, and he was unobserved. Jane euphemistically described what he did next as rather too *loving*. It had happened quickly. Sir Essex Edgeworth had seized her.[36] He made an outrage on her cheek.[37] Jane was quick on her feet. She gave the abominable old man a most mighty knock. "I think," she told her mother and sister, "I made his poor withered arm feel the weight of mine for some time hence."[38]

After Jane told a friend about his insult and assault on her, gossip spread across town, along with speculation she would marry him anyway. But Jane refused to speak to him unless he delivered an apology. He finally did, half-heartedly, pleading intoxication as the cause. He didn't touch Jane again, although he did attempt to win her back by appealing to her as an author. He told her he could arrange a meeting between her and his famous novelist cousin, Maria Edgeworth. Jane said she'd be happy to be introduced to Miss Edgeworth, if she came to Bath, but didn't invite him to visit her in London. She didn't want to continue his acquaintance there.

Everyone in Bath seemed to think Jane would, like Mrs. P., grasp at some old title or old fortune, but she had no intention of it. Fortunately, she found three men of her own age whose company she welcomed, for humor and brilliance. Soon, these three men were constantly at her side and Mrs. Carrol's. The trio met up with the two women daily if they could in the Pump Room. They joined the women on their walks and served as constant shadows at the balls. It was also a form of protective chaperoneship in numbers that Mrs. P. apparently wasn't providing Jane.

Jane dubbed the first man in the trio her sentimental companion. He was the soon-to-be-famous poet Walter Savage Landor. Landor had left Oxford five years earlier, with a reputation for being a mad Jacobin. He'd once shot out another student's windows during college prayers.[39] But when Jane met him, he was around thirty and said to be living in a profuse style at Bath. He had fine-looking eyes, black hair that covered his forehead, and a stubbornness in the upper half of his face with a sweetness and humor around his mouth. He was said to be a man very conscious of his great intellectual powers, without having yet found an opportunity for exerting them.[40] Jane appreciated his excellent literary knowledge and observations.

The second man of the trio was Captain Myers. He was widely thought to be the finest dancer in Bath and was a strong admirer of female genius. Jane told Maria that Captain Myers haunted her like a ghost. She felt some guilt about it because Myers was engaged. He told Jane that, if he weren't, he would have proposed to her directly. One night, as they stepped out of the ball together, Captain Myers took Jane's hand, and whispered in her ear, "I give you my left hand, because that will place you closest to my heart."[41] Jane was not unmoved by this gallantry. Eventually, however, the captain's fiancée wrote him a letter to plead that he not be seduced away from her by Miss Porter's beauty.[42] It stopped the flirtation cold.

The third man of the trio was a cousin and confidential friend of Mrs. Carrol's, Mr. O'Brien, one of the most admired men in Bath. Jane assured Maria she hadn't lost her heart to him.[43] There was too much bustle in Bath to lose one's heart. But Jane reported that she enjoyed so much male attention that the women there were ready to tear her body to atoms. The men were just as ready to take up cudgels in her defense.[44] "I never was in such a whirligig before. How different I am," Jane told Maria, "when sitting by our quiet and care-worn fire-side at home, to the gay, admired creature of a Bath Ballroom! Ah, little do the numerous girls . . . know that I would not give one rush for all that awakens their envy and malice!"[45]

As the Plunketts readied to leave Bath, an opportunity arose for Jane to stay on there with Mrs. Carrol. If Jane were to stay, it meant she'd need seventeen shillings to return home on the night stagecoach from Bath to London. She asked if her family could afford this sum. Permission was granted by Mrs. Porter and seconded by her brothers. They'd have been willing to invest almost a pound in the hope Jane would yet find a husband there.

As happy as Jane was to stay, she was falling behind on her writing. She was sending back to London chunks of the pamphlet for Robert's *Battle of Alexandria*, as she completed them. She and Maria were also working on their new periodical, *The Sentinel*. Even though Jane had been remarkably frugal in Bath, spending money only on sedan chair hires, tea at the balls, and having her clothes washed, the Porter family's financial needs were great.[46] She had to carve out time and space to complete her writing, but as Jane confessed to Maria, the idleness that reigned in Bath often made her a lazy author.[47] With the Plunketts, the problem was made greater by their receiving so many visitors. She'd regularly endured a hundred orders to stop her pen. "Even now, I am scribbling with half a dozen folks chattering in the room," Jane once complained.[48]

The pressure increased when Longman and Rees approved the second edition of *Thaddeus of Warsaw* and sent her twenty-four pounds to complete corrections and additions, which were desired immediately.[49] Despite the public praise she'd heard for her novel in Bath, Jane privately found fault with it and vowed to make it fifty times better in the second edition.[50] Ideas came at her from all sides about how to do it.

Some friends told her to change the book's title or give it a memorable subtitle. Jane was told stupid people were forgetting the title when asking for it at the bookseller. One friend advised retitling it *Thaddeus of Warsaw, or, The Hero*.[51] When Jane asked Maria for her advice, she wrote back with alacrity. "All the world says (truly) that you have drawn the portrait of a hero," Maria pointed out, "but you should not say it."[52]

At least working on the revisions became easier in Jane's new household with the Carrols. Mrs. Carrol had by then been joined in Bath by her husband. Their days had a quiet regularity, which Jane preferred, and she made fast work of the *Thaddeus* corrections. By the end of her two-month stay in Bath, Jane had nearly finished the second edition, but the only person she'd lost her heart to was her friend, Mrs. Carrol.[53]

As she prepared to leave, there was little left to do but marvel at the empty gossip that had circulated for weeks about who might win her hand in marriage. She gave a final accounting to Maria. Jane had been spoken of as the "admired of Captn Meyers, Sir Essex Edgeworth, & c.—And the betrothed of Henry Caulfield—and strange to relate! the engaged to Sir Sidney Smith." "I wonder what Sir Sidney will say when he hears, that I am to be his wife!" Jane joked, "How wild is the world!" She finished off her letter home with a message to give to Henry Caulfield, who'd departed from Bath. "When you see dearest Henry, give him my love, and a box on the ear," Jane wrote to Maria. "I am sure it will be of service to him, so don't be tender in the execution."[54]

But after Jane returned to London in May 1804, she couldn't be so sportive about Henry, who was in trouble. There were financial problems. Robert's diary cryptically recorded his calling on a tradesman a year earlier on Bond Street, to settle what he called "Henry's business."[55] That business was surely debts, and it hadn't been settled to the creditor's satisfaction. The business had moved to the courts. From there, it exploded into national scandal.

Henry's legal problems began, and the scandal came to light, when a tradesman who sold tools on Bond Street sued Captain George Chambers for an unpaid bill. It was for the purchase of household goods by his wife, Mrs. Jane Chambers, which had never been paid for. The tradesman took legal action against Captain Chambers for her nonpayment. It then came out that Captain and Mrs. Chambers were legally separated.

Captain Chambers claimed in court that, because of their official separation, he wasn't responsible for his wife's debts. It was a legal gray area. To strengthen his case, he laid out a far more explosive claim. Mrs. Chambers, he testified, was living under the same roof with Henry Caulfield.[56] Captain Chambers's position was that he shouldn't be responsible for the debts of a separated wife living with her lover. But Henry's being publicly revealed as an adulterer changed the entire conversation.

Mrs. Jane Rodney Chambers had come into Henry's life when he was around eighteen. They met at a ball in Huntingdon. She was then in her early thirties and the mother of ten children.[57] She'd gotten a legal separation from her abusive husband, thanks to the help of her powerful, wealthy relatives, who had extricated her from his household. They also helped her get custody of the children—unusual for the time—and Captain Chambers had agreed to pay a small maintenance for her, which he apparently never delivered.

Even after bearing ten children, Mrs. Chambers was still thought beautiful. Robert, who'd once dined with her and had and stayed at her home with Henry, thought her a "sweet character."[58] Depending on whose account is to be believed, Mrs. Chambers was either a manipulating, selfish jezebel and a bad mother, or a lovelorn, pitiable woman, battered by a villainous husband. Henry saw her only as the latter. Jane wasn't so sure. Either way, Henry's fate was now publicly tied to hers.

By the summer of 1804, gossip about the Chambers-Caulfield affair had gone from snickers and whispers to open statements of support or calumny. Everyone would have anticipated the next step. A wronged husband might bring a charge of criminal conversation (called "crim. con.") against his wife's lover. In effect, the husband would accuse the other man of stealing his sexual property and seek monetary damages from the "thief" for his loss. The stakes for Henry's reputation, and his livelihood, were high.

Jane, out of loyalty and concern for Henry, set out to help him in the summer of 1804. Anyone trying to restore the reputation of an accused adulterer was taking part in a risky endeavor. For an unmarried woman like Jane to get involved was closer to self-destructiveness. Yet Jane didn't waver in doing what she thought right. She considered how she might use her formidable writing skills to defend Henry. Jane wrote to Maria, "I now have no doubt of getting him clear of the Public opinion without *Dishonour*."[59]

Jane's confidence in her powers to fix Henry's problems wasn't unwarranted. She'd gained significant experience in managing difficult literary business behind the scenes. She was used to writing under pseudonyms, as if she were a man. Jane was optimistic, too, because Henry had enlisted the help of a wealthy, powerful woman—Mrs. Mary Campbell—who might help him with legal costs.

At first, Mrs. Campbell seemed poised to be as ardent a champion of Henry as Jane was. She was connected to the Caulfield family by marriage. Her daughter-in-law, Jessie Caulfield Campbell—Henry's younger sister—had married Mrs. Campbell's son, Frederick, a few months earlier. Jessie must have worked on her mother-in-law Mrs. Campbell's sympathies, because she agreed to front the money to pay off Henry's debts and clear his good name. They decided Jane would manage the public relations. On many days that summer, Jane would run from Mrs. Campbell's to a circus manager (perhaps to try to get Henry work) to a male friend, Mr. Fenwick, who knew the editor of a newspaper. The group of them planned to use their influence to get positive coverage for Henry into the papers. "I never rested till half after five, when I sat down to write to you," Jane wrote to her sister, "I have great hopes, thro' Fenwick of setting poor Henry's mind at ease."

Mrs. Campbell's life was at a moment of intense transformation. Her husband was on his deathbed. She confessed to Jane that she didn't love him and would be glad when he died. He'd used her barbarously. At his death, she and her son would inherit an ample fortune. Once Mrs. Campbell had that independence—which she expected any hour—she'd instantly launch Henry

Caulfield forward and clear him of every pecuniary distress. The barbarous husband died in a matter of days, and Mrs. Campbell paid Henry's debts. Jane was sure that, once Henry had money, he'd show himself in his true light. He'd silence perjury and defamation and convince the world he was a man of honor. "By the way, how strange it is," Jane wrote to Maria, "that Women should be the only agents to extricate Henry from difficulties, which the world supposes, women dare hardly look at!"[60]

Jane wasn't just unafraid to look. She was deeply involved. She was secretly helping Henry write a defense of his own conduct, in anticipation of the crim. con. action brought by Mr. Chambers. Jane helped Henry try to place the defense with newspaper editors, but everyone they approached declined to publish it.

The next idea Jane had involved privately printing Henry's defense as a letter that would be distributed by hand at the coffeehouses, where it might be read by London's fashionable men. Jane was sure this method would sway public opinion away from Captain Chambers.[61] A draft fragment of this document survives. It paints Captain Chambers as a very cruel, derelict husband who'd wronged his wife, rather than the other way around, before Henry arrived on the scene. "In 1799," the document Jane ghostwrote for Henry explains, "Mrs. Chambers finally quitted her husband. I will forbear stating her reasons. It is enough to say that they were fully approved by her brothers and her friends. *They had no shadow of a reference to me*. They were such as will ever find an advocate in the breast which is not quite callous to the touch of humanity."[62]

It's unclear if Henry ever printed or circulated Jane's ghostwritten defense. What certainly happened is that the project brought Jane's moral and sexual reputation to an alarming precipice. She was shocked when sly paragraphs impugning her character—although not directly mentioning her by name—began to appear in the *Morning Post*. One such paragraph suggested that a "celebrated novel writer" had the press "shut against her," when she tried to publish some indelicate material about a chamber scene. The use of the word "chamber" served as a double entendre. Jane was terrified that she'd brought infamy onto herself and her family because of what she called her "headlong friendship" for Henry. Jane acknowledged the world would never think what she was doing arose merely from friendship. "Oh! How we have been tortured! How I have stabbed myself! How I have lacerated you! And plagued my family!—A pretty sum-total of my utility!!!!" she wrote to Maria.[63]

Yet Jane smelled a rat in these *Morning Post* paragraphs. At first, she thought Captain Chambers was the informant, but she soon suspected they were placed there by her supposed ally, Mrs. Campbell. Some of the language in these continued insinuating bits in the papers echoed phrases Jane had shared with Mrs. Chambers alone. The motive seems to have been that Mrs. Campbell, widowed just one week, wanted to marry the captivating Henry herself and imagined Jane as her rival. That fear seemed confirmed when Mrs. Campbell somehow intercepted and read a private letter that passed between Henry and Jane. From the intimacy she saw displayed on the page, Mrs. Campbell accused Jane of immorality. In her letter of reply, Jane vigorously defended her own character. She claimed she and Henry were only ever friends, though long in the habit of scribbling to each other under all humors.[64] Then Jane wrote another letter to Henry, explaining what happened. His response convinced Jane that, in this strange triangle with his sister's mother-in-law, he valued her most.

"Would I could deem myself worthy of the regard you lavish on me," Henry wrote to Jane. "I must tenderly cherish your friendship, & can surrender it only with my breath alone." These words buoyed Jane, even if, as she acknowledged, whenever she thought of Henry now, it was with a soul that felt as if it had been beaten and bruised all over.[65]

Captain Chambers's crim. con. case against Henry moved forward in the fall of 1804. In the weeks before the trial, Jane left London on a long-term visit, in part to escape this painful drama. She was in despair from afar. She'd heard gossiping reports, repeated in the newspapers, that Henry had eloped with a wealthy, married woman, Lady B——.[66] Henry was said either to have been seduced by her or to have run off with her for her money, although she was married.[67]

If this rumor were true, it would also ruin Henry's court case. It would be easy to believe a man who committed crim. con. once could do it twice. If it were true, then Jane was determined to drop Henry's friendship. She told Maria to refuse and return any letters that arrived from him. But then, against her resolution, Jane did open her next letter from Henry. He merely told her he was working for a theater in Bristol. He made no mention of Lady B—— or running off with anyone. Jane believed, after reading, that the elopement rumors were false.

Unfortunately, Jane soon learned that Henry was in even deeper trouble than he'd admitted. The diabolical Mrs. Campbell had betrayed Henry and deserted his cause. She'd fired his lawyers (whose fees she'd been paying) and used her influence to tell everyone she knew in the legal world not to take the case, because he'd be unable to pay them. Her rumors had nearly gotten Henry arrested for debt in Bristol. "I am actually on the verge of ruin," Henry wrote to Jane, adding later, "I have hardly a doubt of being undone."[68]

Henry's falling out with Mrs. Campbell, which led to her withdrawing her financial support, turned out to be over an argument about Jane. Mrs. Campbell confronted Henry about what she was still sure was their inappropriate relationship. Henry defended Jane's purity of body and soul. But Mrs. Campbell said she was prepared to besmirch Miss Porter's reputation—to ruin her entirely in the literary world—by spreading word of her and Henry's illicit intimacy. The ultimatum Mrs. Campbell allegedly made was that Henry could either choose her (and her money) and desert Jane, or choose Jane and be deserted by Mrs. Campbell. When faced with the decision, Henry protected Jane's reputation. He forfeited Mrs. Campbell's patronage.

He "*sacrificed all her friendship*, and all her *gold*," Jane told Maria, "to my *honor and justification*."[69]

At first, Henry didn't tell Jane what he'd done. "Delight me more and more," Henry wrote instead to Jane, "with your frequent letters."[70]

Henry promised Jane that he and Mrs. Chambers were through. Jane, relieved at this news at least, wrote to Maria about his breaking away from his married lover, using cryptic language. "That Treacherous Disease, which we so long dreaded would overwhelm him," Jane wrote about Mrs. Chambers, "he declares he has done with it—it has no communication with him."[71]

Members of Jane's family would become distressed by her deep involvement in Henry's problems. John wrote Henry a severe and haughty letter and let it be known about town that he was considering challenging Henry to a duel, over his connection to Jane.[72] Gossip spread that Jane's reputation was damaged because of her obstinate infatuation for Henry.[73] John's challenge never happened, perhaps because he wisely decided, or was fortunately persuaded, that a duel might do more to confirm Jane's guilt than defend her honor in the public eye.

When she learned about this near challenge, Jane was livid with John. He should have known she'd never sacrifice her honor. She wrote to Maria, echoing a hero's rhetoric: "My name shall be written on my Grave, without one spot to sully its brightness! I need no swords, no pistols, to defend my reputation; I want no other weapons, to destroy both it, and my life together."[74]

The trial at large for criminal conversation by Captain Henry Caulfield, with the wife of Captain George Chambers, Esq., was held at the Court of the King's Bench on December 3, 1804, which also happened to be Jane's twenty-ninth birthday. Henry's trial was covered in almost every newspaper in the country. As an actor and skater, Henry had gained moderate fame. As an accused adulterer on trial, he'd become infamous overnight. When the trial began, Jane remained far away from London.

The plaintiff's lawyers laid out the case against Henry. Mrs. Chambers was exquisitely beautiful, perfectly accomplished, and of most fascinating manners.[75] Defendant Henry Caulfield was a man of elegant person and finished address. He was endowed with talents, arts, and powers that easily attracted women, which theatrical experience had only enhanced. He'd put them to use in wooing Mrs. Chambers, who, feeling herself admired, had a revolution in her feelings and left her husband.

Captain Chambers's lawyers called their supporting witnesses, who said the couple's marriage been a happy one before Henry came along. Captain Chambers was a loving husband who went abroad to war only to discover on return that his wife's affections had been stolen by Henry Caulfield. Evidence was presented that Mrs. Chambers and Henry had lived together in several residences over several years, often with separate bedrooms, because the Chambers's youngest children were present. Former servants testified that Mrs. Chambers and Henry sat too close to each other on the sofa. One testified to seeing evidence that Mrs. Chambers and Henry shared a bed.

When it was their turn to present evidence, defense lawyers called no witnesses on Henry's behalf. They acknowledged they couldn't and wouldn't pretend adultery hadn't been proved. This was unusual. The most common defense in crim. con. trials was to claim adultery had never occurred. Instead, Henry's lawyers focused on the fact of legal separation and Captain Chambers's alleged cruelty to his wife. Documents and letters were introduced.[76] The letters, the defense said, would excite astonishment and compassion and would show Captain Chambers deserved to receive no crim. con. damages, because he was a violent man separated from his wife. Her affections hadn't been stolen by Henry. Instead, Captain Chambers ought to be seen as having given up all claim to her, legally and morally.

The most arresting evidence given by the defense was a letter from Captain Chambers himself to his wife. It contained this line:

"With regard to the pistols, I never intended you the smallest injury, and what I uttered was under the momentary influence of hurry and intoxication." Evidence showed that Captain Chambers had drunkenly threatened his wife's life with two pistols. This threat, it was said, had caused her to flee his home and seek a legal separation, with the help of her male relatives. Her husband even signed the deed of separation, acknowledging his wrongdoing. "In consequence of his brutality," the defense argued, "therefore, for any act of infidelity, however successfully shewn," could "maintain no action for damages in a court of justice."

To counter these points, the plaintiff's lawyers claimed Captain Chambers hadn't hurt anyone with those *unloaded* pistols.[77] They argued his good character against Henry's bad character. Henry Caulfield, the plaintiff's lawyers said, was the demon who conducted a lady of noble alliance from town to town and exposed her in a state of prostitution to face ridicule and contempt.

The jury deliberated for less than half an hour. It returned a verdict for the plaintiff. Henry Caulfield was ordered to pay Captain Chambers damages of two thousand pounds. His lawyers appealed and won a temporary respite.[78] The judge told the court he wanted the whole extraordinary case to be sifted to the bottom.[79] On appeal, the plaintiff's lawyers cannily argued that under the law, a separation wasn't a divorce, which meant what Henry had done was still adultery. Captain Chambers told the court he very much hoped to win his wife back. The damages weren't proportionate *enough*, his lawyers said, to the magnitude of Henry's offense.[80] The judgment was upheld.

Jane's hopes for Henry's vindication were dashed. Henry was guilty in the eyes of the law and financially ruined. But she continued to imagine herself as a lone, powerful hero in his life, who might, in the future, come to his rescue.

"*Bad as Henry is*, one day he may *repent*," Jane confided to Maria. "One day he may need *a friend*, when all the gay world has *deserted him*.—*I* shall then reappear."[81]

CHAPTER 10

Taking up a Rose with the Left Hand

The Porter Women Secretly Retrench, as Jane Is Nearly Buried Alive (1804–5)

In 1804, the Porter women decided to leave London behind. Jane declared she had a love-hate relationship with the metropolis. Maria felt it wasted their time. She was tired of visiting Miss This and Miss That and being dragged up and down the mall and St. James's Park.[1] The sisters told themselves they were ready to move. But the real reason was financial.

"Truly my dear Jane," Maria wrote, "to save myself from any one of the miserable hours I have spent in consequence of our dear Robert's undeserved misfortunes and mortifications, I would willingly bury myself in a cavern." This was a joking reference to Sophia Lee's *The Recess* (1783–85), a Gothic historical novel in which the fictional twin daughters of Mary Queen of Scots are secretly brought up in a cave. But it was also accepting reality. The Porter women would be moving to Surrey to save money. It wasn't as dreary as a cavern, but the move was a kind of social burial. The next year would bring even more forced isolation, especially for Jane.

For the Porters, money problems had become so deep that they had no choice but to retrench. Not one of Mrs. Porter's adult sons had fulfilled his expected role as a provider for her in her widowhood or for their unmarried sisters. Maria's and Jane's modest earnings from writing, instead of adding a sweetener to their own living expenses, were wholly supporting themselves and their mother. The sisters were sometimes even shoring up their brothers' losses. Robert had at least said he wanted to help them, which is another reason the sisters clung to him with greater affection than to John or William. That spring, Robert was serving in the Westminster Militia and weighing his next career move.

His misfortunes were also preventing him from marrying. He'd fallen in love with sweet Fanny Dalrymple, daughter of powerful military man Colonel William Dalrymple, who was aide de camp to the Duke of Clarence, the future King William IV. Fanny returned Robert's affections and was beloved by Jane and Maria, but her father objected to the match. Robert was an unwelcome suitor, as the father saw it, unless he brought a fortune. Colonel Dalrymple kept his daughter away from Robert, calling him a "dangerous man."[2]

Robert began to consider going abroad. He'd had dinner once with a Russian man who thought the artist could get rich there.[3] Robert shared the idea with his would-be patron, the wealthy Margravine of Anspach, formerly Lady Craven. The Margravine was so fond of Robert she referred to him as her adopted son, despite having seven grown children. She was supportive of Robert's leaving England, inasmuch as she thought it was no place for talent to flourish. "I advise you to fly this foolish little Island," the Margravine had written to him. Fly, she said, before "you & all the Best Brains & Blood of this Kingdom will be placed to stand before the first Artillery Men in the world."[4]

She referred to the possible attack of the Napoleonic French. It's otherwise surprising she'd encourage Robert to leave. The Margravine enjoyed the young artist's companionship and liked to keep him close—close enough that it was causing tongues to wag, given that she was still married to her second husband, the old Margrave.[5] There had been a Porter family hope that the Margravine might pay off Robert's debts, which would prevent his needing to fly at all.

The Margravine, who talked a good deal about what she might do for Robert, did not do enough in the end. She told him his intentions to go to Russia pleased her and that, if he did go, she'd provide a letter of introduction to Emperor Alexander and his wife. She'd known the Empress as a child.[6] Such a letter might open doors.

The other Porter brothers had made messes of their lives, too. Faraway William, having escaped debts (and arrest) in Scotland, had taken his family to Durham, including their firstborn son, Charles Lempriere Porter. William and Lydia then had a second.[7] They decided to name him Thaddeus Sobieski Porter, after Jane's bestselling novel. That act wasn't enough to win over his sisters. William hadn't yet paid back Robert more than a fraction of the three hundred pounds owed him.

It was left up to John to find his mother and sisters a cheap house to rent. John hadn't endeared himself to them in the year since he'd returned from Antigua. The sisters thought John was haughty, careless, and selfish. He made it obvious that he didn't like their female friends.[8] He pressured his sisters to marry. John, a colonel, had been involved in risky business ventures that failed and seemed to be going nowhere. Despite having won Robert's trust enough to help with his traveling exhibitions, John surrounded himself with young officers who struck Maria as precious fools.[9] His own mother thought her eldest son didn't assimilate with the rest of them.[10]

The new residence John helped his mother and sisters move to was called Soame House, twelve miles from London in Thames Ditton. When the sisters told friends about their impending move to Surrey, they pretended they were doing it for health reasons. Jane didn't want their leaving London to be seen as motivated by worries over money. The fact that Mrs. Porter and Maria had been so poorly recently meant the excuse of their needing fresh air might have been half believed.

The Porters issued invitations to friends to visit them in their new home. Thames Ditton was reachable from London by a carriage or stagecoach ride of at least an hour and a half. To walk would have been four hours each way. A trip by water was the most convenient means to come see them, because Ditton was close to the Thames River. Jane and Maria wanted guests, but Mrs. Porter may have hoped few would come. She'd grown tired of the constant string of people in and out of her home. The disorderly hours of her children and their visitors exhausted her. Then there was the cost of it. Guests might bring meat to share, but hosts were expected to provide wine, which proved a great expense.[11]

Maria moved to Surrey first, with the help of their servant, Betsey, to set up the household. After Robert's financial success at the turn of the century, the Porters had hired two female servants. Robert and John had manservants who traveled with them, and the two Porter brothers sometimes rented separate London lodgings. That meant there would have been space at Gerrard Street for a servants' room. Betsey wasn't a favorite among the Porter family because they thought her bad tempered. When she and another Porter-family servant, Nanny, had disagreements with each other, the Porters referred to it as "the Gerrard Street Storms."[12] But Betsey's inability to keep her cool might be understandable given that she received no wages. The only benefit of her job was free room and board. That also explains why the Porters kept her on, despite the "storms." With their distressed finances, it wasn't yet clear if the Porters would be able to afford to employ servants in Ditton. Even continuing to support Betsey's living expenses may have seemed out of reach.

When Jane was preparing to leave their home in London for the last time, she joked with Maria that perhaps she should have married one of her odious suitors instead. "Don't you think I ought to have married Mr. Rivers?" Jane teased, "There is an amazing sympathy in our minds!—While I submit my right hand to be cut off, I can take up a rose with my left, and smell its fragrance."[13]

It was a satire on mixed feelings, as well as on the married state. It was also an apt description of what moving to Surrey, and leaving London, felt like. Jane and Maria were losing what was crucial to their lives and livelihoods but gaining a little country peace and quiet. In exiling themselves, the Porter sisters were trying to make a virtue of necessity.

Thames Ditton had a population of about thirteen hundred, most of whom worked in agriculture or trade. Some were servants on grand properties, like Hampton Court Palace, just across the river. Beyond the wealthy handful who owned estates, few residents there were educated. Even fewer made a living as artists or authors. Jane and Maria, unusually interesting figures anywhere, would have stuck out like a sore thumb in Thames Ditton and nearby Long Ditton.

Their elite neighbors noticed their arrival and made the expected visits of welcome. A baronet called three times while Maria and Jane were inelegantly occupied, preparing their new home. On his third attempt, he could no longer be ignored, so Jane pretended to be her own servant. She stuck her head out of the window, disguised herself by shutting one eye gravely, and informed his lordship that her ladies were both out.[14]

Although money was tight, Maria felt sure they'd be able to practice cheerful economy. Soame House had a drawing room, a study, and a best bedroom. Maria wanted new curtains for all the rooms, measuring for how much fabric they'd need if they could afford to buy it. Robert promised to send someone from the Lyceum Theatre to paint the walls. Maria assured Jane they'd have "Peace, Quiet, Leisure, Study, Exercise, Health—and my mother's face again dressed in smiles."[15] The garden was beautiful. Maria put flowers in her hair. She sang twenty songs each morning to brighten her mood.

In the study, Maria placed pots of anemones, larkspurs, and roses.[16] She hung up a portrait of Sir Sidney Smith, which one of the cats liked to sit before as if in worship.[17] Mrs. Porter was already fantasizing about Smith visiting them at the cottage, declaring that he was the only visitor she'd welcome.[18] He didn't come, and Maria was surprised at how few friends would go to the trouble to come to Ditton. "I have a comfortable mansion, a beautiful garden, a whole thicket of honey-suckles," Maria told Jane, but there was no one to share them. She complained, "How worthless, how uncared for, I must be! . . . What is John doing? How is he? When does he mean to visit me? When is Robert to dine here?"[19] Even Kearsley, who'd promised to come walk with her under the shade of elms and poplars, hadn't yet visited. At her best moments in the cottage, Maria felt immortal. At her worst, she felt abandoned.

But there was much writing to be done. She corrected the proofs for *The Lake of Killarney*, to be published in summer of 1804. In her preface to the novel, Maria explains to her readers that it was composed over a long period, during which she endured chronic sickness. She dedicated the novel to their old friend Percival Stockdale with the warmest admiration, expressing the hope that his writings would one day be recognized with laurels they'd been unfairly denied. It was at this moment of social isolation that Jane received an invitation from Stockdale himself, asking her to join him in the north of England the following fall, winter, and spring. "You will be amazed at poor Mr. Stockdale's letter," Jane wrote to Maria. "The contents pierced me to the heart."[20]

Stockdale wanted Jane to nurse him in what he feared was his final illness. Her conversation would illuminate the long gloom and horrors of a Northumberland winter. He hoped she'd take on his domestic cares, sort through his papers, and edit his memoirs, to relieve him of anxieties about leaving his works behind in a proper state and in pure hands.[21] Jane, an experienced secretary for her own family, wouldn't have feared the work of an amanuensis. She knew she was good at it, and it made her feel useful. Sorting through Stockdale's correspondence with famous figures of arts and letters and his memories of knowing them would have its pleasures for anyone interested in great writers.

Jane must also have felt a personal debt to Stockdale. Her only proper teacher had been George Fulton in Edinburgh. After that, Stockdale had guided Jane's reading and writing. He was hard on her and didn't mince words. He corrected her grammar, complained about her spelling, and scolded her for indistinct handwriting.[22] He'd once encouraged her to abridge Johnson's dictionary to improve her use of language. Then he praised her for how well she'd done it.[23]

There had been a more recent education from him, too, in the business of literature. Stockdale sent Jane on his literary errands to publishers and booksellers in London. She made arrangements and bargains on his behalf, and he taught her which of them were treacherous.[24] He believed almost all were liars. Stockdale employed Jane as his agent (at no pay) to get his verses placed in newspapers.[25] These tasks became a literary apprenticeship of sorts, introducing Jane to a circle of editors, publishers, and printers. The work taught her to negotiate and publicize.

As grateful as she was for his attention and tutoring, she hadn't always heeded Stockdale's advice. He'd repeatedly told her writing novels wasted her talent. He admired pioneering novelist Samuel Richardson and acknowledged *Clarissa* brought him to tears, but as he wrote to Jane, "very modern novels . . . *I* most completely despise."[26] Yet, putting aside his objections to the genre, he'd praised Jane's *Thaddeus of Warsaw* when it was published, despite what he felt were its fashionable barbarisms.[27]

Stockdale's heavy-handedness, and frequent scolding, tempered with occasional grudging praise, may have filled an emotional void for Jane—a brilliant fatherless girl who'd grown to be an accomplished literary woman. Stockdale feared he was dying. Jane had become a literary celebrity, something that had eluded Stockdale and which he'd so coveted. His request to Jane offered her an opportunity to repay him for his tough nurturing, from her position of success.

More than that, Jane was moved. She strove to do her duty toward family, friends, and humanity. Jane knew Stockdale's feelings for her were complicated. He once said he wished he was young and rich enough to be her suitor.[28] Two years earlier, he had even suggested setting up a household with Jane. He'd written to ask if she'd move in with him and his servant Molly. Jane rejected the idea as injurious to her respectability. She couldn't properly live in a house with a married man, separated from his estranged wife. At the time, Stockdale wrote in reply, "You were quite right in declining from living with me as I foolishly proposed."[29]

But in this second request in 1804, he directly addressed her previous objections. He told her that her reputation—which he called "the only impediment to my wish that may appear important to you"—wouldn't be in danger this time. His conduct as a clergyman, he told her, would protect it. So, too, would the fact that he was so broken in mind and body. He told her directly, "I have long made you my principal object in my life.—and I shall act consistently with that view of you, in my death." He was, in effect, promising Jane a legacy in his will. His clergyman's salary was three hundred pounds a year. Jane had no precise idea what his wealth was beyond that sum. "Any pecuniary advantage I might derive from such a sacrifice has not one jot weight with me," Jane wrote to Maria, "yet I should not be worse for my good friend's forethought for me."[30]

To take away any last objections to her coming to him, Stockdale offered to pay for all her traveling expenses. If he managed to live through the winter, he'd accompany her on the return stagecoach home the following spring to make a visit in Surrey. Jane felt sure she could have no right to expect such care herself at the end of her own life if she didn't give it now to this old man in need.

After discussing it, Mrs. Porter and Maria agreed Jane should go to poor Stockdale. Maria was convinced it was Jane's Christian duty, if her health and spirits had the strength for such a melancholy task.[31] To help a man die was a sad burden. One positive pull was the prospect of seeing her old friends on the journey north, a trip Jane otherwise wouldn't have been able to afford. She could see the Rawlinsons in Grantham. She could lay eyes on Durham, the city of her birth and later childhood, home to friends from whom they'd been separated for fifteen years.

Unspoken among them was the reality that, while living with Stockdale, Jane wouldn't be a drain on the family's finances. He would cover her living expenses. She'd live on almost nothing for eight months, paying only to receive letters and purchase small etceteras. If Jane left home, her mother and sister might be able to afford to keep Betsey as a servant. There would be benefit, too, in Jane's moving farther away from Henry and his troubles. Robert's departure for Russia to paint there seemed likely. The men Jane loved best were passing beyond her reach. Stockdale, however, very much needed her.

Jane told him she'd come. She'd take the stagecoach by herself from London to Durham and then on to Lesbury, to comfort Stockdale in his probable last illness. She'd sort through his papers and write down his final thoughts on his remarkable life and underappreciated literary talent. He sent her ten pounds for travel expenses—a sufficient but not overly generous amount to cover a one-way journey of more than three hundred miles.

Stockdale must have been anxious for his young friend to arrive because Jane decided she couldn't spare more than twenty-four hours to stop and see the Rawlinsons in Grantham—a painfully short visit. As for dear old Durham, the city of her birth, Jane's time would be limited to stopping with the stagecoach as it changed out its horses.[32]

The passing sight of her childhood home proved emotionally overwhelming. On the stagecoach in the moonlit darkness, Jane had her first view of Durham, crossing the Elvet Bridge. It wasn't as calmly picturesque and beautiful as she'd remembered it, but rather arresting and sublime. The stagecoach's brief stop would have been at an inn in the North Bailey, near Mrs. Porter's former boardinghouse and her long-dead Grandpapa Blenkinsop's Star and Rummer. Jane knew she'd have only minutes to alight before her coach would depart.

In those precious moments, she ran to good Mrs. Brocket's, one of her first caregivers as an infant and one of her mother's oldest friends. Whether Mrs. Brocket needed to be told "It's Miss Porter" or not, the dear old woman was so moved when she recognized Jane that she immediately wept a torrent of tears.[33] This momentary moonlit exchange was all the reconnection Jane would have with this formative part of her upbringing.

With the call for passengers to depart, Jane needed to rush back to the stagecoach. She had another fifty miles—six or so hours—remaining of her overnight journey to the remote coastal town of Lesbury, a long, straggling village of fifty cottages, near the market town of Alnmouth and the River Aln, which emptied into the North Sea. Jane arrived at Stockdale's the next morning, October 13, 1804.

Stockdale, like Jane, had spent childhood years in the north of England, but he hadn't necessarily planned to return there as an adult. It was the luck—or rather, to him, the misfortune—of receiving two church livings in Lesbury and nearby Long Houghton, which provided a livelihood. He'd been a vicar there for twenty years. He was a devout man but perhaps not as devoted to parishioners as some clergymen.

Whenever Stockdale wanted to travel, he'd hire curates at rates far less than his own salary to temporarily take over his clerical duties. Stockdale got to pocket the difference and escape for a time. This was perfectly allowable by the rules of the church, although it wouldn't have endeared him to parishioners he abandoned. He rarely put others first.

In advance of Jane's visit, Mrs. Porter had written Stockdale a letter to smooth her daughter's way. She thanked him for inviting Jane and for his long friendship with her family. She wrote proudly of her daughter's many skills and said she hoped, as the girl's mother, she might take some credit for those accomplishments, although, she acknowledged, "I know, unfortunately, I was no favorite of yours."[34] Mrs. Porter could be just as cuttingly direct as Stockdale.

She reiterated a hope that Stockdale and Jane would come to Ditton together on the stagecoach in the spring. Mrs. Porter boasted that they lived in a paradise, in perfect retirement. She offered her remembrance to Stockdale's servant Molly, too, and hoped she would also be kind to Jane. Mrs. Porter had reason to worry. Molly, jealously devoted to Stockdale, would be no ally of Jane's in Lesbury. Mrs. Porter closed her letter by asking Stockdale to let Jane know that a packet had come from the publisher of her periodical, *The Sentinel*. Her mention of this also sent a message to Stockdale: Jane had important literary business of her own to complete while with him, and he shouldn't forget it.

On arrival, Jane would have made her way to St. Mary the Virgin Church—Stockdale's church—and the Lesbury vicarage, his small but pretty house in the churchyard. He greeted Jane, she thought, with the affection of a father, although she almost didn't recognize him. His face struck her as more like the wax effigy of a dead person than anything she ever saw.[35] Stockdale was still strong enough to walk three or four miles a day, but he'd been worn to a shadow. Jane was sure that, if she hadn't come to him, he would have died or at least fallen into what she called a "mental death." She hoped to strengthen him by winter.

In her first days in Lesbury, Jane noticed the beauty of the place. Walking over its hills—which seemed like mountains—she could almost suppose herself in the Scottish Highlands. If she leaned over a gate near the churchyard, she could just make out the sea, with vessels skimming over its surface and birds washing themselves in the waves.[36] But time for sea-gazing would turn out to be scarce. "I find I shall be completely his companion," Jane wrote home, "for he never loses sight of me, from the hour I appear in the morning, until we go to rest at night."[37]

Their days became routine. They rose at eight and breakfasted at nine. Stockdale would talk to her, read to her, and repeat things, or she might read to him, until three, when they dined. After dinner, they followed the same plan until six, when they had tea. After tea, they went on, just the same, until ten. They had a light supper and retired at eleven. This, Jane wrote, was the probable picture of her life at Lesbury for the next eight months. "I am sorry dearest Maria! to be so sparing a correspondent, but it is literally true, that I have not a moment to myself," Jane wrote, because Stockdale shows himself to be "uneasy whenever I engage myself in a way that has no reference to him."

Whenever Jane attempted to leave his parlor, Stockdale would call after her, "You are not going to leave me! I love to have you in the room with me; pray don't leave me!"[38] She tried to scrawl her letters home during the day, in fits and starts, while he walked up and down the room like a man with a fever, looking over at her every moment. She couldn't write in her bedroom in the morning because the sun wasn't yet up. She thought she might be able to steal an hour at night, with a fire in her chamber, if she pretended to go to bed early.

Jane looked forward to some things there, despite what she increasingly thought of as Stockdale's thralldom over her, her chains, and her captivity. She'd learn things from Stockdale. She realized that she could think about other things while reading aloud to him. It was a skill of split cognition she'd acquired reading empty Gothic novels to Mrs. Crespigny. What Jane most looked forward to was the feeling of internal satisfaction she expected to come from this sacrifice of her time. "Once in my life," Jane told her mother, "I have done a positive duty; I have comforted the forlorn and helpless heart, of an old, and almost deserted friend."[39]

The Reverend Percival Stockdale may have been old and deserted, but few retained as much compassion for him as Jane. Many believed he'd earned his neglect. He had a reputation as a vain, ambitious man whose greatest claim to fame was that he'd once lived on fame's fringes. Fifty years earlier, he'd been on visiting terms with the leading men of London's literary, theatrical, and intellectual world and thought of himself as their equal. Yet, despite publishing copious poems, essays, sermons, and a play, Stockdale never achieved as much respect or renown as they did.

Stockdale still believed he deserved greater renown and that he'd been repeatedly and wrongly passed over for it. The single greatest wrong done to him, he thought, was that a publisher had once invited him to create an edition of great English poets, with biographical introductions. Then the invitation was withdrawn from him and handed to Samuel Johnson. The work became Johnson's celebrated *Lives of the Most Eminent English Poets* (1779). Stockdale believed it was a disgrace. Over the years, he became convinced Johnson had stolen acclaim that ought to have been his.

The dramas of Stockdale's love life couldn't be so easily deflected as someone else's fault. When one of his friends wrote to another, to try to explain Stockdale's personal history, it came out like the plot of a Gothic novel:

> He is a strange eccentrick character & has been guilty of great indiscretions . . . He was first in the army,—then in the church—engaged to a young Lady, married an old one—The young one prosecuted & recovered damages, which he paid. They then ran away together—to Nice, leaving the woman behind, who went mad & died. The lovers then returned & married & then separated. For some time he was tutor to Lord Cravens children, but left them in disdain, because her Ladyship would not admit him of her private parties. . . . I believe he can hardly mention a friend or benefactor with whom he has not quarreled for imaginary slights.[40]

This description leaves one almost breathless. Just how much of Stockdale's history Jane knew when she came to stay with him is uncertain. But he was open with everyone about this much: He was estranged from his wife and paid to maintain her in a separate household. He never saw her, described her as a devil, and openly said he wished she were dead.

Stockdale was perpetually seeking revenge on people, both privately and in print. He suffered from a nervous disorder, periods of depression, and perhaps even bouts of psychosis.[41] But he had several admirable and, to some, redeeming qualities. He published on controversial political subjects. He was an advocate for the abolition of slavery. Unlike many white abolitionists, he defended enslaved people's violent attempts to overthrow enslavers. Late in life, Stockdale was writing his memoirs to reassert his importance to literary history. Jane was supposed to make that happen.

Through hour upon hour of monologues, Stockdale told Jane what he planned for his memoirs, after which she would organize his papers, take dictation, and recopy his work. Once the book went to press, he said, he'd live in London to closely oversee the printing and the proofs. He trusted no one to do that for him. As that work progressed, he told Jane, he'd occasionally come to visit the Porters in Surrey. Then, after publication, he planned to move near them in Ditton. He'd be their fixed resident, he said.[42]

Sometimes his fantasized plans involved Jane living in that neighboring cottage with him. At first, she had gone along with the idea, envisioning herself carrying out the illustrious burden.[43] Jane felt that in helping Stockdale, her entire family would be keeping a sad and worthy man alive. She also hoped the tone of his mind would improve by then so he'd be able to amuse himself more often—or at all.

In her first month in Lesbury, Jane was willing to overlook Stockdale's extreme possessiveness and bad temper. He was truly ill. He'd developed a pain in his chest and was spitting blood. As his spirits improved, Jane felt she'd helped him. She was convinced she hadn't given away in vain the bliss of living alongside Maria for nearly a year.

Much of the news arriving from home in the fall of 1804 was difficult, including Robert's ongoing struggle with debt and Henry's legal problems leading up to the crim. con. case. But happier news arrived on occasion. Maria's new novel, *The Lake of Killarney*, was in high repute. It was in demand at the circulating libraries in the north of England, too, Jane learned—and just as popular as her *Thaddeus of Warsaw*.

"What do you think of our *Novelistick* fame?" Jane teasingly asked Maria that fall. "I should have enjoyed living under the shelter of your laurels, and those of Robert's—but to have planted a tree myself, was beyond my hopes, though not without my wishes."[44]

Maria told a story in return, about a married couple fighting in the streets about the Porter sisters' books. They were said to have been loudly arguing over whether Maria's hero in *The Lake of Killarney* was a better man than Jane's hero in *Thaddeus of Warsaw*. The husband supported Maria's as superior, but the wife was for Jane's. "Would you believe it, that two such affectionate sisters, sincere friends, and amicable authors, as you and I are—are very likely to work mortal hate amongst our followers?" Maria mused.[45]

That fall, Jane discovered a way to send large packets of letters back and forth to London at no cost. She introduced herself to an Alnwick bookseller and negotiated his taking a packet of her letters to London on his monthly trips. He'd then bring back any packet left for her in London. Jane's friends were instructed to give letters to John to pass on to Maria, who'd bring them to their London publisher to give to the Alnwick bookseller, who'd hold them for Jane. It was a circuitous route, but it would be free of charge. Once again, authorship allowed Jane and Maria to secure unusual perks.

As she settled in at Lesbury, Jane found she had very little time to write or even to read personal letters. She struggled to cater to infirm Stockdale's every whim. But one day, in November 1804, at a rare moment when he was temporarily away from home, a visitor arrived at the vicarage, looking for him. A gentleman of perhaps thirty-five was announced. When he learned Stockdale was gone for some days, he asked for permission to write a note for him and sat down in the parlor near Jane to do it. He explained that he was a fellow clergyman, staying with a friend in Lesbury. He'd come to announce his arrival.

"Somehow, before he finished a note of four lines," Jane wrote, "he found, by his watch, that he had sat an hour and a half."[46]

His name was Reverend William Terrot. He struck Jane as an elegant scholar, possessed of fine taste. Their conversation was lively. He spoke with candor and imagination on all the subjects of literature and culture—a welcome break from her monotonous exchanges with Stockdale. Over the next several days, Jane and Terrot had further opportunities to talk. By the end of them, she wrote home terribly distressed. She feared she'd brought temporary misery on this amiable man. He'd fallen in love with her.

Terrot was a learned man, with interesting connections. He'd been a schoolfellow of poet William Wordsworth's at St. John's College, Cambridge. Among Wordsworth's known friends, Terrot was the only one to gain academic honors.[47] After leaving Cambridge, he was ordained a deacon, made a curate, and became a priest and a teacher. He'd worked his way up the Church of

England hierarchy to become minister of Haddington, a town seventy miles north of Lesbury.[48]

Sometime in his youth, Terrot had become engaged to be married. It was a rash engagement he hadn't yet fulfilled and now deeply regretted. It vaguely resembled the fictional situation Jane Austen would later lay out for Edward Ferrars in *Sense and Sensibility*. Where it differed was that Terrot almost immediately confessed the whole lamentable story of his engagement in his conversations with Jane. And he hadn't stayed in Lesbury for more than two days before he confessed new violent emotional struggles. He declared Jane was the only woman he could ever love.

He was highly demonstrative. Terrot repeatedly went down on his knees before her. He hung over her chair. He bathed her hands with his tears. Jane was shocked at first, but he explained why he was so sure so soon about his feelings for her. He told her that he felt he'd long known her.

"I was the being," she wrote to her sister, "which had been the subject of his dreams when he was a boy, and which as a man, he never expected to meet with."[49]

Jane tried to talk Terrot out of his passion. She told him that she "esteemed" his excellent qualities, that she "admired" his sweetness of mind, and that she "had compassion" for his distress. She hoped he'd find the qualities he looked for in the lady to whom he was engaged. She pleaded with him to do his duty and marry his betrothed, but this speech didn't convince him. It only drew from him fresh transports of emotion, expressions of tenderness, and admissions of regret. By the third and fourth days they'd known each other, with Stockdale having returned, Terrot was throwing himself on Jane's mercy at the very moment Stockdale left the parlor.

"His emotions, and my own agitated spirits, so overwhelmed me," Jane admitted, that at last, rather than be mistaken by him, she was honest. She confessed to Terrot what was weighing on her own heart. It was November 1804, and Jane had just received the unhappy rumor from London about Henry Caulfield's supposed elopement. Terrot listened carefully to the tangled emotional history of Jane and Henry. She had much to do to convince him they weren't lovers.

Once Jane talked about Henry, Terrot was, if anything, even more moved by her story of woe than he'd been by her rejection of him. He seemed to enter into her pain and pleaded Henry's case with her. While he listened to Jane during a stolen moment in Stockdale's parlor, Terrot's tears ran over her face. He was that close to her because, "he had as it were unconsciously clasped me in his arms," as Jane admitted to her sister.

Jane was truly struck by the romantic passion and incredible goodness of this man. She and Maria later nicknamed him, without sarcasm, "Saint William."[50] He reminded Jane of their melancholy friend Kearsley. She was disordered by him, she said—by his strange, ardent feelings.

Then, when it seemed things couldn't get any more intense, a surprising conversation followed. As Jane told Terrot more about Henry's troubles and his alleged elopement with a woman, she mentioned for the first time the name of the rumored paramour, Lady B——. Terrot started and flushed, turning red as scarlet. He knew her, too. And he said that if Lady B—— had seduced Henry, then he had fallen into the snares of a known she-seducer.

"You know not how you have shocked me!" Terrot cried to Jane. "For that woman once did her utmost to render *me* detestable to myself."[51]

Over just a few days, Jane and Terrot had shared many confidences and coincidences, but Jane acknowledged to Maria that, despite his first-rate qualities, she didn't find him handsome. She also held to her notion that prior engagements to be married must be kept. Yet Jane, who found Terrot so charitable, also came to believe he must have been sent to her from heaven. He was a source of much-needed sympathy and consolation when her heart was pierced and bleeding over faraway Henry's troubles and hovering Stockdale's tight leash.[52]

After those tumultuous days together, Terrot's scheduled visit to Lesbury came to an end. In another stolen moment alone with her, he made Jane promise that if she ever grew distressed about Stockdale's increasing illness, she must send for him immediately, and he would hasten to her, he promised, at a moment's notice. This, too, was a comfort to Jane, who felt so alone in Lesbury, with the worrying burden of the ailing Stockdale.

Terrot also told Jane, in a private exchange at parting, "Most likely, we shall never meet again, until we do so in Heaven.—but should I die first, and the Almighty will grant me permission—Oh! How blest should I be, to stand by your bedside when you are dying, and be the first to lead you into Heaven."

After his return home to Haddington, Terrot decided to do the only thing he knew he could do to please her—seek out information about Henry to share.

Terrot found an acquaintance in the Guards who knew Henry. This friend had compassion for Henry, spoke of him as capable of feeling deep enthusiasm, speculated about his supposed elopement with Lady B——, and described his known affair with Mrs. Chambers.

"I believe sincerely that he *loved* you," Terrot wrote to Jane of Henry's likely feelings, "and would have sought you for his wife, had he been rich enough to marry. And I believe most *firmly* that he *loves you still*, and that in hearts as weak as ours"—that is, men's hearts—"*real love* to a woman like yourself, may *remain*, though obscured (but it is not extinguished) by the smoke of *Infernal passion*."

Terrot told Jane he wanted to meet Maria in London the next time he was there. He'd bought as many of the sisters' books as he could afford and was reading them. He was sure Maria's *Lake of Killarney* used Henry Caulfield as the model for her hero—a suspicion others had voiced. It was recognized by some that the hero's name, Charlemont, was an ancestral surname in the Caulfield family tree. Terrot's letters to Jane showed that he hadn't entirely cooled emotionally toward her and had what she called a "passionate strain." She didn't know how to respond to them at first, though she did decide to reply.

"Had I not," she reasoned to Maria, "I think I should have been arrogating *a sexual power* over him, which he assures me . . . has ceased. He offers me his friendship," prayers, and advice. How, Jane wrote, could she have rejected these from this worthy man?

But Terrot, now a correspondent at a distance, was no longer Jane's principal problem. It was Stockdale. Jane thought she'd seen a cloud gathering on Stockdale's brow when, during Terrot's visit, Stockdale noticed that his fellow clergyman spent hours looking at Jane's face, or at the floor, rather than at the books Stockdale gave him to read. Stockdale suspected something was amiss. The storm didn't burst, however, until one of Terrot's letters to Jane arrived tucked inside a letter for Stockdale. Stockdale gave it to her, but he was incensed.

Jane learned that her old friend couldn't bear to have her admired too much by other men.[53] Stockdale thought it was outrageous that Terrot would insult Jane's honor by sending her a letter, and that she would dare to accept it, despite their short acquaintance. Naturally, this objection wasn't really about his anxiety for Jane's reputation. It was romantic envy, and Jane saw it. Stockdale railed at Jane that he knew there had been an ardor in Terrot's manner and that he didn't like it. It was ungenerous of Terrot, Stockdale said, to seek to deprive him of his only comfort—Jane herself.

Jane was stunned but replied coolly that it was Stockdale himself who'd formally introduced Terrot to her. It was Stockdale who'd led Jane to think of Terrot as almost a married man. She told Stockdale that she'd seen much of the world in great society, and had been around men of all characters, ranks, and degrees of attachment to herself. Did Stockdale think she had any intention of coming to Northumberland to give away her heart?

"Have confidence in me," she told him, "and believe, that you never have seen, and perhaps never may see, the man to whom I would give my hand!"

At this statement, Stockdale burst into a shower of tears. Chastened, not only for Terrot, but also for himself as Jane's potential suitor, he half apologized. But whenever Terrot's name was mentioned, Stockdale would either mutter to himself or storm out of the room. He had made it clear that Jane was the object of his own romantic love. He lamented his evil fate. Had he been free how happy could he have been with Jane for his wife, he told her, even at so remote a place as Lesbury.[54] She laughed to herself at how easily Stockdale seemed to think she could be won as his wife, if he were in a position to ask her. She decided not to shock the old man with the thunderbolt of telling him that, even if he could legitimately propose, she'd never, ever say yes.

Jane was disgusted with Stockdale's forwardness, jealousy, and vanity, but she agreed to stop corresponding with Terrot. The next month, however, when Terrot and Stockdale mended their breech, Jane resumed her secret exchange of letters with the other clergyman, even as she realized she could never mention his name in front of Stockdale, for fear of his wrath.[55]

The experience with Terrot brought Jane to another realization. Terrot had once described the man he thought should be Jane's husband. He thought she deserved a man like David of the Psalms, with beauty, wisdom, valor, music, poetry, generosity in the extreme, exquisite sensibility. He should be a man after God's own heart. Jane wondered if this sort of man was so rare that she might go single to her grave looking for him.

When she contemplated this male ideal, she told Maria, the only picture in her mind's eye was Sir Sidney Smith. Jane had no love, she said, that didn't pulse for Smith. She trembled at her presumption to lift her eyes so high, especially to a man who seemed not to notice her beyond friendship. She knew that the world would think her sentiments absurd, but she refused to feel regret about these secret thoughts of her soul.

"As long as he remains unmarried," Jane mused, "I may indulge my meditations without a crime, and I shall look on that, as all of Sir Sidney, I shall ever enjoy."[56]

The beginning of 1805 brought terrible weather to Lesbury. Jane continued to try to complete her magazine writing, for a pound or two, and rushed materials back to Maria for *The Sentinel*. Stockdale even contributed to their magazine's pages, although Jane and Stockdale mostly worked on his *Memoirs*, housebound as they were by the elements during the month of January.

In Surrey, Maria and Mrs. Porter were also staying indoors, although in their case for reasons of strict economy. They received no visitors and saw no one. Maria wrote to Jane about *The Sentinel* business. She sent reports about her faraway soldier, Frederick, and about their brothers' troubles. Jane replied with reports of how tired she was of being under Stockdale's thumb. Jane counted 150 days until the end of the promised term of her imprisonment, as she came to think of it. Stockdale was trying to make her his property, and she couldn't abide it.

"There is something in my soul, that loves its Liberty, as it does its Life," Jane wrote to Maria, "Bereave me of Liberty, and I am reduced to a wretchedness, I cannot describe."[57]

It was when Jane realized that Stockdale had designs on her freedom that her heart rose against him. It began to dawn on her when Stockdale didn't want her to answer Terrot's first letter.

"I saw, that he wished to clip my wings—to confine me entirely to himself—to fasten me down to his side—to shut me from all the world," Jane confessed. "*You*, my Maria, know my soaring, my excursive, my ardent, my intensely-extended spirit:—Oh, how could I bear this!"

It was a fatal night for Stockdale in Jane's heart. She couldn't love him better than she did her own liberty of heart, soul, and action. It made her vow that were she ever to marry, it would have to be to a rare man who could respect these essentials to her happiness.

She asked Maria to send her a pound from what they'd earned from the first six issues of *The Sentinel*, to pay for her miscellaneous postage. Jane didn't want to lose any more independence by taking a loan from Stockdale, but Maria couldn't oblige. The situation in Ditton was so financially dire that there wasn't one pound to spare.[58] None of the promised monies, Jane learned, had come in yet from *The Sentinel*. The next letter brought worse news: The publishers of their magazine had withdrawn support. It would fold, its editors never having been paid a penny.

"How strangely are all our attempts to make money, traversed by unfortunate circumstances," Maria wrote to Jane, "but God's will be done—I would not be an Atheist in the present state of our affairs, for all the universe!"[59]

Jane couldn't even afford something so small as receiving the occasional letter. But as February arrived, she had another, darker realization. It dawned on her that Stockdale would never recover his strength of mind. As a result, he absolutely could not stay with them, or near them, in Ditton. Her love of liberty couldn't abide it. To regain her personal freedom, Jane had to find a way to return home alone, without Stockdale as her companion, despite what they'd planned and what he desperately wanted. And not only did she need to get on that stagecoach by herself. She also needed to convince Stockdale to pay her way.

Jane concocted an elaborate ruse to extract herself from his grip. She told Maria and her mother how they'd pull it off. Maria needed to write a letter, pretending Mrs. Porter had an illness. They'd plead for Jane's return alone, at the end of her promised eight months, in early summer. Otherwise, Jane said, she feared she'd be Stockdale's prisoner for life.[60] She no longer expected him to die anytime soon.

Her goal was to get through each day. She referred to herself as an "automaton figure" in Stockdale's home. He didn't want her to write for anybody but him—not even letters home.[61] She put her foot down and demanded the right to copy his *Memoirs* alone in a room with a fire for some time each day. It was the one concession she asked for and got from him during all those months together. That meant Jane could finally write to family and friends for a stolen hour.[62] She hoped this reprieve would make the remaining three months with him more bearable.

Having a few hours to herself also let Jane begin dreaming about writing a next book. She was toying with something on Charles Edward Stuart—known as Bonnie Prince Charlie—grandson of the deposed seventeenth-century King James II. Jane could work herself into a passion for such a book, she thought.[63] Then maybe, if it could succeed, her family's financial worries would vanish.

At home, matters weren't improving. No Porter brother sent the women money. The sisters' attempts to earn a steady income from writing in 1804 and 1805 had failed with *The Sentinel*. Out of desperation, Maria decided to secretly take in gown-altering work and odd sewing jobs for the nine thousandth time, as she put it. She thought it would mean the cessation of all literary engagement. But Maria's hands were soon needed for pen work, too. Robert sought Maria's help with researching and writing the pamphlet to accompany his next great historical picture, which Jane would ordinarily have composed. In between her needlework for pay, Maria read every book on fifteenth-century Europe she could find, which surely exhausted her hands and eyes. Even depressing reports like these made Jane long to return home.[64]

When spring arrived, the plan they'd devised to extricate Jane was set in motion. Maria wrote one last conspiratorial letter to her sister. She described precisely how their agreed-upon web of lies might unfold. They decided it made more sense to pretend Maria, not Mrs. Porter, was gravely ill and needed Jane. Their thinking was that Maria might require nursing her mother couldn't provide.[65]

When Stockdale received the first falsehood-filled letter, he refused to let Jane go home, doubting that her sister could possibly need Jane more than he did. He begged her to stay with him a little longer, and she agreed. But then a pattern began. Another letter would arrive, pleading for her in Surrey. Stockdale would ask her to delay a little more. Jane would agree to each slightly later departure date. Each time, Stockdale made a fresh excuse. But the Porters kept hammering away at the original plan. They sent repeated, insistent letters about Maria's illness, begging for Jane's return. Jane, too, kept pleading with Stockdale to leave.

Finally, in June, he relented. Jane's insistence, and the increasingly panicked tone in each successive letter from Surrey, had worked. By then, ironically, nervous Maria had actually become sick.[66] Stockdale agreed to pay for Jane to leave his home in order to arrive on July 1, 1805, to take care of her sister, whose illness also conveniently explained why they couldn't yet have Stockdale join them in Ditton.

"I have lived an age in these eight months," Jane declared. "I have nearly run through all the emotions which Collins paints so well in his Ode to the passions."[67]

Yet even after agreeing Jane could leave, Stockdale argued with her about how she'd shortchanged him. She was supposed to have stayed *until* July 1, he told her, not return home *by* July 1. He complained that she had cheated him out of a promised week of her time. But in late June 1805, Jane nevertheless set off alone on her long trip home by the stagecoach from Lesbury. The moment she put her foot onto the vehicle, she said, she felt relieved of a great weight on her shoulders.[68]

Jane's departure shattered Stockdale. He wrote to tell her he'd gone into her old room on the day of her departure in an agony of grief. He'd burst into a flood of tears.[69] Instead of thanking Jane profusely, he berated her and bargained with her. For months afterward, he wrote letters demanding to see her again. She successfully put him off.

Eventually, Jane's stint in domestic captivity faded into a distant memory. She rediscovered some feelings of admiration for Stockdale's talents and regained some pity for his derangements. When she no longer feared Stockdale might come to Ditton, she received another letter from him. He shared news from his home in Lesbury: He'd gotten a pretty female kitten, he told her. He'd named his sweet little cat "Porter."[70]

CHAPTER 11

Where the Scale Turns

Jane's Warring Passions and Robert's Russian Adventures (1805–7)

The year 1805 had begun with a fall for Robert Ker Porter—a physical fall. It happened while painting *The Battle of Agincourt*, his next great historical picture-in-progress depicting Henry V's glorious victory over the French in 1415. While on a high scaffold, Robert had unthinkingly taken a backward step to view his enormous canvas. He walked onto empty air. Although a projecting board broke his fall, he still hit his knee violently.

Mrs. Porter was the first of them to see Robert after the accident. She thought he walked as if he had a wooden leg.[1] These difficult years of financial struggle were taking a toll on his body and his good looks. When his *Battle of Agincourt* debuted in 1805, it proved yet another financial disappointment. Robert's luck with spectacle paintings had entirely run out.

John, too, was deeply in debt and not living within his means, having taken lodgings in tony Pall Mall. The expense to live there as if he were a gentleman wasn't a trifle, as Robert noted.[2] John seemed unwell. Jane thought that if he was finding his pecuniary difficulties embarrassing, then he should do something to extricate himself. The detached tone she took in describing his struggles was very different from how she talked about Robert's or Henry's.

"As a woman, I can only speculate," Jane wrote to her mother about John. "Had I been a man, I would act.—I can only advise my Brother. I cannot assist him."[3]

Mrs. Porter complained about John, too. She said it was always his failing not to tell the truth. She ruefully concluded he was full of folly and pride, even worse than William. And as for William, he was the only one of her children whose letters Mrs. Porter regretted being charged for when they arrived, because (as she confessed to Jane) she knew she'd only be paying for nonsense.[4]

Robert was the brother whose preservation was most frequently prayed for. He was still ruminating over the long-brewing idea to travel to Russia. He envisioned arriving armed with letters of introduction, painting at the court of Emperor Alexander—or Tsar Alexander, as he was also called—and triumphantly returning to England to clear his debts with riches amassed abroad. Yet Robert wavered. Friends were skeptical a Russian venture would turn out so well, but Robert had another motivation. He needed to get out of the country. His debts were coming due, after the end of a negotiated extension of terms with his creditors. If he left the country, he'd avoid arrest as a debtor.

Tsar Alexander was a good prospect for an English artist's patronage, having been raised by an English nurse, as well as his powerful grandmother, Catherine the Great. He was an imposing figure and a good-looking man, just Robert's age, who was said to care about the arts, as his grandmother did. Russia was allied with the British against Napoleonic France. For these reasons, Robert hoped Alexander might offer artistic opportunities that would prove lucrative.

If that didn't work out, Robert had a second plan. He'd complete a book of Russian sketches and letters for the publisher Richard Phillips, founder of the *Monthly Magazine*. Robert would send back to Jane the raw materials as he wrote them. She'd gather these contrived letters, add historical research, and rewrite them with flourish, just as she'd done for all but one of Robert's pamphlets. The decision was made that his embellished letters would be addressed not to Jane but to Captain Henry Caulfield, perhaps in a bid to burnish Henry's public image, as well as to avoid the odd, feminizing look of writing letters of politics, travel, and culture to a sister.

Robert waffled about his future for some time, but after exhausting every other route to financial solvency in Britain, he obtained six months' leave from the Westminster Militia to travel to Russia.[5] When he set sail in August 1805, only a month after Jane's return from Lesbury, he was armed with artwork to present to the Russian Court and the highest hopes of financial gain. Maria would call Robert's absence their trial of submission.[6]

War, and its losses, weighed heavily on the Porters' minds at this time, as it did on the country as a whole. The naval hero, and Sir Sidney Smith's rival, Vice-Admiral Horatio Nelson had died in October 1805, after being fatally shot at the Battle of Trafalgar. Jane learned of it while dining with her friends, the actors Henry and Amelia Johnston. Johnston predicted Smith would probably be the next hero to die, which left Jane shattered. If it were to happen, she imagined she'd be as inconsolable about Smith's demise as Nelson's wife must have felt then about her husband's death.[7]

Men's dying in wartime was part of the sisters' daily reality, which put their family problems into perspective. Optimistic Maria tried to assure Jane that, even if her own relationship with Frederick ended in the bitterest disappointment—and even if Jane's feelings for Smith came to nothing—there was much to be grateful for.

"We have so much happiness among ourselves my Jane," she wrote. "And if our dearest hopes are cast away we shall still (if God preserves us, and Rob[er]t) save out of the wreck, far more *real* comfort, nay enjoyment, than almost our happiest friends are seen to possess."[8]

In Robert's absence, Jane and Maria, even with Mrs. Porter's small army widow's pension, didn't have nearly enough money to cover rent, taxes, and living expenses at Soame House. They'd heard rumors their landlord was considering selling.[9] So they decided to leave it for a cheaper, smaller cottage on Lord King's nearby property in Long Ditton. Trading a commodious home for a five-room cottage was a downwardly mobile move, but the annual rent of the new cottage was just six pounds, with taxes of fifteen shillings and six pence.[10] Its other benefit was that it was small enough to prevent the ability to host overnight guests, including Percival Stockdale.[11] Its drawbacks were significant. Maria was very concerned about how it might look to others.

"I am also inclined to remind you," Maria wrote, "that it behooves us, not to appear, falling in the world. . . . if it has at all the air of a make-shift and brings Poverty in the least into our visitors' thoughts, our respectability is all over."[12]

The new cottage in Ditton was unremarkable and plain-looking. It's recorded on some maps as an outbuilding.[13] The location was convenient, near the Crown and Anchor Inn, and just across the River Thames from Hampton Court Palace.[14] But the cottage sat cockeyed in relation to the nearby road—a very busy stagecoach route—which meant a great deal of noise and precious little privacy.[15]

The cottage was in sad shape, too, with a shattered roof and fences. Wallpaper was peeling. The house needed paint. Mrs. Porter worried that they wouldn't be able to cover these expenses. They'd also hoped a pump for water might be sunk on the property, but their stingy new landlord refused.[16] The best feature of the cottage may have been its rustic porch, shaded by roses and honeysuckles, with woodbine trained over the walls. The flowers added an air of interest to the otherwise nondescript home, but privately, Maria declared all of Ditton a heartless hole.[17]

The Porters may have been able to keep up outward appearances, but inside the cottage, sadness prevailed by the end of 1805. Robert's first letters home from St. Petersburg were dispiriting. He was still waiting for the unreliable Margravine's promised letter of introduction to Tsar Alexander's wife to arrive. The Tsar himself was away in Berlin. It was rumored that he might be gone for as long as a year.[18] "I feel *somewhat alone*," Robert admitted to Jane.[19]

But no news would have been more depressing to Jane than the report about Henry Caulfield. Robert had managed to evade being sent to debtors' prison by leaving the country. Henry, in staying in England, had played his cards wrong. He was arrested for debt on January 2, 1806, on the order of George Chambers, for his unpaid 2,120-pound crim. con. judgment.[20]

For a full year, he'd managed to avoid prison. After his guilty verdict, Henry had been a man on the run, wandering the country in hiding. The Porters knew from letters and occasional sightings that he was distracted, torn, and tortured beyond all imagination. He occasionally sent unsigned letters, making Jane his confidante.

"I believe that no one knows where he really is, but myself," Jane wrote to Maria, shortly after her return from Lesbury in July 1805.[21]

That summer and fall, Henry sometimes came to Ditton in secret to see Jane on Sundays. He might walk fifteen miles in the rain, arriving at noon and leaving at six, then walk back that night.[22] Jane referred to Sundays as her day of jubilee, not only for praising God but also for giving her a sight of Henry.[23] For his own good, however, she eventually asked him to stop making the visits. She could see he was too fatigued by walking thirty miles in a day.[24]

Henry's Sunday walks were well calculated. Debtors like Henry, if canny about their movements, might escape both repayment and arrest almost indefinitely. It required getting beyond the arm of the law. Leaving the country was the surest way out of trouble. But even for debtors who stayed in the country, there were well-known methods for evading authorities. Bailiffs weren't allowed to arrest at night or on Sundays. They couldn't break into houses to make arrests. So Henry must have been hiding out in homes during the day and wandering at night. Then he'd come to the Porters on Sunday afternoons.

Jane and Maria, upon seeing Henry, found him unrecognizable. He was no longer the man they'd appreciated for his noble, persevering spirit.[25] He was woefully poor. If he could find the money, he told Jane, he thought about leaving the country, perhaps for Hamburg.[26] Jane wanted him to find work acting in Dublin or somewhere in America, at least until his debts were settled and he could safely return to England.[27] Regrettably, he didn't take Jane's advice.

For a time, Henry had a different plan. He hoped to convince a distant relative to give him a borough and make him a member of parliament. As an MP, he'd be protected from arrest for debt.[28] Or, Henry thought, he might go to court to dispute his father's will, in which he'd discovered some villainy. He thought he might be granted an award by the courts. There was also an aunt who might leave him some money when she died. With all these spinning hopes, he never left England, which left him open to making a false step and led to the unlucky moment of his arrest.

Once incarcerated in the King's Bench Prison, Henry faced terrible conditions and few options. The law was complicated for debtors, with many avenues for punishment and redress, most left up to creditors. Captain Chambers, as Henry's creditor—thanks to the unpaid crim. con. judgment—had the ability to call for his debtor's arrest. If a creditor like Chambers brought suit, then either a summons or a writ for arrest might be issued. If, at summons, the debtor paid up, then all was well. But if a writ was issued, and the debtor was found and arrested, then there were two options. Put up bail, or go to prison.

Arrested debtors who didn't make bail might still come to an arrangement for release. Creditors in this era, in bringing legal actions, were often said to be merely trying to scare debtors (or their friends and families) into paying up. Estimates are that, in one year during this period, only one tenth of London's twelve thousand writs against debtors resulted in subsequent imprisonments.[29] Henry was unlucky because his problem was so multilayered. He had a complete inability to pay and a vindictive creditor with a legitimate claim.

After arrest, if a debtor like Henry couldn't arrange for bail, then Chambers, as creditor, had several options. Chambers, to do maximum personal harm, would have proceeded not against Henry's property but instead "against the debtor's body." This meant Henry would have been allowed to keep everything he owned but had to go directly to prison. Chambers's aim would have been to ruin the lives of his estranged wife and her lover. Henry's term of imprisonment was therefore indefinite. No specific sentence needed to be served. Imprisoned debtors could be held until the creditor was satisfied.

There was little logic to debtors' prison. The way for a debtor to be discharged was to satisfy the creditor, but the debtor's ability to make money was curtailed by being in prison. Even more confusingly, debtor-prisoners were charged for their room and board. There was some charitable aid available for the indigent and a few ways for the skilled and able to make a modest living. But for many, finding a way out of debtors' prison was a grim challenge.

In a strange coincidence of life imitating fiction, Jane had described this very dilemma in *Thaddeus of Warsaw.* Halfway through the novel, her indebted hero, facing debtor's prison, asks, "Can it be possible, that for a few guineas, I am to be confined in this place during life? In these narrow bounds, am I to waste my youth, my existence?" Jane had no idea then that her beloved Henry would have to ask these painful questions.[30]

At this time, anywhere from five hundred to one thousand people were confined to the King's Bench, London's largest prison for debtors. During the day, it saw a great deal of foot traffic in and out. Families, lawyers, merchants, sex workers, and delivery people came and went, because the King's Bench's gates were left open. It was up to the prison's turnkey to oversee the process of exiting. He studied the face of every new prisoner, to make sure that all who left the premises were free to go. That would have been one of the first things Henry had to do upon entering—allow his celebrated face to be scrutinized by the turnkey.

It didn't take long for Henry to arrange for special treatment. An imprisoned debtor might receive permission to live just outside the walls of the King's Bench, under better conditions, called "the Rules." The Rules didn't only refer to an alternate set of prisoner expectations. It was the name given to a designated area of blocks, bounded by several major roads surrounding the prison. Anywhere from one fifth to one third of debtors in the King's Bench were granted the right to live outside the prison walls but within the Rules. Henry rented lodgings within those boundaries, at an address in Melina Place. But he—like every other prisoner in the Rules—was expected to be findable at his reported address at almost a moment's notice. As long as he was a prisoner, Henry wasn't ever supposed to go beyond these bounded blocks near the prison. But Henry did leave them, to see Jane.

Jane was willing to sacrifice other pleasures for Henry's company. She even gave up the chance to go to a masquerade ball at a royal residence on July 1, 1806. More than four hundred guests crammed into the rooms at St. James's Palace, including Maria and Mrs. Porter, but Jane decided to stay home for Henry. By all reports, it was quite a party. Maria, in her letter home, cast herself as the heroine of the evening. She described how she'd required a dramatic rescue, after being overcome by the summer heat, because there was so little air circulating in the rooms. "The crowd was so great," she wrote to Jane, "we lost our party, and I was squeezed almost to death—actually into a fainting fit." A group of good-hearted men dressed as dominos, in loose silk cloaks and half masks, were cavorting with a baronet's wife when they noticed Maria collapsing. Amid the throng, the group quickly stepped in to save her.

"I was dragged thro' a window into the open air," Maria wrote to Jane, "after which I recovered and went off, with due éclat and commiseration."[31]

The masked fête had been a grand success, hosted by the Porters' close friends, beloved Mrs. Anne Boscawen and the less-loved Miss Eliza Tickell, who both lived in apartments at St. James's Palace. Mrs. Boscawen, who had gained her apartment through service in the court of Queen Charlotte, often generously invited Jane or Maria to stay with her.[32] The sisters didn't like to accept her hospitality for very long, because it meant sharing a bed with garrulous Eliza, who exhausted bedfellows by talking all night long about fine people and parties.[33]

Yet the Porter sisters had become such regular fixtures at St. James's Palace that their London acquaintances were very curious why Jane hadn't come in, too, for this grand masquerade. Eliza was especially nosy about it. Mrs. Porter—who once declared her a "little meddling presuming forward minx"—hated Eliza and seemed to take special pleasure in lying to her to cover for Jane.[34] Mrs. Porter said there hadn't been enough room on the Portsmouth coach for Jane but that it was just as well, because her daughter had so much writing to do.

That was at least partly true. Jane was frantically trying to finish her next book for Longman and Rees. She'd swerved away from fiction to produce a collection of Sir Philip Sidney's moral sayings, mixed with her own commentary and reflections. The hero of Jane's book was its subject—the sixteenth-century soldier, scholar, and poet who was her favorite childhood author. Jane couldn't have been more prepared to write about Sir Philip Sidney, yet she always worked more slowly than Maria, in part because she spent hours of her day copying and editing other people's writing.[35]

On the night of the masquerade, Jane, back in Ditton, awaited Henry Caulfield as her surreptious guest.[36] By leaving at nightfall on foot from Southwark, he'd arrive at Ditton cottage about one in the morning. She planned to wait up for the "poor pilgrim," as she called him, and receive him with the family's maid. A maid wasn't a chaperone, but Jane's permissive mother knew this illicit rendezvous was happening and hadn't objected. Mrs. Porter and Mrs. Boscawen had very different values. Had Mrs. Boscawen learned of Henry's overnight stay, she would have severed all contact. She'd already forbidden the Porter sisters from saying his name around her or Eliza ever again.[37] But the Porter women couldn't bring themselves to shun Henry. To the world, his behavior that night might have looked a lot like his dalliances under Mrs. Chambers's roof. But Jane wouldn't adhere to that dictate of conventional morality. She refused to imagine Henry's visit as wrong.[38]

The simple fact was that Jane wanted to see Henry, and he needed her. She continued to think of him as innocent, except for his youthful error with Mrs. Chambers. Jane felt strongly that his whole life shouldn't be judged by one mistake. The Henry she remembered was the sort of man who'd rescued a baby bird that had fallen out of its nest by putting it back into the hollow of a tree.[39] To Jane, Henry represented the best of humanity.

Henry was in distress because it was said that Mrs. Chambers—his former, or perhaps current, lover—had fallen grievously ill and was possibly even on her deathbed.[40] In yet another moment of crisis, he sought out Jane's company, comfort, and advice. She never could refuse him. At whatever late hour it was that Henry finally arrived at the cottage, Jane planned to put him directly into her sister's then-empty bed to sleep off his fatigue, "unless your envious spirit, chuses to disturb his dreams," Jane teased Maria.

The next day, Henry would secretly remain at the cottage.[41] The two could talk to their heart's content until he slipped away the next evening. If he came and went under the cover of darkness, no one in the village would see him. Jane refused to record their private conversations on paper for Maria. It was too dangerous. She communicated in euphemisms, until the sisters could see each other again. Maria was worried that whatever it was that Henry had confessed to Jane was some unnamed new offense. If so, she urged Jane to be forgiving.

"I do not judge Henry harshly," Maria wrote, "I pity him from the bottom of my heart, and beseech *you* not to treat him too severely, thro' a mistaken fear that you may treat him too kindly.—so candid as you have ever been with him, it is impossible that any proof of ardent friendship, and compassionate indulgence, can add to his sufferings."[42]

But after Maria read Jane's next evasive letter, she admitted to her sister that she was confused about what Jane was half-saying on two subjects. One was Henry's upsetting, unnamed revelations during their furtive day together. The other was Jane's apparent confession of her continued love from afar for the war hero Sir Sidney Smith.

Addressing Jane's guarded remarks about both men, Maria wrote, "I can scarcely tell you, what emotion your letter created in me.—a painful one it certainly was—because I was perplexed, and knew not whether to believe you happy or unhappy."[43]

It's quite possible Jane herself couldn't decide. For five years, her feelings had ricocheted between her cherished emotional intimacy with beloved, flawed Henry and her distant admiration for the larger-than-life Smith. But in admitting her feelings for Smith at this moment, even to her sister, Jane stumbled. She felt very little guilt about breaking some rules for polite women, but she was tortured by recognizing and expressing, to herself and to Maria, her continued feelings for Smith. They didn't *feel* wrong, she thought, but perhaps continuing to admit them was wrong. And having feelings for both Henry and Sir Sidney Smith at the same time might seem particularly wrong.

"I must feel," Jane told Maria, "before I can *give the preference*—that by so doing, I *transgress* no *honour, virtue, or goodness*!—You now see *where the scale turns*. I often wished that I had never made you privy to this monstrous combat in my breast—and, then, again, I am reconciled to your knowing me, *just as I am*!"

Jane imagined herself as a warrior in love, as a woman who both thought and felt like a soldier.[44] Her monstrous combat between her feelings for Henry and Smith was the foundation of an emotional battle she felt she could share only with her sister.

"Believe me, my dearest Maria, that my Reason, my Justice, my every worthy thing—determines me *against the side*, which is *nearest to me in distance*—I will (please Heaven) have no more weak thoughts that way—& no more rash ones elsewhere."

Her cryptic language is decodable. Jane's romantic thoughts nearest in distance were for Henry. For so long, she'd harbored hopes that he would reform, that his fortunes would be restored, and that he would act on his pure love for her, rather than his vile feelings for Mrs. Chambers. Those were Jane's weak thoughts. She contrasted them to the rash ones for Smith. They were rash, she thought, because he was so far above her in station, expectations, and reason. Smith had showed some inklings of interest in her five years before, but there had been so few opportunities to be in same room together since then. Robert had kept a friendship with Smith, but the sisters hadn't.

Maria believed it was a regrettable accident that kept Smith "out of that circle in which he might clearly see the whole of my sister's character." She felt sure that if he could only know Jane, as Jane knew him, the sentiments between them would be reciprocal.

"So strongly am I impressed with this belief, that I do protest I shall henceforth seek opportunities of renewing our past friendship, and will no longer avoid from a preposterous delicacy, the means of bringing it about," Maria declared.[45]

This approach of bold action was something Jane had briefly tried out before. In the spring of 1805, when she was still in Lesbury, she'd sent Smith anonymous verses and epigrams she'd written in praise of him and his wartime heroics. She had their friend Elizabeth Dillon recopy the poem to disguise her handwriting. Then Jane had done it again, with more verses, using the same pseudonym and means. It seemed to Jane impossible that she'd be suspected by Smith as the author.[46]

That may seem disingenuous. Jane's dedication to Smith in *Thaddeus of Warsaw* fed public gossip, which continued to flare up thereafter. Jane's name would have been on any short list of guesses of women sending anonymous verse tributes to Smith. An Irish friend told Jane that her supposed impending marriage to Smith was the whole talk of Belfast. "How the people have got it into their heads, I cannot tell," Jane told Maria.[47]

Maria wanted Jane to capitalize on the gossip: "I can do no harm by advising you rather to meet than to shun, every new acquaintance likely to restore the intimacy so desired," Maria wrote to Jane. With Robert in Russia, the sisters sent out their two other brothers to make Smith's acquaintance.[48] Mrs. Porter was brought into these maneuvers to throw Jane back into Smith's path. It took little convincing. Mrs. Porter declared she thought Jane shouldn't marry anyone but Smith, because the two of them were formed for each other.[49] Robert, who'd always expressed astonishment at the idea of Jane as a possible wife for Smith, wasn't brought into their plans.

As Jane plotted ways to get closer to Smith, she also worked to bring the *Aphorisms of Sir Philip Sidney* to completion. She told herself that, by recording and illuminating the life and writings of her historical favorite, Sir Philip Sidney, she was once again doing homage to beloved Sir Sidney Smith. Jane connected the sixteenth-century soldier-author to the contemporary naval hero because they were both knights with "Sidney" in their names. In the back of her mind, too, would have been an intention to provide a gift copy of the book about the dead hero to the living one. Sending a copy of her own book was one of the few acceptable ways for a woman in her situation to give a present to a man in his. On its face, it could seem a professional gesture from a grateful author, rather than a romantic step from an improperly desirous woman.

Longman and Rees had expressed an interest in publishing the *Aphorisms*. They'd been exceptionally helpful assisting her research, too. Owen Rees managed to borrow rarely viewed papers of Sir Philip Sidney's in two large folio volumes to share with Jane.[50] She had grouped his sayings into subjects such as "Reason and Wisdom," "Pride and Violence," "Vanity and Flattery," as well as "Curiosity," and "Persuasion."[51]

Some of Jane's curated selections seem almost admonishments to herself: "It is against womanhood, to be forward in their own wishes." And "Force cannot be the school of love." Other selections seem messages chosen for others, including "Nothing can love so heartily as virtue." And "True love would not, for his life, constrain his lady's presence; but would rather die than consent to her absence."

After some of the quotations, Jane added original remarks, daring to put her own voice in conversation with Sir Philip Sidney's. In commenting on the epigram that "Love cannot exist without hope!" Jane added several paragraphs on women, love, and constancy. She wrote, "A virtuous heart can never be totally indifferent to the happiness of a creature it has once regarded with peculiar tenderness."[52] After four pages of his remarks on love, Jane quotes extensively from an unnamed source. That source was the feminist philosopher Mary Wollstonecraft, drawn from her moving unfinished story "The Cave of Fancy," first published in 1798, which investigates women's erotic turmoil. Jane, to veil her original source and its author's sex, changed Wollstonecraft's first-person references from describing loving a man to loving a woman.[53]

Throughout *Aphorisms*, Jane obliquely lays out her own moral philosophy and her personal struggles with passion and desire, as well as her sense (through Sir Philip Sidney and Mary Wollstonecraft) that iconoclastic passions answer to a higher power than conventional morality. Yet, in private, Jane was continually trying to pin down which of her own romantic impulses and feelings were admirable and acceptable in the eyes of God versus the eyes of man. Just as importantly, she struggled with what it meant when such passions were expressed from the hearts, and pens, of women.

Jane negotiated hard for payment for her two-volume *Aphorisms*. Longman and Rees settled on the price she wanted, 50 pounds a volume. At the same time, her publishers shrewdly proposed another bargain. They'd pay her 100 pounds for the third edition—and all future editions—of *Thaddeus of Warsaw*. They'd give her 50 pounds now, they said, and 150 pounds six months after the publication of *Aphorisms*. It was too much of a temptation. Jane unwisely took the deal. She hoped it would put anxious Mrs. Porter at ease.[54] It would relieve Robert from any worry about their finances while he remained in Russia.

When Robert was next in touch, he told them he bore the pain of family separation with resignation, because he knew he was working to advance their economic comfort. Maria privately admitted her fear that he'd find a different sort of comfort in Russia. She was worried he'd abandon his courtship of poor Fanny Dalrymple—who'd become Maria's close friend—and marry a Russian woman.

As the long winter months had passed into 1806, Robert's painting commissions were progressing. He finally met Tsar Alexander and his wife, the Empress, who'd been the Margravine of Anspach's childhood friend. Thanks to this fortunate connection, Robert's immense artistic talent was recognized by the Imperial Family. The Empress rewarded him with an expensive ring for one of his paintings.[55] But he was reaching the conclusion that his hopes for riches weren't going to be realized there. "The Emperor," Robert shared more candidly with Jane, "has no farther wish for my services."

So in April 1806, Robert decided to visit Moscow to add material to the travel book he was drafting and sending back to Jane. He discovered he was quite well liked in Moscow, especially by its ladies. The tenor of his letters home began to change.

"All the people here are much pleased with your stupid brother," he told Jane, "none under the rank of Princess." He'd won these sirens' hearts by sketching their faces. Some were indeed beautiful, he admitted, but none had made an impression on his "cold heart."

Robert then wrote, "There is a Princess who is anxious to visit England," and who "loves the English almost to folly." This princess, Robert said, longed to come to England one day and be introduced to his honored mother and esteemed author-sisters. Robert hoped they'd show her hospitality, if she ever made that trip abroad.

This sensible and interesting princess, Robert said, planned to write a letter to them. He hoped they'd answer her and suggested they sprinkle references to her as "Princess" throughout their letter in reply. Robert called her "not the happiest creature" in the world and admitted his heart was susceptible to sympathy. These would have been arresting lines to his sisters.

"She is not very young nor very beautiful," Robert acknowledged, "but she is a fine woman of perhaps 7 or 8 and 20, which is here by no means young as they marry sometimes at 14."[56] Stories of her began to fill Robert's letters home.

The Princess Mary Shcherbatov was a dark and extremely fine woman, accomplished, musical, with mental intelligence in her countenance. She lived with her very old, and not very good-natured, mother—a source of continual unhappiness. Because the Princess didn't enjoy evening parties or gaiety, Robert told them, he'd begun to spend intimate evenings with her and a female companion at her home. These nights reminded him of those he'd spent with his dear sisters.[57] Robert tried to calm what he suspected would be Jane's growing fears on learning this.

"No love believe me my dear sister makes me thus speak of her," he declared, "as I believe you no [know] too well the state of my heart and what little affections it can boast."[58]

Robert told Maria that he missed them all and wanted to come home.

"I love you so affectionately and that almost totally are my affections yours."[59] *Almost* totally, he'd written.

When Robert decided to return to St. Petersburg in July 1806, his letters home took another turn. He'd changed his mind and had decided to stay in Russia, at least until the following February. He would stay, he said, to finish a large historical painting of Peter the Great at the Admiralty Hall. But another, stronger motivation was revealed. Robert was astonished to report that the Princess Mary he'd mentioned, who continued to write to him in St. Petersburg from her home in Moscow, had declared her love. She wanted to marry him.

"I said that she knew me not—I was a stranger to her—I might be a fortune hunter a man without principle," Robert wrote in his letter home. He'd also learned what, precisely, her fortune was. Her father, when he'd died, had left Princess Mary a large fortune of 125,000 rubles.[60] She wasn't yet financially independent, because her mother had used that amount to buy an entire village, which Princess Mary would inherit whenever she married—if she married with her mother's consent.[61]

The Princess believed her mother intended to object to her daughter's ever marrying and planned instead to give the village to her other daughter's children. But the village, the Princess told Robert, ought to be hers when her mother died. Perhaps her mother's death would take place soon. Until then, Princess Mary admitted, her mother was unlikely to allow her to marry Robert or any man, even if the Emperor himself—who had very close ties to her family—interceded on her behalf. Her mother would break her arms and legs to stop her merely from writing to Robert, she claimed, if she knew about their clandestine letters.[62]

Princess Mary had a fantastical plan to escape to England and live with Robert, Mrs. Porter, and his celebrated literary sisters. She felt she could exchange her own place in life for that of the least fortunate peasant woman, despite never having had any experience living as a peasant. She had a little wealth at her own disposal, including a house in Moscow and 10,000 rubles worth of diamonds.[63] It was wartime, and values were in flux, but these diamonds alone were worth more than Robert had ever had an inkling of.

To his family, Robert would describe the Princess's expected future fortune as approximately twenty thousand pounds.[64] Most of it was in "estates and slaves," as Robert rightly called Russian serfs, but the Princess vowed to sell the moment she could. If she were his wife, this amount could not only clear off Robert's debts but also provide his mother and sisters with a secure, comfortable life.

Robert told the Princess he had no palace to offer her in England, only a mother in a cottage with contentment. He stated a thousand objections to her desire to marry him, but he also admitted to his sisters that he thought he might be discovering some feelings for her after all. When Robert wrote to his mother about the possibility of marrying the Princess, he assured Mrs. Porter of his continued love for all of them. This daughter-in-law would be a welcome addition to their family. Robert had seen the bad example of his brother William, in "sacrificing himself," as Robert put it, to the unworthy Lydia.

"Believe me therefore," he said, "I will never either disgrace my heart, my family, or my affections in choosing any other than her I think my sisters and you would love equally with myself."[65]

Princess Mary wrote charming, overwrought letters in French to Mrs. Porter, Jane, and Maria, already describing herself as a daughter and a sister. Mrs. Porter didn't know French, and Jane's ability in the language was poor, so this left the translating to Maria, who read the letters aloud. Princess Mary told Mrs. Porter that she knew, in Robert's mother, she'd have as beloved a parent as her own late father had once been to her. In possessing Robert, she believed she'd gain an inestimable treasure.[66]

Gradually, Princess Mary let her attachment to Robert become known in Russia, and the couple began to seek some path to marriage. They'd need the permission of Tsar Alexander to marry. As well liked as Robert was, objections were raised to his lack of rank. In the army, he was a mere captain. His English friends, getting wind of the need, hinted at a knighthood or even a baronetcy, eventually canvassing the Prince of Wales for some title for Robert.

When a portrait of Princess Mary arrived in England, it revealed her to be bewitching, with a lovely mouth, and large, open eyes, full of expression. She had a glowing, dark, peach-colored complexion. Her countenance was full of goodness, graciousness, and sense, Maria thought.[67] Some reports had said the Princess looked like Jane. Maria thought, if that were true, then the Princess's character must be like her own.

"I flatter myself that Bob complimented me, as well as you, in the choice of a wife," Maria teased her sister.[68]

When Jane referred to the possibility of ending up with this princess for her sister-in-law, she called it "Robert's Fairy Tale."[69] There was even a hidden thought that there might be, in this not-too-distant, fairy-tale future, a double wedding. The first would be Captain Robert Porter to Princess Mary Federovna Shcherbatov. The second would be Lieutenant-Colonel Frederick Luke Gardiner Cowell to Miss Anna Maria Porter.[70] Jane made no mention of her own fate.

CHAPTER 12

Finally in His Arms

The Return of Maria's Sighing Soldier (1805–9)

In Maria's dream, Jane was kissing her, then kissing Frederick Cowell. This happy nocturnal vision started with Maria's fantasy of welcoming Frederick, as he returned from abroad, for a visit to England. Then, in her dream, as she later remembered it, the mood turned from bliss to discomfort. In her unconscious mind, Maria watched with concern as Frederick began merely to endure Jane's kisses. Maria desperately wanted Frederick to love Jane—and Jane to love Frederick.

"O Jane, will you ever see that person, and like him well enough to give him an opportunity of falsifying the latter part of my dream!" Maria wondered.[1]

Frederick Cowell had been the stuff of Maria's fantasies and fears for three years. She granted that the entire affair of their secret correspondence, and her own behavior in it, sounded immature.

"Have the honesty to own to me, my dearest Jane," Maria once wrote, "that I am still Fifteen in credulity and sanguineness!"[2]

She was, at the time, almost twenty-six. Maria called this relationship her "strange, unwise infatuation," which led her "step by step into an interest which is so strong and so irresistible." It tortured her, the *unwiseness* of what she'd done—what she was still doing, in writing to him, after having first watched him, and admired him, from a window and never having once spoken to him.

On some days, over the course of those three years, Maria would express regret at ever having thought of Frederick.

"I am therefore tempted to renounce Apollo for ever!" she'd announce to Jane, using another code name for him.[3] Maria would proclaim she'd live for no one else's sake but her sister's.[4] Then the next day, she'd again be celebrating her love for him, imagining providence having designed them to live together and die on the same day.[5] Frederick seemed just as mercurial in resolutions and feelings. Maria would doubt herself, then doubt him, and then return to certainty, and Frederick would do just the same.

In her head, she traced and retraced their relationship, trying to make sense of how things had gotten so out of hand. Endless ruminating had killed her poetic impulse, she thought. She went months without writing verse.[6] Occasionally, Maria would charge Jane with responsibility for sorting out her mess with Frederick.

"Are you not something to blame, for not having scolded me out of this, when it was possible to have done so with a prospect of success?" Maria asked her sister.[7] Maybe, she suggested, if Jane hadn't spent nearly nine months away from home, living with Percival Stockdale in 1804 and 1805, Maria's relationship with Frederick wouldn't have come so far and foolishly forward. It was during those lonely months in Ditton, without Jane, and with no money, that Maria found herself with nothing to do but daydream or make conversation with her dejected mother. She felt, looking back on it, that she'd had no recourse from distress but thoughts of Frederick.[8]

Jane, however, would have none of this imputation of her own guilt. Indeed, she thought there was probably no need for guilt. "So, you blame me for not frowning upon your attachment to this young man!" she replied. "It is not in my nature, to blight the virtuous affections of the heart."[9] Jane, who read parts of Frederick's letters, which Maria copied into her own, thought she could see in the couple a sympathy of sentiment: "Just such a heart, just such a soul, was formed to make you happy."[10]

Maria sometimes felt guilty at the thought of leaving Jane to make a life with Frederick, but Jane entered into Maria's dream of a life with her humble military husband. Jane imagined herself caring for their future children.[11] Of course, before the couple could marry and start a family, they'd need to have their first in-person conversation. Maria was starting to feel this was about as likely to happen as her finding a hidden treasure of gold.[12] But being in the same place wouldn't resolve their difficulties—far from it.

In the eyes of the world, the two of them didn't know each other. No honest explanation could be given for how they'd met. No common friend could invite them to dinner. No mutual acquaintance could pretend to introduce them in a drawing room. These obstacles aside, Maria also couldn't get out of her head the frightening idea that Frederick might not be a man of upstanding character. Jane called it Maria's "suspicious temper."[13]

To gauge Frederick's goodness, Maria decided she needed to learn more about his family. She asked around, as delicately as she could. She learned that his uncle had been a colonel in the Royal Regiment of Foot. He'd commanded four companies in the West Indies and was said to have a fort named after him. Maria asked her brother John if he knew any officers in the Royals, without revealing why she was interested. Remarkably, it turned out John had served alongside Frederick's uncle—now Colonel Cowell—and had known him intimately.

She pressed her brother for more information. She listened to his glowing reports of Colonel Cowell. John worried Maria had fallen in love with the colonel, at least until she revealed she'd heard that he'd recently married and that she'd never met him. There was a lot at stake in a woman's asking her brother a few simple questions about an unmarried man of his acquaintance.[14]

Maria's questions elsewhere had a similar effect. From her deepening interest in current events, her neighbor Mr. Dozy rightly guessed she must be in love with an officer abroad.[15] Maria was mortified. Rather than risk detection by further veiled questions to men, she and Jane again drew on their trusted female network. They contacted Jane's friend from her Bath adventure, Mrs. Carrol, to ask her to find out anything she could about the Cowells in Ireland. The sisters also used their clever writer-friend, Elizabeth Benger, who'd been sending and receiving Maria and Frederick's letters.

What would have been gleaned was this: Frederick Luke Gardiner Cowell was a younger son, one of six born in Harristown, County Kildare, Ireland. The extended Cowell family's men mostly went on to military careers—majors, captains, and lieutenant-colonels. Most married respectable women in Ireland. There were a handful of landed estates but no titles in the extended family.[16] Everything pointed to Frederick's being what he said he was—a low-ranking officer from an honorable family on the fringes of the gentry class. Nothing untoward was discovered about his personal reputation. The sisters did learn that Frederick's powerful military uncle (now retired) wasn't rich.[17] Maria already knew Frederick had no future financial expectations, by his own admission.

She tried to help him advance professionally by inspiring him. She sent him printed portraits of her brother Robert and Sir Sidney Smith, in case he wanted to reflect on the images of good and great men she knew.[18] Maria and Jane lobbied behind the scenes for a promotion for Frederick. Maria even considered that, once he could be revealed as her suitor, she might try her luck asking for a favor for him from the Duke of Clarence, the younger son of King George III, to whom she had connections through friends.[19]

Frederick remained desperate to get out of Jamaica and the Black Troops. It wasn't his regiment but the "abominable country," as he called it, that he wanted out of.[20] It was a country of brutality and inequity. He told Maria he thought only of her and of their time on the Isle of Wight. But returning to Britain was proving a challenge. A process called an "exchange" was a common way to set a new geographical course for oneself in the military. It was used when an officer wanted to leave the location where his regiment was posted (or about to be posted) or wanted different commanding officers. An exchange required one individual's finding another who wanted to make a direct switch. But very few officers posted in Britain or the rest of Europe wanted to exchange for a post in the West Indies and especially not in the Black Troops. With an exchange unlikely, Frederick looked for another way out of Jamaica.

He appealed to his uncle, but there were Cowell cousins serving in Jamaica, too. The uncle couldn't grant favors to every needy nephew. Frederick's cousins teased him endlessly about his failed attempts to get out of the West Indies. They said they could tell he was in love with some European fair and threatened to reveal it their uncle.[21] He eventually requested a leave of absence, due to supposed ill health. His request was denied.

Frederick's poor health may have been a fiction, but Maria's wasn't. In addition to her chronic female troubles and headaches, she struggled with physical debility, some of which must have stemmed from severe anxiety. At one point, she wondered if she might have gout.[22] She felt faint, weary, and sinking. She was exhausted at the slightest action. She had violent pains in her back.[23] She'd become very, very thin.[24] For one bleak period, she reported crying ten times a day.[25] The uncertainty of her future with Frederick was taking a physical and emotional toll. About her lovesick worries, Maria wrote to Jane, "The fear that we should never meet again in this world, used to haunt me like a spectre . . . I daresay that dreadful apprehensions increased my disorder, since the Dr. tells me, it has solely risen from my mind. Who would have thought that an anxious Heart could have caused an inflamed Liver?"[26]

Maria admitted other worries to Jane. Perhaps Frederick wouldn't love her as much as she loved him.[27] Perhaps she wasn't lovable enough. Jane admonished her sister, "Vanquish this mortal contempt which you seem to have conceived against yourself."[28]

Maria worried that Frederick would reject her, because her family was poor, and she brought no dowry.

"Remember, we are not obscure people," Jane told Maria. "We have enough about us to satisfy moderate pride—we are the daughters of a gentleman, & the sisters of a man who is admired all over Europe—Besides, we are not Moles ourselves; our characters have seen the light, and most respectably."[29]

Yet Maria tortured herself with dark thoughts. Maybe Frederick would one day accuse her of having ensnared his heart at too young an age.[30] Maybe her anxiety about him had aged her prematurely and her beauty had waned. Jane thought it ridiculous that Maria doubted her attractiveness. Jane wrote, "Pray recollect. I am three years your senior, and upon my word, I don't think I looked so 'fat & handsome' three years back!"[31]

Maria also worried in the other direction—that Frederick might have lost his looks.

"Trust me," Jane wrote. If when Mr. Cowell returns, "you find him otherwise then you wish, your affection will die a sudden death.—the first shock would kill it."[32] Every worry Maria had, Jane tried to assuage.

Maria's friendships suffered, too, especially her once-close connection to Kearsley. She worried that he'd dropped her acquaintance. But in the winter of 1805, when she visited London, Kearsley heard of her arrival in town from her brother John. Maria hadn't planned to see Kearsley, but she ended up spending time with him every day. Once again, the two of them had strange conversations. He proposed moving to Ditton to be nearer to her. Maria worried that his romantic inclination for her had resumed.[33]

"He professed not to be able to exist without frequently conversing with me," she told Jane, "and delighted me with the assurance that since he had seen me again, he felt an inward certainty that a very few days more, would completely recover him, make his mind what it *never* had been, and enable him to produce some fine and beautiful works."[34]

Kearsley was so devoted to Maria that he risked his own safety for her. During that visit to London, she received an urgent letter, telling her that her mother was sick. Maria was desperate to go back to Ditton immediately, but she knew the last stagecoach home was about to leave. Kearsley ran ahead of her. He put his body in front of the moving vehicle and stopped the stage for her. He'd entered into her cause with so affecting a zeal that she felt she could never adequately thank him.

Mrs. Porter's illness turned out to be nothing, but reflecting on it all afterward, Maria worried that her conduct toward Kearsley was censurable. If she encouraged his moving to Ditton, and allowed strange attentions from him again, then she might be encouraging more than she meant to. Kind, sad, talented Kearsley had no idea that her heart was pledged to another man. Eliza Tickell was spreading rumors that Kearsley was Maria's accepted lover. Maria finally decided she couldn't allow him to move to be nearer to her. She confidently believed she could cure him of his sadness, and she thought Kearsley's was the finest mind in the universe, but she couldn't bring herself to imagine him as her proper suitor.

"How I wish the poor fellow had been born our Brother," Maria wrote to Jane.[35]

While the sisters schemed for Frederick's return, they were also finishing new books. As Jane's *Aphorisms of Sir Philip Sidney* came into its final form—to be published in 1807—she vowed not to fatigue herself, calling such hurrying her "bane." Maria, having just finished one novel, was working rapidly on her next. It would be her seventh published book, and it centered on heroic soldiers.

Maria's *The Hungarian Brothers* was about two military siblings, fighting against the backdrop of post-Revolutionary France. She negotiated with Longman and Rees for twenty guineas a volume for the first edition, for a total of sixty guineas. There would be a further ten guineas a volume should it go into a second and third edition. Jane wrote the memorandum of agreement.[36]

Maria took Jane's help in other ways, too. Like Jane's *Thaddeus of Warsaw*, Maria's *Hungarian Brothers* was designed as a new species of historical romance. It entwined domestic and military contests with real people and history of the 1790s. But Maria's story featured two brothers of opposite personalities, Count Charles Leopolstat and his younger brother, Demetrius, the orphan sons of a Hungarian nobleman. The novel uses the phrase "sense and sensibility," later made famous by Jane Austen. Maria's novel describes Demetrius as having an exquisite sensibility that makes him warm, impetuous, and impulsive. Charles, by contrast, has superb sense and deliberate judgment. The heroes' contrasting temperaments might be seen as fictionalized masculine versions of Maria's and Jane's personalities.

In *The Hungarian Brothers*, the brother-heroes face adversity and adventures, in love and war. Charles, a military genius, guides his brother (whom he's shielded from the realities of the family's debts and troubles) in his career and relationships. The brothers fight the French in different locations, Charles in Switzerland and Demetrius in Italy. Maria was using her novel to comment on the damage and devastation wrought by war. Other parts of the novel were drawn from life, such as when Charles receives anonymous letters from a secret female admirer. The admirer declares her interest in the soldier, despite never having seen him. She turns out to be surprisingly skilled in military matters. Of this admirer, Charles writes to his brother, "It seemed to me as if the fair writer had designed me the honour of her hand; and yet I could hardly reconcile such an explicit declaration, with my ideas of female delicacy."[37] Maria created a moving story of wartime violence and family honor that also explores the most confusing psychological aspects of her own epistolary relationship with Frederick Cowell.

As Maria was writing *The Hungarian Brothers* in 1806, what once seemed almost impossible—a first meeting with her fiancé—appeared within reach. Word came from Frederick that he'd begun to forge a path back to England.

"If he should return my dear Jane!" Maria wrote, "My heart beats as much at writing that if, as tho' it were certain I should see him tomorrow—'tis like a new world opening before me—as if I were entering upon a fresh life."[38]

Frederick had managed an exchange with another officer. It meant transferring into the Eighty-Fifth Regiment of Foot, also posted in Jamaica. But the Eighty-Fifth had become so reduced in numbers that its officers expected the regiment to be ordered home in the spring. Frederick hoped he and Maria might finally see each other by summer. This exchange of regiments had involved some use of his uncle's influence. Frederick worried that he'd forfeited any further patronage. He took the chance anyway, to return to his beloved Maria.

Frederick knew his new regiment would present its own problems. It might eventually be sent to the East Indies. If so, by then, he would have hoped, he'd be going off with his new bride at his side. Maria was less than happy with this plan, but she told Jane she wasn't anxious about it. If she and Frederick ever met, she'd either talk him out of going or discover that his desire to get away from her was so strong that she wouldn't want him to stay.[39] Maria had no intention of moving to the East Indies. She envisioned a life in Britain with Frederick, her mother and sister, and Robert, whenever he might return from Russia.

More immediately, Maria needed to figure out how she and Frederick could meet upon his arrival. The sisters decided to set up a secret code in their letters to signal Frederick's return to England. If Maria said that their friend Elizabeth Dillon had liked Maria's sixth book, *A Sailor's Friendship, and a Soldier's Love* (1805), better than her other novels because it had a better conclusion, that would mean Frederick had arrived.[40] *A Sailor's Friendship,* Maria's short anonymous novel, consisted of fictional ruminations on the famous Lord Nelson and Lady Hamilton's love story. It was written during the early days of Maria's relationship with Frederick and was a perfect choice for this coded purpose. The rehearsed line had a clever second meaning—that Frederick's return to England was *A Soldier's Love* with a better conclusion.

"O Jane, Jane, what a winter this may be to me—either the happiest or most miserable of my life!" Maria wrote. "One interview may destroy the illusions of months, I may now say of years."[41]

The rendezvous had been arranged only to be postponed and then postponed again, but Maria and Frederick were finally able to set up their first meeting in London in November 1806. He was staying there with an uncle, where he was waiting, not at all patiently, for Maria's arrival from Ditton. Maria would come to town and stay with her friends Colonel Charles and

Mrs. Elizabeth Dillon. Once she'd arrived, Frederick would write a note, find a way to get away from his uncle, and come to her.

Maria knew she could safely receive Frederick as her guest at the Dillons'. The Dillons' own relationship flouted conventional morality. They were living together as if man and wife but were apparently not legally married. The pretense of it was notorious enough that Robert didn't like Jane and Maria to be seen consorting with the them.[42] But Robert was still out of the country, and the Dillons' willingness to turn a blind eye served Maria's needs perfectly.

Maria reached London on a Wednesday. She found two letters from Frederick already awaiting her at the Dillons'. One letter had been sent four days earlier. The other had arrived the day before. Mrs. Dillon told Maria that a messenger had been repeatedly sent by this correspondent, over the past four days, asking if their guest had arrived yet and if there was a response to these two letters. Frederick had shown not only his eagerness for Maria's arrival but also that he was unafraid to let the Dillons know just how eager he was.

Maria read his letters. She replied with a short note, inviting him to call on her the following morning, a Thursday. Frederick sent back an immediate reply—really, more of an entreaty. He asked if he might see her sooner—that very Wednesday night. Maria refused.

"I was unable to do so," she told Jane, "for indeed surprize and a thousand strange feelings made me very ill.—You may guess what a night I spent—what a morning, till he was announced."

When Frederick arrived the next morning, he was shown into the Dillons' drawing room. Flouting convention yet again, Maria went in to see him alone.

"I saw nothing," Maria told Jane, "but his agitation, and I was so agitated that I was scarcely able to speak."

She recovered herself well enough to look on this man to whom she'd pledged her love and a married life. Her first feeling was sinking disappointment.

"He was so altered in appearance," Maria confessed to Jane, "that I should have passed him in the street—his complexion entirely faded, his fine hair cropt quite close, and his figure completely changed—he is grown fat—and I confess I was so weak as to feel my heart recede from the alteration in his person."

Maria had trouble hiding her shock. She realized she'd even mistaken the color of his eyes. They weren't blue.

"To add to my mortification," Maria admitted, "a very slight impediment which he has in his speech, was so increased by his emotion, that it gave an air of restraint to his manner. He scarcely spoke—I scarcely spoke—but what he said heightened my distress."

Maria discovered Frederick's heart was completely oppressed by a strong fear of his inferiority to her. Her proud soldier, the man she'd watched so confidently march before her window in his uniform, was collapsing in front of her.

"I was indeed in a tumult of frightful feelings," she told Jane. "I should blush to own them, for I confess [my] preference for him, seemed no longer to have a share in them."

As Maria tried to speak her mind, she was perhaps too blunt. The words she used to describe her feelings, now that they were finally sitting, face to face, were far cooler than what she'd used in her letters. She'd referred out loud to her "liking" him.

As she told Jane, "In answer to a few words of mine, he said in a tone that pierced my heart, 'I foresaw this always.'"

Frederick continued, "I knew you would cease to love me, the moment we met.—Maria, if you are always to express your feelings toward me by that cold word, I wish to God I had died in Jamaica. I see how it must end—after this day, we shall never see each other again."

Maria objected, "How can you think this Fred[eric]k? How can you suppose I can ever be indifferent to you?"

He said, "I don't suppose that . . . But I see you cannot continue to love me—in a few hours to change from *love* to *liking*, to use no term but *that* when you speak to me. O how I wish that I had staid in the West Indies for ever, as I should then have deceived myself still, or you would still have loved me."

"I will never change," Maria said, "if you follow the advice I have just given you.—if instead of resigning yourself to despair, and wasting your youth in regret, you pursue with resolution the plan in life I have painted out."

Maria learned that Frederick hadn't read the books she'd recommended or sent. She lectured him on it.

"Promise to prove your attachment to me," she implored him, "by *studying* for my sake, instead of *thinking* about me." It was perhaps a little too like the lecture her brother William had asked Maria to deliver to Lydia a decade earlier.

Frederick confessed, "While there is a possibility of losing you, I feel it will be out of my power to think of anything else.—I could read and think of what I read, if I might but see you beside me—but if we are to remain separate, I know all my endeavors to obey you, will be useless."

Then Maria delivered a dagger to Frederick. She told him, "You know my affection always was conditionally given. I repeat the conditions—and assure you, it will be solely in your own power to preserve or lose me."

As she spoke, Maria watched Frederick's despondency increase. Tears gathered in his eyes. He declared he wouldn't be selfish. But he wanted a promise from her. If they were going to stay together, he wanted her to pledge she'd never part from him, forever.

Maria thought this speech was as impudent as it was unexpected. She reiterated her promise to remain his but only upon her conditions. Frederick worried that she must be trying to break it off with him. If she weren't, he wanted to go public with their love and tell their families. The couple had, by this point, spent three hours alone together, "in painful perplexity," as she called it.

"I prophesied some disappointment," Maria wrote to Jane, "and I found it where I least expected it, but you must not imagine my disappointment extreme. I know that I have acted with great folly, and ought to pay the price of a little regret."

Maria and Frederick agreed to meet again the next day—a Friday. They took a walk together with Mrs. Dillon as their chaperone. They then found themselves alone again. It was an easier conversation the second time around. The first surprise was over. They were both now less embarrassed, although more positively agitated. Maria heard and received Frederick's declarations and his feelings for her differently, just one day later.

"I then saw sufficient of his tender and diffident heart," Maria wrote to Jane, "to feel myself again entirely his.—I am sure he loves me to an excess which will make all things easy to him, which I may find necessary to command."

Maria let her renewed tenderness toward him show itself gradually. As that tenderness became more evident, it awakened in Frederick the hope of her becoming his wife. With this hope, his mind seemed to return to greater clarity. The two met again on Saturday. By the time he left, Maria felt she'd had a complete revolution from her first negative impression of him on Thursday morning.

"He left me, still more satisfied with the destiny, which only two days ago, I contemplated with terror," she wrote to Jane. "If the most unbounded love, can ensure my happiness I believe it will be certain to me, with him."

"Altho' this love is more passionate and extravagant, less governed than I expected," Maria wrote, "I assure you, it bears no marks of a *vulgar* passion, of which the *person* is the principal object."

As Maria saw it, she had only two things to struggle with. One was his regret at how much time they'd lost between falling in love at first sight and their first conversation. The other was his fear that he'd lose her after all. She decided that she still wanted to keep the existence of Frederick a secret from her mother. She also worried about introducing him to Jane. She begged her sister to try to love Frederick, "tho' his Beauty is gone, and his mind has lain waste so long." Love him, Maria implored, "for indeed he merits it."[43]

Back in Ditton cottage, Jane couldn't wait to hear from Maria about her meeting with Frederick. She began a letter to her sister even before she'd learned any details about their first meeting.

"How can you manage with Mrs. Dillon? Has she no eyes?" Jane wrote.[44]

Jane had, in fact, already learned, through the gossip chain, that Maria and Frederick were interrupted in some intimate pose in the Dillons' drawing room. The information had come in a letter from their friend Mary Cockle, governess to the ten illegitimate children of the Duke of Clarence and his famous actress-mistress, Mrs. Dora Jordan. Mrs. Cockle, though an accomplished poet, was also an untrustworthy, chattering simpleton.[45] It was frightening to Jane that she'd gotten a glimpse of Maria in a compromising position with a strange man. Despite this worry, she told her sister that she believed she already loved Frederick like a brother. He is worthy, Jane concluded, "*of the proudest woman's love.*"

"I have him already in my heart," Jane wrote, "so don't be jealous if I receive him almost into my arms when we meet."[46]

Jane reminded Maria that if she hadn't found Frederick, she may have given hope to Kearsley. Frederick, Jane said, had therefore been a saving angel to Maria, in preventing her from attaching herself to that poor, melancholy artist. She instructed her sister to see Frederick every day she could. She called him her "brother elect." She pushed Maria toward this man she'd never met, just as powerfully as she'd once pushed her sister away from Kearsley.

On the following Monday, Maria wrote to Jane again. She apologized for her previous incoherent letter. She'd feebly tried to capture the strangest feelings she'd ever felt. She hoped, whatever her last letter said, this much came through. Despite Frederick's changed person and almost unmanageable self-contempt, she wouldn't exchange his heart for any heart in the whole world. Every meeting since then had taken away the pains of the first one. "I perceive," she wrote, "that there is nothing he would not suffer or do, to attain the certainty of passing the future of his life with me."

Frederick begged Maria to tell her mother about him. Otherwise, he feared, they'd have to see less of each other. Maria dreaded what Mrs. Porter would have to say about Frederick, a man of no money and few prospects. Her mother might denounce him. Mrs. Porter was a romantic but also a woman whose opinions were shaped by hard experience. In her youth, she'd been engaged for five years, waiting for her husband to make enough money to marry and support a family.

Maria told Frederick they'd need to wait until Robert returned from Russia with his princess bride and made it financially possible for them to marry. Robert, she promised, could smooth the way, too, with Mrs. Porter. Although Jane had warned her sister not to reveal it, Maria couldn't keep the family's secret to herself. Robert's engagement to Princess Mary was news not yet known in England. Maria hoped Frederick would share in her joy, but his response was complicated.

"I rejoice in it with my whole soul," he said, "as it will I trust add to all your comforts—but I fear when your Mother has such a daughter, she will never accept such a poor fellow as I am, for a son."

"O you shouldn't be poor, then," Maria replied. "Surely you will not refuse the friendship of my Brother, and the services that friendship may render you?"

"When you have made me his Brother, Maria," Frederick said, "I will accept anything from him, for your sake, but never till then."

This response wasn't what Maria was expecting, but she heard it with happiness. She rejoiced in Frederick's proud spirit. She thought it was noble that he'd refuse help from Robert until he was already Maria's husband. Shortly after that meeting, a letter from Robert arrived. Although it would turn out to share positive prospects about his anticipated future marriage to the Princess, Maria was incredibly agitated as she opened it. Her future life with Frederick hung in the balance. As she scanned the letter's pages, she admitted to Jane, "Fred[eric]k was forced to hold me in his arms, to keep my poor frame from trembling itself to atoms."

Through these tumultuous experiences, Jane had been a support, and Maria thanked her sister for her tenderness.

"How can I attempt to thank you, my dearest, fondest Jane! My heart is full of what it owes to you—may you ever love me so—ever love so, the objects dearest to *me*."[47]

Jane, who formed plans and solved problems, turned her full attention to settling Maria and Frederick's future. She referred to herself as like Don Quixote, thinking of her sister day and night and going on mad adventures to advance her cause with her secret fiancé.[48] Jane devised new stratagems. She tried to further Frederick's military prospects. When Robert was eventually brought into the secret of Maria's engagement, Jane wanted him, too, to work his military connections to get Frederick a company to lead.

The sisters launched two plans at the end of 1806 that might introduce Jane and Frederick. Both failed due to unforeseen circumstances, but their cancellation again awakened Frederick's fears of inferiority. He confessed to Maria that he prayed to God that he wouldn't see anyone from her family until after they were married. He was sure that, if they were in their right senses, they wouldn't let Maria throw herself away on him.

Jane introduced Frederick into conversations with Mrs. Porter to smooth the way for an eventual meeting. She decided the best way to convince Mrs. Porter that he was the right man for Maria was to compare him to one of her own former beaux, the attentive Mr. Terrot. Mrs. Porter had once hoped Terrot would break it off with his fiancée and become Jane's husband. So Jane decided to warm Mrs. Porter to the idea of Frederick by saying he was just as tender to Maria as Terrot once was to her.[49]

Jane gave Maria ideas about how to mention him in her letters home. Do the thing by degrees, she advised. Jane, in following this advice in her conversations, felt she'd nearly managed to get Mrs. Porter to embrace the idea of Maria becoming Mrs. Cowell.[50] Maria's only duty now, Jane reminded her, was to feel hope—and love Frederick.

A third plan was devised to introduce Jane and Frederick at last—this time at a ball hosted by the Porters' distant relative and new neighbors, Sir Frederick Morton Eden and his wife. The baronet was a noted insurance company manager, philanthropist, writer, and expert on poverty. An invitation for Frederick from the Edens had been difficult to wangle, but Jane managed. Then, surprisingly, Frederick refused it. Jane suspected he'd somehow gotten the idea the Porters were mighty terrific personages. She told Maria that he was going to need to learn to sacrifice his moods to his love.

After that missed opportunity, Jane and Frederick couldn't find another easy way to meet. Jane's trips to London were delayed by rain. Frederick's planned trip to Ditton cottage never came off. Maria felt the loss of her sister's presence in these decisive scenes of her life: "I am a timid, terrified creature, you know, Jane, and now vainly look round for you, my customary support, and counsellor."[51]

Nothing could be settled. Without ever meeting Jane, Frederick had to leave London to visit family in Ireland. From there, he'd need to return to military duties. There was as yet no firmly settled plan for his and Maria's marriage. It was put on hold.

There were other matters to occupy the sisters while they waited. Both were racing to finish books. "If your book proceeds with the celerity of mine, it will appear this time twelvemonth!" Maria told Jane.[52] Maria's *The Hungarian Brothers* and Jane's *The Aphorisms of Sir Philip Sidney* would both be published in 1807. They were largely uncelebrated milestones, although *The Hungarian Brothers* would become one of Maria's best known and most admired works. As she finished her story of two soldiers, Maria felt despondent about Frederick's seeming neglect of her. He was with his regiment by necessity, but when he wrote to her, he often asked if it would be more honorable to end their engagement. So the couple broke off, and then renewed, their engagement several times.

One moment Maria would hope Frederick would make Mrs. Porter "as fond a son at least, if not quite so admirable" as Robert.[53] The next she'd lament that, because of Frederick, "my time and my powers waste away."[54] By April 1807, five months after first meeting in person, Maria considered returning Frederick's letters to him.[55] She thought she could live without ever seeing him again.[56] Crisis, however, had a way of producing profound changes in Maria's feelings.

News arrived that Frederick had been hurt falling from his horse. The horse was killed, and Frederick severely injured his arm.[57] His letter delivering this news, characteristically laconic, moved her. Maria again longed to save him—and marry him.

Jane continually worked on Frederick's career advancement in the military. The sisters asked to have Frederick made a lieutenant in Robert's regiment, where he might gain favors. Jane figured he could become a barracks master with an income of two hundred to three hundred a year, a house free of taxes, and an allotment of coals. That situation, Jane figured, would be just enough for Frederick and Maria to live on.[58] This hope soon fizzled.

Maria felt, in June 1807—four years after they'd met—that she could never be happy without Frederick.[59] Jane began to have her doubts. She began gently to suggest to Maria that perhaps it was the Almighty's will that Maria and Frederick never marry.[60]

Maria's Frederick problem was tied to Robert's Princess Mary problem. The plan to link the two marriages wasn't advancing. The Porters were desperately trying to get Robert knighted, in order to remove Russian objections to his rank and clear the way to his nuptials. Maria feared Robert would think her wickedly selfish for continuing to make her own marriage her principal aim, rather than trying to work for his happiness alone.[61]

Grand historical events also got in the way of a double wedding. In the summer of 1807, Robert was forced out of Russia when Tsar Alexander changed political allegiances, allying the country with Napoleonic France in the Treaty of Tilsit.[62] The Russians, having thrown over Britain and Sweden as allies, made Robert an enemy of the state in one stroke. He hurriedly left Russia for Sweden, without his princess fiancée, and tried to plot his next move.

Robert spent months there, working on his book *Travelling Sketches in Russia and Sweden During the Years 1805, 1806, 1807, 1808.* He was knighted by the King of Sweden, just as Sir Sidney Smith had been before him. Then Robert was knighted by the Order of Saint Joachim in Württemberg, a somewhat more acceptable self-styled European knighthood, previously awarded to Lord Nelson. He could call himself "Sir Robert Ker Porter."[63] But foreign knighthoods were often derided in Britain, seen as the sham or lesser version of the real thing. What Robert wanted were legitimate British honors. Even with a "real" knighthood, he might not be able to secure the permission of Tsar Alexander to marry Princess Mary, at least while Britain and Russia were at war. Circumstances and connections led him from Sweden, briefly back to England, and then to Spain, where he planned to fight, write, and draw, while hoping for victory and peace with France.

Eventually, likely through military circles—and certainly through his sisters' machinations—Captain Robert Ker Porter and Lieutenant-Colonel Frederick Cowell were introduced to each other. They apparently liked each other. There was still a hope that the Porter family's two fairy-tale marriages might come off. It would take until September 1808 for Mrs. Porter and Jane to properly meet Frederick. When he came to call on them at Ditton cottage, he was with Robert, and Maria was away from home. To their amazement, Frederick's hair was almost completely gray. Both men were said to be brown toned—no doubt from marching in the sun—although Frederick wasn't so thin as Robert.[64] Jane declared herself "much, very much delighted with him & only regret that I could not see more of him." Mrs. Porter liked him, too, and had a long conversation with him. She sent Maria a kiss through him.[65] Mrs. Porter had previously considered Lieutenant Cowell a rash and selfish young man.[66] But, having met him in person, she declared he seemed different from other men—tender and amiable.[67]

During this period, Robert made attempts to bring about his sister's and Frederick's happiness, as he strove to make his own way back to Russia and Princess Mary. He promised that as soon as he was married, he and his new wife would settle some money on Frederick, to allow him to marry Maria. This pledge, Jane pronounced, should allow Maria to consider herself absolutely engaged to Frederick.

"I hope that all this will so calm both your minds," Jane wrote, "that you will not have any more distractions."[68]

But Britain's attempts at peace with Napoleonic France, and therefore the reunion of Robert and Princess Mary, were continually scotched. Robert couldn't return to Russia while it was at war with Britain. Princess Mary might lose her fortune if she moved to England. The abysmal exchange rate of rubles to pounds, combined with the fact her property might be confiscated if she left Russia, meant she couldn't fly off without sinking terribly in standard of living.

Mrs. Porter wrote to Jane that Maria's golden dreams had vanished and that she was taking it very hard.[69] By the following spring, May of 1809, Jane was writing letters to Maria, offering suggestions that would help her sister find a way out of this long engagement to Frederick. Maria was by then staying at an estate in the lap of luxury, as a female companion to Robert's still-fond patron the Margravine of Anspach. It was just the sort of place Maria might no longer be socially received, if she were merely Mrs. Frederick Cowell.

While Maria struggled with how to proceed, it was Jane who forcefully shifted her tone. She became painfully direct with her sister about Frederick, describing their love as at an end.

"You need never blame yourself for the love you once bore him," Jane wrote, "but certainly from all he has for this long time been doing, he demonstrates that his once great love for you has now subsided." She then took out another rhetorical weapon—perhaps a fatal one. Jane, whose opinion Maria held so dear, told her sister that Frederick wasn't good enough for her.

"In fact, my dear Maria, your character has been too weighty for his," she wrote. "Your sensibilities are of a more tender kind; and your mind being endowed so far beyond most men's, no wonder that under the circumstances he has been in, with his peculiar character he should shrink from what he might suppose would over-power him."[70]

Jane wrote her opinion that Frederick had been cold and unkind in his recent visits. His letters were becoming few and unequivocally indifferent. Jane told her sister she now believed that the two of them would be joyless together.

"You know another yielding would only be the sealing of your days to wretchedness. I entreat that you will be firm," Jane admonished her, in advising her sister to break it off.[71]

Jane also gave Maria language to copy out for use in a letter to Frederick to set him free. If these words were used, then it was Jane who penned the conclusion to Maria's love story with the sighing soldier. Maria apparently didn't keep a copy of that letter. and little of Frederick's writing has survived.[72] From that point forward, almost all references to Frederick disappear from the sisters' correspondence.

One exception is a cryptic comment from Jane to Mrs. Porter in 1812. She wrote to her mother from London: "I shall attend to Mr. Cowell, when I have the pleasure of seeing him; which will indeed give me pleasure to shew him that we always consider him as a friend.—But I think we had best not invite him to Ditton. I think dear Maria's spirits could not bear it."[73]

Frederick Luke Gardiner Cowell married Isabella Johnston on September 8, 1811, in Downpatrick, County Down, Ireland. He died on December 7, 1815, leaving his widow and their only daughter, Frederica, to eke out a living on a modest army widow's pension. He was twenty-nine years old.

CHAPTER 13

He Must Be Closed Up

The End of Jane's Henry (1807–9)

During the five-year period Maria was focused on a future with Frederick, Jane was not only helping forward her sister's secret courtship and editing her family's manuscripts into publishable books. She was also facing her own longstanding emotional conflicts, managing Henry Caulfield's messes, and trying to put herself back in the path of elusive Sir Sidney Smith. As Jane ricocheted between Henry and Smith, from 1807 to 1809, she began a brilliant new book.

Where Sir Sidney Smith was concerned, Jane and Maria held out hope that he might yet choose Jane for a wife when he was ready to tie the knot. His movements, dictated by war, could be loosely tracked, because they were often reported in the newspapers. His whereabouts, however, might change at a moment's notice. Undeterred by that unpredictability, Jane took matters into her own hands.

In attempting to get closer to Smith, Jane could have gone in several directions. Smith had rivals and enemies everywhere, but he was also very highly placed among the hangers-on of the British royal family. It was Smith, after all, who'd brought the Princess of Wales and the Duke of Gloucester into the Porters' home. But the Porters were also making their own further inroads to cordial relations with royalty in Britain and abroad.

The closest the sisters had gotten to intimacy with the British royal family so far was through Maria. It had happened three years before, after a night at the Richmond theater, which Maria had attended with military and theatrical friends. Thanks to her friends, she had been swept into the royal carriage and invited as an overnight guest at Bushy Park, the estate of the Duke of Clarence. He'd later become King William IV, but when Maria met him, the royal line seemed destined to bend away from, not toward, this younger brother of the Prince of Wales. That night at Bushy Park, His Royal Highness had taken a special interest in Maria, among his other visitors. On arrival, she'd been led into a magnificent salon, where she was introduced to his lover, Mrs. Dora Jordan, the actress Maria so admired. Maria was even seated next to Mrs. Jordan at dinner.

Although she'd expected an entertaining evening, Maria discovered the gathering to be solemn, formal, and cold. It wasn't the Duke of Clarence's fault. Everyone had responded to his questions so mechanically, as if they were clocks he was striking. Maria thought they gave him lifeless answers straight out of a geography textbook, afraid to hazard a remark, lest it be construed as high treason. She must have tried not to behave too stiffly, because the cordial Duke singled her out for special attention. He drank two glasses of wine with her, and she'd felt the honor of it with pleasure.

Then, after everyone had gone to bed, His Royal Highness did Maria another "honor." He came to visit her in her bedchamber. He asked her if she felt comfortable. Then he wondered if her candle had been put out.[1] In telling this story later to Jane, Maria seemed to take the polite Duke's solicitous nocturnal bedroom visit to her at face value. Jane, for her part, mentioned only how lucky Maria was to have had this sort of experience, because "Such spectacles . . . are useful for us as scribblers.[2]

As a result of these brushes with royalty, nobility, and other powerful people, Jane may well have hoped that eventually she or Maria would be invited to some gathering where Smith would also be a guest. The Porter sisters' close friendship with Mrs. Boscawen at St. James's Palace might have prompted an invitation that put them and Smith in the same room, for instance. Jane was becoming a sought-after personage in her own right. Sales of *Thaddeus of Warsaw* soared, as did critical acclaim. By 1806, her novel reached its fourth edition, moving her into a stratospherically successful literary category, alongside the likes of best-selling novelists Frances Burney and Ann Radcliffe.

Among the literati Jane's reputation had also risen. She'd gained some credibility among the novel-wary elite with the *Aphorisms of Sir Philip Sidney*, which had been positively reviewed. It was deemed a work of good sense, pure morality, and amiable piety by the prestigious *Monthly Review*.[3] Friends wrote to Jane to praise *Aphorisms*. Even the persnickety Lady de Crespigny (recently elevated in title when her husband become a baronet) was impressed to find that Jane could discriminate so properly on morality and science at her age. She wondered at what Jane might become in twenty years![4]

None of her friends were more filled with praise for the *Aphorisms* book than dear Elizabeth Benger. The tall, thin writer had by then transformed herself into a turban-wearing London salon impresario, who was sometimes mistaken for a fortune teller.[5] Benger had declared she fell in love with Sir Philip Sidney after reading *Aphorisms*.

"Wicked one that you are," Benger wrote to Jane, "you have excited in me a longing desire to cultivate the acquaintance and I am already willing to make a pilgrimage to his tomb—I love him much—and I love him more for reflecting that I owe my introduction to you."

According to Benger, Jane not only admired heroes but also created them. Among women writers, she said, Jane was remarkable in being able to bestow upon her male characters an impressive valor and virtue.[6] Jane had what Virginia Woolf would later call in *A Room of One's Own*, "the magic and delicious power of reflecting the figure of man back at twice his natural size."[7] Woolf rightly pointed out how this talent might keep women in an inferior station, but in Jane's era, such an ability was prized. Jane activated her literary powers to capture worthy historical men's supposed perfections, in a nation desperate for heroic role models during wartime. Benger, more deeply and directly engaged in progressive political causes than Jane, appreciated Jane's labors.

Benger also prided herself on hosting the famous and making significant introductions. Her London salon made dozens, if not hundreds, of connections possible for the Porter sisters during this period, so it's fitting that it would be Benger and her close friend Sarah "Sally" Wesley who allowed Jane and Maria to insert themselves back into Sir Sidney Smith's life. Miss Wesley knew Smith's widowed aunt, Mrs. Delamain. Someone had learned that Mrs. Delamain was a fan of *Thaddeus of Warsaw*, dedicated to her beloved nephew. It led to a correspondence between her and Jane.

"The door seems now to be opening, which is again to lead us on to intimacy with that love-creating Hero," Maria wrote to Jane, "and we must not stand at the threshold, bowing and hesitating like country bumpkins till it is fairly clapp'd to, on us."[8]

Jane actively pursued the friendship. Mrs. Delamain invited Jane to stay with her in Dover, the port town on England's southern coast, just across the English Channel from Calais, France. Arrangements unfolded quickly in the spring of 1807. Hopes were very high for this new friendship, not only because it might throw Jane in Smith's path again but also because it could benefit the Porter brothers, too. Mrs. Delamain might help forward their military advancement. So the family took on an unanticipated travel expense and sent Jane to Dover.

Dover's population was small, at just seven thousand, but it was an important city, where at least four hundred soldiers and sailors were stationed.[9] It was so close to France that it had long held strategic importance. Dover also had literary significance, through Shakespeare's *King Lear*, and historical interest because of its medieval castle. Jane would stay with Mrs. Delamain at the Smiths' property, nicknamed the Caves, located just beneath the famed white Dover cliffs, near Bunkers' Bridge and the beach.

Mrs. Elizabeth Smith Delamain, then in her late seventies, was the widowed female scion of the famous Smith family. The Smiths were well known for having produced several generations of successful military men, who—without the advantages of inherited wealth or title—gained significant political power. Mrs. Delamain had been married for fifty years to her late husband, the barrister Thomas Delamain, who'd been an abominable husband. He'd beaten and abandoned his wife, before leaving her penniless. Somehow, Mrs. Delamain had survived into old age. It was said she'd done so without depressed spirits.[10] She shared a home with her brother, the widower Captain John Smith, Sir Sidney Smith's well-connected father.

While staying in their beautifully situated home at the Caves, Jane had a view from its windows of the troops doing exercises each morning. Unfortunately, Sir Sidney Smith wasn't among them. Jane was disappointed to learn that she'd see the hero at the Caves just once during her intended stay. That discovery upset Maria.

"Put some little force into your delicate reservedness, for my sake, if not for your own," Maria wrote, "and let no excessive timidity appear, to frighten Sir Sidney from pressing your company with him."[11]

Despite Maria's encouragement, Jane didn't win Smith's heart during that visit. She did, however, win his aunt's. At their emotional goodbye, Jane felt she was treated by the old woman as if she'd been her own departing child.

"This dear woman loves me in a way I cannot describe," Jane told Maria, "I feel that I am rooted in her affections for ever."[12] Jane could now count herself an intimate friend among the illustrious Smith family. Maria wrote back, "The world contains numberless rare creatures, and we know many of them."[13]

After Jane left Dover, Mrs. Delamain extended an invitation to Maria to join her at the Caves. The sisters couldn't both visit at once. Mrs. Porter, in her early sixties and nervous about being left alone, increasingly required a domestic companion at the cottage. Maria went to Dover. Once again, the travel costs stretched the Porters financially. But Maria was determined to ask and say things about Smith's inclinations and intentions to Mrs. Delamain that Jane felt she couldn't. Then, too, perhaps Maria could observe and speak to Sir Sidney Smith himself while she was there, surreptitiously advancing her sister's marital prospects. Unfortunately, Maria's visit to Mrs. Delamain would prove poorly timed.

"I am very, very impatient to see him again," Maria wrote.[14] Her impatience served no purpose. Maria gained only secondhand information about Smith and his love life.

"I have learned so much of him from dear Mrs. Del, as to be able to assure you, that if he never thinks of the person I wish him to think of, he is not at all likely to dispose of himself to any woman he now knows," Maria wrote to Jane. "Both Miss Cook's attachment and Lady Cosby's were unsolicited, and unreturned by him—and it is not very long ago, since he refused the hand of a Countess."[15]

These rumored rejections only raised the war hero in their estimation, but the information came at an unfortunately large cost. Staying at the homes of others had usually proved a way for the Porter sisters to economize. But Maria's stay at the Caves, instead of being cheap, was proving very expensive. She wrote to Jane and begged for a contrived reason to come home. In a short time, Maria had spent the extravagant sum of ten pounds—on clothing, hairdressing, transportation, tea, gratuities, and the other things necessary for balls. She felt she couldn't afford to be invited to even one more ball there, but as their houseguest, she couldn't say no without being rude. To feign illness would only have roused other kinds of activity and expense. As soon as she could, Maria found a way to return home.

Despite this second round of failure at Dover, Jane and Maria hadn't yet given up the chase for Smith. They may have been inspired to push forward more assiduously when their friend Miss Sally Wesley reported that she'd recently spent time with him. One report had it that Miss Wesley was claiming Smith was in love with *her*, although she professed that she didn't return his feelings.

"I laughed outrageously when this story was first told me," Maria wrote to Jane, declaring that Miss Wesley had dwindled in her eyes enough to become ridiculous.[16] But these reports about Miss Wesley's encounters were emboldening. If Smith were in a frame of mind for courting, then they needed to set Jane in his path again as fast as they could.

In late July 1807, Jane maneuvered her way to London, and she managed to arrange a visit with Smith himself, at the home of her friend Mrs. MacLaurin, with whom she was staying. Smith told Jane he'd come to see her and her hostess at four P.M. The visit came and went too quickly. When Jane wrote home about it, she begged her mother not to tell anyone the details.

"His frame is a little more etheralized—but his face is, as it was wont to be, 'magnificent.' Rich in the treasures of Honour, Virtue, & Benevolence," Jane wrote of Smith. From there, however, her account became mechanical, even melancholy.

"I think him a very pleasing man," she wrote. "He said a great many civil things of Robert, & hoped our acquaintance, tho' begun on business, would continue in sociability."[17]

It had been a short, disappointing encounter. But the sisters didn't give up. Finally, in the fall of 1807, Jane got her long-sought tête-à-tête with Smith. She had taken up temporary residence at St. James's Palace with Mrs. Boscawen. There in London, she reconnected with dear Mrs. Delamain and accepted her invitation for a day visit to one of the country's most prominent banking families, the Goldsmids. When the parlor door flew open at the banker's home, Jane saw the great Smith stride in, along with young Mr. Goldsmid.

"Sir S was indeed very 'cordial' to me," Jane reported to Maria afterward. "There was nothing 'stranger-like' in his manner—the moment he came in, he took me by the hand, and said many kind things . . . and then turning to Mr. G. said something very gratifying about myself—but would you believe me, I cannot distinctly repeat what it was."

Jane, nervous and rattled, thanked Smith for the troubles she'd given him of late. She'd previously written to ask him to do military favors for several men of her acquaintance. Smith, who would have received letters of this sort constantly, told Jane that he was always happy to obey her commands. Jane found she had his full attention, but Smith's words were a blur. Her memory was indistinct. She remembered that he mentioned her intimately, by her Christian name.

Then he said to her, "Am I right? It is Jane, is it not?" And, of course, she said yes.

She was sitting next to young Mr. Goldsmid, with Smith on the other side of him. Everything the hero had said to Jane was spoken across that unfortunately located young man. The conversation was unremarkable, but it was pointed. Smith spoke no more than five words to anyone else in the room but Jane. She felt noticed.

At the end of the visit, Mrs. Delamain suggested her hero-nephew ought to drive Jane home to Ditton with him, when he went that direction. That would have been quite an opportunity, to have time alone together in the carriage, as well as to have Smith visit her sister and mother. But Jane didn't think Smith's response to this suggestion left much hope it would happen. The conversation was over in twenty minutes.

Afterward, Jane wrote to Maria, she felt that this star was far, far out of her reach. She thanked heaven for introducing her to the gates of paradise that day—for seating her so near to him—which was more than she ever could have expected. Jane told Maria she just wanted Smith to respect her more than most of her sex. She wanted his real esteem. That would quite satisfy her, she said.

"Not presuming to hope for more, I do not desire it," Jane wrote, resignedly. She told Maria she must teach herself to contemplate Smith's probable marriage—to someone else—with ease.[18] When Jane next saw Smith, a week later, he told her he was about to begin a secret expedition for the government.

He apologized for not being able to drive her to Ditton, as his aunt had suggested. He delivered his goodbyes to the three women in the room, Jane, Mrs. Delamain, and his sister, Miss Philippa Smith.

"He quite treats me like one of his family," Jane said, "and called me 'my cousin!' "[19]

As Jane came to accept the reality that she would not really be joining the Smith family, her own family was becoming a greater burden. All three Porter brothers, but especially John and Robert, were taking up a great deal of her energy. Over the years, Jane had, of necessity, learned how to negotiate and bargain, mostly with male publishers. Her skills had been tested beyond that realm, too, especially during the previous summer of 1806. With Robert gone in Russia, evading his creditors and possible arrest, Jane had tried to keep him and John from ruin. She negotiated on their behalf, in secret, during protracted trips to London.

"John does not like that I should leave the business until it is finally settled," Jane told their mother, explaining her delay in returning home. "He looks upon my voice as decisive, in the whole, & to prevent any mismanagement" between the creditors.

Jane had stayed with their attorney friend, Christopher Chrisop, while they negotiated with John's creditors. Jane asked Chrisop to bargain for repaying a portion of his total debt, offering three hundred, then four hundred, then five hundred pounds, but no more, in return for securing an agreement to give John eighteen months of freedom from arrest. She worked to bring John himself in to talk to attorneys, partners, and creditors, securing his ability to do so without threat of arrest or harm.[20] At the same time, Jane had requested from Chrisop a secret and complete accounting of absent brother Robert's debts. When her bold request produced an estimate of a thousand pounds, Jane faced it head on.

"Our present intention," she wrote home, "is to propose dividing 6 or 700 pounds amongst all" of the creditors—so getting them to agree to a payment of 10 shillings or so on the pound—and then also getting their "written promise, not to molest either of my Brothers for the rest, during a term of eighteen months, or two years," from June 1806 to 1808.

This was remarkable work for a woman. Her celebrity and good reputation certainly helped these creditors take her seriously, but she had handled it shrewdly. She got the terms she sought. The creditors, with the promise of getting paid half of what they were owed, agreed not to try to have Robert or John arrested and put in debtors' prison. It was tricky, because their debts were owed to a range of friends, individuals, and bankers, and in John's case, apparently also the government.

Among his debts to several bankers, Robert owed a small sum of money—twenty-six pounds—to Austen and Maunde, the bank of Henry Austen, the brother of then-unknown and unpublished novelist Jane Austen.[21] Henry Austen's bank would fail a decade later, thanks to bad credit it had extended, well beyond the small amount advanced to Robert. Debts of tens of thousands of pounds brought down banks. That's another reason Robert's and John's creditors would have agreed to Jane's bargain. To get a little something, with the promise of more, was better than having a debtor arrested and getting nothing.

Jane's brokering of this agreement meant Robert could safely return to England from Russia, and John could stop wandering the country to evade the authorities. Both brothers could enter into unfettered new efforts to earn and make repayments until summer 1808. Their debts had been a combination of bad luck and their own foolish doing, but Jane was the liberating hero who masterfully brokered their freedom.

With a reprieve for her brothers secured, Jane also sought legal advice on pursuing action against the publisher of *The Sentinel*, the sisters' defunct magazine. Mr. Dale had never paid the promised twenty-five pounds for the six published issues or what he owed to Robert for illustrations. The lawyer Jane consulted wasn't encouraging.

"A counsellor says, that my suit against Dale & Co. won't friz!—so that's gone," she wrote home.[22]

Jane was mastering how to negotiate financial affairs, but it was proving far more challenging to manage her interests in matrimony. By the end of 1807, although she maintained genuine friendships with the Smith family, Jane was cutting her emotional losses. She was attempting to detach herself from her long-held fantasies of becoming Lady Smith. By 1808, she found herself once again throwing herself into Henry Caulfield's messes.

Over the previous two years, Jane had seen Henry irregularly. He'd remained an outcast, incarcerated for his large crim. con. debt to his lover's husband. Henry still lived in the King's Bench Rules, in rented lodgings at 15 Melina

Place, next door to a mental asylum. Jane apparently visited him surreptitiously.[23] She certainly knew exactly where he lived.

During this period, Jane sometimes stayed in London with her dear friend and mentor the Quaker doctor and progressive activist John Coakley Lettsom. From Jane's guest room window in Lettsom's nearby home, she could just make out Henry's house on Melina Place. She watched it from her window, but on one particular occasion, staying with Lettsom, she denied herself the pleasure of Henry's company.

"Am I not a heroine, to abstain so long?" Jane wrote home. "I shall say adieu to him, before I quit London."[24]

Henry had continued to correspond with Jane under false names, echoing pseudonyms for *The Quiz*.[25] Jane angled for Henry to break off with Mrs. Chambers, which he repeatedly promised to do. He continued to be tormented by Captain Chambers. Chambers, if he really wanted the court judgment paid, might have allowed Henry out of prison to try to make a living as an actor. That he didn't do so suggests money was not his only object. Nor did Chambers pursue a divorce from his wife. His plan seems to have been to keep Henry locked up perpetually, with his estranged wife legally under his control and unable to remarry.

Captain Chambers didn't stop there. His tactics became even more aggressive. He once sent his attorney to Melina Place to demand a sight of Henry in the King's Bench Rules. This was legally allowable. Henry, in being granted official permission to live in a dwelling near the prison, was required to remain within the strict boundaries of the Rules. If his appearance was demanded, then he was obliged to appear within a small window of time. When Chambers's attorney demanded the prisoner's presence, Henry didn't show up. The attorney then tried again another day with the same results. So Chambers filed another lawsuit, this time against the prison's marshal, alleging that the marshal was liable for Henry's unlawful absence from the Rules.

That lawsuit was in process when Henry became ill. Henry's sister Jessie and her husband, Frederick Campbell, were Henry's closest family allies during those dark years. Compassionate, loving Jessie secretly removed Henry from Melina Place in July 1808. She brought him to a more salubrious spot fifteen miles away to nurse him back to health.[26] The Campbells rented a house at Hampton Court, just across the Thames from Ditton Cottage and the Porters.

At the Campbells' invitation, Jane secretly went across the river to stay with them, hoping to help revive Henry.[27]

Jane's leaving Ditton Cottage for this purpose meant that her labors on Robert's next book, *Travelling Sketches in Russia and Sweden*, came to a temporary halt. Her work stoppage would delay the promised five-hundred-pound payment Robert would get from the publisher. Jane and Maria had also recently each made a separate bargain with Longman and Rees to deliver two as-yet-unwritten four-volume novels in one year. For their labors, Jane would receive three hundred pounds and Maria two hundred, an increase in pay over their previous arrangements. There was a further—and unusual—agreement this time. Longman and Rees had immediately advanced the sisters two hundred pounds as a loan.[28] The Longmans must have recognized the Porter family was in dire financial straits. Advancing such a sum, and requiring them to pay interest, was one way to make sure the sisters could (and with the loan, must) keep writing.

Although Robert had directed his sisters to hold on to the money for their own living expenses, Jane and Maria used much of their two-hundred-pound loan to cover their brother's most pressing bank debts.[29] They thought they'd kept back just enough money to survive until they'd finished their novels. But Jane hadn't counted on setting aside her writing obligations to care for the sick Henry Caulfield. Although the 1808 deadline Jane had negotiated with Robert's creditors was looming, and the money from Robert's book and the sisters' novels much needed, she put down her pen.

Henry's convalescence in Hampton Court must be kept secret, Jane warned her family. Previously, when he'd left the confines of the Rules, it was perhaps done through an under-the-table bargain with prison officials. This time, his absence—especially because he was under close watch by Chambers's attorney—was surely unsanctioned.

At the first sight of her beloved friend in his sickbed, Jane found Henry's looks inexpressibly altered. He was no longer the man whose face resembled Shakespeare's, with an animated, open, inspired air.[30] The Campbells feared he was suffering from consumption, or tuberculosis. Their excellent friend and physician Dr. Blackburne—who'd inspired a character in Jane's *Thaddeus of Warsaw*—personally came to examine and treat Henry.[31] Dr. Blackburne diagnosed him with an abscessed lung.

For a time, Henry's condition seemed to improve.[32] Then it deteriorated. Doctors didn't know yet that lung abscesses arose from bacterial infections, although surgical interventions were understood to be dangerous. The commonly prescribed treatment was fresh air and rest. As fluid built up in the patient's lungs, he was encouraged to sit up, for better drainage and sleep. But once the patient's coughing and chronic thirst became severe, outcomes were usually fatal.

When Henry's condition worsened, Jessie and Jane were approached by a third woman who asked to join them at his bedside: Mrs. Chambers. Jessie and Jane agreed that Henry's lover could come to him. This was the woman Jane felt had ruined his life, and it would have been difficult to nurse Henry alongside her, but Jane felt they must.

"This was not a time, dear Maria, when we all feared the hand of death was upon him, for any of us to say, you shall not come near! Or, I will not associate with you!" As they nursed Henry together, Jane found herself surprised by Mrs. Chambers's care and sympathized with her plight. Jane wrote, "I pity her from my soul—and see that she fancies the deep injuries she has sustained, must prevent her from being mingled with the fallen of her sex."[33]

For some days, as they nursed him, Henry retained his ability to speak. Jane was the last one with him before he lost consciousness. Then she stayed beside him until he took his final breath.

"I was the last object, the eyes of my Henry looked upon," she told Maria, "and even when life was fled, they still were fixed on me, till I closed them, with my hand."[34]

In his dying days in Hampton Court, Henry had been surrounded by the women who loved him most—his sister, his lover, and Jane, who was neither and both. Unfortunately, Henry died in the wrong place. He was supposed to be in prison. They tried to pretend he had been. The Campbells surreptitiously returned Henry's corpse to Melina Place in a light coffin, probably under the cover of night. They deceived the coroner, or possibly paid him off, to get him to attest that Henry had died within the Rules of the King's Bench. When Jessie went to Henry's lodgings to quell rumors and take care of her brother's effects, Jane returned to Ditton Cottage to grieve. She believed in the value of shedding tears in sorrow, rather than suppressing them.[35]

Although it should have been a time for all who loved him to mourn Henry Caulfield unmolested, Chambers kept up the legal pressure. He started a rumor that Henry hadn't died a natural death. If the death were thought a suicide, then that perceived sin ("self-murder," it was called) could prevent him from being buried on consecrated ground. Any scrutiny of the circumstances of Henry's death would have been unwelcome.

"We were therefore particularly anxious to have the Funeral as soon + as private as possible," Frederick Campbell wrote to Jane.

Henry's sister Jessie, despite her fragile state, found herself criticized by two of her own siblings, the unstable, mercurial Kitty Caulfield—the sister who'd so long ago been in love with Robert—and her brother, Captain James Caulfield. Frederick Campbell desperately wanted Jane to be there with them in London as they readied for Henry's funeral. It was customary for a family's women to help prepare a body for burial, and to spend time with the corpse in their home, although far less common for them to attend a funeral. Frederick offered to have his chaise sent to Ditton Cottage to carry Jane to town so she could have a last viewing of Henry's body and support poor, despondent Jessie.

"I wish you were also her sister," Frederick confessed to Jane, in a line that carried so much weight and many layers of meaning.

The Campbells were planning to hold the funeral that night.

"Keep the chaise till you are ready," Frederick wrote, "it being sent only for you."[36]

But Jane couldn't bring herself to get in. She sent word that she was indisposed.

The closing up of Henry's coffin went on without Jane. It proved a messy ordeal. There'd been a small hole in the inner coffin, which held water, and gave off a disagreeable smell. The hole had to be repaired. To help with the smell, and in Henry's honor, they'd strewn his dead body with flowers. Then the body had been put into a larger, outer coffin. The final viewing of his corpse had been dreadful.

Henry Edwin Allen Caulfield was laid to rest on September 17, 1808, at the magnificent St. James's Church in Piccadilly. A decade earlier, his brother Wade had been buried far away from his family, but Henry (his angry father now dead) would be interred in the Caulfield family vault. Sometime later, a modest memorial was erected in the south vestibule of the church. It read, HENRY E. A. CAULFEILD, LATE LIEUTENANT AND CAPTAIN IN THE 1ST REGIMENT OF GUARDS, 8 SEPT. 1808. He was twenty-nine years old.

Even after his death, Henry's name continued to appear in the scandal pages. Captain Chambers sued the prison marshal for two thousand pounds, arguing that since the marshal had allowed Henry to escape and die outside of the Rules, the prison should be responsible for his unpaid debt. The marshal denied the charge. But compelling testimony showed Henry had died with Mrs. Chambers at Hampton Court. Luckily for Jane, this report kept her name out of the newspapers. Captain Chambers won his case. Henry's unpaid crim. con. debt was charged to the King's Bench Prison's marshal in December 1808.[37]

Henry's name appeared in the newspapers once again a year later, when Captain Chambers finally sued his wife for divorce. He presented three dozen articles of her alleged acts of adultery committed with the late Henry Caulfield. In response, Mrs. Chambers's lawyers charged Chambers with cruelty. It was the only basis for a wife to sue her husband for divorce. In addition to the story of his threatening her with pistols, new allegations were added.[38] Mrs. Chambers said her husband had committed adultery with the family's female servants. She also said her husband committed incest with her sister, Miss Rodney, under the family roof while she was at home.[39]

The court sided with the husband. In January 1810, the judge found Captain Chambers had proved adultery against his wife but that she'd proved nothing against him. His divorce was granted. He no longer needed to honor their separation agreement or pay her maintenance. Two centuries later, the *Chambers v. Chambers* divorce case is still cited in legal textbooks for its odd complexities.[40]

When Jessie Caulfield Campbell died in 1812—of grief for her brother Henry, it was said—her husband, Frederick, disinterred Henry's coffin and brought it to Staines Church. Frederick made the unusual decision to leave both his wife and his brother-in-law's corpses next to each other, unburied in the church. The peculiar sight caused a stir, these two unburied coffins, covered in crimson velvet, placed on trestles, said to be visited daily by the lady's widower.[41] The anecdote of this unusual monument was repeated in local histories across the nineteenth century, with some disgust. It was declared that above-ground human remains were a repellent spectacle, without any useful moral lesson.[42]

Jane's personal relics of Henry were literary, not macabre. She asked to borrow her friend the poet Thomas Campbell's copy of her own book, *Aphorisms of Sir Philip Sidney*, because Campbell's copy had Henry's marginal markings.

She planned to render each mark into her own copy, to keep a small trace of Henry's voice.[43] Jane also painstakingly reproduced by hand Henry's commonplace book, a fifty-page collection of epigrams, quotations, and short anecdotes. He began it in 1804, just after he and Jane shared adventures in Bath while rumors of their engagement flew. Jane ended her transcription of his words with her own original poem to Henry. The poem's speaker describes how she still believes she's hearing his unforgettable voice, and how, with his death, her own soul's bright genius had fled.[44]

But this was not at all the case. In 1808, after Henry passed away, Jane's writerly genius became fully reactivated. She returned to the novel she'd promised to Longman and Rees. It centered on a beautiful Christian war hero. In it, the hero fought valiantly, was tempted by married women, refused their advances, and became imprisoned. This hero was based on the real-life late thirteenth-century Scottish warrior William Wallace. After losing his wife to murder early in the novel, he ends up dying with a strong, modest heroine at his side.

That Jane-like heroine, Lady Helen Mar, sacrifices everything for Wallace, except her virtue. At the novel's end, as the imprisoned Wallace's enemies are preparing to execute him on a scaffold, he's dying a natural death. One of his last acts is to take the faithful, virtuous Helen as his everlasting "virgin bride," in an unconsummated marriage of two loving souls.[45] They share their first and only kiss on his would-be deathbed, but Wallace isn't allowed to die in his cell. When he's taken to the scaffold for execution, he dies there before he can be hanged, in his chaste wife's arms.

Jane carried her memories of Henry Caulfield across her life and always deeply mourned him. She'd come to describe him as having died of a distempered mind and a broken heart.[46] Eventually, remembering him no longer brought her distress. "This Beauty of his is imperishable," she later wrote to Maria, "and is ever before my eyes, and so in my heart, that it makes me smile when others weep."[47] Jane made sure Henry's beauty didn't perish. She secretly preserved it, in the pages of her books.

CHAPTER 14

Champagne, Orange Juice, and the Margravine

Maria's Year of Luxury and Love (1809)

During the year that Maria's relationship with Frederick Cowell was irretrievably breaking down, and as she and grieving Jane worked furiously on new novels to repay the loan from their publisher, Robert finally came home. His return to England, early in 1809, had been harrowing. He was supposed to have come back to help Jane finish and publish his Russian travel book, but he'd decided at the spur of the moment to accompany British forces fighting Napoleon in Portugal and Spain. There he planned to write another travel narrative and draw landscapes. Instead, he was drawn into bloody battle.

Robert experienced war in the very place that Maria was setting her next novel. Longman and Rees were pressing her to finish it quickly because Britain's eyes were fixated on that part of the globe. Her historical novel-in-progress, *Don Sebastian*, took place in sixteenth-century Portugal. Robert had actually gone into the war zone there, using some of Maria's generously shared advance money for her next novel to cover his expenses. That's how he wound up on the fringes of the Battle of Corunna, on January 16, 1809.

Many died in that disastrous conflict. Lieutenant-General Sir John Moore and thousands of others—along with most of the horses and mules—were sacrificed before the British forces could make their delayed escape by ship. Robert, who'd had his horse shot out from under him, went five days without food.[1] He'd lost his belongings but emerged unscathed.[2] He grieved the loss of General Moore, who'd been his friend since their recent meeting in Sweden.

General Moore did much in his career that deserves to be harshly judged. He specialized in putting down righteous rebellions—by American colonists, enslaved people in the West Indies, and colonized Irish. But Moore had also amassed a domestic militia to protect Britain from French invasion. Among many Britons, news of his death produced a national shock and collective grieving. The Porter women were among those who mourned him. They were gratefully stunned when Robert returned home looking so well that his mother thought no one would believe he'd been in combat.[3]

It was fortunate Robert looked well. He had business to carry out, currying favor with powerful men and secretly managing his creditors. Because Jane had previously negotiated his freedom from arrest for debt only into the year 1808, his old debts were past due. With his book *Travelling Sketches in Russia and Sweden* set to appear in early 1809, and with payments promised to arrive in increments thereafter, his creditors might be mollified. To earn more needed money after that, they'd have to rely on Jane's and Maria's next novels, as well as on Robert's planned next book on General Moore and British military skirmishes in Spain and Portugal. Jane promised once again to reshape Robert's notes into a book and postponed the completion of her novel about William Wallace. This time, they decided to publish Robert's book anonymously, for fear of angering Princess Mary's Russian friends who sided with Napoleon.

Robert was welcomed back to Ditton Cottage as if he were a war hero rather than a fortunately safe observer of war. His family's friends and acquaintances in Surrey, having heard about Robert for years, were eager to lay eyes on him. There were constant visitors at the cottage, which made Mrs. Porter joke that they should hire a servant to turn people away at the gate whenever Robert was around. Providing refreshments for visitors was expensive, and, as Mrs. Porter bluntly put it to Jane, "We are poor."[4] Robert informed his mother and sisters that he planned to change careers, much to their surprise and dismay. He wanted to remake himself into a statesman to please his fiancée, and apparently the Russian Imperial Family, who thought an artist was an inappropriately low profession for the husband of one of its princesses. Robert, who needed a British title to make himself marriageable, was trying to get an audience with the Prince of Wales to advance his case.

He couldn't rely on that avenue alone. Robert was also ingratiating himself with the Margravine of Anspach, his rumored paramour and self-declared mother figure thirty years his senior. The Margravine wouldn't have been able to helpe Robert much with titles because she wasn't on good terms with the British royal family, although they were cousins. She could, however, do Robert other kinds of favors. She invited him to stay at Brandenburgh House, her lavish seventeenth-century residence on the Thames River in Hammersmith, just west of London. Robert wanted to remain in the Margravine's good graces. He would have hoped she'd help him navigate his creditors, or perhaps even pay off his debts, as well as work her connections in Europe and Russia for him, but he had other things to do than swan around her estates. He declined her invitation, which led the Margravine to invite his charming sister Maria to come to her instead.

Before that winter of 1809, the eccentric, talented Margravine had shown only a passing interest in her "adopted son" Robert's sisters. But with Robert engaged to Princess Mary, his sisters' prospects would have seemed on the rise. If Robert were to marry royalty and ascend to riches, then his sisters, too, might become sought-after company in high society. The Margravine would have had less prejudice than most against literary women. She was a published author herself, with her travel narrative, *A Journey through the Crimea to Constantinople* (1789), which may well have influenced Robert to try that sort of writing. She'd published *Letters from a Peeress of England to Her Eldest Son* (1784), a book that denounced oppressive husbands and unfair marriage laws, in which her identity was only thinly veiled. She also wrote plays, but it doesn't seem the Margravine had much knowledge of Maria's and Jane's novels.

In February 1809, Maria left home for a visit of several weeks at the Margravine's Brandenburgh House. It was a grand, redbrick neoclassical mansion with a ridiculous number of rooms. One room held nothing but Chinese porcelain. Another was full of musical instruments, all of which, it was said, the Margravine could play. There was a library on the main floor. A separately built theater along the river was attached to the great house by a long corridor that was heated by stoves in winter.[5] The theater was well used, because the Margravine was, in effect, its manager, director, playwright, and star, all in one. Her private theatricals had become legendary. Reports of them ran in the newspapers. She often costarred with her son Keppel Craven, and Robert himself had previously trod the boards there, before her large and enthusiastic invited audiences. The Margravine's social gatherings at Brandenburgh House included as many nobles as she could round up and whichever of her seven grown children she happened to be on speaking terms with. She was a rich woman, with plenty of nieces, nephews, and other willing hangers-on. There would never be a shortage of company around her, if she wanted it.

The Porters had high hopes for Maria's visit. If the Margravine could be persuaded to loan—or, better yet, give—a thousand pounds to Robert, he could satisfy his creditors and remain in England without threat of arrest. He could send for Princess Mary to come to England, bringing some portable fortune, such as jewels. The couple could marry and settle down, perhaps near the Margravine. She might even offer them the use of one of her many properties! The Porters' fantasies ran wild, but they weren't based on nothing. The Margravine had begun to refer to Robert not only as *like* her child but also *as* a child of her own. Maria, too, was being courted as an almost-daughter.

The Margravine's true financial situation was murky. She'd previously claimed she was too cash poor to help Robert out of his difficulties. But, in the years since her first refusal, her wealthy second husband, the Margrave of Anspach, had died, putting the widow in control of a large fortune. The Porters believed that lovely, generous Maria could soften the Margravine's heart to open her purse and solve Robert's difficulties.

Maria quickly became a necessary and accepted fixture at Brandenburgh House. Her planned visit of several weeks became a longer visit—and then a longer one still. She stayed because she hadn't yet gained her point, as the Margravine didn't immediately reveal a concrete plan to help Robert. At least Maria wasn't suffering. The Margravine's way of life involved unbelievable luxury in comparison to the privations Maria was used to at Ditton Cottage. When her stay was extended, she hoped to use her time there to finish her novel during the day and join the Margravine and her revolving door of guests in the evenings.

At first, Maria was able to carve out time to write. But as the months unfolded at Brandenburgh House—and then at the Margravine's country house, Benham House, in Berkshire—Maria found herself enmeshed in a set of clever, selfish rich people whose sophistication and capacity for cruelty and harm were worlds beyond her own. She wasn't sufficiently prepared, least of all for the Margravine herself.

In her youth, the Margravine of Anspach—née Lady Elizabeth Berkeley—had been a beautiful heiress, the third daughter of an earl. At age sixteen, she'd been something between tricked, pushed, and forced to marry the older, boorish William Craven, the Sixth Baron Craven.[6] When they wed, he got her thirty thousand pounds. She got an unhappy marriage that produced seven children. But any sympathy Lady Craven might have won from the world was lost when she and her husband both embarked on a series of affairs.

The marriage broke down, and Lady Craven separated from the earl. He refused to allow her to see her six eldest children but gave her permission to take their youngest son, Richard Keppel Craven, with her when she left England for a self-imposed exile in Continental Europe. Beautiful little Keppel, as the little boy was called, was supposed to be returned to his father at age eight. Instead, his mother educated the exceptionally bright boy herself and gave him the nickname "Elève"—French for pupil.

Lord Craven kept the six older children out of their mother's reach, especially her daughters, who were taught to renounce her. Rifts were only intensified when, on the Continent, she became attached to the Margrave of Brandenburg-Anspach, a married man fifteen years her senior. He separated from his spouse to travel and live with Lady Craven. He unpersuasively claimed to the world that she was his adopted sister.

In 1791, the Margrave's wife died. On the heels of that, Lord Craven died, too. Lady Craven married the Margrave. That these two deaths and the remarriage happened within the space of eight months only added to the scandal, since the conventional period of grieving was a year. The newly married couple made no pretense of mourning and, of course, stopped referring to themselves as brother and adopted sister.

They decided to resettle in England. The childless Margrave, who sold his margraviate to the King of Prussia in return for a large annuity, kept using his title. The Margravine sought further, grander titles for herself. She got the Holy Roman Emperor Francis II to declare her the morganatic Princess Berkeley. Naturally, some found her title-seeking risible. Many declared the couple's behavior immoral.

On their return to Britain, the Margrave and Margravine were snubbed by royalty, including by the Margrave's cousin King George III. Thanks to the Margrave's large annuity, he and his wife had money enough not to care much about who snubbed them. Together, the couple enjoyed breeding horses. The Margrave kept enormous dogs. With her own private theater, the Margravine attracted a circle of fawning thespians, including her "son" Robert Ker Porter. Most of her grown children kept her at arm's length.

Craven family infighting was constant. The Margravine's eldest son, the present Lord Craven—a military man who'd married a penniless actress—fought with his mother over land and loyalty. The Margravine distrusted and disliked him. She thought he made everyone in the country hate him, except for a few dependents who laughed at or bullied him.[7] She didn't seem to recognize that others said the same of her. Her most loyal dependent was her youngest son, Keppel, twenty-nine at the time of Maria's visit, whose company his mother prized but rarely got enough of to suit her.

In the winter of 1809, when she went to stay with the Margravine, Maria was thirty. Her host was three years into her second widowhood at age fifty-nine. At first, Maria and the Margravine got on famously. Maria felt at perfect liberty, with the household made up of just the two of them and a large number of servants.[8] The level of comfort on the estate, Maria admitted, was to her taste, although she told Jane the luxury made her less industrious with her pen than she liked.

At Brandenburgh House, the two women lived by a schedule. They breakfasted together at nine. Then Maria would go out for a walk between ten and eleven. While she was out walking, the Margravine's housemaid would make up Maria's room. Upon returning from her walk, she'd write until one, then take another walk, until luncheon. She admitted to Jane, somewhat sheepishly, that she'd then often lie down on the sofa. She didn't sleep but instead tried to compose her spirits so she could handle the remainder of the day. Then she'd write more, until dressing for dinner at five.

Evenings with the Margravine were pleasant if intense. They involved conversation, music, and cards, although no gambling. They'd go on together until eleven, with Maria entertaining her host. Usually, Maria would be in bed by midnight and sleep soundly until eight. She was grateful for this "sober arrangement," as she called it.[9] But the Margravine often became restless. When that happened, she'd ask Maria to go with her to London.

One day in March 1809, when the two women went into town to shop, Maria got a full and frightening taste of what it meant to be seen publicly with someone of the Margravine's great wealth. The sight of the Margravine's carriage stopping on busy Oxford Street would have been spectacular with her vehicle's crown emblems and servants' fine livery.

Maria and the Margravine went into the shop as people gathered to gawk. They mistook the carriage as belonging to the Duke of York, the second son of King George III and commander of the British Army. That first error led to a more dangerous second one. By the time the two women exited the shop, the crowd had jumped to the conclusion that one of them must be the Duke's mistress.

"Which is Mrs. Clarke?" someone cried out.

"That with the blue eyes!" another yelled back.

Mary Anne Clarke, a tradesman's daughter, had famously left her debtor husband to become a royal courtesan. Maria bore some slight resemblance to Mrs. Clarke. Both were porcelain-skinned women in their early thirties, with long necks, ample bosoms, and fashionable, face-framing curls.

"Look how frightened she looks," a third person shouted, as Maria tried to escape to the carriage, while the throng gathered closer.

"Damn her!" the mob jeered, crowding in. Maria feared they'd tear her to pieces. She dropped to a supplicating curtsy, which led a gentleman to take off his hat to her. She wasn't sure whether he meant it sarcastically. The servants tried to explain who the women were—or rather who Maria wasn't. The footmen worked to strike out a path from the shop to the carriage, probably by using whips to move the crowd back. With the servants shouting explanations about the mistaken identity, Maria and the Margravine finally got into the carriage and out of harm's way.

"To think your sister Maria should live to be mistaken for that infamous wretch," she had written to Jane. "To remember the incident is laughable, but I protest it was no joke while it existed."[10] Future outings to London in the carriage weren't so dramatic. On one trip, the Margravine bought Maria a lovely straw hat.

The Margravine did seem to be treating Maria almost like a family member. At the Margravine's two principal residences, Brandenburgh in town and Benham in the country, bedrooms were kept ready for her son Keppel. But when Maria arrived, the Margravine had put her guest into Keppel's Brandenburgh bedroom. It was a little agreeable hole, almost a nest, in a turret, which seemed to suggest her host's maternal feelings toward Maria.[11] Those maternal feelings extended to trying to cure Maria's sickly disposition. The Margravine loved to play amateur doctor and try out unusual treatments on the attractive, curable, and mildly ill.

"The Margravine makes me drink champagne now at dinner instead of Madeira, and orange gruel at night, which really does me good I think," Maria wrote home. "Besides this she insists on my taking her orgeat thro' the day, so that literally I never eat a meal, but am always eating or drinking."

Orgeat—a sweet almond or barley syrup, flavored with orange flower water, mixed with water, milk, or brandy—was believed curative. After some trial and error, the Margravine put Maria on a diet of cold liquids. Even without proper food, Maria declared she felt better. She swore off hot tea for life.[12] She reported she was positively fatter from this expensive fruit-and-alcohol regimen.

Being a female companion to a wealthy older literary woman was a role and performance Maria had perfected. She knew how to go along with her host's whims, errands, and excursions. She knew to be agreeable and not make waves. But with the Margravine, Maria's duties expanded so much that it left little time for her own work. "I creep on with my book, when I can write," she reported in a letter home, "so I hope my time will not be quite wasted as I feared—every one is attentive and civil so that I cannot but be chearful.—I only wish for all our sakes that my pen could stamp off all my thoughts at once."[13]

Their established daily routine began to break down further. At first, the Margravine thought the two of them should spend mornings apart. Maria would write, while the Margravine managed her estate, toward which she took a very hands-on approach. But then the Margravine decided they'd take morning airings in her carriage.[14] Next, the Margravine offered to teach Maria to ride a horse.[15] Mornings came to be disturbed by constant interruptions from "Her Highness," as Maria and the servants were expected to refer to the Margravine. She found she had so many ideas that came to her that she simply couldn't wait to share them with Maria.[16]

"It is impossible for me to get on with my novel from frequent visits of her Highness to my room," she wrote, "Then going frequently to town—two dressings—exercise & c.—I shall fairly lay the idea aside."[17]

Jane wrote back, telling Maria to stay put in the Margravine's household, for the sake of her health and to write as she could with the goal of completing her *Don Sebastian* by summer 1809. Jane was busy with Robert's Spanish campaign narrative. She assured her sister that others would help with the historical research Maria usually did for Robert's books. William would provide needed translations. Friend Anna Middleton would help Jane with annotations. Jane planned to get back to her own William Wallace novel after she'd completed Robert's work.[18] In the meantime, Jane encouraged Maria to focus on advancing Robert's interests. In turn, Maria determined to be more assertive in what she'd come there for. She spoke plainly with the Margravine about Robert's money problems.

"I distinctly stated his situation," Maria wrote home, "frankly told her we had no other dependence in the world save him and our own talents—as she has never led to the subject again with me, it must be Robert's task now, to introduce it himself when first he finds himself alone with her."

With Maria's objective carried out, she looked for ways to detach herself from unpleasant daily obligations. When the Margravine decided to go to her house in the country, Maria saw her chance. She used the need to complete her book as an excuse to request staying behind at Brandenburgh House for three days. The Margravine agreed to it.[19]

Upon the Margravine's return, Maria could sense her host was sinking into a gloom. But that gloom cleared immediately when news came that her favorite son Keppel was expected. Maria hoped it might be just the window of opportunity she was looking for to gain permission to return home. Her advocacy for Robert was done, and she was staying in Keppel's bedroom.

Maria asked the Margravine, "How shall I dispose of myself dear M'am—I have Mr. Keppel's chamber—would you not like to receive him alone?"

"O no," the Margravine said. She wouldn't hear of Maria leaving. She wanted her to stay to see Keppel and to witness her maternal happiness at their reunion. The Margravine had already ordered other rooms to be readied for Keppel and his friend Mr. William Gell.

"So now I shall stay," Maria wrote home, exasperated, "till it is decent and proper to go away."[20]

Maria didn't know Keppel and his friend Gell, except by reputation. Her brother Robert and Keppel had, in years past, traveled in the same circles of fashionable men and acted alongside each other in the Margravine's private theatricals. Robert and Keppel were close in age, both known as brilliant and likable figures who kept company with other well-known men of fashion. That's where their similarities ended. Robert was a man of great talent, deep ambition, and hard work. Keppel possessed immense learning but little direction.

His mother was partly to blame. She'd actively discouraged him from pursuing any profession. This wasn't unusual, given his birth and wealth, but it meant he had nothing to occupy him. Keppel was financially dependent on the Margravine. The Margrave, before he'd died, had talked about giving Keppel a fortune of his own, but his mother quashed the idea. By controlling Keppel's access to money, she might ensure he remained on friendly, intimate terms.

Keppel had *some* freedom. Like his mother, he traveled on a whim, visiting siblings and friends. He'd appear at one of his mother's homes, accompanied by whichever hangers-on were alongside him, for stays of indeterminate lengths. The Margravine enjoyed Keppel's spontaneous visits, as well as most of the wits and dandies he brought. She referred to Keppel's young male friends of the moment as the "Banditti"—the outlaw bandits.[21]

When the day of his homecoming arrived, Maria found Keppel wasn't at all what she'd expected. He was shy, which gave him an air of coldness. But once that air was pierced through, he had a heart just as warm as his air was cold. He had a passionate admiration of books. He and Maria had animated discussions of their literary likes and dislikes.[22] They discovered they were admirers of the same novels and collections of letters.

More members of Keppel's entourage arrived. At one breakfast, Maria was seated between Lord Clinton and Keppel. Maria noticed Keppel blushed at improper innuendos made by his male friends, especially those from the celebrated dandy Sir Lumley St. George Skeffington, a rhyming, playgoing, comedy-writing, coquettish baronet, known as "Skiffy."[23]

Maria had known Skiffy for years. When the Porters lived in London, Skiffy seemed to be everywhere the sisters went, especially in theatrical circles. Skiffy, a playwright and close friend of the Kembles, was said to go to four theaters a night. He was a clotheshorse who gave fashion advice to the Prince of Wales. But Skiffy was best known to Maria as the over-the-top admirer of her sister. He always greeted Jane in ecstatics.[24] He called her, in characteristically high-flown rhetoric, a "potent enchantress."[25] Maria noticed that Keppel blushed at Skiffy's off-color, ridiculous bon mots. It would only have raised Keppel in her estimation.

The presence of these men transformed the atmosphere at Brandenburgh House. Maria thought she had finally become less necessary to the Margravine's happiness and might be allowed to leave, but once again, her intention to go home faltered. Not only was the Margravine adamant that Maria must stay. She also tried to pull Jane into the household, too.

Maria wasn't opposed to the idea of Jane joining them. She told her sister that if she were to come for a visit, she must be in her best looks, because the Margravine frequently told her son about Jane's beauty. Keppel turned out to be a great lover of flowing tresses, and Maria thought he would admire her sister's long, dark hair.[26] But Jane, busy with literary work and the care of Mrs. Porter in Ditton, begged off.

After having some time to observe the young men and hear more stories, Maria declared that the Margravine had vipers rather than children in all but Keppel.[27] She also recognized the depths of Keppel's problems with his doting mother. He was in an impossible position, thrust between the Margravine and her wars with his older siblings. Keppel alone tried to stay on good terms with everyone.[28] Maria thought he was sensible, with accomplishments and fine taste, despite his quietness and reserve.

"Perhaps a fellow feeling makes me favor timid people," Maria mused about Keppel in a letter home.[29]

Keppel wasn't entirely bashful. He was also a performer. He sang and danced and played whatever Spanish music his friends asked him to. Witnessing these evening scenes was proving inspirational to Maria's novel. She used the material as she could. She noticed, too, that Keppel seemed to make her his prime audience and to address his remarks and descriptions to her rather than his mother. Maria was flattered.

These attentions to Maria didn't seem to bother the Margravine, who was less willing to part with Maria than ever. At least, with Keppel and his Banditti there, time to write materialized once again. Maria would relish having several days in row to herself to work whenever the Margravine went to Benham House in Berkshire. Maria often stayed back in town at Brandenburgh House. By such opportunities, she'd dashed off two thirds of the next volume of her novel. She hoped that she might finish *Don Sebastian* by the end of summer after all.[30] With that work progressing well, and the young men's occasional visits making the Margravine's household so lively, she felt increasingly at home, with little inclination to return to her mother and sister.

Maria's life at Brandenburgh House contrasted sharply with the genteel poverty and constant anxieties of Ditton Cottage. Brandenburgh House was close enough to Ditton that Maria could make occasional day visits to her family and friends, sometimes with guests, using the Margravine's carriage. Once, Keppel himself had accompanied her to visit her family on the way to a dinner at Lord Douglas's home. Maria thought he appeared exceptionally tongue-tied around Mrs. Porter.

Maria began to appreciate the Margravine's collection of clever guests as much as she did the luxuries of her host's estates. She sent long letters home to Jane and her mother, describing the wit and antics of Keppel's friends Skiffy, Gell, and a new arrival, Charles Kirkpatrick Sharpe. Sharpe—a nervous and talented poet with a strong Scottish accent—was a friend of Walter Scott's.[31] But among them all, Maria felt her heart move toward Keppel.

At his birthday celebration in April, it had been dismal outside, yet they'd had an animated party for twelve, with tea and dinner in the pavilion. The Margravine proved a happy, doting mother that day. Robert came to visit that night, somehow managing to make himself lively again, despite what Maria knew to be the cloud of his continued money and Princess Mary problems. Guests drank to Keppel's health with Tokay wine that was almost sacred because it had been the gift of Prussia's Frederick the Great to the late Margrave.[32]

Maria not only observed but also participated in this whirl of gaiety. She discerned that, in this little group of young men, Gell was the most powerful figure. Skiffy and Sharpe could provide a constant supply of wit and comic relief, but it was Gell whose strong personality directed them and set the tone. Privately, Sharpe complained to Maria that although Gell wanted to be thought a dry wit, his wit was barely perceptible.[33]

At first, Maria liked Gell. He was an author of books on Greece, with charming powers of conversation. He was a classical scholar and, she thought, intelligent and good. He was the heir of a baronetcy, though with no expectation of a fortune. She knew she ought to have preferred him among the company, but she didn't.

"I prefer Keppel to Gell, tho' the latter is more brilliant, much handsomer, and evidently as humane and good as his friend," Maria wrote home.

Maria found fault with Gell, a man too completely at his ease. His jests and witticisms, although not exactly ill natured, were pretentious.[34] Maria tried to approve of Gell's smooth arrogance. Everyone said he intended to marry a woman of fortune.[35] This rumor wouldn't have endeared him to Maria, but she attempted to like him because Keppel did.

"Keppel makes his Eulogium [to Gell] every day with as much ardour as if he were a woman in love with him," Maria reported. "Consequently I conclude Gell to be worthy [of] so animated a friendship."[36]

Watching these joyful young men together reminded Maria of the days when she, Jane, and Robert first befriended the Caulfields. It had been so long since she'd witnessed pure brotherly affection among young men. It brought back sweet recollections, watching them drape their arms over one another and refer to one another as "My dear Charles!" or "My Dear Keppel!"[37] Maria especially enjoyed watching Keppel and Gell, with their complementary personalities. They were opposites, she saw, in much the same way she and Jane were said to be. Keppel was the more thoughtful one. His reserve made him more like Jane. Gell was quick, lively, and free—more like Maria.

"This light and shade makes them charming together, and renders them almost necessary to each other," Maria wrote. "Friendship now-a-days is so uncommon, particularly between men of fashion, that the heart loves to behold it."[38]

Maria developed even deeper feelings for Keppel through watching him interact with a delightful little boy of three or four years old. This gorgeous child, Maria soon learned, was Keppel's illegitimate son. The Margravine privately accepted that Augustus was her biological grandson, yet she always referred to the boy as Keppel's godson during his visits.[39]

Whenever Augustus came to visit, he was accompanied by his nurse, Mrs. Stringer, never by his mother, who went unnamed. It was said she was a Frenchwoman, Madame D'Erville, apparently genteelly born and with some education—but already married.[40] The D'Ervilles had several older children. Augustus appears to have been baptized as if he were their legitimate child, surely understood among them as a fiction. Although Keppel somehow became intimately connected to Madame D'Erville, his natural son seemed all that remained of the relationship.

Maria was broad-minded about children born out of wedlock. She didn't share the era's common cant that illegitimacy sullied a child's potential for moral goodness. She loved children, and little Augustus took an immediate shine to her. The Margravine, who complained loudly whenever Augustus wasn't there, never spent more than five minutes a day with him. Maria was expected to play with the boy. She declared him a pretty little tyrant, demanding her constant attention.[41]

This new household obligation with young Augustus cost Maria writing time, but what began as another effort to please the Margravine became a fond preference. Augustus was a playful child, Maria wrote, although never noisy and unusually docile. Sometimes she'd get her daily exercise by trotting like a horse and playing hide and seek with him.[42] Or Keppel might join them in playing soldiers.

"If all children were like him," Maria declared to Jane, "Mothers would have no pains."[43]

In this odd collection of people around the Margravine, Maria fit in almost seamlessly. She proved a favorite of Augustus's nurse, Mrs. Stringer. Even Keppel's huge dog, Pero, took a liking to Maria, which Mrs. Stringer found remarkable.

"I don't see but what anything, and anybody, likes you, m'am," Mrs. Stringer once told Maria. "You're so kind and considerate. All the Margravine's servants—and all Mr. Craven's too, hope you'll marry the best Gentleman in the world."[44]

That spring and summer of 1809, the Margravine became restless. She began to insist on taking Maria with her as she shuttled between Brandenburgh House, Benham House, and a third property she kept in Southampton. Keppel and his male friends came and went at will, too, from these places. The Margravine began to say that Maria was like a member of her family. She encouraged her to think of Brandenburgh as her second home and to tell Jane the same, so that they might come and go from it as they pleased. The Margravine declared she didn't want to separate from Maria.

"For indeed, you make my happiness, my dear Miss Porter," the Margravine told her. "I believe your society will save my life—without it I should have broken my heart by this time."[45]

The Margravine may have been angling, through these invitations to the Porter sisters, to spend more time with Robert, but perhaps his engagement to Princess Mary had transformed the kind of affection the Margravine had for him. Her heart, in any case, was roaming elsewhere. She had made Maria privy to the secret of her romantic feelings for a man of much lower rank.[46] Maria was careful not to name him in her letters home, but gossip spread that it was the Margravine's steward and that she meant to marry him.[47] Others said it was her butler.[48] Yet another report claimed it was the fashionable architect Capability Brown.[49]

Whatever the truth was, Maria wondered if the Margravine also wanted to extend the boundaries of her family through another marriage. The Margravine told Maria that she was determined to shut the door against everybody but those she really loved.

"Indeed if I had always you and Keppel," the Margravine told Maria, "I should never desire any others' society."[50]

Did she mean to make Maria her daughter-in-law? At some moments, the Margravine seemed to encourage an attachment to her son. But even if that were the Margravine's wish, it would depend on Keppel having romantic feelings for Maria. Maria felt Keppel's behavior toward her was inscrutable. He went so frequently from warm to cold.

Whenever Keppel was away from the Margravine's homes and wrote to his mother, he ended his letters by saying "my regards to Miss Porter, if she is still with you." Maria took this as a sign that the Margravine never wrote about her to Keppel, which suggested she was merely an afterthought.[51] But when they were all together, Keppel showed a great preference for her. She wanted to test his feelings.

His preferences were noted by others. Sharpe told the group that Keppel seemed to be in love, although he didn't know with whom.[52] It was Miss Mary Temple—the Margravine's sister's niece, sometimes part of their circle—who made sport of Maria and Keppel liking each other.[53] Maria thought she detected jealousy in the teasing. Once, when all of them took three vehicles to Richmond for a picnic, Miss Temple jumped in at the last minute to prevent Maria from riding in Keppel's carriage. She thought it was a monstrous good joke, declaring, too, that Keppel was compelled to be her companion throughout the day. Maria inwardly seethed. But Keppel seemed to take his revenge when he declared that, although Miss Temple would be his day companion, he'd sit next to Miss Porter at dinner.

"I had then all the gaiety at the table," Maria wrote home, triumphantly, because Keppel had "introduced a droll game after dinner that killed us with laughing."[54]

Maria, having also eaten and drunk voraciously, may have won that battle with Miss Temple, but she often felt she was losing the war against the rest of the group's insinuating comments. She particularly hated their sly remarks about her as a future wife and about Keppel as a future husband. They seemed to make Keppel so uncomfortable.

Gell was the first to deal with Maria with gross unfairness. His vigorous teasing of Maria and Keppel about their signs of preference for each other went beyond Miss Temple's scheming jealousy. Gell's teasing seemed designed to hurt Maria. He dubbed her, in front of all of their set, "outrageously virtuous." He gave her a nickname, too: "the Griffin." Maria was confused at being called the Griffin, entirely unsure what Gell meant by it. But Keppel, on seeing how distressed she was, tried to reassure her. He told her, in front of the others, that it was actually a compliment.

"Indeed," Keppel told Maria, "he calls you so because a Griffin is my Crest, and you know you are always good enough to protect me:—and because I think a Griffin the most amiable and delightful of animals."

Maria, although ashamed, was mollified. The griffin, that fantastical animal with the head and wings of an eagle but the body of a lion, was in the Craven family crest and part of its coat of arms. But Keppel's gentle defense of Maria as the Griffin only seemed to make Gell work harder to ridicule her. Gell came up with an entire new crop of nicknames for her. One of them was Goose.[55]

Despite enduring these raillery-filled evening revels, Maria pushed herself hard during the day to finish her novel. Back in Ditton, Jane was doing the same. Maria was thrilled when her sister reported new progress on her Wallace novel, although Maria worried about Jane's health and hoped she would take a holiday. Maria could feel, in her own body, that intense labor on *Don Sebastian* was proving a slow poison to her strength. She wrote, "Till my book is done, I am miserable."

Nevertheless, when Maria was invited to travel again with the Margravine in July 1809, she acquiesced. The pair would attend a grand ball at Arundel

Castle, sixty-five miles south, just west of Brighton. Maria felt she couldn't refuse the Margravine too often with her continual excuses of needing to write. Then, after Maria had accepted, Keppel changed his mind. He decided he would go, making Maria's company unnecessary.

At first, Maria considered backing out. She needed just six more sheets of manuscript paper from home to finish her book. Her money was almost gone. But overruling all other considerations was Keppel.

"These things interrupt my book, but I could not refuse when she asked me because then Keppel did not mean to go—and now that he has changed his mind, I could not withdraw my promise, without looking pointedly rude to him."[56]

Jane had somehow found and sent a bit of money to allow Maria to make the trip, as well as the needed paper. Maria set aside the completion of her novel, with mere days left to go, to attend a ball. The Margravine took Keppel and Maria in her grand carriage and made the trip south, stopping overnight at inns. They arrived at Arundel Castle, a medieval fortress high on a hill in West Sussex. Their host, the Duke of Norfolk, was a patron of the arts nicknamed the "Drunken Duke." He'd assembled a splendid mob for his ball, "a perfect barrack of Lords and Ladies," Maria thought.[57]

Maria wore a much-admired dress of emerald green. Keppel's graceful clothing showed his elegant shape to greater advantage than she had ever seen it. Even among this grand company, Maria thought the Margravine and Keppel were two of the handsomest creatures in the room. But, as she privately admitted to Jane, she felt almost polluted being in the same atmosphere with people who seemed swallowed up in voluptuousness.[58]

Maria and Keppel were in sync that night. The Margravine mingled with her titled friends, but Maria and Keppel hung back from the crowd. Together, they watched and made fun of people in low voices. Yet Maria was afraid to appear too forward with Keppel.

"I was too timid to dance with Mr. Craven," Maria wrote to Jane, "so he did not dance at all thus I lost the very thing I went for."[59]

There were encouraging signs of Keppel's growing feelings for her. He never left her side throughout the day. The next day he'd asked Maria for a rose out of the bouquet the Duke of Norfolk had given her. Keppel wore her rose on his breast. Whenever she turned her eyes toward him, he put the rose to his lips and gave her a look filled with regard. She couldn't tell if he was sincere. Maria returned from the trip as confused as ever.

"Keppel is vastly odd," she told Jane.[60] "He is very capricious—for one day he makes me fancy that he loves me extremely, and the next, that he does not care whether I live or die."[61]

Maria narrated for Jane an endless series of trifles and puzzles that she hoped her sister's cooler judgment might untangle. But across that summer, as Maria ruminated over Keppel, she pushed herself punishingly hard to finish *Don Sebastian*. After finally sending it off to the printer, Maria declared herself weak from lack of exercise.[62] All of the gains she'd made in her health under the Margravine's care had been reversed, yet she'd stopped asking to go home. As Keppel came and went, and little Augustus came and went, Maria's resolve to leave the Margravine faded away. She imagined herself not as a fixture exactly but as having a future among them.

"Keppel really is attached to me," she told Jane. "I feel more interested than I ought in the nature of Keppel's feelings: what would I not give to know them for a certainty![63] At the end of July, the Margravine's household began to break up. Keppel announced he'd leave for Cornwall to see cousins with no fixed date of return. Little Augustus, too, was to leave. A crowd of relatives came to replace the Banditti, but the Margravine must have been displeased. She proposed taking Maria to Southampton, to cure her health. She informed Maria it would be a short visit, with warm sea bathing, so Maria packed light. But then the Margravine wrote to Nurse Stringer to have Augustus join them. Suddenly, there were day excursions, trips to the races, and balls. A short junket for rest and relaxation became a long, busy stay. The Margravine's reason for taking the trip, to cure her ailing companion, was forgotten. Exhausted Maria felt so low she was ready to sink into the earth.[64]

Her weakness was compounded by news from home of Mrs. Porter's illness and her brothers' continued problems. Robert was waiting for a clarifying letter from the Margravine. On July 31, 1809, his postponed debts had once again come due. If he couldn't raise the needed money immediately, his plan was to escape to Scotland, take a walking tour, and live under a false name.[65] The Margravine was putting him off, but there was no time to lose.

Meanwhile, brother William was on the point of taking a second wife. After Lydia's death at age thirty-six, two years earlier in 1807, William had left his young sons behind in Durham to be raised by her mother. He was avoiding the rest of the family and couldn't be counted on to help his sick mother in Ditton.[66] John's movements, too, were mysterious—in debt, hiding from creditors, under threat of arrest, wandering, indolent.[67]

Everything that Maria's stay with the Margravine had been leading up to, in their hopes for Robert, was coming to a climax. But when the Margravine finally replied to Robert's supplicating letter, she offered no money. She told him she was busy in Southampton. She'd hoped she might see him for just a moment, until he could bring his Princess Mary to meet her.

"Your sister is pretty well," the Margravine concluded her letter to Robert, "but who can be quite well with such weather.—I am very busy trying to get rid of some of my property here. Believe me yours aff[ectionately] Elizabeth."[68]

This rhetoric was characteristic of the self-involved Margravine, but it was a complete blow to Robert's hopes. He made plans to leave the country to avoid arrest, working around the clock to sell his drawings at a fixed price. He left directions to sell his oil paintings and remaining panoramas—the repaired *Agincourt* and the cleaned and varnished *Seringapatam*. He hoped to get 150 pounds for them.[69]

Then, at the last possible moment, the Margravine came through. She loaned Robert enough to keep his creditors satisfied for another eighteen months.[70] Robert, relieved, had a very large obligation to the Margravine.[71] It fell to Maria to show the family's gratitude through continued companionship. Amid this happy chaos, Maria's *Don Sebastian; or, the House of Braganza: An Historical Romance* was published in four volumes and advertised in August 1809.

There was little fanfare among the Porters for Maria's eighth book. The Margravine, Maria knew, would likely neither read nor appreciate *Don Sebastian*, because she thought moral lessons in romances were hateful.[72] One of *Don Sebastian*'s first readers was Mrs. Porter, who complained the story was dismal. Maria told Mrs. Porter that she was very sorry to hear that, because she hadn't intended to write a dismal novel.[73] Jane suspected its hero was modeled after Keppel Craven, although Maria initially denied it.[74] On reflection, she wrote, "He must have been in my mind when I drew it. Indeed it is very like him."[75] The novel's Don Sebastian is a young man for whom everything is a passion—his friendships, his love for people—yet these passions often flame out. And despite his temperate example among other other lively young men, the narrator explained, the hero didn't understand women, because he'd never yet been in love.[76]

In September, when the Margravine left Southampton for her country house in Berkshire, she invited Maria to stay another four months, until just after Christmas. Maria learned Keppel and the Banditti were going to make Benham House their base of operations that autumn. There she could investigate whether Keppel had feelings for her. She told her mother and sister that her conscience wouldn't allow her to stay past the end of 1809. She'd then have lived apart from them for the better part of a year. Surely, Maria wrote, she wasn't supposed to act as if she'd given herself to the Margravine for the rest of her life.[77]

No sooner had they arrived at Benham than the Margravine promptly left Maria alone for a fortnight. Maria appreciated this rare opportunity of having to neither speak nor listen.[78] It turned out the Margravine had dashed off to catch a glimpse of Keppel, whereabouts then unknown. The Margravine, who detested Keppel's frequent mysterious wanderings, often tried to use his male friends to find him.[79] This time, she had accidentally met Keppel's groom on the road. She learned her son had lied to her about his travels, which incensed her. He responded to his mother's anger by postponing his arrival to Benham House until mid-October.

Maria felt sure that, if only the Margravine would allow Keppel some financial independence, he'd choose to come to her out of generosity, rather than out of obligation. Then his mother would never again suspect her son of loving her out of necessity alone. Maria wasn't entirely disinterested in this desire. A Keppel in command of his own fortune could make life decisions on his own, including about marriage.

As solitary Maria wandered the property and wondered whether Keppel might want to marry her, she also browsed the shelves of his library. When she came across a copy of her novel *The Hungarian Brothers*, she took it down and inspected it. It showed tell-tale signs of having been read by Keppel himself, with every third or fourth leaf doubled down.[80] Maria had previously noticed that Keppel, while reading a book, would fold down pages with passages he liked. She looked carefully at the pages he'd marked with folds and noticed an odd pattern. All of them were love scenes. One page folded down with particular vigor was the section when Maria's hero fearfully takes the hand of the heroine to walk her to a carriage. Both characters hesitate, unable to look into each other's eyes. The heroine blushes, as their hands tremble. The description ends, "Are not true love and respect inseparable?"[81]

Maria remembered that she'd had that same experience with Keppel, both of their hands trembling when getting into a carriage. She wondered if his folding down this page might be meant as a sign to the book's author. Could this be his way of declaring his affection?[82] Sometimes he seemed capricious or indifferent to her, but it was possible the powerful, controlling Margravine made Keppel fear the consequences of showing regard for any other woman.[83]

The date of Keppel's and the Margravine's separate returns back to Benham kept fluctuating. When Keppel finally came back, he greeted Maria very strangely. First he'd started and joyfully caught up her hand. Then he'd immediately changed his manner. He said to her nonchalantly, "O how do you do Miss Porter," as if they'd just seen each other the day before. Then he turned away to notice his just-returned mother and Gell. Keppel looked at Maria two or three times earnestly, but then he didn't look at her again the rest of the night. In the morning, he ignored her.

His first advance to Maria the next day seemed truly bizarre. He sat in the corner, very near her, without speaking, for more than an hour. Then he abruptly got up, left the room, and returned with a pile of his own drawings and invited Maria to inspect them. As they talked, he asked which room she was staying in at Benham. He approved of her choice. It was the first room he'd occupied there. She didn't understand what he really meant.

The following days went on in this confusing way, with one change. Sometimes Maria felt as if she were talking to Keppel through Gell. It was Gell who privately explained Keppel's fear that his mother might leave him without a farthing. The Margravine made Keppel one promise after another about giving him money but reneged each time. Maria decided that the most submissive husband to a devil of a wife was nothing compared to what Keppel was forced to be to his mother.[84]

"I don't doubt but that she would give her consent tomorrow to my becoming his wife with all sorts of promises of independence & c. but she never would fulfill one of them," Maria wrote to Jane. "I augur then that he and I have met to approve and esteem each other, and to part."[85]

But slowly and gradually, Keppel reestablished a close connection to Maria. He read and admired her new novel, *Don Sebastian*, and its perfect tone.[86] The two spent many hours alone together. He gave her a gift, a Spanish necklace. In return, she gave him an amber toothpick case.[87] It was a level of intimacy Maria hadn't expected. These were the sort of gestures couples made just before declaring their love and becoming engaged.

In October 1809, more guests joined them at Benham House, including Gell's sister. Miss Gell was welcome enough company, although far too nosy. Once, at dinner, Maria had worn her Spanish necklace and Miss Gell asked about it. Keppel proclaimed to all that it was his gift to Maria. Later, Miss Gell asked, too, about Keppel's amber toothpick case. It seemed always in his hand, she said. Keppel hesitatingly handed it to Miss Gell to inspect.

"There are two names upon it, you see," he told her. "It was given me."

Miss Gell took it and read the names aloud quietly: "Maria—Keppel."

Without saying another word, Miss Gell returned the toothpick case to him. Maria was stunned.

"You may be sure that I was scarlet," she wrote to Jane. "I could not guess how those two names could be on it."[88]

Maria had put her own name on the case because it was her gift to him. She learned only at that moment, thanks to Miss Gell's close questioning, that Keppel had secured a piece of gold and put his own name on it, too. He revealed his partiality for Maria in declaring this fact to their circle.

The Margravine also noticed her son's growing intimacy with the novelist but didn't show any change of attitude. Maria felt, if she were to become Keppel's wife, it might be because she was the opposite of his mother. Having a half-censurable, half-admirable mother-in-law like the Margravine would be a small tax for gaining a husband like Keppel, she told Jane.

As October wore on, Gell resumed hurling insulting mock-compliments at Maria. She would get angry. Then Keppel would grow sullen and not speak. These days proved difficult. Maria had become so used to Keppel's seeking out her eyes whenever he spoke. But after Gell's teasing, he wouldn't look at her for the whole day. How should she act, she asked Jane. If she gave Keppel more attention, then she'd be charged with indelicacy. If she behaved coldly to Gell, he'd dislike her more. If she didn't show attention to Keppel, their intimacy might wither. She wasn't trying to play the coquette, she told her sister. It was just so painful and confusing.

These little misunderstandings would pass, and Maria, Keppel, and Augustus would end up playing soldiers together again in the mornings. One day, when Augustus was sitting on Maria's lap with Keppel beside them both, he suddenly turned to his father and said, "My presus tsild." Keppel asked why the boy would call him "precious child."

"It is what Miss Porter calls me," Augustus replied.

Keppel replied, "No one loves you like Miss Porter, I believe."

There wasn't much competition at Benham House. Gell continually referred to the boy as "anybody's."[89]

The Margravine watched Maria in such affectionate scenes with increasing skepticism. Once she treated her to a private lecture about the coldness and vanity of men who amuse themselves by drawing forth proofs of a woman's fondness, when in reality they care nothing for them. Her meaning wasn't difficult to parse.

A few days later, the Margravine delivered another, more direct private lecture before breakfast. Maria was as innocent as a child, she said, but everyone could tell she was in love with Keppel, and she'd soon be an object of ridicule for it. No young woman who'd ever stayed with them had failed to fall in love with her son. But once Keppel notices, the Margravine warned her, he'll avoid you. Afterward, in her room, Maria cried heartily.

While she was crying, Keppel came to see her. It was an unusual, intimate, and highly inappropriate thing for a man to show up at a woman's chamber, but Keppel had brought little Augustus with him. On finding Maria in tears, he had put Augustus into her arms. She held the child tight. Keppel stood there for a moment, looking at them both. Then he left, without saying a word.[90]

For a time, Maria had cried even harder. She tried to compose herself, for Augustus's sake, and played with the boy. Then, suddenly, Keppel returned, asking her where he might have put a drawing of his and if she'd seen it. It was clear he wanted to be asked to stay. She resolved not to notice him. He eventually left.

With the Margravine's words ringing in her ears, Maria tried to avoid Keppel in the days that followed. The Margravine's attitude had changed completely toward her former favorite. She stopped asking Maria to come out

JANE PORTER (1775–1850)

ANNA MARIA PORTER (1778–1832)

Celebrated sister novelists Jane Porter (left) and Anna Maria Porter (right) resembled real-life precursors to the fictional Dashwood sisters of Jane Austen's *Sense and Sensibility* (1811). Reserved, rational Jane was said to be the more strikingly beautiful one, but gregarious Maria (as she was called) won many admirers through her compassionate enthusiasm.

JANE PORTER, DEPICTED AS A GIRL

SURGEON'S SQUARE, EDINBURGH

BISHOP COSIN'S LIBRARY, DURHAM

The Porters moved to Edinburgh in late 1779. Their newly widowed mother ran a boarding house in Surgeon's Square (upper right) and found her children places in a charity school. By 1785, the family returned to Durham, Mrs. Porter's hometown. Young Jane (left) and Maria received no further schooling, but their mother got them access to Bishop Cosin's Library (lower right), where the girls read voraciously.

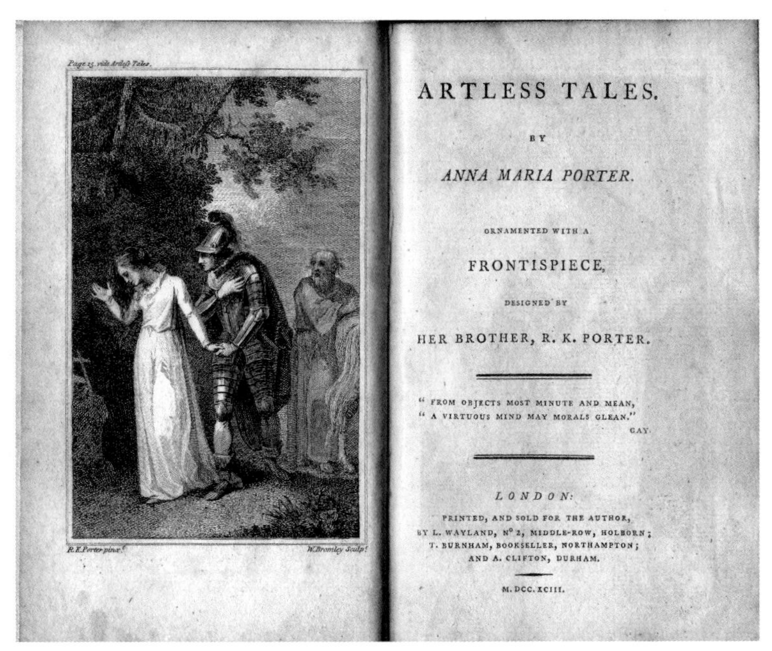

ARTLESS TALES.

BY

ANNA MARIA PORTER.

ORNAMENTED WITH A

FRONTISPIECE,

DESIGNED BY

HER BROTHER, R. K. PORTER.

" FROM OBJECTS MOST MINUTE AND MEAN,
" A VIRTUOUS MIND MAY MORALS GLEAN."

GAY.

LONDON:

PRINTED, AND SOLD FOR THE AUTHOR,
BY L. WAYLAND, N° 2, MIDDLE-ROW, HOLBORN;
T. BURNHAM, BOOKSELLER, NORTHAMPTON;
AND A. CLIFTON, DURHAM.

M. DCC. XCIII.

ANNA MARIA PORTER'S *ARTLESS TALES* (1793), WITH FRONTISPIECE BY HER BROTHER ROBERT

ANNA MARIA PORTER

ROBERT KER PORTER

The struggling Porter family relocated to London, where artist brother Robert Ker Porter (lower right) won a spot in the Royal Academy Schools in 1791. Jane and Maria (lower left) sold writings to support the household. Maria published her first book, *Artless Tales* (1793), at age fourteen (top). Brother Robert provided the frontispiece illustration for Maria's short stories.

MARY CHAMPION DE CRESPIGNY

MARY ROBINSON

ELIZABETH BENGER

ELIZABETH GUNNING

Female mentors offered the Porter sisters publishing advice and social invitations. Prim society matron Mrs. Crespigny (upper left) and famous iconoclastic feminist Mary Robinson (upper right) made conflicting demands that tested Jane's and Maria's loyalties. Young writers Miss Elizabeth Benger (lower left) and Miss Elizabeth Gunning (later Mrs. Plunkett, lower right) helped the sisters navigate literature, courtship, and love. Robert Ker Porter painted Miss Gunning's portrait.

CHARLES KEMBLE AS CASSIO

MARIE-THÉRÈSE DE CAMP AS URANIA

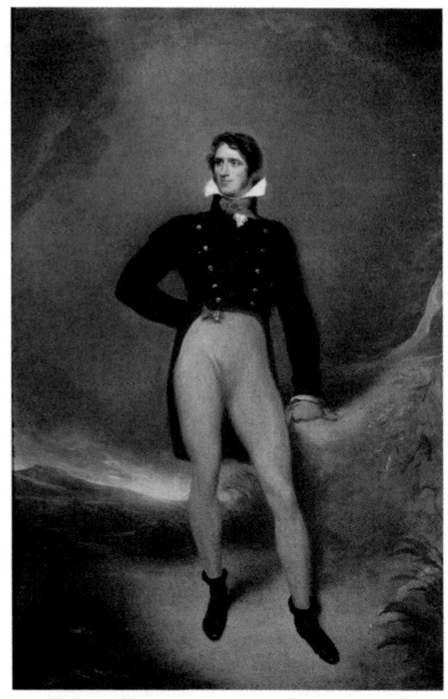

CAPTAIN HENRY CAULFIELD

GERRARD STREET, LONDON

Jane and Maria were immersed in the London theater world in the late 1790s, in their new Gerrard Street lodgings (lower right). The sisters befriended famous actors, including Charles Kemble (upper left) and Miss Therese De Camp (upper right), who pulled Jane into a love triangle. The Porter sisters' favorite thespian was the charismatic, rakish Captain Henry Caulfield (lower left), whose intimacy with Jane raised eyebrows.

PERCIVAL STOCKDALE

SIR SIDNEY SMITH, BY ROBERT KER PORTER

SIR PHILIP SIDNEY, BY ROBERT KER PORTER

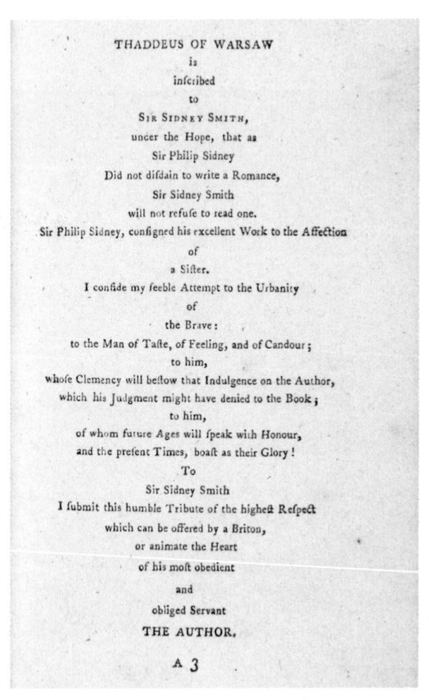

THADDEUS OF WARSAW
is
inscribed
to
SIR SIDNEY SMITH,
under the Hope, that as
Sir Philip Sidney
Did not disdain to write a Romance,
Sir Sidney Smith
will not refuse to read one.
Sir Philip Sidney, consigned his excellent Work to the Affection
of
a Sister.
I confide my feeble Attempt to the Urbanity
of
the Brave:
to the Man of Taste, of Feeling, and of Candour;
to him,
whose Clemency will bestow that Indulgence on the Author,
which his Judgment might have denied to the Book;
to him,
of whom future Ages will speak with Honour,
and the present Times, boast as their Glory!
To
Sir Sidney Smith
I submit this humble Tribute of the highest Respect
which can be offered by a Briton,
or animate the Heart
of his most obedient
and
obliged Servant
THE AUTHOR.

A 3

DEDICATION PAGE OF JANE PORTER'S *THADDEUS OF WARSAW* (1803)

Jane's pioneering historical novel, *Thaddeus of Warsaw* (1803), became a bestseller. She dedicated it (lower right) to war hero Sir Sidney Smith (upper right), with whom she was falling in love. Jane idolized Smith as much as she did her favorite author, Sir Philip Sidney (lower left). In 1804, she traveled north to help her old mentor Percival Stockdale (upper left), whose suffocating, unrequited love made her almost a prisoner in his home.

THE PORTER WOMEN'S COTTAGE, LONG DITTON, SURREY

Jane Porter —

JANE PORTER

SARAH SIDDONS AS LADY MACBETH

The three Porter brothers' debts led Jane (upper right) and Maria to move to a rented, run-down Surrey cottage (upper left). There the sisters took turns escaping its privations for friends' houses or keeping their mother company. Jane was recognized with the Order of Saint Joachim's gold cross, which, with her signature veils, led to her being mistaken for a nun (lower right). Jane was said to resemble famed actress Sarah Siddons (lower left).

Painted by G. Harlowe.
Engraved by J. Thomson.
JANE PORTER,
AS A LADY CANONESS.
Jane Porter

JANE PORTER AS A LADY CANONESS

THE MARGRAVINE OF ANSPACH
From an engraving by H. Meyer after Reynolds

THE MARGRAVINE OF ANSPACH

BRANDENBURGH HOUSE & THEATRE,
Middlesex.

THE MARGRAVINE'S BRANDENBURGH HOUSE AND THEATRE, HAMMERSMITH, NEAR LONDON

European Magazine.

BENHAM NEAR NEWBERY.
The Seat of her Serene Highness the Margravine of Anspach.
Published by I. Asperne at the Bible, Crown, & Constitution, Cornhill, May 1, 1808.

THE MARGRAVINE'S COUNTRY HOUSE, BENHAM, NEAR NEWBURY, BERKSHIRE

Engraved by R. Page.
THE HONBLE KEPPEL CRAVEN,
Vice Chamberlain to Her Majesty.

KEPPEL CRAVEN

Maria, publishing book after book to keep the family solvent, was physically weak when she went to stay with the powerful Margravine of Anspach (upper left) in 1809. Maria lived luxuriously at the Margravine's Brandenburgh House in town (upper right) and Benham House in the country (lower right). There Maria met the Margravine's favorite son, Keppel Craven (lower left), and was drawn into viperous family dramas.

JANE PORTER

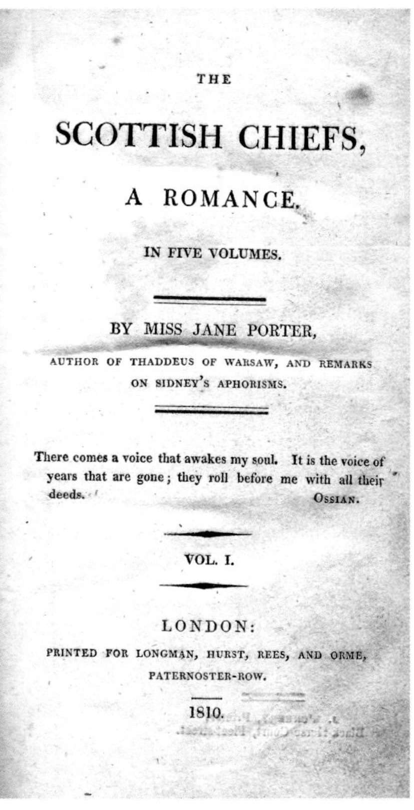

THE

SCOTTISH CHIEFS,

A ROMANCE.

IN FIVE VOLUMES.

BY MISS JANE PORTER,

AUTHOR OF THADDEUS OF WARSAW, AND REMARKS ON SIDNEY'S APHORISMS.

There comes a voice that awakes my soul. It is the voice of years that are gone; they roll before me with all their deeds.

OSSIAN.

VOL. I.

LONDON:

PRINTED FOR LONGMAN, HURST, REES, AND ORME, PATERNOSTER-ROW.

1810.

TITLE PAGE OF JANE PORTER'S *THE SCOTTISH CHIEFS* (1810)

THE PRISON AT CASTLE RUSHEN, ISLE OF MAN

The Scottish Chiefs (1810)—a historical novel of William Wallace at war, in love, and in prison—proved a second bestseller (upper right) and cemented Jane's public reputation for genius (upper left). Privately, she was managing brother John's debts, leading to his imprisonment at the Isle of Man's Castle Rushen (lower left), and beloved friend Henry Caulfield's crim. con. trial and incarceration in the King's Bench Prison (lower right).

KING'S BENCH PRISON, SOUTHWARK, SOUTH LONDON

EDMUND KEAN AS SIR GILES OVERREACH

THEATRE ROYAL IN DRURY LANE, LONDON, 1813

SIR ROBERT KER PORTER

COLONEL DANIEL "DAN" MACKINNON

In the 1810s, the Porters sought financial stability and domestic happiness. Jane wrote plays for famed tragic actor Edmund Kean (upper left), for performance at the Drury Lane theatre (upper right). Brother Robert pulled off an astonishing marriage to a Russian princess and was knighted (lower left). Anna Maria, by then author of thirteen books, was captivated by Colonel Dan Mackinnon, a war hero and dandy (lower right).

CARLTON HOUSE, PALL MALL, LONDON

SIR WALTER SCOTT

SIR ANDREW HALLIDAY

JAMES STANIER CLARKE

The Porter sisters, in the shadow of Walter Scott (upper right), believed he copied their innovative methods in historical fiction without credit. After Scott was knighted by King George IV, Jane and Maria visited Carlton House (upper left), hosted by Royal Librarian James Stanier Clarke (lower right). There Jane met the royal physician and flatterer Sir Andrew Halliday (lower left), who persuaded her to write a historical novel about the monarch's ancestors.

THE PORTER WOMEN'S COTTAGE AT ESHER, SURREY

A cypress flourishes at the head of the grave; and the following touching inscription is carved on the stone:

HERE SLEEPS IN JESUS A CHRISTIAN WIDOW
JANE PORTER
OBIIT JUNE 18TH, 1831, ÆTAT. 86;
THE BELOVED MOTHER OF
W. PORTER, M.D., OF SIR ROBERT KER PORTER,
AND OF JANE AND ANNA MARIA PORTER,
WHO MOURN IN HOPE, HUMBLY TRUSTING TO BE BORN
AGAIN WITH HER UNTO THE BLESSED KINGDOM
OF THEIR LORD AND SAVIOUR.
RESPECT HER GRAVE, FOR SHE MINISTERED TO THE POOR.

MONUMENT TO MRS. PORTER AT ST. GEORGE'S CHURCH, ESHER

FROM LEFT TO RIGHT: ROBERT KER PORTER, JANE PORTER, AND TWO PORTER COUSINS

JANE PORTER'S LONG LETTERS

The Porter women moved to a more comfortable rental cottage in Esher (upper left) in 1825, thanks to promised support from brother Robert, newly made a South American diplomat (lower left, with Jane and two Porter cousins). But after Mrs. Porter's death in 1831 (upper right), followed by Maria's the next year, Jane was left without a home. She described her peripatetic life in long letters to far-away Robert (lower right).

JANE PORTER IN *FRASER'S MAGAZINE* (1835)

NATHANIEL PARKER WILLIS

JANE PORTER IN LATE LIFE

"THE OLD LADY" IN *THE AGES OF FEMALE BEAUTY* (1838)

In the 1830s, Jane lived as a celebrity showpiece in friends' homes. She mentored young writers, including the American N. P. Willis (upper right), whose company she preferred to that of her brother William, a selfish Bristol physician. After Jane was ridiculed in a sexist, ageist magazine profile (upper left), she published a story celebrating older women, which was run alongside an unidentified portrait (lower right) that resembles her own late-life image (lower left).

COUGHTON COURT, NEAR ALCESTER, WARWICKSHIRE, WHERE JANE STAYED AS A GUEST

ST. PAUL'S CHURCH, PORTLAND SQUARE, BRISTOL, NEAR BROTHER WILLIAM'S HOME

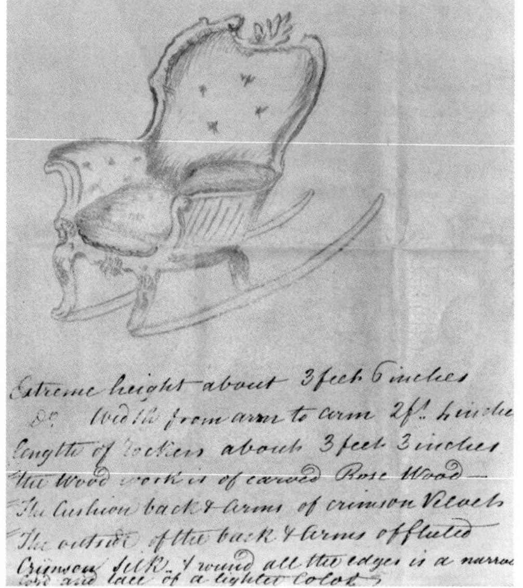

By the 1840s, Jane's books had sold at least a million American copies without payment to her. New York publishers sent an armchair as a token gift (lower left), although she had no fixed residence. She began a book on England's old homes, including Coughton Court (upper left), where she was a guest. When Robert died unexpectedly, Jane moved in with William, perhaps to ensure a final resting place with Maria at Bristol's St. Paul's Church (middle).

SKETCH OF THE CHAIR THAT AMERICAN PUBLISHERS SENT TO JANE PORTER

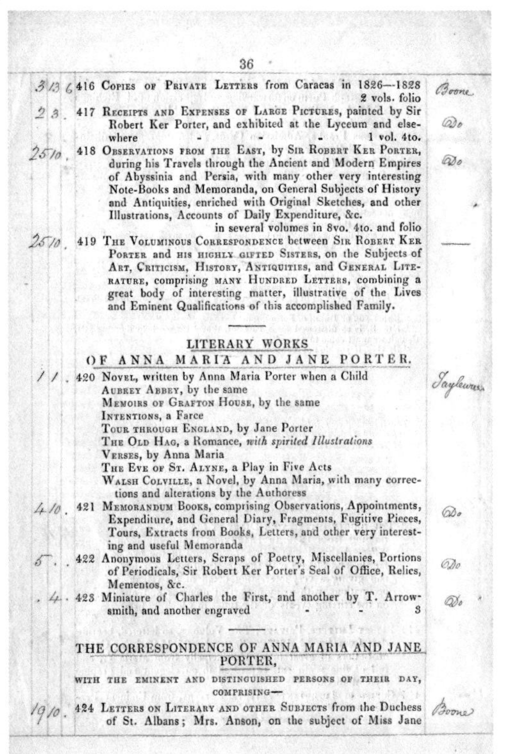

36

416 COPIES OF PRIVATE LETTERS from Caracas in 1826—1828 2 vols. folio

417 RECEIPTS AND EXPENSES OF LARGE PICTURES, painted by Sir Robert Ker Porter, and exhibited at the Lyceum and elsewhere - - - 1 vol. 4to.

418 OBSERVATIONS FROM THE EAST, by SIR ROBERT KER PORTER, during his Travels through the Ancient and Modern Empires of Abyssinia and Persia, with many other very interesting Note-Books and Memoranda, on General Subjects of History and Antiquities, enriched with Original Sketches, and other Illustrations, Accounts of Daily Expenditure, &c. in several volumes in 8vo. 4to. and folio

419 THE VOLUMINOUS CORRESPONDENCE between SIR ROBERT KER PORTER and HIS HIGHLY GIFTED SISTERS, on the Subjects of ART, CRITICISM, HISTORY, ANTIQUITIES, and GENERAL LITERATURE, comprising MANY HUNDRED LETTERS, combining a great body of interesting matter, illustrative of the Lives and Eminent Qualifications of this accomplished Family.

LITERARY WORKS
OF ANNA MARIA AND JANE PORTER.

420 NOVEL, written by Anna Maria Porter when a Child
AUBREY ABBEY, by the same
MEMOIRS OF GRAFTON HOUSE, by the same
INTENTIONS, a Farce
TOUR THROUGH ENGLAND, by Jane Porter
THE OLD HAG, a Romance, *with spirited Illustrations*
VERSES, by Anna Maria
THE EVE OF ST. ALYNE, a Play in Five Acts
WALSH COLVILLE, a Novel, by Anna Maria, with many corrections and alterations by the Authoress

421 MEMORANDUM BOOKS, comprising Observations, Appointments, Expenditure, and General Diary, Fragments, Fugitive Pieces, Tours, Extracts from Books, Letters, and other very interesting and useful Memoranda

422 Anonymous Letters, Scraps of Poetry, Miscellanies, Portions of Periodicals, Sir Robert Ker Porter's Seal of Office, Relics, Mementos, &c.

423 Miniature of Charles the First, and another by T. Arrowsmith, and another engraved - - 3

THE CORRESPONDENCE OF ANNA MARIA AND JANE PORTER,
WITH THE EMINENT AND DISTINGUISHED PERSONS OF THEIR DAY, COMPRISING—

424 LETTERS ON LITERARY AND OTHER SUBJECTS from the Duchess of St. Albans; Mrs. Anson, on the subject of Miss Jane

THE PORTER SISTERS' PAPERS SOLD AT AUCTION BY SOTHEBY'S, 1852

After Jane and William died in 1850, his paramour put a memorial to the Porter family in Bristol Cathedral (right). (The once-prominent tablet was later moved to an obscure vestibule.) Several sea chests of Jane's and Maria's papers were auctioned off for a pittance in 1852 (above), then squirreled away for a century by an indiscriminate collector. When the papers finally reached auction again, the sisters' once-great fame had faded away.

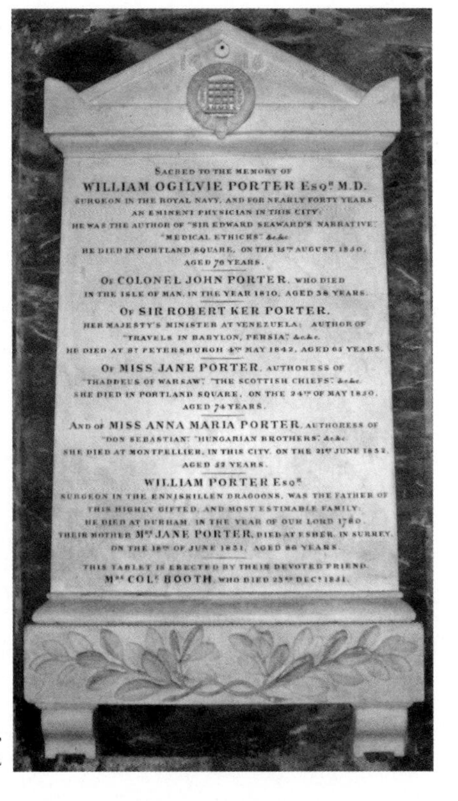

THE PORTER FAMILY MEMORIAL TABLET, BRISTOL CATHEDRAL

CIGARETTE CARD OF JANE PORTER (C. 1910)

THE

SCOTTISH CHIEFS.

BY

JANE PORTER,

Author of " Pride and Prejudice," "Sense and Sensibility," etc., etc.

LONDON:

WARD, LOCK & CO., LIMITED,

WARWICK HOUSE, SALISBURY SQUARE, E.C.,

NEW YORK AND MELBOURNE.

THE SCOTTISH CHIEFS, BY THE AUTHOR OF PRIDE AND PREJUDICE (C. 1890)

THE

SCOTTISH CHIEFS

By JANE PORTER

EDITED BY

Kate Douglas Wiggin *and* Nora A. Smith

Illustrated By N. C. WYETH

N. C. WYETH'S COVER ILLUSTRATION FOR *THE SCOTTISH CHIEFS* (1921)

CLASSICS ILLUSTRATED NO. 67, *THE SCOTTISH CHIEFS* (C. 1950S)

During the Porter sisters' slow posthumous forgetting, errors crept in. A cigarette card featured Jane's face but Scott's quotation (upper left). A misprinted edition of *The Scottish Chiefs* was said to be by the author of *Pride and Prejudice* (lower left). It was repackaged as a children's book (upper right) and a comic book (lower right). Critics wrongly dismissed Jane's claim that she, not Scott, invented the modern historical novel.

with her for morning airings. Maria wrote home to beg her mother and sister to send her advice as November neared.

Just when it seemed things couldn't get worse, tensions at Benham soared higher. Gell resumed his cruel teasing of Maria. But Sharpe, who'd recently rejoined them at Benham, began loudly to take Maria's side. Privately, Sharpe told Maria he absolutely despised Gell. The man was vulgar, bad natured, and possessive of Keppel, Sharpe said, and Keppel seemed almost to have been put under powerful Gell's spell.

Keppel's private diary suggests it was close to the truth. In it, he describes Gell as "a person in whom I Have found most of the qualities that constitute perfection in a human being, & fewer of the faults that are the share of all such."[91]

By then, the Benham social circle had become its own pit of vipers. Sharpe wanted Maria's help in detaching Keppel from the controlling Gell. Gell, meanwhile, seemed to be attempting to detach Keppel from Maria and Sharpe. Maria acknowledged that Sharpe could sometimes be a bit too sharp, but she far preferred him as a friend, both for herself and for Keppel.[92] It was shaping up to be a war over Keppel, as the Margravine—who must have hoped both sides would lose—awaited their mutual destruction.

Sharpe and Maria discovered they agreed, too, on the Margravine's bad character. He was, if anything, more damning. He wanted to open Maria's eyes to the reality of the Margravine. He thought her mad—literally insane. Sharpe claimed she had once sent Keppel a letter accusing him of having attempted to poison her. In reporting this back to Jane, Maria asked, "Can you wonder that Keppel's heart was estranged from such a mother?"[93]

Perversely, Gell and Sharpe seemed strengthened by these perpetual domestic conflicts. By contrast, the anxieties made both Keppel and Maria sick. Naturally, the Margravine tried to reassert her own power. She finally succeeded in truly shocking Maria with a lecture railing against female chastity. Then she insisted on starting a course of extreme medical treatments on her physically weakened son.

When Keppel complained of pains in his chest, the Margravine brought in Dr. Pierse Hackett to bleed him. Dr. Hackett agreed to carry out the treatment, but he confided in Maria his conviction that Keppel's sickness was in his mind. Maria couldn't understand why the Margravine would try to kill her favorite son. She'd leave Keppel with endless numbers of fanciful concoctions but then neglect to give him his actual medicines or help him remember to take them. Maria felt she'd finally seen the Margravine for what she really was. She entirely believed circulating gossip about her host's immorality.

"I find that I have grasped a cloud for a goddess," Maria wrote home.[94]

Keppel eventually recovered, and the conflicts boiling at Benham House were reduced to a simmer. One November day, when Maria took her regular morning walk, she was surprised to find Keppel there, halfway into the woods. He and Gell both knew the route Maria took. She felt sure Keppel had been looking for her. They walked, just the two of them, for two hours. Keppel told Maria intimate details about his mother, his family's conflicts, and his chronic illnesses. He claimed his mother always took an aversion to anyone who liked him. For that reason, he hoped Maria might conceal her liking. He told Maria the Margravine's feelings had changed toward her and that it would be wise not to stay much longer. A few days before, she had cryptically told Keppel there was some person who liked him more than she wanted.

She'd told her son, "If they love you, they must hate me—we are so different."[95]

Maria heard in Keppel's voice how trapped he felt. She put plans in motion to leave the Margravine in January. But then, after that first hours-long clandestine walk, there came many others. Keppel and Maria talked about literature. He recommended favorite books, including Isaak Walton on angling or fishing.[96] Once, as Maria and Keppel emerged from the woods, the Margravine caught the two of them together. Keppel had walked boldly up to his mother. Then he'd avoided the woods for the rest of the week.

The following week, Keppel came to Maria's bedroom once again with Augustus. This time, after he came in, Keppel shut the door. "Conceive my coolly admitting a gentleman into my bed-chambers!" Maria wrote to Jane, although she admitted nothing had happened. Their conversation contained little of importance.

Soon after, their secret long walks resumed. Day after day, Maria and Keppel walked together until they were both physically weary. Keppel never said anything to her he might not say to another friend. There were no declarations of feelings. He complimented her only with his eyes and actions. Maria worried about having given consent to Keppel for these confidential rambles. She knew it wasn't proper. But she didn't refuse.

"I do believe he has taken our unspoken-of walks as a sort of compact between us," she wrote to Jane. "He and I perfectly understand each other about his mother."[97]

There were innocent moments of physical intimacy, too. Keppel, known for his reserved manner, enjoyed shaking hands. Whenever he took Maria's hands, she felt as if he were almost putting a kind of speech into the pressure of it. It made her blush all over.

The Margravine treated Maria with a sort of graciousness to her face, but behind her back, she'd begun to write disturbing letters to the rest of the Porter family. The Margravine expressed a concern that Maria had formed an inappropriate, unrequited love for Keppel. Jane, Mrs. Porter, and Robert were perfectly in on the secret, thanks to Maria's confessional letters home. Robert had practically wished Maria joy on her anticipated marriage to Keppel. But none of the Porters revealed to the Margravine they had any previous inkling of the matter.

First, the Margravine wrote a series of enigmatical letters to Robert, eventually assuring him that, where Maria was concerned, "I shall take care nothing I can prevent shall ever hurt her," despite complaining that although she'd been like a mother to her, Maria never confided in her.[98] The Margravine told Robert she needed to talk to him. She asked him to come to her as soon as possible and bring three brace of pheasants. Robert struggled with this last command. He couldn't afford six birds.

The Margravine's letter to Mrs. Porter must have been even more to the point, judging by Mrs. Porter's disingenuous reply: "My Maria is the last in the world who I should have expected would have given way to such a prepossession as your Highness describes," she wrote. "She was always, though generally affable with gentlemen, particularly insensible to any individual preference; I therefore am the more affected by what your truly parental feelings have confided in me."[99]

Mrs. Porter told the Margravine the best thing would be to send Maria home just after Christmas, as they'd long planned. The Porters lived more than fifty miles away. They'd have wanted the Margravine to let Maria go with as little gossip, rancor, and expense as possible. Above all, Robert needed to stay on good terms with the Margravine, his secret creditor. Maria's next discovery, however, made it impossible for her to slink quietly away from Benham House. She wrote home in a panic.

"All our letters have been opened," Maria wrote, "O Jane, how heavy my heart is!"[100]

The Margravine had been secretly reading Maria's intimate letters before they were sent out. She'd been opening some of Jane's letters to Maria, too, before passing them on to her guest. It meant the Margravine would have known about Maria's feelings for Keppel for months. What seemed to prompt the Margravine to come clean about her snooping were Maria's letters accusing her of being crazy, cruel, and a bad mother.

Maria was no longer welcome at Benham, and after this shocking revelation, every instant she remained there was a misery.[101] She claimed the Margravine had turned into a spy and had secretly lain in wait for two hours in Maria's room, just to see if Keppel would come to her. Maria must have expected he would. She believed their unspoken feelings were mutual. She would have hoped for a warm goodbye from him, at least, if not a declaration of love. But Keppel didn't come. He had made his choice. Maria assured her sister that she'd eventually recover her peace of mind. It was just crushing to think of Keppel's friends gossiping about her and scoffing at her feelings.

"I, I must remain the sacrifice," Maria dramatically, selflessly—and not inaccurately—concluded.[102]

Maria, shattered in looks and spirits, left Benham for the Dillons' home in London in mid-December 1809. She unburdened herself to her hosts and to her dear friend Elizabeth Benger. Benger assured Maria that the Margravine's character was so bad that no ill conduct of hers could surprise anyone. As for Keppel, Benger believed he couldn't have acted otherwise with such a mother.[103] His mind, she thought, seemed capable of becoming Maria's other self.[104] Perhaps one day, Benger thought, he'd prove his true love for Maria.

But if Keppel had strong feelings for Maria, he didn't reveal them in his private diary. It's entirely possible, of course, that Keppel knew his mother surreptitiously read its pages, just as she'd read Maria's private letters. One puzzling passage refers to an unnamed female friend: "There is indeed another female whom a long intercourse, many excellent qualities, and gratitude & habit have attac'd me to, but with her I am never totally at ease."[105]

Keppel's only direct mention of Maria in his diarywas on December 22, 1809. "We have had, & have still a House full of company, and have celebrated my Mother's birthday, with much glee & festivity," Keppel wrote. "Miss Porter has left us."[106]

In the winter of 1810, Maria returned to Ditton Cottage from London, after an absence of almost a year. Both sisters were numb and grieving. Maria was so sick she was spitting up vermillion-colored blood.[107] Mrs. Porter was worried the world would think Maria was lovesick, not physically ill. She asked Jane to caution Maria never to mention the Margravine's or Keppel's names in public.[108]

Robert sent Maria a sympathetic, reassuring letter. He told her he'd learned the Margravine opened her guests' letters as a regular household practice. Robert apologized for his inability to break off his friendship with her. The Margravine, he noted, had twice saved him from debtors' prison.[109] Yet he planned to drop her once Princess Mary paid back the loan.[110]

The Margravine wrote several rage-filled letters to Robert and one long lecture-letter to Jane, using an imperious tone like that of *Pride and Prejudice*'s Lady Catherine de Bourgh. She said the Porter sisters should let this debacle be a lesson to them. She was shocked—*shocked*—at the behavior of two such young women. She couldn't believe they'd set themselves on a level with, or even above, the Margravine (who referred to herself in the third person). That the sisters would so undermine and condemn the Margravine, a caring mother they had long flattered for their own purposes! Her letter claimed the sisters misread every sign before them. Keppel wasn't sighing after Maria, she claimed. He was cold. He himself wasn't lovesick—merely sick.

"Could not Miss P. know that a romance in real Life, must at least have the Hero of it in the Plot," the Margravine wrote. "The M. hopes this will be a warning to the Miss Porters to confine their Compositions to Novels, where only sentiments of gratitude & respect are found in those young Ladies."[111]

If, during this humiliation, Maria had been paying any attention to the reviews of her new novel, she'd at least have seen her powers positively praised there. The *Critical Review* described *Don Sebastian* as an achievement that added a thousand charms to her historical characters and interested readers extremely in their fates. The reviewer declared Maria was entitled to be ranked among the best living novelists.[112]

When rumors circulated that the Margravine intended to remove Keppel to the Continent, allegedly for his ill health, Maria couldn't help but think it was to get him completely out of her orbit. The gossiping world assumed Miss Anna Maria Porter's feelings for Mr. Keppel Craven had arisen without any sign of preference from him. Maria felt that was untrue. Yet she decided she'd never claim there was a mutual affection, unless Keppel first declared feelings for her.

Some months after the dramatic break with the Margravine, Gell sent a kind letter to Maria. He told her she'd been mistaken about Keppel's feelings, that he'd never meant anything more than friendship. In reply, Maria told Gell that she blamed the Margravine, first for encouraging her to think of Mr. Craven as a romantic figure, and then for using the snare of opening her letters to call her to account for it. Maria said she felt she'd paid a full penalty for her folly, including making this final humiliating confession to Gell.

She told him, "Could you see what an agony of shame and sorrow I am suffering at this moment, you would pity me."[113]

Eventually Keppel himself sent a letter of some kind about Maria, either to Robert, or to Jane, or to Maria herself. The letter doesn't seem to have survived. Its contents, whatever they were, fully satisfied Jane when she read them.

"You see he avowes that you were not deceived in his partial sentiments of you," she wrote to her sister. "This letter then, leaves you fully in possession of your own self-respect—and what must add to your quiet, gives you conviction of his respect also."[114]

Jane encouraged Maria in her hopes for Keppel, certain their feelings for each other would eventually win out. Time, Jane said, would prove Keppel's honor to Maria, and Maria's entire innocence to him.[115] Maria hoped one day Keppel would again visit their home. He didn't. Over the years, she grew less certain of his romantic love, but she longed, still, for an imperfect friendship with him. Perhaps somewhere, in the back of her mind, was the feeling that, once the Margravine died, Keppel would be free to come for her. In the future, whenever the sisters referred to the Margravine in their letters, they called her "Pandora." It was a superb joke. In Greek mythology, deceitful Pandora opens a jar or box and releases evil into the world.

For Maria, the breach with the Margravine remained total. But through a mutual friend, she learned that little Augustus often asked for her. Maria made shoes to send him.[116] Then friends brought the boy to her for a visit. At their reunion, he ran right up to her. She couldn't believe she had the chance to hold him in her arms again. They played together for four hours. He'd grown taller and could read, write, and dance. Maria thought him "so like, so very like Keppel."[117]

With the approval of the boy's mother, she made regular visits to Augustus, who had begun to attend a nearby school. He would sometimes come to the Porters' cottage for dinner. "My precious Augustus," Maria called him.[118] She treated him as if he were hers, rather than nobody's, or anybody's. She stayed close to him for years.

Eventually, Keppel did right by Augustus, acknowledging him as his son and giving him the Craven surname. Two decades later, after he came of age, Augustus Craven became the rumored suitor of actress Fanny Kemble, the daughter of Charles Kemble and Therese De Camp Kemble.[119] But Augustus instead chose a London-born Frenchwoman as his wife. Pauline Marie Armande Craven later became an acclaimed novelist.

Long before that, in the mid-1810s, Keppel and Gell went into the service of the Princess of Wales, before she became Queen Caroline. It was the only job Keppel ever held. Unfortunately, it wound up giving him a supporting role at her unprecedented and nationally riveting adultery trial. That's what Keppel is now best known for in histories of this period.

The Margravine and Keppel, who always remained closely enmeshed, left England to resettle in Italy, at Craven Villa in Naples. They took Gell with them and into their home, although the Margravine was said to have despised him. Keppel and Gell lived together for the rest of their lives in a same-sex partnership.[120]

After the Margravine died in 1828, she left everything to Keppel in trust, for the remainder of his life. She stipulated that if Keppel died without legitimate children, then at his death, the fortune would go to her brother's children. The Margravine cut off the rest of her own offspring. She left nothing to her "adopted son," Robert Ker Porter. When Sir William Gell died in 1836, he left his belongings to Keppel. Keppel had Gell's body buried next to his mother's. At Keppel's death in 1851, his remains joined theirs.[121]

CHAPTER 15

Family Misfortunes and Jane's *Scottish Chiefs* (1810)

During the dramatic, painful year of 1809, while Maria dangled in the viselike grip of the Margravine of Anspach, Jane endured problems of her own. One of the things she had to contend with was the fallout from the reemergence of Percival Stockdale, her former mentor and would-be keeper.

Stockdale's memoir, the work Jane had spent those captive months editing four years earlier, was finally published in March 1809. He gave it the long-winded title *The Memoirs of the Life, and Writings of Percival Stockdale Containing Many Interesting Anecdotes of the Illustrious Men with Whom He Was Connected. Written by Himself.* It was a two-volume, 943-page book, published by Longman and Rees and dedicated to Jane.

Jane wasn't pleased. Stockdale's book, she reported to Maria, is "most flamingly dedicated to me."[1] He had recently declared, in a private letter, that Jane was his best friend.[2] But the book's dedication didn't have her best interests at heart. It was written by an old married man, estranged from his wife, who called attention to his strong feelings for a much younger, single woman.

Stockdale's four-page dedication to Jane used the language of a lover while diminishing her efforts by describing her as his "humble copier."[3] He revealed she'd once lived in his Northumberland home, which didn't have the look of propriety. Stockdale declared that the present age couldn't adequately understand Jane's goodness, which was more characteristic of long-past, romantic, heroic ages than the fallen world of the present. His worship was on view for all to see. Jane didn't admit it to herself, but Stockdale's dedication to her wasn't unlike what she'd done in dedicating *Thaddeus of Warsaw* to Sir Sidney Smith. That had also aroused gossip and prompted speculation. Thanks to Stockdale's dedication to her, she was imagined as the paramour of a man some considered cock-brained and one of the worst poets of the present age.[4]

In the five years since Jane escaped Stockdale's home in Lesbury, she'd maintained a regular correspondence yet kept him at arm's length. They'd reconnected in person in the winter of 1809, when he traveled to London to oversee the printing of his *Memoirs*. Despite all Jane had endured with him, she still felt sympathy for this frail man in his early seventies who'd taught her so much.

When Stockdale's *Memoirs* were published, *Thaddeus of Warsaw* was in its fourth British edition, and Jane was trying to write another great novel. They needed the two hundred pounds she'd be paid when she delivered her next book. While Maria was living with the Margravine, Jane was at Ditton Cottage, researching and writing her five-volume masterpiece about the legendary life of thirteenth-century Scottish hero William Wallace. Maria called Jane's book "her Wallace." When they composed novels, Jane and Maria fully immersed themselves in the moments, people, and worlds of their chosen settings. Jane later described their approach in an anonymous letter to the *Gentleman's Magazine*. They intended for the stories to excite an interest beyond themselves. They wanted readers to pick up the nonfiction books their novels drew on so "the door of romance" would open up a world of "interesting Historical fact, and traits of celebrated Biography."[5] It's precisely what Jane was striving for when finishing up her Wallace, but as she was reconstructing a favorite hero from the past, her favorite hero of the present, Sir Sidney Smith, took an irrevocable step.

"I see by the papers that Sir Sidney is married," Robert wrote home to his mother. "It surprized me a little as Lady Rumbold was the last I should have thought he would have pitched upon."[6]

Smith, forty-five, had married a baronet's widow, also forty-five, on October 11, 1809. Her first husband had been a diplomat. She was a dashing mother of six, and at her age, a second marriage wasn't likely to produce children. Although she wasn't exceptionally wealthy, the widow had money, with property in Hyderabad, India.[7] Lady Rumbold was an adventurous and well-traveled woman. In that sense, she and Smith were similar.

The world hadn't expected this marriage. It was whispered the couple had been having an affair. As one man put it in a private letter, Sir Sidney Smith "had for years been supposed to have obtained all he could wish or expect from the lady."[8] The gossiping world also said Smith had gone directly from the church ceremony to be presented to King George III, implying he had more interest in status and career than love and marriage. Reputable accounts indeed place him at the church and the private royal levee on the same day.[9]

Maria was sure Smith must have been persecuted into the marriage.

"When women are determined to have a man at the expence of his *esteem* and *respect*, they always succeed," she wrote to Jane, "but what virtuous woman could bear a husband so gained? My heart aches for him, and his, and for all that love him."[10]

Jane wrote an obligatory letter to congratulate Smith on his marriage, which must have pained her. She invited Sir Sidney and Lady Smith to Ditton. A bridal visit, in which the groom introduced his new wife, would put all parties on visiting terms with one another and establish a new intimacy.

Smith's terse response arrived in mid-November.

"My dear Miss Porter," he wrote, "If you could but conceive how I am surrounded beset & overpowered by personal application visits & letters beyond the number that falls to the same of most men in society you would pity rather than blame me for my apparent negligence with regard to your most admissible & reasonable expectation of an answer from me." He thanked her for the lovely invitation and made inquiries after Robert.[11] He didn't mention his new wife or relay any message from her or express any wish they'd ever meet. These omissions spoke volumes.

Eventually the Smiths did make their obligatory visit to the cottage. The couple came at a time when they knew only Mrs. Porter would be home. Jane warned her sister not to tell anyone these details. She didn't want others to know how rudely the Smiths had behaved. Maria saw it more clearly than Jane—what must have been his wife's jealousy and her refusal of the connection. Maria would later say she often thought of Smith but lamented him as if he'd passed into the grave.

"What a sad, sad collapse of all his brightness," she wrote.[12]

Jane couldn't entirely blame Smith. He remained her ideal of the perfect hero, for his having saved a nation at war and put it on a path to its own brighter future.

"With all poor, dear Sir Sidney's infatuations and failures," she wrote later of Smith, "I love him so sincerely."[13]

Indeed, she once had a chance to prove it, on an occasion that Smith himself would never know about. An unnamed lady came to visit Jane at Ditton Cottage and handed her friend a gift she thought would please her. It was a packet of confidential letters written by a woman who'd recently died. This woman had been passionately attached to Smith. Her letters, Jane was told, were of the most interesting nature imaginable—a euphemism for adultery. Jane didn't hesitate a moment. She took the packet out of the hand that had offered it to her. The two friends were sitting together in Jane's parlor, near the fire.

"I drew close to it," she wrote, "and immediately thrusting the packet into the midst of it, & poking it down into the flame with the poker—I then said to my astonished visitor—'Thank you for giving them to me—for this is the use I make of them.'"[14]

Jane said she'd just as soon as tear up out of the grave the heart of the dead woman who wrote these love letters than read one line of what she had to say about Sir Sidney Smith.

Miss Jane Porter's *The Scottish Chiefs*: *A Romance* was advertised as forthcoming in December 1809, but the ad was premature. She was still finishing the fifth volume. As late as February 1810, she was frantically corresponding with the printers and creating an errata sheet.[15] She went to London to oversee the printing process, an attention to detail she'd learned from Stockdale. Jane's five-volume novel made its long-awaited debut in March 1810, shortly after Maria's return to the cottage, heartbroken over her betrayal by the Margravine of Anspach and Keppel Craven. Maria rallied with excitement, however, for the publication of her sister's book. She read it aloud to friends and neighbors.[16]

The Scottish Chiefs begins happily, with William Wallace and his pregnant wife. It quickly shifts to a story of murder and war. Jane rewrote late thirteenth-century Scottish history and the William Wallace legend. She brought her hero through the requisite battles, with the friends and enemies recorded in standard histories. But she changed some of his known enemies into secret allies. She added new characters and twists to the familiar plot, including betrayals, kidnappings, escapes, alliances, and love intrigues.

Some of the story was set in places Jane knew well. For the section in which her character Robert the Bruce is imprisoned in Durham Castle, Jane was on very familiar childhood ground in her descriptions. Other settings were gleaned through consulting books, especially for scenes set in rural Scotland and France, where she'd never traveled. Jane recast her William Wallace as a modern-day Christian hero, drawing on her wide knowledge of contemporary men and their experiences, especially on Sir Sidney Smith's stories of war and Henry Caulfield's struggles in debtors' prison.

"Nothing gratifies me more than that you see my ever-beloved Henry in Wallace," Jane wrote to Maria. "His noble soul was too truly part of my own, (its best part, my dear Maria),—for me not to breathe its spirit into all I would picture of excellence."[17]

The Scottish Chiefs, though ostensibly built around a tragic, male-centered legend, struck many readers as a joyful story, relevant to the present. It also gave centrality to the actions of women in wartime. Jane breathed new life into legend, following the contours and sources of history and biography, adding in fictionalized social history. She created domestic backstories and real and imagined medieval characters. She developed significant new parts for women. For instance, she gave extended attention to her hero's grief over, and desire to vindicate, his wife's murder—an invented fiction. Then she gave Wallace further invented love intrigues and war intrigues by entangled turns throughout the tale.

In her preface, Jane told her readers, "I have spared no pains in consulting almost every writing extant which treats of the sister kingdoms during the period of my narrative." She'd done her research. She acknowledged that in creating her Wallace, she'd added strokes to fill the space and unite the whole. She thanked her friend Thomas Campbell for his suggestions—a canny acknowledgment, as he was a respected poet from a Scottish clan.[18] She argued Britons shared a common national ancestry. Her preface charts out a more clear, compelling, and innovative method and rationale for historical fiction than had been previously seen in the British literary tradition. She acknowledged drawing heavily on the famous fifteenth-century poet Blind Harry, who had written *The Wallace*, a century after the hero's death. In March 1810,

Longman printed 2,000 copies.[19] The standard number for a first edition was 500 to 750. The publishers were anticipating great demand, and Jane was confident she'd created something significant. She was right. Readers had outsized responses. One man, when he reached the part where Lady Wallace dies, was said to have rushed out into London's Bond Street, his eyes overflowing with tears. He was stopped by half a dozen people who asked him what the matter was.[20] The novelist Mary Ann Hanway told Jane *The Scottish Chiefs* beguiled her of many tears and that its style of writing placed Jane among the first claimants of literary fame.[21]

"I could have no doubt of Wallace being preferred to Thaddeus," Maria wrote. "It is transcendentally so—and the sentiment of approval appears gaining ground."[22] Maria did regret one thing, however—that Jane had been forced to write the novel under such anxiety and strain.

"When I know all that you could have made of this work under different circumstances," she told her sister, "I feel that my Jane proved kindred heroism with her Hero, in publishing it at this period."[23]

Not everyone was so kind. Some contemporaries objected to the book's unconventional form. Scottish novelist Mary Brunton was determined not to read *The Scottish Chiefs*, believing Porter must have been disingenuous about dramatizing history only a little. Poet Walter Scott, the Porters' childhood acquaintance, later wrote to a friend about Jane's hero, "Lord help her! . . . It is not safe meddling with the hero of a country and of all others I cannot endure to see the character of Wallace frittered away to that of a fine gentleman."[24]

But most readers proved more willing to accept Jane's mixed-genre characters and methods. The novelist Mary Russell Mitford, an early admirer of Jane Austen's fiction, found Porter's achievement in *The Scottish Chiefs* remarkable: "Indeed, I scarcely know one héros de roman, whom it is possible to admire, except Wallace in Miss Porter's 'Scottish Chiefs.' "[25]

Reviews began to appear. The *British Critic* wrote, "We do not recollect to have read a romance, which was to us more interesting, than the *Scottish Chiefs*."[26] Many editions of it would surely be "called for soon."[27] The praise kept coming, not just for months but for years. One writer dubbed it an epic poem (though denominated a romance) that hadn't been equaled for years, with its leading characters, "superior to any thing ever written." The reviewer claimed, "Milton or Virgil do not surpass it in sentiment."[28] When Jane went to stay with friends, she became the traveling attraction. In Clifton, people again expected her to speak oracles, as they had years before in Bath.[29] Acquaintances hung on her every word. She didn't always enjoy the attention. She called it her "flattering distress."[30]

The book was selling out rapidly.[31] Jane was just as pleased as she was surprised that *Chiefs* was thought superior to *Thaddeus*. Her previous novel, too, was still selling briskly and was soon once again out of print. But by the terms of the agreement she'd signed, Longman and Rees weren't obliged to pay her anything for the next edition of *Thaddeus*—and didn't. She hoped for better treatment for *The Scottish Chiefs*. Jane wrote to Maria, "Between ourselves, my publisher wants generosity." She'd hoped they might share windfall profits from *The Scottish Chiefs*, the way the publisher Joseph Johnson had given Maria Edgeworth an extra four hundred pounds for strong sales of her *Popular Tales*. Jane thought Longman and Rees should offer her another hundred pounds for *The Scottish Chief*'s extra fifth volume.[32] That much they did, whether at her suggestion or not. When Jane received the money, she gave it to Robert, despite knowing perfectly well that it was her brother John who needed it more.[33]

John Blenkinsop Porter's descent into crippling debt was gradual. Although Jane had secured temporary agreements with creditors for him and Robert in 1806, she doesn't seem to have helped John again. There was a warrant out for the arrest of one John Porter in April 1807.[34] It was a common name. Whether the warrant referred to him or not, John would shortly be in great trouble. When Robert was out of the country in 1808, John wrote to ask his famous brother to give him a thousand pounds. Robert refused. He thought John was bewitched by dreams to imagine Robert had this sum.

"I forgive him," Robert wrote to Jane, "and regret most sincerely that I am not rich enough to make him as easy as I wish him."[35] But then, without permission, John had drawn on Robert's bankers for one hundred pounds. When the bankers inquired about the sum advanced, Robert balked and said he no longer had anything to do with his brother.[36] Behind John's back, Robert called him "the black Sheep of the family."[37]

John owed money to others as well. He'd recently been imprisoned for a debt of a mere twenty pounds. It was hushed up, after a friend paid off the sum. Then he had gotten legal help from a Fleet Street attorney, which meant he owed that man money, too. John quickly left town and resorted to sadly typical desperate measures for debtors, including drifting around the country incognito.

He eventually turned up on the Isle of Man.[38] John had somehow relocated three hundred miles northwest, halfway across the Irish Sea. The Isle of Man may have been his destination because conditions for debtors on the self-governing, crown-dependent island were more forgiving. Manx laws stipulated debtors who surrendered all property might go free. Unfortunately for John, that law applied only to *native* inhabitants of the island. By May 1810, John was in debtors' prison at the Isle of Man's dilapidated Castle Rushen Gaol. He sent Robert a letter declaring this time that his brother *owed* him a thousand pounds and demanding repayment. Robert denied any debt. He told Jane that even if he'd had money to spare, it wouldn't have gone to John but instead to his mother and sisters.

"I pity him," Robert said of John. "His experience ought to have placed him at the head of his family as their protector and father instead of calling on the youngest son to support both his own extravagances and be to his mother and sisters what he ought to have been."[39]

The rest of the Porters may have hoped John would remain silent about his faraway incarceration. Instead, he wrote several letters, describing the brutal privations of prison life. He sent them to the day's foremost prison reform writers, who published them. At first, his letters were semi-anonymous, in the form of collaboratively written petitions to the government for debtor relief. Then John wrote at least two epistolary reports, published in a regular column in the *Gentleman's Magazine*'s series "On Prisons" by John Coakley Lettsom and James Neild, two national leaders on prison reform and Porter family friends. The first of John's letters was anonymously excerpted in the December 1810 issue.

Jane, who was especially close to Lettsom, may have been told or privately realized that the man described in the *Gentleman's Magazine* as a mournful correspondent in a miserable situation in Castle Rushen Gaol was her imprisoned brother. If so, the irony of the location wouldn't have been lost on her: John was incarcerated in a castle with historical ties to Robert the Bruce, the Scottish warrior-king who'd played a part in *The Scottish Chiefs*. Robert the Bruce had victoriously laid siege to Castle Rushen in 1313, some years after the principal events depicted in her novel.

By 1810, however, Castle Rushen, despite its grand history, was exceptionally run-down. John described its conditions for the magazine's readers: On admittance, an incarcerated man surrendered all his property. No public funds were made available for food, beds, fuel, or medicine, let alone to support any wives and children. Because the toilet wasn't sunk below ground, the smells were offensive. The courtyard became unusable from sewage in warmer weather. The water pump didn't work. Many rooms had neither roofs nor floors. Apartments held up to a dozen people, most compelled to sleep in the ground, because they couldn't afford to rent a bed. There was no light in the evening. There was no heat, unless an imprisoned man could afford his own coals. The incarcerated foraged for food and cooked it themselves.

When John wrote to Neild and Lettsom, there were nine people incarcerated at Castle Rushen, all imprisoned for debt. They were starving yet were expected to work, pulling fibers out of old rope or breaking up stones.[40] His letter concludes, "The darkness of the room I sit in, must apologize for the badness of my writing; the state of my mind, for the incoherence of my letter; and my poverty, for *this paper*."[41] When it was published, John's letter led to charitable donations. Neild sent the imprisoned people at Castle Rushen Gaol ten tons of coal (enough to last the winter), many candles,[42] and bedsteads.[43]

Only a few lines about John remain in the Porters' extensive surviving correspondence from this period, including in an 1811 letter from Jane to her mother: "We must hope, that God will grant him life, to return from his unhappy errors."[44] This line doesn't suggest the family sent John any relief. In contrast, Jane had never ignored Robert's debts or Henry Caulfield's imprisonment. She even treated her fictional characters better when they were incarcerated. In *The Scottish Chiefs*, the heroine, Helen, visited Wallace in prison in the Tower of London. "I came to minister with a sister's duty to my own and my father's preserver," she tells Wallace, "and while he abides here, I will never consent to leave his feet."[45]

But John's timing was bad in needing his siblings' help, and trust in him was broken. As Jane launched her new novel into the world to rave reviews, and as Robert tried to secure a marriage to a Russian princess, John was anonymously describing in print that he was starving in prison and living amid excrement. These stories could not easily be squared. Things became more complicated still when, in the August 1811 issue of the *Gentleman's Magazine*, John's anonymity was compromised. In Neild and Lettsom's prison letter number 72, readers learned that the former Castle Rushen correspondent, named as "John B. Porter," had tragically died. Whether the Porters were surprised by this news or not, they must have been grateful that at least the widely circulating magazine didn't spell out John's middle name.

On the Isle of Man, however, the local newspaper, *The Manks Advertiser*, printed a more specific death notice on August 24, 1811: "Died, suddenly, on Monday the 19th inst., John Blenkinsop Porter, Esq., aged 39 years; he had been for a year and a half confined in Castle Rushen, and is universally regretted by his brother prisoners."[46] He was buried in Malew Churchyard on August 22, 1811 in an unmarked grave.

"He was not brought up with us like Robert," Jane privately wrote of John, after learning of his death. "Nevertheless we loved him as a brother, and mourn him as such."[47]

Like Wallace in *The Scottish Chiefs*, John Blenkinsop Porter died an imprisoned man. Life would imitate art in yet another way, too. It seems John, like Jane's fictional Wallace, took a prison bride. This marriage, however, wasn't chaste like Wallace and Helen's. It may not even have been legally binding. The *Gentleman's Magazine* communicated that John B. Porter had died "in the most distressing circumstances, leaving a wife and infant child, without one farthing to procure the smallest necessary of life."[48]

This distinction between a legitimate or illegitimate marriage, and a legitimate or illegitimate child, was momentous. In 1811, Robert, still trying to wed Princess Mary, sought permission from a reluctant Tsar Alexander. A report circulating about Robert having a brother who'd just died in a debtors' prison, and who left behind a supposed wife and child, who may or may not have had the benefit of Christian rites, would have been, at the very least, inconvenient. In the past, Jane and Maria had shown charity to children born out of wedlock, including Keppel Craven's son, Augustus. The sisters had socialized with the Duke of Clarence's mistress, the actress Mrs. Jordan, and their many Fitzclarence children. But the Porter family lacked the buffer of wealth and status that those natural children's parents had.

Jane tried to ascertain whether John and his prison bride were truly married. A Mr. Cowell on the Isle of Man was asked to help them. Quite possibly, this was Frederick Cowell, Maria's former fiancé. It may have been one of his brothers. Whoever it was would have had to be someone they trusted. When Maria heard back from Mr. Cowell, she reported, "He has not the least doubt of the woman's assertion being false; for if she had really been his wife, she would have been known as such, in the Isle of Man, and he never heard of her, but as his mistress."[49] The Porters seem to have turned their back on the penniless woman and baby, just as they had John. No further mention of her or the child seems to have been recorded in the Porters' letters. Yet the family couldn't forget John entirely. For years after he died, Robert was still receiving letters inquiring about his late brother's debts.[50]

A few weeks after John's death, Jane was confronted with another loss. Percival Stockdale passed away in Lesbury on September 14, 1811, at age seventy-four. His death was regretted, of course, but the Porter family also hoped he'd left enough of a legacy to make Jane independent. Stockdale mentioned Jane three times in his will. First, she and two other men were given the right to share in any profits that might result from the future publication of his manuscripts. That turned out to be nearly valueless. The will's second mention of Jane included fulsome praise of her having "acted towards me with the most disinterested and exalted friendship."[51] This was in a clause naming a dozen others, each of whom was promised five guineas to buy a ring to remember him by. The will's final mention of Jane was its most disappointing. After having promised specific bequests that totaled nearly two thousand pounds, Stockdale declared that the remainder of his fortune should go to Jane.[52] Unfortunately, he overestimated his estate and vastly overpromised his would-be heirs. It's not even clear whether Jane ended up with the little bequest for buying a ring.

Before this outcome was perfectly understood, Jane published a long, generous memorial to him in the *Gentleman's Magazine*. It was signed "J. P."[53] This meant that from 1810 through 1811, the *Gentleman's Magazine* had published several significant pieces of anonymous writing by and about the Porter family. John's letters about the horrors of prison were followed by the notice of his death. Jane's long memorial to Stockdale celebrated the man who'd once virtually imprisoned and then flamingly dedicated a book to her. The *Gentleman's Magazine* had also published a positive review of *The Scottish Chiefs*, praising the manner in which Miss Porter's novel had interwoven private occurrences with political acts.[54] Few would have understood the difficult, connected personal and political stories behind these three texts.

A year after its publication, *The Scottish Chiefs*, having sold out its large initial print run, went into a second edition. Longman and Rees printed fifteen hundred more copies.[55] Jane had a second bestseller on her hands. Tens of thousands of copies appeared once again in pirated editions across North America. Napoleon became so concerned about the possible influence of *The Scottish Chiefs* on his ability to retain power, presumably because of its celebration of those who resist invasion, that he commanded the French edition be destroyed.[56] Maria, as ever, was Jane's greatest admirer. She compared the pure passages of beauty in her sister's novel to the writings of Shakespeare.[57] Across the nineteenth century, *The Scottish Chiefs* never fell out of print.

CHAPTER 16

Horror Princess

Russians in Britain, Maria's Recluse, *and Jane's Redoubled Fame (1811–14)*

With the runaway success of *The Scottish Chiefs*, Jane had proved herself once again her family's brightest shining star. By 1811, she couldn't be brushed off by skeptics as a flash-in-the-pan, one-lucky-strike novelist. At thirty-five, with two global bestsellers, Jane was a phenomenon. Fame had begun to afford the Porter sisters access to a wide readership and the opportunity to tell their life stories, but the biographical accounts that appeared were misleading or at least selective in their facts. It was presumably at the sisters' own direction. Jane and Maria set out to shape these stories of their lives in the same way that their novels reshaped history—adding or omitting details to entertain or uplift readers, where it suited their purposes. One 1810 memoir of Jane in the *Monthly Mirror* declared *Thaddeus of Warsaw* was her "first work," leaving out both *Two Princes of Persia* and *The Spirit of the Elbe*. From there, the misleading claim was regularly repeated.

In the same memoir, Jane's *Thaddeus of Warsaw* was lauded as "a new species of composition," for its combining "ancient romance, and the domestic interest of a modern novel." This is a more supportable assertion, although anything declared to be a literary origin tends to prompt claims of predecessors and to raise hackles. In 1810, however, few argued with this statement. Readers and critics alike credited Jane with something refreshingly inventive, in a new combination, that produced a different literary kind. The greatest praise, however, was reserved for *The Scottish Chiefs*. Jane's "second" novel (as it was called) was declared a book read throughout the kingdom that "fixed her as it were in an exalted hemisphere, where her imitators, as minor planets, shine with diminished brightness."[1] The Porter sisters were called "true champions" in the cause of moral and religious restraint and the beauty and propriety of women's modesty, as well as encouragers of men's virtue.

Yet Jane and Maria, cast as paragons and wonders, were certainly not living in exalted circumstances during these years. They were still trying to eke out a living writing for magazines, providing for the family through their own hard work. Both sisters, and even brother William, were contributing to *La Belle Assemblée*, one of the era's most prominent women's magazines. Jane was the most productive, publishing untold dozens, or likely hundreds, of separate unsigned pieces, for a fee of three guineas a month.[2]

Maria, although chronically ill, was working on two books. The first she completed was a collection of her verses, *Ballad Romances, and Other Poems* (1811). The poems in the book's first half tell glorious tales of knights, princes, and Scottish heroes. The second half's "Miscellaneous" poems took more chances, including verses like "Epistle from Yarico to Inkle," which use the white trader and "Indian maiden" characters from the well-known opera *Inkle and Yarico* (1787) to give greater agency to the female Yarico. The poem rails against slavery as a "decree of selfish power" and "base perfidy" that creates "life-consuming woe."[3] Other poems were more personal, including the "Sonnet: On Jane," which celebrates her sister's virtue, thought, piety, and "still gracious heart."

Maria's *Ballad Romances* had only a so-so showing with the public. Two years after its publication, Longman and Rees told her that of the 1,000 copies they'd printed, just 350 had sold. As Owen Rees bluntly put it, "The sale of the volume of Poems is considerably short of the expenses of the work."[4] The all-important reviewers weren't ecstatic. The *Critical Review* put Maria in what it called "the second class of the lesser poets of the day."[5]

The other book Maria was working on was a collection of short stories for children, which Longman apparently didn't want. It was eventually published elsewhere as *Tales of Pity on Fishing, Shooting, and Hunting, Intended to Inculcate in the Mind of Youth, Sentiments of Humanity Toward the Brute Creation* (1814). She signed the book "AMP," giving it a veneer of anonymity. *Tales of Pity* included three stories—one each on fishing, shooting, and hunting—told from the perspective of anthropomorphized animals who seek humane treatment as God's living creatures. The first thing Maria did upon the book's publication was send a copy to Keppel's son, Augustus.

Yet amid this substantial amount of new writing and publication, including the success of *The Scottish Chiefs*, the Porter family's primary focus remained Robert's hoped-for marriage. Robert and Princess Mary had been separated by thousands of miles since 1807, as the Napoleonic Wars raged on. A plan was concocted to have her secretly bolt from Russia to England by ship and take along as many valuables as she could sneak away with. They understood the real possibility that her estates would be confiscated if she left the country to marry without Tsar Alexander's permission.[6]

"I am ready to sacrifice all for thee," she wrote to Robert, "to fly to thee and to prove to thee my Love; I will send over my property before I come."[7]

Princess Mary was supposed to transmit twenty-five thousand rubles and bring twenty thousand rubles' worth of diamonds with her, which might fetch three thousand pounds, Robert calculated. After that, he hoped they'd convince Tsar Alexander to let them keep the annual proceeds from her estates, estimated at twenty-five thousand rubles.[8] On that sum the couple could live nicely, though not extravagantly, in England. But when, at the last minute, Princess Mary was told by a trusted adviser about the precise exchange rate from rubles to pounds, she didn't get on the ship. By the time Robert learned she'd stayed behind, he'd waited for her for weeks at an English port, at no small expense to himself.

Princess Mary came up with an alternate plan. Robert should secure a long leave of absence from his military post—his one remaining source of secure income—to return to Russia and marry her. She'd send him money to pay off his debts and provide a subsistence for his mother and sisters for while he was gone.[9] She was working on a petition that would give him special leave to return to Russia as well as official permission to marry her. Meanwhile, Robert was still trying to get a British title to help their case for matrimony succeed with Alexander. Maria declared she'd abhor the thought of Robert's angling for a knighthood, if it weren't so necessary to his happiness.[10] And so she and Jane put a new spin on the Porter family's modest, unknown ancestry. Jane wrote letters to an antiquarian ally, trying to establish, or manufacture, more advantageous family origins, no matter how many generations back or how distant the cousins were.

Jane's ally helped her establish maternal connections to two ancient Northumberland families, the Blenkinsops and the Edens. This illustrious pedigree could be plausibly passed off as true, although it was a stretch. The modest personal origins of Peter Blenkinsop—their Wilkite innkeeper grandfather in Durham who'd sung in the cathedral—would be swept farther under the rug. They had long avoided mentioning his profession and, when asked, responded with dubious accuracy that their respected grandfather's profession was "in the church."[11]

"We had all the Eden pedigree," Jane wrote to her mother, whose own ancestors she was describing. "And almost to a certainty we have fixed my Grandmother's degree of relationship with that family—a question or two, which you can answer will decide the thing." On her father's side, Jane wrote, "I have more hopes from Ireland than I thought it likely I could have." Her source had "hardly a doubt . . . if he gets any accounts whatever of the origin of our family in Ireland, of his tracing them to the old stock of Porter's in England—He seems rather to fix us Endymion than on Sir Charles."[12]

Any connection to any famous historical Porter would do, whether to Sir Endymion Porter—the seventeenth-century courtier of King Charles I—or to Sir Charles Porter, the seventeenth-century Irish Lord Chancellor. The family would eventually claim a connection to Endymion, although, as Robert admitted, "I know not whether we are related to Endimion Porter or not."[13] By hook or crook, they needed to claim noble descent in England. In actuality, their Irish family ancestors were notorious rather than famous—at least in British circles. Their Irish Presbyterian clergyman cousin, the Reverend James Porter, had been hanged for treason for his participation in the 1798 uprising against British rule in Ireland. This branch of the family, of which they must have had some knowledge, went unclaimed in the Porter pedigree.[14]

Other family associations were downplayed. William's sons, for instance, were shaping up to be sad cases. Jane and Maria suspected their two nephews, Charles and Thaddeus, weren't getting loving, solid, or education-oriented upbringings. In the winter of 1811, Robert got a rare sighting of Thaddeus as he went through Durham with his regiment. Thaddeus lived there with his maternal grandmother, Mrs. Betts, the only living family member to whom the seven-year-old boy could possibly have been attached. No one else, not even his father, apparently, had made the trip north in years. Mrs. Betts complained to Robert that she'd written William some time ago to ask him to send old clothes to refashion into dresses for his son. William never answered her letter.[15]

William's attention was focused instead on his new wife, the former Mrs. Phoebe Moody, who was said to have five hundred pounds a year. William may not have known the history of the woman he'd tied himself to. Phoebe, who'd spent time in Southampton and London, lived much of her adult life in North America, where she left quite a reputation behind her. A recent historian describes her as the period's "most litigious woman" in Nova Scotia.[16] By 1811, she'd been involved in forty-nine lawsuits in its Supreme Court and six more at the Court of Common Pleas in Halifax County. She had sued everyone who owed her money, from poor to elite, including garrison officers, farmers, fishermen, sailors, saddlers, and boat builders. She had been involved in many civil cases of trespass, ejectment, and slander, and one civil case for harboring an enslaved person—extremely rare. The last charge is the only one in which Phoebe comes out looking even a little bit in the right.[17]

William had once again chosen an appalling wife. At first she was kind and attentive to her in-laws. But as Mrs. Porter got a closer look at her new daughter-in-law, it made her doubt William's chances for marital happiness. She opined there was such a thing as having been too long one's own mistress, with domestics to tyrannize over. Mrs. Porter thought Jane's heart would have been pained by what she'd witnessed in William's home, implying that Phoebe was beating one of their servants.[18]

Phoebe Moody Porter's money had allowed William to buy a home in Bristol in April 1812—a four-story Georgian row house on Portland Square, a newer section of town, for 1,500 pounds. Finally flush with his second wife's fortune, William began to lend to others, including giving 350 pounds to Robert. That September, William learned Robert couldn't pay him back until the following May. Given Phoebe's approach to debtors, this couldn't have been welcome news and would have driven a deeper wedge between the two brothers. It certainly lowered Robert's already low opinion of Phoebe.

"I fear his Lady is the Devil," he wrote to his mother.[19]

Then Robert got his chance to prove he could choose a better wife. With Tsar Alexander's permission, Sir Robert Ker Porter married Princess Mary Federovna Shcherbatov in Russia on February 7, 1812 (O. S.). In his letter home announcing the marriage, he called it the "sealing of the union of two most sincere hearts." The couple also decided to marry twice, in the Princess's house, among friends, according to the rites of the Church of England, and in a more splendid and imposing ceremony in the Greek Orthodox Church. The chapel was crowded with friends, and "as you can imagine, my Marie was most deeply affected," Robert wrote, using his nickname for his new wife.[20]

"It will satisfy my dear Mother to see how truly her daughter is beloved and respected by the first personages of the Empire," he continued, listing the notables at the wedding, including Tsar Alexander's chief prosecutor, minister of police, and countless princesses, princes, dukes, admirals, senators, generals, and ladies. By British standards, nuptials with more than forty attendees were grand. These numerous guests were among the most powerful people in the Russian military and court. The wedding day ended with a ball, with members of the Imperial Family in attendance.[21]

After the wedding, Princess Mary—now officially Lady Porter—and Sir Robert spent months on her principal estate in Ryazan. He reminded his family to address letters to him as "Sir Robert Porter" and to call Mary the "Princess," "as with us she is so and amongst my countrymen here she is so." He assured his mother and sisters he was truly happy and that they'd all meet his new bride soon. Robert, then thirty-four, also warned them, "You must not expect to find her half so handsome as her picture. Five years in a Russian Lady makes great alterations particularly after 30. However do not let me alarm you. Her heart is the same. And I am contented and blessed."[22]

They'd planned to return to England, until war again turned the world upside down. In June 1812, Napoleon invaded Russia, a former ally, with half a million troops. Terribly outnumbered, Russian forces pulled back. Entire cities were decimated. France took Moscow in September, and Napoleon expected Alexander to fold. But fleeing Russian troops and peasants burned crops and properties so as not to leave anything for the invading French to live on. Several of Princess Mary's estates were devastated, including in Moscow, although she was said to have begrudged nothing to secure her country's future. The Russians successfully starved out the French, over a long Russian winter.

This meant Russia and Britain once again had Napoleon as a common enemy. Early in 1813, Robert planned to return alone to England to rejoin his regiment, keep his military commission, and resume his officer's salary, after his leave of absence. He'd also planned to complete and publish another book, with Jane's help. These books had proved money-making ventures, and he sought a repeat performance. At home he'd also seek future advantage or employment, perhaps as a British diplomat abroad. Princess Mary stayed behind in Russia.

"Her situation is such that I fancy she will not be able to follow me until the summer ensuing," Robert wrote to his sisters. Princess Mary was pregnant.

Jane's work to burnish the Porter family background had paid off. A month after Robert returned to England, he was knighted by the Prince Regent.[23] He rejoined his regiment, then in Peebles, Scotland, guarding French prisoners, and set out to write his next book in off hours. Each week, Robert sent Jane fifteen or sixteen sheets of writing to embellish, edit, and recopy. Together, the two of them readied his *Narrative of the Late Campaign in Russia* with original documents, as an eyewitness account of the war.

"Pray do not curb your own ideas in re-copying it," he told his sister, "Yet I am ashamed to take from you what neither my hand nor reputation merits, pray add as much painting as you can to the horrors of Moscow when in the possession of the Tyrant."[24]

Robert was anxious for Jane to finish quickly, but he also told her that he didn't want her to stint on the work's quality. In effect, he was asking her to sacrifice neither speed nor skillfulness. At least Robert told her this was the last time he planned to be an author. The book was published by Longman and Rees in August 1813 as *A Narrative of the Campaign in Russia, During the Year 1812*. It was further advertised as "Containing Information Drawn from Official Sources, and from Intercepted French Documents Hitherto Unknown to the British Public by Sir Robert Ker Porter."[25] The timely book proved popular with the public and went through several editions.

In July 1813, Robert learned by letter of the safe birth of his child on May 27 (O.S.). Their daughter was called Mary, after her mother, but also after the Dowager Empress—Tsar Alexander I's mother—who stood as the baby's godmother. The baby's godfather would be Alexander himself. It was said the Tsar liked Sir Robert and was partial to Princess Mary. The next step was to arrange for mother and baby to come to England. Jane was preoccupied with

Robert's book, so Maria took responsibility for finding a suitable house for Robert and the Princess to rent. Robert told her he needed to stay with his regiment in Scotland as long as possible, to keep that position and income.[26] Robert asked Maria to find a furnished house for perhaps 200 to 350 pounds a year.

It was settled that the Princess would depart from Russia just after baby Mary's smallpox vaccination in August.[27] Princess Mary asked her sisters-in-law to have some peas dried and ready for her, along with salted cucumbers. She also told them she needed cabbage prepared precisely according to a recipe she was sending.[28] With Robert's book now published and his princess and their baby on their way to England—not to mention Napoleon seeming nearer to defeat—the Porter family's fortunes appeared to have turned.

It was late in 1813 when Robert, the Princess, and the baby moved into their rented home at 39 Weymouth Street, Portland Place, in the stately Marylebone section of London. They rented the house for a year, with payment due quarterly to their landlord, a decorated officer. Jane joined the household as a female companion. Servants would have been hired, too, including a nurse for the baby. The house was similar in style to the one William had recently purchased in Bristol—a Georgian, multistory row house with a carriageway in the rear and the comfort of equally well-off neighbors. Robert hired a carriage, so transportation would be available for visits and trips. The newlyweds proved sought-after company. Jane's presence was useful, in that when Robert needed to be out, she could keep the Princess company. But the Princess's English language skills weren't strong, and Jane's French was entirely too weak.

To be a Russian in Britain at this time proved fortuitous. When Russia defeated French forces at the end of 1813, and—as many saw it—freed the world from the tyranny of Napoleon, all Britain seemed ecstatic. The Russians were cast as global heroes. It was a special point of pride to the Porters that Princess Mary had given up many of her estates and fortune to support the war effort.[29]

"Ten of the princess's estates lay in the track of the contending armies, as you may see by the map; the one being near Tambow, and the other near Tula—they have been materially injured," Maria wrote to a friend, "But her most considerable one, in the Government of Ryazan, was far out of the way, and is as flourishing as ever."[30]

The Porter sisters expressed pride in Princess Mary when speaking about her to others, but behind the scenes, Jane and Maria discovered they couldn't love this new sister. Her company was a burden. She was moody, flighty, and self-centered. Her temper really needed to be—"ameliorated," as Jane delicately put it. Such a change was needed for her own sake, her husband's, her child's, and their own.[31] Princess Mary also often couldn't make—and could only rarely keep to—a plan. Once, on a Wednesday morning, the Princess invited Jane to leave London to go to Oxford with her, intending to stay until the following Monday. Then, a short time later, she told Jane she'd decided not to go to Oxford at all. Days were regularly like this, with unpleasant chaos and foul moods.

"You know her way," Jane admitted to Maria. "I had rather be anywhere than with her while under pain of mind."[32]

When Jane wrote home, just after Christmas 1813, she laid the situation out with clarity. If Maria intended to join the Weymouth Street household, she needed to understand what to expect.

"I cannot promise you many pleasurable sensations here," Jane wrote. "The old stupefying plan goes on from morning till night."

The stupefying habits involved an abundance of calling cards, visits made and received, and a circuit of parties, followed by more calling cards, more visits, and more parties. The winter weather occasionally prevented the carriage from going out. In that case, it was just calling cards and home visitors in a whirl. Jane found that, with all the cards and visitors, she didn't have even half an hour a day to read or write. The company of the Princess was no solace.

"The captivity is wretched," Jane confessed, "when there is no soul in the prison with you."[33]

This was one of the greatest insults Jane could have leveled, especially as someone with previous experience of wretched domestic captivity. Percival Stockdale, at least, had had a soul, although a troubled one. Jane implied the Princess was soulless. Worst of all, this Anglophile Russian princess, who'd fallen in love with and married an Englishman and professed her grand desire to visit his country, declared she disliked British customs.

To add to the absurdity, one of the Princess's favorite complaints to her sisters-in-law was that the English character was very selfish.[34] She wasn't nice to others, especially not anyone she saw as her social inferior, which was most people. About visiting someone of the Porters' acquaintance, Maria wrote to Jane, "Pray let the P [Princess] appear civil, if you can make her seem so."[35] But mostly, the Princess and Robert simply refused to acknowledge the sisters' circle of friends.

"Robert seems pretty well reconciled to the whole," Jane wrote, "and more hostile than ever against our acquaintance."[36]

Robert and the Princess were unwilling to be on visiting terms with Jane's friends. Jane didn't name the friends, but they would have included Elizabeth Benger, Mary Cockle, Eliza Tickell, Anna Middleton, and possibly Elizabeth Dillon, as well as perhaps the mutual theatrical and artistic friends of the siblings' shared youth. The Princess would also refuse to visit with the Porters' Ditton neighbors, who'd been so loyal, charitable, and true during so many years of the family's pain, sickness, and need.

These friends had listened endlessly to Mrs. Porter, Jane, and Maria praising Robert and promising they'd all soon see him again and meet his cherished princess, of whom the family had long kept two portraits in their home. When the time finally came to meet her in the flesh, Robert wasn't only pushing away anyone in his sisters' circles but displaying to Jane his open hostility. His rejection of her friends would have added to Jane's sense of alienation—so near to them in London, yet being kept away from them by family duty and her brother's fiat.

"As such is the state of the case," she told Maria, "I the less urge you to make a push to join us, before you must."[37]

Maria wrote to Elizabeth Dillon, very worried about Jane. She told Mrs. Dillon how miserable she was for her sister and hoped there would be a bright season in heaven to repay her for her suffering for others on Earth.

"I pity our darling Robert," Maria wrote, "but he has the horror in his own hand—he is the horror's Lord and Master, and he ought to conquer her."[38] What most needed conquering, however, was not the horrible princess's snobbery or foul moods. It was the household budget. The horror Princess was terrible with money. To his sisters, Robert tried to pass off his wife's inabilities as a cultural difference. Jane had so much to do in this spendthrift household as its only competent manager. When she wasn't attempting to moderate the conditions of life on Weymouth Street, or receiving cards, or maintaining the correspondence, she was being dragged along to a constant round of parties and dinners. Jane was pleased to attend only a few of these events. Among them were her opportunities to see Madame de Staël, famed author of the novel *Corinne*.

De Staël, on a trip to Britain with her daughter Albertine, seems to have actively sought out acquaintance with British women writers she respected.[39] She'd learned Jane Austen's hidden identity, for instance, and expressed an interest in meeting her. Austen declined. Germaine de Staël was a controversial Frenchwoman who'd raised a daughter conceived out of wedlock. But Jane and Maria—less fastidious about that part, perhaps—agreed to meet this brilliant writer.

Jane wrote to Maria about a large party she'd gone to at Madame de Staël's. Although Jane hadn't talked much to her host, she'd spent time with the famed actress she was said to resemble, Mrs. Sarah Siddons. Her time at this fascinating party was cut short, however, by Robert and the Princess needing to leave to attend a diplomatic dinner. At that dinner, there was one man Jane was interested in talking to, but the Princess froze Jane out of the exchange.

"I should have learnt a great deal from him," Jane lamented, "had my sister-in-law not engaged him so much in the French language. I more & more regret my stupidity there."[40]

The people Robert and the Princess spent time with were principally his titled friends, to whom he owed an obligation or from whom he wanted a favor. One of those was his "second mother," the Margravine of Anspach. Robert had remained quite literally indebted to her. Robert, the Princess, and Jane went to see the Margravine at home, in a large party. Keppel Craven and Augustus were there, along with Madame de Staël. Jane knew that telling Maria these details would bring her sister some pain, but she couldn't resist sharing one story. Robert had found himself in conversation with the Margravine and Madame de Staël. De Staël had asked the Margravine if she knew the Misses Porter and then launched into singing their praises. Robert reported that the Margravine reddened. Then she was silent for some time. Finally, she interrupted de Staël and changed the subject, asking if the celebrated writer could speak German.[41]

A handful of such parties were bright spots in these months of misery for Jane. Whether Robert was happy may have been harder to discern. But at a crucial point, he decided to travel to the Continent. He left the Princess, baby Mary, her nurse, the servants, and Jane in their rented London home without him. Ostensibly, Robert's was a business trip. He went to Holland, hoping to cross paths with the Duke of Clarence and other noblemen who had the power to appoint him to a diplomatic post. From Holland, he somehow wound up in war-torn France. Maria couldn't understand why he'd left London at all. "I am only amazed he is so fond of wasting precious time & money," Maria wrote to Jane, in an unusual fit of exasperation with their brother.[42]

Robert was hoping to meet with Tsar Alexander there, to thank him for being Mary's godfather and to ask if he had any orders for Her Imperial Highness Catherine, Grand Duchess of Russia. The Grand Duchess, Tsar Alexander's sister, was visiting England. She'd been attentive to Princess Mary during their time in London.[43] It would have seemed a promising angle for Robert to work for the advancement of his diplomatic career. Robert's trip was a success, in that he met up with the Russian and the British delegations. But it was a failure in that no one helped him professionally.

Back in England, Princess Mary had become Jane's problem alone to manage. Jane, the internationally celebrated author, was treated as an upper servant by her sister-in-law, but she didn't complain to Robert. She didn't want to be seen as sowing dissension between the couple.[44] Yet there was good reason for Jane to be uncomfortable and even afraid. The Princess wasn't a careful woman. Their Weymouth Street house was in the headlines. One night, in February 1814, the "Lady the Princess Scherbettor," as the newspaper mistakenly called her, went "into the room between seven and eight o'clock with a candle, and by accident, [set] fire to the curtains." The servants and some other unidentified person—surely Jane—got the flames under control before the arrival of the fire engines. In the chaos, the Princess's gold watch was stolen.[45] To make matters worse, that sordid detail, too, was widely reported in the newspapers.

The Princess also strained her relationship with her mother-in-law during this time by refusing to allow the baby to travel to Ditton, worried about her exposure to "country air." Mrs. Porter wrote to Jane that perhaps it was just as well, since she feared she might have become too attached to her only granddaughter. The Princess didn't even answer the letter that Mrs. Porter had sent to her granddaughter on her birthday. Mrs. Porter had new complaints, too, about Robert.

"We are apt to be selfish," she told Jane, "yet I had very little of his society when I was in Town, for by his always talking French, it left me out of all converse with him & neither could derive any pleasure from hearing him speak." Mrs. Porter believed the Princess had forgotten such beings as her mother-in-law and Maria existed and worried about Robert's future chances for happiness.[46]

Robert's thoughts of his mother were of a different kind. From France, he wrote a letter to the Princess, suggesting he was looking for an appropriate place so that she and daughter Mary could join him on the Continent. Returning to England to say goodbye to his mother, he thought, might prove too much for Mrs. Porter to bear, so he'd simply avoid the problem by not returning. In the event, Robert thought better of that plan of surreptitious departure.

Back in Ditton, Maria—clear of much of this turmoil, although not its anxieties—was turning in earnest to her next novel.

"My mother is good enough to say she is interested in my book," Maria told Jane, "but I fear it is sombre-hued, compared with my others. Often we have toiled and suffered, the images of our Fancy are far less pleasing than when we first began the race of life—but I hope my book will animate as it goes on."

Maria also hoped her own quick progress would give Jane a choice to postpone writing her next novel. It would have been impossible, Maria thought, for Jane to write three volumes that year, given all she'd been asked to manage. There were good reasons, too, for Jane to stay in London just then. Maria reminded her that it would be useful to be introduced to more people who might be likely to befriend her.[47] Jane agreed that she needed to keep up her literary reputation, for the sake of their finances.

"I would not, now, trouble myself one finger to tarry one hour in the mob of society," she wrote to Maria, "if I did not think that making one's self known, adds to the notoriety of one's name, and therefore to the profit of the pen. Otherwise, I should shake hands and part with all but a few fast friends and our dear little humble cottage."[48]

Jane's days in London became far more interesting with the influx of illustrious Russians. The first to come was young, vivacious, recently widowed Catherine, Grand Duchess of Oldenburgh, sister of Tsar Alexander. After the victory over Napoleon, the Tsar himself decided to travel to Britain, too. He was greeted with boisterous gratitude wherever he went. Everyone seemed interested in these cordial meetings among three royal families—Britain, Russia, and Prussia—gathering to mutually admire and entertain each other. The newspapers were filled with reports of their comings, goings, ceremonies, and military uniforms.

Jane found herself on the fringes of royal splendor, but the sisters found it difficult to explain to their untitled friends, and even to their own mother, that they were not invited to these grand events. It wasn't personal, they tried to communicate. It wasn't about looking fine. It wasn't a matter of getting an invitation or a ticket. There simply was no allowable way for the untitled to get more than the same glimpse of these royal families from a street or a carriage as the rest of the country. Mrs. Porter felt especially slighted. There had been talk of Tsar Alexander coming to Weymouth Street, but Princess Mary informed her mother-in-law that, if she wanted to see the Tsar, Mrs. Porter should try to do it at one of her own friend's houses.

"That satisfied me, to know she did not invite me to her house," Mrs. Porter indignantly reported.[49]

Princess Mary's behavior contrasted especially sharply with that of her visiting brother, Prince Theodore Shcherbatov. Robert's brother-in-law took the trouble to go to Ditton, to meet the Porter women at home and convey his respects. Prince Shcherbatov told them (in French, translated by Maria) that he planned to prevail on his sister to come to Ditton with baby Mary—something she hadn't yet done.[50] They found the Prince delightful, graceful, and of real worth. No one said "unlike his sister," but that was certainly implied.

Jane's close looks at the Russian Imperial Family seem to have made their way into print.[51] Long eyewitness descriptions of Tsar Alexander and the Russian delegation appeared anonymously in the magazines, including *La Belle Assemblée*, to which both Porter sisters contributed. One account there reported how Alexander appeared on the balcony of his London hotel and "bowed in the most condescending manner, which he occasionally continued to do until eleven at night, the people rending the air with their shouts of applause."[52] Surely some of these accounts were by Jane. These events may have been seen with her own eyes, rather than reported secondhand.

Robert, after basking in victory celebrations in his home country, decided it was time to leave for his wife's. They packed up their Weymouth Street household and readied to depart for Russia in summer 1814. The exchange rate remained low, so Robert told the Princess that they'd need to live as economically as they could once they returned to Russia, "to make up for my folly in bringing thee to England."[53] The part of Robert's folly that most disturbed Jane and Maria was the vast overspending. Robert still hadn't repaid his debts from a decade ago, stemming from the Lyceum Theatre debacle. Now he'd added to them significant new debts from life on Weymouth Street. He couldn't have been surprised by this. From a very early point in their visit to England, Robert had tried to curtail their enormous expenses.

"Since you were with us," he'd earlier confessed to his mother, "we have brought things into more regularity and consequently it does not cost so much per week."[54] But he and the Princess hadn't economized nearly enough. Everything would have been far worse, Maria thought, if Jane hadn't been there to deal with Robert's London bills throughout the visit and brought some order to them. Maria didn't want to accuse her brother of intentionally defrauding people. He lacked discretion, she thought, not principles. The Princess, however, was hopeless. Jane, who rarely admitted any fault in her brother, declared Robert had mental cowardice. He refused to be direct with the Princess about the necessity for financial moderation.

Not only that, but "He has his old trick," Jane told her sister, "of appearing not to like to listen to any kind of business information what ever."[55]

Maria agreed: "This marriage for which all wished so much believing it would join affluence with affection to our Robert's destiny, has on the contrary brought him more cares for money, and deprived him of domestic peace."[56]

The stress on Jane proved immense. Maria worried her sister was unwell. She suspected Jane was hiding the extent of her misery from living with the Princess and the labor of trying to bring order to a reckless household. To Jane, one bright spot promised to lift the sisters out of trying circumstances.

"I am reading your Novel," she wrote to Maria, "and find the interest so deep that I sat up till one last night reading it."

Maria had started this novel a year earlier, in the winter of 1813. She was ill then and trying to recover under the care of her physician brother William in Bristol. William had recommended Maria stop writing entirely and rest. Maria had been calling her next novel "The Recluse," and, as William noted, she was now herself a recluse, at his medical recommendation. Maria's room was to remain always dark. She never sat up, even in bed.[57] She was trying so hard to follow William's medical advice that she didn't even read letters that came to her. But as she recovered, work on her novel advanced. By the spring of 1814, it was halfway done.

"The characters, tho' true to nature, are new in the world of novels," Jane wrote.

Maria decided to honor her Russian brother-in-law by naming her hero Theodore. But Jane also told Maria that she recognized Augustus Craven in the sections on Theodore's childhood. "It must end well," Jane warned Maria "I am convinced unhappy catastrophes are the ruin of success.—For myself, I would rather not read a Novel which so ends."[58] The plan was to ask Longman once again for an advance of fifty guineas for each completed volume, to pay off their medical bills and other household debts, followed by the rest of the payment on delivery of the manuscript.

Maria wrote back, "If you think it may pass, send them to Longman... They must give me my hundred pounds or guineas—and may begin advertising and printing."[59]

Maria pushed herself to complete her novel in order to support the Ditton household. The sisters were, at this point, in personal debt themselves. They owed fifty pounds to the apothecary Mr. Baker for their mother's accumulated medical bills. Maria's expected fifty-pound advance from Longman was needed in several other places, too, including Robert's debts.

Robert's financial obligations on Weymouth Street surely contributed to the stealthy way in which he and the Princess finally exited the country, never advertising the true date of their departure. Some of his creditors would already have suspected there was new trouble ahead. Their Weymouth Street landlord was on his guard. Not only had the Princess asked to be released six months early from their year-long rental agreement. They also hadn't paid him their last quarter's rent.[60] Few people would have been fooled by these shenanigans. Mrs. Porter understood what this sneaky behavior by her son and the Princess meant. Robert, in once again absconding from the country and his creditors, would likely find it very hard to safely return to England. But while Mrs. Porter worried that Robert and the Princess wouldn't be able to come back, Maria worried that they would.

"All that we have suffered from the Princess," Maria wrote to Jane, "overbalances the comfort of our Robert's society and the delight of seeing the dear child."[61]

Maria had grave concerns, too, about baby Mary's future with such a mother. The sisters were grateful the child seemed to have her father's disposition, rather than the Princess's.[62] As the date of their departure approached, Robert softened some toward his mother. Before he and the Princess slipped away, he finally brought his baby daughter to Ditton. For this small favor from her son, Mrs. Porter was immensely grateful. She felt sure it would be the last time before she died that she'd see her granddaughter.

"Oh! my loved Jane what I felt when I gave it the last kiss," Mrs. Porter wrote. Mrs. Porter also fatalistically called this her "final separation from my son."[63] Maria wondered what exactly Robert had forfeited his country for. Not real comfort, she feared.[64]

"I cannot bear the Idea & the thought, that he is with his talents, to be buried Alive in Russia," she wrote.[65]

After the Princess and Robert left England in June 1814, he gave his sisters the onerous task of finding someone to sublet their Weymouth Street house for the final six months of their lease, during London's unfashionable summer months. They couldn't find a taker. Rent—and back rent—was owed. The landlord struck the sisters as an angry, and perhaps vocal, man who might be willing to ruin Robert's reputation among his titled and military sets by advertising this failure to pay.[66] The sisters decided it would be better for Robert to owe them a sum of money, rather than the landlord. So they planned to use one hundred pounds from *The Recluse of Norway*—half of Maria's earnings for her next book—to pay the rent on the house that Robert and Princess Mary had abandoned. They were so preoccupied with debt that it would have been difficult to celebrate the publication of Maria's book in September 1814.[67]

"The extravagance of the Princess will cause Rob. to be years in liquidating what he owes in England," Mrs. Porter wrote later to Jane. "How his character will suffer for want of principle & will confirm his enemies in their opinion that he cannot be an honest man."[68] The long-held fantasy of Robert's Russian princess wife, who'd bring the family into wealth, ease, and status, had been destroyed. Instead, Jane and Maria found themselves doggedly working themselves to pay off their royal sister-in-law's extravagances. The sister novelists would need to continue to write, quickly, to support themselves and Mrs. Porter.

The work and worries of authorship once again made them sick. Jane ended up with full paroxysms of pain in her face. She told Maria she wanted to take anything for it but opium. She was wrapping her head for treatment.[69] Jane consulted several doctors, including her brother William, who at least provided his medical advice for free. Just as he'd prescribed for Maria, William insisted Jane take a rest cure. She went for this purpose to Brighton with Mrs. Dillon, who agreed they'd travel cheaply.[70] Jane admitted she'd lost her health by the constant disquiet in the Princess's household.[71] The Princess, Jane later concluded, was selfish and unjust, even in comparison with their other sister-in-law, Mrs. Phoebe Porter. "I think Mrs. P. as much superior to her, as perhaps Robert may be to our other brothers," Jane wrote to Maria. "And as I speak so freely, you had best burn this letter when read."[72]

Maria focused on the positive. It was lucky they'd had so many pecuniary blessings in 1814. There'd been subsequent editions of their works with five- or ten-pound-a-volume payments as gifts from their publishers. The sisters had continued their magazine writing. Finishing *The Recluse of Norway* had provided Maria with great relief. But because the two sisters took turns writing books, it was now Jane's turn. Maria pitied Jane for having to begin a new novel. Jane's planned book would be called *The Pastor's Fire-Side* and would follow the Duke of Ripperda, in seventeenth- and early eighteenth-century Madrid and Vienna. To begin it, Jane needed to gather historical materials. In the meantime, Maria recommended that Jane should read an excellent new historical romance by an anonymous author. It was called *Waverley; or, 'Tis Sixty Years Since.* Maria thought it the most spirit-stirring and living book she'd read in ages. She was very surprised it was meeting with such a tepid reception.

"I am out of patience with the Public," Maria wrote to Jane. "Good novels, excellent novels multiply, and they receive them, as a spoiled child does a new plaything, dashes them away, and cries for another."[73]

CHAPTER 17

Monstrous Literary Vampires

Jane and Maria, After Walter Scott (1814–16)

After Princess Mary stormed into the Porter sisters' lives—leaving wreckage behind her when she and Robert fled from Britain in 1814—another and very different storm was brewing, a literary one. The anonymous publication of Walter Scott's bestselling historical novel *Waverley* (1814), and everything that happened after it, would change the course of Jane's and Maria's careers and legacy. They saw it coming but didn't understand its magnitude.

"Tell Miss W[esley]—if she does not read 'Waverley' before I see her again," Jane wrote to Maria in March 1815, "I shall think her so great an insensible that I would doom her ever afterwards to reading nothing but Coelebs for the rest of her life."[1] To punish a friend by dooming her to read only Hannah More's exceptionally dull novel, *Coelebs in Search of a Wife* (1809), was a great joke. More, a celebrated moralist, was a dreadful novelist. Jane had even published a hilarious, anonymous spoof of More's book called "Hymenaea in Search of a Husband."[2] Yet there was nothing funny or self-satisfied in the sisters' conversations about the acknowledged excellence of the historical novel *Waverley; or, 'Tis Sixty Years Since.*[3]

Waverley follows the adventures of a fictional man caught up in the Jacobite uprising of 1745, that unsuccessful attempt by Bonnie Prince Charlie—the deposed King James II's grandson—to regain the British throne for his father. But *Waverley*'s protagonist, rather than being a legendary historical hero like Jane's Wallace or a glorious fictional one like her Thaddeus, was a wavering upper-class English everyman, blown about by the winds of history. Edward Waverley meets his heroine, Rose Bradwardine, in Scotland. Thanks to his growing closeness to Rose's landed family, he also meets Bonnie Prince Charlie and ends up taking part in the historic uprising. When it's quelled, Waverley—impossibly successful at playing both sides—survives to return to the Hanoverian-supporting English. He mends rifts through his marriage, friendships, and political interventions, thus doing his own unheralded, personal part to heal Great Britain's wounds.

There were significant similarities in method among Walter Scott's *Waverley* (1814), Jane's *Thaddeus of Warsaw* (1803) and *The Scottish Chiefs* (1810), and Maria's *The Hungarian Brothers* (1807). All had interwoven fictional stories of domestic strife and romantic love with horrific battles, moving prison scenes, and inspiring male friendships. The novels included important historical figures deftly mixed in with fictional characters, all living through momentous past events. These obvious similarities might even have been seen by the sisters as a flattering imitation, if the *Waverley* author had acknowledged their influence.

The anonymous afterword to *Waverley*, "A Postscript, which Should Have Been a Preface," would have been a fine place to mention the Misses Porter and their works. Instead, that essay renders them almost unnecessary to the tale of the book's composition. The author claims *Waverley* was begun long ago and then mislaid, unfinished with his waste papers. This convenient claim allows him to suggest he had the idea for this historical romance many years before Jane's *Scottish Chiefs*, around the time of her *Thaddeus*. Perhaps the claim of starting and mislaying it was true. Even so, there would have been other ways to honor the innovations of the Porters.

Oddly, Scott (his identity yet veiled) does give some credit to other women writers in his postscript. He mentions the "admirable" Irish portraits of Maria Edgeworth, which he acknowledges he had "in some distant degree" tried to "emulate." He notes his book's similarities to works by Scottish authors Elizabeth Hamilton and Anne MacVicar Grant. But he claims his novel was begun before their works. In the guise of praise, he points out that his own story isn't "confined" to rural Scotland like Hamilton's. He moves beyond the "traditional records" used by Grant.[4] He entirely neglects to mention Jane and Anna Maria Porter, authors who deserve mention just as much as or indeed more than the others.

Today, we might call Scott's naming of Edgeworth, Hamilton, and Grant a kind of "signal boosting." In ignoring the Porter sisters in his postscript, Scott condones their erasure, after engaging in a literary imitation of method that falls somewhere between borrowing and theft in the novel itself. At least that's how the Porter sisters saw it, and it remains a plausible charge. Whether Scott's sidelining of Jane and Maria was intentional or not, the damage was eventually done.

At first, Jane and Maria didn't understand that the author of *Waverley* was Scott, their acquaintance from their Edinburgh childhood days. He was already famous as a poet, and some immediately suspected him as the author of *Waverley*. Jane Austen, for instance, assumed Scott wrote *Waverley* and joked that he was a threat to her livelihood: "Walter Scott has no business to write novels, especially good ones. . . . He has Fame & Profit enough as a Poet, and should not be taking the bread out of other people's mouths."[5] But even for those who didn't recognize the hand of Scott in *Waverley*'s pages, this much was clear. The ground of the literary marketplace for fiction was shifting in 1814, thanks to that powerful book.

The Porter sisters were formidable figures, having earned a high place among Regency London's "literary lions." Noted writer-celebrities then were likened to kings of the jungle—and animals in a zoo. One of Jane's letters home described attending a party of four hundred people, chock-full of celebrities. A young woman had come up to Jane and complimented her, telling her she looked "like a queen of kingdoms." Jane cheekily informed her mother of the compliment, saying, "You see I do not quite look like a dowdy old maid."[6] It was a disarming quip, meant to draw a laugh, but it also shows her sensitivity to the ways she was scrutinized and the stereotype she was being slotted into.

Jane and Maria had each reached the threshold at which an unmarried woman was depreciated as a spinster. After age thirty, a single woman of means was supposed to dwindle into a humble helpmate to her extended family. Jane Austen joked about it: "By the bye, as I must leave off being young, I find many Douceurs in being a sort of Chaperon for I am put on the Sofa near the Fire & can drink as much wine as I like."[7] The little pleasures of social invisibility open to Austen were, however, closed to the Porter sisters. Fame meant that, even if seated on a sofa, Jane and Maria were being closely watched. They also had a fraught relationship to remaining single. Spinsters might be ignored, pitied, or scorned, but spinster-authors were routinely blamed for having brought supposed unmarriageability on themselves. Maria saw it very differently. She thought the problem was those doing the blaming.

"Public fame," she argued in a heartbreaking letter to a friend, "is the death blow to private happiness" for a woman. "Whatever draws her out of the shade, drags her into hosts of enemies, Enviers and ridiculers—and it is so natural to men to start at the idea of a woman making herself a public talk—that perhaps the very best of them consider delicacy injured, when a woman voluntarily does it." The best of men were harmful, but "inferior men" were vicious. They disliked public women.

Maria wrote, "because wishing to keep women subservient from a belief of inferiority, they look upon any approbation of their talents as putting arms into the hand of a slave."[8] Her likening of majority-white women writers to enslaved Black people is rightly controversial today. The institution of slavery isn't comparable to the profession of authorship. What Maria's comparison offers is further insight into what it meant for white women to liken their pens to swords. She recognized that many elite white men of her day sought to keep down the disempowered not only by state-sanctioned violent force but also by withholding recognition of their intellectual powers.

Maria created ideal heroes, but she'd lost faith in real men. As she wrote to Jane, "My heart begins to fail me now—indeed cruel experience makes me distrust all men."[9] Jane, however, retained her belief in men's capacity for goodness. She even hoped there might be more love, perhaps even romantic love, awaiting her in middle age. She wrote to her sister, "all worth was not bound up in the too-beloved Idols of my youth.—God, who made them, has made others also, worthy of being loved."[10] Yet it was Maria, not Jane, who expressed twinges of regret about not marrying, especially because she loved children.[11] Husbands seemed another matter. Maria believed that by not marrying she and Jane had likely escaped many kinds of pain.

"Thank God, my dearest Jane," she wrote, "that although you and I are but too likely to be amongst that despised set of old maids, we are no longer in danger of being tempted to link ourselves for life to a living lump."[12] Maria told a female friend that, when she looked around her, she felt she ought to congratulate herself for not tying her life's work and meaning to the hearts of man.[13] The world was less willing to offer its congratulations, although it remained nosy about how these unconventional celebrity sisters were managing—and how their beauty and talents were holding up—as middle-aged spinsters.

One person who sought out the Porter sisters for closer inspection was John Hamilton, the First Marquess of Abercorn. In late 1814, he and his wife invited Jane and Maria to stay at Bentley Priory, their grand home in Stanmore, north of London. Eccentric Lord Abercorn, then in his late fifties, had a reputation for collecting celebrities around him, especially attractive women, as if they were curiosities—or pets. "All the guests," said one contemporary, "shot, hunted, rode or did what they liked, provided they never spoke to Lord Abercorn except at table. If they met him, they were to take no notice."[14] Walter Scott had previously stayed there, as had novelist Sydney Owenson (later Lady Morgan), famous for *The Wild Irish Girl: A National Tale* (1806). Jane and Maria accepted the Abercorns' invitation. It was snickered behind their backs that they'd agreed to come only on the condition that he paid for their transportation.

What happened after the sisters' arrival at Bentley Priory became the stuff of legend. As soon as the sought-after sisters were received by servants, Lord Abercorn was said to have stolen a secret look at them through a peephole. He allegedly then ran up a private staircase to find his wife and exclaimed to her, "Witches! My lady. I must be off." Lord Abercorn then snuck away from his property to avoid meeting these frightful new guests.[15] This tale, however, can't possibly be true. Surviving letters prove it's a wicked myth of patriarchal literary history. The Porter sisters did visit Bentley Priory, but their host had already met Jane. When Lord Abercorn wrote in December 1814 to invite them to come to his home, he told Jane he wanted to see her *again* and make the acquaintance of her sister.

"I hope you will make such arrangements as will enable you to make us a long visit," he told Jane, "as it w[oul]d be impossible after having had the pleasure of seeing you once not to wish for an opportunity of being better acquainted with you."[16] This line alone gives the lie to the "Witches!" legend. But further evidence points to the sisters not having been ignored at all but perhaps too warmly welcomed.

Lord Abercorn's attentions seem to have put the sisters on edge. After their arrival, he singled out Maria, who feared her host was imagining her as if she were a heroine from one of her novels.[17] Realizing this, she kept a reserved distance. Abercorn may well have had designs on her person. Just two years before, a baroness hosting a ball had been so astonished at Maria's attractive bosom that she'd accused the novelist of manufacturing her chest. (Some women did so then with wax prosthetics.) When Maria assured her ladyship that her bust was real, the baroness had thrust her own hands down the front of Maria's dress in front of the entire company, to determine whether she was telling the truth.[18] She was.

If Regency noblewomen were willing to take such liberties in full view with famous female authors, then it doesn't take much to imagine what titled and entitled men might do on their own estates if they thought no one was looking. The Porter sisters, staying together, hadn't allowed Lord Abercorn to get too close to them during their visit. They swore to avoid him in the future, especially after stories circulated that he was pursuing (perhaps successfully) a naval officer's wife.

"It is impossible," Maria wrote to Jane, "to consider Lord Abercorn with any other sentiment than aversion—so ends our acquaintance at the Priory."[19]

Instead of Lord Abercorn's having rejected Jane and Maria for being hideous spinsters, it seems the sisters found themselves needing to step away from him. The predatory Abercorn apparently then cast aspersions on his would-be prey, spreading rumors about their poverty and ugliness. His insult would eventually, through others' retelling, make its way into print. It then became the century's most ubiquitous story of the Porter sisters in middle age. The "Witches!" remark not only circulated in dozens of books of literary anecdotes. It even made its way into Jane's first entry in the *Dictionary of National Biography*.[20] The Porter sisters' side of the story has never been previously told. At the time, they had no way of knowing Abercorn's malicious lies would become the recorded history of their uncomfortable acquaintance at Bentley Priory.

Jane and Maria understood perfectly well that female authors' personal and literary reputations were fragile and required management. Jane's popularity was so massive there was almost nowhere to go but down. She was described as one of the era's three most recognized literary women, with poet and dramatist Joanna Baillie and novelist Maria Edgeworth. The two were a decade Jane's senior and respected also for unimpeachable feminine modesty as single women. At a crowded party a few years before, Jane had looked on as everyone gazed rudely at Maria Edgeworth. Some did more than gaze. They attacked her, as they "clambered over each other's backs like sheep at the water trough" to exchange a word.[21] Jane's response seems to have been "Watch and learn." Across the 1810s, she was especially anxious that she not be accused of self-conceit or arrogance. She managed her comportment and did everything she could to avoid such a charge.[22] Jane and Maria both set out to be unfailingly polite and humble in public.

As part of her approach to reputation management, Jane was also careful about allowing herself to be formally introduced to others at parties. To be introduced meant being known to each other as acquaintances who might speak to, write to, and visit each other. If the initial introduction could be avoided, then it might prevent such connections. Jane once avoided a significant introduction, much to her eventual regret. It was at a party hosted by poet William Sotheby, a flatterer who'd previously apparently embarrassed Jane by calling her the writer of "the best and grandest historical romance that was ever or will be written!"—*The Scottish Chiefs*. Jane thought Sotheby was absurd. She wondered how anyone could bear to have such outrageous things said to one's face.[23] He was, however, a leading host. Making appearances at his dazzling gatherings was to her professional advantage. Then one night, at Sotheby's, Jane was struck by a beautiful male voice.

"I was arrested from listening to the person conversing with me by the Sounds of the most melodious Speaking Voice I had ever heard," Jane later recorded. "It was gentle and beautifully modulated . . . I turned round to look for the Speaker, and then saw a Gentleman in black of an Elegant form . . . and with a face I shall never forget. The features of the finest proportions. The Eye deep set, but mildly lustrous; and the Complexion . . . a Sort of moonlight paleness. It was so pale, yet with all so Softly brilliant."

Jane learned it was the great poet and notorious libertine, Lord Byron. She wasn't aware he was in the room or even that he'd been invited. She was astonished. She saw nothing of the proud spirit said to be part of his dangerous reputation.[24] Nor was there any scorn on his brow, as she might have expected from his acerbic satires.[25]

Maria, charmed with Jane's eyewitness account, chastised her sister for not getting someone to introduce her. Maria felt sure Byron would have been attracted to Jane. Once they knew each other, Maria thought, Jane would have had a positive influence on Byron, because his mind had the same sort of character and genius as Henry Caulfield's.[26] But Jane reminded Maria she'd once advised her sister never to be introduced to Byron, because of his bewitching immorality.

"I had forgot my advice about Lord Byron," Maria sheepishly admitted, "but it arose from the same dread of being charmed—I think he seems now so rapidly receding from ill, that I wish you to know him—so do not avoid it."[27] Maria wasn't accurate about Byron's imminent reformation, but it didn't matter. Byron soon left England, never to return.

Jane and Maria, who met most Regency authors of note, recorded their candid perceptions of the fellow famous. These celebrities included Romantic poet William Wordsworth (called "elegant" and "rational"), poet and critic Anna Letitia Barbauld (a rare creature who "listens to everything that is said to her"), novelist Maria Edgeworth (lively and unaffected, although "terribly plain"), and poet Thomas "Anacreon" Moore ("the very murmuring melodious voice of Love itself").[28] The sisters' unpublished letters include private observations of dozens more. People recorded their impressions of Jane and Maria, too. Novelist Mary Russell Mitford privately described Jane as one of the few literary ladies who didn't look like a scarecrow.[29] Maria was appreciated for her countenance, which was "gentleness and sweetness itself." It was said that their response to an explosion of compliment and praise was to almost run out of the room.[30] This was how authoresses were supposed to perform genius, and during these years, the Porter sisters obliged the public by conforming.

If one were to try to pinpoint the precise moment of the pinnacle of the Porter sisters' fame, the year 1814 might be it. Sixty-five novels were published in Britain that year, including titles by the era's best-regarded novelists—Frances Burney, Maria Edgeworth, Mary Brunton, Sydney Owenson, and Jane West. But the two novels that gained the most long-lasting reputations were anonymous. One was Austen's *Mansfield Park*, which failed to attract reviews and sold poorly. The other was Scott's bestselling *Waverley*.

Maria, too, published a novel that year: *The Recluse of Norway*, her eleventh book. It did well, was published in America, translated into French, and earned a second British edition by 1816.[31] Maria had chosen eighteenth-century Norway as her setting because it was "ground untrodden by other novel writers." Its location was a timely, canny choice. Norway, having just gained independence from Denmark, correctly anticipated an attack from Sweden and was in the news. Treating historical events in geopolitically buzzing locations had become a winning formula in the Porters' fiction.

Maria's *Recluse of Norway* stuck to the method she and Jane innovated. Parts are beautifully written, but the novel shows evidence of being rushed to completion. Maria again included a self-deprecating preface designed to lower expectations, but readers seemed perfectly pleased. Critics, however, complained. The *Monthly Review* discovered the very falling off of powers many looked for in a female author's works—and body—as she aged. The reviewer complained Maria's novel didn't measure up to her former productions.[32] That review stands in stark contrast to a positive one *The Recluse* received in the *Augustan Review*, perhaps because it was secretly written by Jane.

Conflicts of interest in reviewing weren't something editors felt deeply about then, especially because book review culture assumed anonymity. The *Augustan Review*'s editor had invited Jane to anonymously review *The Recluse* and provide a biographical sketch of Maria.[33] Jane accepted, sharing Maria's opinion that "Our point now is to sell what we write well."[34] Her review set out to do that, describing the sisters' brand and laying out their claims to fame. She begins by noting that the early nineteenth century was proving a great age for novel-writing, following the genre's mid-eighteenth-century origins with the works of Henry Fielding, Samuel Richardson, and Tobias Smollett. Conditions had changed by 1814, however. Jane, writing anonymously, explains why the novel's excellence and status, after a slow start, has grown by leaps and bounds since: It was all thanks to women.

"The principal cause of its tardy excellence," she argues, "will be found in the late elevation of the female sex, who form at once its most delightful subjects and its ablest votaries."

"Among the female novelists," she continues, "there is, perhaps, none who more strikingly proves the truth of these observations, than the lady before us, or her sister."[35] It's important to remember that, in this hidden act of sisterly love and self-praise, Jane was elevating her own status only slightly, having moved herself up from one of the country's three most recognized female authors to one of its best women novelists—while bringing her sister up beside her. Jane credits the Misses Porter with creating works that are remarkable because they're simultaneously ideal and true to nature—romantic and morally uplifting, while probable and historical. She also faces head-on the imperative to measure aging women writers' allegedly waning powers, insisting Maria's *The Recluse* isn't at all inferior to her previous works.

This fascinating review reveals that, while in person Jane and Maria performed expected feminine modesty, they behaved quite differently under cover of anonymity. Jane unreservedly praises Maria's remarkable achievements and her own as pioneering professional women writers. What Jane didn't seem to understand was how quickly the history of the novel she was asserting was fading away. The story of British women's great giftedness in novel-writing was eroding, thanks to the sensation of *Waverley*.

Walter Scott hadn't been a part of the Porters' lives since their Edinburgh childhoods. In the thirty years since, he had married, had children, and was working as a lawyer and sheriff in Edinburgh where he also published verse translations and original ballads. He'd published a long narrative poem with a medieval setting in 1805. It was a commercial and critical success, and his subsequent historical romances in verse sold brilliantly, too. Scott became the most popular poet in Britain until Lord Byron burst onto the scene in 1812.

In creating his historical poems, Scott mined previously published events, characters, and materials. He wasn't the only poet doing so, but the Porter sisters thought they saw in Scott's books many traces of the methods used in their historical novels. "Borrowing," Jane had once privately called it. Maria used a stronger word—"theft." One of Scott's poems, *The Vision of Don Roderick* (1811), used similar historical source materials about Portugal as Maria's *Don Sebastian* (1809). Another, *Lord of the Isles* (1815), had Scott picking up where Jane's *Scottish Chiefs* (1810) left off. While the Porter sisters' reputations (and sales) still soared, this might have seemed just an annoying part of doing literary business. Once they were being measured for a decline in their literary talents, their sense of things may have begun to shift.

By April 1815, Jane had become irate. Poet Robert Southey, like Scott, had published a Portuguese history–inspired poem, *Roderick, the Last of the Goths* (1814). Jane complained to Maria that both Scott and Southey were doing for historical verse what Jane and Maria had done for historical fiction. Each man had lifted his characters from Maria's *Don Sebastian* and Jane's *Scottish Chiefs*, while commenting on current events through historical material, mixed with domestic romance.

"It is monstrous how these poets play the vampire with our works," Jane wrote to Maria. "Some time or other, I think I shall be provoked to give the public the real Genealogy of these matters."[36]

It wasn't a coincidence that Jane got so angry that month. Two weeks earlier, she'd been reunited, for the first time since her childhood, with Walter Scott himself, while he was staying in London. She learned of it and sought him out. He was a famous poet. She was a famous novelist. Their families had known each other. Reconnecting must have seemed obvious—at least to Jane.

"I knew him instantly at the door he was coming out of," Jane told her sister. "His picture, but more the face as I had remembered it in Scotland, assured me it was him. He kindly expressed much pleasure in seeing me. I was in Mrs. Patterson's carriage; & tomorrow I call on his wife."[37]

That week, Jane visited more than once, found Mrs. Scott pleasing and animated, and liked Walter Scott. Maria hoped she might soon be introduced, too, as an avid admirer of Scott's poetic genius. She was also hopeful Scott would make things right with Jane. She told her sister, "I doubt not, now he has seen you, he will repent his literary sins against you."[38]

The vampirism they charged him with must have been what Maria refers to her as his literary sin. What his repentance might look like went unsaid. Presumably it would have involved some expressed debt of gratitude for the inspirations of their novels. It's possible that a private compliment would have sufficed. A public one would have been even more welcome. The Porter sisters weren't unrealistic. They knew literary history was full of imitation and recycling and that the literary marketplace thrived on it. It didn't seem to bother them, as long as it furthered, or at least didn't hamper, their own reputation and fame—or as long as there was a gracious acknowledgment.

The very week Jane reconnected with Scott, a performance of *Wallace, or the Hero of Scotland*, billed as a "New Grand Equestrian Spectacle," had been mounted at the Royal Circus.[39] Jane declared it a ballet, but it was a choreographed horse performance—and seemingly a tribute to *The Scottish Chiefs*. A horse-infused ballet wasn't a threat to her livelihood, as it might even have enhanced sales of her original novel, but Scott's poems were different. They were imitations in direct competition with the Porter sisters' book sales. Their era's best fiction, most of it female-authored, had sparked famous men's subsequent work.

Yet it was the women novelists who were beginning to be wrongly described as weak or derivative, rather than foundational or inspirational.

After several visits between Jane and Mrs. Scott that week in April 1815, Walter Scott returned Jane's visit and spent a full hour in her company. "He was very kind," she wrote to Maria, "inviting me to visit him in Scotland." Jane wasn't entirely impressed, however.

"He wants grace of manner," she said. "He looks, & speaks like a scholar—but not like a poet.—This is all entre nous.—and he wants a certain air of frankness which I love.—In short, he looks like a man, who could play the literary part, he has done to me.—Again, I repeat, this to yourself alone."[40] Whatever Scott had said to Jane, it must not have involved any appreciation, gratitude, or remorse. And at this point, it was only in Scott's poetry that Jane and Maria felt there had been a wrong done to them.

The Waverley novels—there would grow to be more than two dozen of them—proved a phenomenon from the first. *Waverley* had been published in July 1814. By September, two editions had sold out with a call for a third. Editions just kept selling out. Then, astonishingly, seven months later, in February 1815, the *Waverley* author was back with *Guy Mannering*. It sold out on its first day. In the spring of 1815, just before Jane reconnected with Scott, she and Mrs. Porter were reading it: "We have now finished Guy Mannering & do not think that the author has lowered his fame an inch," Jane declared. "The story is totally different from Waverley, though laid about the same period—Its interest is very great—and is, altogether an admirable performance."[41] Maria was somewhat less enthusiastic, finding the book desultory and crammed with low horrors, although acknowledging it made her vividly feel.[42]

For Jane, the *Waverley* author prompted reflections about differences between men and women as novelists. "The more I read men's works of this kind," she wrote, "the more I am convinced that theirs is the province of observation, woman's of imagination."[43] It wasn't a compliment. What's a novel with inferior imagination? But critics would increasingly claim that the Waverley novels had elevated the genre of fiction—and especially historical fiction—bringing to it a superior new (masculine) excellence, while correcting supposed previous (feminine) faults.

Speculations about the *Waverley* author's identity added a frisson of excitement to his books. It would be thirteen years before Scott publicly confirmed he was the author who came to be called "the Great Unknown," proving right those who'd long suspected it. The Porter sisters had an inkling but were skeptical for years that Scott alone was behind the novels, particularly as titles multiplied, with ten books appearing in five years. Maria was a very fast writer who'd published ten books in twenty years. She knew the time and effort required and couldn't believe the novels came from one pen.

"I persist in thinking that the works are from a manufactory," she told Jane, "that there is as regular a firm of writers there."[44] She thought *Tales of My Landlord* must be by Scott but that the rest came from others' hands. Maria wasn't entirely wrong. Just as Robert secretly relied on others to complete the painting of his great historical pictures and the elaborating, embellishing, and editing of his travel books, so Scott secretly relied on assistants, collaborators, and a secretary. He was known to have dictated a novel. Maria recognized, too, that the works varied in quality. She thought *The Antiquary* (1816) was "as good of its kind as the former works" but that "the author paints Love with a pencil died [i.e., dyed] in water gruel."[45]

Maria predicted that public taste for antiquarian-infused Waverley novels—thick with event but thin on feeling—would fall off.[46] She was wrong. Public taste lasted. And as it hung on, critics began to forget, ignore, or downplay the inventions of the Porters in historical fiction, crediting instead the Great Unknown. Jane, who watched Scott, in his poetry, and the Waverley novels in fiction, gain credit for what she and Maria had invented, became more brazen in her public relations. She redoubled efforts to get Porter family achievements inserted in newspapers. She attended fashionable parties she knew would be covered in the press. Maria's attitude, by contrast, often sounded more sadly defeated.

"To you I may say, what to others would be folly and scarcely understandable, that I am somewhat vexed at the unfairness of this concealed writer," Maria wrote of the Great Unknown. "He evidently uses *our* novels as a sort of store house from which . . . he draws unobserved whatever odd bit of furniture strikes his fancy for his own pompous edifice."

"I do not say he steals the thing itself," Maria continued, "but the idea & fashion of it, and if he had the honesty to shew that he thought well of our writings, by a word or two of such commendation as he liberally gives to works that have no resemblance to his own, I should say the conduct was fair and allowable. But I quarrel with the self-interestedness of valuing the hints we give him, yet never owning that he does."[47]

She shared her vexation with the Great Unknown's selfishness with Jane alone. Jane would eventually go directly to the public to set the record straight, just as she'd threatened, after she grasped the extent of Scott's neglect, borrowing, theft, or vampirism—whatever it might be called. It would take fifteen more years for her justified anger to reach that boiling point.

CHAPTER 18

Beware of Imagination

Jane's Pastor, Maria's Two Novels, and Colonel Dan (1816–18)

Ditton Cottage was damp and extremely cold in the winter of 1816. It came to be called the "Year without a Summer," after the eruption of Mount Tambora brought on severe weather across the globe. The month of February produced one of the heaviest snowfalls and coldest conditions on record in England, with rare below-zero Fahrenheit temperatures.[1] The Porters' glass thermometer showed it wasn't much warmer indoors, although Maria tried to put a happy face on it.

"The glass is at 30 in my mother's bed room at night—in mine at 10!—would you believe it?" she wrote to Jane. "We don't feel it, being quite warm in bed, and using her fire to dress and undress by."[2]

Jane was temporarily away, but that winter, she, Maria, and Mrs. Porter were living in such a spartan manner that one of their concerned neighbors, Lady Mary Sullivan, wrote to Dr. William Ogilvie Porter in Bristol, despite being little more than a stranger to him. Lady Sullivan must have described that his mother and sisters were suffering from overwork and deprivation. She asked William to contribute fifty pounds a year to their maintenance. William was so incensed at Lady Sullivan's audacity in writing to him to suggest this that he wrote Jane to defend himself. He explained that he'd lost Phoebe's money and had gone into debt after a failed investment in a brewery. It might have seemed he was wealthy because he kept a carriage, but he was required to have that vehicle to practice as a physician. It wasn't a sign of real prosperity, he assured his sister.[3]

It would have been humiliating for William to be accused of failing to provide for them. Observant neighbors weren't supposed to care more actively for the area's dependent middle-class women than the men of their own family, yet that was the situation of the Porter women. Lady Sullivan twice offered to lend money to make it possible for them to move into a more comfortable home, but Jane felt she couldn't accept the loan, because she had no prospect of repaying it.[4] Ditton Cottage was home to two of the country's most celebrated novelists, yet they lived in dank quarters alongside their increasingly hard-of-hearing mother. The cottage itself had become significantly more run-down after a decade without maintenance. Mrs. Porter called their stingy landlord, Lord Peter King, "a base man."[5]

"I fear it is the stupid life we lead & the confined society we have & our oeconomical manner of living," Mrs. Porter wrote, "which all tends to encrease Maria's delicate constitution, which is all nerve & all bilious, but situated as we are, I see no remedy—for a much dearer house we could not attempt to have."[6]

Because their own home was so inhospitable, the sisters often accepted invitations to visit well-off friends for long periods of time. Leaving the cottage inevitably improved their overall health.[7] Such visits were rest cures, writers' retreats, and opportunities to save money on food and coal. Not all hosts were so understanding of the sisters' fragile health or their pressing need to write. Jane saw the entire structure of dependence and hospitality as sexist and elitist.

"As society is constituted," she wrote to Maria, "only men can, untrammeled, keep up a social acquaintance with widely different ranks." Or, she added, "persons, who have their own house in Town, and power of locomotion." Dependent women, on the other hand, "on visits, are captives to the set of their hostess; hence, we are tethered, in general, every where."[8] Jane and Maria needed to be very careful not to end up in the households of overly jealous hosts who wanted to control their time. Their livelihood depended on carving out daily hours to put pen to paper.

On balance, these long visits with friends were worth the trouble. In the early summer of 1816, Jane went to stay with dear friend Charlotte Hugonin Murchison at Nursted House in Hampshire. Charlotte, more than a dozen years younger than Jane, had recently married and was on her way to becoming a pioneering geologist. At Nursted House, Jane enjoyed learned conversation, along with space and time to write, and opportunities to strengthen her body after being unwell that winter.[9] When she was strong enough, she was writing between five and six hours a day. She was disciplined and mechanical about it.[10]

Jane hadn't published a novel in six years, while Maria had published three. It wasn't that Jane had been idle. She'd also been secretly trying to turn to writing for the stage, but so far, playwriting hadn't worked out. Maria begged her sister to complete her next work of fiction, *The Pastor's Fire-Side*, an early eighteenth-century Jacobite story set in the north of England and the courts of Europe and Africa that was close to half done. But the *Pastor* manuscript was proving a chaos, while the pressure on her to maintain her reputation was coming up against the family's desperation for income. Longman had advertised the novel prematurely. Mrs. Porter tried to shame Jane into completing her novel, saying that if the *Pastor* didn't make his debut in the coming year, nobody would take either Jane' or her publisher's word again.[11] Jane compared writing her *Pastor* to a difficult pregnancy, and she anticipated a monstrous birth.

"The good Lady, who brought three hundred & sixty five children at a birth," Jane wrote, "never was so delighted at being relieved of her burthen, as I shall be at the delivery of mine."[12]

This was a humorous quip, comparing her book to a baby, but it was, of course, still possible that the sisters might marry and have children. Maria was then thirty-seven and Jane forty. It was widely known that famed novelist Frances Burney had married for the first time at age forty-one and had a son. Jane and Maria discovered that men's romantic attentions of various kinds had continued into their middle age. Their letters describe several admirers and hangers-on, but so far, the sisters hadn't taken any of them very seriously as suitors.

When Jane was away at Nursted House, a letter arrived for her from the wealthy Mackinnons, then in Portswood, near Southampton. Maria opened it—because it was the sisters' permitted habit to do so with each other's letters—and found an invitation for Jane to visit. Maria wrote back to the Mackinnons and offered herself as a companion instead, which they approved.[13] It was difficult for both sisters to be away from home. Mrs. Porter preferred to have one of her daughters with her always at the cottage, particularly Jane.

"You are so absolutely necessary to my own existence that I am anxious every moment you are absent for your return," Mrs. Porter once wrote to her eldest daughter. She called Jane her "better half and the best part of myself."[14] But all three would have agreed it was in Maria's best interest to escape the cottage's unhealthy atmosphere, even if it meant leaving Mrs. Porter. In the end, Mrs. Dillon came to stay in the cottage for a time as a companion to Mrs. Porter, and Maria left the privations of the cottage for the comforts of Portswood.

Her host, Mrs. Emma Mackinnon, had met the Porters through her late father, the Irish writer Joseph Budworth Palmer, who'd published many anonymous pieces in the *Gentleman's Magazine*. Before Mr. Palmer died, Maria had showed her gratitude for his long mentoring friendship by dedicating *The Recluse of Norway* to him. Emma Palmer—handsome, clever, and rich—was sole heiress of her late father's estates and had proved a catch on the marriage market several years before. That summer in Portswood, she was in her late twenties and the mother of two young children, with a third on the way.

Emma's husband, Mr. William Alexander Mackinnon, had inherited his father's estates in Scotland and had come into money of his own, principally made from Antiguan plantations run on the labor of enslaved people. Mackinnon seems to have accepted that ill-begotten portion of his wealth without hesitation, and Jane and Maria showed no scruples about accepting his hospitality. Mackinnon was a rigid but jovial Cambridge-educated man. He was an antiquarian, on his way to membership in the Royal Society, and a noted activist for animal welfare, who'd become a Whig politician.

Mrs. Mackinnon, although not an intellectual herself, was a lively, social woman, undeterred from activity by her successive pregnancies. Shortly after Maria arrived, the two went out on a boat ride so jostling that Maria worried her host would miscarry. At first, the two women filled their days with separate activities. Mrs. Mackinnon studied Italian.[15] Maria had been working on two novels, *The Fast of St. Magdalen* and *The Knight of St. John*. She'd found *The Fast of St. Magdalen* too difficult to research, given the complexities of its setting in sixteenth-century Italy, so she'd set it aside to write the first volume of

The Knight of St John.[16] That novel was set in sixteenth-century Malta, in the circle of French Christian hero Jean de Valette. It was another story about a fictional war hero active in battle and love.

One evening, early in her stay, Mr. Mackinnon said to Maria, "A gentleman who I am told is a very warm admirer of yours, I don't know whether of yourself or your writings, is coming to Southampton next week, and I mean to ask him here." Maria began to laugh. She planned to respond in her gayest manner, surely with something flippant about male admirers. But then Mr. Mackinnon said the name of this man: Keppel Craven.

"When those few words fell on me like a thunderbolt, I felt every drop of blood fly from my face, and I know not what I said," Maria later told Jane.

Mr. Mackinnon observed enough to lead him to abruptly drop the subject. After dinner, Mrs. Mackinnon told Maria she looked like death when her husband had said Keppel's name. Maria felt she owed it to her friend to try to provide an explanation for her overwrought response. Mrs. Mackinnon expressed shock after hearing the sordid details of 1809, but what she was most surprised at was Maria's having been allowed to visit the dissolute Margravine in the first place.

"I pleaded my poor mother's ignorance of the world," Maria told Jane, and that was easily believed.[17]

"O my Jane how it annihilated the last six years," Maria confessed. "Now shall I stay or go?—Shall I stay to see if Providence will clear up the mysterious past of that sad transaction—namely Keppel's acquiescence in it?—shall I stay to ascertain whether my reason is as much master of my weak partiality, as I was beginning to think it?" Maria mused, with pain, "O how carefully should we avoid real love, when it is so hard, so very hard, to eradicate it from the heart."

In reply, Jane told her sister it wasn't possible to offer her advice, because anything she said would produce painful consequences. Only Maria could be the judge how of far her strength would stand up to seeing Keppel. After declaring her hesitancy, however, Jane wrote three more pages laying out a course of action for her sister.[18] Maria first sought out confirmation of the report of Keppel's coming to Southampton. She asked the Margravine's physician, Dr. Hackett, also in Southampton, who told her the report was true. She tried to gather as much information as she could about Keppel's recent movements and learned he likely had no idea she was there. He was returning from the Continent with Gell, who was sick with jaundice. Maria asked Dr. Hackett whether he thought she should stay or leave the Mackinnons' home. Dr. Hackett, who knew Maria's romantic history with Keppel, encouraged Maria to stay but warned her Keppel might yet be insincere with her. He was still entirely financially dependent on his mother.

The next day, while Maria was sitting in the Mackinnons' carriage, Dr. Hackett ran up. He pushed his way through the other men at the side of the vehicle and said, "I wish for you to read this letter." Maria took it, expecting it to be from Keppel, but it was from the Margravine to the doctor, asking him to take a house in town for her because she was coming to be with her son. Reading this steeled Maria's resolve to remain near Southampton. She didn't want the Margravine to think she could be driven away. At the same time, knowing the Margravine would be around, too, dampened Maria's hopes for a joyous reunion with Keppel.

"In truth, my Jane," Maria wrote, "What could follow any happy explanation between Keppel and me, but a life of separation from each other?—his mother is likely to outlive us both—at least our youth—and he is still a son."[19]

After Maria's emotional response to the mention of Keppel's name, Mr. Mackinnon thought better of inviting him to dinner. Maria wrote Jane with the anticlimactic outcome a week later: "They are come and gone, and I have not seen them." The circumstances of Keppel's Southampton visit were difficult for Maria to piece together. The Margravine, who'd only just returned to the country and was said to be planning to resettle in England, had suddenly decided to leave for Germany with Keppel in tow. Maria felt sure the change in plans was due to the Margravine's fear of nearby Maria's power over her son.

"But, what power," Maria wrote, "when hers can so counteract it!—there must be some frightful reason for all this. However, *now*, I must banish them both, from my letters and my thoughts, and if remembering them, do it with an awful impression, that *Heaven forbids* our meeting in this world."[20]

In the brief window between when Maria was expecting Keppel, when she knew he was in town, and when he'd hastily left, another man arrived at Portswood: Mr. Mackinnon's fascinating younger brother, Colonel Daniel Mackinnon. At first, Maria's thoughts of the Colonel were bound up in Keppel, because she thought the two men similar. But it wasn't many days before all mention of Keppel disappeared from her letters. She declared Colonel Dan an extraordinary personage.[21]

From the first moment, Maria had been encouraged by Mrs. Mackinnon to admire Colonel Dan. Even before he'd arrived, her friend had expressed a most earnest wish that this handsome brother-in-law and Maria might fall in love with each other.[22] But she'd also been warned about him. "I hear he is the most amiable coxcomb in the world—and tormented with Alexander's rage for conquest—but not over kingdoms—over hearts," Maria wrote to her mother. "I defy him, so I shall sit quietly by, and speculate on such a mixture of absurdity and such dissipation and domestic affection;—for such, they say, he is."[23]

Colonel Daniel Mackinnon, a dashing officer in the Coldstream Guards, was a very eligible bachelor. He frequented the ultrafashionable White's Club, had been the constant companion of Lord Byron, and was a jokester. Stories circulated of his having once plunged his head into a punch bowl at a state dinner. He was also very athletic. His male friends made bets about whether he'd be able to climb up to the ceiling or over a rooftop.[24] He'd amuse them by racing over the tops of furniture in a room, like a monkey. It was said the famed clown Joseph Grimaldi believed if the Colonel put on a costume, "he would totally eclipse me."[25]

Colonel Dan had come to visit his brother and sister-in-law's Portswood home via Paris. He'd served with the Duke of Wellington's victorious regiment during the recent Napoleonic Wars, lost three horses, and was shot in the knee.[26] He'd walk with a limp for the rest of his life, so there would be no more climbing over furniture. "I wish you and Jane could have a sight of this interesting young man," Maria wrote to her mother, "for so he is, being just six and twenty, and one of the three heroic Colonels that so gallantly defended the position of Hougoumont, at the battle of Waterloo." When the Colonel told the story of the battle, Maria thought, it seemed as if every word he spoke were an image.[27]

She was also taken with his manners and looks, especially his elegance, strength, air, and animated actions. She thought he resembled Keppel Craven in his eyes, complexion, and hair and Henry Caulfield in his fine figure. Maria saw dangers in his similarities to Henry.

"I looked at Colonel Mackinnon with pity as well as pleasure," she wrote to her mother, "for I remembered how fatal all these precious gifts had been to our poor friend . . . how handsome men can escape the snares of life, I guess not."[28]

To Jane, she put it slightly differently.

"He is Keppel and Henry in one—but still more of Henry."[29]

Maria's separate letters to her mother in Ditton and Jane at Nursted House had them both immediately worried that Maria had lost her heart to this amiable coxcomb.[30] Many other women were smitten. Mrs. Mackinnon regaled Maria with stories about the ways that married and single women alike set out to attack her brother-in-law's heart and honor, sending him endless pictures, bracelets, and letters. He laughed at his "fair wooers."[31] But as Maria got to know Colonel Dan, she found him more than what others said he was. He seemed to listen to her without gallantry. They argued hotly with each other about men and women—and lust and love.

"I could weep when I think how he is beset by the vile passions of women who think only of his beautiful person," Maria told Jane, "but I tell him, he is destined to love some virtuous woman, who will teach him what I preach, that a virtuous woman's love 'is strong as death'—and the only *constant* love."[32]

So Maria set aside her work on *The Knight of St. John* to try to convert a real-life war hero to the side of virtue and religion and perhaps help him find the chaste heroine he deserved. The danger was that Maria began to wonder, along with Mrs. Mackinnon, whether that heroine might be herself. Maria was aware that she was fully ten years older than Colonel Dan and not then in her best looks. She blamed her days of worry about Keppel Craven, as well as having pushed herself to write and publish three books in three years. Yet she knew she still had charms. "I often wish for Beauty," Maria told Jane, "and yet my experience has shewn me that Beauty is not necessary to invite affection."

Maria's stay at Portswood was supposed to last two weeks, but Mrs. Mackinnon begged her, with tears, to stay longer. She said Maria would be necessary to her happiness during her upcoming confinement in late pregnancy. Maria agreed to stay another month.[33] New guests joined them at the house—an aunt, cousins, spouses, children, and their servants. Although Maria's company was much in demand, she began to spend most of her days with Colonel Dan, with the express intention of reforming his rakish faults. Maria thought that, with just a few more inspired principles, the Colonel would be irresistible.

"You must imagine that he has a few notions about our sex, that make a conscientious woman grieve," Maria told her mother. "We have most amicable debates on the subject.—and sometimes he abandons his opinions."[34] After several such conversations, Colonel Dan confessed to Maria that he liked to make experiments to test a woman's character and gauge her real value. With her, he declared, he'd now stopped playing a part.[35]

Maria watched as the ladies of Southampton tried various tricks to capture his attention. When Maria and Colonel Dan went out on town drives in his pretty barouchette, she couldn't help but remark on how the women behaved. "The two Miss Onslows," Maria wrote, "seem every day to snip their petticoat a little shorter, to display legs like stumps, and to disgust him. For I am admitted behind the scenes of his opinions about women's dresses and manners; and I see with pleasure that altho' their flattering attentions may rather turn his head, they cannot warp his heart."

Maria became convinced Colonel Dan was far more than a shallow man of pleasure when, one day, he noticed a poor little quail almost drowned in the water. "He brought it home," Maria wrote, "and nursed it by his bedroom fire . . . till it came to life, and then transferred it to me. I cottered it in my blanket and bed half the night, but alas, it died after all." Maria felt she could see the tender man beneath Colonel Dan's "mask of worldly manners."[36]

"I am not a morsel in love with him," Maria had assured her mother, "tho' I give myself the utmost credit for not being so, since he has already made me some animated haters amongst the other young ladies, by entertaining them solely with my praises."[37] In her letters to Jane, she was more forthright. "Pardon me," Maria wrote, "if I confess that it will cost me an effort to keep my interest in him, under the control of reason? I am ashamed to confess this.—Yet you shall ever know me as I am."

From him and his family, Maria learned his whole history. He'd gone into the Guards at fourteen and managed to live debt-free on a private fortune of thirteen hundred a year. He kept a small, elegant house in London, furnished with exquisite taste. He kept a carriage. He dressed better than any man. But he was most proud of not having incurred debts. After Maria learned that Colonel Dan's library held twelve hundred volumes of the best books that he'd collected himself, and that he was deeply read, they began to discuss books.

Soon, Maria was declaring that the beauty of his person was the least of Colonel Dan's recommendations. She knew he wasn't perfect. He had two fatal flaws: First, he'd never had a single religious principle implanted in him, and second, the male company he kept was a bad influence. It harmed him to be the favorite of the Duke of Wellington.

"He has read Hume & Voltaire," Maria wrote, "and his opinions are all chaos." Colonel Dan decided to put himself in her hands, on what she felt the most important of all subjects—religion. He wasn't usually a churchgoer, believing it to be a mere form, but he went to church with Maria.

"Is it not sweet to assist in saving a soul?" she wrote to her mother.[38]

She suggested a new course of study. They began to read the New and Old Testaments together. She promised to suggest more books for him to read, which she'd buy—gifts she couldn't really afford to give. Colonel Dan assured her that his libertine inclination wouldn't be a problem after he married. He confessed he'd recently taken up with a French girl of rank. He claimed she'd thrown herself at him, again and again, and loved him to a mad excess. She was at the point of agreeing to become his mistress when another woman poisoned herself, on account of being rejected by the Colonel.

"And dare you after this, think of offering such a polluted heart to a virtuous woman?" Maria asked.

He answered, "Never! Till the fire has burnt long enough to purify it.—but the woman I wish to marry, must know all my faults, before she loves me and takes me.—then all she will know of me afterwards will be a completely changed life."[39]

Maria and Colonel Dan spent a month constantly together. His military leave expired in late July 1816, requiring him to return to the Duke of Wellington and the Guards, still stationed in France. The Colonel asked Maria if she'd stay with the Mackinnons until he could return there, in two months' time. Then he revised this plan. He asked if he could come see her at Ditton Cottage in three months' time.

"I said, 'Yes!'" Maria told Jane.

Maria's head must have been swimming. Such a visit to Ditton Cottage would be the action of a suitor. Although Colonel Dan had never professed his love for Maria, he did seem to have preferred her company to all others, in the many weeks they'd spent continually together. Maria's proof of the depth of Colonel Dan's feelings for her was this: When they'd parted, "He kissed my hand so earnestly that the pressure made his lip bleed."[40]

Maria felt the support of the Mackinnon family behind the connection.

"I wish he could marry, directly, and would let me choose a wife for him!" Mrs. Mackinnon had said to Maria, who replied that she should *never* persuade

Colonel Dan to marry without the most perfect love. Mrs. Mackinnon said in response, "And don't you think I am sure he *does* love the person I would chuse for him?" Maria couldn't answer her. It wouldn't have been polite. Yet the two female friends understood each other: Mrs. Mackinnon wanted Maria for a sister-in-law and believed Colonel Dan wanted it, too.

In the week after Colonel Dan left Portswood, however, Mrs. Mackinnon had a change of heart. It began when Mr. Mackinnon suggested that his brother was probably off, at that very moment, jesting about Miss Anna Maria Porter among the officers. That remark stung. Then the Mackinnons had a late-night private conversation about Maria and Colonel Dan, lasting until three in the morning. The next day, Mrs. Mackinnon talked to Maria and expressed her alarm at having encouraged Maria's romantic feelings. Maria assured her friend she didn't allow herself to fall in love so quickly but admitted she'd developed a strong regard. The tone of their conversations changed dramatically after that.

Mrs. Mackinnon began expressing doubts to Maria about Colonel Dan's sincerity in his attentions to women. She warned Maria that he may have been trying to attach himself to a virtuous woman to impress the world. His vanity, too, may have been stroked by success with Maria. "It might be the determination of conquering a favor hard to win," his sister-in-law explained, "of pleasing a person in defiance of their knowledge and disapprobation of his faults."

Mrs. Mackinnon's suspicions went further still. She told Maria that Colonel Dan had such a naturally caressing manner that he'd surely already been carried back into dissipation. She said she'd blame herself all her life if she didn't warn her friend not to rely upon him.

Maria heard what her friend was saying, but it was emotionally difficult to process. "In spite of a woeful headache and a good fit of crying by myself," Maria wrote, "I managed to . . . talk as composedly as usual." Whenever the subject of Mrs. Mackinnon's dangerous brother-in-law came up, Maria let it drop. She told Jane she was prepared for future disappointment. She tried to confine her wishes into making Colonel Dan a sincere Christian.

"Let some happier woman reap the benefit of the seed I have sown," Maria declared. "It would be joy." She continued, "I am sure you must have a contempt for me . . . If you do but *see* him, you will but pardon me."[41]

Jane replied, "Why should we not know every feeling of each other's hearts? . . . Yours are always so virtuously directed, their communication, can only encrease my respect and love for your character."[42]

Maria was secure in Jane's love for her. Of Colonel Dan's, she was deeply unsure. She held out hope that Mrs. Mackinnon was wrong and Colonel Dan returned her feelings. As days went by, she resigned herself to waiting to see what things would be. If he came to visit her on his return to England, it would prove his constancy. Unfortunately, however, Mrs. Mackinnon's feelings toward her Maria cooled over the next month. Mrs. Emma Mackinnon—like Jane Austen's fictional Emma Woodhouse—was perhaps made deeply aware of the damage she'd done to her friend in a scheme of matchmaking.

"His amiable sister-in-law has had no small share in creating this folly," Maria wrote to Jane, "and now she appears alarmed at her work, and desirous of undoing it."[43] As Maria prepared to leave Portswood, she felt certain she'd done nothing to bring on the change in Mrs. Mackinnon's feelings for her.[44] The withdrawal of her friend's affections hurt.

Jane, still a guest at Nursted House, was writing nonstop and inching ever closer to finishing *The Pastor's Fire-Side*. The first volume had already been submitted to Longman and Rees at 300 pages. The second volume was 404 pages. Both were already printed. But by summer's end, Jane hadn't quite finished the last two volumes, despite her strict daily writing goals. She confessed to Maria, "It must be the worst or the best I ever wrote (though I much doubt the latter,) for it has given me more trouble than all the rest put together.—It sticks, like an apple-core in my throat.—but I hope to disgorge it at last."[45]

In August, Maria returned home. With the help of Jane and their friend Reverend Richard Raikes, Maria chose books about Christianity to send to Colonel Dan in France. Then Maria waited and hoped. If Colonel Dan were going to visit her on his next return to England, she needed to be waiting at Ditton Cottage.[46] Jane was surprised, in late August, to get her own invitation from Mr. and Mrs. Mackinnon to come stay with them. It had been their original intention, but after Maria left on cold terms with Mrs. Mackinnon, the sisters didn't expect to hear from them. Jane accepted, planning to finish her novel there while she awaited Colonel Dan's return and the chance to gauge the true nature of his feelings for Maria.

Back in Ditton, Maria began to wonder if her experiences with Colonel Dan hadn't been just a dream. In settling back into life at the cottage, she made a round of visits to neighbors, including the dear Sullivan family, whose head of household, the widowed Lady Mary Sullivan, had previously shown such care and concern for the Porters. Maria had come to think of the Sullivans' villa as her second home.[47] It was a large mansion, known as Ditton House, with extensive grounds situated close to the river and across from Hampton Court Palace.

The Sullivans, a large family with seven grown children, had long treated the Porter sisters almost as cousins. None of the offspring were more kind to Jane and Maria than the surviving eldest son, Sir Charles Sullivan. He was a naval man in his late twenties, with a reputation for sensitivity and good character. He was the sort of man who used far too many exclamation points in his letters and who shook other men warmly by the hand.[48] He was the proverbial single man of good fortune. He, too, was ten years younger than Maria.

In autumn 1816, Maria wrote to Jane with a significant revelation she'd uncharacteristically kept to herself.

"I blame myself in some disgrace in another matter, about which I was silent to you," Maria confessed to Jane. "I am much mistaken if the dear Sullivans do not reckon confidently upon me, as one of their family hereafter. You must be amazed at this.—so was I, first surprized to see Sir Charles most unequivocally in love with me—and astonished, affected, tortured beyond measure."

The previous spring, while Jane was away at Nursted House, Maria had led the Sullivans to believe she might accept Sir Charles's hand, if he'd offered it. He was known to be actively hunting for a wife, visiting his friends who had sisters. Although it had been a surprise to find herself beloved, Maria had briefly warmed up to Sir Charles as a suitor. It was at the time when William was so unkind, refusing to contribute to their mother's maintenance, and Lady Sullivan had taken up their cause. Maria had so much lively admiration and gratitude for Lady Sullivan. She'd had a constant, near view of Sir Charles's amiable heart. A general idea had formed among all of them that Maria might be his wife. Maria didn't discourage the idea.

"I was trying to reason myself into accepting him," she admitted to her sister, "believing I should never love again."[49]

Then, without warning or explanation, Sir Charles had left for the Continent. Maria decided she must be out of the running for an offer of marriage. But, on his return to Ditton that fall, Maria observed signs that his feelings for her were unchanged. When they were all together at the villa, Lady Sullivan asked Maria to temporarily move in with them. That's when Maria suspected things must be moving toward a proposal. She declined his mother's invitation to buy herself more time. The next morning, when she woke up with a sore throat, she used it as an excuse for not joining them. She was in a difficult position. Much had happened since the previous spring, when Maria believed herself incapable of loving. Marrying for comfort had seemed possible before she'd opened up her heart in Portswood.

"I dread the offer and the refusal," Maria told Jane.

Maria longed to be able to tell Sir Charles she was engaged to Colonel Dan. Of course, she wasn't. Jane sympathized with her sister over this dilemma, but it's clear where she wanted to steer her sister's head and heart.

"I own, that however Col. M. may love you, I have not a hope of your ever being his," she wrote. Jane knew his fortune wasn't large enough for him to marry a woman without a substantial one herself. On the other hand, Jane noted, "Sir C—— S—— amiable heart devoted tenderness and blameless life, would have been essential to your happiness." Most importantly, Maria's marriage to Sir Charles Sullivan "would have set you free from every care, for the evening of your days—when, to struggle with the world, is bitterness."

Jane, in focusing on the money, might have said, the evening of *our* days. Maria's freedom from care and struggle would free her and Mrs. Porter, too. Jane, then scrambling to finish her novel, would never have to rush to write for money again if she were the beloved sister-in-law of a generous neighboring baronet.

"Oh, my Maria, how I grieve over this," she wrote. "I beseech you, consider well, before you refuse him.—Consider how far Imagination may have carried you on in your feelings towards Col. M."

The sisters decided together that Maria's next course of action must follow directly from what Jane observed when she met the dashing Colonel Dan in Portswood.

"If I find that his happiness is not dependent upon my preference of him," Maria wrote, "I trust the delightful dream of one month, may be forgot at least, in calmer but still most valuable certainty."[50] Meanwhile, Maria said, she'd try to deal honestly with Sir Charles Sullivan, if there were a need. The baronet, apparently scared off by her lack of encouragement, planned another retreat to Paris.

"He comes and goes and never calls," Maria reported.[51] She was left to sort out her feelings for Colonel Dan. With these relationships hanging in the balance, Maria took ill again. In October, Jane received a letter describing her sister's weakened physical state. The Mackinnons' clueless response to this distressing news was to offer to send Maria the gift of a pony. Jane explained that simply couldn't be. There was no one to ride with Maria, and they had no stable.[52] Maria's disorder was bilious, but based on all she'd endured in 1816, Mrs. Porter suspected her daughter was also lovesick, understood then as a physical ailment. The family worried about paying for Maria's medical care. Maria begged Jane to finish *The Pastor's Fire-Side*.

"You well know that your Book must be finished, or the very means of getting me well, will fail," she wrote to her sister. "So if no other argument can prevail with you, let that do it."[53]

Jane assured Maria she was getting writing done. Maria, however, wasn't. Her progress on *The Knight* stalled. She'd become increasingly cynical about novel-writing and her own talents.

"Take a sprinkling of Taste, an ounce of Observation, a whole pound of early Experience bought *at as dear rate as possible*, then add the very smallest pinch of Book-learning, and you have the talent of a Novelist," she wrote to a friend.

"Pray remember," she continued, "that I pretend to no higher title."[54]

By November 1816, Maria's health had taken a positive turn. She reported to Jane, "I begin to look like a living thing once more."[55] The Mackinnons were surprised Jane hadn't returned home immediately to nurse Maria, but both sisters were in agreement: Jane must meet Colonel Dan, although she used the need to complete her book as an excuse for staying on.[56]

"Who would guess, that I stay away to serve you?" Jane asked Maria.

In late November, two long-awaited things happened. Jane finished her novel, and Colonel Dan returned. Finishing the novel was a great relief, like letting go a precious burden.[57] Colonel Dan's arrival was more fraught. There had been a death in the Mackinnons' extended family that darkened the mood at Portswood. Jane nevertheless wrote to Maria with her promised first impressions of the dashing officer.

"He was standing in the drawing room, and, after the first common salutations, he asked immediately after you," she wrote. Jane recorded in her letters every time Maria's name was mentioned. At dinner, when Mr. Mackinnon said something kindly about Maria, Colonel Dan immediately turned to Jane and said, "She is quite a favourite of mine." Jane said she could see how delightful Colonel Dan would be but had no warmer words.

Later, the Colonel thanked Jane for the religious books Maria sent. He'd read one volume immediately but had only recently received the packet and still hadn't acknowledged her gifts. "He would not venture to write," Jane wrote, "because he did not think, you would think it proper . . . but now that he had seen me, he hoped I would express his gratitude to you." When Maria's name came up in conversation, Jane thought his face showed "something better than the transitory flame of admiration, which is given to a fascinating woman."[58] She declared Colonel Dan must have a tender reverence for Maria. He was enjoying reading *The Recluse of Norway*, but his interest in its author never extended beyond discussing her novels. He didn't mention his former intention to visit her at Ditton Cottage. Jane discovered no signs of his love for her sister. A week later, with Jane's sleuthing completed at Portswood, she returned home to nurse Maria back to health and see her *Pastor* through the press.

The Pastor's Fire-Side was published in January 1817.[59] It centered on male protagonists, but included a heroine, Cornelia, who struck their friends as very Jane-like.[60] Her friends expressed surprise that, in the end, Cornelia would marry a reformed rake, the Duke of Wharton. These readers couldn't imagine that Jane would allow a reckless man to take a chaste woman as his wife. Those who knew Jane well might have seen some wish fulfillment at work, imagining the late Henry Caulfield as her favorite rake. What they wouldn't have known is that she'd written the end of her book while contemplating her sister's favorite object for reformation, Colonel Dan Mackinnon.

On the publication of Jane's *Pastor*, she got the much-needed second payment—two hundred guineas. Longman and Rees again printed a large run of two thousand copies. *The Pastor's Fire-Side* sold well enough to go into a second British edition in 1817, this time of three thousand copies, and editions were also printed in New York and France.[61] This was literary success, and it would have paid off debts. Yet *The Pastor's Fire-Side*, Jane's first book published after the emergence of the Waverley novels, did not become another bestselling literary sensation.

Reviews were mixed. The *Literary Gazette*'s reviewer wrote, "The literary reputation of Miss Porter has already risen to a height above that of any contemporary female writer of adorned history."[62] The "female" part would have been emphasized to bracket off her work from the *Waverley* novelist. Readers and critics both took issue with the *Pastor*'s happy ending. Many thought the destructive Wharton ought to have died. Jane had initially thought so, too, but Maria—immersed in her hopes to reform Colonel Dan—had talked Jane into letting what she called a "gay and gallant fictional creature" live.[63] It was forgiving and tolerant but not true to history and also seemed out of keeping with the didactic strain of the sisters' previous fiction.

Finally, Maria, too, settled down to write. Upon recovering her health in late 1816, she quickly finished *The Knight of St. John*.[64] Longman and Rees paid her three hundred guineas and printed some eighteen hundred copies the next year, in October 1817.[65] Maria's half-finished novel, *The Fast of St. Magdalen*, followed fast on its heels, published in November 1818.[66] This time they paid her even more handsomely—four hundred guineas—and printed two thousand copies. From 1817 through 1818, the Porter women would have been able to pay off debts and live on Maria's productivity.

Maria's *The Fast of St. Magdalen* follows two young heroines, close friends of very different personalities, who support each other in much the same way Jane and Maria had in 1816. Modest Ippolita, nicknamed the "Beautiful Statue," has a talent for conciliating. She maintains her power by never seeking to display it. Ippolita becomes the nurse and adviser of the second heroine, Rosalia. Rosalia—said to have the naïveté of childhood, with the delicate tact of matured sensibility—had a weak constitution.[67] In the end, strong Ippolita marries Rosalia's honorable brother, the brave war hero, Valombrosa. Then Rosalia marries a Medici prince.

Perhaps it was crafting a naïve heroine that finally opened Maria's eyes to Colonel Dan. Before *The Fast of St. Magdalen* was published, Maria acknowledged to Jane that something had happened to change her sense of her interactions at Portswood. She came to see herself as cruelly toyed with by both flippant Colonel Dan and matchmaking Mrs. Mackinnon. It had taken two years, but

Maria now imagined all that had transpired as driven by their vanity and her credulity. She felt cheated by the Mackinnons and frustrated by herself.[68]

In 1819, Sir Charles Sullivan, the young neighbor who had seemed poised to propose to Maria if she'd encouraged him, married another neighbor—the heiress Jean Anne Taylor, only daughter of Surrey sheriff Robert Taylor, Esq., of Ember Court.[69] After Mr. Taylor's death, Sir Charles and his wife moved into Ember Court, the oldest estate in the district, with its thirteen bedrooms, nine dressing rooms, six rooms for servants, coach houses for four carriages, and stables for thirteen horses.[70] Sir Charles married exceptionally well, choosing a woman whose circumstances couldn't have been more different from Maria's.

In 1823, more than six years after Maria's visit to Portswood, word arrived in Ditton that Colonel Dan Mackinnon was engaged to Miss Dent, heiress daughter of John Dent, Esq., banker and member of Parliament. Mrs. Mackinnon wrote to inform Maria that Colonel Dan had finally "offered himself up at the shrine of Love."

"But I hear the young lady has a fine fortune & is very pretty and agreeable," Maria told Jane, "so I trust he will be happy, and made all that Heaven in its bounty formed him capable of being."[71]

CHAPTER 19

Played by Kean

Jane's Dramas at the Drury Lane Theatre (1817–19)

One reason it had taken Jane so long to finish *The Pastor's Fire-Side* was because she was also throwing herself into writing a play. Maria had given up on that genre long before, after her failed comic opera, *The Fair Fugitives* (1803). But Jane had never tried her hand at it, at a time when a third of women novelists were also dramatists.[1] When Jane decided to write for the stage, Maria worried that her honorable sister was walking into a cutthroat world like a lamb among foxes.[2]

Jane would have felt she had the material for it. In the 1810s, the sisters were spending time among people of the era's highest and lowest status. This zigzagging between the haves and have-nots struck Maria as comical.

"What a strange state is ours," she wrote to Jane, "from dining at the table of a Marchioness to a seat in a Stage Coach."[3]

But what Maria saw jauntily, her sister saw in loftier terms.

"We just see enough now, into all circles, as to give us a general idea of mankind in all ranks of life," Jane wrote to Robert, "and that is our study, as the human form, and the science of colours, may be to a painter."[4]

In February 1816, just a few months before Maria met Colonel Dan Mackinnon, Jane had gone to stay in cold, snow-dusted London as the guest of wealthy friends, Captain Robert and Mrs. Patterson. The Pattersons lived in a commodious house on York Place, which Mrs. Porter derisively called the "vortex of fashion."[5]

The price of staying with the Pattersons was that Jane had to accompany Mrs. Patterson on her regular round of morning visits, taking her carriage from one drawing room to the next. Visits might last fifteen minutes or an hour and were made and returned in almost regimental rounds that were usually quite dull. But on one of these visits, Jane found herself face to face with the man believed by many to be the greatest living tragic actor, Edmund Kean—still considered one of history's best Shakespearean actors.[6] Jane's conversation with Kean, and Kean's wife, changed her life.

Edmund Kean had exploded onto the London stage two years before, in January 1814. He was a radical performer, a theatrical revolutionary. Almost overnight he overturned the dominant acting style of the Kemble family, who'd long ruled the London stage with an ordered, patrician approach to roles. Kean brought instead a violent tempestuousness. Audiences mobbed the Drury Lane theatre's doors to see him. Carriages and pedestrians brought traffic to a standstill outside of it to get a ticket or just a glimpse.

Some scoffed at his popularity and denied his talent. To skeptics and enemies, Kean's acting flouted classical taste with performances that were low, vulgar, and without dignity or elegance.[7] The man himself was similarly depreciated. It was all very politically charged. The old Kemble style was favored by conservative Tories, but Kean became the favorite of the liberal Whigs.[8] The Kembles stood in for high culture, whereas Kean was low. The Porter family had ties to both sides. It was said their friend Eliza Tickell was the one who'd first discovered Kean when he was acting in a barn in Devon.[9]

Before Kean's explosive arrival on the London scene, the Drury Lane theatre was on the verge of financial collapse. After Kean, it again enjoyed packed houses, with 2,400 people a night. Almost singlehandedly, Kean pulled Drury Lane back into profitability. During the regular performance season of November through May, nearly half a million seats were sold.[10] This success altered Kean's career, as well as, it seems, his personality. In 1816, when Jane first met him, he'd gained a reputation for megalomania.[11] He thundered through London's streets on one of his fast black horses.[12] He had a pet lion he walked around town. Offstage, he'd formed a drinking society, the Wolves Club.[13] On the stage, he would rewrite entire sections of a play to increase his own role, without consulting the playwright.

The famous actor was then thirty years old, wealthy and debauched, jealously guarding hard-won celebrity and power. After a spectacularly fast rise, he was already experiencing a slow decline in both popularity and health. Audiences were dwindling. It's possible Kean was suffering from tuberculosis or venereal disease. Some said he had syphilis and gonorrhea simultaneously. Nearly everyone believed he drank excessively.[14] Perhaps because she projected her own morality onto those around her, Jane believed she saw a better person.

"He is a much younger man than I expected to see," she wrote home, about first meeting Kean, "with a face whose prevailing expression is sweetness and melancholy."

With Jane in tow as her companion and celebrity prop, Mrs. Patterson had called on Mrs. Mary Kean, the actor's wife, at her home, on a routine morning visit among ladies. As they chatted, the actor himself walked in. He was introduced. Jane complimented him for the impressively wide range of his talents.

To that, Kean smiled and said, "The Publick think I play villains best; and so they must have me!"[15]

What Jane learned in that brief first exchange was that Kean longed to play characters of milder, or rather nobler, stuff. He told her he planned to revive Philip Massinger's *The Duke of Milan* to play the lead. When the morning visit ended, Jane and Mrs. Patterson left with the Keans' promise to attend an upcoming dinner.

"Luckily for me, he and his wife consider me *as a personage*," Jane wrote to Maria. "So I shall have part of his converse to myself."[16]

The dinner party at the Pattersons' home was the sort of evening at which wealthy and famous guests sang, recited poetry, and held forth in general eloquence. In that elite company, Kean would have been even less at ease than reserved Jane.

"His manners are peculiarly quiet," she wrote. "He talks little.—but his countenance speaks volumes.—It answers in the sweetest smiles, and the most intelligent glances, to the discourse of others."[17]

Kean was the type of man who'd more than once captured Jane's attention—an immense talent with a riveting demeanor and a bad reputation. He was hailed as a wonder and disparaged as a libertine. Jane, wary of gossip, was certain the gifted Kean couldn't truly be a man of vice. She observed, instead, a bearing that spoke of virtuous genius. She trusted her own observations over idle, jealous chatter.

She heard from his wife and sister-in-law that Kean kept early hours and had studious habits. Then, too, she had the proof of their evening together. Mr. Patterson said Kean hardly took any wine at all. Of course, in high society, Kean was being watched—and knew it. Elsewhere, he was rumored to behave quite differently. But Jane chose to believe her own eyes.

Kean reminded her of Henry Caulfield. They didn't look alike, Jane admitted. They shared only the most distant personal resemblance. But she found she'd experienced an inexplicable association between them, which filled her with painful pleasure. To Jane, Henry had been a superman, larger than life, but with Kean, she saw an arresting, authentic everyman. She described him in raptures.[18] She felt, too, that she'd connected well with Kean's wife, who'd invited Jane to see her husband play the lead in Shakespeare's *Richard III*. Jane declined, although she didn't reveal why. She secretly felt it would be too overwhelming to watch anyone but Henry Caulfield in that role. She'd vowed never to see it again, as a tribute to him. Not long after this declined invitation, Mrs. Patterson and Jane called on Mrs. Kean at her home. The conversation there stopped her cold.

"When I had the pleasure of sitting with you in Clarges Street," Jane wrote afterward to Mrs. Kean, in early March 1816, "you talked to me of a sort of character which Mr. Kean greatly desired might be written for him. You described it so minutely, and with such effect, that when I left you, it still haunted me—and indeed, I could not get rid of the impression that you meant I should think of it."[19]

Jane felt called to this opportunity for playwriting. She shut herself up in her room and literally worked from morning until night to write a play expressly for Kean. Her character, Count Egmont, was based on Mrs. Kean's description of her husband's wishes for a new tragic hero. Jane asked Mrs. Kean to have her husband decide whether this idea was worth putting forward.

"If he does not approve it," she said, "I shall then quietly consign it to the oblivion it deserves."

Jane also requested something in return: that her authorship of this play be kept secret. She wanted to avoid rivalries and jealousies on one side, she said, and indiscreet friends on the other. She told Mrs. Kean that her sister alone was her confidante.[20]

A month later, Jane finished a complete draft *Count Egmont*, a dramatization of fictional characters caught up in Dutch protests of the Spanish Inquisition in the sixteenth century. Jane asked Kean, through his wife, whether he'd be willing to play the part: Count Egmont, son of a famous politician, whose love interest was named Camilla. In Jane's play, Count Egmont is convinced to betray the Netherlands to the Spanish, after which he himself is betrayed by tyrants and goes mad.[21] It was a multilayered, noble yet tragic part—just the kind Kean said he wanted to play.

"Assure Mr. Kean," Jane wrote, "from *my heart*, that I shall not be offended with him, if he frankly tells me—*It will not suit him*! I shall value him the more, for believing of me, that I must always be best pleased *with perfect candour*."[22]

For the play to be officially brought forward, Jane needed the Drury Lane Committee to approve it. Such decisions were made by two powerful men: George Lamb, who functioned as artistic director, and Peter Moore, who handled administration. But the all-important voice was Kean's. He had the power to choose his parts. Jane promised to leave Kean alone to consider the matter at his leisure. But three weeks later, she couldn't resist writing him again. When he failed to respond, she turned to a member of the royal family, the Duke of Gloucester, the nephew and son-in-law of King George III, who'd become her friend.[23]

The duke, close to Jane in age, had long been single. But in the summer of 1816, he'd married his first cousin, one of King George III's daughters, securing his power and status. That fall, when Jane wrote to congratulate him on his marriage, she also asked for his assistance on a matter crucial to her future economic livelihood—her play *Count Egmont*, under consideration at Drury Lane. The Duke told her he'd never advocated for a play before but couldn't refuse her.[24] His advocacy continued into the next year, because Jane's play wasn't approved for performance. Early in 1817, the Duke even surprised Jane with an in-person visit. She was then staying in London with the Baron and Baroness de Montesquieu and had just returned home with them, when she discovered a letter from the Duke, announcing an intended visit that day. Jane, wearing only a thin, cotton pelisse dress, had just thrown off her bonnet in a panic when the Duke's carriage drove up to the door.

"In the next two minutes," Jane told Maria, "I heard him on the stairs; and, hastening down, even in my disordered trim, I found him & the Baroness curtseying & bowing to Each other, with a world of compliments." The baroness exited, and Jane's royal visitor told her about conversations he'd had with a member of the Drury Lane subcommittee. He always spoke of Jane as "my Friend."

"Had I thousand tongues, I could never fully express my feelings of gratitude to him," she told Maria, "and had I thousand hearts, they must all be filled with love towards his most efficient goodness."[25]

The Duke asked Jane to let him know how the business of the play proceeded after she received Mr. Lamb's criticisms. He and the Duchess had also begun reading her just-published novel, *The Pastor's Fire-Side*, and were enjoying it very much. With the Duke's help, Jane's *Egmont* cleared the first hurdles at Drury Lane. Lamb gave Jane two pages of remarks to guide her revision.[26] Edmund Kean, too, gave her comments, but not directly. He'd only communicate with Jane through Mrs. Kean. Jane returned the revised manuscript with the changes Kean wanted and sent him a possible costume. She'd also begun to behave as a friend to the Keans. Once, she visited their young son at school to check on the boy's well-being when he was recovering from a cold.[27] Another time, Jane sent them a present of rabbit meat.[28]

Her efforts, and the Duke of Gloucester's, paid off. Kean agreed to *Egmont*'s advancing to possible future production. Both Kean and Lamb were full of praise for her play, likening Jane's work to Shakespeare's.[29] What she needed to happen next was for *Egmont* to get a reading in the Green Room. There, the script would be read through, with actors encouraged to state any objections to it. If the reading went well, the play would be scheduled for production.[30]

In May 1817, when *Count Egmont* got its Green Room reading, it went poorly. The official word was that her play was sent back for its lack of action. Jane heard from a source behind the scenes that jealousies and misunderstandings prevented it from getting its fair chance.[31] Actors read the parts with buffoonery, apparently mistaking the playwright for someone else they hated.[32] Jane believed these reports, but Maria suspected Kean himself must have sealed *Count Egmont*'s sad fate. He, too, was rumored to have mocked it throughout the reading.[33]

That the play wasn't produced in 1816–17 was a blow to Jane, although Drury Lane's entire season proved disastrous. All three plays Kean chose were failures.[34]

Receipts were down. Kean no longer drew crowds. After Jane was compelled to withdraw *Count Egmont* or, as it had come to be called, *The Eve of St. Alyne*, from consideration for future production, she could have cut her losses and gone back to fiction writing. Instead, she negotiated further with Lamb. She extracted his promise to consider a new play from her for the next season.

Once again, Jane wrote to the Duke of Gloucester to beg for his help. She explained that if she were striving for literary reputation alone, she'd have let playwriting drop. But her reasons for persistence were economic. In one draft letter, she presented herself as an author and daughter in distress, attempting to secure her family's comforts. She admitted she was in a state of deep mental distress.[35]

Jane's new play, *Switzerland, or The Heir of Underwald*, was set in that romantic country (as it was then seen) in the fourteenth century. The plot features mistaken identity, a villainous father, a murder plot, and a castle imprisonment. It includes escapes, accusations, and disguises, as well as two young men in love with the same woman. It ends with the tragic hero, Eugene, dying after being shot by an arrow.[36] As he pulls the arrow from his body, he learns that Underwald (Unterwalden, a member of the old Swiss Confederacy) has gained victory. Then he delivers the play's last lines. Of his blood, Eugene proclaims, "It is not shed in vain!—Underwald, my Country, thou art free!—My Mother—Sweet is the bed of death!"[37]

When Jane submitted *Switzerland* in draft to Drury Lane at the end of 1817, manager Peter Moore suggested tactics for her to maneuver it to the stage. He likened it to a courtship—a model familiar to her from working with booksellers. This time, the committee treated her with greater kindness. They added her to the free admission list for the season.[38] She saw Kean perform in Colman's *The Iron Chest* from her seats in the elite committee box.

"It was the climax of perfect acting," she gushed to Mrs. Kean afterward. "and I rose from my seat, to go away, with an impression of one of the most glorious specimens of human genius which had ever been exhibited before the eyes of man."[39] Mrs. Kean promised Jane she'd always find in her and her husband "truth, candour, and integrity."[40] Kean offered gratifying assurances about *Switzerland*.[41] But once more, Jane's play was completed, revised, considered, promised—and then postponed.

For Drury Lane's 1817–18 season, Kean chose four new plays, which proved expensive to mount. None succeeded, although the plays themselves may not have been entirely to blame. Kean had worked under three different stage managers. One died, one had been fired, and one Kean refused to work with. Then Moore and Lamb decided to make Kean himself the stage manager, although that kind of work wasn't his strength. He had a habit of forcing out anyone poised to upstage him.[42] Members of his company grew to hate him.[43]

By the summer of 1818, when Jane revised *Switzerland* again, Drury Lane's financial problems had become public knowledge. Mrs. Porter feared the theater might close.[44] In October, Jane's luck improved. Drury Lane put *Switzerland* back onto its list of scheduled plays, although management encouraged her to find another leading man. Kean told the committee twice that he couldn't play Eugene. But Jane, who insisted on Kean in the role, also wanted him to apologize to her for the shabby way he'd treated her play the previous season. When relations seemed ready to break down, Eliza Tickell, friendly to both parties, served as a go-between. It was Eliza who assured Jane that the Keans had friendly feelings toward her.[45] They were now, she reported, willing to serve Jane's interests and support her play.[46]

In January 1819, *Switzerland* was finally approved for production at Drury Lane. Jane felt secure enough in it that she decided to tell the public she was its author.[47] The *Times* reported, "A new tragedy has been read in the green-room of Drury-Lane Theatre: it is from the pen of Miss Jane Porter. Mr. Kean and Mrs. West are to be the hero and heroine."[48] While *Switzerland* was in rehearsals, Jane turned to publicity. Short pieces about the upcoming play appeared in the *Sun*, a newspaper operated by a friend.[49] Enough buzz was created that poet John Keats planned to attend *Switzerland* in its first week.[50] As opening night approached, the Porter family debated who should sit with Jane in the committee box.

"My mother's feelings could not be trusted in an exposed box—yet should I but half enjoy your success if she were not in the house to share it," Maria wrote.[51] Mrs. Porter's nerves, deafness, and discomfort traveling to London needed to be considered. If she and Maria stayed in London, they'd also need to inconvenience friends by asking them to provide a bed. They worried, too, about introducing Mrs. Porter into their circle. In recent years, the sisters had struggled with their "dear indiscreet mother," as they called her. She had a tendency to blurt out inappropriate things.[52]

After weighing their options, they decided against having Maria or Mrs. Porter in the audience on *Switzerland*'s opening night. They'd stay in Ditton and attend the play on its second or third night.[53] Or they'd wait until Jane had a benefit night, when she'd personally collect the proceeds from admissions, perhaps as much as a thousand pounds, and gather as many people as possible to come then.[54] Some Porter allies took boxes for opening night and planned to stock them with friends. Their wealthy neighbor, Sir Charles Sullivan, who'd just married, postponed a newlywed trip to see Jane's play.[55] Maria worked hard to get titled allies into the play's first audience.[56]

Jane, who'd seen the first week's rehearsals, returned to Drury Lane for the very last one. Kean looked gloomy, she thought. She whispered her concerns to the manager's wife, who told Jane not to be afraid. Kean knew what he was about, and all would be well.[57]

The London newspapers advertised Jane's play for Monday, February 15, 1819. As it told the public, at the Theatre Royal, Drury Lane, this evening would be presented a new tragedy in five acts, called *Switzerland*. The ad listed its principal characters, starting with Kean. The afterpiece that night—the short comic play performed after the main fare—would be *High Notions*.[58]

On that Monday night, the house was overflowing. "One of the most brilliant audiences ever assembled at a theatre," it was called.[59] The curtain rose, and the play began. Most of the first act consisted of exposition concerning Eugene's past military exploits and Switzerland's present national difficulties, interwoven with romance and domestic strife. The audience listened attentively. Yet it became clear that Kean wasn't exerting himself. He read the part in a flat tone, apparently intentionally.[60] The script called for Kean to deliver a few tortured, tongue-twisting phrases, such as "a panoply of usurpation." Kean didn't deliver one word in ten that Jane wrote.[61] Jane knew by the end of the opening scene that her play was dead.

"It was so bad, from the first," Jane told her mother and sister, "that if I could have dropped the Green Curtain at the end of the first act, I would have done it."[62]

Jane watched as Kean made nonsense of everything he was supposed to say. The entire cast, Jane thought, was thrown off balance, lacking the cues for their own lines. The consequence was total confusion. Only the female leads even tried to play their roles as written. Mrs. West and Mrs. Glover made an effort, with West acting as if the piece depended solely on her efforts.[63] The audience occasionally applauded her bursts of strong and true passion.[64] There were technical problems, too. When the scene shifters were moving one of the pieces of the set, scenery tumbled down onto the heads of the actors, who fell down around it.[65] Tragedy had inadvertently become comedy. "It would seem," one reviewer put it, "as if the whole theatre had conspired against it, even to the scene shifters." The audience ran out of patience. When, in one scene, a set of bandits apparently transformed into heroes, an unruly spectator yelled that they should be given a month's hard labor. Some applauded the heckler.[66]

The third act saw continual cries from the audience of "Off! "Off!" Acts four and five were almost inaudible over the jeering. Kean faced a storm of hisses.[67] After the epilogue was read, when Henry Johnston came forward to announce the play for repetition the following night, the audience revolted. Some said that the "Ayes" had it for the play to be repeated. Others claimed that not a word Johnston spoke could be heard over the objections.

The crowd called, "Manager! Manager!"

The curtain dropped. No manager came.

The crowd was said to have continued to shout "Manager!" for a full thirty minutes. Then, finally, the orchestra struck up and went through the overture, announcing the beginning of the afterpiece. But when the curtain rose, and the actors attempted to begin the musical farce *High Notions*, the audience threw orange peels and compelled the curtain to be lowered. For ten more excruciating minutes, the audience called "Manager!" They thumped sticks at the sides of the boxes. They howled.

The curtain rose again, with another attempt to start *High Notions* and calm down the riled-up spectators. Then the entire pit of nine hundred playgoers was said to have risen up in a fury. This time, instead of just throwing orange peels, they hurled whole fruit. The actors beat yet another hasty retreat. A few minutes later, the Drury Lane manager Stephen Kemble stepped onstage. He was immediately struck in the forehead by an orange. This prompted a cry of "Shame!"[68]

With some difficulty, Kemble called for the audience's attention.[69] "Gentlemen," he said, "It is for you to prescribe laws, and it is our duty to obey them." This statement provoked a new set of audience jeers: "Then why did you not obey us before?" and "Why were you so long in coming?" as well as "Withdraw the Tragedy!"[70]

Kemble continued, "I cannot but regret the failure of this piece: we have brought forward several novelties this season, all of which have been honored with your approbation; we cannot, therefore, for an instant doubt of your kind disposition towards us."

"This Tragedy," Kemble said, "since it has not proved equally fortunate, shall certainly be withdrawn." A burst of applause followed.[71] Kemble bowed and left the stage.[72] Jane's *Switzerland* was officially and tragically dead. *High Notions* began and was met with applause.[73] The evening ended.

Jane had remained in the committee box until the end of her play. One source reported that before the manager came out, he'd consulted with the author. Jane agreed her play should be withdrawn.[74] Gossip circulating after that night declared Kean ungallant at best and abusive at worst. His defenders claimed he was putting his foot down to demand literary quality. His detractors said Kean himself organized the rowdy clique in the audience that shouted down Jane's play.[75] Jane learned Kean had complained to Stephen Kemble during the week before the performance that the part was the longest he'd ever had, longer even than Hamlet.[76] He said he needed another week to prepare. Kemble had rejected Kean's request.

After the dramatic failure of opening night, Jane was in misery. Her heavy cold returned. She confined herself to her room for part of every day. In the remaining hours, she was pressed by acquaintances who came to grieve with or gawk at her. They assured her that, among respected circles, the unanimous conviction was that, as Jane herself put it, "The Lightning of my Switzerland, was lost by its non-Conductor!"[77] Kean had refused to light up the part.

During that first week after the failed play, Maria grieved heavily over *Switzerland*'s demise. She felt sick that Jane had lost so much of her time, spirits, and health on this play, which Maria called "a frustrated object." Had it been successful, the financial windfall would have made their lives comfortable. Maria worried her sister would feel self-reproach."[78]

At first, Kean suffered for his nonperformance. Two nights after the *Switzerland* debacle, when he returned to the stage to play Hamlet, the audience was slender.[79] But a month later, the fickle public welcomed him back as

Hotspur. Kean, the actor, was redeemed, while Jane, the playwright, was ruined.[80] Kean never explained himself to Jane. He never apologized. Mrs. Kean's assurances of integrity proved hollow. Perhaps Kean used Jane to show management that he wouldn't tolerate any interference or allow plays to succeed without his approval.[81] He proved that no committee, no manager—no famous novelist and no duke—could force a play to succeed without the star actor's cooperation.

Jane was left to try to pick up the pieces. Across the country, newspapers carried the story of *Switzerland*'s spectacular failure. Most coverage, though lingering over sensational details, leaned pro-Porter and anti-Kean. Porter should publish her play, they wrote, to vindicate herself. At first, Jane agreed. The day after the play, she wrote a short, angry preface.

"The author of this unfortunate Play, was Spectator of its fate on Monday night," she wrote. "To her, it expired even before the conclusion of the first scene . . . She now publishes this Play itself as it was written; and with those passages marked with inverted commas which alone, she had sanctioned to be omitted." Jane acknowledged in the preface that the play, as it was performed, entirely deserved the fate it received. She thanked Drury Lane manager Mr. Stephen Kemble for his "unwearied attentions, during the preparations of the Play." She thanked eight of the actors. She didn't mention Kean by name.[82]

On Thursday, "Miss Porter's New Play" was advertised for publication. Jane wanted to strike while the iron was hot and while the public might buy the play. But then debates and disagreements began among her inner circle. Mrs. Porter was in favor of publication.[83] Maria and Lady Sullivan were against it.[84]

"If it is not printed," Maria wrote, "the thing will pass away from men's minds and have no record in Libraries." Maria argued that an unsuccessful piece would be read with prejudiced feelings against it. Readers would be prepared to find fault. Jane was persuaded by her sister and neighbor. She put a halt to the presses.

After *Switzerland* was withdrawn from the stage and then from publication, Jane herself began to withdraw. She went into a sort of hiding that seems to have been a depression, perhaps the very self-reproach Maria had predicted. Mrs. Porter worried Jane's body might be unable, from perpetual weakness, to shake off this illness.[85] Indeed, that year Jane became chronically ill. By July 1819, she was convalescing in Brighton, after a friend gave the family a much-needed ten pounds to allow Jane to try to recover her health.[86] She described feeling nervous and languid all over. She told Maria her condition was caused by the culmination of two long years of suspense and agitation over her play.

"When the whole was violently cut asunder, at one blow," she wrote of February's performance, "it is not to be wondered at that the flesh and the fibres should continue trembling, long after the mental sense of the Injury was gone."

Jane, who began to refer to *Switzerland* as her "old disaster," couldn't afford to stay in Brighton very long. But what hurried her home was learning that Kean planned to visit Brighton the following week. Above all, she was determined to avoid a chance meeting with the actor on the streets.[87]

CHAPTER 20

Tortured for Others

Maria, Jane, and the Royal Librarian (1819–24)

After the failure of *Switzerland* and Jane's sinking depression, Maria promised to write a new book to support their household.

"I feel all the ability in myself, of my verily completing another 3 volume romance," she assured her sister.[1]

So as Jane convalesced, Maria made progress on *The Village of Mariendorpt*, a historical romance set in seventeenth-century Bavaria. Its backdrop was the Thirty Years' War, rife with bloody battles between Catholic and Protestant factions. Maria told Jane one reason she was getting on so pleasurably with it was because she was trying to make her hero, Rupert Roselheim, resemble their darling Robert in the days of his ingenious, endearing youth.[2]

Rupert's love interest was Meeta Muhldenau, the blooming, sensitive daughter of a government minister. In fashioning Meeta, Maria didn't look to her brother's real-life princess-wife. Instead, Meeta was in the mold of the woman Robert had loved but hadn't married—Fanny Dalrymple. In the story of Robert's life, Fanny was the one who got away, thanks to her military father's preventing contact between the smitten couple. During Robert's long engagement to Princess Mary, Fanny had stopped waiting for him. She'd married a knight descended from a marquis. Maria called Fanny's husband "good enough but duller than stagnant mud."[3]

Despite her optimistic sense of her capabilities, Maria's fatiguing labors on this novel once again had damaging physical consequences. She feared her constitution had broken down. She was diagnosed with a disorder of the spine. Then doctors found she had too much blood in the head.[4] Maria also developed a new recurring problem of occasional blurred vision. "My eyes are so very bad that I literally can no longer see my needle and thread when I am hemming muslin," she admitted.[5] She hated her brother William's recommended treatment of sitting idle for hours on end so as not to strain her eyes. She was convinced her recurring eye problem was temporary, arising from nerves, rather than a condition that might end in blindness.[6] She'd turn out to be right, although her eyesight was deeply affected, for many years.

Even with these obstacles, Maria had pushed ahead with the book. By April 1820, Longman and Rees were describing *The Village of Mariendorpt: A Romance* by Miss Anna Maria Porter as in the press.[7] It was nearly finished, but her health never rallied enough that spring or summer to complete the work. Jane blamed the harsh conditions of their home. Ditton Cottage's bedrooms weren't just cold and damp.[8] They were often wet. When nights were rainy, some bedrooms became unfit to sleep in.[9] Only one room, Mrs. Porter's, could support a fire. The three women took turns sleeping there, giving the warmest bedroom to the two who were the most ill. The healthiest was left with a small, often soggy bed.

That winter, Jane declared that if they were forced to remain another year at Ditton Cottage, it would constitute an act of collective suicide. They were constantly on the lookout for other temporary spaces for sleeping and writing, at the homes of friends, but it wasn't possible to become anyone's houseguest when seriously ill. Maria, so often sick that year, found herself obliged to stay in the very home Jane believed had ruined her health.

The sisters wanted to move to a nearby town called Esher, three miles from Ditton. It was situated on a hill, unlike their low-lying cottage next to the Thames River.[10] Moving to Esher would take them closer to medical care, in trusted surgeon Mr. Henry Neville, while keeping them near friends.[11] Another advantage was Esher's proximity to Claremont House, home to the country's most famous newlyweds, Princess Charlotte and Prince Leopold of Saxe-Cobourg-Saalfeld. Then, sadly, Princess Charlotte unexpectedly died there, in November 1817, after complications from giving birth to a stillborn son. The Porters grieved deeply, along with the rest of the nation, and were especially moved to learn Princess Charlotte had been reading aloud from Maria's *The Knight of St. John* the day before she died.[12] The Prince was said ever afterward to have kept the page turned down where his late wife left off.[13] The Porter sisters weren't on visiting terms with Prince Leopold, but they felt a kinship with him and had sent him copies of their books as gifts.

These gifts were also given with hope that Jane might gain a position in the royal Claremont household. For a time, Eliza Tickell had tried to make it happen.[14] To be given a royal role, with a free apartment, could mean securing a comfortable roof over one's head for life. Even after Princess Charlotte died in childbirth, Jane thought she might be asked to care for the Prince's niece, who'd recently moved in with him—a baby named Victoria.[15] There was as yet no inkling that events would transpire to make her Queen Victoria.

By this point, Robert had been away from England for six years. He'd failed to find a profession in Russia, in part because the Princess disapproved of a career in the arts or the military. So Robert did something entirely unexpected. He left on a junket that Maria called "only one of his old fantasies" and his mother said lacked common sense.[16] He traveled to the Near East and spent three years wandering around Persia. He was trying for a diplomatic position there while writing his next book. There's evidence to suggest he was also doing some freelance espionage—or at least intelligence gathering—to curry favor with the British, the Russians, or perhaps both.[17]

After this extraordinary travel, when Robert visited England in the summer of 1820 with his Persian journals and sketches in hand, it was like the return of the prodigal son. His mother and sisters rejoiced. But William, true to biblical form, played the role of the long-suffering home brother. He was passive-aggressive about the fuss being made over Robert.

William wrote to Robert, "I am truly happy that our mother has lived to see you return laden with the spoils of intellectual conquest, achieved through much danger and accomplished only by great bodily fatigue, and the possession of adequate genius."[18]

For the rest of the Porter family, the reunion was joyous. Maria was shocked at Robert's unkempt looks, but he remained an attractive man and sought-after company. He took London lodgings on Welbeck Street, near the Russian consulate. Jane joined him in the metropolis, while Maria and Mrs. Porter remained back in Ditton. Robert entered a whirlwind of society visits, sharing his recent adventures and purloined artifacts, seeking a diplomatic post, and describing his planned next book. Robert's book was, once again, dumped in Jane's lap to complete. She'd quickly become overwhelmed with the length and state of his notes. She also felt a great pressure. Robert's future prospects—and the clearing of his mammoth, lingering English debts—depended on the book's publication. Jane worked so tirelessly on it that she temporarily lost the use of her fingers.[19]

After months of dining and socializing in London, Robert received disappointing news from recently crowned King George IV that there was no possibility of making him a diplomat at the British Embassy in St. Petersburg. So Robert sought other avenues for advancement or pay.[20] He decided to travel to Paris to try to sell a simultaneous French edition of his Persian travel book, through direct negotiations with publishers in Paris. While there, Robert could continue to angle for a diplomatic position in Europe.

He invited Jane to join him on the trip. At first, she'd excitedly agreed to go. But as the month of July 1820 began, she thought better of it. She needed to keep working on his manuscript.[21] Maria, however, convinced Jane to go to France with her brother. Neither she nor Jane had ever been abroad.

"Every year, will render it more difficult for you to leave my Mother," Maria told Jane.[22] As a result, her sole object should be visiting public places and works of art, as a kind of research. Jane was persuaded. So Maria stayed back in Ditton to care for Mrs. Porter, while Jane left for six weeks in France with Robert in the summer of 1820. They were joined by Elizabeth Dillon as Jane's female companion. It proved one of the happiest times of Jane's life.

In Paris, she was fêted as a celebrity.[23] She met almost everyone of literary significance, reconnecting with Madame de Staël, meeting author Madame de Genlis, and spending time with noted intellectual Alexander von Humboldt. Jane wrote long, happy letters home, describing with color and gusto all she'd seen.[24] There had even been a reunion with Sir Sidney Smith and his wife, who were living in Paris. Robert, Jane, and the Smiths spent a great deal of time together. Jane was surprised to discover that she didn't find Smith nearly as attractive a man as she once had.

When Jane and Robert returned to England, it was with the greatest hope for future prosperity, although with a punishing amount of literary work ahead. In London, Jane thought, they'd need to work tooth and nail—Robert in completing his second volume and Jane in "transcribing," as she called her editing, organizing, and polishing, the first volume.[25] Robert's work went slowly, hampered by traveling and visiting. Then, in autumn of 1820, before the work was nearly done, Robert returned to his Russian family. His future financial hopes were bound up in this Persian travel book, which he'd left in Jane's temporarily paralyzed hands. Robert, and his creditors, were counting on the expected profits.

It was the fourth time Jane had done this uncredited work on a book of Robert's. She understood the labor it required, but this project proved even longer and more difficult than the others. Her efforts were slowed by Maria being unable to help with research because she continued to struggle with illness, as she pushed through on *The Village of Mariendorpt*. At the end of 1820, Maria estimated she'd had only five weeks of good health that year.

Longman and Rees were worried enough about Maria that they wrote her a letter. "You should not *kill* yourself by over exertion in writing the novel," they said.[26] Theirs was a personal relationship, with care and concern on all sides, and Maria was a star author. After many delays, she finished the fourth and final volume of *The Village of Mariendorpt* in December 1820, having brought her story of Rupert and Meeta to a neat conclusion.

Maria dedicated her work to her valued and kind neighbors, "The Principal Inhabitants of Ditton and Thames-Ditton," who'd been so generous during her long, recent bouts of illness. She thanked the friend who came to her sickbed as her nurse. She apologized to neighbors in advance for her family's intention to seek a change of situation—a new home—for her better recovery.[27] In private letters, Maria put it all much less delicately.

"I am scarcely alive," she confessed to a friend, after finishing *The Village of Mariendorpt*.[28]

Longman and Rees prepared a robust print run of 1,750 copies.[29] But when the novel appeared in February 1821, readers didn't immediately take to it, certainly not the way they had to Scott's recent work, the anonymously published *Kenilworth*. Perhaps Maria's book had suffered from a feverish composition under her chronic illness. Unfortunately, her announcement in her preface of her family's intention to leave Ditton was a plan spoken of too soon. The Porter women couldn't yet afford to move. Jane doubled down on her work on Robert's Persian travel book to secure his future, while sacrificing her own.

"You deserved a better fate than to be tortured for *others*," Mrs. Porter had once written to Jane.[30] Although this comment wasn't about Jane's literary labors for Robert, it applied just as well there. Mrs. Porter did complain that Robert, when he next looked at his sister, ought to say to himself, "I have been the occasion of this wreck of my dear Jane's once beautiful face."[31]

In 1821, Jane continued to work without rest to transcribe and edit Robert's Persian tour. She also pursued another angle for its future success. Robert wanted Jane to gain permission to dedicate his book to King George IV. She had every hope of succeeding, although she had conflicted feelings about the King, an open libertine, who'd wronged her old friend, the late Mary Robinson. During the years he was Prince Regent, he'd racked up excessive debts, even as part of one of the richest families in England. At one point he was said to have owed the unthinkable sum of 650,000 pounds. But he also had a reputation as a generous patron of the arts. Robert's book about Persia was her brother's most ambitious yet, and it deserved (the Porters felt) royal notice.

Getting permission for a royal dedication turned out to be a long-term project. Jane began to correspond with the man poised to make it happen: the Royal Librarian, Reverend James Stanier Clarke.[32] To win Clarke over, the Porter sisters went on a charm offensive. They visited Clarke multiple times over the course of six months, trying to convince him to approach the King. Clarke told Jane he needed assurances that Robert's work wouldn't give offense to Russia or Persia, so as not to jeopardize British interests there.[33] Jane promised Clarke that, as the book's editor, she'd make sure nothing of a political nature appeared in its pages.

Even with that promise, getting Clarke to make a move proved difficult. His surviving letters suggest he was a man with an abundance of self-regard. He was a short, plump, and single fifty-year-old clergyman with a penchant for chatting up authors, especially female ones.[34] He eventually invited Jane and Maria to Carlton House, when the King was out of town, encouraging them to bring female friends with them. Clarke had invited Jane Austen to visit there half a dozen years earlier, when she'd dedicated her novel *Emma* by permission to the Prince Regent, as King George IV was then. No record exists of Austen's visit to Carlton House in the fall of 1815, but a colorful letter describes what happened when the Misses Porter visited on April 26, 1821.

Carlton House, the sprawling, neoclassical town residence of the King, was a palace in everything but name. Clarke would have been eager to display to the sisters its brightly colored state rooms, with gilding, good lighting, and large windows said to be among the finest in Europe. On the day of their visit, however, Clarke ended up showing only Maria around. Jane insisted she felt too weak to take his tour. She asked if she might rest in the library. The Carlton House library wasn't just for show. His Majesty was an avid book collector and novel reader. Jane would have known some of the treasures this library held, from books and newspapers to rare clocks. Its ebonized wooden chairs and sofas dated back to King Henry VIII. The doors to the library were decorated to fool the eye and look as if they, too, were bookcases.

If Jane's ulterior motive involved exploring the library on her own, then her plan was thwarted. Also enjoying it that day was Sir Andrew Halliday, a learned, warm-hearted Scotsman in his late thirties, whom Jane had never met before. She immediately appreciated his blunt manner and friendly way.[35] Halliday was an author of military and historical books, as well as serving as the personal physician to the King's brother, the Duke of Clarence. Halliday told Jane he admired *The Scottish Chiefs* and asked her questions about her William Wallace.[36]

He also had a story to tell her. A year earlier, in 1820, Halliday had been in that very room, he said, in the company of the King and Sir Walter Scott, who had recently been made a baronet. Everyone there had admired the anonymous Waverley novels, reputedly by Scott, although Scott continued to deny authorship. At some point in the conversation, Halliday challenged Scott about the literary influences of the "Great Unknown" *Waverley* novelist.

"Well Sir, who ever may be the author of those Novels," Halliday said, "you, Sir Walter, must allow that the foundations of them all, were laid by Miss Porter in her Scottish Chiefs."

"I grant it," replied Scott, "There is something in what you say."[37]

To hear this story would have felt vindicating to Jane. For so long, she and Maria suspected the *Waverley* author had taken his inspiration and method from their books without giving them credit. Sir Andrew Halliday's report affirmed it as true. And to imagine that Scott had acknowledged it right there in the library, before the King!

Halliday suddenly asked Jane whether she'd ever considered writing a book about King George IV's Hanoverian ancestors. Jane replied she hadn't. The King's Hanoverian ancestors were a hobbyhorse of Halliday's. His favorite hero was Duke Christian of Brunswick Luneburg, born in 1566, a great uncle of Britain's first Hanoverian king, George I, who was George IV's great grandfather.

"I can assure you," Halliday told Jane, "nothing would please the King so much, as your writing a romance on that hero!"

This line, and Halliday's manner in delivering it, struck Jane forcibly. There, in Carlton House, she felt Providence was laying an opening before her for some future royal advantage for herself and her family. Jane promised Halliday she'd consider whether she could manage the subject to the King's satisfaction and her own.

Jane told him, "Nothing would delight me more, if the subject really struck my feelings; for without the sort of inspiration which enthusiasm gives, I could do nothing."[38] The two agreed not to mention the matter to anybody, except Clarke and the King.

A month after Jane and Maria's Carlton House visit, in May 1821, Jane finished the first volume of Robert's Persian travels. It ran to an enormous 720 pages.[39] She finally secured permission for the royal dedication. She decided to move ahead with a new historical novel of her own, as Halliday worked quickly to advance the project through Clarke.

In June 1821, Clarke wrote to tell Jane the good news. The King had also given "that ingenious and most delightful Writer," Miss Porter, permission to dedicate to His Majesty her intended novel on his ancestor Duke Christian.[40] It had taken Jane ten months to get permission to dedicate Robert's book to the King. It took just a handful of weeks to secure it for her own as-yet-unwritten historical novel about his Hanoverian ancestors.

Jane had no way of knowing it, but she wasn't the first author invited to write such a book. Six years earlier, Clarke had asked Jane Austen if she'd write a historical romance based on the German ancestors of the Prince Regent's soon-to-be son-in-law, Prince Leopold of Saxe-Cobourg. Austen famously declined, writing back to Clarke, "I could not sit seriously down to write a serious Romance under any other motive than to save my Life."[41] But for Jane Porter, an invitation to write a novel about the King's ancestors was galvanizing. She saw her entire family's brighter economic future in it.

"I have a hope, that hereafter Maria's old age & mine may be rendered moderately independent by some pension from His Majesty," she wrote to Robert, "should my work really please him."

She'd been told the King was an admirer of her work. Her hope for a government or royal pension wasn't unreasonable. A number of celebrated literary figures had received them. Jane hoped that, with a pension from the King, they'd never have to ask Robert for financial support again.[42] The Porter sisters, in their forties, felt the creep toward late life and deteriorating health. They worried about how they'd make a living, because, as Maria noted, "God knows how long either of us may be able to write."[43]

Jane couldn't start on her promised new novel immediately. Volume one of Robert's Persian tour appeared in June 1821, under the unwieldy title *Travels in Georgia, Persia, Armenia, Ancient Babylonia, &c. &c. During the Years 1817, 1818, 1819, and 1820*. Jane's name appears nowhere on the book, yet her voice regularly enters its pages. There was also a second volume, yet to be transcribed and edited. For Jane to go directly from Robert's first volume into his second frightened her publishers. In May 1821, Owen Rees wrote to her, "Since I find it is quite out of the question to give you aid"—probably meaning help with her transcribing—"you must then proceed your own way: but I have only this injunction to make, that, whether the second volume be published in November, or January, you must not kill yourself." It was the same language he'd used in his worries about Maria.

Rees offered Jane an advance of one hundred pounds on *Duke Christian*. On the same day, Longman and Rees wrote Maria, to tell her that the sale of *Village of Mariendorpt* "fully answered our expectation," so she should draw on them for another one hundred pounds. That meant that Longman and Rees had paid Maria a total of five hundred pounds for the book, an amount finally equal to Jane's rate of pay.

It's probable Rees wasn't being entirely straightforward. *The Village of Mariendorpt* had only been out two months and the publisher wouldn't have been able to tell whether it would turn a significant profit. They hadn't called for a second edition yet because the first hadn't sold out. Sending Maria what was, in effect, bonus pay may have been her loyal publishers' surreptitious act of charity, a means to keep afloat two popular authors on Longman's list, privately known to be in weak health and in significant financial distress.

These payments of hundreds of pounds sound large, and were, especially when a clerk made between fifty and one hundred pounds a year, and when less celebrated novelists were paid a fraction of that. But for the Porter women—living off their mother's small army widow's pension and loans or advances on their novels—the money wouldn't go far. They were renting a home, buying coal, and paying doctor's bills, as well as helping with Robert's debts and interest payments. The sisters' visits to more salubrious places, in search of better health, were particularly expensive, even if a host were offering a free place to stay. If these large amounts were funding present costs or could be laid away for future ones, all may have been well. The problem was that these payments were needed for past debts.

It's possible there was another thing motivating Longman and Rees to make these payments to the Porter sisters: the realization that Robert's *Travels* weren't going to succeed. Jane's labor for Robert may have been for love, but it wouldn't turn out to be for money. Owen Rees had the difficult task of writing to inform Robert that the first volume's moderate sales hadn't offset its great production costs of more than two thousand pounds. Profits had been less than three thousand pounds. Robert had an advance of one thousand pounds, more than what either of his sisters were getting, in what may look like pay discrimination. The second volume of Robert's *Travels* would finally appear in May 1822, at a gargantuan 869 pages, but there would be no further payment.

"It is therefore very uncertain of our having it in our power to pay money to any of the claimants upon you," Rees had written.

That was sad news. The claimants Longman referred to were Robert's creditors, who'd taken more aggressive measures and actively sought repayment through his publisher. After Robert promised them a settlement from the profits of his book, several had gone directly to Longman and Rees, to cut out the middleman. One creditor had laid an attachment—a kind of garnishing—on any sums realized from Robert's books, up to the amount of his debt. Another claimant was in line behind him.

"If there were prosperity" from Robert's book, Rees wrote, "we have not the power of paying a shilling of it to any one till the Attachments are removed." Robert must have asked his publishers if there might be some monies available to pay Jane, because Rees also responded, "I need not tell you how readily I would pay money to Miss P. were it in my power to do so, knowing the time & labour she bestowed on the work."[44]

The book's great expense and middling showing was upsetting in another way. It meant any terms negotiated for a future book Robert might sell to Longman and Rees would have to go first to his creditors. Robert's previous method of paying living expenses through advances on a promised future book couldn't continue. That may explain why *Travels* was the last one he published.

With his *Travels* a disappointment, Jane eventually turned to negotiating with Longman and Rees for the terms for her next novel, *Duke Christian of Luneburg*. They made a bargain more lucrative than any previous deal she'd had. The publishers agreed on six hundred guineas. Jane felt the payment wasn't only proof of her labor's value but also of something "yet more valuable—the friendship of the House" of Longman. It was precious to her, she told them, as the place her name as an author had found a home from her girlhood.[45]

Duke Christian began to take shape. With Maria so frequently ill, Jane found a research helpmate in Halliday instead. Regular letters and visits were exchanged, and he quickly became one of Jane's favorites. When Clarke left the post of the Royal Librarian, replaced by the Reverend Charles Sumner, it was Halliday who became the chief means of communication between Jane, Sumner, and the King.

Jane began writing her Germanic hero in a mode similar to her Polish and Scottish ones, but when her progress stalled, Maria again came to the financial rescue. She quickly completed another novel—*Roche-Blanche; or, The Hunters of the Pyrenees: A Romance* (1822). At least, that was its corrected title. Maria was embarrassed to discover that the original title she'd given it, "Roche Blanc," was incorrect French. Maria had gotten confused because of "Mont Blanc," the title of a poem by Percy Bysshe Shelley. Her blunder was corrected on the title page, with a note to the reader to "substitute the name of Roche-Blanche, for Roche Blanc, throughout this work." The novel shows other evidence of hurriedness. She acknowledges in her preface that it shares features with *The Village of Mariendorpt*, placing dissimilar characters in similar situations.[46] *Roche-Blanche* was a sixteenth-century French and English story, set in the days of Mary, Queen of Scots. It had Maria's usual interwoven stories of romantic entanglements, historic people, and battles over religion and territory.

Roche-Blanche, although not among Maria's great literary successes, brought needed income.[47] The money helped pay their living expenses and enabled the Porter women to send Maria away from the cottage to recover her damaged eyesight and strength. Then, with Maria having earned enough to give them the ability to support themselves for a time, it was Jane's turn to write. Over the next two years, from the summer of 1822 to the winter of 1824, Jane worked diligently on *Duke Christian*. As the novel lurched toward completion in the fall of 1823, Jane made an inquiry about whether the King wanted to suggest a title for her book. Word came back through Halliday that it was to be called *Duke Christian of Luneburg: or, Tradition from the Hartz*.[48] In letters to Maria, Jane again described her authorship in military terms: "When I get into the press, I shall feel myself on the field"—charging into battle—"and Heaven generally gives me a braver hand there, than in bringing up my forces."[49] She mustered confidence and readied to do battle with royals, readers, and reviewers. At the end of January 1824, she finished it. She wrote to Maria, "The toil is over, and I feel light as a feather."[50]

Duke Christian of Luneburg follows the adventures of a man who honors his parents, succeeds on the battlefield, encounters obstacles to love, and attracts admiration for his high moral character, especially from women. The hero of the novel's title is one of seven sons. At their celebrated father's deathbed, the sons draw lots to see which one will carry on the family line. Their dying father insists only one of them should marry. Young Christian, who doesn't win, is devastated, because he's already secretly engaged to Adelheid, an orphan raised as his sister. Christian reneges on their secret engagement, rather than betray his dying father's wish. He declares Adelheid will be the only woman he'll ever love. When she dies before the end of the first volume, it clears the way for Christian to be fruitlessly pursued by other women for the rest of the novel.

The parts of *Duke Christian* that are set in England are interesting for their fictional introduction of William Shakespeare as a character. He and Duke Christian become each other's mutual admirers. Christian is impressed by Shakespeare's having "a mind, royal, noble, in all but the trapping and the power!"[51] When Duke Christian returns to the Continent, Shakespeare serves as his guide back to Dover.

The novel ends with the pronouncement that George I's grandmother, Sophie, will grow up to give birth to a race of princes who will inspire the people's love, not just their vassalage. The novel describes in rosy terms the origins of the Hanoverian line, but the book wasn't much of a love story. As it couldn't marry off its hero, the greatest love on display in its pages may be the love of one's country.

Anticipating *Duke Christian*'s success, Jane, Maria, and Mrs. Porter dreamed again of having enough money to move out of Ditton Cottage. Jane sought advice about how to present her work to the King. She fantasized about how he might reward her. She hoped for a pension for herself, a diplomatic position in Continental Europe for Robert, or both. If it were both, Jane mused, then "how it would smooth our paths every where!"[52]

Jane's advisers thought it likely, if she could handle it prudently, that her great objects might be gained. It was built on the expectation that, after the presentation of *Duke Christian* by Jane's emissary, the King would ask to see Jane. Jane would then tell him that Robert had married more to honors than wealth. She'd rouse the King's sympathy, gently leading him to give Robert a paid position of some kind, not just another knighthood.

But late in 1824, as Jane was trying to figure out how best to present her book, she learned that the King was in Brighton, recovering from gout. He wouldn't be back in London in time to receive her novel. So Halliday arranged for his own employer, the Duke of Clarence, to send a dispatch to the King, informing His Majesty that Miss Porter's work was ready for presentation.

Perhaps if the King were well enough to see her, then Jane could still give him the book in person. She looked into ways to travel fifty miles to Brighton the next week—an expensive venture. Once there, she'd have to find a genteel way to be brought to the convalescing King at the Royal Pavilion, so she asked a Porter cousin if she might borrow his carriage. But this planning turned out to be needless. Jane was further advised that she ought not to be the one to present her book to the King after all. The only ways to get the book into his hands would be at an elite levee or through the royal librarian.[53] After that, Jane could be presented as the book's author, but she required a male emissary to send it first.

"Whoever it may be," Jane told Robert, "the K[ing] must be given to understand, when he leads the way on the subject, that I should prefer a pension to honorary titles . . . [H]e must lead the way, before the thing can be mentioned.[54]

Jane decided her mother's cousin Sarah's son, Harry Gill, should be the man. Harry was a good-looking, low-ranking ensign, barely into manhood. In uniform, he'd be an interesting object and could capture the King's attention. Harry, as a relative, could speak on behalf of the Porter family. Jane hoped for some advancement for Harry as well. She had become attached to him and felt Harry loved her like a second mother. In mid-February 1824, Harry Gill presented several copies of Jane's book to the royal family. He began his errand not with the King but with the successful delivery of copies to the Duke of York and Duke of Gloucester.[55] But then the rest of Harry's mission faltered. He couldn't gain admission to see the King, bedridden still with gout.

There was no way to get the book into King George IV's hands other than through the new royal librarian, Sumner. The feeling among Jane's advocates was that delivery couldn't be delayed any further. So Sumner had unceremoniously handed Jane's book over to the convalescent King. The librarian dutifully reported back to Halliday that he'd presented Miss Porter's new work to His Majesty, who'd graciously received it and had immediately opened the novel to read it.[56] There was no further communication of any sort from the King.

It must have been difficult for Jane to let go of the vision she'd had of a pension. *Duke Christian* was supposed to have made her financially secure in old age. One remaining hope was for a better response from the reading public. Longman and Rees prepared an enormous print run of three thousand copies, in anticipation of brisk sales.[57] Buyers, however, were few. The novel received just a handful of reviews and proved a failure—or, as Longman and Rees would later euphemistically refer to it, a "non success."[58]

By the summer of 1824, Robert and Maria were trying to convince Jane that the blame for the novel's failure didn't belong on her shoulders but on their own. Maria told friends that the completion of *Duke Christian* had been slowed because of her own poor health and Jane's great worries over it.[59] Robert blamed the King first and himself second.

"What can I say to you about the K——?" Robert wrote to Jane. "It is a painfull thing to find that Individual, whom a subject ought to hold up to others as the model of generosity, patriotism, and liberality, fall so woefully short of any of these virtues."[60] What Robert most wanted was that Jane not blame herself.

"I am the culprit," Robert wrote, "and you are the victim. The hours you dedicated to my service, and the cruel Effects such had on your health—engendered the long delay ere the Duke was ready, and thus the real truth stands."[61]

To try to make up for these cruel effects, Robert helped Jane send a presentation copy of *Duke Christian* to Tsar Alexander, in the hope that the Russian emperor might offer her a gift of some value in return. Alexander did, in due course, respond very generously to the plight of the Porters, although it was to Princess Mary, rather than to Jane. In the late 1810s, after returning from her visit to England, the Princess had contracted extensive debts in Russia, too. She'd also discovered that her estates were being defrauded by an unprincipled steward. That prompted her to appeal to Alexander for assistance, both with her debts and with Robert's stalled career. The Tsar offered Princess Mary a large advance, of an amount referred to only as "a sum."[62] Robert estimated she'd need to keep a third of it back, to pay off her Russian debts, but a portion of the Tsar's monies could go toward paying off Robert's English debts.

Robert wrote to Jane requesting that she again work with his creditors. He wanted to get them to agree to his paying off only his original debt of a thousand pounds, without providing them any interest whatever. It was a considerable shortchanging, but if they'd agree to that payment, then Robert could again return to England without threat of arrest.

"When they see the little chance of getting more," he wrote to her, "I trust they will come into the offer."[63]

So Robert, having just apologized to Jane for keeping her tied up with his transcribing and editing for several years, sent his sister off to do more work for him. At the same time, Princess Mary made one further request of the Tsar. She asked him to advocate for Robert's professional advancement in Britain. So Alexander had his ambassador write an extraordinary letter to King George IV's ambassador, asking, from one sovereign to another, that a diplomatic post be provided for Sir Robert Ker Porter.[64]

In August 1824, Robert set sail again for England, bringing money to begin to pay his debts, along with that unusual letter from the Russian ambassador to the British one, meant to communicate from the Tsar to the King.[65] Robert rented a house in London and worked to advance his prospects with the Foreign Office. It took some months, but the letter from Russia finally reached the people it needed to reach, and its influence was felt. Robert learned he'd be given a British diplomatic position, as a favor to Alexander: Sir Robert Ker Porter was offered a post in South America.

He'd be sent to Caracas, the capital of Venezuela, part of Gran Colombia, as a chargé d'affaires to head the British mission there in absence of a stipulated minister. Venezuela wasn't yet an independent country. The area was politically volatile. More than 4,600 miles separated London and Caracas, with more than 6,000 between Moscow and Caracas. Robert didn't speak Spanish. This was a difficult, undesirable position in a faraway place. Yet Robert felt compelled to accept it.[66] The position's regular salary was 1,250 pounds a year.[67]

"Go to it with a cheerful face," a powerful friend advised Robert. "Do what you can do, & not one jot beyond—never mind the given direction."[68]

Once there, Robert hoped he might save up enough money to support both his Russian and English families. After having proved himself in South America, he might be offered a better ministerial position in Europe. He wrote to let his wife know he'd be leaving her and their daughter, without a fixed date of return.[69] This would have come as a shock, even after his multiyear junket wandering around Persia. It was shocking to his mother and sisters, too.

One important thing Robert managed to do before his departure was help move Mrs. Porter, Jane, and Maria into a more livable cottage in Esher, the nearby desirable village they'd long been eyeing.[70] The publisher's generous payment for Jane's *Duke Christian* and Maria's *Roche-Blanche* would have helped make the move possible, but it was Robert's promise that he'd send a regular allowance from his diplomatic salary that gave his sisters the confidence to make the leap to a more expensive house.

As a moving present, Robert bought his mother and sisters a set of chairs for their sitting room so they could have guests in this more solid home. Then, on October 19, 1825, Mrs. Porter said goodbye again to her beloved son, upon his departure to South America. She put a rose in his breast, which he pressed and kept for the rest of his life.[71] Robert left Jane with his power of attorney, putting her in charge of his still unsettled and messy business affairs in England. Although she had once fantasized about serving as Robert's private secretary, this surely wasn't what she'd envisioned. Adding to the disappointment, her visions for financial independence through *Duke Christian* had proved chimerical. It was the only one of her novels after *Thaddeus of Warsaw* that didn't reach a second edition.

Jane didn't blame Sir Andrew Halliday for having first encouraged her in the failed venture of *Duke Christian*, but through pushing Jane to write the novel, he had contributed to three wasted years of her life as an author. It seems he'd nudged her to write *Duke Christian* at least in part to feed his own interests and vanity, rather than to fulfill the King's supposed wishes. In 1821, Halliday had made vague promises to Jane about a material return for her literary labors, which would never be delivered from the King. Halliday's own results, however, proved far better. He, too, would eventually dedicate a book by permission to George IV—*Annals of the House of Hanover* (1826).[72] Halliday's fulsome, public praise of the King in his dedication resulted in several distinctions and promotions. The lessons of Jane's failure surely smoothed the way for Halliday's better success.

After *Duke Christian* was published and came to naught, and during Robert's stint in South America, Jane and Sir Andrew Halliday remained friends. Mrs. Porter was the first to think she detected some remorse from Halliday over the role he'd played in Jane's flop.

"I think he now feels rather ashamed," Mrs. Porter wrote to Jane, "that all his speeches are now nothing but empty wind."[73]

CHAPTER 21

Strange, Unworthy Brother

Jane and Maria Publish Together and William Writes Away (1824–31)

Jane may have put too romantic a spin on their new home in Esher by calling it a "little rambling old dwelling."[1] It was a regular-looking two-story house, perched atop a hill, on a shop-filled street lined with elm trees, but there's no question that the Porter women's move in autumn 1825 brought greater comfort. Jane was almost fifty, Maria nearly forty-seven, and Mrs. Porter was eighty years old.

Their dry, spacious cottage had a double drawing room with folding doors to entertain guests. It had a library with a stove, done up in green and mahogany, with green-striped calico curtains. The dining parlor had a rose-flowered carpet, a stove, and a green-painted table. The cottage had attic rooms to accommodate servants. There were three cellars, a scullery, and a wash house. There was even a water closet—which needed to be filled by pails of water from the pump, once a week—and a privy in the garden. The sisters hired a second female servant, which meant they wouldn't always need to manage callers. In the past, Jane or Maria had answered the door whenever the maid was out. With two servants, the sisters might finally be able to write without constant interruption. They could control their own time and whether visitors were allowed in.

Jane took to the newfound solitude, but Maria often felt bored. She had a pleasant room with a fireplace and "the power of shutting out all their neighbors," as she put it.[2] But sometimes life proved too quiet for her, without even village gossip to share.[3] Whenever Jane traveled to London on business, Maria would write during the day while Mrs. Porter read books or knitted.[4] In the evenings, Maria couldn't see well enough to read or do needlework, and Mrs. Porter couldn't hear well enough to talk with her lively daughter. Maria might ask Mrs. Porter ten questions in a row but get only one answer. Her mother would ask "What?" the other nine times.[5] So the two women would either sit in silence or interact through card games.

The property's low, ivy-covered fence bordered the rich woodlands of Claremont Park, still home to Prince Leopold, who proved a good neighbor. If his pheasants crossed into their little garden to eat Mrs. Porter's gooseberries, the incursion was repaid with gifts of fruit and game.[6] Prince Leopold had once given Mrs. Porter a portrait of himself, a gift she felt to be an honor. But the member of the Claremont household they most liked to see was six-year-old Victoria—a girl no one yet guessed would be queen—rambling in the park with her governess. The Porters enjoyed watching the child with glossy fair ringlets running like an antelope over the Claremont lawn.[7]

When the Porters first moved to their rented cottage in Esher, its long lease and greater expenses seemed manageable. It cost them 30 pounds a year in rent, plus 10 pounds in taxes and church fees. Robert had promised to send them an allowance from his new salary. They wrote out a careful accounting of anticipated expenses. They'd spend 177 pounds on subsistence, like coal and food, adding medical expenses (15 pounds a year), clothing (30 pounds), wages for their two maids (16 pounds), and two pounds for laundry. They didn't include the cost of books, travel, or assisting with Robert's continued debts and interest. Perhaps that was captured in the modest 20 pounds estimated for miscellaneous expenses. Their proposed annual budget came to 280 pounds.

Three women living on less than three hundred pounds a year wasn't poverty, but it was a lean budget, especially considering Jane's and Maria's global celebrity and their supposedly wealthy princess-in-law. Indeed, the sisters' fame created unusual financial pressures. Visitors were supposed to be treated to generous hospitality, including expensive meat and wine. These expectations were yet another reason why they needed a maid to control who came into their house and how often. A servant to turn people away would save the sisters money as well as time. Unfortunately, their frugal estimates of how little they might live on proved too optimistic.

Even before they understood they couldn't live within their income, Porter family happiness was shaken by a series of deaths. Word came from Russia that Tsar Alexander had passed away at age forty-seven, in December 1825. Alexander's death hit Robert hard, because the Tsar was by then his personal friend and benefactor, as well as Princess Mary's. He'd also been their daughter's sponsor or godfather. Robert privately declared the loss a blow to his future hopes and prospects in Britain and Russia.[8]

There was one small thing to be grateful for. Before he died, Tsar Alexander had cleared the way for Robert's daughter, Mary—Mashinka, as she was called—to inherit her mother's Russian estates.[9] By Russian law, children born to a foreign father were classified under their father with no legal claim on a mother's Russian property. To override that law, the Tsar had issued a special decree that Mashinka would be granted the noble rank of her mother, although not her title.[10] Jane and Maria's niece had her future as an heiress secured, just in the nick of time.

It was becoming clear that Robert wouldn't be sending his wife and child, or his sisters and mother, any of his diplomatic salary for at least two years. To succeed in his new role, Robert needed to present himself as a gentleman, without "any appearance of poverty peeping out," as Jane put it.[11] He had to set up an attractive house in Caracas. Not only would the Porter women need to do without Robert's promised allowance; they also knew William wouldn't send much more than free medical advice from Bristol.

To earn 300 hundred pounds a year, Jane and Maria would have to take turns publishing a novel every two years at their present rate of pay. In the fall of 1825, Maria's eyesight had improved enough to resume writing. But the sisters decided, for the first time, to publish a book together, to share the necessary literary effort. They decided on a co-authored, two-volume work, *Tales Round a Winter Hearth*, with separately written stories of England, Scotland, and Ireland.[12] The sisters knew the volumes were short when they approached Longman and Rees to sell it. Rees nevertheless offered them the same rate as for *Roche-Blanche*—140 pounds a volume. He advanced 100 pounds, with the rest to be paid when the book was delivered.[13]

Maria's half was done by December 1825, in three short stories with Scottish and Irish settings. Jane's tales were inspired by a visit she'd made to Burnham Abbey, with historical and antiquarian detail and color. She drew on her vast knowledge of Turkey and Armenia, gained through editing Robert's *Travels in Persia.* On the publication of *Tales Round a Winter Hearth* in the spring of 1826, Rees informed them the book was selling well enough, yet they'd received few reports from friends or admirers.

"As we mix now so little with society," Maria wrote to Robert, "we hear scarcely anything about [the *Tales*] otherwise."[14]

The sisters needed their book to succeed. With greater living expenses in Esher, the Porter women had recently joined Robert in carrying personal debt. Mrs. Porter worried their creditors would band together to take legal action.[15] As for the debts she owed, Mrs. Porter declared, "I am ashamed of mine."[16]

Jane, Maria, and Mrs. Porter had each spent on credit, assuming they'd be able to repay it all from an expected bequest in the will of their late cousin William Blythman Blenkinsop of Rochester. But that legacy became tied up in the infamous Court of Chancery. They would ultimately receive only a small fraction of the five hundred pounds they'd expected to inherit. They also hadn't understood Robert's salary from the government would often be delayed. Then, too, when his three-hundred-pound quarterly payment came in, most of it was already spoken for by his previous spending. Robert's English creditors were again becoming restless and threatening legal action.

Jane got creative. She asked their publishers to serve as the family's shadow banker, to make direct payments to Robert's most aggressive creditor, paying the money off from their book advance. But even this wasn't enough to get out of the red. So in March and April of 1826, Jane borrowed large sums from two old friends, Anna Middleton and Elizabeth Dillon. Anna's father and brothers continued to run the lucrative art supply business on St. Martin's Lane. She generously loaned Jane and Maria five hundred pounds. Jane promised to pay Anna five percent quarterly interest until the total was repaid at some unnamed future date.[17]

Their other lender, their sterling-hearted friend Mrs. Dillon, loaned the sisters two hundred pounds with interest and no fixed term of repayment. Mrs. Dillon could be trusted to keep confidences about debt, because she herself was trying to hide a notorious past. When the man who'd pretended to be her husband became a viscount, he cast her off and married elsewhere. He'd given her permission to keep using his surname and granted her an annual allowance of two hundred pounds. Mrs. Dillon loaned the Porter women a year's worth of her former lover's hush money. These loans saved the Porter women from public shame but meant Jane and Maria couldn't afford to take a break from writing.

In the first half of 1826, Maria was determined to finish her next novel, *Honor O'Hara*. In negotiating the sale, Jane instructed Maria to say "We are obliged to make every possible exertion, to get us this year through the consequent difficulties."[18] That way, Jane said, Longman and Rees wouldn't be surprised when the sisters approached them with another pressing request for an advance on a next book soon afterward. Longman and Rees were more generous than expected. For her three-volume novel, they paid Maria 140 pounds per volume, for a total of 420 pounds.[19] That would have been a windfall, had much of it not already been spoken for to pay previous debts and interest and had their household expenses not been three hundred a year.

Maria's *Honor O'Hara: A Novel*—a story of domestic manners, set in England's recent past—was a departure. Heroine Honor may have been inspired by the late Jane Austen's protagonists. Honor is an independent woman who delights in the ridiculous, like Elizabeth Bennet, yet has extreme sensibility, like Marianne Dashwood. Honor is a lover of nature who enjoys solitary walks and curling up with the latest book of poems. There's a bit of Maria and Jane, too, rolled into Honor's personality, although more of Maria, who'd drawn on her experiences of failed courtship in narrating Honor's adventures. One of Honor's beaux in the novel has similarities to their neighbor Sir Charles Sullivan. He's described as a pleasant, inoffensive caller and a silent wooer, who spends months visiting Honor's home. He never manages to come to the point and propose.

The hero of *Honor O'Hara* is a sensitive captain of dragoons, Delaval Fitz Arthur, perhaps inspired by men she'd formerly admired, although Maria's Captain Fitz Arthur was clearheaded, generous-spirited, and steady in principle. Honor is slow to realize Fitz Arthur's excellence. Before she meets the real man, she sees his portrait at his father's estate and thinks he looks like a hideously plain, ill-favored, glum schoolboy. Honor eventually overcomes this "prejudiced imagination" and gives up her enthusiastic quest for love at first sight to marry him.[20]

Privately, Maria doubted the tone and quality of *Honor O'Hara*. "You will not wonder that I can only write such light stuff at present," Maria admitted to Robert. "It is the sort of thing which sells now, Romance being out of fashion, and luckily may be spun by a mechanical operation almost, when a better manufacturer would call for a free heart and mind to do the task properly."[21]

Although Maria undersells this finely written, entertaining novel, it's no wonder that neither her heart nor mind were free to write. *Honor O'Hara* was published in November 1826, just six months after the appearance of *Tales Round a Winter Hearth*. It was Maria's seventeenth book. The publisher printed fifteen hundred copies, but *Honor O'Hara* didn't sell well.[22] It has memorable characters, moving events, and a winning heroine, but it wasn't the sort of work readers expected from Miss Anna Maria Porter. Reviewers were perplexed, disappointed, or both.

There was no time to wallow in poor sales or mixed reviews, because devastating news arrived from Russia. First, they heard Princess Mary had taken ill. Then, in October, the British Ambassador to Russia wrote from St. Petersburg that Princess Mary—or, rightly, Lady Porter—had expired.[23] The Princess's death was a calamity. No one knew what to do with thirteen-year-old Mashinka. The state of the Princess's finances made it worse. She died deeply in debt. Maria understood it had been ten or twelve million rubles, perhaps sixty thousand pounds.[24] Robert wouldn't be able to receive any revenues from his late wife's estates, for himself or his daughter, until the Princess's debts to the crown were paid off.[25] The hope was that these debts could be repaid slowly from the rents on her estates, rather than forcing the sale of her properties.[26] That way, Mashinka would one day grow up to be an heiress of something other than her foolish mother's chronic overspending.

How Mashinka would be supported in the meantime was anyone's guess. There was talk of sending her to her aunts in Esher and leaving the Russian estates in a caretaker's hands. No one suggested the girl should go to Caracas with Robert. The travel expense (with a companion, if one could even be found) would've been enormous, and the political situation in South America was unstable. There was no proper place to educate the girl or, when the time came, to marry her off to someone of a similar class background. Whether Robert wanted her there is another question entirely. It all became moot when the Russian Imperial Family declared Mashinka wouldn't be allowed to leave the country, except in the company of her father.

The motherless girl was enrolled at the School of the Order of St. Catherine, a fashionable institution that specialized in educating the daughters of the nobility. From the very first, Mashinka hated her life at school. She wrote distraught letters to her aunts and grandmother, complaining that she'd received only two letters from her father in the first year after her mother died.[27] Mashinka asked if she could please live in England. Sometimes her letters were so pitiful that Jane kept them back, rather than forwarding them to Caracas, to spare Robert the pain of reading them.

Mashinka began to complain of chest pains and violent headaches.[28] She told her English family she spent her birthdays crying, kissing her parents' portraits, and waiting for her father to return.[29] Each year, she'd remind her father how long it had been. Five years. Six years.[30] Longer. She claimed her teachers were worthless. She wrote to her grandmother, "It will be a great shame if I am a great girl and know nothing."[31] But Jane and Maria received a report that the problem was the girl herself, not the school. The Porter women chose to believe the school.

In the late 1820s, changes were afoot in Britain that had a great impact on Jane and Maria. At a February 1827 event, Sir Walter Scott finally admitted that he'd authored the Waverley novels. Everyone had already assumed this, but Scott's acknowledgment changed the ways he, and his bestselling novels, were publicly discussed. The Porter sisters may have hoped Scott's admission would finally prompt him and others to acknowledge his debt to their historical romances. He didn't. Few others noted it, either.

Something must have shifted in Jane's mind that year. Perhaps her anger couldn't be contained any longer. She wrote a twenty-five-page serialized short story for a magazine that bayoneted Scott's long attachment to anonymity and his unfair literary dominance. Her story ridiculed his nickname, the "Great Unknown," and accused him of snuffing out fellow authors, by turning them from somebodies into nobodies. The story's first installment, published in June 1827, was titled "Nobody's Address" and after that "Nobody's Journal." It was signed by "J. P."

The point of "Nobody's Address" is to turn Nobody into a proper name and a character, through a gag best known in the twentieth century in Abbott and Costello's comedic baseball routine "Who's on First." The conceit allows for J. P.'s tongue-in-cheek assertion that Nobody wrote historical novels before Sir Walter Scott. When the Great Unknown is gone, then Nobody should supply his place.[32] The slippage between known and unknown, nobodies and somebodies, is deeply uncomfortable, if clever. Jane's stories reveal the pain of having been an author-somebody turned into a nobody over the course of a dozen years by the literary omnipresence of Scott's Great Unknown.

In the fall of 1827, the sisters approached Longman and Rees to sell a second co-authored book. It was advertised at first as a follow-up to the last, to be called *Summer Nights at Sea*.[33] When the book appeared, its title was changed to *Coming Out; and The Field of the Forty Footsteps*. Maria's two-volume contribution, *Coming Out: A Tale of the Nineteenth Century*, was a damning indictment of the fashionable world. The third volume was Jane's: *The Field of the Forty Footsteps: A Romance of the Seventeenth Century*. The sisters once again charged into the literary marketplace together.

Maria's *Coming Out* is a tour de force, showing her at full strength as a fiction writer. It draws heavily on her interactions with the Margravine of Anspach. Heroine Alicia is brought under Lady Donnington's thumb. The parallels with the Margravine are many, including that the real woman and fictional character both keep homes in Berkshire, demand complete obedience from their female charges, and show little interest in the feelings or needs of others, except where it serves their self-interest. Lady Donnington, Maria writes, "spoke when she pleased, and what she pleased; broke off when she pleased; did or did not answer, just as it suited her humour or her purpose; let down or pulled up the windows without enquiring the wishes of her companion."

Maria drew from life, too, for inspiration in creating her fictional Polish princess, Princess Azorinski, who speaks in broken English and is described as a good-humored, tin-eyed, mustard-skinned, wide-mouthed, big-toothed, powerful woman, whose own biographer dubs her "The Little Monster." The Princess Azorinski lives in her own house as heedlessly and without management as if it were a hotel. She's called an unapologetically flirtatious, "charming grown baby."[34] It's little wonder Maria waited until her Russian sister-in-law was dead before creating this colorful portrait. The preface disingenuously claims the author hasn't drawn from living characters under feigned names as was fashionable then.

Jane's contribution, *The Field of the Forty Footsteps: A Romance of the Seventeenth Century*, tells the story of a legendary duel, set on a real field near London's Russell Square. Oral tradition said two brothers had once fought there to the death. Superstition had it that their footprints remained stamped there ever after and that grass wouldn't grow over the spot where their unnatural, fatal combat stained the ground. *The Field of the Forty Footsteps* is a single-volume, 680-page work that owes much to the Gothic tradition. Jane implicitly argues that the British national record is fast disappearing, although it remains under foot. In researching the story, Jane had become an antiquarian herself. At Jane's request, Robert also sent his sister a letter filled with recollections of the field and even a chart to find the exact spot.[35] Jane and Maria both drew on their own lives and observations to tell tales designed to guide readers, and the country, to happier endings.

The sisters' two works might have received greater attention and acclaim as separate novels. Jane's *The Field of the Forty Footsteps* could have easily been two volumes and compensated as such. Maria's one-thousand-page *Coming Out* might have easily filled three volumes. By publishing five volumes in three, the sisters lost hundreds of pounds of much-needed potential income. When Jane approached Longman and Rees to negotiate a price, Owen Rees reported that the partners consulted with "every liberal feeling towards you and your sister" but decided to offer the same amount as they had for *Honor O'Hara*—140 pounds a volume, "though the sale of neither that work or the Tales fully warrant it."[36] The sisters got 420 pounds, which, if they hadn't had debts and interest, might have supported them for a year and a half. As quickly as they were writing, it wasn't fast enough to cover their expenses.

Coming Out; and The Field of the Forty Footsteps was published in January 1828. Jane had a copy of the book sent—at her expense—to Sir Walter Scott. Another copy went to their dear old Edinburgh teacher, George Fulton.[37] The sisters often sent books to people they hoped would advance their prospects or to whom they felt special gratitude. Scott was the former, and Fulton the latter. Jane's letter to Scott describes Maria's *Coming Out* as a novel on existing manners and her own, *The Field of the Forty Footsteps*, as a kind of trespass on ground he'd so completely made his own. She told Scott that their book "comes in the light of a tribute, however humble the offering, to the rightful Lord of the Soil!"[38] She told him his work inspired hers. Her letter was precisely the sort of gracious, credit-where-it's-due statement Scott never made to Jane or Maria. For Jane, the footsteps of her long literary duel with Scott made an indelible impression. She was opening the door for him to respond in kind. It seems to have been fruitless.

If Scott acknowledged receipt of the letter or read the sisters' presentation copy of their book, then no record survives of it. By 1828, Scott himself had an enormous, secret debt of 140,000 pounds from a failed publishing partnership. That amount makes the Porters' crippling thousand pounds of debt look laughably small. Jane and Maria's version of becoming house poor was renting a tiny Surrey cottage that was a little beyond their means. Scott's version was having bought a large estate in the Scottish Borders and building a castle on it that he couldn't ultimately pay for, having filled it with furniture, books, and relics. Years of Scott's life were spent publishing manically, trying to dig out of debt and keep Abbotsford House.

Throughout their careers, Jane and Maria had faced sexism. In this latest book, they met with reviews that blatantly coupled sexism with ageism. Reviewers found *Coming Out; and The Field of the Forty Footsteps* old-fashioned and declared its authors merely old. "The taste of the age is so very much altered since our fair authoresses began their literary career," the *Literary Gazette* opined, so that "it is scarcely fair to try their works by the ordeal of modern opinion."[39] Maria had idealistically hoped *Coming Out* would transform the fashionable world by inspiring better morality. She was distressed to learn her novel was having the opposite effect. She heard stories suggesting it was inflaming, not dampening, a mania for vapid dress and hollow amusement.[40] After completing the book, Maria again took ill, having predictably worked herself into exhaustion. At fifty, Maria worried about how much longer her weakened frame would be able to keep up this punishing pace of writing. In July 1828 Maria wrote, "My body is literally my prison."[41] She hoped she and Jane would soon be able to leave off the pains of seeking pay, and celebrity, as authors.

Jane had more literary energy remaining. She wrote dozens of pieces, signed and unsigned, for periodicals.[42] A few were inspired by famous men Robert had gotten to know in South America, including Simón Bolívar. Jane was enthusiastic about Bolívar's bringing liberty there and was proud her brother knew him. Jane's politics were complicated. She told Robert that although she was with the Tory administration—the conservatives—in England, she was a most enthusiastic admirer of Bolívar, the great liberator abroad.[43] She was also relieved that Robert didn't belong to any political party, which she hoped would advance his diplomatic career, because parties in power and prime ministers so regularly changed. Jane worked to place short, uncontroversial, career-enhancing, and anonymous paragraphs about Robert's labors in South America in the newspapers.

Maria was upset to think she and Jane would never meet Bolívar. She told Robert that, if she were reincarnated in the 1920s, then she'd write a historical romance about Bolívar and General José Antonio Páez, another of Robert's new friends, and put Robert in as a character, too.[44] As Maria fantasized about writing a novel in her next life, Jane envisioned becoming a museum curator. She loved the relics of history's notables that she'd been given as gifts or that Robert sent home from the Americas, including items said to be from Bolívar (a ribbon, hair), General Páez (hair), Francisco Pizarro (a flag), and something from "Mrs. Washington," presumably Martha.[45] Jane hoped to set up these objects in a little display to be viewed by visitors in a future household she imagined sharing with Maria, Mrs. Porter, Robert, Mashinka, and perhaps even Robert's nephew, Prince Shcherbatov, a man she hoped Mashinka might one day marry.[46]

Thanks to Robert's contacts in South America, Jane and Maria's circle of acquaintance grew among men recently returned from stints there and the West Indies. One such man was the naval officer Captain Charles Austen.[47] Jane and Maria were excited to get to know Captain Austen, Robert's gallant friend, especially because he was the brother of the late Miss Austen, whose novels they so admired. Captain Austen had read Anna Maria Porter's *Honor O'Hara*, a novel that seems to have been inspired by his sister Jane's success.[48] When he returned to England, he exchanged letters with Jane.[49] The Porter women expected him to visit them in Esher in December 1828, but illness in his household delayed the trip.[50] Perhaps it was never made.

In 1829, Jane proposed to create and anonymously write the contents for a new magazine, *Eminent Women*. The periodical fizzled with its prospective publisher before any issues appeared. That year, Maria started a new novel, *The Barony*, sending the first volume to Longman and Rees. Her publishers disappointed her, however, by offering only 100 pounds a volume.[51] The "indifferent success of your latter works," they said, wouldn't allow them to pay her the previous rate of 140.[52] The sisters' "expected golden-returns" turned into "more empty air," as Jane put it.[53]

In the spring of 1829, Maria went alone to Bristol for a long visit to William and Phoebe as she often did at that time of year, so that her brother could treat her many illnesses. He had occasionally stepped up to help his sisters and mother during Robert's absence in South America in the late 1820s. Mrs. Porter believed William's love must truly be returning to his long-neglected family, especially after he started sending her gifts of game and cheese every fortnight.[54] During that 1829 visit to Bristol, Maria reported a new medical problem to her brother—an extreme weakness of the nerves in her hand. William was little help, but Jane shared that she, too, had once developed the same condition while copying one of Maria's long manuscripts. Jane sent Maria her treatment plan for symptoms that sound like carpal tunnel syndrome.

"The greatest relief I found," Jane reported, "was from writing always in gloves, which prevented the extreme pressure of the pen as on the flesh of the fingers . . . also the sides of the hand on the table & I have some recollection that I washed my hand in Salt & water."[55]

William decided to treat Maria's other illnesses under a new regimen, which consisted of withholding food. While on a starvation diet, she was trying to complete *The Barony*.[56] She told Jane she hoped it wasn't idleness or sloth, but she just couldn't write.[57]

"I pray fervently to Heaven for a renewal of my mental energy," she wrote. "Most likely the fit will seize me, and I shall at once be inspired with ideas & words."[58]

Literary inspiration didn't happen while she was starving, but over the course of two months there, Maria felt her condition improve under her brother's care. However, just two days before Maria's scheduled return to Esher in late May 1829, Mrs. Porter experienced an alarming attack of paralysis.[59] Maria and William rushed back to help. Upon examining his mother, William's opinion was the same as that of Mrs. Porter's Esher surgeon, Mr. Neville. The elderly woman had had a paralytic seizure, causing her to lose the use of her left side.[60] Fortunately, the effects were temporary, and her memory was sound. She eventually walked again.[61]

As Mrs. Porter slowly recovered, the Esher household was anticipating Robert's return to England from Caracas. He'd been granted a short leave of absence by the government, but he left things in such a state in South America that he seems to have hoped he might never return.[62] He traveled to Britain via the United States, as newspapers tracked the celebrated Sir Robert's trek home.[63] When he arrived in England in July 1829, Robert learned about Mrs. Porter's frightening illness. Although his leave of absence had ostensibly been to mend his own weakened health, that was merely a convenient cover story.[64] Robert had planned to go from England to Russia, in order to bring Mashinka back with him to England, to reunite with her aunts and grandmother for the first time since she was a baby. Mrs. Porter's stroke, however, postponed these plans. With his mother's health so perilous, he decided to wait to go to Russia until spring.

Even with these health and travel setbacks, there were happy times during Robert's return home. He and Jane reconnected with old theatrical friends Charles and Therese Kemble and saw their talented actress daughter Fanny Kemble perform. Robert was so impressed he told Jane that if Fanny had been able to act with the late Henry Caulfield, the two of them would have been the living picture of Romeo and Juliet.[65] Robert also renewed his acquaintance with the friendly Duke of Clarence, then second in line for the throne.[66] The duke, Robert felt, had been "more than usually gracious and condescending" to him, as in the days of old. Robert also spent time with George Villiers, the future Earl of Clarendon and British foreign secretary and dined, too, in a large party with Prince Leopold at Claremont House.[67] Much was hoped for from these high connections.

Most of Robert's visits were far less tony. Whenever Jane could get away from Esher, she accompanied him on what he termed "abominable calls of ceremony."[68] Despite these assiduously renewed connections, no new diplomatic opportunity had yet materialized. Then, in late February 1830, he received an urgent directive from the Foreign Office, telling him to return immediately to Caracas.[69] He felt he had no choice but to follow orders.[70] The political situation in South America was changing rapidly, and the British wanted a representative on the ground to protect their political and commercial interests.[71] Robert felt he was promised that, if he could manage these interests, he'd be rewarded. When he broke the news to his daughter Mashinka that he wouldn't be coming to St. Petersburg after all, she replied with letters full of pained feeling.[72] The motherless girl, nearly seventeen, had last seen her father around age ten.

When the day of Robert's second departure for Caracas arrived, he said his melancholy goodbyes in Esher. At this parting, Mrs. Porter thought Robert's last look at her had been such a solemn one.[73] They'd both have been thinking the same thing—that they would likely never lay eyes on each other again in this world. When Robert's ship was delayed at the port by bad weather, Jane ended up with a second opportunity to say goodbye and see him off at the coast. As his ship finally left, she stood on the beach at Southsea, crying and alone, until the last white spot of the frigate disappeared at the end of the western sky.[74]

Upon her return to Esher in May 1830, Jane learned the good news that Maria's novel *The Barony* had been published. In the weeks and months following, the sisters turned their attention to promoting their writing careers, seeking to attract readers and reviewers for Maria's work. Its reception, however, was made challenging by political and personal circumstances.

"I really think it is a most languid performance," Maria wrote, in a private letter about *The Barony*, "and its tone too deeply tinctured by the depressed state of my health & nerves."[75] In this novel, Maria had returned to her familiar ground of historical romance, telling a complex, three-volume story of rival neighboring families in late seventeenth-century Cornwall. In composing *The Barony*, she had drawn on her emotional life in the late 1820s, especially in describing lonely separations and faraway siblings. But the novel's heroine, Aura Trevanion—unlike real-life Maria—is a presumed heiress, nudged to marry a military cousin she isn't interested in.

However, Aura meets the reformed rake, gambler, and atheist Lord Villiers, a member of the real-life seventeenth-century family of that name. Early in the novel, Lord Villiers's wife dies, and the widower Villiers is left with their young son, Charles, whom he sends to be raised in the country. Later, when Aura and Lord Villiers are thrown together, the little boy comes to adore Aura, sits in her lap, and plays with her hair. "I wish you were my mamma!" Charles innocently tells her with Lord Villiers in earshot. Aura blushes, and the father is moved, as she describes experiencing a melancholy feeling while pressing the boy to her breast.[76]

This scene surely comes from Maria's experiences with little Augustus and her love for the boy's father, Keppel Craven. Other personal connections, too, colored the novel's composition. Maria's organizing the book around the historical Villiers family was likely an attempt to please George Villiers, the future Lord Clarendon, Robert's powerful friend who was poised to help him advance in the Foreign Office. At the conclusion of Maria's *The Barony*, Aura and Lord Villiers marry. Long-standing, unresolved claims of illegitimacy and the barony are resolved. It's a happily-ever-after ending, for both Cornish families and for the nation going forward. *The Barony* is filled with incident, intrigue, and skilled characterization, as well as sharp, fluid dialogue.

Friends wrote to the sisters with praise for Maria's achievement. The learned (and as-yet-unpublished) diarist and travel writer Lady Charleville felt it was nearly the best of Maria's beautiful compositions.[77] As the novel was more widely read and reviewed, it become controversial. Some denounced *The Barony* for its supposed harsh treatment of Roman Catholics. Maria was shocked. She felt sure that she'd stated her convictions and objections to the pernicious *doctrines* of Catholicism, not to worthy Catholic people. She hoped she'd presented her Catholic characters with the love and respect she genuinely felt. The Porters were very close to a prominent English Catholic family, the Throckmortons, and demonstrated more religious tolerance than most people of their Protestant faith then did.

Yet there's no question Maria had been unfortunate in the choice of her seventeenth-century source material. The Roman Catholic Relief Act had passed in 1829. That act finally allowed Catholics to serve in Parliament, among other things. Maria's romance of the Glorious Revolution, in which Catholics were excluded from the throne and state, was seen as out of step with the more open-minded views in 1830. She called *The Barony* her "poor abominated book."[78] Its reviewers again employed a tired formula that mixed indirect ageism and sexism. One reviewer remarked on *The Barony*'s "appalling length" and complained that Miss Porter still wrote as she did twenty years ago. It declared that the only readers of *The Barony* who might find it pleasurable would be those of the so-called old school.[79]

The Porter sisters needed to find a next income stream from writing, so they tried to adapt their talents to suit new literary opportunities, including writing one-off pieces for literary annuals. But the sisters became wary of this trendy publishing sensation. They saw that their names might be prominently used to sell a first annual volume but that they, and other celebrated authors, were rarely asked back to contribute to subsequent years of the same title. Magazines, too, were taking advantage of authors, Jane thought, even when their submitted work had been invited. First, she might wait three months to learn whether and when her submission would see print.[80] Then, after publication, it might take another three months—and repeated letters of inquiry—to get paid. Jane once waited six months for a piece to be published and then had to scramble to get a promised payment of five pounds.[81]

The next literary venture that fell into Jane's lap came from a surprising source: her brother William. After Robert's second departure for South America, William had come to Esher, bringing with him the beginnings of a book he was secretly writing. He read aloud to his sisters from what would become his anonymous *Sir Edward Seaward's Narrative* and gave his hearing-impaired mother the manuscript to read on her own. Despite her tired eyes after a day of needlework, Mrs. Porter read *Sir Edward Seaward's Narrative* with a most lively delight.[82] William was in high spirits with their approval, and Mrs. Porter was charmed with her son's rediscovered generosity and affection. When William returned to Bristol, he continued to send his mother and sisters parts of his manuscript as he wrote them over the next year. Mrs. Porter was proud of him. She felt her talented children were good and kind to her—that they were all trying to smooth her pillow of death.[83]

News of a significant death arrived from another quarter. Sir Sidney Smith's wife had passed away. Smith had recently come into a secure and regular income, because one of the first acts of the former Duke of Clarence, who became King William IV in 1830, had been to enact a provision for Sir Sidney Smith's maintenance. The Porters would have celebrated Smith's money, but they little mourned the loss of his wife. They were gratified when, in the summer of 1830, Smith had come to Esher to pay his respects to Mrs. Porter and her daughters. He was animated and erect, Jane thought—the opposite of what he'd seemed a decade earlier when she saw him in Paris. He told them, in confidence, about his own debts and difficulties, which explained why he'd exiled himself in Paris all those years. For four hours, Sir Sidney Smith sat with them.[84] But if Jane harbored any secret hope he might consider her for a second wife, they would've been dashed. Smith made absolutely no romantic overtures to her.

Early in 1831, William approached Jane with the completed manuscript of his *Robinson Crusoe*–inspired novel. She agreed to edit, smooth, and reshape his work, just as she had Robert's before it, and help him find a publisher. William was adamant that Jane must keep his authorship a secret. He felt taking credit for the book would damage his medical practice and reputation. He told Jane not even to tell Robert about it in her long monthly letters to Caracas. So Jane merely told him she was working on a friend's manuscript, which she might be able to sell to Longman and Rees for fifty pounds. She could do the editorial work while caring for their mother, who needed constant attention. It seemed a good time to take on William's project, because Jane felt she couldn't easily pursue her own writing under the circumstances.[85]

"I have not leisure of mind, or time, to set about anything considerable from my own pen," she wrote.

The year 1831 was proving difficult for each Porter sister's peace of mind. Britain was experiencing national upheaval, as a starving working class demonstrated against the country's wealthy overclass. Jane felt torn about how to interpret the events. The sisters were grateful King William IV and Prime Minister Lord Grey were in power. These men, at least, didn't spend the people's money on selfish indulgences, as King George IV had.[86] Jane thought there would have been a hundred times more demonstrations if he were still king and Lord Wellington prime minister. These men, if still in charge, might have violently put down the demonstrations, too, invoking martial law. Jane was relieved for the country and its people that that hadn't come to pass.

But Jane thought the revolutionary orators of the early 1830s were deluding the people. She agreed it was wrong that male laborers were paid so poorly and that they couldn't put a roof over their heads or buy a morsel of bread for their wives and children. She agreed, too, that the working class had been driven to action against the aristocracy because of a desperate lack of ruling-class generosity. But instead of overturning the social order, she thought the problem would best be solved by reforming the ruling class.

The Porter sisters' literary careers benefited from the political upheaval. Economic strife rekindled popular demand for weightier fiction, including historical and didactic stories. Jane rightly suspected her own reputation would be helped by a returned interest in grand political subjects. Positive attention turned back to *Thaddeus of Warsaw*. In the thirty years since that novel's publication, Poland remained partitioned under a series of Russian, Prussian, and Austrian regimes. A bid for independence in Poland in 1830 resulted in a war. Polish patriots were eventually put down, and power was again consolidated under Russian rule. It led many Polish activists and soldiers to immigrate to other parts of Europe by 1831.

"These new events are now making my old Thaddeus be read everywhere afresh," Jane told Robert. That *Thaddeus of Warsaw* was widely and positively talked of was something she was grateful for because "by furnishing up my name in the Republic of Letters, when ever I write again, I may be the more ardently welcomed; and so my price be advantaged."[87]

When Jane decided to speak directly to the political conversation, however, she did it anonymously in the pamphlet *On the Laws and Liberties of Englishmen: Britons Ever Shall Be Free!* Although the title sounds revolutionary, the pamphlet was conservative. Jane argued that the constitution already bestowed on the people all the liberty they required. She advocated for keeping the class structure of Britain in place. Her pamphlet also argued against universal suffrage and therefore against the then-controversial Great Reform Bill of 1832, which proposed to extend the vote to a larger group of men.

Jane held these opinions about retaining class structures despite having herself risen above the station of her birth and overcome the downwardly mobile conditions of her early upbringing. Rather than admitting the unfairness of the economic limitations she faced, it seems Jane imagined herself as the beneficiary of a well-functioning meritocracy. How she could have believed that the system functioned successfully, given the economic conditions her family and friends had faced—even if only taking a hard look at the country's unfairly applied and unfair laws for incarcerating debtors—is puzzling. But in making this rightward turn from earlier views, Jane was following other Romantic-era writers, like William Wordsworth.[88] Aging authors who were formerly sympathetic to revolutionary philosophies worried that Britain might experience the social breakdown, violence, and despotism that France faced in the 1790s. When parliament eventually passed the 1832 Reform Act, and after it the Slavery Abolition Act of 1833, earlier fears of catastrophe, held by Jane and others, were proved unwarranted.

But two years earlier, in 1831, the fate of the West Indies and its enslaved people, as well as the people of Great Britain, seemed to hang in the balance. The Porter sisters knew they had one close family member yet in the West Indies—their eldest nephew, Charles. Charles, raised in Durham, and eventually with his father in Bristol, had long displayed a preference for what Maria thought were evil habits. The boy had been neglected and abused. Maria didn't feel fondly toward Charles, but she was sickened to have once watched William beat his teenage son.[89] Eventually, William had shuffled the young man off to points elsewhere, including the West Indies. News arrived in Esher that Charles, a serial seducer of young women and long estranged from his family, had returned from Jamaica suffering from consumption. Charles died in his father's Portland Place home, fully reconciled to his family and to God, William reported, on February 14, 1831.[90] That death meant William had outlived his first wife and all their children, because his youngest son, Thaddeus, had died of illness several years earlier, at twenty-two, on the Island of Sardinia, as an assistant surgeon in the Royal Navy.[91]

What the sisters found strange is that these deaths were having so little effect on William, especially because, throughout the 1820s, he'd shown far more interest in an orphaned patient than he'd ever taken in either of his sons. This girl, Eliza Clark, was all William could talk about. Maria called it her brother's "infatuated conduct," noting that this wasn't the first time he'd brought shame on his family through a strange fancy for a girl he'd taken a shine to.[92] With this second girl, William seemed on the same disastrous track. He took Eliza into their home and cared for her, putting his wife, Phoebe, into a jealous rage. Then the young woman had died of illness. When Charles died several years later, William reported that he'd buried his son just a few yards from his much-lamented Eliza, at nearby St. Paul's Church in Portland Square. Then William compared the two of them in a letter. He callously told his sisters that he ought not to grieve for Eliza, whose gifts were many, but that he didn't grieve at all for his own son Charles, whose gifts were few.[93] Jane and Maria were appalled.

"Everything relating to this strange unworthy brother, I confess, blinds my eyes so, that I can hardly see to write," Maria wrote to Jane. "Allow me therefore to say no more on the subject. God forgive and amend him."[94]

The only thing William seemed to care about in 1831, after these deaths, was publishing his book. He asked Jane to get on more quickly with her editing of his manuscript.[95] Yet she was working so hard that her arm was numb from overuse.[96] Other women in his life were also helping him finish the book. Maria made an unnamed contribution to its first volume. William's new friend, the widow Mrs. Sarah Booth, recopied the work from its original rough manuscript. William reported that Mrs. Booth had cried when she finished recopying it, because her delightful task had come to an end.[97]

When Jane finished editing *Sir Edward Seaward*, William seemed grateful. He described Jane as both godfather and godmother to "the boy," referring to his book as his child. He admitted Jane's editorial work had improved his writing, although he complained she'd sometimes changed his meanings. He shifted them back to his original prose. Overall, however, William declared that Jane was putting "him"—meaning *Sir Edward Seaward*—forth into the world in a good style.[98] The next thing to do was sell the book. At first, William thought he might publish at his own expense and risk, sharing the profits with Jane, but then they'd decided instead to approach her publishers, Longman and Rees. In negotiating with them, Jane found she could command more money if she allowed her name to appear on the title page as its editor. She asked for three hundred pounds for the three-volume work.[99] The publishers and William approved of this plan and price.

For Jane's trouble in editing and reshaping *Sir Edward Seaward*—for negotiating for its publication, allowing her name to be used on the title page, and correcting its proofs—William gave his sister his 100-pound advance. He also promised that, when he got the remaining 200 pounds on publication, he'd give 50 to his mother and Maria as a gift.[100] The other 150 pounds he'd keep for himself. Once the book was published, William asked Jane to use her network to get *Sir Edward Seaward* into the hands of famous authors, critics, and magazine editors, without ever revealing its author. William wanted Jane to advocate for the fictional book's authenticity, too.[101] Jane used the well-worn trope found in some historical novels, claiming the book's contents were drawn from a manuscript diary that had fallen into her hands. Her preface said she'd recommended the manuscript's owner publish the book as a work of family history.[102] Some readers mistakenly believed this cover story, and therefore the book's contents, to be true.

The work was published as *Sir Edward Seaward's Narrative of His Shipwreck, and Consequent Discovery of Certain Islands in the Caribbean Sea: With a Detail of Many Extraordinary and Highly Interesting Events of His Life, from the Year 1733 to 1749, as Written in His Own Diary*. After its publication, those who mistook it for nonfiction tried to authenticate the supposed location of its tiny, unknown island. Even those who recognized that no such island existed praised the book. One reviewer declared it was the most extraordinary fiction he'd ever read, not excepting Daniel Defoe's.[103] Many assumed Jane must be the author. Another reviewer claimed *Sir Edward Seaward* would have been a much better book if it had been written by a man, but as it had to be by a woman, no female pen could have outdone Miss Porter's.[104] When pressed on the question of whether she was the author, Jane would reply, "Sir Walter Scott had his great secret. I must be allowed to keep my little one."[105]

Sir Edward Seaward proved a sensation—one of those books that everyone seemed to be reading and talking about. William was riding high on its success as well as on his anticipated return to solvency. In addition to the income he'd received for his book, he'd recently been bequeathed some property. Newly flush, William decided to make his own will. He offered to leave some of his wealth to his sisters. Jane assured him that they'd rather have him as a brother than receive a bequest of millions. With this offer to support them, should he die first, William put himself back in their good graces.[106]

He also showed greater generosity and attention to his mother, including making a plan to visit her that July. He pledged to speak to her in short sentences so that she could hear him.[107] This outpouring of love brought Mrs. Porter happiness and hope, in an otherwise difficult year, which had seen the death of her last remaining grandson, alongside such painful national unrest. She felt fortunate by comparison.

"I look round," she wrote to Robert, "& see so many suffering more than I do & with perfect resignation."[108]

Several weeks after William's anonymous book was published, Mrs. Porter became ill. It began with a pain in her side. Maria realized something was very wrong with her mother when a letter arrived from Robert that she didn't have the energy to read.[109] Jane and Maria wrote to William about their mother's new decline. He came to Esher briefly and assessed her, then left her to Jane's dutiful nursing. After William's return to Bristol, the sisters called in the Esher surgeon, Mr. Neville. Soon he was coming three times a day and sometimes at night, too, to care for Mrs. Porter.[110]

When her condition worsened further, the sisters wrote again to William, informing him their mother appeared to be on her deathbed. Jane and Maria expected their brother to rush back to his mother's bedside. Instead, he delayed writing them back for five days. In his reply to Maria, he said he was too busy to make another trip to Esher, sounding callously resigned to whatever might happen next.[111] After that, his letter took an even more shocking turn in its tone. He brought up old grievances against their brother Robert and gloated about the positive attention *Sir Edward Seaward's Narrative* was receiving. He shared with his distraught sisters the great pleasure he was privately taking in his book's success.

When Mrs. Porter's end seemed near, Jane and Maria wrote letters to close friends and loved ones, telling them this was likely to be the close of Mrs. Porter's long life. Cousin Henry Gill, on receiving his letter, immediately left behind his own wife and child to rush to Esher. In riding thirty miles on horseback to say goodbye to his cherished kinswoman, Harry Gill behaved as a son might do.[112] William only sent along a letter he said he wanted his hearing-impaired mother to read to herself on her deathbed. The sisters were beside themselves. Maria felt she and Jane then were like weaker vessels who'd had "many a fracture this life" that rendered them worthless.[113] Yet even hard experience hadn't prepared them for their mother's dying. Jane never left her mother's side, day or night.[114] The sisters arranged for Mrs. Porter to take communion in their home, in preparation for her passing.[115] She seemed to be without pain and even happy.[116] Their mother's last words were, "Prayer. Prayer. Prayer."[117]

Mrs. Porter had always liked to tell people that she came into the world during eventful times, so she figured she'd probably leave it during them, too. She was born on the day the Duke of Cumberland marched through her native Durham on the way to the Battle of Culloden, during the 1745 Jacobite uprising. It seemed only fitting to Jane and Maria that Mrs. Porter died on the anniversary of the Battle of Waterloo.[118]

Jane Blenkinsop Porter, widow, of Esher, age eighty-five, died on June 18, 1831, with her two devoted daughters at her bedside. Her eldest surviving son, Dr. William Ogilvie Porter, was a hundred miles away in Bristol. Her youngest, Sir Robert Ker Porter, was almost five thousand miles away in Caracas. Her only known surviving grandchild, Mashinka Porter, age eighteen, remained in Russia. It would be up to Jane and Maria to share news with them of the loss of their plainspoken, loving, and beloved matriarch, who'd raised such remarkable children, without the benefit of fortune or education.

CHAPTER 22

Separating Sisters

A Pitiless and Cold-Blooded Plan (1831–32)

A month after their mother's death, Jane reported to Robert, "William has most wonderfully failed, through the whole of this trying occasion to us."[1]

Jane and Maria were grieving, floundering, and furious. To acquaintances, they didn't admit it. To dear friends, they described ongoing weakness and anxious nerves, and the feeling of a kind of widowhood, in losing their mother.[2] To Robert alone Jane expressed her great disgust. After refusing to come to his mother's deathbed, despite his previous promises that he'd fly to help her at a moment's notice, William could have redeemed himself by supporting his sisters. Just months before, he'd been giving them small gifts, promising help, and pledging an annuity of one hundred pounds to Jane and Maria, if he should die first. But his lack of care and concern after their mother's death was beyond anything they'd thought possible, even from this self-centered brother.

Mrs. Porter passed away on a Saturday. By the following Tuesday, William's vows to care for his sisters began to unravel. First, he didn't arrive at Esher until Friday. Then, when he finally showed up, he said he could stay only until Monday. He took little interest in the work of planning his mother's funeral or settling her affairs. If he'd asked, he would have learned his mother had died with medical debts of thirty pounds. Jane was grateful that kind, attentive Mr. Neville had behaved like a son and doctor both, but there'd have been no expense at all if William had tended to his dying mother.

Funeral arrangements were traditionally handled by men. With the Porters, such work had predictably fallen to Jane, who, as a friend observed, was looked up to and leaned upon as if she had the strength of a son or brother.[3] An ungenteel funeral service for Mrs. Porter would have been an embarrassment to her daughters. Funerals signaled the departed person's status, wealth, and supposed worth in life. Their costs were rarely made clear until the undertaker's bill was presented. A middle-class funeral could cost fifty pounds.[4]

Emotionally, Jane and Maria had community support to draw on to make up for William's detachment. There was an outpouring of sympathy from friends, neighbors, and tradespeople who knew their mother.[5] Rich and poor alike offered testimonies of Mrs. Porter's beloved character. Yet such support probably expanded the size of the feast traditionally held after the funeral—another expense.

The sisters struggled to afford the cost of Mrs. Porter's death. They sought credit and offered gifts, either in lieu of payment or to forestall it. The undertaker Mr. Shrubsole was given one of Robert's paintings as compensation.[6] After all was said and done, Jane informed William she believed she'd arranged everything her mother would have liked, without incurring any unnecessary expense.

"Ah, well," William answered, "You had better, then, let me have the Bill."

Jane found this faint offer of help so insulting that she told him they couldn't possibly take his money. At the same time, she made sure to tell William that creditors were willing to give the sisters some time to pay off debts. That statement should have communicated to him that his sisters were in need.

"Well," William had said, "let me know if there is anything extra."[7]

William seemed determined to do as little as possible. He brushed off any further expenses. Maria and Jane withered at the thought of there being no monument at their mother's grave. The sisters had prepared their mother's final resting place to be large enough for her two daughters to be buried alongside her after their deaths.[8] William, who had his own family vault at St. Paul's Church in Bristol, showed little interest in his mother's grave in Esher. Sometime later,

Robert paid for the table monument erected at his mother's grave, memorializing her as a Christian widow.[9] RESPECT THE GRAVE, her epitaph read, FOR SHE MINISTERED TO THE POOR. Mrs. Porter's freestone tomb was one of the most striking in the churchyard.[10]

In the days leading up to and just after his mother's death, William sinned by omission, Jane told Robert. She characterized his dealings with them as sterile.[11] When saying his goodbyes to his bereaved sisters, he hadn't so much as said, "I shall be glad to see you at Bristol!" He seemed unconcerned about how they'd support themselves or where they'd go. Jane, in her long letters to Robert during that painful summer, decided to break her promise to William to keep his authorship secret. "I now come to the cause of his over-weaning self-absorption," she wrote, "by confiding to you (for nobody is to know it, not even Longman & Rees know it!) that he is the author of 'Sir Edward Seaward's Narrative.'"

Jane wanted Robert to understand the reasons behind William's inattentiveness at their mother's sickbed and after her death. He had become puffed up with his own extraordinary, anonymous literary fame. He believed he'd already done enough to support his mother and sisters, giving them half the proceeds from the sale of his celebrated book. Having paid Jane one hundred pounds and offering his late mother fifty, he thought he'd done handsomely by them. Had he calculated it honestly, he would have realized his mother's medical bills, funeral, and burial alone came to something near seventy-five pounds.

Jane and Maria had planned to live in deep mourning and seclusion for the first month after their mother's death, but they couldn't keep friends away. "These unceasing visits," and their uncertain economic future, were taking a toll on their bodies. Maria described her and Jane's nerves as shattered by severe anxiety.[12] Jane longed to get her fragile sister away to somewhere quiet, where she might focus on regaining strength.

Now that Mrs. Porter was gone, so was her widow's pension. Jane and Maria knew they needed to find a new income stream, to retrench, or both. Jane continued to publish anonymous stories in magazines about things she'd witnessed, overhead, or learned secondhand. For the *Lady's Monthly Museum* and *La Belle Assemblée*, she wrote pieces about Simón Bolívar and the Dowager

Empress of Russia. She sometimes wrote about herself in the third person. One piece began "A lady, of some literary celebrity, happened to be sitting one day at a small family dinner table."[13]

Jane approached Longman with a proposal for a three-volume book of selections from their letters. The sisters hoped for one hundred pounds a volume.[14] Jane asked Robert to send back letters she and Maria had written him over the years to mine for material about great figures and living heroes of war, history, arts, and letters they'd observed. By the end of the year, however, Jane and Maria gave up on their planned book of letters. They concluded that the material in those letters just wouldn't do.[15] "Should we live, and in future times have leisure," Jane wrote, "when we are all together, such a thing might be selected—for an ultimate record of us!"[16]

Another promising project materialized—reprinting their bestselling works. In March 1831, two months before Mrs. Porter's death, Longman and Rees sold the remaining copyright of some of its popular backlist titles, including the Porter sisters' novels. A pair of eager publishers, Henry Colburn and Richard Bentley, formed a partnership and created a series, the Standard Novels, to bring out new editions of the previous generation's best fiction with new introductions, notes, and revised texts. The Porter sisters' works were among the first literary properties Colburn and Bentley bought, with four of their works included in the series.

Jane described her new prefaces and additions as little *douceurs*.[17] The first of her titles in the Standard Novels was *Thaddeus of Warsaw*, a timely choice. It's surprising Longman and Rees would have sold their financial stake in that desirable literary property, but they'd received a seven-hundred-pound payment for the Porter backlist. Although not obliged to share any of the money with Jane and Maria, they'd given the sisters one hundred pounds. This payment honored—and, in a sense, ended—a thirty-year publishing connection.

For their 700 pounds, Colburn and Bentley got a bargain, because, in addition to the remaining copyrights, they'd purchased all unsold stock—some eight thousand volumes of fourteen Porter novels. Colburn and Bentley sold copies of eleven novels to a publisher for 333 pounds. They sold the copies of *Thaddeus of Warsaw*, *Scottish Chiefs*, and *Hungarian Brothers* at a higher price to another bookseller who dealt in remainders. He paid them nearly

100 pounds. In effect, Colburn and Bentley paid just 230 pounds for the remaining copyright to fourteen of the Porters' novels.[18]

Having gained Colburn and Bentley as their new publisher came with unpleasant surprises. The sisters had occasionally complained about Longman and Rees, but Jane felt they'd treated her with respect and attention.[19] Colburn and Bentley, by contrast, began by ignoring her letters. She couldn't get hard information about upcoming deadlines until after she saw *Thaddeus of Warsaw* advertised. Then she scrambled to finish the needed additions and revisions. Colburn and Bentley hadn't told the sisters what they'd be paid for editing and reintroducing their old bestselling novels. Advertisements claimed new content in the series had been obtained at considerable cost. Yet the publishers offered Jane just ten pounds for her revisions, notes, and preface. It was so insulting a sum that Maria thought Jane should refuse it and give them the preface as a present, rather than set her price so low.[20]

Jane tried to negotiate a better bargain for her next Standard Novels title. She thought twenty pounds would be fair. Colburn and Bentley ultimately agreed to pay Jane some thirty pounds for her revisions and additions to *The Scottish Chiefs*. After that, they promised fifteen pounds for each further revised, republished title.[21] *The Scottish Chiefs* came out in the Standard Novels in the autumn of 1831, three months after *Thaddeus of Warsaw*.[22]

Being asked to write new prefaces compelled Jane to reflect on her literary career during the sad and difficult months of her mother's last illness and death. Jane wrote prefaces that were modeled on Sir Walter Scott's recently published autobiographical essays, prefixed to his Magnum Opus edition of 1829. Scott had been bringing out a volume a month in a new edition of his old works, published as part of his effort to dig himself out of debt. The Standard Novels series echoed that model and pace.

In her prefaces for the Standard Novels, Jane smooths over the rough edges of their lives in describing herself, but she makes bold claims for her literary contributions. She writes that, back in 1803, she'd been reluctant to publish *Thaddeus of Warsaw*, which wasn't entirely true. She more honestly acknowledges that her new preface to her novel emulates Scott's Magnum Opus introductions. In copying his method, however, she claims that she's only doing to him what he did to her. Scott, Jane writes, "did me the honour to adopt the style or class of novel of which 'Thaddeus of Warsaw' was the first:—a class which, uniting the personages and facts of real history or biography, with a combining and illustrative machinery of the imagination, formed a new species of writing in that day." She finally made this powerful claim: she, not Scott, deserves to be known as the innovator in historical fiction. She reminds readers that her historical novels were published "many years before the literary wonder of Scotland gave to the world his transcendent story of Waverley."[23]

Reviews of the Standard Novels' *Thaddeus of Warsaw* began to appear in fall 1831. Many were raves. *The Literary Gazette* concluded, "*Thaddeus of Warsaw* has gone through ten editions; what can a critic say after that?"[24] But the *Aberdeen Magazine* was cruel in its review, published in the form of a long, sarcastic mock letter to the editor, signed "Peter Puff." Puff claims he warmly admires Miss Porter's extreme modesty but suggests she's been too bashful by half in her self-praise in her new preface.

"For what indeed are the Waverley Novels but imitations (as you, unquestionably, Madam, had the honor to discover) of your Standard Novels," he writes. "What is Sir Walter Scott but an imitator of Miss Jane Porter?"[25] Puff sarcastically declares he blushes as red as his morocco slippers for not realizing Scott imitated Jane. Then Puff insults her rank and class. He notes that Scott was made a baronet by George IV, while Miss Jane Porter languishes in untitled obscurity, her works read only by the "discerning devourers" of circulating libraries.

How this line must have rankled. Jane proudly counted lords and ladies, even dukes, among her close friends. She corresponded with princes and princesses. Her brother was a knight who'd been married to a princess. It was said Jane had been enrolled in the chivalric Order of St. Joachim in Württemberg, like Robert before her.[26] But none of her pretensions put her any nearer to Scott's baronetcy, formal education, or exalted literary pedigree—things available almost exclusively to men. If these were the terms used to judge Miss Jane Porter's claims to originality, then Sir Walter Scott would always win.

"Let us hope," Puff writes, "that the world will now do justice to you—that Sir Walter Scott will be ignominiously deprived of his spurious laurels . . . while Miss Jane Porter will float down to posterity in all the splendor of her well-merited fame, and her name be held in remembrance when Homer, Shakespeare, Scott, and the Aberdeen Magazine are all buried in dusky oblivion!"[27] The "letter" ends with a final shot, implying Jane is unfeminine and indelicate.

Undeterred, publishers Colburn and Bentley prepared more Porter-authored Standard Novels. Maria's *Hungarian Brothers* (1807) was republished as volume 11 in December 1831, with a new preface. Maria confessed to Robert that when she'd reread her novels, she was surprised at their faults. "Their stile is better than I expected to find," she wrote, "but the execution is miserable—I mutter to myself all the time I am skimming or rather plodding thro- their pages—'no genius! no genius!' " But when Maria reread Jane's work, it prompted an opposite response. Jane occasionally produced overlong, didactic passages, which Maria called "villainous defects." In every other sense, Maria thought, her sister's work was full of life, energy, and interest—"the very criterion of Genius."[28]

The Standard Novels made Jane and Maria newly popular among a younger set of readers, as the sisters discovered in the winter of 1831–32. Jane and Maria spent time at literary parties in London, where they were sought out as celebrities and approached for advice by aspiring authors.[29] The sisters regularly encouraged the up-and-coming, who in turn expressed awe and reverence.[30] Yet the sisters were so genteelly poor that they couldn't afford the cost of renting a small Esher cottage.

Jane informed William she and Maria planned to find a tenant to sublet the long lease on their property, in order to lessen their expenses. He offered no financial help, although he did invite them to visit for two weeks at Portland Square, while Phoebe was out of town. His wife's jealousy wouldn't bear his sisters visiting for longer periods of time.[31] William also offered to pay to send them back to Esher at the end of the proposed two-week visit.[32]

His next suggestions went from stingy to shocking. The way to solve his sisters' long-term financial problems was, he believed, to separate them. He said he'd be willing to house Maria (the sister he openly preferred) in Bristol. He wouldn't even charge her room and board.

"I will take care of you," William had told Maria, "without feeling that you owe me aught but love."[33]

Jane was a different story. Although she'd been a material help to him and his book, had allowed her name to be put on it, and helped him launch it into the world, William thought Jane should travel alone to live with Robert in Venezuela and that Robert should be responsible for supporting her there. When William offered to pay for Jane's one-way trip, Maria was incensed.

"It is too pitiless," Maria complained about William to Robert, "to divide her and me . . . I can scarcely believe myself awake, whilst I read such a cold-blooded plan written by a brother's pen."[34]

Robert was outraged at the suggestion, too. "Who could believe that the same pen that [wrote] the Seaward Narrative could dictate so senseless and wondring an arrangement?" he wrote back. He begged his sisters not to go into seclusion but told them never again to confide in William or include him in their domestic arrangements.[35]

William then offered another fix. He told Jane perhaps he could loan her fifty or one hundred pounds, discounted and due two months hence—a meager loan on hampered terms.[36] She didn't hide her disdain.[37] She wrote William a businesslike letter, turning down his offer. He was highly offended in turn. The two exchanged another round of testy letters. By the end of the month, William asked Jane never again to refer to her and Maria's financial affairs. He said if his sisters survived him and his wife, and yet needed a home, he'd give them his house. That was that.[38]

Fortunately, in Robert, Jane thought, they had a hundred brothers in one.[39] They wanted peaceful relations with William, however. Through it all, Maria somehow managed to stay on good terms with him, so Jane declared herself determined to put aside all painful things between them and move forward.[40] By the end of 1831, the sisters' financial situation had deteriorated further. This time, their old publishers, Longman and Rees, didn't come through in the typical way. Instead of agreeing to give the sisters an advance on a next book, Rees arranged a fifty-pound loan, without making a promise to publish anything from them.[41] At least the loan was advanced to Jane on better terms than what stingy William had offered.

Their situation required action. They'd incurred new debts of one hundred pounds, excluding Robert's burdens, on top of the seven hundred pounds they owed female friends, to whom they were punctually paying interest.[42] So in the spring of 1832, Jane found a wealthy, titled woman to sublet their Esher cottage for several months. Her payment would allow the sisters to come out ahead on the rent. If they could keep expenses moderate and their travel regular, they might work their way out of debt.[43]

Jane and Maria arranged long stays at the homes of friends. In some homes, there would be little extra space, beyond the bed they'd share, so the sisters made the difficult decision to let go of their maids, Becky and Elizabeth. Jane and Maria vacated Esher Cottage on March 15, 1832, having lined up the first six months of visits, for a planned absence of one year.

"We certainly save by visiting," Maria calculated, as the sisters accepted invitations to places they didn't much like.[44] In London, they stayed with new friends, the fashionable Skinners, and old friends, the Mackinnons.[45] After London, they would stay with three sets of friends outside the metropolis, on a gradual progression of visits leading to a stay in Bristol with William and Phoebe—a necessary, politic choice.

The arrangements in Bristol proved tricky. In years past, only Maria had stayed with William and Phoebe. On this trip in the summer of 1832, both sisters would be there. Jane and Maria could conceivably have stayed together in William's home on Portland Square, sharing a bed. But William surprised them by deciding Jane alone would be staying at Portland Square. Maria should become the houseguest of William's interesting friend and regular patient, Mrs. Sarah Booth, in her home in the affluent suburb of Montpelier, a mile away.

Maria already knew the amiable Mrs. Booth, and Jane didn't, so an invitation was extended to Maria alone. William made it clear that during Maria's stay with Mrs. Booth, he'd visit daily—in his guise as both women's physician. This wasn't the cruel separation of continents he'd once suggested for his sisters, but it didn't sit well.

"I own I felt a cut from my side, when she left me," Jane wrote.[46]

Six days later, the pang turned into a panic. After Jane and Maria had taken a Saturday airing in William's carriage, Jane suggested that Maria share her bed that night at William's so they could go together to Sunday service at nearby St. Paul's Church the next morning.[47] During the evening, Maria felt a swelling in her throat. She returned to Mrs. Booth's. As the illness lingered, Jane went to Montpelier to help nurse Maria. A heavy fever arose. Then Jane took sick, too. William, busy with other patients, sent another physician to attend them, but a week later, Maria's condition deteriorated.

William diagnosed Maria with typhus.[48] Mrs. Booth and Jane had been exposed, and by mid-June, all three women were ill. William stepped in to serve as their very attentive physician. He was an acknowledged expert on treating typhus, having published a pamphlet to calm people's fears of the disease. It described a treatment plan involving tepid baths. According to his pamphlet's directions, the windows in Maria's sickroom would have remained open, day and night. She'd have had frequent changes of linen, to halt the contagion. A constant fire would have been kept going, to circulate the air.

Maria's fever didn't break, so her hair would've been cut very short, to make it easier to wash her head, face, and hands. Any bandages, towels, or clothing that touched her body would have to be taken away and boiled. Jane and Mrs. Booth, recovered enough to be only mildly ill, served as Maria's nurses. Jane would have been forbidden from lying down in bed with or caressing her sister. When visitors left the sickroom, they'd have been instructed to blow their nose and to spit, to remove any "infectious poison" they might have inhaled.[49]

William attended to his sister unremittingly. Ten days after Maria contracted typhus, she told Jane she couldn't live. No human skill, she told her sister, could be brought in to save her. Despite her resignation, William held out hope; Jane responded with an almost frantic despair. The dying Maria tried to comfort her sister like a soothing, "ministering angel," Jane thought. As breath allowed, Maria sang hymns. She gave Jane her parting messages to communicate to family and friends. She blessed and remembered them.[50] Maria then called Mrs. Booth to her bedside. She asked her new friend to witness her last wish—that Jane should never, ever blame herself for having taken Maria away from their old cottage or for having come to Bristol.

"My dear Jane," Maria said to her sister, "you have done all you could do for me, you have tried change of air, and change of scene; in the hope of restoring me to health, you have done all things well."[51]

Then she took Jane's hand and Mrs. Booth's and joined them together.

"Love one another," Maria told them.[52]

Jane, Mrs. Booth, and William were with Maria in her final hours. She had been treated with such affection by Mrs. Booth, Jane thought. William's friend had become like another member of the Porter family.[53] Caring William, too, redeemed himself in Jane's eyes. Maria died, resting her head on William's breast, on June 21, 1832, at age fifty-three.[54]

A feeling of resignation came over Jane. It was as if a heavenly voice told her, "Peace be still!" She'd lost the beloved sharer in all her earthly hopes and comfort in every woe. But Jane told herself that Maria being taken away from her, so soon after losing their mother, must have been God's will.[55]

William took care of Maria's funeral arrangements. He paid every expense. A sermon in her memory was preached at St. Paul's Church, across the square from William's home. Maria's works were presented as innocent productions of literature that contributed to the nation's lasting renown. The church was full of tearful mourners who'd known her, as well as strangers and admirers.[56] Jane wasn't among them. Although it wasn't customary for women in the Church of England to attend funerals then, it wasn't unheard of. But in Jane's case, she couldn't have gone, even if she'd wanted to. She was confined to her bed with a touch of the fever that had proved fatal to her sister.[57]

Miss Anna Maria Porter was buried in Dr. William Ogilvie Porter's vault at St. Paul's Church, with William's unloved eldest son, Charles, and near his beloved object, Eliza Clark. To William, this may have seemed a fitting location for the remains of his favorite sister, but Jane thought about it differently. She preferred to remember Maria's final resting place as not far from the grave of her earliest beloved, Wade Francis Caulfield, in nearby Clifton. Maria was buried just a mile from the soldier who'd loved her in her teens and inspired her first novel, *Walsh Colville*.[58]

After the funeral, there was Maria's epitaph to consider. This time, there was no struggle among surviving siblings over whether there should be a monument. A large stone would already have been in place at William's vault. There was, however, a disagreement over the wording to be engraved on it. When Jane gave William what she'd written for the purpose, he criticized it.

"What you have written," he wrote to Jane, "requires to be better organized, it wants point, you would have done it with more art if your feelings had been less deeply engaged." So William rewrote the words of one of the world's best novelists in his own "improved arrangement," focusing on Maria's pious qualities, rather than on her earthly achievements. His epitaph mentioned none of her books, although it at least refers to her high mental endowments and her pen.[59]

Newspapers worldwide ran notices of Miss Anna Maria Porter's death and tributes to her life. She was called the "Female Sir Walter Scott" and heir to the throne of famed Gothic novelist Ann Radcliffe.[60] Elegies were published in her honor.[61] Her name was included in lists of the distinguished departed of 1832 and as the beloved author read in days of youth.[62] Jane planned to write a memoir of Maria, but it was proving challenging to memorialize this sister who was part of her own soul.[63] Grieving over Maria's death, Jane wrote very little. Instead, she turned her heart, as her sister had directed her, to Mrs. Booth.

CHAPTER 23

Preserve and Destroy

Jane's Friends and Enemies (1832–40)

The idea that Maria might die first had never occurred to Jane.[1] "I trusted in her being yet in the meridian of her life," she wrote to Robert. "I trusted in air—I trusted, in short, in the Hope which Love inspires, for a dear object."[2] Jane was struggling with grief, anxiety, and lingering illness. Without Maria as a companion, she had to rethink where to stay and live and whether she should travel alone. Mrs. Booth—who went by the nickname Boothia—wouldn't hear of Jane leaving her Montpelier home. She told Jane she was welcome to stay under her roof for months.[3]

The hard truth was that there were few fit places for Jane to grieve. William dutifully offered his sister a room at Portland Square. His house, he told her, would always be open to her. Staying there, however, offered no tranquility. She didn't see herself getting along with her sister-in-law, Phoebe—a rugged, rough creature in mind, heart, and manners.[4] Boothia, by contrast, struck Jane as a woman of taste and private habits. A widow of independent fortune, she was an occasional invalid, devoted to caring for her elderly father, who lived with her. Her house was small but comfortable, situated on the side of a rising hill, in a newly built neighborhood. Fields and open land lay behind it, perfect for peaceful walks and fresh air.[5] Jane accepted Boothia's invitation, but even in that home, resting and grieving proved challenging.[6]

Fifty letters of condolence had arrived for Jane in Bristol, letters that were expensive to pay for, and time-consuming to respond to.[7] She could, however, use her obligation to respond to these letters as an excuse not to see acquaintances who pressed her for visits.[8] There was other writing to do, too. Jane had promised Colburn and Bentley a preface and notes for their Standard Novels edition of *The Pastor's Fire-Side*. The publishers initially agreed to pay her fifteen pounds. But in her anguished state, she sent them an abbreviated preface and no new notes, so Colburn and Bentley lowered their payment to five pounds.[9] Jane's brief introduction ends abruptly, with a tacked-on postscript, explaining that a recent heavy affliction prevents her from completing the task.[10]

Maria's death changed everything for Jane. After 1832, she no longer had Maria's encouragement for her writing. She also lost the financial benefit of her sister's quick pen and frequent publication. There were fixed costs, including the thirty pounds of interest a year for the large loans from Anna Middleton and Elizabeth Dillon. Beyond that, Jane would try to live on a budget of thirty pounds or less a year—roughly what a governess made.

Jane hoped Robert might finally return from South America after ten years of service—three years hence—and retire on a half-pay pension.[11] If he could just pay off his debts, he might safely come back to England, where he and Jane could set up a modest household. Imagining this happy future, with a brother she began to describe as almost her twin, she kept going.[12] Until Robert's return, however, she'd need a roof over her head.

Jane wrote to Mrs. Porter's old friend Sir Charles Throckmorton, to ask if she might come to him in Warwickshire with her new companion, Boothia. He agreed. Boothia took the place that would have been Maria's on the seventy-mile trip north to Sir Charles's estate, Coughton Court.[13] Its early sixteenth-century Gothic great house looked as if it had sprung from the pages of Jane's earliest novel, *The Spirit of the Elbe*. Most of the English King Henrys had stayed there.[14] The Throckmortons were a prominent Roman Catholic family that managed, even after Henry VIII's break with Rome, to hold on to their faith and their property.

Coughton Court was so enormous that old Sir Charles lived on its south side and put his guests up on the north.[15] The freedom guests had, along with the hospitality of Sir Charles and his servants, led to Jane's returning there each year, across the 1830s, often with Boothia. What the three most enjoyed was taking sightseeing trips together in Sir Charles's carriage.[16] As they traveled, Jane felt Maria was sometimes with them in spirit, creating an incredible feeling of melancholy pleasure.[17] Maria and Jane had once planned to use Coughton Court as a base of operations to visit Stratford-upon-Avon. She and Jane had often talked about how, one day, they'd sit together by the side of Shakespeare's grave and adore him, but Maria never made it to Shakespeare's birthplace.[18] On the day Jane, Boothia, and Sir Charles visited Stratford, Jane felt emotionally overwhelmed. At Shakespeare's tombstone, she let her tears fall without restraint.[19]

For nearly three months, Jane and Boothia stayed with Throckmorton. By October, Boothia returned alone to Montpelier.[20] Jane was beginning to understand that Boothia and William's relationship went beyond that of doctor and patient. Boothia eventually admitted to Jane that William was her "dearest friend." In later years, Jane raised an eyebrow at Boothia and William's unusually close friendship. Boothia dined tête-à-tête with William, whenever his jealous wife, Phoebe, was traveling.[21] Phoebe, increasingly an invalid, was often conveniently sent away from home by her physician husband to recover her health.

Jane doesn't seem to have believed that Boothia and William's relationship was immoral, but she did wonder if it was proper. Jane saw this sort of platonic love between men and women as a rare, peculiar gift from heaven, but she thought it had to be watched, lest it become too absorbing.[22] William once told Jane that if he were ever free—if Phoebe were to die—he'd marry Boothia. Jane wouldn't have appreciated this bald admission. Boothia's unconventional attachment to selfish William would also have made it difficult for Jane to love her quite as Maria had urged in her dying words.

After staying at Coughton Court, Jane began what would become an annual rotation of friendly visits. She once joked that she might have a shelter and a home, if she wanted one, under the branch of every wayside tree.[23] The problem wasn't in finding enough roofs under which she'd be welcome but in avoiding those with clinging hospitality.[24] She rarely had her own space or much control over her daily schedule. With so little independence, Jane had great difficulty getting writing done. She published a short, anonymous memoir of Maria and made plans for a longer one, with a selection of her letters and poetry.[25] Jane owed a book to Longman and Rees to pay off their fifty-pound loan, so perhaps this was the title she considered giving them.[26] Although she spent hours going through Maria's papers, this book never came to fruition.

Jane estimated she was spending half her day writing letters, many of them about Robert's salary, duties, and prospects with the Foreign Office. She also wrote countless letters on behalf of others, especially women in economic peril. They wrote to her seeking patronage, asking for work, or enlisting her in bids for charitable help. She worked assiduously to help a needy old friend from her teenage years, Selina Granville Wheler Davenport, who'd reconnected with Jane through a frantic, begging letter. Selina's life had spectacularly broken down. The Porter sisters' prediction, forty years earlier, had been that Selina would come to no good, but Jane would have taken no pleasure in their being right.

Selina had gone on to become a novelist, too, although neither so well respected nor so well paid as the Porters. Being deserted by her faithless husband—their old friend, the poet and editor Richard Davenport—sent Selina's life into a tailspin. He'd left Selina and their two daughters for another woman, who'd wrongly usurped Selina's name as Mrs. Davenport and gave birth to an illegitimate son. Jane was crushed to learn Selina was desperately poor, trying to live on a shilling a day. She and her daughters were starving.[27] Their annual income was less than that of a well-paid domestic servant, without the free room and board many servants had.

Jane helped Selina sell her new novel for fifteen pounds—as much as Selina was living on per year. Then Jane anonymously and positively reviewed it.[28] Jane also helped Selina's grown daughter, Theodora, break into the literary business. When Longman and Rees rejected Theodora's novel, depreciating it as a green work by a first-time author, Jane placed it with a lesser publisher. She'd agreed to attach her own name to it as an endorsement and inducement to readers.[29] *Young Hearts*: *A Novel* by a Recluse (1834), was billed as "With a Preface by Miss Jane Porter."[30] For these and other efforts, Selina called her old friend and onetime rival "My dear and beloved Jane."[31] Jane regularly tried to solicit help for others in need, especially for female friends who were experiencing greater poverty than she was. Jane had little money of her own to spare, but she spared nothing in using her influence to assist needy women.

Some pleas for money Jane received failed to arouse her sympathy. An unwelcome request came during her annual autumn visit to Chester to stay with her old friend Reverend Henry Raikes and his family. During that visit in 1832, Jane was drawn back into the affairs of the Great Unknown. Sir Walter Scott had died on September 21, 1832, leaving behind enormous debts. A public subscription was initiated to save his grand estate, Abbotsford House, to preserve its library and many relics. Two powerful literary men wrote asking Jane and Robert to contribute.

"To have shrunk back . . . would appear to all these persons as inexplicably mean on my part," she wrote to Robert, "and strangely disrespectful to the memory of Sir Walter."[32] Yet to give just one pound—more than she could afford—and have that sum advertised, as was customary, was insulting. Jane feared giving them Robert's name instead because his creditors might become incensed, wondering how he could help pay down Scott's debts, while avoiding repaying his own.

Jane didn't want any single Porter name added to the public subscription list. She wanted to show the Porter family's collective support of Scott in as innocuous a way as possible. So she asked her publisher Owen Rees to go on their behalf and record it ambiguously in the donation book as a small tribute to Scott, without naming the sum. She asked him to sign from three friends of Scott's youth—Sir Robert, Jane, and their lamented sister, Maria. The Abbotsford subscription committee would notice the contribution, but how much was given and from whom might be obscured and kept out of the newspapers.

Jane decided on five pounds. Parting with a sixth of her annual budget for living expenses to save Scott's lavish estate was no small sacrifice.[33] To get that sum, she pressed Colburn and Bentley to pay what they owed for her *Pastor's Fire-Side* preface.[34] Having to make this donation to Scott's estate might have upset Jane further if she'd learned what likely became of it. A secretary of the fund allegedly ran off to America with some proceeds. Jane's contribution to help pay down Scott's enormous posthumous debts—a man given credit for her literary innovations—may have ended up lining the pockets of an embezzler.

In early 1833, Jane returned to Bristol, as she'd do most winters thereafter. Her stay with William and Phoebe went so poorly that she briefly considered trying to move back into her old cottage in Esher. The expense of living there dissuaded her. Jane never again lived in Esher, although she traveled there each year in spring or summer to visit her mother's grave.[35] Trips to London became Jane's habit in winter and spring, during the town's fashionable season. She sought flexible, accommodating hosts, who had room for her to sleep alone and write. She didn't shrink from accepting the hospitality of wealthy friends who held opposing political views, even on one of the most polarizing issues of the day—colonial slavery.

Jane believed in Christian charity.[36] She couldn't abide that the British poor were starving or that a branch of fellow creatures in the colonies should live in bondage. She considered herself an abolitionist, yet she rarely questioned class stratification, economic privilege, or the culpability of colonial enslavers. In the mid-1830s, Jane began to stay in London, for some weeks each year, with her Jamaican-born Porter cousins who'd resettled in England. Mr. Robert Porter, Esq., and his wife had three daughters, two of the girls already of marriageable age. Jane hadn't known this family in early life. She may not have realized that during his years in Jamaica, her cousin had gained a reputation for barbarity. Abolitionist writings outed him as a man who'd once branded his initials on the bodies of enslaved men.[37] What Jane did recognize was that these cousins weren't charitable. She believed long years in the West Indies had destroyed their benevolent impulses because of that culture's violent use of enslaved people.[38] Yet she accepted their generosity, as a form of charity to her. They let her use their carriage and stay in their attic, in a room of the home normally designed for live-in servants. Jane saw herself as a moderating force on her young female cousins, who'd been raised excessively addicted to empty pleasures.[39]

Long-standing political debates over slavery were coming to a head in Britain in 1833. In August, the Slavery Abolition Act passed, outlawing slavery in the colonial West Indies beginning in 1834. A shamefully slow dismantling would follow, with many enslaved people "liberated" into years of forced indentured servitude. Jane watched these actions closely and deplored the evils of slavery, but she also expressed racist views sadly typical of Britain's white elite. She believed Blacks were the *spiritual* equals of whites, but she didn't imagine Blacks as intellectual or moral equals. That means Jane likely supported the scheme of slow emancipation and believed former enslavers should be paid for the human "property" they lost during abolition. The government's massive scheme compensated former enslavers at taxpayer expense. Jane's old friends the Mackinnons owned Antiguan plantation properties that had held 276 enslaved people, for which they received government compensation of 3,942 pounds.[40] Her Porter cousins were even more deeply involved, with properties holding 524 enslaved people, for which the family would be paid 8,367 pounds.[41] Jane doesn't seem to have found it unfair that the already rich were paid off by taxpayers, while the poor and formerly enslaved yet suffered.

As these events were transpiring in Britain, Jane's niece, Mashinka Porter, remained in Russia. She expected to live off her late mother's estates, which exploited the forced labor of serfs. The late princess's estates were emerging intact from retrenchment.[42] Mashinka would retain ownership of Shcherbatov family land. After she'd turned eighteen and left boarding school, she'd gone to live with maternal relatives, who managed the process of her coming out. When news came to Jane early in 1835 that Mary Porter (as she was now called) was engaged, the letter announced a period of betrothal so short that the wedding would have taken place by the time the letter arrived in England. There could be no objecting. Jane was overcome with worry.[43] She was afraid the groom was a seducer or fortune hunter.[44] Pierre Kikine turned out to be merely a younger brother of little fortune—a fine young man in person, manners, and morals, although not a person of talents. He was a low-ranking officer in the Imperial Guards and no more.

When Jane learned that young Kikine was related to Mary's extended Shcherbatov family, and that Mary's female cousin had introduced the couple, it raised suspicions.[45] By throwing Mary and Pierre together, the Shcherbatov family had successfully secured Mary's estates to itself. At least, Jane rationalized, Mary hadn't been raised in England, where heiresses on display were offered up to the highest bidder.[46] Reports from the newlywed Kikines seemed happy enough, but it was a disappointment to Jane that her only niece was sacrificed in a marriage to an unremarkable distant relative.

"I confess, I once was ambitious for her!" she admitted to Robert. "I confess, from my youth upwards, until very, very far in my life, I was ambitious on many, many objects!"[47]

As she aged, Jane may have let her personal ambitions recede, but she remained a sought-after celebrity. The greatest hospitality she experienced came through the wealthy Mr. Samuel Skinner and his socialite wife, Mrs. Mary Skinner. Jane enjoyed staying with them because Mrs. Skinner gave Jane full freedom to come and go. She could attend their lavish parties or not.[48] People came to gawk at and idolize modest Jane, who preferred simple dark dresses, wore long sleeves, and used sturdy bracelets as cuffs.[49] Sometimes she wore black feathers in her hats, but dark veils remained her wardrobe signature. A later critic said it gave her the mysterious look of a Gothic heroine. It also confused the Protestant public, who worried Jane had Popish proclivities. Assurances were made she was not a Catholic nun.[50] A portrait of Jane by George Henry Harlow shows her in what looks like a nun's habit, holding a gold cross, although it was said to be the honorary dress of a Teutonic order that had recognized her. Jane chose this ennobling image of herself for reprinting, despite feeling it omitted her best youthful physical attribute—her abundant auburn hair.[51]

In later years, Jane was illustrated wearing veils, including in an 1835 portrait in *Fraser's Magazine*.[52] *Fraser's* told Jane it would be featuring her in its pages and secured her permission for its artist to take a quick sketch. The finished illustration was a striking, full-body, seated portrait, with Jane looking off into the distance. Her solemn face is framed by dark curls escaping out of a long mantilla-style veil.[53] She's holding a cup, because, as the accompanying essay explains, "Miss Jane Porter is depicted in the quiet and ladylike occupation of taking coffee at a *soirée* given, we suppose, by Mrs. Skinner."

The rest of the essay is offensive. It introduces Jane by saying "Handsome the face is *still*. We hope that Miss Porter has sufficient philosophy to pardon us for that fatal adverb." It claims she wears the years well but wryly notes if she hadn't dabbled in publishing, she could have smuggled a dozen years off her true age. The writer compares Jane to a criminal forger and likens her authorship to a crime against femininity. This cruel magazine profile was Jane's reward for allowing the *Fraser's* artist to sketch her.

She did have opportunities for repose, as she neared age sixty. Jane began to stay with the Skinners at their country house, Shirley Park, ten miles south of London. It was through Mrs. Skinner that Jane formed a significant new friendship with the up-and-coming poet Nathaniel Parker Willis.[54] Willis had been declared the most interesting American to visit England since Washington Irving and was popularly recognizable from his dandyish coat and ornate cane.[55] Jane later wrote that, if she were a painter trying to personify youth as a Grecian ideal, she'd have tried to capture an image of Willis.[56]

N. P. Willis was a lively writer of nearly thirty, the self-assured son of a prosperous, religious newspaper owner. He knew how to work a room and particularly charmed older women, who opened their homes and carriages to him. Willis, like Jane, became a fixture at Shirley Park, which was filled with a gaggle of authors, all of whom seemed constantly writing, writing, writing, Jane thought, during the winter of 1835.[57] Willis was admirably disciplined. If his daily routine were interrupted by Mrs. Skinner, he made up for it by staying up half the night to write.[58] It reminded Jane of her and her siblings' striving lives of former days. Willis inspired in Jane a renewed desire to write creatively. The two developed a habit of writing seated next to each other, as Jane and Robert once had.[59]

Jane and Willis spent untold hours walking together at Shirley Park.[60] She cried while telling him about the loss of her sister and absence of her brother, tears she usually reserved for when she was alone in her bedroom.[61] He soothed her. After one of these conversations on the grounds of Shirley Park, she wrote feelingly in her diary, "I could hear Willis' heart beat, as he sat close to me."[62] Willis' way of circulating in rooms, and his facial expressions, reminded her of Robert.

"I will not apologize for writing so much about him," she told Robert about Willis, "because I really love him better than I thought I should ever be moved to love anything *new* to me on this Earth again."[63]

Jane's partiality to Willis opened her up to ridicule.

"He must have bewitched her!" the poet Elizabeth Barrett Browning wrote of Willis's effect on Miss Porter. "He a great writer!! . . . Pretty & fanciful he often is, graceful sometimes, vivacious generally! And there, is said the outside of all . . . & perhaps you may think beyond it! How *wonderful* of Miss Porter!"[64] A few people in England embraced this attention-seeking American poet, but many outright despised him. Some criticism of Willis seemed based in anti-Americanism, which Jane didn't share. She'd also previously seen what tittle-tattle could do to ruin talented, attractive young men, so Jane wouldn't heed any criticism of him. But within two months of meeting Willis, she found herself embroiled in his personal dramas.[65] One of them was his marriage.

That summer at Shirley Park, among the Skinners' guests, Willis found a bride. Miss Mary Stace would have three hundred pounds a year.[66] It was said to be love at first sight.[67] After one week together, Willis proposed to this paragon of femininity and hoped she'd reform him of his bad habits.[68] Rumors flew about what those habits had been. Some had him cohabiting with a widow during a previous sojourn in Italy.[69] Jane refused to believe the reports.[70] In advance of his marriage, Willis received a letter from his mother in Boston asking Miss Porter to please keep her son under her fostering care. So Willis invited Jane to meet his Mary and attend his small wedding as his surrogate mother.[71] On October 1, 1835, Jane joined the Staces and the Skinners for these unostentatious nuptials.

As Willis made plans for his married life, Jane tried to talk him out of being a professional writer. She had come to believe that authorship was like a vampire on a man's life, spirits, and happiness.[72] He soon had proof enough. After he disparaged in print the novelist Captain Frederick Marryat, Marryat challenged Willis to a duel, and Willis accepted the challenge. Jane, terrified for him, asked a war-veteran friend to guide Willis through the mess.[73] The duel never happened. Soon afterward, and perhaps because of this headline-grabbing fight with Marryat, Mr. and Mrs. Willis removed to America in May 1836. Jane admitted that almost every day of the past year and a half of her life had been devoted to this man who reminded her of Robert and Maria rolled into one. She yearned for Willis's voice, but especially his eyes. She felt she could communicate with him through eyes alone, as she had with her family.

"These were my soul's fellowship with my mother, my sister, my Robert," she wrote. But among her faithful friends, she told Willis, "I have found this dear familiar language of that responsive spirit, only in you."[74]

Jane's close friendship with this man she called her "fairy child" was now largely carried out in moving letters exchanged across the Atlantic over many years. Willis later returned to England and did Jane a material favor during that visit. In his meeting with a London publisher, George Virtue, Willis brought up Miss Porter's *The Scottish Chiefs* and the idea of republishing her novels.[75] A lucrative republishing deal with Virtue went forward, thanks to Willis. It paid Jane 210 pounds for each of her three most popular novels.[76] Jane planned to revise her old prose to fit new Victorian mores—and her own more conservative social and political views. This was a very good turn Willis did for her with George Virtue, an advocacy that those who'd known her for decades either wouldn't do or hadn't thought of.

Jane hoped, after she died, that Willis would edit and publish her and Maria's letters and write her memoir. Jane and Willis directly discussed it. He'd urged Jane to write her own life story and told her to prepare her papers for a faithful friend to build a true narrative on. He also pledged to be that faithful friend, if he survived her.[77] Jane wrote an informal will about her hope for a posthumous biography. She said she wanted none of her or Maria's letters to be published. Yet Jane also wrote that, if it were in her power, Maria's letters would be preserved forever. She asked her dear and esteemed friend Mr. Willis to compile a memoir from these papers for the press. At some point, however, Jane scratched out Willis's name and wrote over it the name of her new young historian friend Agnes Strickland.[78] Perhaps Jane preferred a female biographer. Or maybe Jane realized Willis wasn't the admirable man she first thought him.

N. P. Willis is remembered in literary history as a scoundrel. He and Mary had one surviving child, who was raised by a Black nurse, Harriet Jacobs. Jacobs was employed by Willis for more than twenty years before she published *Incidents in the Life of a Slave Girl* (1861). In Jacobs's narrative, the abusive employer, Mr. Bruce, is said to be based on Willis. Others skewered him more directly. The novelist William Makepeace Thackeray published an essay spoofing Willis under the name Napoleon Putnam Wiggins. Wiggins is described as an impertinent, greedy, self-praising American observer of British customs.[79] Willis also later ended up a defendant in a celebrated divorce case. It was said he'd become the lover of a famous American actor's wife. When the angry husband horsewhipped Willis in a public park in New York, it made national news. Jane never knew the worst of Willis's dishonor. By the late 1830s, she occasionally questioned whether he was quite so perfect as she'd once thought. The friendship cooled, but Jane stayed loyal to this deeply flawed man, who treated her kindly but abused many others. Years later, she signed off on her letter to faraway Willis, "Ever to remain, most faithfully, until Death, your affectionate old friend, Jane Porter."[80]

Jane continued to publish short pieces of writing, both fiction and nonfiction, as she entered her sixties.[81] One important autobiographical story, "The

Old Lady," advocated for the value of women's voices in late life.[82] It was published in *The Ages of Female Beauty* (1837), an illustrated gift book. The short story describes the narrator's childhood experiences listening to her Aunt Anna (surely Mrs. Porter's sister Nanny Blenkinsop) and argues that old women are the best preservers and communicators of national history.[83] The portrait published alongside Jane's story features an unidentified older woman, wearing a black mantilla veil and a face-framing frilly bonnet. The woman in the portrait, who resembles Jane, might be said to counteract the scathing *Fraser's Magazine* feature published several years earlier. In *Fraser's*, Jane had been cast as an ugly, old, criminally visible author, an embarrassment to herself and her country. In *The Ages of Female Beauty*, Jane and all old women are said to provide an inestimable national service of carrying forward oral and written histories that must outlive them.

It was a significant time for considering women's power because Queen Victoria had come to the throne in 1837. In the early months of her reign, a timetable finally materialized for Robert's permitted return to England. The Foreign Office granted him a twenty-four-month leave of absence on half pay, starting whenever he'd like.[84] But Robert delayed his trip home, not only for financial reasons, to satisfy his most insistent creditors before landing on British soil, but also to finish his crafting of a treaty to end the slave trade in Venezuela. His successful work there would end up being one of the most important things he accomplished during his years in South America.

In 1839, with the fourteen-year lease on their Esher cottage finally expiring, Jane prepared it for reversion to its owner. She cleaned out the attic and sold their old furniture.[85] She rented a room at the Pantechnicon building, an early storage facility in London, for twenty pounds a year.[86]

"There are boxes of family Papers," she wrote to Robert, "not less valuable, I am sure, by some of the Writers." Jane looked forward to the day when "you and I may have the home leisure to look them through, & class them—preserve!—and destroy."[87] Jane wrote to Robert that she felt like an old but popular and respected daughter in a perpetual drama, impatient to retire. She was tired of taking the stage. What she most wanted was a home of her own, with him.

"You can comprehend the difference, my Robert," Jane wrote, "between being the Guest of even the most kind Host & Hostess, & the placid freedom of one's own home.—It is the constant round of people coming to me, or writing to me on their affairs, & c. & c. & c. which so successfully blocks upon my time from fulfilling my engagements."[88]

One of the most important of these engagements was her publishing deal with George Virtue for the newly revised, illustrated editions of her three best-selling novels. This income made it possible for her to hire Eliza Bullen as her maid at twenty pounds a year.[89] Bullen, as she was called, began to travel with Jane throughout her sixties, when her strength began failing her.[90] In the fall of 1839, Jane became perilously ill and was treated for five months by a respected physician and a surgeon.[91] Such care might have cost sixty pounds.[92] The doctors refused to charge her, out of reverence for the celebrated name she bore.[93]

"I was at the very Gates of Death," Jane admitted.[94]

It was a welcome restoration to health when Queen Victoria sent Jane one hundred pounds from the Royal Bounty Fund at the end of 1839.[95] These charitable funds were immediately needed for the apothecary's bills and Bullen's wages. The remainder would have been deposited with Wright and Company, her bankers. Jane felt a personal connection to Victoria, the sweet girl she'd seen playing in the fields behind Esher cottage. On the day of the coronation, two years before, Jane had been seated in the window of the home of a friend that allowed her to be just yards away from Her Majesty's carriage as it passed by in Pall Mall. Jane expressed awe of Victoria's "perfect, pearl-like purity" and sent Victoria a poem in her honor.[96] Although King George IV hadn't given her a pension in 1824, Jane's hopes renewed that with this new monarch, a royal or government pension might be awarded to her in recognition of her valuable services to literature. She made annual appeals for such a pension, feeling she was just as celebrated and certainly more needy than past recipients.[97]

In the autumn of 1840, with Robert's scheduled return to England finally arranged for the following winter, Jane went on her annual visit to Coughton Court. There she found Sir Charles Throckmorton, eighty-four, looking well. Two weeks into her stay, he came running into her room, with a pale face, carrying an open letter.

"Bad news," he blurted out. Jane stood up immediately. She thought he was going to tell her Queen Victoria had died. Instead, he said, "Wright's House has stopped!" The next step after a bank stopped was usually bankruptcy. Jane dropped back into her chair.

"I fear your Brother must be a great sufferer?" Sir Charles asked her.

"All my Brother's available prosperity," Jane replied, "is with them."[98] She herself must have lost the rest of the Royal Bounty Funds she'd received, but she fortunately hadn't yet deposited her 210-pound payment from George Virtue. She'd been just one day away from transferring it to the bank.[99] Robert's losses were significant, not so much in their amount—others would have been far greater losers—but in that he had already spent the monies that had been stopped. It was like an overdraft, only for a change, the insufficient funds weren't Robert's fault. Jane immediately began to try to negotiate for more time for Robert to pay, so as not to trigger legal action against her brother by a new round of creditors.

These financial crises affected Sir Charles's body. He told Jane he feared he wasn't long for this world.[100] She was a guest in his Coughton Court home when Sir Charles Throckmorton died in his sleep on December 3, 1840—Jane's sixty-fifth birthday. On the day of his funeral, she couldn't even bring herself to look out her bedroom window at his long procession. Sir Charles Throckmorton's will left almost everything to his nephew and heir, with further specific instructions for relief to the poor. An 1835 codicil bequeathed gifts from his library to friends.[101] But Jane, his close companion in the five years since the will's last updating, wasn't named anywhere. When Sir Charles's nephew took possession of Coughton Court, he told Jane she could remain there as long as she liked. She chose to take her leave.

CHAPTER 24

Her Younger Self Again

Jane and Robert Reunited (1841–42)

Jane's head and heart were filled with planning for Robert's arrival back in England in the winter of 1841. Robert would be warmly welcomed—or so Jane declared. He had been away so long he didn't know many of the friends Jane planned to have greet him.[1]

"I thank God my Brother has returned in fair health to me!" she wrote to one of those friends, "and he does not think me quite a withered Heap."

The reunion so excited Jane that she couldn't hold a pen for a week afterward.[2] Officially, Robert planned to return to South America after his two-year leave of absence. Unofficially, his plans—and Jane's hopes—were different. He set out to renew ties with powerful friends to try to secure a retirement pension or a new diplomatic post. He and Jane longed for a placement in Italy—perhaps Rome.[3] He planned to angle for it over the spring and summer in England, before heading to Russia to be reunited with his daughter. It was decided that he and Jane would go to Russia together in the fall of 1841, returning in spring 1842. By then, he would have hoped, there would be a different opportunity lined up and no need to return to Caracas.

In early April, they rented temporary lodgings at 27 Green Street in London's fashionable Mayfair neighborhood. In choosing Green Street, Jane wanted her brother to have an aspirational London address. It also gave her the power, for the first time in a decade, to invite friends to come stay with her, including her historian protégée, Agnes Strickland.[4]

That spring and summer, Jane and Robert reconnected with their old friend Charles Kemble, who'd enjoyed an illustrious theatrical career as an actor, playwright, and theater manager. Kemble and his famous actress daughter, now Fanny Kemble Butler, hosted lively theatrical evenings at their London home. (Therese De Camp Kemble had died two years earlier.) Jane and Robert watched Charles, despite a hearing impairment, brilliantly perform Shakespearean scenes in his drawing room alongside his daughter. At such social events, Jane was an asset. Robert thought her as bright and intellectual as anyone at these parties.

Robert's surest guide through London's complicated social networks was his old friend George Villiers, the Fourth Earl of Clarendon. Lord Clarendon, twenty years younger than Robert, served as adviser to the Foreign Office. Robert and Lord Clarendon had cemented their friendship long ago in Russia, when Villiers (as he was then known) was attaché to the British Embassy, a role Robert had once coveted. The powerful Lord Clarendon directed Robert never to mention that he hoped not to return to Caracas, and the two men discussed how to get him presented to Queen Victoria. Robert wanted to wear his military uniform, but Clarendon said he must purchase a minister's costume—a civil uniform Robert had never needed. These court-compulsory uniforms were purchased by the wearer at his expense. Jane went with Robert to the Foreign Office to get a drawing of the complicated garment to bring to the tailor. The cost was great but being presented at Queen Victoria's levee was a crucial part of professional advancement. Robert bought the uniform on credit and arranged to pay the tailor in a year. Sir Robert Ker Porter was presented to Queen Victoria by Lord Palmerston at St. James's Palace in April 1841. Both Victoria and Prince Albert, who'd been married a little over a year, received him. Robert thought it a hurried affair compared to the relaxed individual attention customary at the Russian court.[5]

Jane had never been presented at court. Seeking to remedy that, her friend Lady Diana Hamlyn Williams worked to put forward Jane's name to the Queen's people. Presentations at court were something wealthy families furiously angled for, especially for debutante daughters, to advance their marriage prospects. For a woman of Jane's age and situation, a presentation at court had different aims. It would cement her as a respectable, accepted, and virtuous member of high society. Presentation lists were vetted with great care. When the request to present Miss Jane Porter to Queen Victoria was approved, Jane likely needed to purchase a new dress. Rules for Victorian court dress for women were exacting. She would have needed something with a train, gloves, and a fan or a bouquet. Queen Victoria insisted that women must come to court décolleté, baring their shoulders, regardless of age.[6]

On June 17, 1841, Miss Jane Porter was presented by a lady-in-waiting to Queen Victoria at St. James's Palace. The palace itself was very familiar ground, because Jane had stayed there so often as a young woman, as the guest of the late Mrs. Boscawen. This time, Jane was presented as one of the most celebrated and esteemed writers in the nation. "Went with my dear sister to Court, to witness her presentation by Lady Barham to the Queen," Robert's diary records. "She was not at all fatigued and looked quite simply her *younger self* again—most simple and beautifully attired."

In July 1841, Jane and Robert took the Great Western Railway to stay with William and Phoebe in Bristol. Phoebe struck Robert as "very old and broken down." The week with William was filled with horrid large parties with his uninteresting friends. At the end of the week, Robert rejoiced to leave Bristol behind, summing up the visit as "a fatiguing duty of relationship paid."[7] There was still no love lost between these two brothers, and it was perfectly clear which one Jane preferred.

Back in London, Jane and Robert left no social stone unturned—as much as Jane's energy allowed. An old friend worried she was living too much in the world for her health or peace.[8] That may be one reason why Robert decided to lay out an enormous sum—147 pounds—to buy a used carriage to take with them on the ship to Russia that fall.[9] He planned to use it to keep Jane in better strength and health during their nine months in St. Petersburg. They would leave before winter and return in spring, when there was less risk of ice hampering their voyage.

In August 1841, Robert booked passage for four to Russia on a steamer, the *Jupiter*, which they'd take across the North Sea and the Baltic the following month. The traveling party would include Jane, her maid Bullen, himself, and his new valet, John Jacobs, a Black servant he'd hired in London, at a rate of pay twice what Bullen earned.[10] This trip would take Jane the farthest distance from home she'd ever traveled. For Robert, of course, it was almost another homecoming.

The Porter siblings had very different emotional responses to arriving in St. Petersburg. Jane's first impression overwhelmed her with sadness. Robert, however, was ecstatic. Within an hour of arrival, he found himself in the arms of his lovely daughter, Mary Porter Kikine. She introduced them to her husband Pierre, an affectionate, warm-hearted man, who wore his Imperial Guard uniform.

"My joy is not to be described in again embracing so dear a dau[ghter] from whom I had been separated seventeen years," he wrote to a friend.[11]

The reality was more complicated. Robert was struck and surprised by Mary's fragile health. "Very, very delicate," he called her in his diary. The couple, especially Pierre, wanted a child, but Mary had already endured at least two miscarriages.[12] They lived in a mansion furnished in the "luxury typical of mansions of its kind," Robert thought. That word "typical" couldn't have been a compliment. Mary was, from all appearances, a virtuous and pious young woman, but her father's absence from her life seemed to have damaged her physically and emotionally.

Faithful monthly letters from Mary during the almost two decades of her father's absence tell the tale. At age six, the girl wrote of his going away: "I wish I was going with him."[13] Motherless in her early teens, she'd begged him, "Come and take me from here."[14] At age sixteen, Mary told her aunts she did nothing all day but think about her father's return.[15] Every summer of her life, she waited. By nineteen, she realized her wishes for his return were in vain.[16] How hard this separation had been on her heart, she once wrote, not to get to see her papa as she was growing up. Very aware of her English relatives, she felt neglected by them. As a teen, she'd read every one of her aunts' novels. She'd been shocked to learn of the death of Aunt Maria from the newspapers, rather than from a family member.[17]

Jane and Robert had been in the country for three weeks when Tsar Nicholas, the anxious and powerful brother of the late Alexander, arrived back in St. Petersburg. Robert found an opportunity to be presented to His Imperial Majesty. It pleased Jane that the Tsar recognized Robert's face, even before his name was announced. Nicholas took both of Robert's hands in his and ardently welcomed him as almost a family member. Robert was similarly greeted by the rest of the Imperial Family, who'd known him personally, twenty years before.

In letters home to England, Jane was quick to tell friends that she herself was impressed by Nicholas and his family, not because of their rank but because they seemed worthy people.[18] Historians would see it differently. Although Tsar Nicholas once considered abolishing the institution of serfdom, he hadn't carried out reforms, due to his worries over how Russia's wealthy nobles would respond. He'd earned a reputation as an autocrat. What Jane would have focused on, in the autumn of 1841, was that the Imperial Family was closely tied to her brother's and her niece's interests. She may also have been conscious of the possibility that any letters she sent home from Russia could have been opened and read.

Whatever her true opinions were of the Russian court, Jane found the country's climate not at all to her liking. She felt weak. At first, Robert believed it was only a typical newcomer's response to the cold.[19] Soon, however, it was clear Jane had developed a chronic condition. She was so perpetually unwell that she saw little of St. Petersburg. She called herself "an almost constant prisoner" of their rented house.

As 1842 began, Jane kept a diary to record their activities. She wrote movingly of having watched a lunar eclipse out of the window of their lodgings on a bright night filled with stars when she and Robert were both homebound with influenza.[20] Jane regretted that illness was making her lose out on so much of her brother's company. He received near daily invitations to dine out, but Jane usually felt too weak to join him. Illnesses prevented her from attending St. Petersburg's splendid balls and parties.[21] She did, however, begin to attend small dinners.

The first mansion Jane dined in, other than Mary and Pierre's, belonged to the powerful Orlovs. The member of the Orlov family best known to history is Grigory Orlov, lover of Catherine the Great, who'd partnered with her to stage a coup against her husband, Tsar Peter III. Grigory's brother, Alexei Orlov, is popularly believed to have been Peter III's assassin. Jane socialized with their relatives. The Countess Orlov Jane met was married to the natural child of an Orlov brother. This particular nineteenth-century Orlov, Alexey, was famous for having helped Tsar Nicholas quash the 1825 Decembrist revolt against his rule. As a reward, Count Orlov would be put in charge of the Third Section, the

Russian secret police, in 1844. These were wealthy, extremely powerful people whose families were central to the country's dramatic, violent history, whether Jane understood it or not.

She liked most of them. She found Countess Orlov cheerful, warm, and kind, especially because she'd seated Jane and Robert on each side of her at dinner—at places of honor. English was spoken that evening, which would have been a relief to Jane, whose French remained weak. When French was spoken, Robert was often compelled to serve as Jane's interpreter.[22] The countess surprised the Porters by raising her glass to offer a welcome toast to each of them, in English. Everyone around the table raised their glasses. The gentlemen stood up. All the people at the table added to the countess's toast their own "Welcome!" Jane felt like royalty. She was used to being gawked at as a celebrity, but this was a deference of rank and status she'd rarely enjoyed before.[23] She learned that her literary accomplishments were highly valued in Russia. At the Orlov dinner, two young men in the Russian Imperial Guard told Jane about their enthusiasm for *The Scottish Chiefs*.

"My dear Jane was respected and honored as a Queen," Robert wrote later in his diary. "[There is] not one of the ladies she meets in society but who have read her *Scottish Chiefs*—and as they ought, are in raptures with the work."[24]

There are frequent mentions in the diaries of Robert and Jane spending time with the late Princess Mary's extended family of Shcherbatovs, as well as with members of the powerful Volkonsky family and with the Volkonskys' cousins, the Tolstoys, relatives of the future novelist. In 1842, Jane and Robert were spending time with the real-life people—and descendants of people—who'd later be mentioned in Leo Tolstoy's *War and Peace* (1869). The Porters also socialized with many of the figures said to have inspired that novel's fictional characters. Jane's and Robert's respective diaries record colorful impressions of many of them.

Jane was befriended by notable Russian women writers of the day, too. She especially loved the poet Countess Yekaterina Rostopchin, about her age. In her journal, Jane compared the countess to her beloved sister, Maria, because both women were "all heart, observation, tenderness, purity."[25] Jane had both surprised and impressed the countess by knowing all about the late Count Rostopchin's exploits in the Napoleonic Wars. Such historical personages, Jane wrote to a friend, and their different descendants, interested her greatly.[26] She believed she could have listened to the countess's stories for hours and thought them minutes.[27] The visit was so exciting and exhausting that Jane was forced to lie down on the sofa for a day to recover her nerves.

Jane occasionally felt well enough to meet other fascinating women, including taking evening tea with the once-celebrated beauty Princess Evdokiya Golitsyna, known as Princess Nocturne, or Princess of Midnight, whom Jane found a surprisingly delightful person. As she explained in her diary, "People suppose she lies in bed all Day; therefore, she receives visitors of an evening, or, occasionally goes out to soirees. They give her the name *Nocturna*." It was said a fortune-teller once predicted the princess would die while sleeping in her bed. Consequently, to cheat death, the princess determined to stay awake all night. Some believed she made up her own legend and nickname out of vanity, so she'd be seen only in soft evening lighting. Rumors flew about her taking lovers and practicing black magic. Jane was eager to judge for herself.

"I expected to find a failed beauty only," she wrote, "with a degree of cleverness. . . . and some eccentricity perhaps from the way she was represented. But I find her quite different from all this."

Jane immediately thought her very intelligent and by the end of the evening concluded that the princess was "a comet" and one of the most extraordinary women she'd ever met.[28] Princess Nocturne declared her high religious principles, too. It's possible the princess became devout in later life, but her earlier years tell a different story. After an unfortunate marriage, she became the mistress-muse of poet Alexander Pushkin. Gossip also connected her romantically to the late Tsar Alexander. In her old age, Princess Nocturne was called a "boring bluestocking," but Jane admired how widely read she was in history and the sciences, as well as being the author of a manuscript on mathematics. Jane—perhaps unsurprisingly from someone so devoted to Mary Robinson in her youth—was entirely won over.

When the warmer weather in the spring of 1842 began breaking up the ice on the Neva River, Jane felt well enough to take walks along the quay, which she found cold but delightful.[29] Her niece, Mary, however, was still perpetually ill. Jane's maid, Bullen, too, had taken sick. Jane, for a change, was feeling more her old self, able to see sights and accept social visits. She took the opportunity to conduct historical research. In April, she made a trip to the Imperial Library, a grand building on Nevsky Prospect. The library's director was a cousin of her late sister-in-law.[30] Perhaps that's how Jane gained permission to read correspondence there from British sovereigns. She copied letters from Queen Elizabeth I and Queen Mary I for Agnes Strickland's next book.[31] Then word came that Jane was granted carte blanche to copy any document she liked—an extraordinary level of access. She wished she'd had more time. She found herself so tired after three hours in the library that she couldn't stir afterward.[32] In her next visit, she took extracts from Queen Mary's prayer book. She also marveled over documents taken as spoils of war after Russia's partitioning of Poland.[33] They would have echoed the brutal stories she'd told in *Thaddeus of Warsaw*.

Despite excitement like this firing her mind in her final weeks in Russia, Jane wrote to a friend that she looked forward to returning to England as a bird would to its mother's nest. She thought Russia a hostile place to anyone used to milder climates. She also worried it would take time to restore Robert to his former vigor.[34] He'd been suffering from violent headaches.[35]

"Both of us having been so victimized by this climate," she wrote, "my Brother has nearly made up his mind to pass the next winter in Italy, in hopes that its balmy atmosphere may undo the mischief."[36] Robert's daughter, Mary, was upset by her father and aunt's resolution to leave her. Robert, however, privately expressed little regret. Spending eight months in her company had convinced him Mary was a hypochondriac. He found it painful to listen to her constant complaining. His diary makes it clear he didn't imagine Mary as a significant part of his future. He had affection for her, but he intended never again to endure a Russian winter.[37]

Robert booked passage back to England on the very first steamer of the spring, in late May 1842. On May 13, he went to say goodbye to Nicholas, who showed him unusual attention. His Imperial Majesty talked to Robert for a long while, holding him by both hands. They exchanged smiles and conversation. Then the Tsar took Robert's hands once more to shake them heartily. An onlooker thought she heard several of the ladies say, "What a frank, independent air Sir Robert Ker Porter has."[38]

The weather was surprisingly warm on the drive back to his lodgings that late afternoon. When his carriage arrived home, a servant opened its door. Sir Robert stepped, then lurched, out of the vehicle. He fell forward. Robert staggered into the house, where he found Jane waiting for him. He didn't speak. He couldn't speak. Something was very wrong. The servants and Jane moved him upstairs to his bed. He was conscious and able to take some water.[39]

Physicians were called immediately. When they arrived, Robert was breathing, but he'd become as pale and motionless as a statue. Every attempt was made to revive him. Jane never left her brother's side. He took his last breath fourteen hours later, early the following morning, on May 14, 1842.[40] The official cause of Robert's death was apoplexy. Jane would always maintain that the stroke that killed him was brought on by the heat of that day, suddenly thawing out the blood in his veins, which had been so strained by moving from a scorching Venezuelan climate to a freezing Russian winter.[41]

"How vain our human plans," Jane wrote in her diary, "My beloved brother was taken from me." She described Robert's death as her "Great Affliction."[42] In the days that followed, a handful of English friends and Russian in-laws called to offer condolences. The Kikines didn't come. Jane's niece, ill again, apparently couldn't bring herself to view her father's body, laid out in his lodgings, as was the custom.

"Yesterday, I looked over him twice on his last bed, in his own room," Jane wrote in her diary, "looking nobly in death, as if the Saviour had given to His Servant his Crown."[43]

The next day Jane went in to see her brother twice more, praying over his remains, just as her chaste Lady Helen Mar had done for William Wallace at the end of *The Scottish Chiefs*. She said, "Amen. Amen. Amen," until it was time to bring Robert's body to the church.[44] But Jane couldn't bring herself to attend his funeral, although it was more common there for women to be present. There had been a group of ladies at the service, headed by Robert's Russian niece. His son-in-law, Captain Pierre Kikine, helped carry the bier. His daughter Mary Kikine was too devastated or ill to attend. Robert's body was then laid to rest in the Protestant burial ground—known as the Smolensky Lutheran Cemetery—in its section for the English dead.

Jane wrote her niece Mary a long, affectionate letter of grief and condolence. She described what she believed were Robert's last wishes for his daughter. She wrote that Robert would have wanted Mary to have his most cherished memorial of her mother—a large gold watch, chain, and key. That beloved possession was a gift from the Princess at the time of their marriage. Jane added, too, a few other memorials Robert wore on his body. The most valuable were a diamond cypher—a gift from Tsar Alexander—and a gold chain, from which he hung his spectacles. Jane sent Mary those three precious things, with the fervent prayer that Robert's daughter would enjoy a long life.

Jane told Mary she planned to keep for herself the three plain gold rings Robert wore, in memory of his lamented friends. Other things, she explained to her niece, weren't hers to give or keep. The insignias of his orders and knighthoods would need to be returned to those who had given them. Then there was the matter of Robert's wardrobe. Jane proposed his clothes be given to his faithful servant, John Jacobs, except for the minister's uniform. That was so expensive, Jane wrote, that she hoped to return it to the London tailor who'd made it, to defray some of Robert's unpaid bill.

In writing this, Jane was gently alluding to Robert dying in debt. Perhaps she hoped the Kikines would offer to cover some costs. Jane would later estimate that her brother yet owed something between one thousand and two thousand pounds in England. She told her niece that every honorable proceeding would need to be made regarding his credit and her own. For that reason, Jane told Mary, she'd had to send Robert's carriage to the undertaker as collateral for the large cost of the funeral. She explained that the carriage had been a gift to her and implied that it was also hers to decide to use for this purpose. There was no mention of who'd pay for the funeral.

"As soon as I became able to enter into these details, my dear Neice," Jane wrote, "I have done so, thinking it my duty that you should know every particular in my power to give, of your Father. I need not describe to you, the sorrow of a sister, over such a Brother! You are his Daughter, and must feel it all."

She signed herself, "Ever dear Mary, your affectionate Aunt."[45]

But the letter's contents, and the loving sign-off, must not have been well received. The next day, Mary sent an unknown friend to call on Jane to deliver a letter asking for the return of more of Robert's possessions, there on the spot. Jane, horrified, absolutely refused and eventually sent Mary a reply.

"The visit of a stranger from you, yesterday my Neice . . . making demands upon me, in purport and stile, anything but like a Daughter of my Brother; after all I had previously sent to you from the affection of an Aunt, of the most valuable relics of your late Father . . . has rendered me incapable of coming to you today; as you knew I intended to do."

Jane was in a frenzy, although she acknowledged the conflict between them may have stemmed from a misunderstanding. One of the gold rings Jane had kept back turned out to be Robert's wedding ring. She said of course she'd give her niece that ring.

"A little patience, Mary; and you would have had it, without the sting now given to the hand that sends it to you," she wrote. Jane then decided to deliver a sting of her own. She compiled, in her neatest hand, the "List of Things sent by Miss Jane Porter, to Madame Kikine by her desire, on the 2nd of May, 1842." She wrote at the end of it, in her own cold prose, "If Madame Kikine will write her name at the bottom of this List, in receipt that she has received them safely, the Bearer will then Deliver them duly in Exchange."

Jane's formal list of returned items included not only Robert's wedding ring and other things Mary had sent her courier to fetch. Jane sent back more than Mary demanded, including coats the Kikines had given to Bullen and John Jacobs and every present they'd given to Jane since her arrival. Then she delivered her own blow. She refused to give Mary three objects she'd demanded—her father's eyeglass, silver pencil, and sword.

"After my death," Jane wrote, Robert's sword "will belong to his country's archives of its great and Good men!" Jane wrote, "None of these, I determinately say, shall ever be separated from me, while I have life."

Jane, who'd gained international acclaim for immortalizing heroes and wars, recast this domestic struggle with her niece as a fight over Robert's heroic legacy. Her letter to Mary was full of righteous anger, with an ultimatum that resembled speeches she'd put into the mouths of her novels' wronged heroines.

"And now, as it may happen, that you and I may never meet again in this world," she wrote to her niece, "believe that I leave my Blessing to my Brother's child—and will ever Pray for her, while on this Earth. I am her Aunt, Jane Porter."[46] Jane's second cold sign-off was unmistakable. She was severing ties. Mary, to her credit, apologized. She sent back a contrite letter, telling her aunt that she was only acting in accordance with the customs of her country. Peace was nominally made, and Jane was grateful for it.[47]

Trust between them, however, was broken. In her final two weeks in Russia, she saw little of Mary. On May 23, 1842, Jane said her final goodbyes in St. Petersburg. Pierre Kikine came with his carriage to take Jane, Bullen, and John Jacobs to the river vessel that would bring them to the seaport of Kronstadt.

Mary didn't join her husband. Half a dozen others came to see Jane off. The next day, the three of them boarded the *Jupiter* for their return voyage. When the steamer finally reached England and entered the Thames, Jane had no idea who, if anyone, might be there to greet them at the ship's landing. On disembarking, she was elated to find Mr. and Mrs. Morgan, her old Ditton neighbors, waiting to welcome her back to her mother country. They whisked Jane and Bullen off to their comfortable home.

CHAPTER 25

A Chair of One's Own (1842–50)

After grief-filled Jane returned to London in summer 1842, she was immediately thrust back into the public eye. It was a mixed blessing. Sir Robert Ker Porter's obituary and the story of his fatal stroke had become international news. So had Jane's bereavement. One paper put the story on its front page: "It is gratifying to be able to announce the safe return of" Miss Jane Porter. "She is at present the guest of her late brother's distinguished friend the president of the Geological Society, in Belgrave-square." While Jane was with these friends, the Murchisons, the newspaper reported that crowds of carriages of those who admired and esteemed Jane and Sir Robert were incessantly at her hosts' door.[1] As the Murchisons' servants turned away carriage after carriage of mourners, Jane received countless letters of condolence.

Charlotte Murchison had generously taken in her old friend while Jane tried to chart a next course. She and Robert had planned to live on his salary, which had stopped at his death, although his debts lingered. Jane would have had no money at all, had not an old friend of Robert's, from the Mocatta banking family, offered her a loan. She began, once again, her old process of lining up places to stay, from one peripatetic month to the next, to save money.

A kind letter came from her brother William, offering her a room in his house in Bristol and mentioning that she also had a place in his fraternal heart. A week later, he traveled to London to reunite with her. During that reunion,

Jane got one important point clarified. William informed her that he would resign all right to Robert's property.[2] William's stepping away from the tangled problems of Robert's affairs wasn't helpful at all, but it did have one silver lining: Jane could work to discharge Robert's debts without revealing anything to unsupportive, judgmental William.

She was left to sort out Robert's estate within a legal and economic system that allowed women little room to maneuver independently.[3] Her brother's debts, and her own, would end up taking her years, not weeks or months, to clear. Jane found a powerful adviser in Robert's "truest friend," Lord Clarendon.[4] He visited Jane and told her he empathized with her calamity.[5] He advised her to write immediately to Prime Minister Sir Robert Peel to again request a civil list or royal pension. Jane did as he suggested. In her letter, she mentioned her advanced age, infirmities, and what she called her "friendless state." She concluded with hope and said she'd respect his judgment.[6] Peel's office responded that day, with a curt, formulaic reply. It told Miss Jane Porter that the sum placed at the disposal of the crown for pensions was limited. The claims upon it were too numerous to hold out any hope the prime minister would have it in his power to comply with her request.[7]

Without a regular income and with Robert's debts to pay off—to save his and their family's honor—it wasn't feasible to rent lodgings of her own. At the advice of another friend, she wrote a begging letter to her old Esher neighbor Prince Leopold, asking if he might give her use of a free cottage on his estate or nominate her for a vacant apartment at Hampton Court Palace. That request went unanswered.[8] She explored other avenues to raise funds. Robert's most valuable work was a large folio volume on Persian geography with information of potential interest as foreign intelligence. Jane wanted the British Museum to pay one thousand pounds for it. That fantastical sum would have paid down most of Robert's debts. After two years, dozens of visits, and countless letters to powerful men in multiple countries, the British Museum finally offered three hundred pounds.[9] Jane used that money to repay her almost twenty-year-old debt to her friend Anna Middleton, to whom she'd been faithfully paying interest each year.[10]

As Jane tried to move forward, she was again in what she called a "pilgrim state," living with great economy, going from house to house.[11] Her friends, increasingly worried about her poverty, decided to take matters into their own hands. Thomas Longman, the namesake son of Jane's longtime publisher, approached the charitable Royal Literary Fund without her knowledge. Longman described Miss Porter as single and sixty, although she was almost sixty-seven. She was left with nothing, he said, because of her late brother's losses in a bank failure. This must have been the little lie Jane told friends had caused Robert's large posthumous debts. In reality, it was only a small, although new, part of the problem. The Royal Literary Fund's committee granted her fifty pounds—a modest windfall that would have once again allowed her to pay Bullen's wages.[12]

Jane's next step was to sell some of Robert's personal property. In the winter of 1843, she auctioned off things stored at the Pantechnicon, unable to afford the 20 pounds a year in rent. She approached auctioneers Christie and Manson, who set the sale for March 30 and April 1, 1843.[13] That auction would disperse much of Robert's original art, as well as his collected works by old masters like Albrecht Dürer and Peter Paul Rubens.[14] Jane parted with unique things her brother had received as gifts. She'd painfully decided to sell portraits of two men she'd once loved—Robert's of Sir Sidney Smith and George Henry Harlow's of Henry Caulfield. Jane held back some of Robert's valuable things from the sale, storing these works of art and jewelry in friends' homes. It was just as well because the prices turned out to be so disappointing. The sale of 284 lots of Robert's property fetched only 380 pounds.[15] The sacrifice of many precious things hadn't been enough to clear away his debts or provide for Jane to rent her own lodgings.

In the spring of 1843, William again offered Jane a room in his home at Portland Square, adding in the sweetener of a separate attic room for her maid, Bullen. He promised her he'd sometimes allow her privacy in the little drawing room near her bedroom. As they negotiated the terms, William conceded that she could admit guests as she chose and offered the occasional use of his carriage. He called Jane "my dear Sister!" and lamented, "We are all that remain—*here*."[16] William also cryptically told Jane that his financial circumstances were tied up. If she came to him, he said, she must be aware that he could do nothing else for her at all. What Jane understood from her brother's caveat was that she must always be prepared to pay her own way in everything—perhaps even food, drink, and coals—and that William would never inquire about her ways and means. With no better options, she took her brother up on his miserly offer.

Upon arriving in Bristol, she discovered that William's home was a changed place. His wife, Phoebe, was fully an invalid. That summer of 1843, Jane and William went to nearby St. Paul's Church together, where they visited Maria's final resting place. Jane lamented that Robert wasn't alongside her and that Mrs. Porter was buried in Esher, 110 miles away. It troubled Jane that her family's remains were so divided.

"My dear & kind Brother Dr. Porter, most probably will 'sleep' with our beloved sister, in his vault at Portland Church," she wrote in her journal. "While I—God only knows, where my mortal Remains may be put in Earth!"[17] One of Jane's greatest fears was that she'd inconveniently die while staying under the roof of one of her generous friends.[18]

News of a death in the extended family came from elsewhere that summer. It was among the kin of her Jamaican-born cousin, the late Robert Porter, Esq., and his three daughters. The three young women—to whom Jane felt she served as an honorary aunt—had married military men. Each couple inherited some of the remains of their late father's ill-begotten and apparently squandered West Indian wealth.[19] A catastrophe had happened as a result of an argument over money between two of the Porter daughters' husbands.[20] It provoked a challenge that resulted in a fatal duel on July 1, 1843, when one brother-in-law killed the other. The tragedy became national news. It inspired political cartoons and vigorous debate in the House of Commons. Laws were eventually amended, with new punishments required for any officer who didn't try to stop a duel.[21] The affair would go down in history as the last duel fought on British soil.[22]

When Jane heard about this senseless death, she pronounced it a melancholy thing. Then her own name was mentioned in the newspapers as a relative of the men's wives. It was a strange coincidence that she'd previously published a novel about the deaths of dueling brothers in *The Field of the Forty Footsteps*. Books like hers had set out to prevent such tragedies from happening again. That a duel occurred among her cousins, to whom she was no longer close, made her sad, as well as terribly angry. "And so has been crushed the Earthly happiness, of a whole family," Jane wrote in her diary, "by This horrible Crime sanctioned by Fashion—and a False Principle of Honour!"[23]

During these years, Jane's name came into the public eye in far happier ways. She recorded in her diary that a friend told her Mrs. Trollope had spoken of her in *The Blue Belles of England* (1841–43).[24] Fanny Trollope—the prolific novelist mother of Anthony Trollope—had done more than speak of Jane; she used her as the basis for a notable character. The character makes a brief appearance in the second volume, when two young women attend a society party and observe a celebrated woman writer, Mrs. Jane Beauchamp. Heroine Constance expresses her surprise to her friend Miss Hartley, upon learning that she's looking at *the* Mrs. Jane Beauchamp: "There is something so unobtrusively quiet in her dress, aspect, and demeanour," Constance notes. Sightings of Mrs. Beauchamp are rare, her more knowing friend says, because the somewhat older woman shows up only often enough to stop the world from saying she's renounced companionship yet rarely enough that she isn't harassed by constant obsequiousness.

"That quiet little lady is decidedly the most remarkable woman extant," Miss Hartley says. "I may stoutly venture, without fear of contradiction, to say that she is the most extraordinary woman that has ever made herself known to fame. That is Mrs. Jane Beauchamp." Constance's face was said to glow as she gazed at this extraordinary woman writer. These passages would have been read by thousands then as direct homage to Miss Jane Porter, under a loosely veiled name.[25]

The most unusual tribute she received during this period was a gift from American strangers. Publishers in the United States had for decades brought out editions of Jane's novels at great profit to them and none to her in the absence of international copyright protection. One publisher acknowledged keeping five presses running throughout the year to print Miss Porter's *Thaddeus of Warsaw* and *The Scottish Chiefs* in cheap editions. They claimed they'd printed upward of a million volumes of her two best-known works.[26] Perhaps only Sir Walter Scott, it was said, had brought more money into the hands of American booksellers than Miss Porter.[27]

As a gesture of thanks, the New York publishers considered sending Jane a gift. At first they planned to get her a golden ink stand.[28] Then they'd changed their minds and decided instead on a large rosewood rocking chair. At about three feet tall, three feet deep, and two feet across, the chair was ornate, sturdy, and dark, covered in crimson velvet and silk. They'd selected one in an Elizabethan style—"a chair for the virgin queen of English romance, made in the style of the virgin queen of English history."[29] The publishers didn't understand that a chair was a terribly inconvenient thing for Jane to receive. These Americans might have taken a clue from the fact that they couldn't find a permanent address to which to direct their gift. Instead, they'd sent it in care of the Lord Mayor of London, who must have been surprised to be asked to accept an enormous wooden box addressed to a famous novelist he didn't personally know. Even he had trouble figuring out where Jane lived. Eventually, Mr. and Mrs. Skinner were contacted. They referred the Lord Mayor to John Shephard, Jane's London friend and lawyer. He received the chair on her behalf and kindly sent her a sketch of it.

This chair, which put Jane's name back in the newspapers, likely drove further sales of her novels. Naturally, it prompted ridicule, too. The *Illustrated London News* made fun of the idea of sending women writers gifts of furniture, speculating about which authors ought to be sent which silly objects.[30] But the American chair may have led to a next gift. In the winter of 1845, Sir Robert Peel finally offered government aid to Jane. He couldn't give her a pension, he said, but he could provide another 150 pounds.[31] Jane used much of it to liquidate Robert's remaining debts.[32] It had taken almost three years, and an extraordinary number of hours of letter writing and behind-the-scenes work, but she was coming close to paying them off.

Amid these bounties came another loss. William's wife, Phoebe, died and was buried in her husband's family vault in St. Paul's Church. Phoebe Porter's epitaph, engraved just after Maria's, was comparatively brief: ALSO PHOEBE, AGED 79, WIFE OF DR. PORTER, PORTLAND SQUARE, WHO DEPARTED THIS LIFE THE 20TH FEBRUARY 1845.[33] The "also," though perfectly common, seems apropos for Phoebe. William, despite having once told Jane he planned to marry Boothia after his wife died, didn't take the opportunity when it arose. Boothia, however, did move into a large house near his on Portland Square. After Phoebe's death, Jane became a permanent resident at William's Bristol home. In the summer of 1845, a few months shy of her seventieth birthday, she gathered some of her stored possessions from her London friends' houses and paid to have them brought to Portland Square. These things may or may not have included her family's precious letters and papers or that inconveniently delivered American chair. Mr. Shephard, as her adviser, continued to help Jane manage her belongings and affairs, probably as a sign of respect and without charge to her.

Jane took a small step toward financial independence, no doubt with Mr. Shephard's help. Between her earnings from Virtue and her new grant from Peel, she'd been able to purchase an annuity for four hundred pounds, which paid out forty pounds a year.[34] A yearly income of forty pounds wasn't enough to set up her own household, but it would have brought peace of mind for covering her own modest expenses in William's home. In her seventies, she'd no longer have to write for a living. Jane lived an isolated life in Bristol. Few old friends came to see her. One who did thought the novelist seemed a shadow of her former self—graceful, dignified, and beautiful in age, although requiring assistance to get up from her couch to greet her guest.[35] Her mobility was limited.

Adding insult to injury, Jane was being excluded from neighboring women's gatherings in Portland Square. There was another powerful woman on the square—a notable female poet and preacher, who led Bible classes out of her home. Such a person should have been a friend and ally, but she disapproved of Jane's past as a fiction writer. Jane longed to get to know her but was consistently rebuffed. The preacher, a devout Methodist, forcefully declared her hostility to novels and declined Jane's many attempts at intimacy.[36] For more than a year, Jane tried to befriend her neighbor, to have the companionship of other educated religious women, but was excluded from the group because of her fiction-writing past.

At the end of 1847, William was so ill that his death had been rumored in the newspaper.[37] He'd actually had a seizure or stroke, like his brother Robert, and perhaps like their father before them.[38] Jane nursed William at his bedside. His mental faculties, she wrote to a friend, were as noble and clear as ever.[39] But six months later, he'd only partially recovered the power of speech.[40] It's doubtful he was able to resume his medical practice. Throughout these difficulties, Jane kept in touch with the new prime minister, Lord Russell. In 1848, when she once again became eligible for charity from the Royal Bounty Fund, Lord Russell awarded her two hundred pounds.[41] That meant she could cover her personal expenses, her maid's wages, and her medical bills, which was fortunate, because there were more bills to come. In the spring of 1849, Jane suffered a heart attack.[42] Without Lord Russell's grant, she wouldn't have been able to afford the necessary medical attention.[43] In early May 1850, with continued health setbacks, she revisited her will. She wrote to her dear, tender friend John Shephard, in handwriting that displayed the strong clarity more characteristic of her letters from earlier days.

"*I completed The Will*," Jane wrote, "according to your directions you had so clearly explained to me; signing it and dating it."[44] She decided to leave everything she had to working women. Two friends were named as executors. Publisher John Churchill would dispose of any remaining copyrights for her, Robert's, and Maria's works. Then she asked Shephard to use the assets of her estate to help the women who'd worked for her family, as well as several middle-class female cousins. The will stipulated that, with the proceeds from Jane's estate, a government annuity should be purchased for her maid, Eliza Bullen, giving her twenty pounds a year for the rest of her life. It was to be done in recognition of her services during years of sorrow and sickness. Jane, who never got the pension she'd sought, made sure her maid got a regular income for life. Jane also wrote into her will that, should Bullen ever marry, this annuity would be paid to her alone, independent of her husband. The money wasn't to be in any way connected to her husband or his debts. Regardless of whether this proviso would have stood up to legal scrutiny, it was a clear indication of what Jane thought of the economic powerlessness of wives under the law.

She asked, too, that a sum be left to Ann Percival, the "attached maid of her beloved mother," and if enough remained, an annuity purchased for her.[45] Jane had kept in touch with Ann over the past two decades since Mrs. Porter's death, visiting her whenever she went to Esher. Ann and her husband had raised two children and endured the deaths of several more.[46] After that bequest, should anything be left, Jane wanted it to go to her cousin Sarah Gill, Sarah's daughter, Emily Gill, or Sarah's grandchildren. One of these grandchildren was Anna Maria Porter Gill, daughter of the late Harry Gill, the young cousin Jane had long ago treated as if he were her son. She planned to leave wishes for her funeral in a sealed envelope with Bullen.[47]

Jane told Shephard that what was most important to her in these final wishes was to use any residue of her existence for the comfort of those who'd been dear to her. Unnamed there were her niece, Mary Kikine, her brother William, or his companion, Boothia. The implication was clear. They were not dear. Jane reminded Shephard that William had once told her that "he could do nothing else for me!" and wrote, "I always kept silence out of delicacy to his feelings with regard to any emolument in my own 'ways and means' & about which he never enquired."[48] If William would share nothing of his wealth with Jane during her life, other than to permit her under his roof, then she'd share nothing of her estate with him after her death.

Jane had a second heart attack on May 12, 1850. She died two weeks later. She spent her last days at 29 Portland Square, cared for by Bullen and two of William's servants, who witnessed her death. Her last moments were spent just across the square from St. Paul's Church where her sister had been laid to rest eighteen years before. Jane's death in Bristol meant she could be buried alongside Maria. Indeed, Jane may have deliberately chosen to spend her late life in Bristol in William's unwelcoming household with this end in mind.

The words to honor Jane on William Porter's vault were undeservedly short, if admirably simple. Jane, one of the nineteenth century's most famous, innovative, and lasting historical novelists, who'd immortalized the lives and stories of so many men and women—living and dead—got an epitaph of just fifteen words:

MISS JANE PORTER, A CELEBRATED WRITER, DIED ON THE 24TH MAY 1850, AGE 74 YEARS.[49]

CODA

Three or Four Closely Packed Sea Chests

The Historic, Confused, and Unsorted Porter Correspondence (After 1850)

Two days after Jane's death, William was feeling well enough to write to his sister's lawyer, John Shephard, to discuss arrangements for her will to be read, acknowledged, and proved.[1] Jane's intentions in that document were perfectly clear. She directed her executors to sell the entirety of her property for the benefit of Eliza Bullen, Ann Percival, and her female cousins, the Gills. Where the document was less clear was in its lack of directions about what ought to be done with Jane's, Maria's, and Robert's unpublished letters and papers.

Her executors, Shephard and Churchill, wasted no time in setting up the sale of her library and miscellaneous effects. Two catalogs were printed of seven and ten pages. The auction was scheduled by Christie and Manson for July 24–25, 1850.[2] The first day's sale auctioned off Jane's many books. All told, it brought in a meager 77 pounds. The next day's sale, the miscellaneous effects, was more lucrative. It turned out that Jane had held back many valuables from the sale of Robert's property eight years earlier, especially art and jewelry. That may have been wise, given the low prices his things fetched then. After her death, Shephard and Churchill engineered better conditions for this sale. Day two raised 430 pounds. It would have been enough to pay off Jane's remaining debts and purchase the annuity for Bullen and perhaps for Ann Percival, too. In fact, the proceeds were almost enough for a single woman to have established a small household of her own for a time.

William didn't have long to contemplate his exclusion from his sister's will or these surprisingly large auction proceeds. On August 15, 1850, he had a fatal stroke at his home in Bristol. At age seventy-six, he'd outlived Jane by three months. His will had been prepared two years earlier. That document assumed Jane would outlive him. His final wishes show that he wanted to maintain control over his famous sister from beyond the grave. Boothia was named William's principal heir in a will that cast Jane as an untrustworthy charity case. He'd planned to transfer Jane's dependence from himself to Boothia. His house was left to Boothia, who was herself not at all needy. Jane was to have been given the option to remain in his former home to the end of her natural life but only if she stayed in her stipulated rooms. The will spelled out in cruel detail how Jane and her friends would, at least, be allowed reasonable right of ingress and egress through the house. It also stipulated terms under which she'd lose access to these rooms.

Excluding Jane from his will in favor of Boothia might have been more understandable if William had married her. He hadn't. It's true that Boothia had once given William a great deal of money to rescue him from ruin stemming from a stockjobbing scheme.[3] The two of them functioned as life partners, and she maintained his correspondence. But Boothia already had a home of her own, purchased near his on Portland Square.[4] In life, William had made it clear to Jane that his love for and sympathy with other women—for Eliza Clark, for Boothia—was greater than what he felt for her. It is only fitting that his will would reveal the choice of a wealthy neighbor as his heir, with no bequest whatever to his famous, dependent sister.

Boothia did, at least, have loyal family feeling toward the Porters as evidenced by her arranging to have a large mural monument to them installed prominently in Bristol Cathedral in 1851.[5] William, of course, was listed first. It read SACRED TO THE MEMORY OF / WILLIAM OGILVIE PORTER ESQ. M.D. / SURGEON IN THE ROYAL NAVY AND FOR NEARLY FORTY YEARS / AN EMINENT PHYSICIAN IN THIS CITY, before revealing him as the author of *Sir*

Edward Seaward's Narrative and a pamphlet on medical ethics. Robert and John were named. So was their father. Jane was described as authoress of *Thaddeus of Warsaw* and *The Scottish Chiefs*. Anna Maria followed, described as the authoress of *Don Sebastian* and *The Hungarian Brothers*.

Boothia, who outlived each member of this "highly gifted and most estimable family," described her contribution at the bottom of the monument: THIS TABLET IS ERECTED BY THEIR DEVOTED FRIEND. Someone later added, MRS. COL. BOOTH, WHO DIED 23 DECEMBER 1851.[6] At the time of her death, Boothia had owned (and lived in) William's house on Portland Square for about sixteen months. A month after she died, the contents of 29 Portland Square were auctioned off by her executors. The advertisement touted the sale of expensive furniture, china, costly jewelry, minerals, shells, coins, wine, rare birds in handsome cages, and a thousand-volume library.[7] Which of these things had originally been Boothia's and which had been William's is unclear. Unknown, too, is who eventually ended up with the Porter family papers.

The public learned about the existence of these papers from a newspaper ad in the winter of 1852. A massive number of autograph letters would go up for auction—the extensive correspondence of Anna Maria and Jane Porter, to and from the eminent and literary personages of their day.[8] The sale, organized by Sotheby and Wilkinson, was announced for March 19–20, 1852. The extent and condition of the Porter sisters' letters were said to be shocking. It was reported that "three or four closely-packed sea-chests of unsorted papers containing what was called 'The Porter Correspondence'" would be sold. The sale was so remarkable that the *Athenaeum* covered in its column "Our Weekly Gossip." It opined, "Never, we believe, has been seen before in an auction-room such a confused mass of Correspondence."

Those stuffed trunks held papers so chaotic it was almost impossible to tell what private, intimate details they held. The *Athenaeum* found this unknowability absolutely tantalizing. "It is difficult to imagine how such a heap of unsorted Correspondence could be sent for sale," it was reported, "otherwise than by legal seizure or by remissness greatly to be deplored of executors."[9] The gossip columnist added portentously that the Porter correspondents had something to dread.

Sale prices proved shockingly low, with the buyers primarily autograph dealers.[10] Five volumes of Robert's diaries went for sixteen pounds. Robert's letters to his sisters sold for twenty-five pounds. Next up was the auction of the sisters' unpublished literary manuscripts, including Maria's works (now seemingly lost) called *Aubrey Abbey*, *Memoirs of Grafton House*, and *Intentions, a Farce*. Papers by Jane included her unpublished plays and an illustrated work by one or both sisters titled *The Old Hag, A Romance*. These manuscripts sold for just one pound to an autograph dealer. His business may have involved cutting them up and selling them off as relic pieces for collectors' scrapbooks.

The longest description in the sale materials was reserved for "The Correspondence of Anna Maria and Jane Porter, with the Eminent and Distinguished Persons of Their Day." The names of a hundred celebrities followed, including John Quincy Adams, the Marquis de Lafayette, and a slew of British prime ministers. Some correspondents' names, like Percival Stockdale's, were followed by the descriptor "long and interesting letters." A few batches were salaciously described as "very interesting." All these letters sold for a mere nineteen pounds.

The same autograph dealer bought the lot of correspondence with actors and actresses for 2 pounds. Correspondence with Sir Walter Scott went for 3 pounds. The thirty-eight "very interesting and important" letters from Edmund Kean and his wife attracted the highest bid at 24 pounds. Notably left undescribed in the sale catalogue are the letters exchanged among Jane, Maria, and Mrs. Porter. In the end, the contents of those three or four highly packed sea trunks sold for a total of 115 pounds.[11] This wasn't an insignificant amount of money, but it was about as much the Porter sisters were paid for just one volume of their novels in their heyday. William's surviving papers and diaries had a different end. Most seem to have been destroyed by a fire at a prominent Bristol bookseller's shop on February 14, 1860.[12]

After this period, the fate of a large portion of the surviving Porter papers becomes more easy to trace. They were purchased by the Victorian bibliomaniac and antiquarian Sir Thomas Phillipps. Phillipps had a ridiculous goal—to own every book and manuscript ever written. He amassed the largest collection of manuscripts known to the nineteenth century and acquired a share of the Porter Correspondence sometime after the 1852 auction. He privately numbered them by order of acquisition and put them into semi-uniform volumes. Then he added these volumes to the rest of his massive collection at his estate at Middle Hill in Worcestershire. The Porter Correspondence found its place somewhere in Middle Hill's sixteen to twenty rooms filled with shelves, boxes, and stacked crates, which could be reached only through tight, stuffy, and blocked passages. It was said that Phillipps would relax at the end of the day by selecting a random manuscript as a figurative dessert, to sweeten his late-night hours.[13] Given the massive number of manuscripts he acquired, it's possible he never took more than a cursory glance at the Porter Correspondence.

As peculiar as this act of literary hoarding was, Phillipps might be seen as almost a heroic figure in the Porter family story because his mass purchase effectively saved these materials for posterity, although it also long hid them from view. Over his lifetime, Phillipps spent nearly a quarter million pounds on fifty thousand books and pamphlets and sixty thousand manuscripts. He often made purchases on credit and ignored his bills. Creditors tried to compel him to pay by court order.[14] That, too, may seem a fitting coda for the traces of the Porter family, who lived so much of their lives on advanced and borrowed money.

Phillipps's purchase of the massive Porter Correspondence, though a fraction of his holdings, had the effect of shutting up the sisters' larger-than-life stories in a dusty castle, like a Gothic novel's captive heroines. After Phillipps's death, his heirs—having failed to negotiate a proposed sale to the British Museum—auctioned these materials off, little by little, over the course of the next hundred years. During that time, a handful of Porter friends, critics, and scholars considered writing full-length family biographies—or biographies of Jane or Robert alone. The works they produced were either short and speculative or ultimately unpublished. They were also usually factually wrong because their writers only had access to the self-mythologizing, unreliable stories Jane herself provided in her late-life prefaces and appendices to her republished novels.

As the nineteenth century turned to the twentieth, and the fame of Jane Austen and the Brontë sisters grew, Jane and Maria Porter's names gradually faded out of literary histories. *The Scottish Chiefs* had its advocates and retained devoted fans, most of whom read and loved the book as children. In 1921, *The Scottish Chiefs* was abridged as a Scribner's Illustrated Classic, featuring the art of the renowned N. C. Wyeth. In the 1950s, the novel was still popular enough to warrant inclusion in the Classics Illustrated comic book series as number 67. But, as it came to be classified more often as children's literature, fewer critics were willing to read it, let alone espouse its importance or value.

Thanks to Sir Walter Scott's towering reputation, mentions of the Porter sisters' fiction became inconvenient. The Porters' existence didn't fit the powerful myth of Scott's invention, singularity, and deserved triumph.

By the time the manuscript-hoarding Sir Thomas Phillipps's descendants got around to auctioning off his Porter manuscripts during the 1950s, '60s, and '70s, few people cared. Thousands of items were divided into lots and sold at auction, once again by Sotheby's. Many were eventually exported to the United States to libraries in California, Kansas, and New York. Smaller batches ended up in London, Edinburgh, Bristol, Durham, and Caracas. Over the past fifty years, these libraries and their staffs—especially at the Huntington Library, the University of Kansas Spencer Library, and the New York Public Library's Pforzheimer Collection—have made it possible for the Porter sisters' history to be preserved, pieced together, and substantially told for the first time.

It shouldn't be controversial to say that Jane and Anna Maria Porter were among the most important fiction writers of the nineteenth century. They were the pioneers of the method of writing historical fiction that Sir Walter Scott would ultimately be credited with having invented. The Porter sisters, not Scott, were the first bestselling authors of that then-emerging genre, which we no longer call "historical romance," "historical tale," or "biographical romance" but refer to by the weightier-sounding masculine label, the "historical novel."

The simple fact that Jane and Maria published twenty-six books, separately and together, should itself have earned them a more prominent place in literary history. In quantity, their output makes them among the most productive sister novelists in literary history. Jane's bestsellers sold millions of copies. Children were named after her novels' characters. Towns were named after some of the heroes the sisters created and helped keep in the public eye. The three Brontë sisters would eventually outdo the Porters in literary impact and numbers of copies sold, but the success of Jane and Maria in marketing themselves as sister novelists unquestionably paved the way for the Brontës, who were just beginning to publish under androgynous pseudonyms around the time of Jane's last illnesses and death.

Jane once wrote to Robert, "What a historian I might be, of the various interesting times in which I have lived—and the still greater variety of interesting persons I have known or seen, if I could ever have energy to sit down to the recollection and pen it down!"[15]

In truth, Jane and Maria *had* found the energy, over many decades, to use their pens for this considerable work of recollection. It wasn't only in their brilliant, innovative historical fiction that they'd documented various interesting times. They also left us the gift of their own razor-sharp, funny, and heart-rending portraits of the nineteenth-century woman writer of genius. The sisters preserved—or perhaps just couldn't bring themselves to destroy—their moving, honest, and still-unpublished letters to each other, so lovingly exchanged across their remarkable lives.

ACKNOWLEDGMENTS

This book was made possible by grants and fellowships from the John Simon Guggenheim Memorial Foundation, the National Endowment for the Humanities (most recently through a Public Scholar award), the Rockefeller Foundation's Bellagio Center, the Huntington Library, the New York Public Library's Pforzheimer Collection, the University of Kansas's Kenneth Spencer Research Library, the American Philosophical Society, and a Big 12 Faculty Fellowship, as well as support from Arizona State University (the Department of English, the Virginia G. Piper Center for Creative Writing, and the College of Liberal Arts and Sciences) and the University of Missouri–Columbia (Research Council, Research Board, and Center for Arts and Humanities).

A staggering number of librarians and archivists also helped make this book possible. Those who've assisted this project—over the course of many years and, in some cases, decades—have gone above and beyond, as consultants and collaborators. Several provided extraordinary pandemic help. Among them I particularly thank Anne Barker (Mizzou), Joe Buenker (ASU), Gayle Richardson (Huntington), Charles Carter (NYPL), Karen Cook (KU), Elizabeth Denlinger (NYPL), Elspeth Healey (KU), Kathy Lafferty (KU), and Julian Pooley (Surrey History Centre). I also thank family historian Vincent Gallagher for generously sharing genealogical research on the Porter family and Joan Afferica for help researching the Shcherbatov family.

I was one of a handful of professors who presented conference papers on the Porters at the Modern Language Association meeting in Los Angeles in 2011. We joked that if natural disaster struck, Porter Studies could be wiped out in an instant. Those three scholars have produced work that's inspired and informed my own—Tony Jarrells, Thomas McLean, and Fiona Price. In the decade since, illuminating new work on the Porters has been published by Peta Beasley, John Bies, Sarah Faulkner, Ruth Knezevich, and Graeme Morton. May the numbers of us restoring the Porter sisters' monumental contributions to literary history continue to grow.

This book wouldn't have been possible without the vision and support of my agent, Stacey Glick, and the heroic efforts of Bloomsbury's senior production editor, Barbara Darko. Most importantly, this book owes its shape to my brilliant editor, Grace McNamee, whose great talents I've had the pleasure of knowing since she became my undergraduate student at the University of Missouri. I'm honored to have had the chance to become her author-student in the making of this book.

Stalwart family and friends also supported me and this project across many years. A more extensive list of acknowledgments may be found on the book's website, sisternovelists.com. That site also includes a gallery of extra illustrations, not found in the book's pages, which further illuminate the Porter sisters' extraordinary lives and legacy.

MAJOR WORKS OF JANE AND ANNA MARIA PORTER

JANE PORTER

The Spirit of the Elbe: A Romance (1799) [anonymous], 3 vols.
The Two Princes of Persia, Addressed to Youth (1801) [as I. Porter]
Thaddeus of Warsaw (1803) [as Miss Porter], 4 vols.
Aphorisms of Sir Philip Sidney, with Remarks, by Miss Porter (1807), 2 vols.
The Scottish Chiefs: A Romance (1810), 5 vols.
The Pastor's Fire-Side: A Novel (1817), 4 vols.
Switzerland, or the Heir of Underwald [Play, in five acts] (1819)
Duke Christian of Luneberg: or, Tradition from the Hartz (1824), 3 vols.

ANNA MARIA PORTER

Artless Tales (1793)
Artless Tales Volume II (1795/6)
Walsh Colville; or A Young Man's First Entrance Into Life: A Novel (1797) [anonymous]
Octavia (1798), 3 vols.
The Fair Fugitives [Opera] (1803)
The Lake of Killarney: A Novel (1804), 3 vols.
A Sailor's Friendship, and a Soldier's Love (1805) [anonymous], 2 vols.
The Hungarian Brothers (1807), 3 vols.
Don Sebastian; or, The House of Braganza: An Historical Romance (1809), 4 vols.
Ballad Romances, and Other Poems (1811)
Tales of Pity on Fishing, Shooting, and Hunting, Intended to Inculcate in the Mind of Youth, Sentiments of Humanity Toward the Brute Creation (1814) [as AMP]
The Recluse of Norway (1814), 4 vols.
The Knight of St. John: A Romance (1817), 3 vols.
The Fast of St. Magdalen: A Romance (1818), 3 vols.
The Village of Mariendorpt: A Tale (1821), 4 vols.
Roche-Blanche; or, The Hunters of the Pyrenees: A Romance (1822), 3 vols.

Honor O'Hara: A Novel (1826), 3 vols.
The Barony (1830), 3 vols.

CO-AUTHORED BY JANE AND ANNA MARIA PORTER

A Defence of the Profession of an Actor (1800) [anonymous]
The Sentinel, or, British Miscellany and Review [Magazine] (1804) [anonymous]
Tales Round a Winter Hearth (1826), 2 vols.
Coming Out; and The Field of the Forty Footsteps (1828), 3 vols.

WORKS BY ROBERT KER PORTER (*Arranged and Edited by Jane Porter, Uncredited*)

Travelling Sketches in Russia and Sweden During the Years 1805, 1806, 1807, 1808 (1809), 2 vols.
Letters from Portugal and Spain, Written During the March of the British Troops under Sir John Moore (1809) [as An Officer]
A Narrative of the Campaign in Russia, During the Year 1812 (1814)
Travels in Georgia, Persia, Armenia, Ancient Babylonia, &c. &c.: During the Years 1817, 1818, 1819, and 1820 (1821–22), 2 vols.

WORK BY WILLIAM OGILVIE PORTER, EDITED BY JANE PORTER

Sir Edward Seaward's Narrative of His Shipwreck, and Consequent Discovery of Certain Islands in the Caribbean Sea: With a Detail of Many Extraordinary and Highly Interesting Events of His Life, from the Year 1733 to 1749, as Written in His Own Diary, Edited by Miss Jane Porter (1831), 3 vols.

LIST OF ILLUSTRATIONS

Page 1, left: Samuel Freeman, after George Henry Harlow, portrait of Jane Porter, c. 1811. Private collection.

Page 1, right: Thomas Woolnoth, after George Henry Harlow, portrait of Anna Maria Porter, 1833. Private collection.

Page 2, left: L. F., portrait of Jane Porter, undated. Jane Porter and Anna Maria Porter Collection, C1174, Manuscripts Division, Department of Special Collections, Princeton University Library.

Page 2, upper right: Thomas Barber, after drawing by Thomas Hosmer Shepherd, Surgeon's Square, Edinburgh, 1830. Private collection.

Page 2, lower right: G. H. Adcock, after drawing by R. W. Buss, "Examination of the Students of the University of Durham," 1842. Reproduced by permission of Durham University Library and Special Collections.

Page 3, upper: Robert Ker Porter, frontispiece and title page of Anna Maria Porter's *Artless Tales* (London: [no publisher], 1793). Private collection.

Page 3, lower left: J. Thomson, after George Henry Harlow, portrait of Anna Maria Porter, 1823. Private collection.

Page 3, lower right: Samuel Freeman, after John Wright, portrait of Robert Ker Porter, published by Vernor, Hood & Sharpe, Poultry, London, 1809. Private collection.

Page 4, upper left: William Ridley, after Emma Smith, portrait of Mrs. Crespigny, printed in the *European Magazine*, vol. 46, December 1804, 402.

Page 4, upper right: George Dance, portrait of Mary Robinson (née Darby), 1793. © National Portrait Gallery, London.

Page 4, lower left: Thomas Charles Wageman, after Thomas Woolnoth, portrait of Elizabeth Benger, 1825. Print Collection, The New York Public Library.

Page 4, lower right: K. Mackenzie, after Robert Ker Porter, portrait of Elizabeth Gunning, London, 1802. Private collection.

Page 5, upper left: Richard James Lane, after Alfred Edward Chalon, portrait of Charles Kemble as Cassio in *Othello*, printed by Jérémie Graf and published by John Mitchell, 1838. Private collection.

Page 5, upper right: Giovanni Vendramini, after Joseph Muller, portrait of Marie-Thérèse De Camp in the Character of Urania, 1802. Music Division, The New York Public Library for the Performing Arts.

Page 5, lower left: George Henry Harlow, portrait of Captain Henry Caulfield, undated. Private collection. Photo © Christie's Images/Bridgeman Images.

Page 5, lower right: After Herbert Railton, "Historic House in Gerrard Street Where Dryden Died," printed in *The Sphere*, September 21, 1901, 349. (The Porters' rented lodgings were near but not in Dryden's former home.)

Page 6, upper left: James Fittler, after John Downman, frontispiece portrait of Percival Stockdale, from Stockdale's *Sermons on Important and Interesting Subjects* (London: John Stockdale, 1774). Private collection.

Page 6, upper right: Anthony Cardon, after Robert Ker Porter, portrait of Admiral Sir Sydney [Sidney] Smith, G. C. B., undated, published by Henry Colburn, London. Private collection.

Page 6, lower left: Samuel Freeman, after Robert Ker Porter, frontispiece portrait of Sir Philip Sidney, from Jane Porter's *Aphorisms of Sir Philip Sidney, with Remarks* (London: Longman, Hurst, Rees, and Orme, 1807).

Page 6, lower right: Dedication page of Jane Porter's *Thaddeus of Warsaw, in Four Volumes* (London: T. N. Longman and O. Rees, 1803). Courtesy of the Huntington Art Museum, San Marino, California.

Page 7, upper left: John Hassell, "Residence of Jane Porter, authoress of *Thaddeus of Warsaw*, etc.," 1823. Original drawing tipped into volume 7, page 178, of Manning and Bray's *History of Surrey*. British Library, General Reference Collection Crach.1.Tab.1.b.1. © The British Library Board.

Page 7, upper right: J. Thomson, after George Henry Harlow, portrait of Jane Porter, undated. Private collection.

Page 7, lower left: George Henry Harlow, portrait of Sarah Siddons as Lady Macbeth, undated. Courtesy of The Huntington Art Museum, San Marino, California.

Page 7, lower right: J. Thomson, after George Henry Harlow, portrait of Jane Porter as a Lady Canoness, undated. Private collection.

Page 8, upper left: H. Meyer, after Sir Joshua Reynolds, portrait of the Margravine of Anspach, from A. M. Broadley and Lewis Melville's *The Beautiful Lady Craven*, vol. 1 (London: John Lane, 1914), xii.

Page 8, upper right: James Lewis, after John Preston Neale, "Brandenburgh House and Theatre, Middlesex," from The Beauties of England and Wales series (London: John Harris, July 1815). Private collection.

Page 8, lower left: R. Page, portrait of the Honourable Keppel Craven, 1821. © National Portrait Gallery, London.

Page 8, lower right: Samuel Rawle, after J. Nixon, Esq., "Benham near Newbery, The Seat of Her Serene Highness the Margravine of Anspach," printed in *European Magazine*, vol. 53, May 1808, 248.

Page 9, upper left: H. J. Harding, portrait of Jane Porter, c. 1822. Reproduced by permission of Karen Ievers of Mount Ievers Court, Co. Clare.

Page 9, upper right: Title page of Jane Porter, *The Scottish Chiefs: A Romance* (London: Longman, Hurst, Rees, and Orme, 1810).

Page 9, lower left: Godfrey, "Rushin [Rushen] Castle, Pl. 1, Isle of Man," from Francis Grose's *The Antiquities of England and Wales* (London: printed for S. Hopper, 1775). Private collection.

Page 9, lower right: Thomas Rowlandson and Augustus Charles Pugin, after John Bluck, Joseph Constantine Stadler, Thomas Sutherland, J. Hill, and Harraden, "King's Bench Prison," plate 9 in Rudolph Ackermann's *Microcosm of London or London in Miniature* (London, [R. Ackermann], 1809. Private collection.

Page 10, upper left: Thomas Charles Wageman, after Thomas Charles Wageman, portrait of Edmund Kean as Sir Giles Overreach, published by Simpkins and Marshall, London, 1818. © National Portrait Gallery, London.

Page 10, upper right: "The present-day Theatre Royal in Drury Lane, sketched when it was new, in 1813," printed in *Survey of London: Volume 35, the theatre Royal, Drury Lane, and the Royal Opera House, Covent Garden*, originally published by London County Council, London, 1970. Wikimedia Commons.

Page 10, lower left: Thomas Woolnoth, after George Henry Harlow, portrait of Sir Robert Ker Porter, published by Dean and Munday, London, July 1822. Private collection.
Page 10, lower right: C. Clark, Colonel Daniel "Dan" Mackinnon. Player's Cigarettes, Dandies Series, No. 27. 1932. Private collection.
Page 11, upper left: J. Pye, "Carlton House, Pall Mall," for The Beauties of England and Wales series, July 1810. Private collection.
Page 11, upper right: Sir Walter Scott, Detroit Photographic Company, 1905. Public domain.
Page 11, lower left: Portrait of Sir Andrew Halliday, undated. Wellcome Collection.
Page 11, lower right: John Russell, Portrait of James Stanier Clarke, c. 1790. Public domain.
Page 12, upper left: "Jane Porter's Cottage at Esher," printed in Mrs. S. C. Hall, "Memories of Miss Jane Porter," *Harper's New Monthly Magazine*, vol. 1, no. 4, September 1850, 437.
Page 12, upper right: Monument to Mrs. Jane Porter (d. 1831), "Here Sleeps in Jesus a Christian Widow," printed in Mrs. S. C. Hall, "Memories of Miss Jane Porter," *Harper's New Monthly Magazine*, vol. 1, no. 4, September 1850, 438.
Page 12, lower left: Augustin Edouart, silhouette portraits of Robert Ker Porter and Jane Porter, with cousins Annie Francis Porter and Eliza Porter, 1829. © National Portrait Gallery of Scotland.
Page 12, lower right: Jane Porter's Letters. Kenneth Spencer Research Library, University of Kansas.
Page 13, upper left: Daniel Maclise, portrait of Jane Porter, printed in "Gallery of Literary Characters, No. LXIX," *Fraser's Magazine*, vol. 11, April 1834, 404.
Page 13, upper right: Archibald L. Dick, after George W. Flagg, portrait of Nathaniel Parker Willis, printed in *Graham's Magazine*, vol. 25, no. 4, April 1844. Private collection.
Page 13, lower left: Portrait of Jane Porter, c. 1838. Reproduced by kind permission of the owner and Julian Pooley, The Nichols Archive Project.
Page 13, lower right: H. T. Ryall after R. Richard, portrait of unidentified woman, accompanying Frederic Montagu, "The Old Lady," and Jane Porter [writing as The Author of Thaddeus of Warsaw], "The Old Lady: A Fragment." In *The Ages of Female Beauty*, ed. Frederic Montagu (London: Charles Tilt, 1838), 57.
Page 14, upper left: William Radclyffe, after John Preston Neale, Coughton Court, near Alcester, Warwickshire, c. 1812–25. Private collection.
Page 14, middle: Newman & Co., "St Paul's Church, Bristol, Portland Square," from *Twenty Four Views of Clifton and Bristol* (London: Newman, 1873).
Page 14, lower left: John Shephard, drawing of Jane Porter's chair from American publishers, 1844. Reproduced by permission of Durham University Library and Collections.
Page 15, upper left: "The Porter Correspondence," in auction catalogue, S. Leigh Sotheby and John Wilkinson, March 19, 1852, with notations in an unknown hand. Private collection.
Page 15, lower right: Porter Family Memorial Tablet, Bristol Cathedral, Bristol, England. Photograph by Devoney Looser.
Page 16, upper left: Cigarette card of Jane Porter (with lines of verse adapted from Walter Scott's *Marmion*), Mogul Cigarettes, c. 1910.
Page 16, upper right: N. C. Wyeth, cover illustration for Jane Porter's *The Scottish Chiefs* (New York: Scribner's Illustrated Classics, 1921).
Page 16, lower left: Jane Porter, *The Scottish Chiefs, by the author of Pride and Prejudice* (London: Ward, Lock & Co., c. 1890). Courtesy of the James Smith Noel Collection, Louisiana State University-Shreveport.
Page 16, lower right: Classics Illustrated No. 67, *The Scottish Chiefs*, c. 1950s. © 2018 First Classics, Inc., ClassicsIllustratedBooks.com.

NOTES

ABBREVIATIONS

AMP	Anna Maria Porter (1778–1832)
JP	Jane Porter (1775–1850)
MRS. JP	Jane Blenkinsop Porter (1745–1831)
RKP	Robert Ker Porter (1777–1842)
WOP	William Ogilvie Porter (1774–1850)

ANCKETILL	Matthew Ancketill, "Strange Destiny: The Rediscovery of Sir Robert Ker Porter: A Life." Matthew Ancketill Collection. GB165-0009. Unpublished manuscript on deposit at The Middle East Centre Archive, St. Antony's College, Oxford University. Copyright Ancketill Family.
BEINECKE	Beinecke Rare Book & Manuscript Library, Yale University
BL	British Library
DBF	[Database of British Fiction] P. D. Garside, J. E. Belanger, and S. A. Ragaz, *British Fiction, 1800–1829: A Database of Production, Circulation & Reception*, designer A. A. Mandal. http://www.british-fiction.cf.ac.uk. Citations include record number.
CARACAS DIARY	Robert Ker Porter, *Sir Robert Ker Porter's Caracas Diary, 1825–1842: A British Diplomat in a Newborn Nation* (Caracas: Walter Dupouy, 1966).
CLARK	William Andrews Clark Memorial Library, UCLA
DURHAM	Porter Family Correspondence, Durham University Library, Archives and Special Collections. https://n2t.durham.ac.uk/ark:/32150/s1qr46r082g.xml
FOLGER	Folger Shakespeare Library
HOUGHTON	Houghton Library, Harvard University
HL, POR	Jane Porter Papers, Huntington Library, San Marino, California
LILLY	The Lilly Library, Indiana University
MORGAN	The Morgan Library & Museum

MORRISTOWN	North Jersey History & Genealogy Center, The Morristown and Morris Township Library, Miscellaneous Manuscripts Collection
NLS	National Library of Scotland
NOTTINGHAM	Special Collections, University of Nottingham
NRO	Northumberland Record Office
ORLANDO	Susan Brown, Patricia Clements, and Isobel Grundy, eds., *Orlando: Women's Writing in the British Isles from the Beginnings to the Present* (Cambridge: Cambridge University Press, 2022). orlando.cambridge.org
PFORZHEIMER	Carl H. Pforzheimer Collection of Shelley and His Circle, New York Public Library
SPENCER	Porter Family Collection (MS 28), Kenneth Spencer Research Library, University of Kansas
UCLA	Collection 715, Special Collections, UCLA Library
V&A	National Art Library, Victoria & Albert Museum

PROLOGUE: TWO SISTERS OF BLAZING GENIUS

1. AMP to JP, 15 July 1820, HL, POR 839.

2. "Testimonial to Jane Porter," *Richmond Enquirer*, November 15, 1844, 1.

3. Graeme Morton, *William Wallace: A National Tale* (Edinburgh: Edinburgh University Press, 2014), 134.

4. Alexander Murdoch, *Scotland in America, c.1600–c.1800* (New York: Palgrave Macmillan, 2010), 156.

5. William Makepeace Thackeray, *The Works of William Makepeace Thackeray*, vol. XXII (London: Smith, Elder, 1886), 234.

6. Jane Porter, *The Scottish Chiefs*, Hartford, 1823, Dickinson Family Library, EDR 231, Houghton; Jane Porter, *Thaddeus of Warsaw*, New York, 1820, Dickinson Family Library, EDR 524, Houghton.

7. Gary Kelly, "Introduction," in *Varieties of Female Gothic*, vol. 4, *Historical Gothic* (New York: Routledge, 2002), xii.

8. AMP to Mrs. JP, 19 August 1793, Spencer, Box 9, Folder 2.

9. AMP to RKP, 21 September 1803, Spencer, MS Q 48:3.

10. JP to AMP, 8 September 1799, HL, POR 1436.

11. AMP to JP, 10 October 1812, HL, POR 684.

12. AMP to JP, 16 April 1795, HL, POR 1427.

13. JP to H. Hindley, 23 May 1833, BL, 74/Tab.438.a.1. vol. 3, 146.

14. JP, "Poetic Epistle," Clark, Porter Folder 1/2.

15. S. C. Hall and Anna Maria Hall, "Memories of Authors," *Atlantic Monthly* 15, no. 89 (March 1865): 336.

16. AMP to JP, 7[?] July 1816, HL, POR 743; JP, "Anticipation—to my Sister, A Home Scene," Poems, Folger, N.a.3.

17. S. C. Hall and Anna Maria Hall, "Memories of Authors," *Atlantic Monthly* 15, no. 89 (March 1865): 336; JP, "Song," Poems, Folger, N.a.3.

18. [Jane Porter], "Miss Jane Porter," in *National Gallery of Illustrious and Eminent Personages of the Nineteenth Century; with Memoirs*, vol. 5 ed. William Jerdan (London: Fisher, Son, & Jackson, 1834), 3.

19. AMP to JP, 5 November 1799, HL, POR 362.

20. Charles MacFarlane, *Reminiscences of a Literary Life* (New York: Charles Scribner's Sons, 1917), 113.

21. AMP to JP, 8–12 September 1803, HL, POR 428.

22. AMP to JP, 7 March 1805, HL, POR 482.

23. AMP to Elizabeth Dillon, 21 May 1824, HL, POR 218.

24. JP to AMP, 28 April 1815, HL, POR 1708.

25. JP to Mrs. JP, 28 February 1806, HL, POR 1915.

26. AMP to JP, 18 May 1808, HL, POR 583.

27. JP to AMP, 23–24 June 1801, HL, POR 1451.

28. JP to AMP, 26 June 1801, HL, POR 1454.

29. AMP to JP, 14 July 1812, HL, POR 284.

30. AMP to JP, 8 December 1805, HL, POR 249.

31. JP to AMP, 17 November 1818, HL, POR 1761.

32. JP to AMP, 4 April 1811, HL, POR 1656.

33. Thomas Hammersley to JP, 28 April 1811, Pforzheimer, PORT 11.04.28.

34. JP to AMP, 4 April 1811, HL, POR 1656.

35. JP to AMP, 14–15 May 1805, HL, POR 1561.

36. JP to AMP, 29 June 1815, HL, POR 1716.

37. "Recent Deaths," *International Weekly Miscellany*, July 1, 1850, 10.

CHAPTER 1: FIVE FATHERLESS PORTER CHILDREN (1779–90)

1. Jane "Jenny" Blenkinsop, the youngest child of Peter Blenkinsop and Mary Adamson Blenkinsop, was baptized on January 25, 1745. Her older siblings were John, Peter, William Blythman, Jane (deceased), Mary, and Anne. Her mother died and was buried in Durham St. Oswald's churchyard on December 7, 1761. See *North Country Diaries (Second Series)* (Durham: Andrews & Co., for Surtees Society, 1915), 160.

2. Roz Southey, "Concert Promotion in Newcastle and Durham, 1752–72," in *Concert Life in Eighteenth-Century Britain*, ed. Susan Wollenberg and Simon McVeigh (New York: Routledge, 2004), 69n95.

3. William Porter, "Catalogue," HL, POR 99.

4. "Last week was married," *Newcastle Weekly Courant*, July 28, 1770, 2.

5. First son William Porter was baptized at St. Mary-le-Bow on June 27, 1771, and died in infancy. A child named Thomas Porter was buried in Durham on March 23, 1772. This may have been the same boy who'd been baptized as William Porter the previous year. If this buried child was indeed William and Jenny's firstborn son, then his name may have been William Thomas Porter. It's also possible that their firstborn son was not laid to rest in Durham. See Durham Record Office EP/Du. SO 156. Son John Blenkinsop Porter was baptized at St. Ann's Manchester in Lancashire on October 19, 1772, with an as-yet-unknown birthdate. Son William Ogilvie Porter was born on an as-yet-unidentified date in 1774. Son Robert Ker Porter was baptized at St. Mary-le-Bow on July 10, 1777, but celebrated his birthday on April 26, with a likely birthdate of April 26, 1777. Anna Maria Porter was baptized twice—first privately at St. Thomas's, New Sarum (Salisbury) on December 25, 1778, and again at

St. Mary-le-Bow in Durham, on September 7, 1779. She celebrated her birthday on December 17, with a likely birthdate of December 17, 1778. See *North Country Diaries (Second Series)* (Durham: Andrews & Co., for Surtees Society, 1915), 160. On Anna Maria Porter's first baptism, see Clark, Porter Folder 1/17. Robert Ker Porter's biographer Matthew Ancketill speculates that these gaps between Porter birthdates and baptisms were related to their parents traveling to namesake patrons to ask them to serve as the infants' sponsors. Ancketill also repeats nineteenth-century rumors that John, William, and Jane Porter were born in County Donegal, Ireland, but that their parents wanted to hide their Irish births and so delayed their baptisms. See Ancketill 6–7. (Ancketill's 822-page biography remains unpublished but survives in typescript.) Jane believed she was born in Durham, in the same room as her brother Robert. See JP to RKP, 20 August 1832, Spencer, Box 4, Folder 13.

6. JP to RKP, 20 August 1832, Spencer, Box 4, Folder 13.

7. William Porter, Sr., to Mrs. JP, 5 May 1777, HL, POR 2627.

8. William Porter, Sr., to Mrs. JP, 16 March 1777, HL, POR 2617.

9. Peter Blenkinsop to William Porter, Sr., 7 December 1778, HL, POR 140.

10. William Porter, Sr., to Mrs. JP, 25 April 1777, HL, POR 2625.

11. Peter Blenkinsop to William Porter, Sr., 25 October[?] 1778, HL, POR 142.

12. Ann Blenkinsop to Lord Crewe's Charity, 9 December 1778, NRO.

13. Kirstin Olsen, *Daily Life in 18th-Century England* (Westport, CT: Greenwood, 1999), 15.

14. JP, 17 December, Diary of 1835, Folger. M.a.18.

15. "Ann Maria," BL, RP 7204.

16. JP to RKP, 12 September 1837, Spencer, Box 6, Folder 32.

17. Samuel[?] Porter to Mrs. JP, 1 September 1779, HL, POR 2606.

18. "Preferments," *Scots Magazine*, vol. 41, April 1779, 223.

19. Fragment, c. 1780., Spencer, Box 38, Folder 48.

20. Prophecy for Mrs. JP, c. 1780[?] HL, POR 124.

21. JP to AMP, 27 May 1805, Spencer, Box 3, Folder 20.

22. William Porter (nephew) to Mrs. JP, 11 October 1790, HL, POR 2611.

23. Leonard Morse to Mrs. JP, 8 November 1779, HL, POR 193.

24. Samuel[?] Porter to Mrs. JP, 1 September 1779, HL, POR 2606.

25. Charles S. Earle and Lawrence A. Body, *Durham School Register*, 2nd ed. (London: Bradbury, Agnew, & Co, 1912), 92–93.

26. Charles G. Harper, *Stage-Coach and Mail in Days of Yore: A Picturesque History of the Coaching Age*, vol. II (London: Chapman Hall, 1903), 157.

27. William Albert, *The Turnpike Road System in England, 1663–1840* (Cambridge: Cambridge University Press, 1972), 184.

28. Advertisement, *Caledonian Mercury*, November 10, 1779, 1.

29. Advertisement, *Caledonian Mercury*, December 6, 1779, 3.

30. H. P. Tait, "Notes on the History of Paediatrics in Scotland," *Edinburgh Medical Journal* 58, no. 4 (April 1951): 185.

31. JP, tribute to AMP, c. 1832, HL, POR 86.

32. William Porter, Sr., to Mrs. JP, November[?] 1777[?], HL, POR 2635.

33. "Visit to Miss Porter," *Chambers Journal of Literature, Science, and Art*, 4th series, no. 3, January 1874, 336; Jane Porter, "A Retrospective Introduction to the Standard Edition of the Scottish Chiefs. A. D. 1831," in *The Scottish Chiefs: A Romance* (London: Henry Colburn and Richard Bentley, 1831), xv.

34. Paul A. Gilje, *Liberty on the Waterfront: American Maritime Culture in the Age of Revolution* (Philadelphia: University of Pennsylvania Press, 2012), 18.

35. Hermit in London, "My First Visit to an Edinburgh Boarding House," in *Angelo's Pic Nic or Table Talk*, ed. Henry Angelo (London: J. Ebers, 1834), 190.

36. Ibid., 191.

37. Judith Bryan, "The Evolution of Black London," in *Black British Writing*, ed. R. Victoria Arana and Lauri Ramey (New York: Palgrave Macmillan, 2004), 70; Hermit in London, "My First Visit," 188.

38. JP to John Churchill, 3 December 1846, Pforzheimer, PORT 46.12.03.

39. Anna Maria Porter, "Supposed Address of a Highland Girl to Charles Edward, the Young Pretender," *The Lady's Monthly Museum*, vol. 14, October 1821, 234–35.

40. "Visit to Miss Porter," *Chambers Journal of Literature, Science, and Art*, 336.

41. Dugald Butler, *The Tron Kirk of Edinburgh or Christ's Kirk at the Tron: A History* (Edinburgh: Oliphant, Anderson & Ferrier, 1906), 364.

42. David Fraser-Harris, *Saint Cecilia's Hall in the Niddry Wynd: A Chapter in the History of Music of the Past in Edinburgh* (Edinburgh: Oliphant, Anderson, & Ferrier, 1899), 2.

43. James Grant, *Cassell's Old and New Edinburgh*, vol. 2 (Cassell, Peter, Galpin & Co., 1882), 239.

44. Butler, *The Tron Kirk of Edinburgh*, 49.

45. Robert Chambers, ed., *A Biographical Dictionary of Eminent Scotsmen*, vol. 4 (Glasgow: Blackie & Son, 1853), 404.

46. JP to AMP, 22–26 January 1805, HL, POR 1539. Jane copied out sections of a letter that had arrived from George Fulton in her own to Maria.

47. Anne Ellwood, *Memoirs of the Literary Ladies of England from the Commencement of the Last Century*, vol. 2 (London: Henry Colburn, 1843), 279.

48. Jane Porter, *The Scottish Chiefs*, 2 vols. (London: Colburn and Bentley, 1831), I:viii.

49. "Visit to Miss Porter," *Chambers Journal of Literature, Science, and Art*, 336.

50. JP to AMP, 27 May 1813, HL, POR 1704.

51. JP to Sir Walter Scott, 5 October 1831, NLS, MS 5317 f. 185–86.

52. In 1831, Scott replied to a letter from Jane, signing off by declaring himself her his kind and delightful friend. He doesn't respond to Jane's claims that her mother delighted in remembering him as a youth. See Caroline McCracken-Fletcher, "Dead Letter? A Walter Scott Manuscript at the University of Wyoming," *The Scott Newsletter*, no. 37 (Winter 2000), 4–5.

53. Mrs. JP to Revd Sir, 5 September 1785, NRO, NRC 452/C/2/127.

54. Mrs. JP to the Trustees of Lord Crewe's Charity, Northumberland Archives, NRO 452/C/2/129; Mrs. JP, October 1785, Account Book of the Executors and Trustees of Lord Crewe, NRO, Ref NRO 452/B/2/2, 200.

55. William Porter (nephew) to Mrs. JP, 11 October 1790, HL, POR 2611; W. O. Porter, "To the Trustees of the Bristol Infirmary," *Bristol Mirror*, March 26, 1825, 3.

56. Lord Banff to Mrs. JP, 1 June 1786, HL, POR 130.

57. Mrs. JP to Revd Sir, 15 November 1786, NRO, NRP 452/C/2/143.

58. Mrs. JP, 27 November 1786, Account Book of the Executors and Trustees of Lord Crewe, NRO, Ref NRO 452/B/2/2, 226.

59. Mrs. JP to John Wilkes, 22 January 1769, BL, Add MS 30870 f. 103.

60. JP to RKP, 31 October 1831, Spencer, Box 4, Folder 1; "Death of Sir Robert Ker Porter, The Painter and Traveller," *The Mirror* 1, no. 23 (June 4, 1842): 360.

61. Jane Porter, "Recollective Preface," in *The Scottish Chiefs* (London: George Virtue, 1840), 15.

62. David Ramage, "The Library Buildings on Palace Green," *Durham University Journal* XXXVIII, no. 3 (June 1946): 94.

63. A. I. Doyle, "John Cosin (1595–1672) as a Library Maker," *Book Collector* 40, no. 3 (Autumn 1991): 345.

64. JP to RKP, 31 October 1831, Spencer, Box 4, Folder 1.

65. JP to AMP, 2 March 1813, HL, POR 1675.

66. JP to Miss Wesley, 7 September 1804, UCLA, Box 1, f. 6.

67. JP to AMP, 17 April 1793[?], HL, POR 1420.

68. Jane Porter, *The Scottish Chiefs* (George Virtue), 15.

69. "Miss Jane Porter," in Jerdan, *National Gallery of Illustrious and Eminent Personages of the Nineteenth Century*, 3.

70. JP, "My Rhyming Follies," 1794, BL, RP 7204.

71. "Obituary: Miss Anna Maria Porter," *Gentleman's Magazine*, vol. CCI, December 1832, 576.

72. William Cullen to Mrs. JP, 19 September 1786, Pforzheimer, PORT 86.09.19.

73. AMP to Mrs. JP, 19 August 1793, Spencer, Box 9, Folder 2.

74. William Page, *Victoria History of the County of Durham*, vol. 1 (London: A. Constable, 1906), 385.

75. Percival Stockdale to JP, 21 July 1797, Houghton.

76. Ina Mary White, "The Diary of Jane Porter," *Scottish Review*, 1897, 327.

77. "Obituary: Miss Anna Maria Porter," *Gentleman's Magazine*, 576.

78. William Henderson, *My Life as an Angler* (London: W. Satchell, Peyton, & Co., 1879), 9–10.

79. Ibid.

80. Mrs. JP to JP, 12 December 1809, HL, POR 1106.

81. JP to Mrs. JP, c. 1790, HL, POR 1884.

CHAPTER 2: LONDON'S COVENT GARDEN AND MARIA'S TEENAGE TALES (1790–96)

1. William Porter (nephew) to Mrs. JP, 14 October 1792, HL, POR 2613.

2. William Porter (nephew) to Mrs. JP, 11 October 1790, HL, POR 2611.

3. William Porter (nephew) to Mrs. JP, 14 October 1792, HL, POR 2613.

4. Sidney C. Hutchison, "The Royal Academy Schools, 1768–1830," *Volume of the Walpole Society* 38 (1960–62): 30.

5. JP to AMP, 7–20 July 1801, HL, POR 1457.

6. Charles Knight, *School History of England: From the Earliest History to Our Own Times* (London: Bradbury and Evans, 1865), 651.

7. JP to RKP, September[?] 1818[?], HL, POR 2042.

8. "Sir Robert Ker Porter," in *Dictionary of National Biography*, vol. XLVI, ed. Sidney Lee (London: Smith, Elder & Co., 1896), 191.

9. Martin Archer Shee, *The Life of Sir Martin Archer Shee*, vol. 1 (London: Longman, Green, Longman, and Brothers, 1860), 149.

10. An Artist [John Varley], "Robert Ker Porter," *Somerset House Gazette*, 1824, 364.

11. Shee, *The Life of Sir Martin Archer Shee*, 151.

12. Thomas Frognall Dibdin, *Reminiscences of a Literary Life*, vol. I (London: John Major, 1836), 175.

13. [Jane Porter], "Miss Jane Porter," in *National Gallery of Illustrious and Eminent Personages of the Nineteenth Century; with Memoirs*, vol. 5, ed. William Jerdan

(London: Fisher, Son, & Jackson, 1834), 8. Some sources suggest Jane sat as a model for Benjamin West. The president of the Royal Academy she sat for may have been Martin Archer Shee.

14. JP to RKP, 20 June 1839, Spencer, Box 7, Folder 31.

15. Quoted in Ancketill, 626.

16. Percival Stockdale to JP, 13 April 1794, Houghton, MS Eng. 1250.

17. Royal Academy of Arts Archive, Attendance Records, RAA/KEE/2/2.

18. JP to AMP, 15 August 1793, HL, POR 1421.

19. AMP to Mrs. JP, 19 August 1793, Spencer, Box 9, Folder 2.

20. AMP to Elizabeth Dillon, 21 May 1824, HL, POR 218.

21. Lesley Peterson, "The Subscription List for Artless Tales," in Anna Maria Porter, *Artless Tales*, ed. Leslie Robertson et al. (Edmonton, Canada: Juvenilia Press, 2003), 129.

22. Porter, *Artless Tales* (2003), 4.

23. Article 45, review of *Artless Tales*, *Monthly Review*, vol. 12, September 1793, 112.

24. Review of *Artless Tales*, *Critical Review*, n.s. 9, 1793, 94–96.

25. "MARRIED In Spanish Town, Dr. Wm. Porter, of his majesty's ship Success, to Miss Lydia Helen Betts," *Postscript to the Royal Gazette*, October 4, 1794, 23.

26. The National Archives, *Tales from the Captain's Log* (London: Bloomsbury Publishing, 2017), 125.

27. RKP to JP, 5 November 1794, HL, POR 2420.

28. "Rochester Dinner," *Kentish Weekly Post*, May 12, 1809, 1.

29. RKP to JP, 12 July 1795, HL, POR 2424.

30. "To The Trustees of the Bristol Infirmary," *Bristol Mirror*, March 26, 1825, 3.

31. AMP to JP, 30 March 1795, HL, POR 337.

32. JP to RKP, 27 March 1833, Spencer, Box 4, Folder 25.

33. AMP to JP, 7 April 1795, HL, POR 339.

34. AMP to JP, 3[?] April 1795, HL, POR 338. The quoted material in this section is taken from this letter.

35. Anna Maria Porter, *Artless Tales; or, Romantic Effusions of the Heart* (London: Hookham and Carpenter, 1796).

36. AMP to JP, 22 February 1820, HL, POR 825.

37. Porter, *Artless Tales.*

38. Review of *Artless Tales, Critical Review*, vol. 15, October 1795, 236.

CHAPTER 3: TWO GIRLS MASQUERADING AS SOCIETY GENTLEMEN: JANE'S AND MARIA'S EARLY FICTIONS AND THE CAULFIELD BROTHERS (1794–97)

1. RKP to JP, 17 November 1794, HL, POR 2421.

2. JP, "Memorandums and Observations in March, 1796," Diary of 1796, Folger, M.a.17.

3. JP, 18 March, Diary of 1796, Folger, M.a.17.

4. JP, 30 June, Diary of 1796, Folger, M.a.17.

5. JP to Nathaniel Parker Willis, c. 1839, Morristown.

6. "War Office, December 10," *Caledonian Mercury*, December 16, 1793, 4; "War Office, Sept. 10," *Kentish Weekly Post*, September 16, 1796, 2.

7. JP, Note on Wade Caulfield, c. 1833, HL, POR 20.

8. "Wade's Hair," Spencer, Box 44, Folder 47; JP to AMP, 18–19 July 1812, HL, POR 1665.

9. "First Regiment of Foot Guards," *Caledonian Mercury*, January 2, 1800, 2.

10. "Domestic Occurrences," *The Athenaeum* 4, no. 23 (November 1808): 455.

11. Thomas Frognall Dibdin, *Reminiscences of a Literary Life*, vol. I (London: John Major, 1836), 144.

12. "Portraits," in *A Guide to the Exihibition of the Royal Academy for 1797, Part I* (London: G. Cawthorn, 1797), 25.

13. AMP, "Beauty: Sonnet to H. Caulfield," January 1797, Clark, Porter Folder 1/18; JP, 13 February, Diary of 1796, Folger, M.a.17.

14. JP, Memorandums, July, Diary of 1796, Folger, M.a.17.

15. JP, Memorandums, August, Diary of 1796, Folger, M.a.17.

16. JP to AMP, 7 April 1795, HL, POR 339.

17. JP, "My Rhyming Follies," 24 September 1794, BL, RP 7204.

18. Maria published more than a dozen poems under her own name in the first four volumes of *The Pocket Magazine*, from 1794 to 96. Several other poems in these volumes are dedicated to her as well.

19. JP to AMP, 7 October 1797, HL, POR 1431.

20. "Selina Davenport," in *Orlando*.

21. JP to Selina Wheler, 14 August 1794, Pforzheimer, PORT 94.08.14B.

22. Ibid., 94.08.11B.

23. Richard Davenport, "To Serena," *Monthly Visitor*, vol. 2, 1797, 55.

24. JP, 12 February, Diary of 1796, Folger, M.a.17.

25. JP to AMP, 16 April 1795, HL, POR 1427.

26. JP, Memorandums, March, Diary of 1796, Folger, M.a.17.

27. JP to Henry Caulfield, n.d., HL, POR 1285.

28. AMP to JP, 13 March 1804, HL, POR 439.

29. RKP to JP, 27 May 1794, HL, POR 2414.

30. Selina Wheler to JP, c. 1797, HL, POR 2653.

31. A Society of Gentlemen, *The Quiz*, vol. 1 (London: J. Parsons and T. Jones), 5, 15, 176.

32. JP to AMP, 14 April 1795, HL, POR 1425.

33. "Obituary: Miss Anna Maria Porter," *Gentleman's Magazine*, vol. CII, December 1832, 578.

34. W. C. [Wade Caulfield] to JP et al., 27 November 1797, Pforzheimer, PORT 97.11.27.

35. JP, 23–24 February, Diary of 1796, Folger, M.a.17.

36. Review of *Walsh Colville*, *Critical Review*, vol. 21, December 1797, 474.

37. Review of *Walsh Colville*, *Monthly Visitor*, vol. 1, 1797, 473.

38. AMP to JP, 14 October 1797, HL, POR 343.

39. JP to AMP, 2 October 1797, HL, POR 1430.

40. Wade Caulfield to Mrs. JP, c. 1798, HL, POR 153.

41. "Died.," *The Monthly Magazine*, vol. 6, September 1798, 234.

42. W. C. [Wade Caulfield] to JP et al., 27 November 1797, Pforzheimer, PORT 97.11.27. Jane added memorializing remarks in her own hand on this letter from Wade, after he died.

43. Will of Wade Francis Caulfield, National Archives, PROB 11/1306/196.

44. Will of Wade Toby Caulfield, National Archives, PROB 11/1346/336.

45. JP, Note on Wade Caulfield, c. 1833 HL, POR 20.

46. JP, "To the Spirit of Dear Wade," Spencer, Box 33, Folder 49.

47. "Selina Davenport," in *Orlando*.

48. AMP to JP, November[?] 1799[?], HL, POR 367.

49. AMP to JP, 14 October 1797, HL, POR 343.

CHAPTER 4: IN SPITE OF THE PRUDISH WORLD: THE SISTER NOVELISTS AND THE GREAT HISTORICAL PICTURE (1798–1800)

1. JP to Percival Stockdale, 22 October 1794, Clark, Porter Folder 1/3.

2. JP, 16 February, Diary of 1796, Folger, M.a.17.

3. RKP to JP, 19 October 1793, HL, POR 2412.

4. AMP to JP, 14 October 1797, HL, POR 343.

5. Ancketill, 31.

6. AMP to JP, November[?] 1799[?], HL, POR 367.

7. JP to AMP, 8 September 1799, HL, POR 1436; AMP to JP, November[?] 1799[?], HL, POR 367.

8. Anna Maria Porter, *Octavia*, vol. I (London: T. N. Longman, 1798), 61. The book was advertised in October 1798 and an edition of five hundred copies printed ("Anna Maria Porter," in *Orlando*).

9. [Reverend James Bannister], Review of *Octavia*, *Monthly Review*, vol. 27, March 1799, 346.

10. Review of *Octavia*, *Analytical Review*, vol. 28, November 1798, 518.

11. Review of *Octavia*, *Critical Review*, vol. 24, December 1798, 472.

12. AMP, "Stanzas on Mary Wollstonecraft's Grave" and "Lines on the Same Subject," 1800, Folger, N.a.4.

13. AMP to JP, April[?] 1804, HL, POR 465.

14. JP to AMP, 1 August 1801, HL, POR 1463.

15. "The School of Eloquence," Clark, Porter Family Scrapbook.

16. "The School of Eloquence," *Morning Chronicle*, April 18, 1799, 1.

17. Amanda Vickery, *The Gentleman's Daughter: Women's Lives in Georgian England* (New Haven: Yale University Press, 1998), 4.

18. AMP to JP, 14 October 1797, HL, POR 343.

19. Henry Caulfield, Commonplace Book, HL, POR 2.

20. "Ithuriel," Spencer, Box 34, Folder 39; Devoney Looser, "Mary Wollstonecraft, 'Ithuriel,' and the Rise of the Feminist Author-Ghost," *Tulsa Studies in Women's Literature* 35, no. 1 (March 2016): 59–91.

21. JP to AMP, 14 July 1801, HL, POR 1458.

22. JP to AMP, 7–20 July 1801, HL, POR 1457.

23. JP to RKP, 22 November 1799, HL, POR 2036.

24. JP to Mrs. JP, 13 December 1799, HL, POR 1887.

25. JP to AMP, 8 September 1799, HL, POR 1436.

26. Harriet Kramer Linkin, "The Citational Network of Tighe, Porter, Barbauld, Lefanu, Morgan, and Hemans," in *Women's Literary Networks and Romanticism: "A Tribe of Authoresses"* (Liverpool: Liverpool University Press, 2017), 199.

27. "Signatures," Jane Porter Poetry Volume, Folger, N.a.3.

28. AMP to JP, 26 December 1800, HL, POR 1073.

29. JP, 8 May, Diary of 1796, Folger, M.a.17.

30. JP, "Imitations," Clark, Porter Family Scrapbook.

31. Jane Porter, *The Spirit of the Elbe*, vol. 1 (London: Longman and Rees, 1799), 4.

32. "This Day is Published . . . *The Spirit of the Elbe*," *The Times*, March 13, 1799, 2.

33. Review of *The Spirit of the Elbe*, *The British Critic*, vol. XIV, 1799, 190.

34. AMP to JP, 5 August 1799, HL, POR 350.

35. JP to AMP, 22 September 1799, HL, POR 1437.

36. AMP to JP, 5 August 1799, HL, POR 350.

37. AMP to JP, 30–31 August 1799, HL, POR 352.

38. JP to AMP, 28 August 1799, HL, POR 1435.

39. JP to AMP, 8 September 1799, HL, POR 1436.

40. Probate of the Will of Elizabeth Rawlinson, Late of Grantham, 1800, Lincolnshire Archives, BRA 513/65.

41. JP to AMP, 26 September 1799, HL, POR 1438.

42. JP to AMP, 26 September 1799, HL, POR 1438.

43. JP to Mrs. JP, 14 December 1799, HL, POR 1888.

44. AMP to Mrs. JP, 27 June 1799, HL, POR 236.

45. AMP to JP, 29 October 1799, HL, POR 359.

46. AMP to JP, 11 November 1799, HL, POR 363.

47. JP to AMP, 11 October 1799, HL, POR 1440.

48. JP to AMP, 26 September 1799, HL, POR 1438.

49. JP to AMP, 14 November 1799, HL, POR 1444.

50. JP to Mrs. JP, 13 December 1799, HL, POR 1887.

51. AMP to JP, 21 December 1799, HL, POR 368.

52. AMP to JP, 8 October 1799, HL, POR 378.

53. AMP to JP, 18 November 1799, HL, POR 365.

54. William Porter (nephew) to Mrs. JP, 12 February 1792, HL, POR 2612.

55. "Obituary of Remarkable Persons," *Gentleman's Magazine*, vol. LXVI, February 1796, 168.

56. Will of Charles Kerr of Antigua, National Archives, PROB 11/1276/320; Vere Langford Oliver, *The History of the Island of Antigua*, vol 2. (London: Mitchell & Hughes, 1896), 119.

57. Ancketill, 42.

58. Ibid., 34–35.

59. Austin Brereton, *The Lyceum and Henry Irving* (London: Lawrence & Bullen, 1903), 27.

60. JP to AMP, 16 October 1799, HL, POR 1441.

61. C. B. Norman, *Battle Honours of the British Army* (London: John Murray, 1911), 87.

62. Earl of Warwick to RKP, 2 February 1800, Pforzheimer, PORT 00.02.02.

63. RKP to Mrs. JP, 26 July 1800, Spencer, Box 1, Folder 2.

64. F. G. Stephens, "William Mulready, R.A.," *The Portfolio*, January 1887, 120.

65. AMP to JP, 8 October 1799, HL, POR 357.

66. "News," *The Observer*, April 13, 1800, 2.

67. Leigh Cliffe, *Anecdotal Remembrances of Distinguished Literary and Political Characters* (London: R. & S. A. Bielefeld, 1830), 66.

68. Thomas Frognall Dibdin, *Reminiscences of a Literary Life*, vol. I (London: John Major, 1836), 145.

69. "Storming of Seringapatam," *Morning Chronicle*, April 23, 1800, 1.

70. Dibdin, *Reminscences*, 147–48.

71. RKP, 26 April 1801, Diary, V&A, SD.813. The Porters may have helped spread misinformation about Robert's age or, at the least, not refuted it.

72. [Mary Robinson], "Robert Ker Porter," in *Public Characters 1800–1801* (London: R. Phillips, 1801), 176.

73. AMP to JP, n.d., HL, POR 369.

74. "Storming of Seringapatam," *Star and Evening Advertiser*, July 15, 1800, 1.

75. "When the Castle Spectre . . . ," *The Observer*, July 15, 1800, 3.

76. RKP, Diary, "Receipts and Expenses," V&A, SD.813.

77. "Lyceum, Strand," *Morning Chronicle*, May 7, 1800, 3.

78. JP to AMP, 24 July 1801, HL, POR 1461.

CHAPTER 5: CUT MY HEART: JANE AND MARIA'S RIVAL MENTORS (1798–1801)

1. Anna Maria Porter, *Octavia*, vol. 1 (London: T. N. Longman, 1798), iii–iv.

2. Agnes Repplier, "The Perils of Immortality," *Harper's Magazine*, 1905, 627.

3. "Mrs. Crespigny," in *Public Characters for 1805* (London: Richard Phillips) 193–94.

4. AMP to JP, October[?] 1799[?], HL, POR 361.

5. JP to AMP, 27 June 1804, HL, POR 1511.

6. E. S. S. to JP, 12 June 1798, Spencer, Box 27, Folder 68.

7. "Mary Robinson," in *Orlando*.

8. JP to Miss Robinson, c. 1799, Pforzheimer, PORT 95A.

9. AMP to JP, 30–31 August 1799, HL, POR 352.

10. Mary Robinson to RKP, 15 April 1797, in *The Works of Mary Robinson*, ed. William D. Brewer et al. (London: Pickering & Chatto, 2010), part II, vol. 7, 308–9.

11. [Mary Robinson], "Robert Ker Porter," in *Public Characters 1800–1801* (London: R. Phillips, 1801), 176.

12. Jane wrote of "the roundabout way of writing thro' the means of your friend" in JP to Maria Elizabeth Robinson, undated, *The Works of Mary Robinson*, part II, vol. 7, 327.

13. AMP to JP, 22 September 1799, HL, POR 355.

14. "Original Poetry," *Morning Post*, June 16, 1800, 1; *The Works of Mary Robinson*, part II, vol. 2, 433.

15. "Lady Dashwood-King's Masquerade," *Morning Post*, June 12, 1800, 1.

16. JP, "Verses that were given in the character of a Flower-Girl, by Miss Myers—at Lady Dashwood's Masquerade. I wrote them to be tied to Flowers," Poems, Folger, N.a.3.

17. Mrs. Robinson, "To Miss Porter, in the Character of a Nun," and "To Miss Maria Porter, as Roxalana," in *The Works of Mary Robinson*, part II, vol. 2, 90–91.

18. Mary Robinson to JP [between 12 June and 16 July 1800] and Mary Robinson to RKP, 3 July 1800, in *The Works of Mary Robinson*, part II, vol. 7, 312.

19. Eliza Fenwick to Mary Hays, c. 29 July, 1800, *The Works of Mary Robinson*, part II, vol. 7, 313–14.

20. Mary Robinson to RKP, 11 September 1800, in *The Works of Mary Robinson*, part II, vol. 7, 326.

21. Ibid.

22. AMP to JP, 24 December 1800, HL, POR 1072.

23. JP, 3–4 January 1801, Diary of 1801–03, Folger, M.b.15.

24. JP to Miss Robinson (copy), 1 January 1801, Spencer, Box 3, Folder 18.

25. JP, 4 January 1801, Diary of 1801–03, Folger. M.b.15.

26. JP, "Lines supposed to be written in Old Windsor Church Yard, at the Grave of the Celebrated Mrs. Robinson," Poems, Folger, N.a.3.

27. Repplier, "The Perils of Immortality," 629.

28. Ina Mary White, "A Page from the Past: Selections from a Diary of Miss Jane Porter," *Cornhill Magazine*, 1902, 216.

29. JP, 13 February 1801, Diary of 1801–03, Folger, M.b.15.

30. JP, "Rise at 6," Clark, Porter Family Scrapbook.

31. JP, 13–20 January 1801, Diary of 1801–03, Folger, M.b.15.

32. JP, 7 February 1801, Diary of 1801–03, Folger, M.b.15.

33. JP, 29 January 1801, Diary of 1801–03, Folger, M.b.15.

34. JP, 3 February 1801, Diary of 1801–03, Folger, M.b.15.

35. In the original, there is an errant "or" after the word "making," AMP to JP, 8 October 1799, HL, POR 357.

CHAPTER 6: GONE THEATRICAL MAD: MARIA'S PLAYS, JANE'S NEW ROMANCE, AND THE ENCHANTING KEMBLES (1801)

1. AMP to JP, 15–16 February 1801, HL, POR 388.

2. Ben P. Robertson, *Elizabeth Inchbald's Reputation: A Publishing and Reception History* (London: Pickering & Chatto, 2013), 116.

3. AMP to JP, December[?] 1799[?], HL, POR 366.

4. AMP to JP, 17 December 1800, HL, POR 373.

5. JP, 23 February 1801, Diary of 1801–03, Folger, M.b.15.

6. "If a Woman," Spencer, Box 42, Folder 10.

7. JP, 11 March 1801, Diary of 1801–03, Folger, M.b.15.

8. AMP to JP, 21 August 1799, HL, POR 351.

9. AMP to JP, October[?] 1799[?], HL, POR 349.

10. AMP to JP, December[?] 1799[?], HL, POR 366.

11. Surviving correspondence suggests that Jane may have been the main author, working with Maria's assistance. In later works by Robert, Maria often contributed in uncredited ways by undertaking historical research that was foundational to Jane's writing. It's likely that it's this kind of research help Maria gave Jane to complete *A Defence of the Profession of an Actor.*

12. [Jane Porter and Anna Maria Porter], *A Defence of the Profession of an Actor* (London: W. Miller, 1800), 3, 6, 13. They wrote, "The bright path in the career of life, which the steadfast step of Mrs. Siddons has irradiated, will make evident to every eye, the truth which animates these pages" (3).

13. [Dr. Charles Burney], Review of *A Defence of the Profession of an Actor*, *Monthly Review*, vol. XXXIV, April 1801, 384–86.

14. AMP to JP, October[?] 1799[?], HL, POR 349.

15. AMP to JP, 22 September 1799, HL, POR 355.

16. Joel L. Gold, "Kearsley, George," in *Biographical Dictionary of Modern British Radicals*, vol. I, *1770–1830*, ed. Joseph O. Baylen and Norbert J. Gossman (Sussex: Harvester Press, 1979), 275–76.

17. AMP to JP, 22 September 1799, HL, POR 355; JP to AMP, 9 August 1801, HL, POR 1466.

18. AMP to JP, 11 November 1799, HL, POR 363.

19. AMP to JP, October[?] 1799[?], HL, POR 349.

20. JP to AMP, 2 October 1799, HL, POR 1439.

21. AMP to JP, 28 September 1799, HL, POR 356.

22. AMP to JP, October[?] 1799[?], HL, POR 349.

23. JP to AMP, 2 October 1799, HL, POR 1439.

24. "Pic Nic Fete," *The Times*, June 28, 1802, 3.

25. "Private Theatricals," *Morning Post*, November 22, 1802, 3.

26. JP, 14 February 1801, Diary of 1801–03, Folger, M.b.15.

27. AMP to JP, 23–28 June 1801, HL, POR 396.

28. AMP to JP, 22 February 1801, HL, POR 390.

29. AMP to JP, October[?] 1799[?], HL, POR 349.

30. JP, 14 February 1801, Diary of 1801–03, Folger, M.b.15.

31. JP, 15 February 1801, Diary of 1801–03, Folger, M.b.15.

32. Material in the above paragraphs is from AMP to JP, 1800[?] HL, POR 379. Dialogue in this section has been slightly modified from the original in capitalization and punctuation for greater readability.

33. AMP to JP, 22 February 1801, HL, POR 390.

34. AMP to JP, 23–28 June 1801, HL, POR 396.

35. AMP to JP, 28 January 1801, HL, POR 384.

36. AMP to JP, 16[?] August 1802[?], HL, POR 413.

37. Jane Williamson, *Charles Kemble: Man of the Theatre* (Lincoln: University of Nebraska Press, 1964), 15.

38. Ibid., 18.

39. "Theatre: Drury Lane," *London Courier and Evening Gazette*, January 1, 1801, 3. The reviewer describes Kemble's performance as best represented by "coldness, languor, and monotony" and says "how little he is qualified" for the part.

40. JP, "The Contest of Venus with Erato," Poems, Folger, N.a.3.

41. Williamson, *Charles Kemble*, 24.

42. AMP to JP, 24 December 1800, HL, POR 1072.

43. AMP to JP, 15–16 February 1801, HL, POR 388.

44. AMP to JP, 7 January 1801, HL, POR 381.

45. JP, 13 March 1801, Diary of 1801–03, Folger, M.b.15.

46. Jane Porter, *Two Princes of Persia: Addressed to Youth* (London: Crosby and Letterman, 1801), xxiii. Extracts from the book were published in magazines ("Jane Porter," in *Orlando*).

47. JP, 20 March 1801, Diary of 1801–03, Folger, M.b.15.

48. JP, 25 March 1801, Diary of 1801–03, Folger, M.b.15.

49. JP, 26 March 1801, Diary of 1801–03, Folger, M.b.15.

50. JP, 6 April 1801, Diary of 1801–03, Folger, M.b.15.

51. RKP, 18 April 1801, Diary, V&A, SD.813.

52. AMP to JP, 4 November 1804, HL, POR 453.

53. JP, 7 April 1801, Diary of 1801–03, Folger, M.b.15.

54. JP, 16 April 1801, Diary of 1801–03, Folger, M.b.15.

55. JP, 22 April 1801, Diary of 1801–03, Folger, M.b.15.

56. RKP, 27 April 1801, Diary, V&A, SD.813.

57. JP to AMP, 30 July 1801, HL, POR 1462.

58. RKP, June–September 1801, Diary, V&A, SD.813.

59. RKP to JP, 11 July 1801, Spencer, Box 1, Folder 9.

60. JP, "A Visit from Aunt Bridget or, Traveling at Home," Spencer, Box 33, Folder 1.

CHAPTER 7: "THE FIRE! THE SPLENDOUR!": MARIA'S OPERA, JANE'S BESTSELLER, AND THE WAR HERO, SIR SIDNEY SMITH (1802–3)

1. Tom Pocock, *A Thirst for Glory: The Life of Admiral Sir Sidney Smith* (London: Pimlico, 1998), 113–14.

2. G. Lenôtre, *Romances of the French Revolution*, vol. 2, trans. Frederic Lees (London: William Heinemann, 1908), 51.

3. RKP, December 1801, Diary, V&A, SD.813.

4. All the above material is from JP, 11 December 1801, Diary of 1801–03, Folger, M.b.15.

5. JP, 2 December 1801, Diary of 1801–03, Folger, M.b.15.

6. Charles Kirkpatrick Sharpe, *Etchings with Photographs* (Edinburgh: Blackwood, 1869), 21.
7. JP, 8 March 1802, Diary of 1801–03, Folger, M.b.15.
8. JP, December 1801–January 1802, Diary of 1801–03, Folger, M.b.15.
9. AMP to JP, 28 August 1801, HL, POR 408.
10. "Anna Maria Porter," in *Orlando*.
11. AMP to JP, 17 December 1800, HL, POR 372.
12. AMP to JP, 8 September 1801, HL, POR 411.
13. AMP to JP, 24–25 August 1802, HL, POR 414.
14. AMP to JP, 28 January 1801, HL, POR 384.
15. AMP to JP, 24–25 August 1802, HL, POR 1802.
16. JP, 25 February 1801, Diary of 1801–03, Folger, M.b.15.
17. JP to AMP, 22 July 1801, HL, POR 1460.
18. "Jane Porter," in *Orlando*; Thomas McLean, *The Other East and Nineteenth-Century British Literature* (New York: Palgrave Macmillan, 2012), 69.
19. Jane Porter, *Thaddeus of Warsaw*, vol. 1 (London: Longman and Rees, 1803), 79.
20. McLean, *The Other East and Nineteenth-Century British Literature*, 69.
21. Jane Porter, *Thaddeus of Warsaw: A Novel*, ed. Thomas McLean and Ruth Knezevich (Edinburgh: Edinburgh University Press, 2019), 228.
22. JP to Mrs. JP, 17 August 1802, HL, POR 1891.
23. Jane Porter, *Thaddeus of Warsaw: A Novel* (Edinburgh: Edinburgh University Press, 2019), 2.
24. "This Day was Published," *The Star* April 4, 1803, 1.
25. "Memoir of Miss Porter," *Monthly Mirror*, vol. 8, December 1810, 403.
26. "The Drama," *Monthly Visitor*, vol. 4, May 1803, 80.
27. "The Theatre," *The Sun*, May 17, 1803, 3.
28. "The Fair Fugitive," *Morning Post*, May 20, 1803.

29. "The Drama," *Monthly Visitor*, vol. 4, May 1803, 80.

30. "Drama," *Monthly Register*, June 1803, 83.

31. "Public Amusements," *Lady's Monthly Museum*, June 1803, 416.

32. "The Fair Fugitive," *Morning Post*, May 20, 1803, 1.

33. "Account of the New Musical Entertainment called 'The Fair Fugitives,'" *The Lady's Magazine*, vol. 34, May 1803, 267.

34. *Airs, Duets, Choruses, & c. In the Fair Fugitives, A Musical Entertainment, as Performed at the Theatre Royal, Covent Garden. The Overture and Music Entirely New, and Composed by Dr. Busby* (London: Longman and Rees, 1803).

35. Review of *Thaddeus of Warsaw*, *Anti-Jacobin Review*, vol. 19, September 1804, 78.

36. Review of *Thaddeus of Warsaw*, *Monthly Register*, vol. 3, May 1803, 16; Review of *Thaddeus of Warsaw*, in *Flowers of Literature for 1803* (London: B. Crosby, 1804), 461.

37. Review of *Thaddeus of Warsaw*, *Imperial Review*, vol. 1, February 1804, 314.

38. "Literature and Polite Arts," in *New Annual Register for the Year 1803* (London: G and J. Robinson, 1804), 329.

39. AMP to JP, 8–12 September 1803, HL, POR 428.

40. WOP to Mrs. JP, 5 June 1804, Durham; WOP to Mrs. JP, 11 September 1804, Durham.

41. RKP, 18 April 1803, Diary, V&A, SD.813.

42. AMP to JP, 13 March 1804, HL, POR 439. Michael Adams estimates that *Thaddeus of Warsaw* went through eighty-four editions and printings across the nineteenth century. See "Jane Porter," in *Dictionary of Literary Biography*, vol. 116 (Detroit: Gale Research, 1992), 264.

CHAPTER 8: HEARTS AND DARTS: MARIA'S SIGHING SOLDIER (1803–4)

1. AMP to JP, 9 January 1805, HL, POR 475.

2. AMP to JP, 3–4 July 1803, HL, POR 420.

3. R. K. Webb, "Aspland, Robert (1782–1845)," in *Oxford Dictionary of National Biography* (Oxford: Oxford University Press), 2004.

4. Robert Brook Aspland, *Memoir of the Life, Work, and Correspondence of Rev. Robert Aspland, Of Hackney* (London: Edward Whitfield, 1850), 120.

5. AMP to JP, 3–4 July 1803, HL, POR 420.

6. AMP, "Poetry: Verses to a Glow-Worm, Which a Gentleman Had Taken from a Hedge, in the Isle of Wight, and Given Into My Care," *Monthly Repository*, vol. 2, October 1807, 551.

7. AMP to JP, 4 July 1803, HL, POR 421.

8. AMP to JP, 14–16 July 1803, HL, POR 422.

9. AMP to JP, 4 July 1803, HL, POR 421.

10. AMP to JP, 3–4 July 1803, HL, POR 420.

11. Ibid.

12. AMP to JP, 14–16 July 1803, HL, POR 422.

13. Anna Maria Porter, *The Lake of Killarney* (London: Longman and Rees, 1804), vol. 2, 254; vol. 3, 63, 76. An American edition was published in 1810, with English editions published in 1833, 1838, and 1839 ("Anna Maria Porter," in *Orlando*).

14. AMP to JP, 14–16 July 1803, HL, POR 421.

15. JP to AMP, 26 July 1803, HL, POR 1482.

16. A Gentleman Abroad [Anna Maria Porter], "The Serenade: or, Green Griffin," *The Sentinel, or, British Miscellany and Review* (November 1804), 294.

17. AMP to JP, 25 July 1803, HL, POR 424.

18. AMP to JP, 24 January 1805, HL, POR 478.

19. AMP to JP, 28 July 1803, HL, POR 425.

20. AMP to JP, 14 January 1805, HL, POR 476.

21. AMP to JP, 9 March 1805, HL, POR 483.

22. AMP to JP, c. 1804, HL, POR 469.

23. AMP to JP, 14 January 1805, HL, POR 476.

24. AMP to JP, December[?] 1806[?], HL, POR 546.

25. "The West India Regiments," National Army Museum, n.d., www.nam.ac.uk/explore/slaves-red-coats-west-india-regiment.

26. David Lambert, "[A] Mere Cloak for their Proud Contempt and Antipathy towards the African Race': Imagining Britain's West India Regiments in the Caribbean, 1795–1838," *The Journal of Imperial and Commonwealth History* 46, no. 4 (2018): 630.

27. In 1808, there was a mutiny among the Second West India Regiment, with fourteen killed, five wounded, two dozen taken prisoner, ten tried, and seven executed. Frederick Cowell was, by then, no longer with the regiment. There were more than three hundred thousand enslaved people in Jamaica during the period Cowell was stationed there. See Frederic William Naylor Bayley, *Four Years' Residence in the West Indies: During the Years 1826, 7, 8, and 9* (London: William Kidd, 1833), 621.

28. AMP to JP, 25 January 1804[?], HL, POR 432.

29. AMP to JP, 29 October–1 November 1804, HL, POR 454.

30. Birth and death records for Frederick Luke Gardiner Cowell, son of George Cowell and Amelia White Cowell, support an estimated birth year of 1786–87. See John O'Hart, *Irish Pedigrees; or, the Origin and Stem of the Irish Nation*, 5th ed., vol. 1 (Dublin: James Duffy, 1892), 395.

31. AMP to JP, 20 July 1804[?], HL, POR 423.

32. AMP to JP, 22 May 1805, HL, POR 497.

33. AMP to JP, 23 March 1805, HL, POR 486.

34. AMP to JP, c. 1804, HL, POR 469.

35. AMP to JP, 24 August 1803, HL, POR 426.

36. JP to AMP, 4 July 1805, HL, POR 1564.

37. AMP to JP, 16 March 1805, HL, POR 485.

38. JP to AMP, 23–24 June 1801, HL, POR 1451.

39. AMP to JP, 24 August 1803, HL, POR 426.

40. JP to AMP, 27 August 1803, HL, POR 1485.

41. AMP to JP, 9 March 1805, HL, POR 483.

42. AMP to JP, March[?] 1806[?], HL, POR 524.

43. AMP to JP, 6–7 September 1804, HL, POR 449.

44. JP to AMP, 5 September 1804, HL, POR 1517.

45. AMP to JP, 13 May 1805, HL, POR 496.

46. AMP to JP, 23 March 1805, HL, POR 486.

47. AMP to JP, 14 January 1805, HL, POR 476.

48. RKP to JP, 7 June 1804, HL, POR 2442.

49. "This Day Was Published," *The Star*, August 6, 1804, 4.

50. AMP to JP, 14 April 1804, HL, POR 444.

51. Ad for *The Sentinel*, *The Times*, August 9, 1804, 1.

52. "For Editing Six Numbers," Clark, Porter Family Scrapbook.

53. JP to AMP, 10 September 1804, HL, POR 1520.

54. JP to AMP, 27 October 1804, HL, POR 1524.

55. JP to AMP, 13 October 1804, HL, POR 452.

56. JP to AMP, 29 October–1 November 1804, HL, POR 454.

57. AMP to JP, c. 1804, HL, POR 466.

58. JP to AMP, 1 September 1804, HL, POR 1516.

59. AMP to JP, 23 March 1805, HL, POR 486.

60. AMP to JP, 8 March 1804, HL, POR 438.

CHAPTER 9: HOW WILD IS THE WORLD: CELEBRITY JANE'S SUITORS AND A DEFENSE OF CRIM. CON. (1804)

1. JP to AMP, 10 February 1804, HL, POR 1494.

2. Algernon Graves, *The Royal Academy of the Arts: A Complete Dictionary of Contributors*, vol. 6 (London: Henry Graves, 1906), 308; JP to Mrs. JP, 4 August 1799, HL, POR 1885.

3. JP to AMP, 17 June 1801, HL, POR 1449.

4. Mrs. JP to AMP, 25[?] June 1801, HL, POR 1050.

5. Charles Rivers to JP, 16 February 1804, Pforzheimer, PORT 04.02.16.

6. AMP to JP, 3 March 1804, HL, POR 437.

7. JP to AMP, 11–13 February 1804, HL, POR 1495.

8. JP to AMP, 25 August 1803, HL, POR 1484.

9. "Died," *Morning Post*, October 4, 1802, 4.

10. "Births, Deaths, Marriages," *Scots Magazine*, vol. 66, January 1804, 78.

11. JP to AMP, 13–27 February 1804, HL, POR 1496.

12. RKP to John Porter, 17 December 1803, HL, POR 2592.

13. AMP to JP, 16 February 1804, HL, POR 434.

14. JP to AMP, 11–13 February 1804, HL, POR 1495.

15. Phyllis M. Hembry, *The English Spa, 1560–1815: A Social History* (Madison, NJ: Fairleigh Dickinson University Press, 1990), 123.

16. JP to AMP, 13–27 February 1804, HL, POR 1496.

17. JP to AMP, 11–13 February 1804, HL, POR 1495.

18. JP to Mrs. JP and AMP, 11–13 February 1804, HL, POR 1495. The quotations in this section have been modified slightly from the original, which presents them only partially in direct dialogue.

19. JP to AMP, 11–13 February 1804, HL, POR 1495.

20. AMP to JP, c. 1804[?], HL, POR 547.

21. AMP to JP, 29 February 1804, HL, POR 436.

22. JP, 3 February 1803, Diary of 1801–03, Folger, M.b.15.

23. "Theatre Royal, Covent Garden," *Morning Chronicle*, February 17, 1803, 3.

24. "Theatre Royal Bath," *Bath Chronicle and Weekly Gazette*, February 23, 1804, 3.

25. JP to Mrs. JP, 18 February 1804, HL, POR 1897.

26. JP to AMP, 13–27 February 1804, HL, POR 1496.

27. "Hon. Mr. Caulfield," *Caledonian Mercury*, January 4, 1800, 3.

28. Anna Maria Porter, *The Lake of Killarney: A Novel*, vol. 1 (London: Longman and Rees, 1804), 239.

29. JP to AMP, 27 February 1804, HL, POR 1497.

30. JP to AMP, 13–27 February 1804, HL, POR 1496.

31. Ibid.

32. JP to AMP, 27 February 1804, HL, POR 1497.

33. JP to AMP, 11 March 1804, HL, POR 1499.

34. JP to AMP, 13 March 1804, HL, POR 1500.

35. JP to AMP, 13–27 February 1804, HL, POR 1496.

36. JP to AMP, 6 March 1804, HL, POR 1498.

37. JP to Mrs. JP, 3 March 1804, HL, POR 1899.

38. JP to AMP, 13–27 February 1804, HL, POR 1496.

39. Keith Hanley, "Walter Savage Landor," in *British Romantic Poets, 1789–1832, First Series, Dictionary of Literary Biography*, vol. 93 (Detroit: Gale, 1990), 200–201.

40. Stephen Wheeler, ed., *The Letters and Other Unpublished Writings of Walter Savage Landor* (London: Richard Bentley, 1897), 18–19.

41. JP to AMP, 13 March 1804, HL, POR 1500.

42. JP to AMP, 20 March 1804, HL, POR 1501.

43. Ibid.

44. JP to AMP and Mrs. JP, 22 March 1804, HL, POR 1900.

45. JP to AMP, 13 March 1804, HL, POR 1500.

46. JP to Mrs. JP, 23 March 1804, HL, POR 1901.

47. JP to AMP, 27 February 1804, HL, POR 1497.

48. JP to AMP, 1 April 1804, HL, POR 1502.

49. AMP to JP, 31 March 1804, HL, POR 442.

50. JP to AMP, 28 March 1804, HL, POR 1503.

51. JP to AMP, 3 April 1804, HL, POR 1504.

52. AMP to JP, April[?] 1804, HL, POR 443.

53. JP to AMP, 11 March 1804, HL, POR 1499.

54. JP to AMP, 5 April 1804, HL, POR 1505.

55. RKP, 10 February 1803, Diary, V&A, SD.813.

56. "*Jones v. Chambers*," *British Press*, May 16, 1804, 3.

57. "Court of Chancery: *Chambers v. Collins*," *The Sun*, August 17, 1805, 4. This piece lists the Chambers's children as William, age nineteen, Auriol, seventeen, Augustus, fourteen, Frederick, Newton, Jane, and Courtney, age seven. Elsewhere they are reported as William, George, Auriol, Frederick, Luke, Augustus, Newlon, Jane Eliza, Courtnay, and Montague.

58. Ancketill, 70.

59. JP to AMP, 2 June 1804, HL, POR 1580.

60. JP to AMP, 3 June 1804, HL, POR 1509.

61. JP to AMP, 6 June 1804, HL, POR 1510.

62. "In Justice to the Lady in Question," Spencer, Box 42, Folder 29.

63. JP to AMP, 19 July 1804, HL, POR 1514.

64. JP to Mary Campbell, 12 July 1804, HL, POR 1298.

65. JP to AMP, 5 September 1804, HL, POR 1517.

66. Anne Boscawen to AMP, 1804[?], HL, POR 145.

67. AMP to JP, 6 December 1804, HL, POR 460.

68. Quoted in JP to AMP, 29 November–1 December 1804, HL, POR 1530.

69. JP to AMP, 15 December 1804, HL, POR 1533.

70. JP to AMP, 27–28 November 1804, HL, POR 1529.

71. JP to AMP, 5 November 1804, HL, POR 1526.

72. JP to AMP, 11 April 1805, HL, POR 1555.

73. AMP to JP, 21 December 1804, HL, POR 461.

74. JP to AMP, 11 January 1805, HL, POR 1537.

75. Richard Johnson, *The Trial at Large of Capt. J.* [sic] *Caulfield, Esq. for Criminal Conversation with the Wife of Captain George Chambers, Esq.* (London: R. Butters, [1804]), 8.

76. Ibid.

77. Johnson, *The Trial*, 9–10, 12.

78. "*Chambers v. Caulfield*," *Public Ledger and Daily Advertiser*, January 28, 1805, 3.

79. "Captain Caulfield," *Leeds Intelligencer*, February 4, 1805, 1.

80. "Chambers v. Caulfield," *Morning Chronicle*, February 11, 1805, 3.

81. JP to AMP, 14–17 December 1804, HL, POR 1532.

CHAPTER 10: TAKING UP A ROSE WITH THE LEFT HAND: THE PORTER WOMEN SECRETLY RETRENCH, AS JANE IS NEARLY BURIED ALIVE (1804–5)

1. AMP to JP, 8–12 September 1803, HL, POR 428.

2. AMP to JP, 29 February 1804, HL, POR 436.

3. AMP to JP, 8 March 1804, HL, POR 438.

4. Margravine of Anspach to RKP, 31 August 1804, Spencer, Box 17, Folder 23.

5. AMP to JP, 2 January 1805, HL, POR 474.

6. Margravine of Anspach to RKP, 31 August 1804, Spencer, Box 17, Folder 23.

7. William and Lydia Porter had three sons. Death records point to a likely birth of Charles Lempriere Porter in 1799 and a likely birth of Thaddeus Sobieski Porter in 1803–4. For Charles, see "Died," *Bristol Mercury*, February 22, 1831, 3. For Thaddeus, see "Deaths Abroad," *Monthly Magazine*, vol. 59, part. 1, no. 407 (March 1825): 185. A third namesake son, William, died in childhood.

8. JP to AMP, 2 September 1803, HL, POR 1487.

9. AMP to JP, 18 February 1804, HL, POR 435.

10. Mrs. JP to JP, 13[?] March 1804[?], HL, POR 1077.

11. Mrs. JP to AMP, 9 July 1804, HL, POR 1512.

12. JP to AMP, 12 September 1804, HL, POR 1521. The Porters kept in contact with "faithful Nanny" who "shared so often in our afflictions" for many years after she left their employment. See AMP to JP, 12–13 June 1806, HL, POR 535.

13. JP to AMP, 11 July 1804, HL, POR 1513.

14. JP to Mrs. JP, 26 May 1804, HL, POR 1903.

15. AMP to JP, 8 March 1804, HL, POR 438.

16. AMP to JP, 6–7 September 1804, HL, POR 449.

17. AMP to JP, 9 January 1805, HL, POR 475.

18. Mrs. JP to JP and AMP, 9 July 1804, HL, POR 1512.

19. AMP to JP, 2 June 1804, HL, POR 447.

20. JP to AMP, 12 September 1804, HL, POR 1521.

21. Percival Stockdale to JP, 8 September 1804, Houghton.

22. Percival Stockdale to JP, 4 December 1798, Houghton.

23. Percival Stockdale to JP, 4 January 1795, Houghton.

24. Percival Stockdale to John Stockdale, 5 October 1801, NLS, MS 967, f. 190; Percival Stockdale to JP, 28 November 1801, Houghton; Percival Stockdale to JP, 30 September 1801, Houghton.

25. Percival Stockdale to JP, 5 May 1796, Houghton.

26. Percival Stockdale to JP, 31 May 1803, Houghton.

27. Percival Stockdale to JP, 31 March 1803, Houghton.

28. Percival Stockdale to JP, 8 March 1795, Houghton.

29. Percival Stockdale to JP, 25 October 1802, Houghton.

30. JP to AMP, 12 September 1804, HL, POR 1521.

31. AMP to JP, 12 September 1804, HL, POR 450.

32. JP to Mrs. JP, 15 October 1804, HL, POR 1905.

33. JP to AMP, 17 October 1804, HL, POR 1523.

34. Mrs. JP to Percival Stockdale, 10 October 1804, HL, POR 1263.

35. JP to Mrs. JP, 15 October 1804, HL, POR 1905.

36. JP to AMP, 17 October 1804, HL, POR 1523.

37. JP to Mrs. JP, 15 October 1804, HL, POR 1905.

38. JP to AMP, 4 November 1804, HL, POR 1525.

39. JP to Mrs. JP, 15 October 1804, HL, POR 1905.

40. William Johnson Temple to Edward Jerningham, 19 July 1785, quoted in Howard Weinbrot, "Samuel Johnson, Percival Stockdale, and Brick-Bats from Grubstreet: Some Later Response to the "Lives of the Poets," *Huntington Library Quarterly* 56, no. 2 (Spring 1993): 109.

41. Quoted in Weinbrot, "Samuel Johnson," 110.

42. JP to Mrs. JP, 15 October 1804, HL, POR 1905.

43. JP to AMP, 2 November 1804, HL, POR 1525.

44. JP to AMP, 17 October 1804, HL, POR 1523.

45. AMP to JP, 5–7 May 1805, HL, POR 494.

46. JP to AMP, 29 November–1 December 1804, HL, POR 1530.

47. Kenneth Neill Cameron, ed., *Shelley and His Circle, 1773–1822*, vol. 3 (Cambridge: Harvard University Press, 1970), 198.

48. "The Annual Meeting of the Stockton Bible Auxiliary Society," *Durham County Advertiser*, May 27, 1815, 3.

49. JP to AMP, 29 November–1 December 1804, HL, POR 1530.

50. JP to AMP, 9 April 1805, HL, POR 1553.

51. JP to AMP, 14–17 December 1804, HL, POR 1532.

52. JP to AMP, 11 April 1805, HL, POR 1555.

53. JP to AMP, 15 December 1804, HL, POR 1533.

54. JP to AMP, 14–17 December 1804, HL, POR 1532.

55. JP to AMP, 2 January 1805, HL, POR 1536.

56. JP to AMP, 14–17 December 1804, HL, POR 1532.

57. JP to AMP, 16 February 1805, HL, POR 1544.

58. AMP to JP, 18 January 1805, HL, POR 477.

59. AMP to JP, 14 January 1805, HL, POR 476.

60. JP to AMP, 22–26 January 1805, HL, POR 1539.

61. JP to AMP, 9–10 February 1805, HL, POR 1543.

62. JP to AMP, 22–24 February 1805, HL, POR 1545.

63. JP to AMP, 1–5 April 1805, HL, POR 1552. Jane didn't write a book with this historical backdrop, but Sir Walter Scott did, with *Waverley* (1814), which he claims he first began in 1805. Interestingly, Jane had a similar idea around the same time.

64. AMP to JP, 5–7 February 1805, HL, POR 480.

65. AMP to JP, May[?] 1805, HL, POR 498.

66. AMP to JP, 12 June 1805, HL, POR 500.

67. JP to AMP, 9 June 1805, HL, POR 1562.

68. Mrs. JP and AMP to JP, [5 September] 1816, HL, POR 1140.

69. Percival Stockdale to JP, 27 July 1805, Houghton.

70. Percival Stockdale to JP, 4 March 1806, Houghton.

CHAPTER 11: WHERE THE SCALE TURNS: JANE'S WARRING PASSIONS AND ROBERT'S RUSSIAN ADVENTURES (1805–7)

1. Mrs. JP to JP, [20 March] 1805, HL, POR 1083.

2. RKP to Mrs. JP, 6 May 1805, HL, POR 2298.

3. JP to Mrs. JP, 13 July 1805, HL, POR 1911.

4. Mrs. JP to JP, [20 March] 1805, HL, POR 1083.

5. Sir H. Clinton to RKP, 16 July 1805, Spencer, Box 20, Folder 38.

6. AMP to JP, March[?] 1806[?], HL, POR 525.

7. JP to AMP, 7 November 1805, HL, POR 1579.

8. AMP to JP, March[?] 1806[?], HL, POR 525.

9. Mrs. JP to Dear Sir, c. 1806[?], HL, POR 1040.

10. T. S. Mercer, "New Facts About Two Famous Authoresses," *Esher News*, February 13, 1959, n.p.

11. Mrs. JP and JP to AMP, 15 November 1805, HL, POR 1581.

12. AMP to JP, 19–20 November 1805, HL, POR 248.

13. Mercer, "New Facts About Two Famous Authoresses," n.p.

14. AMP to JP, September[?] 1822[?], HL, POR 869.

15. "Reminiscences of By-Gone Days," *Surrey Comet*, August 5, 1854, 1.

16. Mrs. JP to JP, 14 April 1806, HL, POR 1085.

17. AMP to JP, 10 January 1809, HL, POR 598.

18. Mrs. JP to AMP, 2–3 December 1805, HL, POR 1054.

19. RKP to JP, 20 October 1805, Spencer, Box 1, Folder 19.

20. *King's Bench and Fleet Prison Discharge Books and Prisoner Lists, 1734–1862*, Piece 144: King's Bench Prison: List of Prisoners (1806), via Ancestry.com.

21. JP to AMP, 13 July 1805, HL, POR 1565.

22. Mrs. JP and JP to AMP, 15[?] October 1805, HL, POR 1573.

23. Henry Caulfield, Commonplace Book, HL, POR 2.

24. Mrs. JP and JP to AMP, 29 October 1805, HL, POR 1576.

25. JP to AMP, 7 September 1803, HL, POR 1489.

26. AMP to JP, 24 January 1805, HL, POR 478.

27. JP to AMP, 29 September 1805, HL, POR 1570.

28. JP to AMP, 23 October 1805, HL, POR 1574.

29. Tawny Paul, *The Poverty of Disaster: Debt and Insecurity in Eighteenth-Century Britain* (Cambridge: Cambridge University Press, 2019), 113.

30. Jane Porter, *Thaddeus of Warsaw: A Novel*, ed. Thomas McLean and Ruth Knezevich (Edinburgh: Edinburgh University Press, 2019), 285.

31. AMP to JP, 2 July 1806, HL, POR 540.

32. RKP to JP, 4 December 1829, HL, POR 2401.

33. Mrs. JP and AMP to JP, 1 March 1805, HL, POR 1082.

34. Mrs. JP and AMP to JP, 26 December 1804, HL, POR 1080.

35. RKP to JP, 14 February 1806, Spencer, Box 1, Folder 23.

36. JP to AMP, 31 May 1806, HL, POR 1590.

37. Anne Boscawen to AMP, c. 1804[?], HL, POR 145.

38. JP to AMP, n.d., HL, POR 1476.

39. JP to AMP, c. 4 May 1815, HL, POR 1711.

40. JP to AMP, 26–27 June 1806, HL, POR 1591.

41. JP to AMP, 27 June 1806, HL, POR 1592.

42. AMP to JP, March[?] 1806[?], HL, POR 525.

43. AMP to JP, March[?] 1806[?], HL, POR 525.

44. JP to AMP, 18 January 1824, HL, POR 1825.

45. AMP to JP, 6 November 1805, HL, POR 510.

46. JP to AMP, 27 May 1805, Spencer, Box 23, Folder 20.

47. JP to AMP, c. 1807, HL, POR 1631.

48. JP to AMP, 21 December 1806, HL, POR 1608.

49. Mrs. JP to JP, n.d., HL, POR 1147.

50. JP to Mrs. JP, 12 March 1806, HL, POR 1917.

51. Jane Porter, ed., *Aphorisms of Sir Philip Sidney, with Remarks, by Miss Porter*, 2 vols. (London: Longman, Hurst, Rees, and Orme, 1807), 1:v–vi.

52. Porter, *Aphorisms of Sir Philip Sidney*, 2:74, 100, 105, and 109.

53. Ibid., 114.

54. JP to Mrs. JP, c. March[?] 1806[?], HL, POR 1918.

55. RKP to AMP, 4 April 1806, Spencer, Box 1, Folder 27.

56. RKP to JP, 4–6 April 1806, Spencer, Box 1, Folder 26.

57. Ancketill, 142.

58. RKP to JP, 4 April 1806, Spencer, Box 1, Folder 26.

59. RKP to AMP, 4 April 1806, Spencer, Box 1, Folder 27.

60. Ancketill, 159.

61. Ibid., 212.

62. Ibid., 160.

63. Ibid., 159.

64. Ibid., 170.

65. RKP to Mrs. JP, July 1806, Spencer, Box 1, Folder 30.

66. AMP to JP, 22 December 1806, HL, POR 544.

67. AMP to JP, 15 December 1808, HL, POR 593.

68. AMP to JP, 8 June 1807, HL, POR 567.

69. JP to AMP, 11–12 November 1806, HL, POR 1596.

70. JP to AMP, 23 December 1806, HL, POR 1609.

CHAPTER 12: FINALLY IN HIS ARMS: THE RETURN OF MARIA'S SIGHING SOLDIER (1805–9)

1. AMP to JP, 24 January 1805, HL, POR 478.

2. AMP to JP, 3–5 December 1804, HL, POR 459.

3. AMP to JP, 24–26 November 1805, HL, POR 512.
4. Mrs. JP and AMP to JP, 31 May 1805, HL, POR 1084.
5. AMP to JP, c. 1804[?], HL, POR 470.
6. AMP to JP, 24–26 November 1805, HL, POR 512.
7. AMP to JP, 3–5 December 1804, HL, POR 459.
8. AMP to JP, 23 March 1805, HL, POR 486.
9. JP to AMP, 14–17 December 1804, HL, POR 1532.
10. JP to AMP, 26 February 1806, HL, POR 1586.
11. AMP to JP, 3 October 1805, HL, POR 1571.
12. AMP to JP, 23 March 1805, HL, POR 486.
13. JP to AMP, 27 June 1806, HL, POR 1592.
14. Mrs. JP and AMP to JP, 6 November 1804, HL, POR 1079.
15. AMP to JP, 14 January 1805, HL, POR 476.
16. John O'Hart, *The Irish Landed Gentry When Cromwell Came to Ireland* (Dublin: James Duffy, 1892), 619.
17. Mrs. JP and AMP to JP, 6 November 1804, HL, POR 1079.
18. Mrs. JP and AMP to JP, 26 December 1804, HL, POR 1080.
19. JP to AMP, 5 September 1804, HL, POR 1518.
20. Mrs. JP and AMP to JP, 15 February 1805, HL, POR 1081.
21. Ibid.
22. AMP to JP, c. 1804, HL, POR 473.
23. AMP to JP, April[?] 1806[?], HL, POR 527.
24. Mrs. JP and AMP to JP, 31 May 1805, HL, POR 1084.
25. AMP to JP, 16 May 1807, HL, POR 562.
26. AMP to JP, 6 June 1805, HL, POR 499.
27. Mrs. JP and AMP to JP, 26 December 1804, HL, POR 1080.

28. JP to AMP, 1 September 1804, HL, POR 1516.

29. JP to AMP, 5 September 1804, HL, POR 1518.

30. AMP to JP, 9 March 1805, HL, POR 483.

31. JP to AMP, 5 September 1804, HL, POR 1518.

32. JP to AMP, 1 September 1804, HL, POR 1516.

33. Mrs. JP and AMP to JP, 26 December 1804, HL, POR 1080.

34. AMP to JP, 21 December 1804, HL, POR 461.

35. AMP to JP, 30 December 1804[?], HL, POR 463.

36. JP, Memo, Pforzheimer, PORT 06.03.24B.

37. Anna Maria Porter, *The Hungarian Brothers*, vol. 1 (London: Longman, Hurst, Rees, and Orme, 1807), 86. According to *Orlando*, *The Hungarian Brothers* went through approximately sixteen printings in England and the United States, prior to 1850, as well as a French translation ("Anna Maria Porter").

38. AMP to JP, 14 January 1805, HL, POR 476.

39. AMP to JP, April[?] 1806[?], HL, POR 527.

40. JP to AMP, 23–25 October 1805, HL, POR 1575.

41. AMP to JP, 6 November 1805, HL, POR 510.

42. Mrs. JP and AMP to JP, 1 March 1805, HL, POR 1082.

43. AMP to JP, November[?] 1806, HL, POR 581.

44. JP to AMP, 11–12 November 1806, HL, POR 1596.

45. JP to AMP, 11 April 1814, HL, POR 1686.

46. JP to AMP, 11–12 November 1806, HL, POR 1596.

47. AMP to JP, c. November 1806, HL, POR 468.

48. JP to AMP, c. November 1806, HL, POR 1601.

49. JP to AMP, November 1806, HL, POR 1593.

50. JP to AMP, 18 December 1806, HL, POR 1606.

51. AMP to JP, December[?] 1806[?], HL, POR 546.

52. AMP to JP, 13 March 1807, HL, POR 548.

53. AMP to JP, June[?] 1806[?], HL, POR 539.

54. AMP to JP, 21 December 1806, HL, POR 543.

55. AMP to JP, 8 April 1807, HL, POR 555.

56. AMP to JP, 18–19 April 1807, HL, POR 557.

57. AMP to JP, 23–24 April 1807, HL, POR 558.

58. JP to AMP, 20 May 1807, HL, POR 1616.

59. AMP to JP, 11 June 1807, HL, POR 568.

60. JP to AMP, 9 June 1807, HL, POR 1620.

61. AMP to JP, 4 July 1807, HL, POR 572.

62. RKP to JP, 10 December 1808, Spencer, Box 1, Folder 40.

63. There were some bumps in the road for him getting this knighthood officially recognized in England. See Jane Porer to Samuel Edgerton Brydges, 29 November 1808, University of Pennsylvania, Folder 8.

64. AMP to JP, c. 1808, HL, POR 594.

65. JP to AMP, 10 September 1808, HL, POR 1637.

66. AMP to JP, June[?] 1806[?], HL, POR 538.

67. JP to AMP, 12 September 1808, HL, POR 1638.

68. JP to AMP, 10 September 1808, HL, POR 1637.

69. Mrs. JP to JP, June[?] 1808[?], HL, POR 1171.

70. JP to AMP, 21 May 1809, HL, POR 1644.

71. JP to AMP, 24 May 1809, HL, POR 1645.

72. Frederick Cowell to AMP, 2 May 1809[?], HL, POR 158; AMP to JP, 23 March 1805, HL, POR 486.

73. JP to Mrs. JP, 15 May 1812, HL, POR 1943.

CHAPTER 13: HE MUST BE CLOSED UP: THE END OF JANE'S HENRY (1807–9)

1. AMP to JP, 21 September 1803, HL, POR 429.

2. JP to Mrs. JP, 16–19 September 1803, HL, POR 1894.

3. "[Ralph Griffiths], Art. 38: Aphorisms of Sir Philip Sidney," *Monthly Review*, vol. 56, August 1801, 443.

4. Mary Champion de Crespigny to JP, 5 June 1807, Pforzheimer, PORT 07.06.05.

5. S. C. Hall and Anna Maria Hall, "Memories of Authors," *Atlantic Monthly* 15, no. 89 (March 1865): 336.

6. Elizabeth Benger to JP, 1807[?], Beinecke, Osborn Shelves d. 162.

7. Virginia Woolf, *A Room of One's Own and Three Guin*eas, ed. Morag Shiach (Oxford: Oxford University Press, 1992), 45.

8. AMP to JP, c. 1804[?], HL, POR 547.

9. H. Moyse-Bartlett, "Dover at War," *Journal for the Society of Army Historical Research* 50, no. 203 (Autumn 1972): 131.

10. Quoted in Anne Powers, *The Female Infidel: The Vindication of Fanny Dashwood* (London: A Parcel of Ribbons, 2018), 103.

11. AMP to JP, April[?] 1807[?], HL, POR 560.

12. JP to AMP, 25 April 1807, HL, POR 1614.

13. AMP to JP, 28 April 1807, HL, POR 559.

14. AMP to JP, 2 July 1807, HL, POR 571.

15. AMP to JP, 15 July 1807, HL, POR 575.

16. AMP to Mrs. JP, 13 June 1807, HL, POR 254.

17. JP to AMP, 22 July 1807, HL, POR 1627.

18. JP to AMP, 20 October 1807, HL, POR 1628.

19. JP to AMP, 27 October 1807, HL, POR 1629.

20. JP to Mrs. JP, 26 May 1806, HL, POR 1922.

21. RKP to JP, July 1806, Spencer, Box 1, Folder 28.

22. JP to Mrs. JP, 28 May 1806, HL, POR 1923.

23. JP to AMP, 14 December 1806, HL, POR 1605.

24. JP to Mrs. JP, March[?] 1806[?]. HL, POR 1918.

25. Desiderius [Henry Caulfield] to JP, 7 September 1807, Pforzheimer, PORT 07.09.07.

26. JP Memo, n.d. Spencer, Box 35, Folder 60.

27. JP to Mrs. JP, c. 1807, HL, POR 1635.

28. JP and AMP to Longmans, 1 June 1808, HL, POR 33.

29. RKP to JP, 18–20 May 1808, HL, POR 2456.

30. JP to Mrs. JP and AMP, 4 June 1811, HL, POR 1936.

31. Jane Porter, *Thaddeus of Warsaw* (London: Richard Bentley, 1831), 190.

32. AMP to JP, c. 1808, HL, POR 594.

33. JP to AMP, c. 1807, HL, POR 1633.

34. JP to AMP, 29 July 1816, HL, POR 1730.

35. JP to AMP, 20 July 1812, HL, POR 1666.

36. Frederick Campbell to JP, 17 September 1808, Pforzheimer, PORT 08.09A.

37. "Captain Caulfield Died," *Gentleman's Magazine* 78, no. 1 (December 1808): 1124.

38. "Bishop's of London's Court, Doctor's Commons, Dec. 8, Chambers v. Chambers," *St. James's Chronicle*, December 9, 1809, 3.

39. "Bishop of London's Court, Doctor's Commons, Dec. 8, Chambers v. Chambers," *Kentish Weekly Post*, December 12, 1809, 3.

40. R. H. Helmholz and William Rodolph Cornish, *The Oxford History of the Laws of England*, vol. 13 (Oxford: Oxford University Press, 2003), 778.

41. J. Norris Brewer, *London and Middlesex; or, An Historical, Commercial, and Descriptive Survey*, vol. 4 (London: J. Harris, 1816), 505–6.

42. *The Steam-Boat Companion* (London: T. Hughes, 1824), 132; the coffins were buried when the new church was erected. Edward Walford, *Greater London*, vol. 1 (London: Cassell, 1883–84), 189.

43. JP to AMP, 4 April 1810, HL, POR 1650.

44. JP, Henry Caulfield Commonplace Book, HL, POR 1.

45. Jane Porter, *The Scottish Chiefs*, vol. 5 (London: Longman, Hurst, Rees, and Orme, 1810), 309.

46. JP, Memo, c. 1836, HL, POR 45.

47. JP to AMP, 22 March 1810, HL, POR 1648.

CHAPTER 14: CHAMPAGNE, ORANGE JUICE, AND THE MARGRAVINE: MARIA'S YEAR OF LUXURY AND LOVE (1809)

1. RKP to JP, 25 January 1809, HL, POR 600.

2. RKP to JP, 23 January 1809, Spencer, Box 1, Folder 41.

3. Mrs. JP to JP, 19[?] February 1809, HL, POR 1103.

4. Mrs. JP to JP, 26[?] February 1809, HL, POR 1104.

5. Julia Gasper, *Elizabeth Craven: Writer, Feminist, and European* (Wilmington, DE: Vernon Press, 2017), 195–96.

6. Ibid., 15–17.

7. Elizabeth Craven to RKP, 27 August 1809, Spencer, Box 17, Folder 45.

8. AMP to JP, 4 March 1809, HL, POR 604.

9. Ibid.

10. Ibid.

11. AMP to JP, 4–5 September 1809, HL, POR 618.

12. AMP to JP, 28 September 1809, HL, POR 622.

13. AMP to Mrs. JP, 20 March 1809, HL, POR 261.

14. AMP to Mrs. JP, 7 March[?] 1809, HL, POR 260.

15. Ibid.

16. Margravine of Anspach to RKP, 12[?] March 1809[?], Spencer, Box 17, Folder 36.

17. AMP to JP, 16 March 1809, HL, POR 418.

18. JP to AMP, 31 March 1809, HL, POR 1643.

19. AMP to Mrs. JP, March[?] 1809, HL, POR 262.

20. AMP to Mrs. JP, 1 March 1809, HL, POR 259.

21. Elizabeth Craven to RKP, 20 November 1809, Spencer, Box 17, Folder 48.

22. AMP to JP, 12[?] April 1809, HL, POR 605.

23. Charles MacFarlane, *Reminscences of a Literary Life* (New York: Scribner's, 1917), 128.

24. JP to AMP, 22 February 1806, HL, POR 1585.

25. Sir Lumley St. George Skeffington to JP, 5 April 1810, Beinecke, Osborn Shelves d. 162.

26. AMP to Mrs. JP, 3 April 1809, HL, POR 263.

27. AMP to JP, 5 August 1809, HL, POR 272.

28. AMP to Mrs. JP, 9–10 April 1809, HL, POR 265.

29. AMP to Mrs. JP, 3 April 1809, HL, POR 263.

30. AMP to Mrs. JP, 3 April 1809, HL, POR 263.

31. AMP to JP, July[?] 1809, HL, POR 615.

32. AMP to Wilhelmina Hole, 17 April 1809, HL, POR 225.

33. Charles Kirkpatrick Sharpe, *Letters to and from Charles Kirkpatrick Sharpe, Esq.*, vol. 1, ed. Alexander Allardyce (Edinburgh: William Blackwood and Sons, 1888), 413.

34. AMP to Mrs. JP, 3 April 1809, HL, POR 263.

35. Sharpe, *Letters*, 413.

36. AMP to Mrs. JP, 3 April 1809, HL, POR 263.

37. AMP to JP, 12[?] April 1809, HL, POR 605.

38. AMP to Wilhelmina Hole, 17 April 1809, HL, POR 225.

39. Margravine of Anspach to RKP, 30 August 1809, Spencer, Box 17, Folder 46.

40. Sharpe, *Letters*, 412. Keppel's son was probably the "Augustus Derville" baptized in February 1806, at St. James's, Picadilly, recorded as the child of Francis and Victorine Derville. See "Baptisms 1806," London Metropolitan Archives, Church of England Parish Registers 1538–1812, Reference Number: DL/T/090/003.

41. AMP to JP, April[?] 1809, HL, POR 609.

42. AMP to JP, 24[?] August 1809, HL, POR 616.

43. AMP to JP, August[?] 1809, HL, POR 617.

44. AMP to JP, 21–22 September 1809, HL, POR 621.

45. AMP to JP, August[?] 1809, HL, POR 617.

46. JP to AMP, 2 July 1809, HL, POR 1646.

47. "The Margravine of Anspach," *Bury and Norwich Post*, February 21, 1810, 2; "The Intended Nuptials," *Kentish Weekly Post*, August 14, 1810, 3; Sharpe, *Letters*, 412; AMP to JP, 27 February[?] 1810, HL, POR 635.

48. JP to AMP, c. 1810, HL, POR 1655.

49. JP to AMP, 4 April 1810, HL, POR 1650.

50. AMP to JP, 12[?] April 1809, HL, POR 605.

51. AMP to JP, 21–22 September 1809, HL, POR 621.

52. AMP to JP, 23 July 1809, HL, POR 613.

53. Gasper, *Elizabeth Craven*, 238.

54. AMP to Mrs. JP, 9 April[?] 1809, HL, POR 264.

55. AMP to Mrs. JP, 16[?] July 1809, HL, POR 271.

56. AMP to Mrs. JP, 9 April[?] 1809, HL, POR 264.

57. AMP to JP, 23 July 1809, HL, POR 613.

58. AMP to JP, 14 July[?] 1809, HL, POR 612.

59. AMP to JP, 23 July 1809, HL, POR 613.

60. AMP to JP, August[?] 1809, HL, POR 275.

61. AMP to JP, 23 July 1809, HL, POR 613.

62. AMP to JP, July[?] 1809, HL, POR 615.

63. AMP to JP, 23 July 1809, HL, POR 613.

64. AMP to Elizabeth Dillon, 19 August 1809, HL, POR 214.

65. RKP to JP, 24 July 1809, HL, POR 2469.

66. RKP to Mrs. JP, 10 August 1809, HL, POR 2317.

67. RKP to JP, 24 August 1809, HL, POR 2472.

68. Margravine of Anspach to RKP, 14 August 1809, Spencer, Box 17, Folder 44.

69. RKP to JP, 24 August 1809, HL, POR 2472.

70. RKP to JP, 6 December 1810, HL, POR 2516.

71. RKP to JP, 17 June 1810, HL, POR 2508.

72. AMP to JP, 13[?] September 1809, HL, POR 620.

73. AMP to JP, 7[?] September 1809, HL, POR 619.

74. AMP to JP, 21–22 September 1809, HL, POR 621.

75. AMP to JP, 28 September 1809, HL, POR 622.

76. Anna Maria Porter, *Don Sebastian*, vol. 1 (London: Longman, 1809), 18–19. It went through many British and American editions ("Anna Maria Porter," in *Orlando*).

77. AMP to JP, 2–5 November 1809, HL, POR 628.

78. AMP to JP, 13[?] September 1809, HL, POR 620.

79. Sharpe, *Letters*, 413.

80. AMP to JP, 4–5 September 1809, HL, POR 618.

81. Anna Maria Porter, *The Hungarian Brothers*, vol. 2 (London: Longman, Hurst, Rees, and Orme, 1807), 18.

82. AMP to JP, 4–5 September 1809, HL, POR 618.

83. AMP to JP, 7[?] September 1809, HL, POR 619.

84. AMP to JP, 6–11 October 1809, HL, POR 624.

85. AMP to JP, 29 September–5 October 1809, HL, POR 623.

86. AMP to JP, 14–18 October 1809, HL, POR 625.

87. AMP to JP, 6–11 October 1809, HL, POR 624.

88. AMP to JP, 14–18 October 1809, HL, POR 625.

89. Ibid.

90. AMP to JP, 25–29 October 1809, HL, POR 627.

91. Keppel Richard Craven, Journal, BL, Add MS 63609, f. 5.

92. AMP to JP, 2–5 November 1809, HL, POR 628.

93. AMP to JP, 6–10 November 1809, HL, POR 629.

94. AMP to JP, 2–5 November 1809, HL, POR 628.

95. AMP to JP, 13–19 November 1809, HL, POR 630.

96. AMP to JP, 23[?] May 1811, HL, POR 661.

97. AMP to JP, 20–23 November 1809, HL, POR 631.

98. Margravine of Anspach to RKP, 25 November 1809, Spencer, Box 17, Folder 49.

99. Mrs. JP to the Margravine of Anspach, November[?] 1809, HL, POR 1039.

100. AMP to JP, 27 December 1809, HL, POR 632.

101. AMP to William Gell, c. 1809, HL, POR 224.

102. AMP to JP, 27 December 1809, HL, POR 632.

103. JP to AMP, c. 1810, HL, POR 1655.

104. Elizabeth Benger to AMP, c. 1810[?] Beinecke, Osborn Shelves d. 162.

105. Keppel Richard Craven, Journals, BL, Add MS 63609, f. 6.

106. Keppel Richard Craven, Journals, BL, Add MS 63609, f. 15.

107. AMP to JP, 27 February[?] 1810, HL, POR 635.

108. Mrs. JP to JP, May[?] 1810[?], HL, POR 1111.

109. RKP to JP, c. 1810[?], Spencer, Box 1, Folder 47.

110. RKP to AMP, 10 January 1810, HL, POR 2231.

111. Margravine of Anspach to JP, 16 December 1809, Chawton House Library, Document #6645.

112. Review of *Don Sebastian*, *Critical Review* 18, no. 4 (December 1809): 356.

113. AMP to William Gell, c. 1809, HL, POR 224.

114. JP to AMP, 19 April 1810, HL, POR 1652.

115. JP to AMP, 22 March 1810, HL, POR 1648.

116. AMP to JP, May[?] 1810, HL, POR 648.

117. AMP to JP, c. 1810, HL, POR 654.

118. AMP to JP, 2 January 1814, HL, POR 694.

119. "Hay-Market Theatre," *Theatrical Observer*, no. 3681, October 3, 1833, 1.

120. Gasper, *Elizabeth Craven*, 241.

121. Ibid., 268.

CHAPTER 15: FAMILY MISFORTUNES AND JANE'S *SCOTTISH CHIEFS* (1810)

1. JP to AMP, 31 March 1809, HL, POR 1643.

2. Percival Stockdale to JP, 20 April 1809, Houghton.

3. Percival Stockdale, *The Memoirs of the Life, and Writings of Percival Stockdale Containing Many Interesting Anecdotes of the Illustrious Men with Whom He Was Connected. Written by Himself*, vol. 1 (London: Longman, Hurst, Rees, and Orme, 1809), vi.

4. Isaac Disraeli, *Calamities of Authors: Including Some Inquiries Respecting Their Moral and Literary Characters*, vol. 2 (London: John Murray, 1812), 320, 315.

5. JP to AMP, 29–30 September 1819, HL, POR 1773; "Miss Porter," *Gentleman's Magazine*, vol. LXXXIX, October 1819, 326; Constant Reader, "Cahets in France," *Gentleman's Magazine*, vol. LXXXIX, July 1819, 8.

6. RKP to Mrs. JP, after 11 October 1809, HL, POR 2322.

7. "The Will of Sir Sidney Smith," in *The Life and Correspondence of Admiral Sir William Sidney Smith*, vol. 2 (London: Richard Bentley, 1848), 497.

8. *The Later Correspondence of George III*, ed. A. Aspinall, 5 vols. (Cambridge: Cambridge University Press, 1970), 64.

9. "On Wednesday," *The Examiner*, October 15, 1809, 665.

10. AMP to JP, 14–18 October 1809, HL, POR 625.

11. Sir Sidney Smith to JP, 18 November 1809, Pforzheimer, PORT 09.11.18.

12. AMP to JP, 3[?] June 1814[?], HL, POR 709.

13. JP to AMP, 10 May 1815, HL, POR 1712.

14. JP to RKP, 26 September 1838, Spencer, Box 7, Folder 12.

15. JP to Mr. and Mrs. McCreary, 3 February 1810, Berg NYPL.

16. AMP to JP, 6 March 1810, HL, POR 636.

17. JP to AMP, 22 March 1810, HL, POR 1648.

18. Jane Porter, *The Scottish Chiefs* (London: Longman, 1810), vi.

19. Impression Book Entry, Longman & Co., March 15, 1810, Longman Impression Book, no. 4, fol. 31, DBF 1810A070.

20. JP to AMP, 8 July 1812, HL, POR 1664.

21. Mary Ann Hanway to JP, 20 May 1811, Pforzheimer, PORT 11.05.20.

22. AMP to JP, 11 April 1810, HL, POR 645.

23. AMP to JP, c. 1810, HL, POR 652.

24. James Hogg, *Familiar Anecdotes of Sir Walter Scott* in *Anecdotes of Scott*, ed. Jill Rubenstein (Edinburgh: Edinburgh University Press, 1999), 71.

25. Mary Russell Mitford, *The Life of Mary Russell Mitford: Related in a Selection from Her Letters to Her Friends*, vol. 1, ed. A. G. L'Estrange (London: Bentley, 1870), 217.

26. Review of *The Scottish Chiefs*, *British Critic*, 247.

27. Ibid., 256.

28. Thomas Dudley Fosbroke, *British Monarchism* (London: John Nichols, 1817), 344–45; Extract, HL, POR 125.

29. JP to AMP, 18–19 July 1812, HL, POR 1665.

30. JP to AMP, 29 August 1812, HL, POR 1660.

31. JP to AMP, 22 May 1810[?], HL, POR 1653.

32. JP to AMP, 10 April 1810, HL, POR 1651.

33. RKP to JP, 27 September 1810, HL, POR 2514.

34. Correspondence and Warrants, Criminal Entry Books, HO 13/18, National Archives, 1806–08.

35. RKP to JP, 12–13 April 1808, HL, POR 2454.

36. RKP to JP, 13 [November] 1809, HL, POR 2476.

37. RKP to Mrs. JP, 11–12 September[?] 1809, HL, POR 2318.

38. RKP to JP, 18–20 May 1808, HL, POR 2456.

39. RKP to JP, 31 May 1810, HL, POR 2506.

40. Karl T. Christian, *History of the Isle of Man Prison Service, 1229–2017* (Douglas, Isle of Man, UK: Manx National Heritage, 2017).

41. James Neild, *State of the Prisons in England, Scotland, and Wales* (London: John Nichols and Son, 1812), 113.

42. "Castle Rushen Prison," *Manks Advertiser*, December 22, 1810, 2.

43. "Second Donation," *Manks Advertiser*, February 9, 1811, 7.

44. JP to Mrs. JP, 18 June 1811, HL, POR 1937.

45. Jane Porter, *The Scottish Chiefs*, ed. Fiona Price (Peterborough, Ontario: Broadview Press), 2007, 683. According to *Orlando*, "At least ten London editions of *The Scottish Chiefs* appeared by 1850, with New York and Philadelphia editions in 1810 and a French translation in 1814" ("Jane Porter").

46. "Douglas, August 24, 1811," *Manks Advertiser*, no. 516, 1881, 2.

47. Quoted in Dunelmensis, "Erroneous Monumental Inscriptions," *Notes and Queries*, June 25, 1864, 529.

48. John C. Lettsom and J. C. Neild, "Letter LXII: On Prisons," *Gentleman's Magazine*, November 1811, 423.

49. AMP to JP, 13[?] May[?] 1812, HL, POR 642.

50. RKP to JP, 11 June 1813, HL, POR 2540.

51. Will of Percival Stockdale, Northumberland Archives, NRO, PROB 11/1529/450.

52. J. C. Hodgson, *Percival Stockdale: Sometime Vicar of Lesbury* (Edinburgh: Neill and Co., [c. 1910]), 4.

53. JP to Sir Samuel Edgerton Brydges, 30 October 1811, Private Collection. Consulted at Surrey History Centre.

54. Review of *The Scottish Chiefs*, *Gentleman's Magazine*, vol. LXXX, October 1810, 346.

55. Jane Porter, *The Scottish Chiefs*, Impression Book Entry, Longman & Co., 21 March 1811, in DBF.

56. Jane Porter, *The Scottish Chiefs: A Romance*, vol. 1 (London: Henry Colburn, 1831), xxvi.

57. AMP to JP, 11 April 1810, HL, POR 645.

CHAPTER 16: HORROR PRINCESS: RUSSIANS IN BRITAIN, MARIA'S *RECLUSE*, AND JANE'S REDOUBLED FAME (1811–14)

1. "Memoirs of Miss Porter," *Monthly Mirror*, vol. 8, December 1810, 404–5.

2. JP to AMP, 9 June 1807, HL, POR 1620.

3. Anna Maria Porter, *Ballad Romances* (London: Longman, Hurst, Rees, Orme, and Brown, 1811), 103.

4. Owen Rees to AMP, 19 January 1814, Longman Letter Book I, 98, no. 121, Longman Group Archive, University of Reading Special Collections.

5. "ART. [Article] VII.—*Ballad Romances*," *Critical Review* 1, no. 2 (February 1812): 164.

6. RKP to Mrs. JP, 25 March 1810, HL, POR 2336.

7. Quoted in RKP to JP, 11[?] February 1810[?], HL, POR 2491.

8. RKP to JP, 23–24 August 1810, HL, POR 2512.

9. RKP to AMP, 15 July 1811, HL, POR 2239.

10. AMP to JP, 13 May[?] 1808[?], HL, POR 584.

11. RKP to JP, 31 July 1803, HL, POR 2435.

12. JP to Mrs. JP, 10 March 1808, HL, POR 1930.

13. RKP to JP, 28 January 1808, HL, POR 2450.

14. C. J. Woods, "James Porter (1752/3–98)," in *Dictionary of Irish Biography*, 2009, www.dib.ie/biography/porter-james-a7432. I'm grateful to researcher Vincent Gallagher for sharing his expertise on this branch of the Porter family. The parentage of James Porter is uncertain, but he was likely a first cousin once removed of Jane and Anna Maria Porter. There has been significant misinformation about Jane Porter and Ireland. See Edward MacIntyre, "Jane Porter's Connection with Lifford Merely a Fable," *The Ulster Herald*, September 20, 1975, 9.

15. RKP to Mrs. JP, 14 March 1811, HL, POR 2350.

16. Julian Gwyn, "Women as Litigants before the Supreme Court of Nova Scotia, 1754–1830," in *The Supreme Court of Nova Scotia: From Imperial Bastion to Provincial Oracle*, ed. Philip Girard, Jim Phillips, and Barry Cahill (Toronto: Osgood Society for Canadian Legal History and University of Toronto Press, 2004), 298.

17. Ibid., 299–300.

18. Mrs. JP to JP, 1 December 1809, HL, POR 1105. Mrs. Porter wrote, of the new marriage and their servant Sally, "O my Jane—it is not the days of married happiness & comfort, as used to be—I know your heart will be paind—happy I am, that you did not witness what I did—poor Sally she has a dismal prospect—Wm loves her as he does them all. but there is such a thing as having been too long ones own Mistress & having domestics under them, to tyrannize over."

19. RKP to Mrs. JP, 23 June 1813, HL, POR 2365.

20. RKP to JP and AMP, February 1812, Spencer, Box 1, Folder 49. Princess Mary was also known as Marie, among her other nicknames. She was an Anglophile, but the language of the Russian court was French, and Marie is the French version of Mary.

21. RKP to JP and AMP, February 1812, Spencer, Box 1, Folder 49.

22. RKP to JP and AMP, May 23/June 5, 1812, Spencer, Box 1, Folder 50.

23. "From the London Gazette," *Caledonian Mercury*, April 8, 1813, 2.

24. RKP to JP, 13 June 1813, HL, POR 2541.

25. "This Day is Published," *Caledonian Mercury*, August 5, 1813, 3.

26. RKP to AMP, 18 July 1813, HL, POR 2241.

27. RKP to Mrs. JP, 11 July[?] 1813[?], HL, POR 2367.

28. RKP to JP, 27 June 1813, HL, POR 2366.

29. AMP to Wilhemina Hole, 29 September 1812, HL, POR 226.

30. AMP to Wilhelmina Hole, 5 December 1813, HL, POR 227.

31. JP to AMP, 27 October 1814, HL, POR 1698.

32. JP to AMP, 23 April 1814, HL, POR 1507.

33. JP to AMP, 29 December 1813, HL, POR 1684.

34. AMP to JP, September[?] 1814, HL, POR 715.

35. AMP to JP, 8 May 1814, HL, POR 707.

36. JP to AMP, 29 December 1813, HL, POR 1684.

37. Ibid.

38. AMP to Elizabeth Dillon, n.d., HL, POR 215.

39. Albertine de Staël and Madame de Staël to JP, 2 December 1813, Pforzheimer, PORT 13.12.02A.

40. JP to AMP, c. 1813, HL, POR 1685.

41. JP to AMP, 29 December 1813, HL, POR 1684.

42. AMP to JP, 17 April 1814, HL, POR 700.

43. RKP to Mary Shcherbatov Porter, 21 April 1814, Spencer, Box 1, Folder 64.

44. JP to AMP, 14 May 1814, HL, POR 1690.

45. "Saturday Morning in the House of Sir Robert Ker Porter," *Morning Post*, February 15, 1814, 3.

46. AMP to JP, 20 April 1814[?], HL, POR 701.

47. AMP to JP, 2 April 1814, HL, POR 696.

48. JP to AMP, 10 May 1814, HL, POR 1689.

49. Mrs. JP to JP, 12 June 1814, HL, POR 1120.

50. AMP to JP, 26[?] April 1814[?], HL, POR 702.

51. AMP to JP, 10 June 1814, HL, POR 710.

52. "Historical Account of the Reception and Pursuits of the Emperor of Russia and King of Prussia," *La Belle Assemblée*, June 1814, 280.

53. RKP to Mary Shcherbatov Porter, 21 April 1814, Spencer, Box 1, Folder 63.

54. RKP to Mrs. JP, c. 1813, HL, POR 2377.

55. JP to AMP, 14 May 1814, HL, POR 1690.

56. AMP to JP, 30 June 1814, HL, POR 288.

57. WOP to Mrs. JP, 28 February 1813, Durham.

58. JP to AMP, 2 May 1814, HL, POR 1688.

59. AMP to JP, April[?] 1814[?], HL, POR 704.

60. Sir Henry Cosby to Mary Shcherbatov Porter, 9 April 1814, Spencer, Box 29, Folder 49.

61. AMP to JP, September[?] 1814, HL, POR 715.

62. AMP to JP, 30 April–1 May 1815, HL, POR 722.

63. AMP to JP, April[?] 1814[?], HL, POR 703.

64. AMP to JP, 10 May 1814, HL, POR 708.

65. AMP to JP, 12 June 1814, HL, POR 711.

66. JP to AMP, September 1814, HL, POR 1697.

67. On the reviews of *The Recluse of Norway,* including one by Anna Letitia Barbauld in the *Critical Review,* see "Anna Maria Porter," in *Orlando.*

68. Mrs. JP to JP, 5 April 1815, HL, POR 1123.

69. JP to AMP, 12 September 1814, HL, POR 1696.

70. JP to AMP, 31 August 1814, HL, POR 1694.

71. JP to AMP, 5 September 1814, HL, POR 1695.

72. JP to AMP, 12–13 April 1815, HL, POR 1704

73. AMP to JP, 5 November 1814, HL, POR 716.

CHAPTER 17: MONSTROUS LITERARY VAMPIRES: JANE AND MARIA, AFTER WALTER SCOTT (1814–16)

1. JP to AMP, 26 March 1815, HL, POR 1702.

2. [JP], "Hymenaea in Search of a Husband," *La Belle Assemblée,* vol. VI, 1809, 72–77.

3. AMP to JP, 4 June 1815, HL, POR 724.

4. [Walter Scott], *Waverley; or, 'Tis Sixty Years Since,* vol. III (Edinburgh: Archibald Constable, 1814), 369–70.

5. Jane Austen, *Jane Austen's Letters,* 4th ed., ed. Deirdre Le Faye (Oxford: Oxford University Press, 2011), 289.

6. JP to Mrs. JP, 14 May 1811, HL, POR 1934.

7. Jane Austen, *Jane Austen's Letters,* 261.

8. AMP to Elizabeth Dillon, 21 May 1824, HL, POR 218.

9. AMP to JP, 22 July 1812, HL, POR 679.

10. JP to AMP, 10 August 1812, HL, POR 1688.

11. AMP to JP, 5 April 1815, HL, POR 720.

12. AMP to JP, 22 July 1812, HL, POR 479.

13. AMP to Wilhelmina Hole, 29 September 1812, HL, POR 1672.

14. John Timbs, *English Eccentrics and Eccentricities*, vol. 2 (London: Richard Bentley, 1866), 286.

15. Benjamin Haydon, *The Diary of Benjamin Robert Haydon*, vol. 4, ed. Willard Bissell Pope (Cambridge: Harvard University Press, 1964), 277.

16. Lord Abercorn to JP, 12 December 1814, HL, POR 2649.

17. AMP to JP, 15 April[?] 1815[?], HL, POR 981.

18. AMP to JP, 24 August 1812, HL, POR 662.

19. AMP to JP, 15 April[?] 1815[?], HL, POR 981.

20. "Jane Porter," in *Dictionary of National Biography*, vol. 46, ed. Sidney Lee (London: Smith and Elder, 1896), 183.

21. JP to AMP, 27 May 1813, HL, POR 1680.

22. JP to [William] Haines, c. 1813, Robert Taylor Collection, Princeton University.

23. Charles MacFarlane, *Reminiscences of a Literary Life* (New York: Scribner's, 1917), 114.

24. Thomas McLean, "Jane Porter and the Wonder of Lord Byron," *Romanticism* 18, no. 3 (2012): 250–59.

25. Ina Mary White, "Art. [Article] VII. Diary of Jane Porter," *Scottish Review*, vol. XXIX, 1897, 332.

26. AMP to JP, 17 April 1814, HL, POR 700.

27. AMP to JP, 20 April 1814[?], HL, POR 701.

28. Wordsworth (HL, POR 1943), Barbauld (HL, POR 1466), Edgeworth and Moore (HL, POR 1680).

29. Mary Russell Mitford, *The Life of Mary Russell Mitford: Related in a Selection from Her Letters to Her Friends*, vol. I, ed. A. G. L'Estrange (London: Bentley, 1870), 376.

30. MacFarlane, *Reminiscences of a Literary Life*, 113.

31. Peter Garside, James Raven, and Rainer Schowerling, *The English Novel, 1770–1829: A Bibliographical Survey of Prose Fiction Published in the British Isles*, vol. II, 1800–1829. (Oxford: Oxford University Press, 2000), 403.

32. "Art. [Article] 27. *The Recluse of Norway*," *Monthly Review*, vol. 77, June 1815, 212.

33. A. J. Valpy to JP, April 4, 1815, Pforzheimer, PORT 15.04.04.

34. AMP to JP, 3[?] June 1814[?], HL, POR 709.

35. "Art. [Article] IV. *The Recluse of Norway*," *Augustan Review*, May 1815, 106–7.

36. JP to AMP, 25 April 1815, HL, POR 1707.

37. JP to AMP, 12–13 April 1815, HL, POR 1704.

38. AMP to JP, 15[?] April 1815[?], HL, POR 981.

39. "Royal Circus—This Evening," *Morning Post*, April 18, 1815, 1.

40. JP to AMP, 19 April 1815, HL, POR 1705.

41. JP to AMP, 1 April 1815, HL, POR 1703.

42. AMP to JP, 4 June 1815, HL, POR 724.

43. JP to AMP, 1 April 1815, HL, POR 1703.

44. AMP to JP, 10 June 1823, HL, POR 819.

45. AMP to JP, 3 June 1816[?] HL, POR 740.

46. AMP to JP, 10 June 1823, HL, POR 819.

47. Ibid.

CHAPTER 18: BEWARE OF IMAGINATION: JANE'S PASTOR, MARIA'S TWO NOVELS, AND COLONEL DAN (1816–18)

1. Luke Howard, *The Climate of London* (London: W. Phillips, 1818), table CXV.

2. AMP to JP, 11 February 1816[?], HL, POR 732.

3. WOP to JP, 31 May 1820, Durham.

4. JP to AMP, before 25 April 1815, HL, POR 1706.

5. Mrs. JP to JP, June[?] 1808[?], HL, POR 1171.

6. Mrs. JP and Elizabeth Dillon to JP, 12 July[?] 1816, HL, POR 1137.

7. AMP to JP, 15 April[?] 1815[?], HL, POR 981.

8. JP to AMP, 3 September 1824, HL, POR 1839.

9. AMP to JP, 3 June 1816, HL, POR 740.

10. JP to AMP, 30 June 1816, HL, POR 1726.

11. Mrs. JP to JP, December[?] 1816[?] HL, POR 1159.

12. JP to Mrs. JP, 29 October 1816, HL, POR 1971.

13. AMP to JP, 3 June 1816, HL, POR 740.

14. Mrs. JP to JP, 7 October 1812, HL, POR 1118.

15. AMP to Mrs. JP, 25–30 June 1816, HL, POR 294.

16. AMP to JP, 14 March 1816, HL, POR 736.

17. AMP to JP, 18 June 1816, HL, POR 741.

18. JP to AMP, 20 June 1816, HL, POR 1725.

19. AMP to JP, 24–30 June 1816, HL, POR 742.

20. AMP to JP, 7[?] July 1816, HL, POR 743.

21. AMP to Mrs. JP, 4 July 1816, HL, POR 295.

22. AMP to JP, 7[?] July 1816, HL, POR 743.

23. AMP to Mrs. JP, 25–30 June 1816, HL, POR 294.

24. Ian Fletcher and Ron Poulter, *Gentlemen's Sons: The Guards in the Peninsula and at Waterloo, 1808–1815* (Staplehurst: Spellmount, 1992), 16.

25. Rees Howell Gronow, *Reminscences of Captain Gronow*, 2nd. ed. (London: Smith, Elder, and Co., 1862), 84.

26. Fletcher and Poulter, *Gentlemen's Sons*, 16.

27. AMP to JP, 12 August 1816, HL, POR 746.

28. AMP to Mrs. JP, 4 July 1816, HL, POR 295.

29. AMP to JP, 7[?] July 1816, HL, POR 743.

30. Mrs. JP and Elizabeth Dillon to JP, [?] July 1816, HL, POR 1137.

31. AMP to Mrs. JP, 4 July 1816, HL, POR 295.

32. Ibid.

33. AMP to JP, 17 July 1816, HL, POR 298.

34. AMP to Mrs. JP, 10 July 1816, HL, POR 296.

35. AMP to Mrs. JP, 17 July 1816, HL, POR 298.

36. AMP to Mrs. JP, 13–14 July 1816, HL, POR 297. Maria is using "cottered" in a nineteenth-century sense meaning entangled or crowded together.

37. AMP to Mrs. JP, 17 July 1816, HL, POR 298.

38. Ibid.

39. AMP to JP, 27 July 1816, HL, POR 744.

40. AMP to JP, 27 July 1816, HL, POR 744.

41. AMP to JP, 31 July 1816, HL, POR 745.

42. JP to AMP, 4 August 1816, HL, POR 1731.

43. AMP to JP, 31 July 1816, HL, POR 745.

44. AMP to JP, 12 August 1816, HL, POR 746.

45. Richard Raikes to JP, 8 August 1816, Pforzheimer, PORT 16.08.08A. Jane included a note to Maria along with this letter.

46. AMP to JP, 24 August 1816, HL, POR 747.

47. AMP to JP, 2 November 1816, HL, POR 758.

48. Sir Charles Sullivan to Lord Hardwicke, 18 September 1852, BL, Add MS 35800 (13 Sep 1852–27 Sep 1852), f. 160.

49. AMP to JP, 29 August 1816, HL, POR 748.

50. Mrs. JP and AMP to JP, [5 September] 1816, HL, POR 1140. JP to AMP, 31 July 1816, HL, POR 1735.

51. AMP to JP, 12–13 October 1816, HL, POR 752.

52. JP to AMP, 8 October 1816, HL, POR 1736.

53. AMP to JP, 29–30 October 1816, HL, POR 757.

54. AMP to [?], 23 October 1816, NLS, ACC 9051.

55. AMP to JP, 14–15 October 1816, HL, POR 754.

56. JP to AMP, 5 November 1816, HL, POR 1741.

57. JP to AMP, 30 October 1816, HL, POR 1740.

58. JP to AMP, 26 November 1816, HL, POR 1745.

59. "Miss Porter's New Novel," *The Star*, January 31, 1817, 1.

60. Anna Middleton to AMP, 18 March 1817, Pforzheimer, PORT 17.03.18.

61. Impression Book Entry, Longman & Co., January 11, 1817, Longman Impression Book, no. 6, fol. 68v., DBF 1817A049.

62. "Critical Analysis: The Pastor's Fire-Side," *The Literary Gazette*, March 8, 1817, 101.

63. Jane Porter, *The Pastor's Fire-Side*, vol. 1 (London: Henry Colburn and Richard Bentley, 1832), xiii.

64. "Miss A. M. Porter's New Work," *The Star*, October 21, 1817, 1.

65. Impression Book Entry, Longman & Co., October 1817, Longman Impression Book, no. 6, fol. 115, DBF 1817A048.

66. "Miss A. M. Porter's New Novel," *The Star*, November 13, 1818, 1.

67. Anna Maria Porter, *The Fast of St. Magdalen: A Romance*, vol. I (London: Longman, Hurst, Rees, Orme, and Brown, 1818), 82; 70; 65. According to *Orlando*, both *The Knight of St. John* and *The Fast of St. Magdalen* went through two English editions, a French translation, a New York edition, and a Boston edition in 1817–19 ("Anna Maria Porter").

68. AMP to JP, c. 1817, HL, POR 784.

69. "Marriages," *Gentleman's Magazine*, vol. LXXXIX, January 1819, 81.

70. T. S. Mercer, *Tales and Scandals of Old Thames Ditton*, enlarged ed. (Thames Ditton: privately printed, 1968), 57.

71. AMP to JP, 9[?] August 1823, HL, POR 900.

CHAPTER 19: PLAYED BY KEAN: JANE'S DRAMAS AT THE DRURY LANE THEATRE (1817–19)

1. Nora Nachumi, *Acting Like a Lady: British Women Novelists and the Late Eighteenth-Century Theatre* (New York: AMS Press, 2008).

2. Mrs. JP to AMP and JP, 29 April 1818, HL, POR 1161.

3. AMP to JP, c. 1816, HL, POR 765.

4. JP to RKP, September[?] 1818[?], HL, POR 2042.

5. Mrs. JP to JP and AMP, 4 May 1817, HL, POR 1151.

6. Jim Davis "Introduction," in *Lives of the Shakespearean Actors, Edmund Kean, Sarah Siddons, and Harriet Smithson, by their Contemporaries*, ed. Jim Davis et al. (New York: Routledge/Pickering & Chatto, 2009), xix.

7. Jane Moody, *Illegitimate Theatre in London, 1770–1840* (Cambridge: Cambridge University Press, 2007), 230.

8. Davis "Introduction," in *Lives of the Shakespearean Actors*, xxii.

9. John Arthur Roebuck, *Life and Letters of John Arthur Roebuck*, ed. Robert Eadon Leader (London: Edward Arnold, 1897), 4.

10. David Worrall, "Jane Austen Goes to Drury Lane: Identifying Individuals in a Late Georgian Audience," *Nineteenth Century Theatre and Film* 47, no. 1 (2020): 4.

11. Giles Playfair, *The Flash of Lightning: A Portrait of Edmund Kean* (London: William Kimber, 1983), 70.

12. Moody, *Illegitimate Theatre in London*, 229.

13. "Mr. Kean & Mr. Buck: Drury Lane Theatre," *The Observer*, March 21, 1819, 2.

14. Raymund Fitzsimons, *Edmund Kean: Fire from Heaven* (New York: Dial Press, 1976), 118.

15. JP to AMP, 9 February 1816, HL, POR 1719.

16. JP to AMP, 12 February 1816, HL, POR 1720.

17. JP to AMP, 21 February 1816, HL, POR 1722.

18. Ibid.

19. JP to Mary Kean, 6 March 1816, HL, POR 1357.

20. JP to Mary Kean, 6 March 1816, HL, POR 1357.

21. Thomas McLean, "Offstage Dramas: Jane Porter, Edmund Kean, and the Tragedy of Switzerland," *Keats-Shelley Review* 25, no. 2 (2011): 147–59.

22. JP to Mary Kean, 19 April 1816, HL, POR 1358.

23. JP to the Duke of Gloucester, 8 May 1817, Pforzheimer, PORT 17.05.08A.

24. JP to AMP, 10 November 1816, HL, POR 1742.

25. JP to AMP, 27 January 1817, HL, POR 1749.

26. JP to Mary Kean, 22 April 1816, Pforzheimer, PORT 16.04.22A-B.

27. JP to Mary Kean, September[?] 1817, Houghton.

28. JP to Mary Kean, 20 March 1817, HL, POR 1360.

29. McLean, "Offstage Dramas," 151; AMP to JP, 12 April [1818], POR 814.

30. "Mr. Kean & Mr. Buck: Drury Lane Theatre," *The Observer*, 2.

31. JP to Duke of Gloucester, 8 May 1817, Pforzheimer, PORT 17.05.08A.

32. JP to George Lamb, 3 May 1817, Pforzheimer, PORT 17.05.03.

33. McLean, "Offstage Dramas," 151.

34. Fitzsimons, *Edmund Kean*, 119.

35. JP to Duke of Gloucester, 8 May 1817, Pforzheimer, PORT 17.05.08A.

36. McLean, "Offstage Dramas," 156.

37. Ibid.

38. Drury Lane Theatre to JP, 10 January 1818, Spencer, Box 28, Folder 61.

39. JP to Mary Kean, 23 January 1818, Morgan, MA 4500.

40. JP to My Dear Friend (including copy of a note from Mary Kean), February[?] 1818[?] HL, POR 1403.

41. JP to Mary Kean, 23 January 1818, Morgan, MA 4500.

42. "Mr. Kean & Mr. Buck: Drury Lane Theatre," *The Observer*, 2.

43. Fitzsimons, *Edmund Kean*, 122.

44. Mrs. JP to AMP and JP, 29 April 1818, HL, POR 1161.

45. JP to AMP, 17 November 1818, HL, POR 1761.

46. JP to AMP, August[?] 1818[?] HL, POR 1758.

47. JP to John Taylor, 18 January 1819, Pforzheimer, PORT 19.01.18.

48. "A new tragedy," *The Times*, January 26, 1819, 3.

49. JP to John Taylor, 11 February 1819, Pforzheimer, PORT 19.02.11.

50. John Keats, *The Letters of John Keats* (London: Reeves & Turner, 1895), 284.

51. AMP to JP, 5 February 1819, HL, POR 804.

52. AMP to JP, 29 August 1816, HL, POR 748.

53. AMP to JP, 5 February 1819, HL, POR 804.

54. AMP to JP, 11[?] February 1819[?], HL, POR 806.

55. AMP to JP, 5 February 1819, HL, POR 803.

56. AMP to JP, 12 May 1818, HL, POR 793.

57. JP to AMP, 22 February 1819, HL, POR 1766.

58. "Theatre-Royal Drury-Lane," *Morning Advertiser*, February 15, 1819, 2.

59. "Mr. Kean & Mr. Buck: Drury Lane Theatre," *The Observer*, 2.

60. "Drury Lane Theatre," *Evening Mail*, February 17, 1819, 2.

61. JP to My Dear Friend, 18 February 1819, HL, POR 1402.

62. JP to AMP, 16 February 1819, HL, POR 1764.

63. "Drury-Lane Theatre," *The Times*, 3.

64. "Mr. Kean & Mr. Buck: Drury Lane Theatre," *The Observer*, 2.

65. Mrs. JP, "Extract from the Champion," 28 February 1819, HL, POR 110.

66. "Drury-Lane Theatre," *Morning Advertiser*, 3.

67. Ibid.

68. Ibid.

69. "Drury-Lane Theatre," *Morning Chronicle*, February 16, 1819, 2.

70. "Drury-Lane Theatre," *Morning Advertiser*, February 16, 1819, 3.

71. "Drury-Lane Theatre," *Morning Chronicle*, February 16, 1819, 2.

72. "Theatre: Drury-Lane," *Morning Post*, February 16, 1819, 3.

73. "Drury-Lane Theatre," *The Times*, February 16, 1819, 3.

74. "The Theatre," *Sun*, February 16, 1819, 3.

75. Fitzsimons, *Edmund Kean*, 125.

76. JP to AMP, 22 February 1819, HL, POR 1766.

77. JP to John Taylor, 18 February 1819, Pforzheimer, PORT 19.02.18.

78. AMP to Elizabeth Dillon, 8 February 1819, HL, POR 217.

79. F. W. Hawkins, *Life of Edmund Kean*, vol. I (London: Tinsley Brothers, 1869), 68.

80. Ibid., 69.

81. Fitzsimons, *Edmund Kean*, 125.

82. JP to AMP, 16 February 1819, HL, POR 1764.

83. Mrs. JP to JP, 18 February 1819, HL, POR 1168.

84. AMP to Elizabeth Dillon, 8 February 1819, HL, POR 217.

85. Mrs. JP to JP, 23[?] February 1819, HL, POR 1169.

86. Mrs. JP to JP, c. 1819[?], HL, POR 1175.

87. JP to AMP, 21 July 1819, HL, POR 1771.

CHAPTER 20: TORTURED FOR OTHERS: MARIA, JANE, AND THE ROYAL LIBRARIAN (1819–24)

1. AMP to JP, 12 April [1819], HL, POR 814.

2. AMP to JP, c. 1820, HL, POR 827.

3. AMP to JP, 10 December 1817, HL, POR 780.

4. AMP to Wilhelmina Hole, 3 December 1820, HL, POR 230.

5. AMP to JP, 17 September 1818, HL, POR 796.

6. AMP to Mrs. JP, 18[?] January 1824, Clark, Porter Folder 1/19.

7. "In the Press," *Morning Post*, February 10, 1820, 2.

8. JP to RKP, 30 June 1823, HL, POR 2063.

9. JP to AMP, 21 July 1819, HL, POR 1771.

10. JP to AMP, 24 February 1830, HL, POR 1782.

11. Mrs. JP to Dr. Neville, 16 November 1817, HL, POR 1048.

12. AMP to Wilhelmina Hole, 26 December 1817, HL, POR 228.

13. Agnes Strickland, *Queen Victoria from Her Birth to Her Bridal*, vol. I (London: Henry Colburn, 1840), 94.

14. AMP to JP, 2 November 1816[?], HL, POR 845.

15. JP to AMP, 24 January 1820, HL, POR 1778.

16. AMP to JP, 12–13 April 1817, HL, POR 775; Mrs. JP to JP and AMP, 8–9 May 1817, HL, POR 1152.

17. Elizabeth Renne, "Artist Sir Robert Ker Porter (1777–1842) in Russia," *Our Legacy*, no. 63–64, 2002, 151–63.

18. WOP to RKP, 20 July 1820, Durham.

19. Mrs. JP to Elizabeth Dillon, July[?] 1820[?], HL, POR 1043.

20. RKP to Lord Cathcart, 13 August 1820, Spencer, Box 1, Folder 74.

21. JP to AMP, 27 July 1820, HL, POR 1786.

22. AMP to JP, 7 May[?] 1820, HL, POR 833.

23. AMP to Wilhelmina Hole, 3 December 1820, HL, POR 230.

24. JP to AMP, 28 August 1820, HL, POR 1788.

25. JP to Mrs. JP, 27–28 September 1820, HL, POR 1989.

26. Owen Rees to AMP, 27 December 1820, Longman Archives, Longman I, 101, no. 69, DBF 1821A061.

27. Anna Maria Porter, *The Village of Mariendorpt: A Tale*, vol. 1 (London: Longman, Hurst, Rees, Orme, and Brown, 1821), iii–iv.

28. AMP to Wilhelmina Hole, 3 December 1820, HL, POR 230.

29. Impression Book Entry, Longman & Co., February [1821], Longman Impression Book, no. 7, fol. 110, DBF 1821A061.

30. Mrs. JP to JP, November[?] 1824[?] HL, POR 1219.

31. Mrs. JP to JP, July[?] 1824[?], HL, POR 1213.

32. James Stanier Clarke to JP, 14 August 1820, Pforzheimer, PORT 20.08.14.

33. Owen Rees to JP, 14 March 1821, Pforzheimer, PORT 21.03.14.

34. Chris Viveash, *James Stanier Clarke: Librarian to the Prince Regent, Naval Author, Friend of Jane Austen* (privately printed, 2006), 59.

35. JP to RKP, 22 October 1822, HL, POR 2056.

36. JP to RKP, 21 September 1821, HL, POR 2045.

37. Ibid.

38. Ibid.

39. Sir Robert Ker Porter, *Travels in Georgia, Persia, Armenia, Ancient Bablyonia, &c. &c. During the Years 1817, 1818, 1819, and 1820*, vol. I (London: Longman, Hurst, Rees, Orme, and Brown, 1821), iv.

40. James Stanier Clarke to JP, 2 June 1821, Pforzheimer, PORT 21.06.02.

41. Jane Austen to James Stanier Clarke, April 1, 1816, *Jane Austen's Letters*, 4th ed., ed. Deirdre Le Faye (Oxford: Oxford University Press, 2011), 326.

42. JP to RKP, 21 September 1821, HL, POR 2045.

43. AMP to JP, April[?] 1819[?], HL, POR 817.

44. Owen Rees to RKP, 19 June 1823, Longman Letter Book, I, 101, no. 373, University of Reading.

45. JP to [Longman & Co.], 11 September 1823, Pforzheimer, PORT 23.09.13.

46. Anna Maria Porter, *Roche-Blanche; or, The Hunters of the Pyrenees: A Romance*, vol. I (London: Longman, Hurst, Reeds, Orme, and Brown, 1822), vii.

47. Owen Rees to [JP], 10 December 1824, Longman Archives, Longman I, 101, no. 519B, DBF 1822A062. Rees notes that they paid AMP 140 pounds per volume for *Roche-Blanche*, a three-volume novel.

48. JP to [Longman & Co.], 11 September 1823, Pforzheimer, PORT 23.09.13.

49. JP to AMP, January[?] 1824[?], HL, POR 1828.

50. JP to AMP, 25 January 1824, HL, POR 1826.

51. Jane Porter, *Duke Christian of Luneburg: or, Tradition from the Hartz*, vol. 2 (London: Longman, Hurst, Rees, Orme, Brown, and Green, 1824), 269.

52. JP to RKP, 20 November 1823, HL, POR 2067.

53. William Knighton to Andrew Halliday, 31 January 1824, Pforzheimer, PORT 24.01.31.

54. JP to RKP, 25 January 1824, HL, POR 1250.

55. JP to AMP, 16 February 1824, HL, POR 1830.

56. JP to RKP, 28 February 1824, HL, POR 2069.

57. Longman Archives, University of Reading, Reel 39 H11 22.

58. Letter from Longman & Co. to JP, 17 May 1825, Longman Archives, Longman I, 101, no. 507B (draft), DBF 1824A078.

59. AMP to Wilhelmina Hole, 10 November 1823, HL, POR 231.

60. RKP to JP, 2 July 1824, HL, POR 2565.

61. Ibid.

62. Ancketill, 462.

63. RKP to JP, 2 July 1824, HL, POR 2565.

64. Ancketill, 460.

65. Brown, Longman, and Rees to JP, 13 October 1824, Spencer, Box 25, Folder 72.

66. Ancketill, *Strange Destiny*, 472.

67. Henry Rolleston to RKP, 18 October 1825, Pforzheimer, PORT 25.10.18.

68. Charles Bagot to RKP, 20 May 1825, Pforzheimer, PORT 25.05.20.

69. RKP to AMP, 27 June 1825, HL, POR 2246.

70. JP to Lady Charlotte Bury, 3 November 1825, NLS, ACC 10033.

71. Dried plant, Spencer, Box 44, Folder 43.

72. Sir Andrew Halliday, *Annals of the House of Hanover*, 2 vols. (London: N. Sams, 1826).

73. Mrs. JP to JP, 19 August 1824, HL, POR 1216.

CHAPTER 21: STRANGE, UNWORTHY BROTHER: JANE AND MARIA PUBLISH TOGETHER AND WILLIAM WRITES AWAY (1824–31)

1. Agnes Strickland, *Queen Victoria from Her Birth to Her Bridal*, vol. I (London: Henry Colburn, 1840), 93.

2. AMP to RKP, 15 April 1826, HL, POR 1014.

3. AMP to RKP, 12 May 1826, HL, POR 1015.

4. Moyle Sherer to AMP, 3 November 1827, Spencer, Box 29, Folder 14.

5. Mrs. JP to JP, 11 October[?] 1828[?] HL, POR 1238.

6. Strickland, *Queen Victoria*, 94.

7. Strickland, *Queen Victoria*, 100; AMP to JP, July–August[?] 1826, HL, POR 956.

8. RKP to Prince Lieven, 6 February 1826, BL, Add. 47293 A f. 6.

9. "Petersburgh, Sept. 28," *The Times*, September 19, 1825, 2.

10. "It Being a Law in Russia," *Morning Post*, October 28, 1825, 3.

11. JP to RKP, 15 February 1826, HL, POR 2071.

12. Jane Porter and Anna Maria Porter, *Tales Round a Winter Hearth*, vol. I (London: Longman, Rees, Orme, Brown, and Green, 1826), v–vi. This book went into a German edition the following year ("Anna Maria Porter," in *Orlando*).

13. Owen Rees to [JP], 10 December [1825], Longman Archives, Longman I, 101, no. 519B, DBF 1826A064.

14. AMP to RKP, 12 May 1826, HL, POR 1015.

15. Mrs. JP to JP, 1826[?] HL, POR 1231.

16. Mrs. JP to JP, 1826[?] HL, POR 1232.

17. Loan from Anna Middleton, Spencer, Box 36, Folder 39.

18. JP to AMP, 27 July 1826, HL, POR 1850.

19. "Coming Out," *Archives of the House of Longman, 1794–1914*, Reel 39, H11 145.

20. Anna Maria Porter, *Honor O'Hara: A Novel*, vol. I (London: Longman, Rees, Orme, Brown, and Green), 57, 60, 113.

21. AMP to RKP, 14[?] April 1828[?], HL, POR 1024.

22. Impression Book Entry, Longman & Co., October 1826, Longman Impression Book, no. 8, fol. 144v, DBF 1826A063.

23. Daniel Bayley to Mrs. JP, 10 October 1826, Pforzheimer, PORT 26.10.10A.

24. AMP to JP, 10 December 1826, HL, POR 969.

25. RKP to Mrs. JP, 5 December 1829, BL, RP 1415/1.

26. AMP to JP, c. 1826, HL, POR 965.

27. Mary Porter to Mrs. JP, 15 October 1827, Spencer, Box 15, Folder 18.

28. Mary Porter to RKP, 9 September 1828, Spencer, Box 15, Folder 23.

29. Mary Porter to Mrs. JP, 15 July 1829, Spencer, Box 15, Folder 27.

30. Mary Porter to RKP, 29 December 1829, Spencer, Box 15, Folder 25.

31. Mary Porter to Mrs. JP, 27 May 1827, Spencer, Box 15, Folder 17.

32. J. P., "Nobody's Address," *Ladies' Monthly Museum*, July 1827, 336; Thomas McLean, "Nobody's Argument: Jane Porter and the Historical Novel," *Journal for Early Modern Cultural Studies* 7, no. 2 (Fall/Winter 2007): 91.

33. "Ad: Summer Nights at Sea," *Morning Post*, October 9, 1827, 1.

34. Jane Porter and Anna Maria Porter, *Coming Out; and The Field of the Forty Footsteps*, 3 vols. (London: Longman, Rees, Orme, Brown, and Green, 1828), vol. I, 229, 321–23, 342, vol. II, 2. This book was soon afterward published in a New York edition as well as in French and German translations ("Anna Maria Porter," in *Orlando*).

35. JP to AMP, 2 May 1827, HL, POR 1860.

36. Owen Rees to AMP, 29 November 1827, Longman Archives, Longman I, 102, no. 60C, DBF 1826A063.

37. "Coming Out," *Archives of the House of Longman, 1794–1914*, Reel 39, H11 194.

38. JP to Sir Walter Scott, 8 April 1828, NLS, NS 3906 ff. 196–97.

39. Review of *Coming Out; and The Field of the Forty Footsteps*, *Literary Gazette*, vol. 575, 1828, 52.

40. AMP to RKP, 3 June 1828, HL, POR 1026; JP to Mrs. JP, 27 June 1828, HL, POR 2028.

41. AMP to JP, 2 July 1828, HL, POR 980.

42. Thomas McLean, "Jane Porter's Later Works, 1825–46," *Harvard Library Bulletin* 20, no. 2 (Summer 2009): 45–63.

43. JP to RKP, 4–5 March 1828, HL, POR 2081.

44. AMP to RKP, 19 March 1827, HL, POR 1021.

45. JP to RKP, 17 January 1827, HL, POR 2078; RKP to JP, 28 February 1828, Spencer, Box 2, Folder 27; JP to RKP, 17 October 1826, HL, POR 2074.

46. JP to RKP, 16–17 April 1827, HL, POR 2080.

47. *Caracas Diary*, 467.

48. Ruth Knezevich and Devoney Looser, "Jane Austen's Afterlife, West Indian Madams, and the Literary Porter Family: Two New Letters from Charles Austen," *Modern Philology* 112, no. 3 (2015): 564.

49. Ibid., 554–68.

50. AMP to RKP, 30 November 1828, HL, POR 1027.

51. Owen Rees to AMP, 20 January 1829, Spencer, Box 29, Folder 6.

52. Longman & Co. to AMP, 13 January 1829, Longman Archives, Longman I, 102, no. 98D (draft), DBF 1826A063.

53. JP to RKP, 4–5 June 1832, HL, POR 2088.

54. Mrs. JP to RKP, 4 January 1829, HL, POR 1251.

55. JP to AMP, 7 April 1829, HL, POR 1863.

56. AMP to Mrs. JP, 9[?] April 1829, HL, POR 326.

57. AMP to JP, 20–21 April 1829, HL, POR 327.

58. AMP to Mrs. JP, 9[?] April 1829, HL, POR 326.

59. JP to Thomas Joseph Pettigrew, 10 July 1829, Beinecke, General MSS 265, Box 1, Folder 11.

60. JP to RKP, 4 September 1834, Spencer, Box 5, Folder 18. In this letter, Jane recollects her mother's stroke in comparison to that of a neighbor's.

61. AMP to Wilhelmina Hole, 15 October 1829, HL, POR 232.

62. JP to RKP, 3 June 1831, Spencer, Box 3, Folder 67.

63. "The National Gazette," *Philadelphia Inquirer*, June 23, 1829, 2; "Joseph Bonaparte," *Morning Post*, August 25, 1829, 4.

64. RKP to King William IV, 18 January 1831, Spencer, Box 2, Folder 34.

65. RKP to JP, 8 December 1829, BL, RP 1415/1.

66. RKP to Mrs. JP, 16 September 1829, BL, RP 1415/1.

67. RKP to Mrs. JP, 16 September 1829, BL, RP 1415/1; *Caracas Diary*, 450.

68. RKP to Mrs. JP, 18 March 1830, BL, RP 1415/1.

69. JP to RKP, 1 December 1830, Spencer, Box 3, Folder 58.

70. *Caracas Diary*, 455.

71. RKP to King William IV, 18 January 1831, Spencer, Box 2, Folder 34.

72. AMP to JP, April[?] 1830[?], HL, POR 985.

73. Mrs. JP to RKP, 24 May 1830, HL, POR 1255.

74. JP to Nathaniel Parker Willis, 26 June 1836, Morristown.

75. JP and AMP to RKP, 4 May 1830, Spencer, Box 9, Folder 15.

76. Anna Maria Porter, *The Barony*, vol. 3 (London: Longman, Rees, Orme, Brown, and Green, 1830), 556–57.

77. Lady Charleville to JP, March 6, 1831, Pforzheimer, PORT 31.03.06.

78. AMP to RKP, 3 May 1831, Spencer, Box 9, Folder 19.

79. Review of *The Barony*, *Monthly Review*, vol. 10, October 1830, 466.

80. JP to RKP, 30 July 1834, Spencer, Box 5, Folder 15.

81. JP to RKP, 30 October 1834, Spencer, Box 5, Folder 20.

82. JP to RKP, 6 April 1831, Spencer, Box 3, Folder 64.

83. Mrs. JP to RKP, 6–7 July 1830, HL, POR 1257.

84. JP to RKP, 31 August 1830, Spencer, Box 3, Folder 56.

85. JP to RKP, 5 January 1831, Spencer, Box 3, Folder 59.

86. AMP to RKP, 17 February 1831, Spencer, Box 9, Folder 18.

87. JP to RKP, 5 January 1831, Spencer, Box 3, Folder 59.

88. William Wordsworth to RKP, 23 February 1832, Berg Collection, New York Public Library.

89. AMP to JP, 30 April–1 May 1815, HL, POR 722.

90. WOP to JP, 22 February 1831, Durham.

91. Will of Thaddeus Porter, National Archives, PROB 11/1722/127.

92. AMP to JP, April[?] 1826[?], HL, POR 922.

93. WOP to JP, 22 February 1831, Durham.

94. AMP to JP, April[?] 1824[?], HL, POR 922.

95. WOP to Mrs. JP, 28 December 1830, Durham.

96. JP to RKP, 3 June 1831, Spencer, Box 3, Folder 67.

97. WOP to Mrs. JP, 1 March 1831, Durham.

98. WOP to Mrs. JP, 24 May 1831, Durham.

99. WOP to Mrs. JP, 1 March 1831, Durham.

100. JP to RKP, 4 May 1831, Spencer, Box 3, Folder 66.

101. Fiona Price, "Jane Porter and the Authorship of *Sir Edward Seaward's Narrative*: Previously Unpublished Correspondence," *Notes and Queries*, March 2002, 55.

102. [William Ogilvie Porter], *Sir Edward Seaward's Narrative*, vol. I (London: Longman, 1831), v.

103. "Review of New Publications," *La Belle Assemblée*, August 1831, 79.

104. Review of *Sir Edward Seaward's Narrative*, *Metropolitan*, July 1831, 502.

105. "Miss Jane Porter," *Gentleman's Magazine*, vol. XXXIV, August 1850, 222.

106. JP to RKP, 4 May 1831, Spencer, Box 3, Folder 66.

107. WOP to Mrs. JP, 24 May 1831, Durham.

108. Mrs. JP to RKP, 5 April 1831, HL, POR 1260.

109. AMP to RKP, 28 May 1831, HL, POR 1036.

110. JP to RKP, 2 August 1831, Spencer, Box 3, Folder 69.

111. WOP to AMP, 15 June 1831, Durham.

112. JP to RKP, 2 August 1831, Spencer, Box 3, Folder 69.

113. AMP to WOP, 13 June 1831, HL, POR 1038.

114. AMP to RKP, 5 July 1831, Spencer, Box 9, Folder 20.

115. AMP to JP, 20 December 1831, HL, POR 999.

116. JP to Samuel Carter Hall, 28 June 1831, UCLA, Box 1, f. 6.

117. JP to RKP, 25 April 1837, Spencer, Box 6, Folder 25.

118. JP to Sir Walter Scott, 5 October 1831, HL, POR 2144.

CHAPTER 22: SEPARATING SISTERS: A PITILESS AND COLD-BLOODED PLAN (1831–32)

1. JP to RKP, 2 August 1831, Spencer, Box 3, Folder 69.

2. AMP to RKP, 5 July 1831, Spencer, Box 9, Folder 20.

3. Moyle Sherer to JP, 28 July 1832, Spencer, Box 28, Folder 16.

4. Julian Litten, "The English Funeral, 1700–1850," in *Grave Concerns: Death and Burial in England from 1700 to 1850*, ed. Margaret Cox (York: Council for British Archaeology, 1998), 8–16.

5. AMP to RKP, 5 July 1831, Spencer, Box 9, Folder 20.

6. JP to Mr. Shrubsole (copy), July 1831, HL, POR 2155; JP to RKP, 1 November 1832, Spencer, Box 4, Folder 15.

7. JP to RKP, 2 August 1831, Spencer, Box 3, Folder 69.

8. [Jane Porter], "Miss Jane Porter," in *National Gallery of Illustrious and Eminent Personages of the Nineteenth Century; with Memoirs,* vol. 5, ed. William Jerdan (London: Fisher, Son, & Jackson, 1834), 7.

9. Almost two years after Mrs. Porter died, Jane ordered "the simple table monument" using fifteen pounds of Robert's funds. See JP to RKP, 23 May 1833, Spencer, Box 4, Folder 28. Jane gave five shillings a year to the church clerk for the care of her mother's grave. See JP to RKP, 13 June 1840, HL, POR 2110.

10. JP, Grave Inscription for Mrs. Jane Porter, 11 May 1833, HL, POR 44; JP to RKP, 25 April 1833, Spencer, Box 4, Folder 27; Mrs. S. C. Hall, "Memories of

Miss Jane Porter," *Harper's New Monthly Magazine* 1, no. IV (September 1850): 438.

11. JP to RKP, 7 September 1831, Spencer, Box 3, Folder 70.

12. AMP to Mrs. Bain, 28 June 1831, Clark.

13. J. P., "British Heroism," *La Belle Assemblée*, vol. 6, n.s. 35 (November 1827): 214.

14. JP to RKP, 29 September 1831, Spencer, Box 3, Folder 72.

15. JP to RKP, 7 December 1831, Spencer, Box 4, Folder 3.

16. JP to RKP, 31 January 1832, Spencer, Box 4, Folder 4.

17. JP to RKP, 4 May 1831, Spencer, Box 3, Folder 66.

18. "Works of Jane and Maria Porter," Reel 47, Bentley Papers, University of Illinois.

19. JP to Samuel Carter Hall, 28 June 1831, UCLA, Box 1, f. 6.

20. JP to RKP, 4 May 1831, Spencer, Box 3, Folder 66.

21. JP to Samuel Carter Hall, 10 August 1831, Bentley Papers, University of Illinois.

22. JP to Colburn and Bentley, 12 October 1831, Houghton.

23. Jane Porter, *Thaddeus of Warsaw*, rev. ed. (London: Colburn and Bentley, 1831), vi.

24. Review of Standard Novels IV: *Thaddeus of Warsaw*, *Literary Gazette*, June 4, 1831, 360.

25. Peter Puff, "Letters to Certain Persons: Epistle I: To Miss Jane Porter," *Aberdeen Magazine*, October 1831, 553. This review is reprinted in Jane Porter, *The Scottish Chiefs*, ed. Fiona Price (Peterborough, Ontario: Broadview Press, 2007), 754–61.

26. Graeme Morton, "The Social Memory of Jane Porter and her 'Scottish Chiefs,' *The Scottish Historical Review* 91, no. 232 (October 2012): 330.

27. Puff, "Letters to Certain Persons," 554–55.

28. AMP to RKP, 9 December 1831, Spencer, Box 9, Folder 25.

29. AMP to RKP, 28 March 1832, Spencer, Box 9, Folder 29.

30. Julia Pardoe, "Father and Son," *Abroad and at Home: Tales Here and There* (London: Lambert & Co., 1857), 176.

31. JP to RKP, 7 September 1831, Spencer, Box 3, Folder 70.

32. WOP to JP, 13 August 1831, Durham.

33. JP to RKP, 7 September 1831, Spencer, Box 3, Folder 70.

34. AMP to RKP, 5 September 1831, Spencer, Box 9, Folder 22.

35. RKP to AMP, 22 October 1831, Spencer, Box 2, Folder 36.

36. JP to RKP, 29 September 1831, Spencer, Box 3, Folder 72.

37. JP to RKP, 7 September 1831, Spencer, Box 3, Folder 70.

38. JP to RKP, 29 September 1831, Spencer, Box 3, Folder 72.

39. JP to RKP, 31 October 1831, Spencer, Box 4, Folder 1.

40. JP to AMP, 17–18 October 1831, HL, POR 1875.

41. JP to RKP, 7 December 1831, Spencer, Box 4, Folder 3.

42. AMP to JP, 7–8 January 1832, HL, POR 1007.

43. JP to RKP, 31 October 1831, Spencer, Box 4, Folder 1.

44. AMP to JP, 2–3 January 1832, HL, POR 1006.

45. JP to RKP, 31 January 1832, Spencer, Box 4, Folder 4.

46. "Jane's Journal to the 28th of May 1832," Spencer, Box 4, Folder 10.

47. JP to RKP, 3 July 1832, Spencer, Box 4, Folder 11.

48. JP to Charles Denham, 28 July 1832, Houghton.

49. W. O. Porter, M.D., *Remarks on the Causes, Prevention, & Management of the Present Prevailing Epidemic, Commonly Called Typhous Fever, For the Use and Benefit of the People* (London: Baldwin & Craddock, 1819), 40.

50. JP to Charles Denham, 12 July 1832, Houghton.

51. Sarah Booth to RKP, 4 July 1832, Spencer, Box 4, Folder 11.

52. JP to RKP, 26 July 1832, Spencer, Box 4, Folder 12.

53. JP to Charles Denham, 12 July 1832, Houghton.

54. JP to RKP, 3 July 1832, Spencer, Box 4, Folder 11.

55. JP to Charles Denham, 28 July 1832, Houghton.

56. JP to RKP, 3 July 1832, Spencer, Box 4, Folder 11.

57. JP to Lady Charleville, 23 July 1832, Nottingham, MY 560/4.

58. JP, Note on Wade Caulfield, c. 1833 HL, POR 20.

59. WOP to JP, 20 August 1833, Durham.

60. "Anna Maria Porter," *World of Fashion*, no. 102, September 1, 1832, 214; "Miss Anna Maria Porter," *New York Spectator*, August 20, 1832, 1.

61. "Obituary: Miss A. M. Porter," *Gentleman's Magazine*, vol. CII, December 1832, 578.

62. "The Departed of Thirty-Two," *Fraser's Magazine*, vol. 6, December 1832, 752.

63. Jane Porter, *The Scottish Chiefs: Revised, Corrected, and Illustrated* (London: James S. Virtue, 1840), 24.

CHAPTER 23: PRESERVE AND DESTROY: JANE'S FRIENDS AND ENEMIES (1832–40)

1. JP to RKP, 1 November 1832, Spencer, Box 4, Folder 16.

2. JP to RKP, 3 July 1832, Spencer, Box 4, Folder 11.

3. Ibid.

4. JP to RKP, 24 September 1833, Spencer, Box 4, Folder 35.

5. JP to RKP, 26 July 1832, Spencer, Box 4, Folder 12.

6. JP to Caroline James, 7 July 1832, Houghton.

7. JP to RKP, 26 July 1832, Spencer, Box 4, Folder 12.

8. JP to Eliza Vanderhorst, 18 July 1832, Bristol Record Office, 8032/89.

9. JP, Account Book, 10 July 1832, UCLA.

10. Jane Porter, "Introduction," in *The Pastor's Fire-Side* (London: Colburn and Bentley, 1832).

11. JP to RKP, 27 November 1833, Spencer, Box 5, Folder 2.

12. [Jane Porter], "Miss Jane Porter," in *National Gallery of Illustrious and Eminent Personages of the Nineteenth Century; with Memoirs,* vol. 5, ed. William Jerdan (London: Fisher, Son, & Jackson, 1834), 3.

13. JP to Lady Charleville, 23 July 1832, Nottingham, MY 560/5.

14. Jane Porter, *The Scottish Chiefs: Revised, Corrected, and Illustrated* (London: James S. Virtue, 1840), 45.

15. Charles Lines, *Coughton Court and the Throckmorton Story* (Manchester: Whitehorn Press, 1974), 21.

16. Jane Porter, "Miss Jane Porter's Tour," Spencer, Box 38, Folder 38.

17. JP to RKP, 20 August 1832, Spencer, Box 4, Folder 13.

18. JP to Lady Charleville, 28 August 1832, Nottingham, MY 561/1.

19. Ibid.

20. JP to RKP, 20 October 1832, Spencer, Box 4, Folder 15.

21. Sarah Booth to JP, 31 October 1835, Durham.

22. JP to RKP, 28 September 1836, Spencer, Box 6, Folder 12.

23. JP to RKP, 28 June 1836, Spencer, Box 6, Folder 7.

24. JP to RKP, 12 October 1833, Spencer, Box 5, Folder 1.

25. JP to RKP, 5 August 1833, Spencer, Box 4, Folder 32.

26. JP to RKP, 27 November 1833, Spencer, Box 5, Folder 2.

27. S. C. Hall, *A Book of Memories of Great Men and Women of the Age* (London: Virtue & Co., 1871), 131.

28. JP to RKP, 25 August 1834, Spencer, Box 5, Folder 17.

29. JP to RKP, 30 July 1834, Spencer, Box 5, Folder 15; Saunders and Otley to JP, 4 May 1834, Pforzheimer, PORT 34.05.04.

30. [Theodora Davenport Peers], *Young Hearts: A Novel, By A Recluse, With a Preface by Miss Jane Porter* (London: Saunders & Otley, 1834).

31. Selina Wheler to JP, 21 March 1837, Pforzheimer, PORT 37.03.21a.

32. JP to RKP, 26 December 1832, Spencer, Box 4, Folder 20.

33. JP, December 15, Diary of 1835, Folger, M.a.18.

34. JP, Account Book, 8 December 1832, UCLA.

35. JP to RKP, 28 June 1836, Spencer, Box 6, Folder 7.

36. [JP], "To My Countrywomen," *Gentleman's Magazine*, vol. LXXI, December 1811, 501–2.

37. Rev. R. Bickell, *The West Indies as They Are: or, A Real Picture of Slavery: But More Particularly as it Exists on the Island of Jamaica* (London: J. Hatchers and Son, 1825), 41.

38. JP to RKP, 25 June 1834, Spencer, Box 5, Folder 12.

39. JP to RKP, 1 April 1834, Spencer, Box 5, Folder 9.

40. "William Alexander Mackinnon," Legacies of British Slavery database, accessed June 7, 2021, www.depts-live.ucl.ac.uk/lbs/person/view/44859.

41. "Robert Porter," Legacies of British Slavery database, accessed June 7, 2021, www.depts-live.ucl.ac.uk/lbs/person/view/22676.

42. JP to RKP, 31 January 1832, Spencer, Box 4, Folder 4.

43. JP, 7 February, Diary of 1835, Folger. M.a.18.

44. JP to RKP, 18 February 1835, Spencer, Box 5, Folder 25.

45. JP to RKP, 28 April 1835, Spencer, Box 5, Folder 28.

46. JP to RKP, 12 September 1837, Spencer, Box 6, Folder 32.

47. JP to RKP, 28 January 1838, Spencer, Box 7, Folder 1.

48. Mary Skinner to JP, 9 March 1833, Spencer, Box 28, Folder 29.

49. JP to RKP, 12 October 1833, Spencer, Box 5, Folder 1.

50. Agnes Repplier, *A Happy Half-Century and Other Essays* (Boston: Houghton Mifflin, 1908), 14–15.

51. JP to RKP, 26 January 1836, Spencer, Box 6, Folder 1.

52. JP to James Fraser, 4 August 1834, Houghton.

53. JP to RKP, 24 December 1838, Spencer, Box 7, Folder 17.

54. JP, 22 December, Diary of 1835, Folger, M.a.18; JP to RKP, 18 February 1835, Spencer, Box 5, Folder 25.

55. Glenn Hendler, *Public Sentiments: Structures of Feeling in Nineteenth-Century American Literature* (Chapel Hill: University of North Carolina Press, 2003), 159.

56. JP to RKP, 27–28 November 1835, HL, POR 2097.

57. JP to RKP, 18 February 1835, Spencer, Box 5, Folder 25.

58. JP to RKP, 21 July 1835, Spencer, Box 5, Folder 33.

59. JP to RKP, 19–31 March 1836, HL, POR 2100.

60. JP to RKP, 21 July 1835, Spencer, Box 5, Folder 33; JP to RKP, 23 May 1836, Spencer, Box 6, Folder 6.

61. JP to RKP, 23 May 1836, Spencer, Box 6, Folder 6.

62. JP, July, Diary of 1835, Folger. M.a.18.

63. JP to RKP, 28 August 1835, Spencer, Box 5, Folder 34.

64. Elizabeth Barrett Browning, Letter 133, 11 January 1842, in *The Letters of Elizabeth Barrett Browning to Mary Russell Mitford, 1836–1843,* vol. 1, ed. Meredith B. Raymond and Mary Rose Sullivan (Waco, TX: Browning Library of Baylor University, 1983), 327.

65. JP to Lady Charleville, 28 April 1835, HL, POR 1289.

66. Henry A. Beers, *Nathaniel Parker Willis* (Boston: Houghton Mifflin, 1892), 172.

67. JP to Mrs. Robert Porter, 3 October 1835, HL, POR 1419.

68. Beers, *Nathaniel Parker Willis*, 177.

69. JP to Mrs. Holmes, 12 August 1835, HL, POR 1352.

70. JP to RKP, 28 August 1835, Spencer, Box 5, Folder 34.

71. JP to RKP, 24–28 September 1835, HL, POR 2093.

72. JP to RKP, 26 September 1836, Spencer, Box 6, Folder 11.

73. JP to RKP, 26 January 1836, Spencer, Box 6, Folder 2.

74. JP to Nathaniel Parker Willis, 21 October 1837, Morristown.

75. Nathaniel Parker Willis to JP, 24 October 1839, Beinecke.

76. Nathaniel Parker Willis to JP, 1 November 1839, Beinecke; JP to RKP, 13 June 1840, HL, POR 2109.

77. JP to RKP, 25–30 April 1836, HL, POR 2102.

78. JP to RKP, 19–31 March 1836, HL, POR 2100.

79. [William Makepeace Thackeray], "Notes on the North What-D'Ye-Callem Election," *Fraser's Magazine*, vol. 24, September 1841, 352.

80. JP to Nathaniel Parker Willis, 13 April 1843, Morristown.

81. Thomas McLean, "Jane Porter's Later Works, 1825–46," *Harvard Library Bulletin* 20, no. 2 (Summer 2009): 45–64.

82. Frederic Montagu to JP, 13 July 1837, Pforzheimer, PORT 37.07.13.

83. The Author of Thaddeus of Warsaw [Jane Porter], "The Old Lady: A Fragment," in *The Ages of Female Beauty: Illustrated in a Series of Engravings*, ed. Frederic Montagu (London: Charles Tilt, 1837), 58–62.

84. RKP to Mrs. Spicer, 16 August 1837, Spencer, Box 2, Folder 43.

85. JP to John Churchill, 25 January 1839, Beinecke.

86. Jane Porter Account Book, 1830–39, UCLA, Box 1, Folder 3.

87. JP to RKP, 12 May 1839, Spencer, Box 7, Folder 28.

88. JP to RKP, 13 July 1839, Spencer, Box 7, Folder 32.

89. JP to Nathaniel Parker Willis, 1 February 1841, Morristown.

90. JP to RKP, 13 June 1840, HL, POR 2110.

91. Porter, *The Scottish Chiefs* (1840), 49.

92. JP to RKP, 27 January 1840, Spencer, Box 8, Folder 11.

93. JP to RKP, 12 December 1839, Spencer, Box 8, Folder 8.

94. Ina Mary White, "The Diary of Jane Porter," *Scottish Review*, vol. XXIX, January and April 1897, 333.

95. JP to Lord Melbourne, 20 January 1840, HL, POR 1386.

96. JP to RKP, 20 June 1838, Spencer, Box 7, Folder 9; on the poem, see Graeme Morton, *William Wallace: A National Tale* (Edinburgh: Edinburgh University Press, 2014), 133.

97. Devoney Looser, "Jane Porter and the Old Woman Writer's Quest for Financial Independence," in *Women Writers and Old Age in Great Britain, 1750–1850* (Baltimore: Johns Hopkins University Press, 2008), 141–67.

98. JP to [Belinda Morgan], 28 November 1840, HL, POR 1312.

99. JP to RKP, 27 November 1840, Spencer, Box 8, Folder 32.

100. JP to RKP, 11 December 1840, Spencer, Box 8, Folder 33.

101. Will of Sir Charles Throckmorton, National Archives, PROB-11-1941-388.

CHAPTER 24: HER YOUNGER SELF AGAIN: JANE AND ROBERT REUNITED (1841–42)

1. JP to RKP, 10 March 1841, HL, POR 2112.

2. JP to Mrs. Brooke Taylor, 27 March 1841, BL, Add. 52343 f. 85.

3. *Caracas Diary*, 1116, 1160.

4. Agnes Strickland to John Adamson, c. 1841, Private Collection.

5. *Caracas Diary*, 1115, 1116, 1119, 1124, 1126, 1140.

6. Philip Mansel, *Dressed to Rule: Royal and Court Costume from Louis XIV to Elizabeth II* (New Haven: Yale University Press, 2005), 135.

7. *Caracas Diary*, 1126, 1130.

8. Moyle Sherer to JP, 20 March 1841, Spencer, Box 28, Folder 28.

9. *Caracas Diary*, 1116, 1131; RKP Receipts, July–August 1841, Spencer, Box 32, Folder 40.

10. *Caracas Diary*, 1132.

11. RKP to Colonel Burwood, 17 February 1841, BL, RP 1415/1.

12. Mary Porter Kikine to RKP, 3 October 1840, Spencer, Box 16, Folder 23; Mary Porter Kikine to JP, 3 October 1840, Spencer, Box 16, Folder 22.

13. Mary Porter Kikine to Mrs. JP, c. 1820, Spencer, Box 15, Folder 6.

14. Mary Porter Kikine to RKP, 27 May 1827, Spencer, Box 15, Folder 17.

15. Mary Porter Kikine to Mrs. JP et al., 15 July 1829, Spencer, Box 15, Folder 30.

16. Mary Porter Kikine to JP et al., 15 July 1829, Spencer, Box 15, Folder 53.

17. Mary Porter Kikine to RKP, 8 September 1832, Spencer, Box 15, Folder 56.

18. JP to Nathaniel Parker Willis, 12 February 1842, Morristown.

19. RKP to Colonel Burwood, 17 September 1841, BL, RP 1415/1.

20. JP, 26 January, Diary of 1842, UCLA, Box 1, Folder 5.

21. WOP to JP, 17 February 1842, Durham.

22. JP to Lady Charleville, 31 March 1842, Nottingham, MY 565.

23. JP, Diary of 1842, Notes for February, UCLA, Box 1, Folder 5.

24. *Caracas Diary*, 1136.

25. JP, Journal, March–April 1842, Spencer, Box 36, Folder 4.

26. JP to Lady Charleville, 31 March 1842, Nottingham, MY 565.

27. Jane Porter, Journal, March–April 1842, Spencer, Box 36, Folder 4.

28. JP to Lady Charleville, 31 March 1842, Nottingham, MY 565.

29. JP, 1 May, Diary of 1842, UCLA, Box 1, Folder 5.

30. Alexis Olenin to JP, 14 October 1825, Spencer, Box 27, Folder 3; RKP to Alexey d'Olenin, September 1818, Spencer, Box 1, Folder 60.

31. *Caracas Diary*, 1181.

32. JP, 18 April, Diary of 1842, Notes for April, UCLA, Box 1, Folder 5.

33. JP, 26 April, Diary of 1842, UCLA, Box 1, Folder 5.

34. JP to Nathaniel Parker Willis, 12 February 1842, Morristown.

35. *Caracas Diary*, 1173.

36. JP to Lady Charleville, 31 March 1842, Nottingham, MY 565.

37. *Caracas Diary*, 1172, 1173.

38. JP, entry for May, Diary of 1842, UCLA, Box 1, Folder 5.

39. "Sir Robert Ker Porter," *Bristol Mercury*, May 21, 1842, 8.

40. JP, entry for May, Diary of 1842, UCLA, Box 1, Folder 5.

41. [Jane Porter], "Memoir of the Late Sir Robert Ker Porter, K. C. H.," *United Service Journal*, October 1842, 264.

42. JP, 4 May, Diary of 1842, UCLA, Box 1, Folder 5.

43. JP, 5 May, Diary of 1842, UCLA, Box 1, Folder 5.

44. JP, 7 May, Diary of 1842, UCLA, Box 1, Folder 5.

45. JP to Mary Porter Kikine, 9 May 1842, HL, POR 1366.

46. JP to Mary Porter Kikine, 2 May 1842 (O. S.), HL, POR 1367.

47. JP, 15 May, Diary of 1842, UCLA, Box 1, Folder 5.

CHAPTER 25: A CHAIR OF ONE'S OWN (1842–50)

1. "After Our Melancholy Communication," *English Chronicle and Whitehall Evening Post*, June 28, 1842, 1.

2. JP, 9 June, Diary of 1842, UCLA, Box 1, Folder 5.

3. JP, 6 June, Diary of 1842, UCLA, Box 1, Folder 5.

4. JP to Lord Clarendon, 4 May 1842, Lilly.

5. Lord Clarendon to JP, June 1842, Lilly.

6. JP to Sir Robert Peel, 10 June 1842, BL, Add. 40510 f. 75.

7. Sir Robert Peel to JP, 10 June 1842, Pforzheimer, PORT 42.06.10.

8. JP, 29 June and 10 July, Diary of 1842, UCLA, Box 1, Folder 5.

9. JP to Robert Ingles, 26 September 1843, HL, POR 1354.

10. JP to Messrs. Drummond, 19 December 1843, Spencer, Box 36, Folder 41.

11. Jane Porter, Journal Entries, 1843, Spencer, Box 35, Folder 46.

12. "Jane Porter," File no. 1055, Reel 35, Archives of the Royal Literary Fund, 1790–1918, BL, M1077/35.

13. Jane Porter, "Mr. Christie Questions," c. 1843, HL, POR 30.

14. *The Catalogue of the Very Interesting Original Works, and the Collection Formed by that Distinguished Amateur and Highly Accomplished Traveler Sir Robert Ker Porter, K. C. H., Deceased*, Spencer, Box 39, Folder 21.

15. Mr. Drummond to JP, 17 April 1843, Spencer, Box 37, Folder 32.

16. WOP to JP, 11 June 1843, Durham.

17. Jane Porter, Journal Entries, 1843, Spencer, Box 35, Folder 46.

18. JP to Emerson Tennant, 20 June 1844, BL, Add. 40547 f. 147.

19. "The Late Fatal Duel," *Freeman's Journal*, July 19, 1843, 2.

20. "Alleged Cause of the Duel," *English Chronicle and Whitehall Evening Post*, July 11, 1843, 7.

21. Stephen Banks, *A Polite Exchange of Bullets: The Duel and the English Gentleman, 1750–1850* (Woodbridge, UK: Boydell & Brewer, 2010), 231, 286.

22. "Duelling," *Montreal Gazette*, December 14, 1904, 6.

23. Jane Porter, Journal Entries, 1843, Spencer, Box 35, Folder 46.

24. JP, 26 June, Diary of 1842, UCLA, Box 1, Folder 5.

25. Elizabeth Barrett Browning to Mary Russell Mitford, 23–25 December 1841, in *The Brownings Correspondence, January 1841–May 1842*, vol. 5, ed. Philip Kelley and Ronald Hudson (Winfield, KS: Wedgestone Press, 1987), 193.

26. "Testimonial to Jane Porter," *Richmond Enquirer*, November 15, 1844, 1.

27. Nathaniel Parker Willis, *Prose Works of N. P. Willis* (Philadelphia: Carey & Hart, 1849), 726.

28. JP to RKP, 3 May 1834, Spencer, Box 5, Folder 10.

29. Willis, *Prose Works of N. P. Willis*, 726–27.

30. "Our Commentaries for the Week, In Prose and Verse," *Illustrated London News* 6, no. 142, January 18, 1845, 42.

31. Robert Peel to Lord Aberdeen, 12 March 1845, Pforzheimer, PORT 45.03.12A.

32. Lord Clarendon to JP, 9 April 1846, Lilly.

33. "The Porter Family of Bristol," *Gloucestershire Notes and Queries*, vol. 3, January 1885, 31.

34. JP, Memo, 28 January 1846, Spencer, Box 36, Folder 53; JP, Memo, 29 April 1847, Spencer, Box 36, Folder 54.

35. S. C. Hall, *A Book of Memories of Great Men and Women of the Age* (London: Virtue & Co., 1871), 131.

36. Myrtle Hill, "Lutton, Anne (1791–1881), Wesleyan Methodist preacher," in *Oxford Dictionary of National Biography*, September 23, 2004, accessed March 15, 2022, www-oxforddnb-com.ezproxy1.lib.asu.edu/view/10.1093/ref:odnb/9780198614128.001.0001/odnb-9780198614128-e-52703.

37. "Dr. Porter's Illness," *Bristol Mercury*, December 25, 1847, 8.

38. Lady Clarendon to JP, 5 January 1848, Lilly.

39. Lady Clarendon to JP, 10 January 1848, Lilly.

40. G. M. J. Crawford Bromehead to JP, 17 July 1848, Pforzheimer, PORT 48.07.17.

41. William Law to JP, 26 May 1848, Pforzheimer, PORT 48.05.26.

42. "Death of Miss Jane Porter," *Bristol Mercury and Daily Post*, May 25, 1850, 8.

43. JP to John Shephard, 27 December 1849, HL, POR 2150.

44. JP to John Shephard, 8 May 1850, HL, POR 1301.

45. JP to RKP, 26 December 1832, Spencer, Box 4, Folder 20.

46. JP to RKP, 27 March 1833, Spencer, Box 4, Folder 25.

47. Will of Jane Porter, Spinster, PROB 11-2118-428, National Archives.

48. JP to John Shephard, 22 April 1850, Pforzheimer, PORT 50.04.22.

49. Bristoliensis, "The Porter Family, of Bristol: Monumental Inscriptions, etc.," in *Gloucestershire Notes and Queries*, vol. 3 (London: William Kent & Co., 1887), 31.

CODA: THREE OR FOUR CLOSELY PACKED SEA CHESTS: THE HISTORIC, CONFUSED, AND UNSORTED PORTER CORRESPONDENCE (AFTER 1850)

1. WOP to John Shephard, 26 May 1850, Pforzheimer, PORT 50.05.26.

2. "Library and Miscellaneous Effects of the Late Miss Jane Porter," *Morning Chronicle*, July 15, 1850, 8.

3. JP to RKP, 21 February 1837, Spencer, Box 6, Folder 21.

4. Sarah Booth to JP, 9 May 1843, Pforzheimer, PORT 43.05.09.

5. William George, "263. Porter, Dr. W. Ogilvie," *Antiquarian Magazine and Bibliographer* 5, no. 114 (1884): 10; "Mural Monument," *Bristol Times and Mirror*, March 29, 1851, 5.

6. Bette Burke, *Cinderella Square: A History of Portland Square* (Bristol: BRB Publications, 2004).

7. "Continuation and Close of Sale," *Bristol Mercury*, February 28, 1852, 1.

8. "Rare, Curious, and Interesting Collection of Manuscript and Autograph Letters," *The Times*, March 15, 1852, 16.

9. "Our Weekly Gossip," *The Athenaeum*, March 27, 1852, 355.

10. "The Porter Correspondence," *Notes and Queries*, 8th series, vol. VII, no. 2, February 1895, 87; "Porter Correspondence," *Notes and Queries*, 8th series, vol. VIII, no. 9, March 1895, 191.

11. "Gossip of the Literary Circles," *The Critic*, vol. 11, April 1, 1852, 189.

12. W. George, "Sir Edward Seaward," *Notes and Queries*, 6th series, vol. I, no. 31, January 1880, 100.

13. A. N. L. Munby, *The Formation of the Phillipps Library From 1841 to 1872,* vol. IV (Cambridge: Cambridge University Press, 1956), 165, 171.

14. Munby, *Formation of the Phillipps Library*, vol. IV, 166–69.

15. JP to RKP, 25–30 April 1836, HL, POR 2102.

INDEX

A NOTE ON THE AUTHOR

DEVONEY LOOSER is Regents Professor of English at Arizona State University and the author or editor of nine other books on literature by women, including *The Making of Jane Austen* and *The Daily Jane Austen: A Year of Quotes*. Her writing has appeared in the *Atlantic*, the *New York Times*, *Salon*, the *Times Literary Supplement*, the *Washington Post*, and *Entertainment Weekly*, and she's had the pleasure of talking about Austen on CNN and in a series of video and audio lectures for The Great Courses. Looser, who has played roller derby as Stone Cold Jane Austen, is a Guggenheim Fellow and a National Endowment for the Humanities Public Scholar. She lives in Phoenix, Arizona, with her husband and two sons.

Further acknowledgments and additional supporting images for *Sister Novelists* may be found at sisternovelists.com.